COMMANDERS

COMMANDERS

HISTORY'S GREATEST MILITARY LEADERS
R.G. GRANT

LONDON, NEW YORK, MELBOURNE,
MUNICH, AND DELHI

DK PUBLISHING
Senior Editors Sam Atkinson, Paula Regan
Editor Ferdie McDonald
US Editor Margaret Parrish
Senior Art Editor Gadi Farfour
Designer Amy Orsborne
Jacket Designer Duncan Turner
Cartography Merritt Cartographic,
Simon Mumford
Production Editor Phil Sergeant
Production Controller Rebecca Short
Creative Technical Support
Adam Brackenbury
Managing Editor Camilla Hallinan
Managing Art Editor Karen Self
Art Director Phil Ormerod
Associate Publisher Liz Wheeler
Reference Publisher Jonathan Metcalf

TOUCAN BOOKS LTD.
Senior Editor Alice Peebles
Editors Natasha Kahn, Amy Smith,
Donald Sommerville, Anna Southgate
Art Editor Mark Scribbins
Designers Nick Avery, Phil Fitzgerald,
Thomas Keenes, Ralph Pitchford
Picture Research Tam Church,
Sarah and Roland Smithies
Picture Manager Christine Vincent
Managing Director Ellen Dupont

CONSULTANTS
Lindsay Allen, Roger Collins, Richard Overy,
David Parrott, Brendan Simms

First American Edition, 2010
First Paperback American Edition, 2013
Published in the United States by
DK Publishing
375 Hudson Street
New York, New York 10014

13 14   10 9 8 7 6 5 4 3 2 1
178691—04/13

Published in Great Britain by Dorling Kindersley Limited.

A catalog record for this
book is available from the Library of Congress.

ISBN 978-1-4654-0225-7

DK books are available at special discounts when
purchased in bulk for sales promotions, premiums,
fund-raising, or educational use. For details, contact:
DK Publishing Special Markets, 375 Hudson Street,
New York, New York 10014 or SpecialSales@dk.com

Printed and bound in China by Leo Paper Products

Discover more at
www.dk.com

CONTENTS

FOREWORD

Military commanders have been a diverse collection of individuals and their job has altered radically over time through the impact of technological innovation and social and political changes. The men profiled in this book range from all-conquering warriors to cautious dedicated career soldiers, from the rulers of kingdoms and empires to ordinary citizens thrust by circumstance into the forefront of war. Some were men who delighted in combat and slaughter, while others were often sickened by their own trade and would agree with the Duke of Wellington that "next to a battle lost, the greatest misery is a battle gained."

Military command has always been, in all historical situations, a complex task. It is true that, during the American Civil War, President Lincoln described General Grant as indispensable simply because "he fights." But this does not mean the conduct of battles is the sole essence of generalship. The military commander has to look to the morale and training of his soldiers, and see that supplies are provided for the men, their animals, and their machines. He must gather and sift intelligence before preparing coherent plans and clearly communicating them to his subordinates. If he is cunning, he will ensure that battle is only joined when his army has the advantage—a general who repeatedly wins close-run victories against the odds is not doing his job properly. Bold risk-taking fighters, from Alexander the Great through Richard the Lionheart to George Patton, have always caught the eye, but some of the most successful commanders have been of an altogether different temperament—the intellectual and cultivated Moltke the Elder, for example, or the cool and diplomatic Dwight D. Eisenhower.

Writing in the 1960s, Israeli general Moshe Dayan expressed nostalgia for "the good old days" when, at the approach of battle, "the commander got on his white horse, someone blew the trumpet, and off he charged toward the enemy." Certainly it was possible for Alexander the Great to lead from the front, charging the enemy at the head of his Companion cavalry. Even a more level-headed commander of the ancient world, such as Julius Caesar, would have been close enough to the action to shout encouragement to his fighting men. A location just behind the fighting zone remained the normal battle position for a commander into the 19th century, when it was still just possible to survey a whole

battlefield with the aid of a telescope. But the increasing size of armies, the growing power and range of weapons, and new means of communication, such as telephone and radio, imposed remoteness on the field commander. By the early 20th century, the German general, Alfred von Schlieffen, could foresee a future in which "the warlord will be located… in the rear, in a house with spacious offices… seated in a comfortable chair, in front of a large desk." He could not have predicted that by 2001 it would be possible for an American general to command operations in Afghanistan from a headquarters in Florida.

The managerial complexity of modern military command, regretted by General Dayan, has often made it difficult to identify the individual to be credited as the commander of a particular operation. There was no doubt whatsoever that Hannibal led the Punic army campaigning in Italy in the third century BCE, or Nelson the British fleet at Trafalgar in 1805. But at Passchendaele in World War I, Canadian General Arthur Currie held command under British General Herbert Plumer, who himself was under Field Marshal Douglas Haig. In selecting entries for this book, an attempt has been made to identify hands-on commanders of armies and fleets, excluding both those too bureaucratically high-placed for field command and those too lowly to qualify. Military commanders who were also political leaders—the majority, in fact, up to the 18th century—are included, but political leaders who interfered in military operations, without being military commanders in their own right, are not.

Respect for military commanders as role models has declined in recent times. Heroes such as Alexander the Great and Julius Caesar, once universally admired, have been the subject of revisionist biographies focusing on their massacres and lust for power. Yet the men surveyed in this book showed many and varied human qualities, including moral fortitude, decisiveness, resilience under pressure, physical courage, humane concern for the welfare of their soldiers, and the ability to shoulder a great burden of responsibility. Our societies may yet find that, in the future, they need the martial virtues more than they expect.

R. G. GRANT

1

1500 BCE—500 CE

HEROES OF THE ANCIENT WORLD

THE CAMPAIGNS OF THE GREATEST GENERALS of ancient times—Alexander of Macedon, Hannibal, Julius Caesar—have provided lessons in strategy and tactics to be studied and admired through millennia. At a time when no army enjoyed a technological advantage, the human factor in warfare was paramount. It was the commander's ability to provide leadership, maintain morale among his troops, and seize the initiative on the battlefield that determined the narrow margin between defeat and victory.

The first organized warfare known to history took place among the Mesopotamian city-states (in present-day Iraq) some 4,500 years ago. Rulers such as Sargon of Akkad and Eanatum, king of Lagash, commanded small but effective armies that fought for control of neighboring states and scarce resources. As other societies capable of large-scale organization emerged in various regions of the globe—around the shores of the Mediterranean in Egypt, Greece, and Rome, in the Indus Valley, the river valleys of China, and central America—states expanded through warfare to create empires whose rulers commanded impressive armies. The pharaohs of New Kingdom Egypt (c. 1570–1070 BCE) led armies that numbered in tens of thousands, while the Persian emperors (c. 500 BCE) reportedly deployed several hundred thousand men. These figures were no doubt exceeded in ancient Chinese warfare.

LINES OF COMMUNICATION

Large armies raised fundamental problems of command. In simpler tribal societies the war leader was the bravest and strongest fighting man—a warrior who led his men weapon in hand. The rulers of the civilized empires often aspired to imitate this model. Egyptian pharaohs had themselves depicted as solo charioteers slaughtering their enemies with bow or mace. But in practice, large armies called for more detached management. The ruler's war chariot was more likely to function as a command platform behind the front line, screened off from attack by an entourage of elite troops.

The technology available for command and control was basic and largely unchanging. Communication was by messenger on foot or horse. The Greek author Xenophon noted that a Persian ruler generally positioned himself in the center of the line of battle because "if he has occasion to dispatch any necessary rider along the lines, his troops will receive the message in half the time." Signals by trumpets or by flags could deliver additional basic battlefield

Sumerian helmet
This helmet dates from c. 2600 BCE and was found in excavations of the ancient Mesopotamian city of Ur (in present-day Iraq). Forged from gold sheet, the ornate curving relief mimics hair.

orders, but these had to be simple and prearranged. Devolution of command was essential. Generals of the Roman empire benefited from experienced subordinates at lower levels of command—for example, centurions—who could be relied upon to execute plans faithfully and show initiative if required.

FRESH CHALLENGES

Although commanders in the ancient world were aware of the importance of logistics, out of necessity armies often lived off the land when on campaign. A commander who waged campaigns over long distances had to overcome the obstacles presented by poor or nonexistent road systems. Some empires, including Assyria, Persia, and Rome, built impressive networks of roads and bridges. From 500 BCE to 500 CE commanders often faced the added challenge of coping with warfare that was asymmetrical—that is, fought between armies and cultures with sharply different

approaches to combat. The large, complex forces of the Persian empire were puzzled by the small, compact citizen armies of Greek city-states. Generals of ancient Rome had to learn to fight Celtic and Germanic tribal warbands in Europe, and Parthian and Sassanian mounted archers in Asia.

RECIPE FOR VICTORY

Some of an ancient commander's roles were religious—he had to make sacrifices and read omens before battle. But sophisticated practical traditions of military command also evolved, based on accumulated experience of warfare and reflection upon the performance of famous generals. Much of this was passed down by word of mouth and by example—learning on the job—but a substantial literature of military history and theory also thrived. Analytical works such as the Chinese thinker Sun-tzu's *Art of War* (c. 500 BCE) and the Roman writer Vegetius's *De Re Militari* (c. 400 CE) displayed penetrating insights into the fundamentals of warfare. But the art of generalship probably gained more from written accounts of actual conflicts, such as the Greek historian Thucydides' account of the Peloponnesian Wars or Julius Caesar's commentaries on his campaigns. Through the study of such works any adept commander would be expected to know how to conduct a siege and arrange infantry and cavalry for battle, to grasp the importance of surprise and of reconnaissance to keep from being surprised himself, and to know how crucial it was to maintain supplies to one's own army and deny them to the foe. Only an exceptional commander, however, would have the moral and intellectual qualities to translate such knowledge into victorious campaigns.

Tutankhamun in battle
This scene from Tutankhamun's painted chest, 14th century BCE, shows the pharaoh in his war chariot firing arrows at his enemies. The inscription calls him "the good god… who tramples hundreds of thousands."

1500 BCE—500 CE

1500—100 BCE

GREECE AND THE ANCIENT EMPIRES

> WE MACEDONIANS ARE TO FIGHT MEDES AND PERSIANS, NATIONS LONG STEEPED IN LUXURY, WHILE WE HAVE NOW LONG BEEN INURED TO DANGER BY THE EXERTIONS OF CAMPAIGNING. IT WILL BE A FIGHT OF FREE MEN AGAINST SLAVES.

ATTRIBUTED TO ALEXANDER THE GREAT, SPEAKING AT THE BATTLE OF ISSUS, 333 BCE

FROM AT LEAST 3,000 years ago, western Asia and the eastern Mediterranean was an area fought over by competitive empire-builders. The rulers of Egypt, Assyria, Babylon, and Persia evolved highly organized, complex, professional armies of impressive size capable of campaigning over long distances. In Greece, by contrast, city-states developed small tight-knit citizen forces. The success of the Greeks in combat against the Persians in the 5th century BCE was one of the turning points of European history.

Modern archeology and research into the inscriptions found on the monuments of ancient Egypt make it possible to begin to reconstruct the strategy, tactics, and weapons of warfare from the 15th century BCE. Under rulers such as Thutmosis III (ruled 1479–1425 BCE) and Ramesses II (ruled 1279–1213 BCE), Egyptian armies campaigned from Syria in the north to Nubia in the south. Records show that Thutmosis won history's first recorded battle at Megiddo (c. 1457 BCE), thanks to a carefully worked-out battleplan. The kings of Assyria, whose empire was based in northern Mesopotamia, took the exercise of military power to a new level between c. 900 and 600 BCE, adding cavalry to chariots and perfecting the art of siege warfare. But the Achaemenid Persian rulers surpassed all their predecessors, conquering Mesopotamia, Egypt, and Anatolia (present-day Turkey) in the 6th century BCE, thanks to the superb large-scale military organization created by Cyrus the Great.

The resistance of the Greek city-states to control by the expanding Persian Empire led to the dispatch of a Persian punitive expedition to Greece in 490 BCE, followed by a full-scale invasion under Xerxes I ten years later. The city-states, including Athens and Sparta, succeeded in uniting for long enough to resist the invaders, largely through their superiority in naval warfare—as demonstrated at the battle of Salamis in 480 BCE. They were also effective on land because of their highly motivated armored infantry spearmen, or hoplites.

NEW EMPIRES

After defeating the Persians, the Greeks fell to fighting one another in a series of wars that chiefly set the naval power of Athens against the land power of Sparta. Over time, these conflicts fatally weakened the city-states of Greece, and in 338 BCE, they succumbed to conquest by a new breed of warrior from the north—the kings of Macedonia.

Riding into battle at the head of their cavalry "Companions," the Macedonian rulers also recruited and trained disciplined infantry forces. They found in Greece a cultural mission to fuel their desire for conquest. Philip of Macedon bequeathed to his son Alexander the Great the ambition to attack and destroy the mighty Persian Empire, a process that would carry Greek culture to central Asia and northern India.

Dying young, Alexander failed to leave a unified empire, but his successor dynasties, including the Seleucids in Asia and the Ptolemies in Egypt, commanded armed forces on a truly imperial scale during their internal squabbles. It was not until the 2nd century BCE that the rise of a new Mediterranean military power, the Roman Republic, rendered the Greek military tradition obsolete.

Greek hoplites
Ancient Greek infantry, known as hoplites (from *hoplon*, the type of shield they used), fought in a tight phalanx formation, stabbing overarm with their spears from behind a wall of shields. This impenetrable formation left little scope for variety in battlefield tactics.

Hoplite headgear
The Corinthian helmet, named after the Greek city-state of Corinth, was worn by hoplites, who valued maximum protection for head and face more than all-around vision.

LEADERS OF THE ANCIENT EMPIRES

THE RULERS OF THE ANCIENT EMPIRES of pharaonic Egypt, Assyria, and Achaemenid Persia were military leaders who regularly campaigned with their armies, although they also employed trusted generals to lead forces on their behalf. Among the pharaohs, Ramesses II stands out because he left behind the clearest record of his military deeds. Tiglath-Pileser III is preeminent among the many battling Assyrian kings for founding a strikingly successful military system. The two centuries of the Achaemenid empire were framed at the outset by the brilliance of its founder, Cyrus, and the defeat of Darius III at its end.

Extending borders
This statue of Ramesses II was carved at Abu Simbel in Nubia, a region in which he campaigned to extend Egypt's southern borders.

RAMESSES II

EGYPTIAN PHARAOH
BORN 1303 BCE
DIED 1213 BCE
KEY CONFLICTS Nubian Campaign, Syrian Campaigns
KEY BATTLE Kadesh c. 1275 BCE

Ramesses II occupied the Egyptian throne for 67 years, from 1279 BCE. He waged many campaigns in his long reign but his reputation rests on a single battle, at Kadesh in about 1275 BCE. There he set out to challenge the Hittites, an Anatolian people, for control of Syria. He marched north to the Bekaa Valley with his army organized into four divisions, but was almost undone by poor intelligence and the superior generalship of the Hittite king, Mutwallah, who sent agents to misinform Ramesses about the position of the Hittites. Believing his enemy to be far to the north, Ramesses let his troops spread out on the march. He encamped outside the city of Kadesh while the rear of his army was still advancing. The Hittites made a hidden flanking move, striking the Egyptian rear with a mass chariot charge. Ramesses' men were scattered and the enemy turned to attack the camp, threatening the pharaoh himself. He reportedly led a counterattack on his chariot and drove off the host. His propagandists ensured that records of the battle stressed his action in averting disaster, rather than the boldness that had led him into a trap.

TIGLATH-PILESER III

KING OF ASSYRIA
BORN Unknown
DIED 727 BCE
KEY CONFLICTS Wars Founding the Neo-Assyrian Empire
KEY BATTLES Siege of Arpad 743–740 BCE, Siege of Babylon 734 BCE

Tiglath-Pileser III was a usurper who seized the Assyrian throne in 745 BCE at a time of weakness and disunity in the kingdom. He reformed the Assyrian armed forces, creating a well-supplied regular army in which the infantry was mostly foreign prisoners of war or mercenaries, and the cavalry and charioteers were Assyrian. Under skilled generals this army provided a powerful instrument for Tiglath-Pileser's expansionist ambitions. His ruthless campaigns established the Neo-Assyrian empire and laid the foundation for renowned successors such as Sennacherib (ruled 705–681 BCE) and Ashurbanipal (ruled 669–c. 630 BCE).

Ruthless leader
Like other Assyrian rulers, Tiglath-Pileser III was noted for his delight in the torture and mass deportation of conquered peoples.

CYRUS THE GREAT

PERSIAN KING
BORN Unknown
DIED 530 BCE
KEY CONFLICTS Conquests of Media, Lydia, and Babylonia
KEY BATTLES Sardis c. 545 BCE, Opis 539 BCE

Founder of the Achaemenid Persian Empire, Cyrus the Great ranks as one of history's greatest conquerors and state builders. According to the Greek historian Herodotus, when Cyrus became ruler of the Persians in 559 BCE they were dominated by their Iranian neighbors, the Medes. He not only threw off this overlordship, but in 549 BCE also took the Medean capital, Ecbatana. As king of the Persians and Medes, he then attacked Lydia, a rich Anatolian empire ruled by King Croesus. Cyrus seized Croesus and his capital, Sardis, in c. 545 BCE. Babylonia, a resurgent empire in Mesopotamia, was next—after his victory at Opis in 539 BCE, Cyrus declared himself "king of the four corners of the world."

Cyrus's army was a multinational force of great size. It included Arabs and Armenians, and used camels as well as horses. The army was also capable of considerable engineering feats, such as constructing the canal to divert the course of the Euphrates during the Babylonian campaign.

PUBLIC IMAGE

Unlike the Assyrian kings, who used their reputation for massacre to terrorize enemies, Cyrus projected an image of tolerance. For example, his sympathetic treatment of the defeated Lydians was widely publicized. But it was essentially because of his recent victories that Babylon surrendered almost without a fight. Herodotus records that Cyrus died on campaign, fighting the Massagetae in central Asia.

Tomb of Cyrus the Great
Cyrus was buried at Pasargadae (in present-day Iran), the original capital of his empire. His tomb is a stark memorial to his greatness.

DARIUS III

PERSIAN KING
BORN Unknown
DIED 330 BCE
KEY CONFLICTS War against Alexander the Great
KEY BATTLES Issus 333 BCE, Gaugamela (Arbela) 331 BCE

Sometimes military commanders are truly unfortunate in the opponents they encounter. This was undoubtedly the case for Darius III, whose defeats at the hands of a military genius, Alexander of Macedon, brought Achaemenid rule in Persia to an inglorious end.

TAKING ON ALEXANDER

Known to us primarily from Greek sources, Darius has inevitably been presented in the most pitiful light, yet there is strong evidence at least for his physical courage. As a young man he distinguished himself in single combat against a champion put forward by the Cadusii, an Iranian mountain tribe in rebellion against the empire. His route to the Persian throne was tortuous, for he was only a minor scion of the royal family, posted far from the center of power as satrap (governor) of Armenia. But a rash of poisonings engineered by the palace courtier, Bagoas, cut a swathe through the ruling elite and opened his path to imperial rule in 336 BCE.

When Alexander invaded the Anatolian Empire in 334 BCE, Darius could be excused for treating this as a local difficulty to be handled by the regional satraps. When he did respond to the invasion, advancing with his army into Syria in 333 BCE, he seemed to have maneuvered Alexander into a disadvantageous position, emerging behind the Macedonians on the coastal plain at Issus. Darius drew up his army in a strong defensive position, then tried an outflanking move—tactics that might have succeeded against a lesser foe. The Persian forces were shattered, however, and Darius had no option but to flee the battlefield to avoid capture.

Darius's second great battle against Alexander at Gaugamela (Arbela) proved just as disastrous (pp.22–23). Fleeing to Ecbatana, Darius intended to raise another army to continue the fight, but a rebellious subordinate, Bessus, satrap of Bactria, held him prisoner and killed him.

The Alexander Mosaic
This Roman mosaic from Pompeii shows Darius III (right) being driven away from the battlefield—possibly at Issus—by his charioteer, as he is threatened by the spear-wielding Alexander of Macedon (left).

ANCIENT GREEK COMMANDERS

FIGHTING ON SEA AND LAND, whether against the Persians or against one another, the ancient Greeks earned a formidable reputation as skillful and tenacious warriors. In the city-state era, up to the 4th century BCE, their citizen armies were led by commanders who were "first among equals"—leaders who often fought on foot alongside fellow citizens. The rise of the Macedonian king, Philip II, and his son, Alexander (later, the Great), transformed Greek warfare and political life. After Alexander's conquests, Hellenistic commanders had large, complex professional armies at their disposal and sought imperial power as their goal.

THEMISTOCLES

ATHENIAN COMMANDER
BORN 524 BCE
DIED 459 BCE
KEY CONFLICTS First and Second Greco-Persian Wars
KEY BATTLES Marathon 490 BCE, Artemisium 480 BCE, Salamis 480 BCE

Described by the Greek historian Thucydides as a "natural genius," Themistocles was the man most responsible for the repulse of the Persian invasion of Greece in 480 BCE. A prominent politician in democratic Athens, Themistocles took military command in times of crisis. He served in the defeat of the Persians at Marathon in 490 BCE and persuaded the Athenians to build a fleet of triremes (warships) to meet the larger-scale Persian attack he foresaw would follow. He devised the strategy with which Athens and its allied city-states met the invasion: the

Voting tablet
An Athenian citizen scrawled Themistocles's name on this piece of pottery, voting for his exile from the city of Athens.

Spartans carried out a delaying action on land at Thermopylae, while the Athenians led the naval defense at Artemisium. Unable to command the quarrelsome allies, Themistocles used persuasiveness and cunning to impose his own strategy, inducing the Athenians to abandon their city as indefensible and the allies to allow him to position the fleet at Salamis, where enclosed waters would give the advantage to his nimble triremes. Plying the Persian king Xerxes with misinformation, he tempted him to send his ships into a prepared trap. Victory at Salamis saved Greece, but little thanks was given to Themistocles. He was eventually driven into exile by his political enemies, ending his life, ironically, at the Persian court.

KEY BATTLE
SALAMIS

CAMPAIGN Greco-Persian War
DATE September 480 BCE
LOCATION Straits of Salamis, Greece

When Persian ruler Xerxes occupied Athens in 480 BCE, the Greek fleet lurked nearby at Salamis. Themistocles initiated a plan to destroy the Persians' numerically superior navy. He sent an agent to Xerxes to make him believe the Greek fleet was about to withdraw. Thinking his enemy on the run, Xerxes sent part of his fleet to attack the Greek anchorage and the rest to block the escape route to the west. As the Persian ships entered the enclosed waters of the Salamis strait, they were surprised by the Greek triremes with a series of savage ramming attacks. The Persians lost around 200 warships in the encounter.

EPAMINONDAS

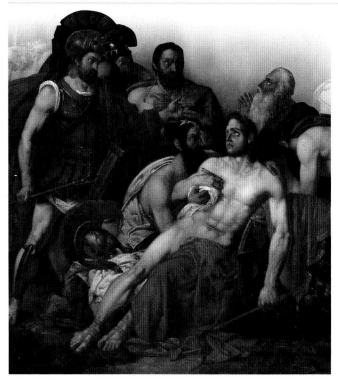

THEBAN GENERAL
BORN 410 BCE
DIED 362 BCE
KEY CONFLICTS The Theban Wars
KEY BATTLES Leuctra 371 BCE, Mantinea 362 BCE

Of the many commanders who fought in the wars between Greek city-states, the Theban, Epaminondas, was the most inspired innovator. The Spartans had long been the dominant military power in Greece when they faced Epaminondas on the battlefield at Leuctra in 371 BCE. Greek-versus-Greek encounters were traditionally trials of strength between bodies of hoplite infantry formed up in lines eight ranks deep. However, at Leuctra Epaminondas massed his hoplites on

The death of Epaminondas
Epaminondas died from a wound that he sustained at the battle of Mantinea. His last words are said to have been: "I have lived long enough, for I die unconquered."

the left of his line in a powerful body some 50 lines deep, while his center and right avoided combat, screened by cavalry and lightly equipped skirmishers. The Thebans crushed the Spartan right and weighed into the rest of the enemy line from the flank with devastating effect.

GROWING OPPOSITION

Epaminondas then pursued a subtle strategy of undermining Spartan power by freeing the subject states from which Sparta drew its slave workforce. His success inevitably led to the formation of alliances to oppose him. In 362 BCE, Epaminondas faced not only Sparta but Athens and the Peloponnesian city of Mantinea. He gambled on a pitched battle outside Mantinea, where a repeat of his strategy at Leuctra was successful once more, and the enemy was driven from the field. Epaminondas himself was fatally wounded leading the advancing infantry and died soon after the battle.

PHILIP II OF MACEDON

KING OF MACEDON
BORN 382 BCE
DIED 336 BCE
KEY CONFLICTS Third Sacred War,
War against Athens
KEY BATTLE Chaeronea 338 BCE

Macedonia was a backward kingdom on the northern fringe of the Grecian world when Philip came to the throne in 359 BCE. A ruler of exceptional energy and vision, he created a world-class army as the vehicle for his ambitions. Its strike force was the Companion

cavalry, a body of Macedonian aristocrats who formed the king's personal entourage and were usually led by him in battle. There was also an aristocratic Macedonian infantry elite, equipped like Greek hoplites, but the majority of Philip's infantry were light-armored professionals with long spears known as "sarissas." Operating in a phalanx of great depth, they were trained to carry out disciplined maneuvers. In the course of expanding his kingdom,

Gold victory medal
Struck at Tarsus, Turkey, in the 2nd century BCE, this medal bears Philip's portrait. The beard and furrowed brow signify maturity.

Philip also co-opted light horseman from Thessaly into his forces. The Greek city-states proved incapable of resisting Philip's forces, although his campaigns cost him an eye in the siege of Methoni.

SEEKING REVENGE

At Chaeronea, in 338 BCE, Philip decisively defeated the armies of Athens and Thebes. He assumed leadership of the Greek cities and had himself authorized to lead a campaign of revenge against the Persian Empire in the name of Greece. His advance guard had already crossed into Asia when Philip was assassinated by one of his bodyguards at Aegae.

PYRRHUS OF EPIRUS

**KING OF EPIRUS AND MILITARY
ADVENTURER**
BORN 319 BCE
DIED 272 BCE
KEY CONFLICTS Pyrrhic War
KEY BATTLES Asculum 279 BCE, Beneventum 275 BCE

Worthy leader
Hannibal is said to have described Pyrrhus of Epirus as second only to Alexander the Great as a military commander.

Pyrrhus of Epirus was a Greek military adventurer who fought for wealth and power in the unstable Mediterranean world of the post-Alexander era. As a young man, he took part in the struggles between Alexander's successors—the Macedon Antigonids and the Ptolemies of Egypt—switching sides as it suited his interests. His campaigns in Greece, where he was established as king of the small state of Epirus, created a reputation that traveled far.

In 281 BCE Tarentum, a Greek city in southern Italy, asked Pyrrhus to help defend it against the Romans, whose expansionist republic was threatening the independence of all the region's cities. Pyrrhus, who would have barely heard of Rome, doubtless sensed an opportunity for easy victories and personal conquest. He arrived in Tarentum in 280 BCE with 25,000 men and 20 elephants—these animals already commonplace in battles farther east, but previously unknown in Italy. At first, the strength of his cavalry and the shock effect of his elephants gave him a comfortable win over the Romans at nearby Heraclea. But the following year, at Asculum, he was victorious only at the expense of huge losses. This is the battle that gave rise to the term "Pyrrhic victory."

AN IGNOBLE END

At this point, Pyrrhus was distracted from the struggle with Rome by a new invitation, to aid the Greek cities of Sicily against the Carthaginians. He campaigned on the island for three years and had himself proclaimed king of Sicily, but failed to reduce the most stoutly defended Carthaginian strongholds and alienated local Greeks through dictatorial policies. In 275 BCE, he returned to southern Italy for yet another round against Rome. At Beneventum, fighting an enemy that was no longer shocked by elephants, the most he could claim was a draw. Short of money and troops, Pyrrhus returned to Greece, where he seized the throne of Macedon. However, his campaigns were brought to an abrupt end during street fighting in the city of Argos. An old woman threw a tile down on his head from a rooftop and a soldier severed his unconscious head from his shoulders.

War elephant
The Greeks discovered the value of war elephants through their encounters with the armies of Persia and northern India.

> ## ONE MORE SUCH VICTORY AND I AM FINISHED!
> **PYRRHUS OF EPIRUS,** AT THE BATTLE OF ASCULUM, 279 BCE

TIMELINE

- **340 BCE** Aged 16, Alexander rules Macedon as regent in the absence of his father, Philip II; he crushes an uprising in Thrace.

- **338 BCE** At the battle of Chaeronea Alexander heads the decisive cavalry charge that leads to the defeat of Athenian and Theban forces by the Macedonian army.

- **336 BCE** Alexander succeeds to the Macedonian throne after the assassination of his father.

- **335 BCE** Alexander has the city of Thebes razed to the ground as a punishment for rebelling against his authority.

THE BATTLE OF GRANICUS

- **334 BCE** Advancing with his army into Asia, Alexander's personal leadership wins a victory in his first encounter with the Persians at the battle of Granicus (May).

- **333 BCE** Advancing across Anatolia into Syria, Alexander, though vastly outnumbered, defeats the Persian ruler, Darius III, at the battle of Issus (November).

- **332 BCE** To halt Persian naval operations in the Mediterranean, Alexander continues south along the coast to capture their ports. His progress is delayed by hard-fought sieges of Tyre and Gaza. He eventually enters Egypt, where he founds the city of Alexandria (331 BCE).

- **331 BCE** Marching east from Egypt into the heart of the Persian empire, Alexander encounters Darius III for the second time at Gaugamela (October). The Persians are routed.

- **330 BCE** Alexander occupies the Persian ceremonial capital, Persepolis, which is destroyed by fire. He claims the succession to the Persian throne on the death of Darius.

- **329–327 BCE** Alexander campaigns in Sogdiana and Bactria in central Asia, taking a Bactrian bride, Roxana.

- **326 BCE** Alexander invades northern India and defeats Parvataka (King Porus) at the battle of the Hydaspes (July). Alexander wishes to advance farther into India but his veteran Macedonian troops refuse to go any farther. He is badly wounded during the siege of Multan (December).

- **325 BCE** Alexander sends a fleet to explore the Persian Gulf while leading his army back to Persia overland.

- **324 BCE** Alexander faces down a mutiny by the Macedonian veterans at Opis.

- **323 BCE** His constant campaigning ends when he dies of a fever in Babylon (June 13).

ALEXANDER THE GREAT

KING OF MACEDON AND EMPEROR OF PERSIA BY CONQUEST
BORN 356 BCE
DIED 323 BCE
KEY CONFLICTS Conquest of Persian Empire, Invasion of India
KEY BATTLES Chaeronea 338 BCE, Granicus 334 BCE, Issus 333 BCE, Gaugamela (Arbela) 331 BCE, Hydaspes 326 BCE

Arguably the most successful military commander of all time, Alexander of Macedon conquered an empire extending from Greece to India in a life that lasted a mere 32 years. His father, Philip II, ensured that he was blooded in war at an early age. At the battle of Chaeronea, the key encounter in Philip's campaign to establish Macedonian dominance over the Greek city-states, the 18-year-old Alexander was awarded command of the left wing of Philip's line of battle. He came through the test with flying colors, the first to force a breach in the enemy line.

Alexander inherited from his father the ambitious project for an invasion of the Persian empire. As soon as his hold on the Macedonian throne was secure, he campaigned in the Balkans and Greece to quell opposition before leaving for Asia.

ATTACKING PERSIA

Alexander's infamous destruction of the rebellious city of Thebes was the first of many examples of his ruthless use of terror to deter potential revolt. By 334 BCE he was ready to cross the Hellespont into Persian-ruled Anatolia, heading an army consisting of some 40,000 infantry and 5,000 cavalry. The expedition was carefully prepared,

Alexander at Issus
In a relief from c. 320 BCE, Alexander (left) is shown wearing the lion's-head helmet of his "ancestor" Heracles.

with siege equipment in support and supply ships shadowing the army's moves along the coast. At the River Granicus in Anatolia, Alexander encountered an army assembled by the local Persian governor. It was nearly his last battle for, recklessly leading the cavalry charge across the river, he was surrounded by enemies and almost killed. His boldness, nonetheless, carried the day.

The fate of the expedition looked very uncertain for a time. Some of the Greek cities of western Anatolia proved less than enthusiastic about being liberated by Alexander's army.

A city founded
The building of the Egyptian city of Alexandria, fancifully depicted here by a Renaissance artist, was decreed by Alexander in 331 BCE. He founded 16 cities bearing his name, most of them in Asia.

Meanwhile, the Persians delivered a potentially deadly strategic counter-punch, employing Greek mercenary forces to thrust through the Aegean toward Greece and Macedon itself.

DEFEATING DARIUS

When Alexander's army marched into Syria in the winter of 333 BCE, it was reasonable for the Persian emperor, Darius III, to believe that the Macedonians were falling into a trap, for his much larger forces were advancing westward to crush the invaders. But Alexander was confident that if he could bring the Persians to battle, he would defeat them. The two armies met on the plain at Issus. Darius adopted a prudent defensive posture; Alexander gambled on all-out attack. The superior aggression of the Macedonian cavalry, led by Alexander in person, carried the day, driving in the Persian left flank. Darius fled to avoid capture, his army totally shattered. Alexander found the whole eastern Mediterranean opened up

HE DISPELLED THEIR FEAR IN THE MIDST OF DANGER BY HIS OWN FREEDOM FROM FEAR.

ARRIAN, *THE ANABASIS OF ALEXANDER,* c. 145 CE

to conquest. Pressing south into Egypt, he was greeted as a successor to the pharaohs. For most leaders this would surely have been the moment for consolidation after an already awesome triumph. Alexander thought only of total victory over Persia. He forced Darius to give battle at Gaugamela (pp.22–23), where the Macedonian cavalry again achieved a victory against great numerical odds.

RULING STYLE

Alexander continued to campaign, asserting his authority over the Persian empire's provinces farther to the east. His relations with his followers, changed by the scale of his success, became intermittently fraught. His style of command had always been like that of a tribal warband leader. He fought shoulder to shoulder with his companions, and ate and drank with them (the latter to excess). Yet his style of leadership—as an "equal" with senior authority—sat uneasily alongside the triumphant Alexander's pretensions. He claimed descent from the demigod Heracles and the legendary hero Achilles. There were plots, fights, and mutinies. Alexander had his second-in-command, Philotas, executed and

Bronze weapon
Dating from the 4th century BCE, this type of arrowhead would have been used by Alexander's forces.

killed another close companion, Clitus the Black, in a drunken argument between the two men.

Nothing sated Alexander's thirst for military adventure. In 326 BCE, he invaded northern India, overcoming stiff resistance at the battle of Hydaspes, where the Macedonians learned to counter Indian war elephants. Losses in the battle were severe and, soon after, Alexander's army refused to follow him any farther. The soldiers forced him to turn back along the Indus to the sea. En route Alexander suffered a severe wound while leading an attack on Malli near the River Hydraotes. He finally arrived back in Persia in 325 BCE after a harrowing desert march unwisely undertaken. His mind was still full of plans for fresh campaigns into Arabia and north Africa, but his body had repeatedly taken vicious punishment. Scarred with the marks of his numerous wounds, Alexander succumbed to a fever. He died at the palace of Nebuchadnezzar II in Babylon without having secured the succession to his empire.

Godlike features
An idealized marble portrait of Alexander, the earliest version of which dates from the Hellenistic era, depicts him in classical style as the god Apollo.

KEY TROOPS

THE COMPANION CAVALRY

The Macedonian aristocracy formed an elite body of horsemen known as the Companion cavalry. Numbering several thousand, they formed the royal entourage and were led into battle by the king in person. Each horseman was equipped with a long lance and a *kopis*—a short curved sword—and wore a metal cuirass and helmet. The Companion cavalry occupied the place of honor on the right of the line of battle, while light cavalry from Thessaly was positioned on the left. Alexander used the Companion cavalry as a shock force to deliver a killer blow, typically aiming to charge into the flank of the enemy line and target the center where the opposing commander was stationed.

A MEDIEVAL ARTIST'S IMPRESSION OF ALEXANDER'S COMPANION CAVALRY

ALEXANDER: LEADER AND LEGEND

ROMAN COPY OF A 3RD-CENTURY BCE
GREEK BUST OF ALEXANDER

"His life was one long dream of glory."

Iskander (19th century) by Abai Qunanbajuly.
This Kazakh poem reflects the high, even idealized, repute of Alexander in central Asian cultures.

ALEXANDER WAS AN INSPIRATIONAL leader of men. The Roman historian Plutarch described how, during a hard desert march, some soldiers brought Alexander scarce water in a helmet. In full view of the army he refused to drink, declaring that he intended to share the sufferings of his men. The army responded by proclaiming that it would follow such a king anywhere.

Alexander thoroughly understood the effectiveness of such theatrical gestures in winning the support of his men when conditions were hard. He made the ordinary soldier feel that he identified with their hardships, while at the same time stirring their pride with a consciously cultivated image as their heroic and exceptional leader. He is also described as taking special care with morale-building gestures after battles, conducting elaborate funeral ceremonies and distributing reward to soldiers who had performed well in combat. The fact that he usually had wounds of his own gave greater force to the bond between the army and its charismatic commander.

His soldiers shouted out to Alexander to lead them forward boldly… declaring that they would not regard themselves as weary, or thirsty, or as mortals at all, so long as they had such a king.

The Life of Alexander *(c. 100 CE) by Plutarch*, which describes an incident that took place during the pursuit of Darius III after the battle of Gaugamela.

Alexander plunged into the river with 13 cavalry squadrons. He was now advancing through a hail of enemy missiles toward a steep and heavily defended bank, while negotiating a current that swept his men off their feet and pulled them under. His leadership seemed foolhardy and reckless rather than prudent. Yet, he persisted and, with great effort and hardship, reached the opposite bank of the river, which was wet and slippery with mud. He was at once forced into a chaotic battle, man against man…

The Life of Alexander *(c. 100 CE) by Plutarch*, in which the historian describes the opposed crossing of the Granicus River by Alexander and his cavalry in May 334 BCE.

ALEXANDER'S NATURAL PLACE in war was at the head of his cavalry. This style of command, leading from the front, was imposed on him by his society and culture. The ruler of Macedonia was the leader of a warband, required to prove himself and dominate his followers by the evidence of his fighting prowess.

But Alexander's boldness went beyond this basic requirement. By leading a charge across the Granicus River to attack an enemy in a strong position, Alexander seriously put at risk his army's key asset: himself. He was nearly killed in the melee and was only saved by the timely intervention of a companion. Ancient historians often criticized Alexander for his impetuousness and his unnecessary risk-taking, although sometimes they excused these faults on the grounds of his relative youth.

Yet Alexander was also an acute judge of the psychology of warfare, recognizing that confident boldness would usually triumph in the face of an overcautious enemy. Shock and surprise were key elements in his strategy and tactics, as he wrong-footed opponents through his speed and unbridled aggression.

HEROES OF THE ANCIENT WORLD

ALEXANDER NEVER HESITATED to use maximum force to achieve his goals. He showed no special respect for human life and saw little distinction between civilians and combatants. He could show mercy when it was politically desirable, but terror was also a weapon in his arsenal. His campaigns in the Indus Valley in 325 BCE have been characterized by some historians as "genocidal," but to Alexander such laying waste was no more than a suitable punishment for those who resisted his progress and a practical means of imposing his authority.

> **M**uch country was wasted, so that every spot was filled with fire and devastation and… the number of persons killed reached many myriads. By the destruction of these tribes, all their neighbors were terrified and submitted to Alexander.

Library of History (60–30 BCE) by Diodorus Siculus, on Alexander's crushing of the Orietae tribe during the Indus campaign in 325 BCE.

> "No mortal on Earth excelled or equaled him."

Anabasis of Alexander (2nd century CE) by Arrian, part of the historian's final assessment of Alexander's career.

Defeating great beasts
In the battle of Hydaspes, fought in India in 326 BCE, Alexander triumphed over Indian ruler Parvataka (known as King Porus), defeating his army of war elephants.

ALEXANDER VS. DARIUS

AFTER HIS HUMILIATING DEFEAT at Issus by Alexander in 333 BCE, the Persian ruler, Darius III, resolved to fight the Macedonians again and crush them. He assembled a considerable army from his Asian satrapies and waited in Mesopotamia for Alexander to come to him. In the summer of 331 BCE, Alexander, equally eager for a second battle, marched from Egypt through Syria to the Euphrates. Darius sent cavalry under the satrap Mazaeus to deny him supplies and fodder in the Euphrates valley, so Alexander had to continue northeast to the Tigris. Darius awaited his enemy's much smaller army at Gaugamela (near Arbela) on the far side of the river.

ALEXANDER

Alexander crossed the Tigris unaware of the position or size of Darius's army. After four days' march along the river, prisoners taken in a clash with Persian cavalry revealed Darius was on a plain some 6 miles (10 km) distant, hidden by intervening hills. Alexander set up a fortified camp and spent four days preparing for battle.

On the evening of September 29, he drew up his army and advanced toward Gaugamela, intending to attack at dawn after a night march. But, on reaching the crest of the hills above the plain, Alexander ordered a halt. Probably the sight of the Persian campfires, revealing the full scale of his enemy's forces, made him hesitate.

PREPARING FOR BATTLE

After inspecting the field the next day, Alexander finalized his plans. He rejected a night attack, an obvious tactic for an inferior force, saying, "Alexander does not steal his victories." Instead, he adjusted his usual dispositions—infantry phalanx in the center, the Companion cavalry on the right, a light cavalry left wing— with measures to combat a possible envelopment. On the wings, cavalry and skirmishers would counter any outflanking moves and a second line of infantry was stationed to the rear, ready to turn around and defend the backs of the front line. Thus prepared, Alexander slept soundly that night.

ALEXANDER TRIUMPHS

The following morning he brought his army down on to the plain, riding at the head of the Companion cavalry and supported by the best of his infantry. He led the whole army to the right, across the face of the Persian line. Alexander attacked the Persian left with his Companions, while the Persian cavalry tried outflanking moves but were beaten back.

Amid the chaos of combat, utterly obscured by dust rising from the dry plain, Alexander next turned his heavy cavalry, with infantry support, to strike toward Darius in the Persian center. As the Persian king fled, Alexander's instinct was to pursue, but his horsemen were needed to aid his forces engaged in furious combat on other parts of the battlefield. The Persian army was scattered with huge casualties. Victory was total.

Macedonian triumph
A 17th-century painting shows Darius, standing terrified in his chariot, as Alexander's troops hack their way toward him.

ALEXANDER

| **Evening** Alexander orders his army to equip for battle and marches from the camp toward the enemy's position | **Night** Alexander halts, abandoning his plan for a dawn attack | **Daytime** Alexander and a contingent of Companion cavalry ride around the battlefield to inspect it for obstacles and observe the Persian dispositions | **After nightfall** Aided by his seer, Aristander, Alexander carries out the necessary sacrifices to the gods | **Night** At a council of war, senior Macedonians recommend a night attack, but Alexander rejects this and opts for battle the following day |

331 BCE: SEPT 29   SEPT 30

DARIUS

| **Darius** waits at his chosen battlefield, while cavalry scouts under Mazaeus keep watch on Alexander's camp, 6 miles (10 km) distant, from a hill between the two armies | **Evening** Darius is informed by Mazaeus of Alexander's approach; the scouts pull back and Darius readies his army for battle | **Dawn** Surprised by the failure of the Macedonians to press home their attack, Darius sends scouts to observe the arrangement of Alexander's line | **Evening** Darius orders his troops to stay armed and alert for a second night, fearing that the Macedonians will launch a surprise night attack | **Night** Accompanied by his generals, Darius tours his troops and offers them words of encouragement |

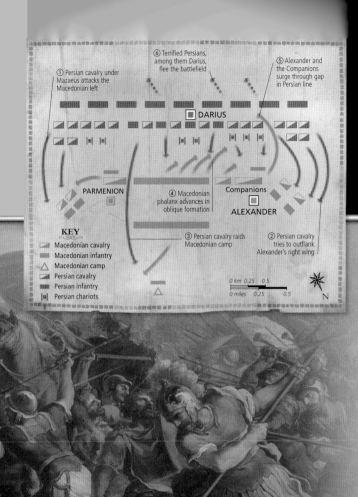

Battle map key and labels

① Persian cavalry under Mazaeus attacks the Macedonian left

⑥ Terrified Persians, among them Darius, flee the battlefield

⑤ Alexander and the Companions surge through gap in Persian line

DARIUS

PARMENION

④ Macedonian phalanx advances in oblique formation

Companions
ALEXANDER

③ Persian cavalry raids Macedonian camp

② Persian cavalry tries to outflank Alexander's right wing

KEY
- Macedonian cavalry
- Macedonian infantry
- Macedonian camp
- Persian cavalry
- Persian infantry
- Persian chariots

0 km 0.25 0.5
0 miles 0.25 0.5

N

LOCATION Uncertain: probably near Arbela in the Kurdistan region of northern Iraq

CAMPAIGN Conquest of Persian Empire

DATE October 1, 331 BCE

FORCES Strengths disputed by historians; Persians: perhaps 95,000, about half cavalry; Macedonians: perhaps 50,000, including about 8,000 cavalry

CASUALTIES Persians: up to 50,000 dead; Macedonians: fewer than 1,000 dead

DARIUS

Darius made no effort to prevent Alexander from crossing the Tigris. He had already chosen his battlefield, a broad, flat expanse where his superior forces would be able to envelop Alexander's shorter line on both flanks. His dispositions were long prepared: a line of 2,000 chariots in front of the army, massed cavalry forces on the wings, and Darius himself in the center with his bodyguard of infantry Immortals and 15 war elephants. He had the surface of the plain flattened and cleared to aid his chariots and horsemen. Despite the ill-omen of an eclipse of the Moon on September 20, Darius believed he must win if Alexander attacked him in daylight. His greatest fear was a surprise night attack.

Informed by his cavalry scouts of Alexander's every move, Darius put his troops on full alert as soon as the Macedonians broke camp on September 29, but Alexander's surprising delay before giving battle meant that Darius's force ended up staying awake and battle-ready through two tiring nights.

Alexander's advance to the right as battle was joined disconcerted Darius, who understandably rushed his cavalry force left to block this maneuver. This opened up a weak point left-of-center in his line into which Alexander thrust, forcing his way ever closer to Darius himself. Whether panicked by this threat or regarding himself as a vital strategic asset, Darius rapidly fled the field, abandoning his army to its fate.

> ❝ DARIUS, WHO HAD ALREADY LONG BEEN IN A STATE OF FEAR... WAS THE FIRST TO TURN AND FLEE. ❞
>
> **ARRIAN**, *THE ANABASIS OF ALEXANDER*, 2ND CENTURY CE

Dawn Alexander wakes after a sound sleep, dons his armor and rides up and down the line, exhorting his troops to fight the enemy bravely

Midmorning The Macedonians march down into the plain. Alexander leads from the right, pressing farther to the right as he advances

Alexander leads a combined cavalry and infantry charge against the Persian center where Darius is positioned

Alexander prepares to give chase to Darius, but pulls back to aid his center and left, which are in difficulties

OCT 1

Darius sends his cavalry farther left and it clashes with Alexander's flanking units. Mazaeus leads a strong advance on his right. Darius's chariots charge without effect

As the Macedonian attack strikes home, Darius panics, abandons his army, and flees the battlefield on his chariot

Persian troops break through to the Macedonian camp but are then savaged by Alexander's cavalry and infantry. The Persian army flees the field

509 BCE—500 CE

ANCIENT ROME
AND ITS ENEMIES

"WITH THE ROMANS, THE INCENTIVES TO VALOR WERE THEIR HABIT OF VICTORY AND INEXPERIENCE OF DEFEAT, THEIR CONTINUAL CAMPAIGNS AND PERPETUAL TRAINING, THE MAGNITUDE OF THEIR EMPIRE."

JOSEPHUS, *THE JEWISH WAR*, c. 75 CE

ROME DEVELOPED one of the most efficient fighting forces in the ancient world, its army evolving from a citizen militia into regular professional legions. High command was mostly entrusted to aristocratic amateurs—powerful politicians but only part-time soldiers, often without training or much military experience. Despite this haphazard system, commanders as inspired as Scipio Africanus and Julius Caesar emerged in the course of Rome's endless warfare against enemies ranging from Carthaginians to Parthians to Celtic tribal warriors.

Roman commanders did not lead from the front in the reckless manner of Alexander of Macedon, but they did generally share most of the risks and hardships of their men. Emperor Constantius, in 355 CE, wrote that a commander should "inspire by example without being rash" and "go as a brave man to lead other brave men."

Commanders directed sieges and engineering works in person, as well as carrying out the essential religious functions of sacrifice and the reading of omens. In battle their position was just behind the front line, ready to intervene where troops needed encouragement or support. In the words of a 1st-century CE writer, the general's chief duty was to "show himself to those in danger, praise the brave, threaten the cowardly, encourage the lazy… bring aid to the wearied." Tenacity was probably the most striking quality of Roman leaders. A commander might be forgiven for losing a battle after an honorable fight, but he was expected to regroup his forces and renew the campaign until he eventually won.

THE POWER OF THE LEGIONS

The close bond that often developed between Roman legionaries and their immediate commander, rather than the central government, was one of the causes of the repeated coups and civil wars that scarred Roman history. Power in the Republic and the empire ultimately rested with the legions.

Tactically, Roman armies were limited to a small range of battlefield maneuvers drilled into the troops, enlivened by the occasional ambush.

Discipline was mostly excellent and lower level officers could be trusted to display resolution and initiative. Engineering skills were at a premium, seen in the construction of roads and defensive fortifications all across the empire in peace and war, as well as in siege works on campaign. Strategically, the Romans were bold and aggressive in their expansionist phase, making ample use of terror to ensure the submission of their enemies. At a later stage they adopted a subtle diplomatic approach, as they became dependent on alliances and the incorporation of "barbarian" troops into their fighting forces.

ROME'S OPPONENTS

The enemies the Romans encountered—when not fighting one another—were varied indeed. In the 3rd century BCE the Carthaginians, based in north Africa, challenged the rising Roman Republic in the Punic Wars, a conflict that began as a contest for control of Sicily and ended as a fight to the death between two civilizations.

Extending its power next into the eastern Mediterranean, Rome proved its superiority to the states that had succeeded to Alexander's empire, but was often beaten by the armies of western Asia—Parthians and Sassanids—which depended chiefly on mounted warriors. In western Europe, Celtic and Germanic tribes put up stiff resistance to Rome, inflicting the occasional severe defeat. Mounting incursions by migrating Goths, Vandals, and the fierce Huns eventually put the western Roman empire under impossible strain.

Fighting on horseback
Defeats at the hands of Hannibal's cavalry led Rome to strengthen its own mounted troops. By the 2nd century BCE its cavalry force was made up of a mixture of wealthier Roman citizens (*equites,* or knights), contingents from Rome's allies, and mercenaries.

Roman sword
At the height of Rome's power in the 1st and 2nd centuries CE Roman centurions used short swords like this *gladius,* designed for stabbing in close combat.

COMMANDERS OF THE PUNIC WARS

IN THE 2ND CENTURY BCE, the Roman Republic and Carthage—a city-state in north Africa—vied for dominance of the western Mediterranean. From 264 to 241 BCE. they fought for control of Sicily in the First Punic War. The Romans won, but Carthage wanted revenge. In 218 BCE, the Second Punic War began. Carthaginian general Hannibal crossed the Alps into Italy and defeated the Romans three times in major battles. Yet Rome fought on. In Scipio Africanus the Romans found a military genius to match Hannibal and, in 202 BCE, forced the Carthaginians to surrender. In a Third Punic War, Carthage was utterly destroyed in 146 BCE.

HAMILCAR BARCA

CARTHAGINIAN GENERAL
BORN C. 270 BCE
DIED 228 BCE
KEY CONFLICTS First Punic War, Mercenary War
KEY BATTLES Siege of Drepanum 244–241 BCE, The Saw 239 BCE

Father of the famous Hannibal, Hamilcar was the commander of Carthaginian forces in Sicily during the last crucial phase of the First Punic War. From 247 BCE, he waged a skillful campaign with inadequate forces. He succeeded in tying down Roman troops around Drepanum and was still undefeated when a Carthaginian naval catastrophe ended the war.

Hannibal negotiated passage for his mercenaries to Carthage but, deprived of his leadership and denied their pay, these tough soldiers soon mutinied. Joined by Libyans and Numidians, they threatened to destroy Carthage.

Hamilcar was by far the most effective Carthaginian general in the brutal suppression of the uprising, known as the Mercenary War. Atrocities were common on both sides—Hamilcar is said to have executed 40,000 rebels after the battle of the Saw. He spent the final years of his life invading Hispania (Spain) and endowing Hannibal with a mission of revenge against Rome.

Father and son
The young Hannibal (in a blue sash) swears eternal enmity to Rome as his father looks on, as imagined by an 18th-century artist. Few Carthaginian historical sources survive to give a contemporary view of such events.

FABIUS CUNCTATOR

ROMAN CONSUL AND DICTATOR
BORN C. 280 BCE
DIED 203 BCE
KEY CONFLICTS Second Punic War
KEY BATTLE Tarentum 209 BCE

Quintus Fabius Maximus, known as Cunctator (delayer) because of his war strategy, was an unlikely Roman hero of the long struggle against Hannibal in the Second Punic War.

A member of Rome's aristocratic elite, Fabius had a minor military reputation won as consul in 233 BCE, when he crushed the Ligurians, a tribal people from northern Italy and southern Gaul, and drove them into the Alps.

If Fabius played any part in the First Punic War, it has not been recorded. But when Hannibal destroyed an army led by Consul Gaius Flaminius in June 217 BCE, it was to the sexagenarian Fabius that the panicking Romans turned for leadership. He was made dictator, a six-month appointment that carried extraordinary powers to cope with an emergency.

Taking command of the Roman army, Fabius immediately adopted the delaying approach for which he is famed, shadowing Hannibal's army and harassing his

Thoughtful leader
Fabius Cunctator was an unusually mild-mannered military commander, with a gift for long-term strategic thinking rather than the cut and thrust of the battlefield.

foragers, but refusing pitched battle. Understandably, his tactic did not satisfy most Romans, since it involved the army doing nothing while Hannibal plundered fertile terrain.

Discontent soon found a focus in Fabius's second-in-command, Marcus Minucius Rufus. After a humiliating episode in which Hannibal gave Fabius the slip under cover of darkness, Minucius restored some Roman pride with a successful attack on Carthaginian forces outside Gerunium. Although only a skirmish, it confirmed the general opinion that Fabius was the wrong man for the task. At the end of his six-month dictatorship he was not reappointed and his tactics were abandoned. The result was the defeat at Cannae in 216 (pp. 30–31), probably the worst military disaster in Roman history.

Fabius's military genius was now evident to all. He was elected as a consul for the next two years, and was to play a leading role in restoring Roman morale and rebuilding the army. The war against Hannibal was continued by others along the lines that he had laid down. Denied the chance of a decisive victory in battle, the Carthaginians' position weakened over time and Rome grew stronger.

FINAL TRIUMPH
Elected consul for the third time in 209 BCE, Fabius achieved a last victory in the recapture of the major southern Italian city of Tarentum, lost to Hannibal three years earlier. He never led an army again, although he did later oppose Scipio's plan to invade Africa—fortunately for Rome, his caution did not prevail.

SCIPIO AFRICANUS

ROMAN GENERAL
BORN 236 BCE
DIED 183 BCE
KEY CONFLICTS Second Punic War
KEY BATTLES Ilipa 206 BCE, Zama 202 BCE

Publius Cornelius Scipio, known as Scipio Africanus, was the Roman commander who won the Second Punic War. He was 17 years old when the war began and fought in an army commanded by his father, also named Publius Cornelius Scipio, at the Ticinus River in the opening skirmish of Hannibal's Italian campaign. He came through the battle of Cannae unscathed, distinguishing himself in the rallying of survivors after the Roman debacle, but his career remained in the shadow of his father until the elder Publius was killed in 211 BCE while on campaign in Iberia.

Scipio took over his father's command under unpropitious circumstances, for Roman fortunes in Spain

Scipio's demise
Although one of the greatest Roman military commanders, Scipio Africanus was poorly rewarded for his services to the Empire, forced into retirement in Campania by his political enemies after accusations of corruption.

were at a low ebb. In just four years, he extinguished the Carthaginian presence in Iberia. A bold and charismatic leader, he pursued an aggressive strategy, using speed of movement to put Carthaginian forces at a disadvantage. He took their main base at New Carthage by assault in a surprise attack in 209 BCE, following up with a victory over Hannibal's brother, Hasdrubal Barca, at Baecula.

The Carthaginians responded by sending reinforcements into southern Spain. This led to the major battle of Ilipa in 206 BCE, seen as Scipio's tactical masterpiece. Both armies consisted

KEY BATTLE
ZAMA

CAMPAIGN Second Punic War
DATE 202 BCE
LOCATION northern Tunisia

The climactic battle of the Second Punic War was fought on October 19, 202 BCE at Zama in Tunisia. Despite having many hastily trained recruits, Scipio Africanus's army was laying waste to Carthaginian territory, forcing

Hannibal to give battle. Hannibal tried to disrupt the Roman line with his elephants, but the legionaries made gaps for the beasts to pass through their ranks. The Roman infantry then attacked while their cavalry swept all before them on the wings. When the horsemen returned to hit the Carthaginians from the rear, the battle was won for Rome.

> ❝ HANNIBAL SET SCIPIO APART FROM OTHER COMMANDERS, AS ONE WHOSE WORTH WAS INCALCULABLE. ❞
>
> **LIVY,** *HISTORY OF ROME*, 9 BCE

of troops of various origins and capabilities. Normal policy was for both sides to arrange their battle lines so that like fought like. But Scipio unexpectedly switched his formidable legion infantry from the center to the wings, where they faced the Carthaginians' least effective troops. Maneuvering with consummate skill, these legionaries smashed the Carthaginians' line, moving inward from the flanks.

VICTORY AT ZAMA

With Iberia conquered, Scipio returned to Rome a hero. He was elected consul and given permission to lead an army to Africa, where he planned to threaten Carthage. Crossing to Tunisia, he established himself outside the city and refused to be driven off. This brought Hannibal back from Italy and to his defeat at Zama, which forced the Carthaginians to sue for peace. Aside from supporting his brother, Lucius, in the defeat of Antiochus III of Syria in 190 BCE, Scipio carried out no further military deeds of note.

HANNIBAL

CARTHAGINIAN GENERAL
BORN 247 BCE
DIED 182 BCE
KEY CONFLICTS Second Punic War
KEY BATTLES Cannae 216 BCE, Zama 202 BCE

Hannibal Barca was introduced to warfare at an early age, learning military wisdom from his father, Hamilcar. As a youth, he fought in the Carthaginian campaigns in Spain, which were effectively a Barca family enterprise. He inherited supreme command of the army in Spain in 221 BCE. Roman sources also tell that he inherited his father's burning desire to avenge Carthage's defeat by Rome in the First Punic War (264–261 BCE).

INVADING ITALY

Whether or not Hannibal deliberately provoked war with Rome by attacking the city of Saguntum in 219 BCE, the daring invasion of Italy that followed was well prepared, with the route across Gaul and over the Alps scouted in advance. Hannibal took the Romans by surprise—they had assumed that he would stay in Spain and await their counterattack. The journey was hazardous in the extreme. Along the way Hannibal's army was harried by local tribes. The crossing of the Alps was tough for men and animals, especially for Hannibal's war elephants. Only a fraction of the forces that had left Spain finally reached northern Italy. A first clash at the Ticino River revealed the quality of Hannibal's

Punic armor
This gold Carthaginian breastplate, dating from around the time of Hannibal, would have been worn by a senior commander for ceremonial display.

Hannibal on the move
This representation of Hannibal by a 16th-century Italian artist attempts to capture the exoticism of a commander from Africa. The type of elephants he used is disputed, although they may have been a small African forest species.

Numidian horsemen, who drove the Roman cavalry into flight. An aura of success began to gather around him, and local Celtic tribesmen flocked to join his forces. The Romans intended to stamp on this invasion before it went any further. They shifted an army north to confront Hannibal at the Trebia River, but the Roman leaders were tactically naive and over-optimistic.

KEY TROOPS

HANNIBAL'S ARMY

Hannibal's force in Italy was an amalgam of mercenaries from Carthage's north African allies or tributary states and from Spain. Each group had its specialty, whether sturdy Libyan foot soldiers, nimble Numidian horsemen armed with javelin and spear, slingshot skirmishers from the Balearic Islands, or Spanish hill tribesmen with distinctive short swords. This multicultural array was united by a common allegiance to its charismatic general, who was supported by a number of lieutenants drawn from the Carthaginian aristocracy, including Hannibal's own relatives.

Cavalry tactics
The encounter at the Trebia River in December 218 BCE was Hannibal's first significant victory in his Italian campaign. His cavalry played a major part, provoking the Romans with a succession of attacks on their boundaries.

Hannibal drew them into an attack across the river, then crushed their wings with his cavalry, while concealed troops emerged to strike the advancing Romans from the rear. The Roman legionary infantry had to smash through Hannibal's center and abandon the battlefield to escape from being massacred.

The Romans failed to learn from this reverse. The following year, Hannibal moved rapidly south into Etruria. For a second time, a Roman army hastened north to give battle. Hannibal selected the perfect site for an ambush, where the road passed

> OF ALL THAT BEFELL THE ROMANS AND CARTHAGINIANS, GOOD OR BAD, THE CAUSE WAS ONE MAN AND ONE MIND—HANNIBAL.

POLYBIUS, *THE HISTORIES*, LATE 2ND CENTURY BCE

between steep hills and the shore of Lake Trasimene. The Romans marched into the trap and were massacred as Hannibal's army moved down from the heights, catching them with their backs to the lake.

After this crushing defeat, Fabius Cunctator took charge, signaling a change of tactics. By refusing to be drawn into battle, Fabius left Hannibal with the task of keeping his army and its animals supplied with food and fodder for an extended period in hostile territory. At the end of the campaigning season, Hannibal faced being trapped for the winter on a plain that his troops had already stripped bare of supplies. He escaped only by slipping past Fabius and his army at night, reportedly creating a diversion using cattle with torches tied to their horns.

FRUITLESS VICTORY

In the summer of 216 BCE Hannibal and the Roman leadership, eager for battle, engaged at Cannae (pp. 30–31). This proved the greatest triumph of Hannibal's career, but its aftermath has puzzled historians, for Hannibal made no effort to occupy and destroy the city of Rome, although it lay open to attack. Indeed, from that

point onward, Hannibal's campaign lost its clarity of purpose. He had achieved his original objective: the humiliating defeat of Rome. But since the Romans would not make peace, Hannibal was left to campaign around southern Italy for years, making alliances and capturing or losing cities, winning indecisive battles, and somehow keeping his army united. The last chance of a truly decisive victory was lost when his brother, Hasdrubal, commanding a fresh invading army, was killed in northern Italy at the battle of Metaurus. Afterward, his head was thrown into Hannibal's camp.

In 203 BCE, after 16 years in Italy, Hannibal was recalled to defend Carthage against a Roman invasion. He faced Scipio Africanus at Zama with an army of raw recruits, while the invaluable Numidian cavalry was now fighting for the Romans. Hannibal was defeated, and Carthage was forced to make peace on humiliating terms. Hannibal spent the remainder of his life fleeing Roman vengeance around the Mediterranean. In his last battle in 190 BCE, he commanded the Syrian fleet of Antiochus III against Rhodes. Finally, Hannibal chose suicide rather than submit to Roman captivity.

TIMELINE

■ **237 BCE** Nine-year-old Hannibal accompanies his father, Hamilcar, on campaign in Spain; he reportedly vows to fight Rome with "fire and steel."

■ **221 BCE** Hannibal takes command of the Carthaginian army in Spain after the death of his brother-in-law, Hasdrubal the Fair.

■ **219 BCE** Hannibal besieges and captures the Spanish city of Saguntum, an ally of Rome; the Romans respond with a declaration of war on Carthage.

■ **218 BCE** Marching from Spain through Gaul, Hannibal leads an army across the Alps into northern Italy. He defeats the Romans in a skirmish at Ticinus (November) and in a larger encounter at Trebia (December).

■ **217 BCE** Hannibal loses the sight of an eye through an infection. He successfully ambushes the army of Roman consul Flaminius at Lake Trasimene (June 24), killing some 15,000 Roman soldiers.

■ **216 BCE** Roman forces suffer a catastrophic defeat at Cannae (August 2), but Hannibal chooses not to march on Rome, instead establishing himself at Capua.

■ **212 BCE** Hannibal seizes the city of Tarentum, although a Roman garrison holds out in its citadel.

HANNIBAL BUST FOUND AT CAPUA

■ **211 BCE** Hannibal advances to the walls of Rome but is forced to withdraw south after failing to break the Roman siege. Capua falls to the Roman forces.

■ **207 BCE** Hannibal's brother, Hasdrubal, leads reinforcements to join him in Italy, but is defeated and killed at the battle of the Metaurus.

■ **203 BCE** Hannibal is recalled from Italy to north Africa, where Roman general Scipio Africanus is threatening Carthage.

■ **202 BCE** Scipio's army defeats Hannibal at the battle of Zama (October 19); the Carthaginians are forced to accept punitive peace terms.

■ **195 BCE** Forced into exile by his political enemies in Carthage, Hannibal becomes a general in the service of Antiochus III, the Seleucid ruler of Syria.

■ **190 BCE** The Romans defeat Antiochus III at the battle of Magnesia; Hannibal moves on to avoid falling into Roman hands.

■ **182 BCE** While at the court of King Prusias of Bithynia, Hannibal commits suicide, taking a fatal dose of poison to keep from being handed over to the Romans.

1500 BCE–500 CE

HANNIBAL AT CANNAE

LOCATION
Apulia, southeast Italy
CAMPAIGN
Carthaginian invasion
of Italy, during the
Second Punic Wars (218–201 BCE)
DATE August 2, 216 BCE
FORCES Carthaginians c. 56,000; Romans
c. 86,000
CASUALTIES Carthaginians c. 6,000–8,000
killed; Romans c. 48,000 killed, c. 20,000
taken prisoner

At the start of August 216 BCE,
Hannibal's army faced a much larger
force of eight legions led by the
Roman consuls Lucius Aemilius
Paulus and Gaius Terentius Varro.
Hannibal had captured a key supply
depot at Cannae, near the Aufidus
(Ofanto) River, hoping to draw
the Romans into attacking him.
The Romans needed no urging to
give battle, confident that they were
strong enough to defeat the invader.

TAKING POSITIONS

On the morning of August 2 the
Roman forces crossed the Aufidus
and took up a confined position
between the river and high ground.
Although Hannibal could see that
this might prevent his superior
cavalry from outflanking the Roman
line, he also crossed the river and
formed his army for combat.

Hannibal knew that the Romans
would try to win the battle in the
center through the strength of their

legionary infantry. He saw that this
tactic offered the potential to spring
a trap. Opposite the legionaries he
positioned Spanish and Gallic foot
soldiers—fierce tribal fighters but
no match for the Romans—in close
combat. On each flank of these
lightly clad troops he placed his
disciplined Libyan infantry, wearing
Roman-style armor and packed
in dense formation. Both sides had
their cavalry on the wings.

RESOUNDING VICTORY

When battle was joined, the Roman
infantry beat a path forward into the
Carthaginian center, where Hannibal
had positioned himself. The opposing
heavy cavalry fought on the wing next
to the river, the Carthaginians under
Hasdrubal breaking through to the
Roman rear. On the other wing,
Hannibal's swift Numidian horsemen
chased the cavalry of Rome's Italian
allies from the battlefield.

The Romans still appeared to be
winning the battle in the center, but
as the legionaries pressed forward,
Hannibal ordered his Libyans to
turn inward and squeeze the now
disorganized Roman infantry from
the flanks. The legions were already
being crushed by this attack when
Hannibal's victorious cavalry charged
in from the rear, completing a double
envelopment. Few Romans escaped
the ensuing slaughter. Hannibal's
battleplan passed into history and
was admired by later commanders.

② On the left, Hasdrubal
routs the Roman cavalry,
then sweeps around the
rear of the Roman lines

⑥ The densely packed
Roman infantry is encircled
and slaughtered

⑤ Carthaginian infantry
advances to close the trap
around the Romans

PAULUS

VARRO

④ The cavalry
of the Roman
allies is driven
from the field

HASDRUBAL

MARHABAL

HANNIBAL

① Hannibal's infantry
adopts a crescent formation,
drawing the Roman infantry
into the center

③ In the center
Hannibal orders his
infantry to execute
a controlled retreat

Aufidus

Aufidus

Cannae

0 km   0.5   1
0 miles   0.5   1

KEY
Hannibal's infantry
Hannibal's cavalry
Hannibal's camp
Roman infantry
Roman cavalry
Roman camp

1500 BCE—500 CE

A medieval view of Cannae
This 15th-century manuscript illustration shows the combatants in medieval armor but gives a realistic impression of the closeness and brutality of the fighting.

ROME FROM REPUBLIC TO EMPIRE

DURING THE 1ST CENTURY BCE Rome completed the transition from a citizen militia to an army of career soldiers recruited from the Roman poor. It also changed from a Republic headed by elected officials into a state governed by an emperor, whose power rested ultimately upon the legions. This political transformation was brought about through an intermittent series of civil wars. The victor in the Roman power struggles looked to be Julius Caesar, until his rule was cut short by assassination in 44 BCE. It fell to his successor, Octavian, to found the imperial system as Emperor Augustus in 27 BCE.

MARIUS

ROMAN GENERAL
BORN 157 BCE
DIED 87 BCE
KEY CONFLICTS Jugurthine War, War against the Cimbri and Teutones, Social War
KEY BATTLES Aquae Sextae 102 BCE, Vercellae 101 BCE

Born into an obscure provincial family, Marius made his reputation in the war against the Numidian king, Jugurtha, in north Africa between 107 and 105 BCE. His renown was confirmed when he saved Rome from a barbarian invasion by the Cimbri and Teutones, with victories at Aquae Sextae and Vercellae. Marius was noted as a commander who shared the hardships of his troops on campaign. At Aquae Sextae he led his army into battle sword in hand—unusual for a Roman commander. He encouraged recruitment from the poor, stressing professional training, fitness, and endurance. His men were known as "Marius's mules" because of the great weight of their packs.

In the Social War (91–88 BCE) against Rome's rebellious Italian allies, Marius was eclipsed by the rising star Sulla. At the war's end Sulla and Marius, each backed by their loyal soldiers, fell into dispute over who should command a potentially lucrative campaign in Asia. Sulla seized military control of Rome, then left for Asia, after which Marius took the city with his army. He died soon after, but the power struggle between Sulla's allies and enemies continued.

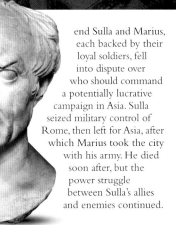

Disciplinarian
Marius brought rigor to the Roman army and campaigned relentlessly in defense of Rome.

POMPEY

ROMAN GENERAL
BORN 106 BCE
DIED 48 BCE
KEY CONFLICTS Spartacus's War, Third Mithridatic War, Roman Civil Wars
KEY BATTLES Dyrrachium 48 BCE, Pharsalus 48 BCE

Gnaeus Pompeius Magnus is known as Pompey the Great, a name that reflects his high ambition and superior military skills. Although from a rich family, Pompey displayed the dynamic opportunism of a self-made man. Sulla's return from Asia in 83 BCE reignited civil war with Marius's former supporters. Pompey raised an army at his own expense and led it vigorously in support of Sulla. With Sulla installed as dictator in Rome, Pompey's reward was to command first in Sicily and then in north Africa, suppressing opposition to the regime.

After Sulla's retirement in 80 BCE, Pompey remained an active supporter of the status quo against various revolts. For five years he campaigned in Spain, defeating the forces of the rebel general Sertorius. He returned to Italy in 71 BCE in time to take much of the credit for crushing Spartacus's slave revolt. Pompey was made consul alongside Crassus the following year and became a popular hero. He confirmed his reputation by clearing the Mediterranean of pirates in an organized, wide-ranging naval campaign in 67–66 BCE. This was followed by four years' campaigning in Asia. There he crushed Rome's long-term enemy, King Mithridates of Pontus, and took Jerusalem.

RISE AND FALL

Returning to Rome in 61 BCE, Pompey celebrated a spectacular triumph that marked the zenith of his fame. He then ceased campaigning, settling down to a commanding role in Roman politics as one of a triumvirate with the wealthy Crassus and junior partner Julius Caesar. The death of Crassus in 53 BCE and the rise of Caesar through his victories in Gaul set the scene for renewed civil war. When Caesar invaded Italy in 49 BCE, Pompey did not try to defend Rome, but withdrew across the Adriatic to Macedonia. There he unwisely gave battle at Pharsalus and was routed. He fled to Egypt but, as he landed, he was assassinated on the orders of Ptolemy, who feared Caesar's wrath if he gave refuge to the fleeing general.

Presentation to Caesar
After Pompey was assassinated in Egypt in 48 BCE, the perpetrators presented his severed head and his seal to Julius Caesar (shown here wearing Egyptian dress). In response, Caesar had the assassins executed.

AUGUSTUS

ROMAN EMPEROR

BORN September 23, 63 BCE

DIED August 19, 14 CE

KEY CONFLICTS Roman Civil Wars

KEY BATTLES Philippi 42 BCE, Actium 31 BCE

Known as Octavian in his youth, the Emperor Augustus was the adopted son of Julius Caesar. Only 19 years old when Caesar was killed in 44 BCE, Octavian was not expected to prove a major player in the ensuing power struggle. In 43 BCE, he formed the second triumvirate (an alliance of three men) with Marcus Aemilius Lepidus and Caesar's right-hand man, Mark Antony. His decision to join Antony in his campaign to avenge Caesar's death put him in a subordinate role. When the pair faced Caesar's assassins, Brutus and Cassius, at Philippi in 42 BCE, his military inexperience was only too evident. He escaped capture when his camp was overrun by Brutus, but put up a determined defense while Antony routed the enemy.

Over the following years, Octavian's ruthlessness and single-minded pursuit of power proved more crucial than his command skills, which could be supplied by deputies such as Agrippa.

Augustus in glory
The *Gemma Augustea*, a cameo carved for Augustus, shows him as Jupiter, with the god's emblematic eagle at his feet. On his right sits the goddess Roma.

> ❝
> ## THE TWO FAULTS THAT [AUGUSTUS] CONDEMNED MOST STRONGLY IN A MILITARY COMMANDER WERE HASTE AND RECKLESSNESS.
>
> **SUETONIUS**, *THE TWELVE CAESARS*, 121 CE
> ❞

Octavian's increasing rivalry with Antony culminated in a public quarrel in 33 BCE and the triumvirate ended the next year. His conduct of the civil war after Antony and Cleopatra's defeat at Actium and the annexation of Egypt in 30 BCE showed implacable willpower, organizational ability, and a clear grasp of overall strategy.

A NEW TITLE

In effect, this victory made Octavian sole ruler of the Roman empire, although republican forms were kept up. He was awarded the title Augustus, meaning "revered," in 27 BCE.

Augustus's throne had been won in war and rested on the support of the army. He turned the legions into permanent formations with a strong sense of identity, while ensuring they were mostly employed far from Rome and were well rewarded. Augustus's four decades of absolute rule brought expansion of the Roman empire and much fighting at the periphery, but he no longer campaigned in person. However, this did not stop him from taking credit for his legions' victories.

AGRIPPA

ROMAN GENERAL AND ADMIRAL

BORN C. 63 BCE

DIED 12 BCE

KEY CONFLICTS Roman Civil Wars

KEY BATTLES Naulochus 36 BCE, Actium 31 BCE

Marcus Vipsanius Agrippa was a close companion of Octavian (the future Emperor Augustus) from childhood. A more gifted combat commander than Octavian, Agrippa was his right-hand man during the wars that followed Caesar's death. He initially campaigned on land, but in 37 BCE the threat posed by Sextus Pompeius, youngest son of Pompey the Great, turned him into a naval commander.

A SUPERIOR FLEET

Based in Sicily, Sextus had control of the Roman fleet, which he used to blockade the Italian coast. Agrippa responded by turning Lake Avernus (near present-day Naples) into a naval base, linked to the sea by a canal. In this safe harbor he built a new fleet and trained crews in the use of heavy on-board artillery, including rock-throwing catapults and the *arpex*,

Thoughtful commander
Busts of Agrippa show a stern, resolute, and reflective commander. His loyalty to Octavian and his devotion to duty never wavered, and he adapted his battle skills to naval warfare with seeming ease.

which hurled a grappling iron. In 36 BCE, Octavian led an army to Sicily, backed by Agrippa's fleet. Sextus sent out his own fleet to give battle, but Agrippa outmaneuvered him and trapped him against the shore at Naulochus. Sextus's fleet was almost totally destroyed. Agrippa went on to command Octavian's ships in

the blockade of Antony and Cleopatra at Actium, winning a decisive victory. He continued to serve Augustus to the end of his life, fighting in campaigns that stretched across the far-reaching corners of the empire—against the Cantabrians in Spain, the Cimmerians in Crimea, and the Pannonians on the Danube.

KEY BATTLE
ACTIUM

CAMPAIGN Roman Civil War
DATE September 2, 31 BCE
LOCATION Ionian Sea, off Western Greece

The battle of Actium was the climax of the struggle between Mark Antony and Octavian for control of the Roman world. Forces commanded by Antony and the Egyptian queen, Cleopatra, were blockaded by Octavian on land and by Agrippa at sea. Running short of supplies, Antony led his fleet out of the harbor in an attempt to break through the blockade and forge a passage to Egypt, but Agrippa's nimble war galleys savaged Antony's larger quinqueremes. As

battle raged, Cleopatra was able to slip away to sea with her treasure-laden transport ships. Antony abandoned the battle to join her, leaving his warships to be harried into surrender. Octavian pursued the fugitives to Egypt, where both committed suicide.

Glorious Caesar
This 18th-century neoclassical statue of Caesar reflects his status at that time as an inspiration to European kings and generals. He is crowned with a laurel wreath, symbol of military triumph.

JULIUS CAESAR

ROMAN GENERAL AND DICTATOR
BORN July 13, 100 BCE
DIED March 15, 44 BCE
KEY CONFLICTS Gallic Wars, Roman Civil War
KEY BATTLES Alesia 52 BCE, Pharsalus 48 BCE, Zela 47 BCE, Thapsus 46 BCE

According to Caesar's biographer, Plutarch, the general was "the equal, as a soldier and a leader of men, of any commander that has ever been." Born into a patrician (elite) family in Rome, as a young man Caesar served with the Roman army in Asia, but he was not driven by purely military ambitions. He came to generalship as an essential element in a high-flying Roman political career. In 59 BCE, on the back of a successful governorship in Spain, Caesar was elected consul and persuaded by the two most powerful men in Rome, Pompey and Crassus, to join them in an unofficial triumvirate dominating Roman politics. The following year he was appointed proconsul responsible for territories that included Transalpine Gaul (roughly present-day France and Belgium). It was an appointment that promised glory and profit, an opportunity that Caesar grasped to the full.

A GROWING POWER

Rome ruled only the south of Gaul, protecting its interests through alliances with the Celtic tribes that controlled the rest. These tribes were often at war with one another and with Germanic tribes pressing from the east. It was a fluid situation that provided Caesar with pretexts for piecemeal military intervention that in time built up into a full-scale campaign of conquest.

In his first year as proconsul Caesar defeated the Helvetii, a tribe that was trying to migrate from Switzerland, and crushed Germanic forces led across the Rhine by the warrior-king Ariovistus. In the ensuing years Caesar extended his military operations ever wider, from the Atlantic to the

KEY BATTLE
PHARSALUS

CAMPAIGN Roman Civil War
DATE August 9, 48 BCE
LOCATION Thessaly, Greece

At Pharsalus Caesar defeated his great rival Pompey, despite being heavily outnumbered. He used his infantry against Pompey's cavalry, ordering them to thrust their spears into the horsemen's faces. This routed the cavalry and was followed by a vigorous and decisive infantry push that drove the Pompeians from the field.

Rhine. In 55 and 54 BCE he even sailed across the Channel in punitive raids on the Celtic tribes of Britain. These campaigns were his personal project—he had no mandate from Rome to wage aggressive war in Gaul. Part of his motivation was financial. The plunder enabled him to pay off his immense debts and to reward the loyalty of his legionaries. But Caesar also wanted to build a reputation as an outstanding general to bolster a future claim to political power, and he wrote eloquent memoirs of his campaigns. However, his victories were accompanied by massacres and enslavement—a deliberate use of terror to subdue resistance.

GALLIC DEFIANCE

The Gauls responded to the mounting threat to their independence with large-scale revolts. In the winter of 54–53 BCE an uprising of the Belgic tribes led to desperate fighting. Caesar then confronted the even larger revolt of an alliance led by the chieftain of the Averni tribe, Vercingetorix. With no real superiority over his Gallic enemies, Caesar required outstanding

HE TOOK OVER 800 CITIES AND TOWNS BY STORM, SUBDUED 300 TRIBES, AND KILLED A MILLION MEN.

PLUTARCH, *LIFE OF CAESAR,* 75 CE

Roman crested helmet
Caesar's legions would have worn helmets like this bronze replica, which has guards to protect the cheeks. Roman helmets had a horse-hair crest for decoration or to denote rank.

qualities to gain victory—speed of movement, calculated risk-taking, endurance, and the ability to motivate his men under pressure. After the siege of Alesia in 52 BCE, Gallic resistance was crushed.

By 49 BCE, when his extended 10-year proconsulship drew to an end, Caesar controlled Gaul as a celebrated commander of loyal, battle-hardened legions. He was in a strong position to claim high political office. But in Rome, Pompey, the only man to rival Caesar's reputation as a general, was plotting his downfall with the Senate's backing. When Caesar led troops across the Rubicon River, the border with Gaul, he was raising the standard of revolt.

FACING POMPEY

Pompey boasted that he could easily recruit enough legions to crush the intruder, but Caesar was aggressive and decisive. In a lightning two-month campaign he occupied the whole of Italy. Pompey withdrew across the Adriatic to Macedonia, where he could build up his forces

protected by a large fleet. It was an intelligent move that forced Caesar to take an outrageous risk to recover the momentum of his campaign. In January 48 BCE, he ferried part of his army across to Macedonia. He could not rely on supplying or reinforcing his men by sea against an enemy with naval superiority. Pinned down by six months of attritional warfare outside the port of Dyrrachium, Caesar's legions were weakened by intermittent fighting, food shortages, and disease. In July, Caesar succeeded

in disengaging to march off into northern Greece, but his situation looked desperate. Instead of maintaining a policy of attrition, however, Pompey allowed himself to be tempted into a decisive pitched battle at Pharsalus in Thessaly, where Caesar's superior generalship carried the day. Even Pompey's subsequent death in Egypt did not bring an end to either the civil war or Caesar's campaigning. Caesar fought in Egypt to aid Queen Cleopatra, who became his mistress, in her struggle to take the throne. He crushed Pharnaces, king of Pontus, at the battle of Zela, which gave rise to his famous boast: *"Veni, Vidi, Vici"* ("I came, I saw, I conquered"). In the north African expedition against the Pompeians in 46 BCE, a desperate struggle to establish an army on land ended in triumph at the battle of Thapsus. Caesar regarded his final victory over Pompey's son at Munda in Spain in 45 BCE as possibly the hardest-won of his career.

Assassination of Julius Caesar
Caesar was murdered on the Ides of March (March 15) in 44 BCE by a group of republican senators outraged by his adoption of the position of dictator-for-life. The assassination triggered a fresh round of civil wars.

COIN SHOWING CAPTURED GALLIC ARMS

TIMELINE

■ **80 BCE** Serving with the Roman army in Asia, Caesar is awarded the Civic Crown for bravery during the siege of Mytilene.

■ **c. 72 BCE** Caesar is elected as a military tribune and probably serves against Spartacus in the Slave War.

■ **61–60 BCE** Caesar is sent to govern part of Spain, where he carries out punitive actions against local tribes.

■ **59 BCE** Caesar is appointed consul, forming a political alliance of three men (the triumvirate), with Crassus and Pompey.

■ **58 BCE** Made proconsul of Gaul, Caesar defeats the Celtic Helvetii at Bibracte and the Germanic Ariovistus at the Vosges.

■ **57 BCE** Caesar defeats the Belgic Nervii tribe at the battle of the Sambre.

■ **55 BCE** Caesar bridges the Rhine for the first time. He also mounts an expedition across the English Channel to land in Kent.

■ **54 BCE** A second, larger-scale invasion of Britain reaches north of the Thames River, but fails to establish a permanent Roman presence.

■ **53 BCE** Crassus is killed at Carrhae while invading Parthia, terminating the triumvirate.

■ **52 BCE** Vercingetorix leads a rebellion of Gallic tribes; Caesar is checked at Gergovia but triumphs at the siege of Alesia.

■ **49 BCE** Caesar crosses the Rubicon into Italy, initiating a civil war against Pompey.

■ **48 BCE** Crossing the Adriatic, Caesar is worsted at Dyrrachium but crushes Pompey at the battle of Pharsalus. Caesar pursues Pompey to Egypt, where the latter is killed.

■ **47 BCE** Caesar secures the Egyptian throne for Cleopatra VII; he also defeats Pharnaces, king of Pontus, at the battle of Zela.

■ **46 BCE** A military expedition to Tunisia almost ends in disaster at Ruspina, but Caesar recovers to defeat Pompey's supporters at the battle of Thapsus.

■ **45 BCE** Caesar achieves his final victory over supporters of Pompey at Munda in Spain; he becomes dictator-for-life.

■ **44 BCE** Caesar is assassinated in Rome as he prepares to embark on a campaign against the Dacians and Parthians.

1500 BCE—500 CE

CAESAR: DARING TACTICIAN

> ## "He inspired an incredible loyalty and affection in his troops."

The Life of Caesar *(c. 110 CE)* **by Plutarch.**
The Greek historian contrasts Caesar with Alexander the Great in Parallel Lives.

BUST OF CAESAR, 27–20 BCE,
AFTER A CONTEMPORARY LIKENESS

Caesar crosses the Rubicon
When Caesar crossed the Rubicon in 49 BCE he committed treason. A law prohibited any general from traversing the stream with an army—to do so made war inevitable.

"It is a disputable point which was the more remarkable when he went to war: his caution or his daring… Sometimes he fought after careful tactical planning, sometimes on the spur of the moment— at the end of a march, often, or in miserable weather, when he would be least expected to make a move."

The Twelve Caesars (121 CE) by Suetonius opens with a biography of Julius Caesar that includes an analysis of his military strengths and weaknesses.

THE EXAMPLES THAT SUETONIUS offers of Caesar's caution include, in general, his use of reconnaissance to avoid falling into ambushes and, in particular, his careful gathering of information about British harbors before attempting his first crossing of the English Channel. To exemplify Caesar's daring, Suetonius tells how the general crossed enemy lines in disguise to join Roman troops in Germany besieged by tribal warriors.

THIS PASSAGE DESCRIBES the battle of the Sabis in which Caesar routed the Belgian Nervii tribe on the banks of the Sambre River in 57 BCE. While making camp, the legions were surprised and nearly overrun by tribal warriors attacking out of the forest. Caesar and his legion commanders rallied their men to fight in improvised formation around their standards. The Nervii were defeated with heavy losses. Caesar would not usually expect to find himself in the front line of a battle, but it was normal for him to be close behind, encouraging the troops by his presence and urging them to give their best.

"As the situation was critical and no reserves were available, Caesar snatched a shield from a soldier [and] made his way into the front line… His coming gave them fresh heart and hope; each man wanted to do his best under the eyes of the commander-in-chief, however desperate the peril."

Commentaries on the Gallic Wars (c. 50 BCE) by Julius Caesar. Caesar wrote his account of his campaigns in Gaul in the third person.

"If Caesar's troops gave ground he would often rally them single-handedly, catching individual fugitives by the throat and forcing them around to face the enemy again, even if they were panic-stricken."

A PHYSICAL CLASH BETWEEN a commander and a fleeing soldier was not surprising given Caesar's relationship with his troops. This was not a relationship distanced by formal hierarchy, as was the case in other military forces, but had the gritty intimacy of shared effort and hardship on campaign. Caesar impressed the legionaries with his physical endurance as well as his mental qualities. When they mutinied, as sometimes happened during the civil war, he faced them down in person. He always addressed his troops as "comrades," rather than as "soldiers," to emphasize his identification with these rough and rugged men.

The Twelve Caesars (121 CE) by Suetonius is possibly here referring to an incident during a clash at Ruspina in 46 BCE.

"Caesar was powerful in speech and action, audacious in every way."

The Civil Wars (c. 150 CE) by Appian. A Greek born in Alexandria, Egypt, Appian wrote extensively on Roman history.

1500 BCE–500 CE

JULIUS CAESAR VS. VERCINGETORIX

IN 52 BCE, **ROMAN PROCONSUL** Julius Caesar quashed a rebellion of tribes in Gaul led by Vercingetorix, a chieftain of the Arverni. A Roman attack on Vercingetorix's principal forces at the hill fort of Gergovia had ended in a sharp defeat for Caesar's army. But a subsequent attempt by Vercingetorix to harass the Romans on the march went desperately wrong. The discomfited Gauls sought safety on another unassailable hilltop at Alesia. The setback at Gergovia had taught Caesar not to risk a frontal assault again. Instead, as he himself recorded, he laid siege to Vercingetorix's army in order to starve the Gauls into submission.

JULIUS CAESAR

Caesar's legionaries excelled in the construction of field fortifications, but the scale of the work he required of them to enclose the hill at Alesia was exceptional. About 11 miles (18 km) of ditch and earth-and-timber ramparts were built, modified, and strengthened, under the general's instructions, to include turrets and booby traps such as concealed sharpened stakes.

Caesar ordered a second, outer line built to defend against a Gallic relief force launching a counterattack. This was even longer, at around 13 miles (21 km). Between the lines, Caesar accumulated supplies for his forces, in anticipation of his besiegers becoming the besieged.

STRONG LEADERSHIP

Once the Gallic relief force arrived, the combats were fought along both sides of the line and gave Caesar the chance to demonstrate his superb skills as a battlefield commander. The general and his legionaries had been placed on the defensive, and, yet, Caesar's approach was positive and aggressive at all times. Every attack from Vercingetorix's men was met with a savage counterattack.

As the conflict raged, Caesar would ride to a high point within the lines so that he could survey the progress of the fighting. He would spot where trouble was developing and direct his officers to lead reserves to strengthen those units that were under the greatest pressure.

SURPRISE ASSAULT

By his own account, at the climax of the battle on October 2, Caesar headed a counterattack in person. The general gathered a force of infantry and cavalry from a quiet sector of his siege line and led these troops to the decisive point in the combat, his distinctive scarlet cloak proclaiming his presence to friend and foe alike.

To coincide with his attack, Caesar ordered a second cavalry detachment to ride around the outer siege line and mount a surprise attack on the enemy's rear. The Gauls were put to the flight, suffering heavy losses under dogged Roman pursuit. The following day, Caesar accepted Vercingetorix's surrender.

Proud surrender
According to Plutarch, the defeated Vercingetorix emerged from Alesia "on horseback, wearing his most splendid armor and with his horse richly caparisoned." Julius Caesar accepted the surrender of the Gauls while seated in front of his camp.

CAESAR				
Caesar orders his men to begin construction of a fortified siege line around Alesia	Caesar begins construction of an outer ring of fortifications to defend against the probable return of Vercingetorix's cavalry with a Gallic relief force		Caesar places his infantry on the defensive and sends out his cavalry to conduct a successful spoiling attack on the Gallic relief force	

VERCINGETORIX	52 BCE			SEPT 28	SEPT 29	SEPT 30–OCT 1
	Vercingetorix positions his army outside the hill town of Alesia, fortifying his camp	Vercingetorix sends away his cavalry by night to escape the siege, finding their way through the incomplete Roman line	Vercingetorix executes a collective decision to remove women, children, and the elderly from the town	Vercingetorix observes the arrival of the Gallic relief force outside the Roman lines and places his men in forward positions, ready for a coordinated assault on the Roman defenses		**Night** The Gallic relief force launches an attack, but Vercingetorix is slow to join in engaging the Romans and the attack is repulsed

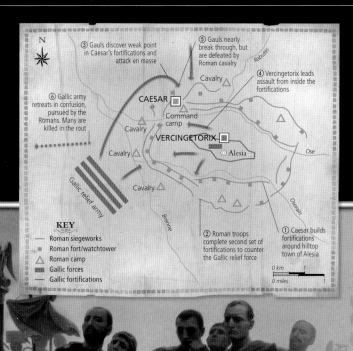

③ Gauls discover weak point in Caesar's fortifications and attack en masse

⑤ Gauls nearly break through, but are defeated by Roman cavalry

④ Vercingetorix leads assault from inside the fortifications

⑥ Gallic army retreats in confusion, pursued by the Romans. Many are killed in the rout

CAESAR

Command camp

Cavalry

VERCINGETORIX

Cavalry

Cavalry

Ⓐ Alesia

Cavalry

Gallic relief army

Rabutin

Ose

Oserain

Brenne

KEY
- — Roman siegeworks
- ■ Roman fort/watchtower
- △ Roman camp
- ■ Gallic forces
- • Gallic fortifications

② Roman troops complete second set of fortifications to counter the Gallic relief force

① Caesar builds fortifications around hilltop town of Alesia

0 km   1
0 miles   1

LOCATION
Near Dijon, east-central France
CAMPAIGN Julius Caesar's Gallic Wars
DATE July–October 52 BCE
FORCES Romans: 45,000; Gauls: unknown
CASUALTIES No reliable estimates

VERCINGETORIX

Vercingetorix at first used his cavalry to harass the Romans as they built their siege line, but in clashes with Caesar's horsemen the Gauls came off much the worse. The chieftain then dispatched his mounted warriors to slip through the enemy line and ride to their various tribes to seek help.

The waiting period that followed was desperate, with food supplies dwindling rapidly, while the Roman fortifications became ever stronger. The eventual appearance of a relief army outside the siege lines stimulated Vercingetorix to fresh efforts, however, and he prepared his men for an assault on the Roman fortifications by making ladders and grappling hooks. But the besieged Gauls had no effective means of communicating with their relief force commanders. When warriors outside the fortifications mounted a night attack, Vercingetorix's men inside the siege lines were as taken by surprise as the Romans.

TOO LITTLE, TOO LATE
The Gauls' major effort came on October 2. As the relief force massed against the weakest point in the Roman defenses—a poorly sited camp—Vercingetorix dispersed his men cleverly to overstretch the defenders by pressing at many points along the inner line. But even when they penetrated the fortifications, the Gauls could not hold on to their gains. The rout of the relief force left Vercingetorix no option but to surrender the next day.

> **I DID NOT UNDERTAKE THE WAR FOR PRIVATE ENDS, BUT IN THE CAUSE OF SHARED LIBERTY.**
>
> VERCINGETORIX, QUOTED IN BOOK VII OF CAESAR'S *COMMENTARIES ON THE GALLIC WARS*, C. 50 BCE

Caesar orders his officer Labienus to reinforce the sector under attack from the relief force. He tours his inner defensive positions, urging the men to resist Vercingetorix's onslaught

Caesar first sends subordinates to repel Vercingetorix's incursion and then leads reinforcements there in person. The Gauls are driven back

Caesar directs a counterattack against the Gallic relief force. After fierce fighting, the relief force is repulsed with heavy losses

Caesar orders his cavalry to mount a pursuit of the fleeing remnants of the relief force

OCT 2   OCT 3

12 Noon The relief force attacks a weak point in the Roman line. Vercingetorix orders his men to sortie en masse to engage the Romans

Vercingetorix changes his point of attack, concentrating on lightly held sectors protected by steep slopes. His men penetrate the Roman defensive lines

Seeing the relief force defeated, Vercingetorix pulls his men back into the town

Vercingetorix rides down from Alesia to surrender

Emperor in action
Trajan's Column was built in 113 CE to celebrate the emperor's conquest of Dacia. Sculpted scenes show Trajan leading troops and supervising legionaries and auxiliaries.

FROM ZENITH TO DECLINE

THE ROMAN EMPIRE REACHED its territorial limits during the 1st and 2nd centuries CE, with the Roman army showing ruthless professionalism in the suppression of revolt and the expansion of frontiers. But the military forces also intervened in Roman political life, and from the 3rd century, the empire was racked by civil wars between ambitious individuals with a following among the legions. To defend the far-flung borders, it became necessary to sacrifice unity and divide rule between two or more emperors. The absorption of "barbarian" Germanic tribes into Roman forces postponed the fall, but by 476, the empire in the west was at an end.

TITUS

ROMAN GENERAL AND EMPEROR
BORN December 30, 39 CE
DIED September 13, 81 CE
KEY CONFLICTS Roman Civil War, Jewish Revolt
KEY BATTLE Siege of Jerusalem 70 CE

The capture of Jerusalem
This 15th-century Flemish portrayal of Titus's taking of Jerusalem shows the Romans as armored knights terrorizing the local people.

Titus Flavius Vespasianus saw military service in both Germany and Britain. At age 27, he accompanied his father, the General Vespasian, to suppress a revolt in the Roman province of Judaea. When Emperor Nero died in 68 CE, there was a brief civil war, from which Vespasian emerged victorious. He was declared emperor in 69.

With his father now ruler, Titus was left to pacify Judaea alone. At the head of four legions, he laid siege to Jerusalem, employing classic Roman tactics. He rode forward in person to reconnoitre the walls, led reserves to counter sorties by the defenders, and terrorized his opponents by crucifying prisoners within sight of the beleaguered city. When it fell, Titus ordered wholesale destruction of the city and slaughtered the population.

After Jerusalem, Titus was granted a triumph in Rome and an arch was erected in his honor. Titus briefly succeeded his father as emperor before his early death at age 42.

TRAJAN

ROMAN EMPEROR
BORN September 18, 53 CE
DIED August 8, 117 CE
KEY CONFLICTS Dacian Wars, Parthian Campaign
KEY BATTLES Sarmizegetusa 106 CE, Ctesiphon 116 CE

Although Trajan was born in Spain, his father became a Roman senator and he was brought up as part of the Roman ruling elite. He showed an early aptitude for the military life and distinguished himself as a legion commander campaigning on the Danube. His reputation as a general led the army to support his adoption as heir to the imperial throne, which fell to him in 98 CE on the death of Emperor Nerva. Between 101 and 106 Trajan carried out two major campaigns in Dacia, an area east of the Danube ruled by the warlike Decebalus.

The first campaign inflicted sharp punishment on the Dacians, who sued for peace. But Decebalus broke the peace terms and on the second campaign Trajan achieved the total conquest of Dacia—including its capital, Sarmizegetusa— the death of its leaders, and the enslavement or massacre of its population.

WAR MEMORIAL
Trajan's Column was erected in Rome to commemorate his victory over the Dacians. The monument's scenes depict him accompanying the legions, drawing up plans with his senior officers, supervising engineering works such as bridge-building, directing sieges, conducting religious ceremonies, rewarding soldiers for bravery, and accepting the severed heads of his foe laid at his feet in tribute. Roman historian Cassius Dio emphasizes that "he always marched on foot with the rank and file of the army… and he forded all the rivers that they did." Trajan returned to active campaigning late in life, heading east to lead a large-scale invasion of Parthia in 114 CE. He first annexed Armenia and pushed farther, taking the Parthian capital, Ctesiphon, and occupying the area in 116–17 CE. The occupation did not last, as Trajan faced a series of revolts in Parthia and internally. He died of natural causes at Cilicia, returning from the campaign, having extended Roman power to its limits.

Strengthening the empire
Trajan's effect on the empire's infrastructure was total. He realized a vast building program in Rome and the provinces, creating new roads, bridges, and aqueducts.

Enemy weapon
Trajan's enemies would have favored double-edged, ring-pommeled daggers like this Sarmatian weapon. The wooden scabbard has oxidized, but the decorative gold mountings and semiprecious stones have survived.

JULIAN

ROMAN EMPEROR
BORN c. 332
DIED June 26, 363
KEY CONFLICTS Defense of the Rhine, Invasion of Persia
KEY BATTLES Argentoratum 357, Ctesiphon 363

By the 4th century CE, the Roman empire could only be governed and defended by dividing imperial power between several emperors, each with regional responsibilities. Flavius Claudius Julianus, a fresh young scion of the reigning imperial family, was declared Caesar (junior emperor) in Gaul in 355.

Julian faced an emergency on the Rhine frontier, where Germanic tribes, the Alamanni, were raiding deep into Roman territory. During 356–359, he led a series of punitive expeditions against them. When the Alamannic king, Chnodomarius, confronted him with a large army

Pagan ruler
Emperor Julian is known as the Apostate because during his short reign he sought to de-Christianize the Roman Empire, reversing Emperor Constantine's religious policy.

of confederate tribes at Argentoratum (present-day Strasbourg) in 357, he carried off a hard-won victory against the numerical odds.

Julian was proclaimed Augustus (senior emperor) in 360 by his men, who lifted him up on their shields. Fortunately, the ruling emperor, Constantius, died before Julian was obliged to uphold his claim by civil war. Sole ruler of the empire, in 363 he launched a campaign against the Sasanian Shapur II, invading Persia with an army of over 80,000 and advancing to the capital, Ctesiphon. He was forced to withdraw and was killed fighting off enemy skirmishers.

STILICHO

ROMAN GENERAL
BORN c. 358
DIED August 22, 408
KEY CONFLICTS Roman Civil War, Roman-Visigothic War
KEY BATTLES Frigidus 394, Pollentia 402

Flavius Stilicho rose to prominence under Emperor Theodosius I, ruler of the eastern half of the Roman Empire. Stilicho's father was a Vandal (of Germanic descent), but Stilicho himself was thoroughly Romanized and made a prominent place for himself at Theodosius's court in

emerged as military commander of the western empire, dominating the ineffectual Honorius. The rest of Stilicho's life was a desperate struggle to halt the breakdown of the empire.

Stilicho's bitterest enemy was the Visigoth warlord Alaric. The Visigoths, a Germanic tribe, had fought with Stilicho as allies of Theodosius at Frigidus, but after the battle Alaric turned to plundering the empire rather than serving it. Stilicho led an army into Thrace to confront the Visigoths and defeated them in Macedonia in 397. Four years later,

> ## THE PRUDENCE AND VIGOR OF STILICHO WERE CONSPICUOUS, [REVEALING] AT THE SAME TIME THE WEAKNESS OF THE FALLING EMPIRE.
>
> **EDWARD GIBBON**, *THE DECLINE AND FALL OF THE ROMAN EMPIRE*, 18TH CENTURY

Constantinople, even marrying into the imperial family. His role as a military commander dated from 392. That same year Arbogast, the Frankish general in charge of the imperial forces in the western empire, placed his own candidate on the throne in Rome. Stilicho organized and trained an army for Theodosius, who led the force to Italy in 394, defeating Arbogast at the battle of Frigidus.

BARBARIAN INVASION

The victory at Frigidus allowed Theodosius to reunite the eastern and western halves of the empire, although they were again divided between his sons, Arcadius and Honorius, on his death the following year. Stilicho, who had performed well at the battle,

allied with the Ostrogoths under their leader Radagaisus, Alaric invaded Italy. Stilicho gathered an army in Gaul and in spring 402 led it across the Alps to attack the two tribes, who had placed Emperor Honorius under siege. At Pollentia Stilicho was victorious, driving Alaric out of Italy.

But Stilicho was powerless to stop the tribal invasions and military revolts that swept through the western empire from 406. He was deposed by his enemies, and in 408 captured by Honorius and executed. Two years later, Alaric's Visigoths sacked Rome.

Stilicho the soldier
This resin replica carving may depict Stilicho. He holds the traditional arms of a Roman soldier of the late empire—a spear and an oval shield.

TRIBAL WARRIORS

THE INHABITANTS OF NORTHWESTERN Europe encountered the Romans as ruthless conquerors, expanding through Gaul to Britain by 43 CE. The Celts and Germans were warlike peoples and they produced leaders capable of taking on the Romans, who were by no means always victorious.

Resistance mostly failed not because of military inferiority but because of disunity—Celtic or Germanic warriors were as likely to fight for the Romans as against them. By the 5th century CE, swamped by tribal migrations from the east, Rome's western empire had become a bloated target to be preyed on rather than a dominant force to be feared.

VERCINGETORIX

GALLIC TRIBAL CHIEF
BORN C. 82 BCE
DIED 46 BCE
KEY CONFLICTS Gallic Revolt
KEY BATTLES Gergovia 52 BCE, Alesia 52 BCE

The Arverni, a powerful tribe in what is now France's Auvergne region, initially cooperated with Roman general Julius Caesar in his various campaigns in Gaul. Vercingetorix, a junior member of the Arverni elite, may have fought as an ally of the Romans against Germanic warriors in 58 BCE. But over succeeding years Vercingetorix came to be alienated by the massacres and enslavement imposed by Caesar on the tribes of Gaul. His strident agitation for resistance to Rome brought him into

conflict with the cautious Arverni tribal leaders, who expelled him from their key town, Gergovia, to avoid angering the Romans. Vercingetorix amassed a band of followers, returned to Gergovia and seized control.

During the winter of 53–52 BCE, Vercingetorix's call for rebellion was heeded by most tribes across central and western Gaul, and by a mixture of force and persuasion he won the command of an intertribal rebel army. Vercingetorix called for guerrilla warfare, denying the Romans supplies by harassing foragers and destroying crops and food stores. Although this strategy was broadly accepted, the Gauls felt they could not leave their key towns. Against his advice, Avaricum, the main city of the Bituriges, was

Gallic metalwork
Found at the site of the ancient Gallic town of Alesia, this bronze helmet might have been worn by one of Vercingetorix's warriors. The Gauls were expert at metalworking.

defended; the Romans captured it after a siege and massacred its inhabitants. Vercingetorix himself felt bound to stand and fight when the Romans threatened Gergovia, and here Caesar suffered a rare defeat. Vercingetorix showed unusual control over his forces, preventing them from pursuing the fleeing legionaries and exposing themselves to a counterattack.

A COSTLY ERROR

After this success, Vercingetorix made a serious error of judgment. Thinking Caesar was leaving, he led his army out to harass the Romans. Caesar then threatened Vercingetorix, who was forced to take up a defensive position on another hilltop, at Alesia. Defeated after an epic siege, Vercingetorix surrendered. He was held prisoner in Rome and exhibited in chains in Caesar's triumph of 46 BCE, after which he was strangled.

Patriotic monument
In the 19th century Arminius came to be celebrated as a German national hero, his statue appearing on the Hermannsdenkmal monument erected in the Teutoburg forest.

ARMINIUS

GERMANIC TRIBAL CHIEF
BORN C. 18 BCE
DIED 21 CE
KEY CONFLICTS Roman-Germanic War
KEY BATTLES Teutoburg Forest 9 CE, River Weser 16 CE

During the reign of Emperor Augustus much of Germany east of the Rhine seemed in the process of absorption into the Roman Empire. Arminius, a chieftain of the Cherusci tribe, was prominent among the Germans collaborating with the Roman army, as a trusted leader of local auxiliaries accompanying the legions. But like many Germanic people, Arminius was in truth hostile

to the Roman intruders, and he plotted with other tribal leaders to rebel against the Roman presence.

In the summer of 9 CE, Roman legate Quinctilius Varus led his forces, including Arminius's auxiliaries, on campaign in central Germany. A tribal enemy revealed Arminius's intended treachery, but Varus did not believe him. As the Romans, numbering some 10,000, marched toward their winter quarters through the mountainous Teutoburg forest, Arminius deserted with his warriors.

He returned, strengthened by allies, to ambush Varus among the trees and annihilate the legionaries. Five years later, a Roman army found gruesome evidence of this—heaps of bones and human skulls nailed to trees.

According to the historian Tacitus, the Romans reacted at once to this humiliation. Between 14 and 17 CE, Germanicus, nephew of Emperor Tiberius, pursued Arminius to seek revenge, defeating the Cherusci chief at Idistaviso on the Weser River. Nevertheless, the Romans abandoned efforts to expand beyond the Rhine. Arminius survived only to be later assassinated by tribal opposition.

> ## THREE LEGIONS WITH THEIR GENERAL AND OFFICERS AND AUXILIARIES WERE MASSACRED TO A MAN.
>
> **SUETONIUS** ON THE TEUTOBURG FOREST DISASTER, *THE TWELVE CAESARS*, 121 CE

BOUDICCA

CELTIC TRIBAL LEADER
BORN Unknown
DIED c. 61 CE
KEY CONFLICTS Revolt of the Iceni
KEY BATTLES Camulodunum (Colchester) c. 60 CE, Watling Street c. 61 CE

Queen of the Iceni, a tribe in eastern England, Boudicca was mistreated by the Roman authorities after the death of her husband, Prasutagus. She raised a revolt in which the Iceni were joined by their neighbors, the Trinovantes. The rebels crushed a detachment of the Ninth Legion and burned the Roman cities of Colchester, St. Albans, and London, massacring their populations. The Roman governor of Britain, Suetonius Paulinus, hastened back from campaigning in Wales to confront Boudicca. His efficient legion infantry destroyed the tribal army. Boudicca survived the battle but committed suicide soon after.

Boudicca's chariot in London
The Celtic Britons used chariots to move warriors around the battlefield but did not, as legend suggests, have scythes on their wheels.

ATTILA THE HUN

EMPEROR OF THE HUNS
BORN 406 CE
DIED 453 CE
KEY CONFLICTS Invasions of the Balkans, Italy, and Gaul
KEY BATTLES Châlons 451 CE

In 434 CE, the Huns, Asiatic nomads who had migrated into territory along the Danubian frontier of the Roman Empire, came under the leadership of the charismatic Attila. A ferocious warrior described by his enemies as "keen of judgment," Attila at first accepted tribute payments from the Romans and campaigned only in regions farther east. However, the wealth of Roman lands eventually proved too tempting. In 441–3 and 447, Attila rampaged through the Balkans and threatened Constantinople. Four years later, he switched his attention to Gaul.

With his fast-moving force of Hun horsemen augmented by Ostrogoths and other Germanic tribesmen, Attila swept away all before him, laying waste to towns

Papal triumph
According to Christian legend, Attila's Hunnic hordes were turned back at the Mincius River in northern Italy by Pope Leo I armed only with the Cross.

and cities. Only his shock defeat at Châlons prevented Gaul from being overrun. During 452, he struck into northern Italy; Rome lay defenseless before him. Reportedly, Pope Leo I rode out to parley with Attila and persuaded him to withdraw. But the spread of plague and famine in Italy threatened to destroy the Hunnic army more certainly than any battle. Attila withdrew never to return, dying the following year in a drunken stupor. However, he left behind him a terrifying reputation for savagery, summed up in the informal title, "Scourge of all lands."

KEY BATTLE
CHÂLONS

CAMPAIGN Hunnic invasions
DATE 451 CE
LOCATION Northeastern France

During Attila's invasion of Gaul he besieged Orléans. An army led by Roman general Aetius, consisting largely of Franks and Alans, and of Visigoths under their king, Theodoric, interrupted the siege. Attila withdrew to the Catalaunian Plains, near Châlons-en-Champagne, where he gave battle. Theodoric was killed, but the Visigoths fought with ferocity, driving back the Huns to their wagons. Aetius held off from a costly final assault so Attila survived, but he had suffered a serious reverse.

1500 BCE–500 CE

350 BCE—400 CE

ANCIENT ASIA

❝ THERE WERE IN HIS ARMY HEROES BEARING ARMOR, WITH
DIVERSE BANNERS AND CHARIOTS... AND THE CREATURES OF
THE EARTH FELT OPPRESSED AND THE EARTH TREMBLED
UNDER THE TREAD OF HIS TROOPS. ❞

THE *MAHABHARATA* EPIC, DESCRIBING THE ARMY OF SALYA, KING OF MADRA, 400 BCE–200 CE

Infantry on the march
The battle of Kurukshatra is the central episode of the ancient Hindu epic the *Mahabharata*. This scene, showing helmeted infantry armed with arrows, is from a temple at Angkor Wat in Cambodia.

TWO MAJOR STREAMS FED into the military tradition of ancient Asia: the nomadic tribes of the steppe were the world's most accomplished warriors on horseback, while the settled civilizations—China, northern India, and Iran—at times achieved high levels of organization and technology. Sophisticated principles of tactics and strategy evolved through centuries of continuous warfare, often blending the tricks and stratagems of the steppe horseman with "civilized" concerns such as provision of logistical support and the conduct of sieges.

Much of the warfare in ancient China resulted from the tendency of central authority to disintegrate for long periods of time. During the Warring States Period (475–221 BCE) and the Three Kingdoms Period (184–280 CE), the large armies of rival Chinese states fought for supremacy within the country. The Qin and Han dynasties saw eras of greater unity but even these were not necessarily times of peace. China was always threatened by incursions of nomadic horsemen from the north and east, defending its land frontier by building the famous Great Wall, which began as a series of earthen fortifications in the Warring States Period.

At their strongest, Chinese rulers were tempted into foreign campaigns to extend the borders of their empire; Han generals of the 1st century CE penetrated as far south as Vietnam and as far west as the Persian Gulf. Chinese commanders fielded vast peasant infantry forces equipped with crossbows and spears, and learned from the steppe nomads the use of cavalry. Generals of the Three Kingdoms Period, such as Cao Cao and Zhuge Liang, became legendary figures whose tactical stratagems were endlessly studied and discussed. During the Warring States Period *The Art of War*, a treatise on strategy and tactics by philospher Sun-tzu, also held an important place in Chinese Taoist culture and is still regarded as a military classic today.

EPICS AND ELEPHANTS

India never developed a tradition of military operations on the scale of China, although battles were central to the country's enduring myths and legends, such as the *Mahabharata* epic poem. The unique Indian contribution to the development of warfare was the taming of elephants for use as heavy chargers, weapons platforms, and mobile command posts. States such as the Maurya Empire, which dominated much of the Indian subcontinent from the 4th to the 2nd century BCE, and the later Gupta Empire (320–550 CE) had sophisticated armed forces. But India was always liable to disruption by waves of invasion from the north, whether by Macedonians and Greeks or by nomadic Scythians and White Huns.

CAVALRY EMPIRES

As the center of military power from the time of the Achaemenid Persian Empire, Iran was heavily influenced by the central Asian nomadic tradition of warfare. Its armies tended to rely on cavalry armed primarily with bows serving as their shock troops.

The Parthian Arsacid dynasty ruled Iran for more than four centuries, from 247 BCE. It extended its rule over a vast area that included Mesopotamia and parts of central Asia. The Parthians were constantly at war, subduing various vassal states and resisting the pressure of infantry-based Roman armies along their western borders with considerable success. The Sasanians displaced them in 224 CE. Fighting Rome and its successor, Byzantium, in the west and campaigning deep into central Asia, the Sasanians ruled until 651 when the rise of Islam ushered in a new era in western and central Asia.

Han dynasty weapon
This bronze spearhead from Han dynasty China (206 BCE–220 CE) is decorated in a macabre fashion—figures of captives dangle from the spearhead.

ANCIENT ASIAN GENERALS

AMONG THE MANY INTERESTING commanders of ancient China, Qin Shi Huangdi stands out for the scale of his achievement in uniting the country, after many centuries of civil war, under the rule of a single individual and a centralized bureaucracy. Many Sasanian rulers in Persia were successful war leaders, and Shapur I, who reigned from 241 to 272 CE, was notable as the founder of the dynastic empire. Yet none could claim to equal the scope of the campaigns conducted by Shapur II. In Indian history, the great Maurya emperors have a special place as conquerors of exceptional moral and spiritual distinction.

QIN SHI HUANGDI

CHINESE EMPEROR
BORN 259 BCE
DIED 210 BCE
KEY CONFLICTS Wars of Unification, Campaigns Against the Xiongnu
KEY BATTLE Conquest of Chu 225 BCE

Ying Zheng inherited the throne of Qin, one of the kingdoms that had been vying for power in China for more than two centuries. Exhibiting remarkable organizational ability, he improved the recruitment, training, discipline, and equipment of the Qin army, turning it into a vehicle for his drive to conquest. In just 10 years, from 230 to 221 BCE, he defeated all six rival states—Han, Zhao, Yan, Wei, Chu, and Qi. The conquest of Chu was the largest military operation, involving hundreds of thousands of men. Unifying China under his rule, Zheng declared himself the First Emperor as Qin Shi Huangdi.

A centralized administration and the concentration of military force in the imperial army allowed the emperor to pacify China, but his general, Meng Tian, conducted campaigns against the Xiongnu nomads on the northern frontier and supervised work on the Great Wall to shut out the steppe horsemen. The emperor's death was followed by a brief period of civil strife before the Han dynasty was founded in 202 BCE.

Lasting reputation
Despite having ruled as emperor for just 10 years, Qin Shi Huangdi remains one of the most significant figures in China's history.

BIOGRAPHY

SUN-TZU

The Art of War is the most famous ancient treatise on strategy and tactics. It may have been written by Sun-tzu around the 5th century BCE, during China's Warring States Period. Nothing is known of Sun-tzu's life, but his writings suggest a personal knowledge of command in war. His precepts call for a subtle indirect strategy designed "to break the enemy's resistance without fighting." He advises that the correct use of deception, espionage, and disinformation will allow an army to "avoid strength and strike weakness." Further, a commander should be "serene and inscrutable," not only exercising leadership through his moral and spiritual qualities, but also through more practical skills, such as ensuring that his soldiers are well cared for and are appropriately rewarded for their efforts.

Terra-cotta Army
Emperor Qin Shi Huangdi's vast mausoleum houses an army of thousands of terra-cotta figures, which give a detailed impression of the forces he must have commanded in life.

SHAPUR II

PERSIAN SASANIAN EMPEROR
BORN 309 CE
DIED 379 CE
KEY CONFLICT Roman-Persian Wars
KEY BATTLE Ctesiphon 363 CE

Sasanian ruler of Persia, Shapur II was crowned while still in his mother's womb. Thus, he ruled from birth to death, a period of 70 years. He inherited a crumbling empire that was suffering incursions from Arabs and central Asian nomads and had lost much of Mesopotamia to the Romans.

On coming of age, he first led an army on a punitive expedition into Arabia and then struck eastward into Transoxiana and Afghanistan. With threats from these directions quelled, in 337, he ended a 40-year peace with Rome, occupied Armenia, and marched against Rome's Mesopotamian

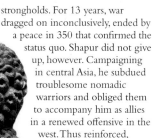

> ## HE TEMPERED THE GREATNESS OF HIS SUCCESS WITH HUMANITY AND COURTESY.
>
> **AMMIANUS MARCELLINUS**, ON SHAPUR II IN *ROMAN HISTORY*, 4TH CENTURY CE

strongholds. For 13 years, war dragged on inconclusively, ended by a peace in 350 that confirmed the status quo. Shapur did not give up, however. Campaigning in central Asia, he subdued troublesome nomadic warriors and obliged them to accompany him as allies in a renewed offensive in the west. Thus reinforced,

Royal regalia
A bust possibly representing Shapur II, excavated at Kish, shows the elaborate regalia of the Sasanian kings, including the typically crenellated crown.

Shapur was more successful, capturing the Roman fortress of Amida (Diyarbakir) on the Tigris River after a siege of 73 days.

Emperor Julian counterattacked in 360, leading an army as far as the walls of the Sasanian capital Ctesiphon. But Shapur kept his nerve and instituted a scorched-earth policy, harassing the Romans mercilessly. Julian was killed in a skirmish and Shapur was able to demand all territory east of the Tigris in return for allowing the surviving Romans safe passage home. For the rest of his reign, Shapur campaigned in central Asia, especially against the Kushans. By the time of his death in 379, the Sasanian Empire stretched from northern India to Mesopotamia.

CHANDRAGUPTA MAURYA

FOUNDER OF THE INDIAN MAURYA EMPIRE
BORN c. 340 BCE
DIED 290 BCE
KEY CONFLICTS Nanda War, Seleucid War
KEY BATTLE Siege of Pataliputra c. 310 BCE

Around 321 BCE, Chandragupta Maurya established himself as the ruler of the Indian kingdom of Magadha, supplanting the long-established and powerful Nanda dynasty. Although little historical evidence has survived of this conflict, it appears that Chandragupta took inspiration from Alexander the Great, whom he may even have met. His campaign against the Nanda was probably fought using popular guerrilla tactics. His forces drew a noose gradually tighter around the Magadha capital, Pataliputra (now Patna), until the overwhelmingly superior Nanda army was defeated.

EXCELLENT MORALE

Once in possession of the resources of a kingdom, Chandragupta seems to have used them to create a highly organized regular army, plentifully supplied with weaponry, chariots, war elephants, and horses. A Greek envoy to India, Megasthenes, was impressed by the high morale of Chandragupta's soldiers, whom he described as "of good cheer," a state

of mind perhaps sustained by the high wages that they were paid in peace as in war. Although Magadha was in northeastern India, roughly in the area of modern-day Bihar and Bengal, Chandragupta extended his rule far to the west and south. He fought a war against Seleucus Nicator, Alexander's former general, who ruled the northwest of the Indian subcontinent, taking from him an area stretching from Punjab and Kashmir north into Kandahar and Baluchistan. In later years, he led his armies south into the Deccan.

Chandragupta's armed strength can be gauged from his gift of 500 elephants to Seleucus to seal their peace agreement in 303 BCE—an astonishing number of valuable animals for a ruler to feel able to spare. In old age, Chandragupta abdicated in favor of his son, Bindusara, bequeathing the most extensive empire seen in India up to that date.

ASHOKA

INDIAN MAURYA EMPEROR
BORN 304 BCE
DIED 232 BCE
KEY CONFLICT Kalinga War
KEY BATTLE Kalinga c. 263 BCE

The grandson of Chandragupta Maurya, Ashoka was the ruler who expanded the Maurya Empire to its greatest extent through military conquest. He is best known, however, as a military leader who regretted the practice of war. He made his views clear during a campaign against Kalinga, a state in eastern India. After a battle fought near the Daya River in around 263 BCE, an inscription records that 150,000 Kalingans were deported and about 100,000 killed. Even if these figures are exaggerated, there was clearly savage slaughter. Ashoka's inscription expressed revulsion at the suffering caused through "violence, murder, and separation from their loved ones." In a reign that lasted 40 years, he does not seem to have disbanded his army or renounced the use of war. But his concern for defeated enemies became an official morality, making him unique among Asian rulers of the ancient world.

Ashoka pillar
These lions were carved to top the Ashoka pillar, which records a visit by the Maurya emperor to the sacred Buddhist site of Sarnath, near Varanasi in India.

2
500—1450

KNIGHTS
AND NOMADS

THE WARRIOR ETHOS, THE BELIEF THAT WARFARE was the rightful occupation of a man, flourished in the period known in European history as the Middle Ages. Members of ruling elites—kings, princes, and the hereditary aristocracy— were destined from birth to command in war. Armed conflicts proliferated and military adventures, from the crusades of Christian Europe waged by knights to the conquests of nomadic Mongol horsemen, gave scope to the energies of gifted leaders.

Between 500 and 1450, cultures of great diversity flourished in different parts of the world. From the Maya civilization in central America to the Ming Empire in China, from the Vikings of Scandinavia to the samurai of Japan, styles of warfare were as varied as their practitioners. Broadly, though, most states had difficulty attaining the levels of military organization that had been achieved by empires in the ancient world. Armies were smaller and often temporary. In western Europe rulers who could not afford standing armies depended on regional lords, who had a sworn obligation to provide troops when required to form a royal army. The elite of these troops were knights whose duty was to serve their lord and fight on his behalf.

There were no fundamental technological breakthroughs to distinguish warfare in this period from the ancient world. The military textbook written by Vegetius in the late Roman Empire, *De Re Militari*, continued to serve as an instruction manual for European commanders throughout medieval times, offering advice on subjects ranging from the laying of ambushes and

conduct of sieges to the choice of a good site for a battle—with due attention paid to terrain, the position of the Sun, and the direction of the wind. Commanders in all societies, however, mostly learned their skills on the job, seeing more or less constant military activity from an early age in a world where, for men of their status, campaigns were often a routine annual feature of life.

TACTICS AND WEAPONRY

Mounted warriors tended to dominate medieval warfare, whether they were heavily armored European knights or more lightly equipped Mongol horsemen armed with bows. Widespread insecurity

The trebuchet
This medieval siege engine was used for slinging projectiles at, or over, enemy castle walls. Weighing as much as 350 lb (140 kg), it wrought much havoc.

led to a heavy concentration of resources on building fortifications. Castles and town walls evolved into highly complex stone structures that could only be attacked with an elaborate array of siege engines, such as catapults and movable towers.

Both swords and armor improved through progress in metalworking. By the late Middle Ages, the suits of armor worn by European knights offered an impressive combination of protection and mobility. Crossbows and longbows increased in effectiveness, while incendiary devices and various weapons using gunpowder came into use. Under skillful commanders, the combination of foot soldiers with cavalry and the intelligent deployment of missile weapons produced battlefield tactics with a measure of genuine originality.

COMMUNICATIONS

In terms of command and control, however, technology had little or no progress to offer. Communications on and off the battlefield remained primitive, and may have declined in places because of a fall in the level of literacy that reduced the use of written messages. Orders were conveyed by a man

on horseback or on foot; banners or musical instruments transmitted simple, prearranged signals. Command was only possible because armies were small. Maintaining supplies of food, fodder, and water tested a commander operating in unfavorable terrain or with an army too large to live off the land.

CAMPAIGNS OF CONQUEST

Campaigning involved leading troops across unmapped landscapes into encounters with enemies whose position and strength were mostly unknown. Yet great feats of conquest were achieved and campaigns of some complexity sustained over long distances.

The explosion of Arab armies across Asia and north Africa and into southern Europe in the 7th and 8th centuries, inspired by the new militant faith of Islam, was a remarkable exercise in the reshaping of the world by military means. The crusades that sent bodies of Christian knights from western Europe to the eastern Mediterranean in the 11th to 13th centuries were in their way equally remarkable military enterprises, although less successful. But the greatest campaigns of conquest were carried out by the hardy nomadic and seminomadic peoples of central Asia. Their horsemen could outfight the armies of any settled civilization and, when inspired by ambitious leaders such as the Mongol Genghis Khan or the Tatar Timur, they became unstoppable. Genghis's descendants for a brief period ruled a vast area from the Pacific to eastern Europe.

THE ROLE OF A COMMANDER

Empire-building was exceptional among the military activities of the period. More commonly, warfare was a relatively endemic state, fought between traditional enemies in interminable and indecisive conflicts.

Order of the Temple
A fresco showing Christian Templar Knights in pursuit of the fleeing enemy. Founded in around 1119, the Templar Knights—identified by their white mantle with a red cross—were among the most skilled horsemen of the medieval crusades.

Established codes of honor suggested that commanders should fight in person, but in practice common sense dictated that these high-status figures keep out of harm's way. Indeed, commanders tended to avoid pitched battles because they carried too great a risk of death or capture. Similarly, they rarely made costly assaults on castles or city walls, preferring to apply pressure in a prolonged siege and achieve a negotiated surrender. By far the most common military activities were laying waste and plunder, which both intimidated enemies and were a direct source of profit. This was the often inglorious reality of an era in which military glory was unreservedly admired.

500—1095

EARLY MIDDLE AGES

"HE WOULD FOLLOW HIS PRINCE, HIS LORD TO THE FIGHT.
HE BORE FORTH SPEAR TO THE BATTLE. HE HAD GOOD
THOUGHT AS LONG AS HE HELD BRIGHT SWORD. HIS BOAST
HE FULFILLED, FIGHTING BY HIS LORD."

FROM THE ANGLO-SAXON POEM, *THE BATTLE OF MALDON*, c. 1000

OR WESTERN EUROPE, THE EARLY MIDDLE AGES were a time of slow recovery from the chronic insecurity that followed the breakdown of the Roman Empire. The Christian kingdoms of the Franks and Anglo-Saxons faced up to the incursions of fierce raiders such as the Scandinavian Vikings. But farther east the tradition of Rome was continued by the Byzantine Empire, ruled from Constantinople, while the rise of Islam brought a new vitality to the Mediterranean zone and west and central Asia.

In the 6th century, it still seemed possible that under Emperor Justinian the Roman Empire might be restored to its full glory. Despite the brilliance of Justinian's general, Belisarius, however, the attempt failed. The Byzantine Empire instead found itself engaged in a defensive fight for survival, dependent on the unassailable walls of Constantinople to hold off aggressors. The greatest threat to Christian Byzantium came from the Muslim Arabs, whose religiously inspired campaigns destroyed Rome's old enemies the Persian Sasanians and narrowly failed to overrun the Byzantines.

By the mid-8th century, Islam had been spread by the sword from Spain to Afghanistan. Coming from opposite directions, Arab and Tang Chinese armies clashed at the battle of Talas in central Asia in 751. But the Arabs did not maintain their military dominance of the Muslim world for long. Arab rulers recruited Turkish warriors from central Asia as slave soldiers to fight wars for them. The Turks soon produced military commanders of high skill and ambition, such as Mahmud of Ghazni, and the formidable Seljuk Dynasty, which created its own Muslim empires in Asia.

THE CAROLINGIAN DYNASTY

In western Europe, the Franks, originally a Germanic tribal people, emerged as a dominant force, their warband leaders evolving into Christian kings. Under the Carolingian Dynasty they stamped their military authority on a large area, including northern Italy and most of modern-day Germany. Their greatest leader, Charlemagne, claimed the succession to the Roman Empire in 800, having himself crowned as emperor by the pope. But the Frankish Empire was a fragile entity, prone to disintegration and long periods of civil strife. Power was largely devolved to counts—local lords who in theory owed service to their king but often served themselves. Their key fighting man, the knight with mail armor, shield, sword, and spear, was an effective warrior, but there was no financial system to support a full-time professional army. The Franks struggled, often in vain, to secure their borders against raiders and invaders.

RAIDERS AND SETTLERS

The most menacing incursion into western Europe was made by the Arabs, who overran the Iberian peninsula and penetrated as far as central France in 732. Seaborne Viking warriors from Scandinavia carried out destructive coastal raids from the 8th century and later settled as migrant conquerors through much of the British Isles and northern France. The Anglo-Saxons, themselves originally migrants into post-Roman Britain, resisted Viking invasions with mixed success, but at their peak the Scandinavians created a brief empire around the North Sea. Anglo-Saxon England eventually succumbed to invasion by descendants of the Vikings—the Normans.

Anglo-Saxon warrior
This decorative panel shows a horseman wielding a spear and trampling an enemy underfoot. It appears on a replica of a helmet found at the Sutton Hoo ship-burial site in eastern England. This rare and finely wrought piece dates from the 7th century.

500–1450

Precious weapon
For the Vikings, a sword was a mark of status as well as a much-prized weapon. This example from 1000 CE in York, England, has a rounded pommel and double-edged blade attached to a crossguard.

BYZANTINE COMMANDERS

WITH ITS CAPITAL AT CONSTANTINOPLE, the Byzantine Empire evolved out of the Roman Empire in the East. During the early medieval period, it was by far the leading Christian military power, reflecting its superior resources and level of bureaucratic organization. Its armies, commanded by the emperor in person or by his generals, failed in a valiant effort to restore imperial rule in Italy, but were ultimately successful in a centuries-long contest with the Persian Sasanian Empire. From around 630 CE to its fall in 1453, the Byzantine Empire stood in the front line of the confrontation between Christian Europe and Islam.

 KNIGHTS AND NOMADS

BELISARIUS

BYZANTINE GENERAL
BORN c. 500
DIED 565
KEY CONFLICTS Byzantine-Sasanian Wars, Vandalic War, Gothic War
KEY BATTLES Dara 530, Tricamerum 533, Rome 536, Constantinople 559

The greatest of Byzantine generals, Belisarius rose to prominence by sheer ability. He was born into an obscure family in the Balkans and, as a young man, served as a soldier in the Byzantine imperial guard. In 527, Emperor Justinian entrusted him with a command in the East, where the empire faced incursions by the Persian Sasanians. Belisarius did so well that by 530 he was in charge of Byzantine forces in Mesopotamia.

BIOGRAPHY

JUSTINIAN

Ruling the Byzantine Empire from 527, Justinian aspired to recover imperial control of the western Mediterranean, including Italy and Rome itself. Despite the efforts of his generals Belisarius and Narses, this goal was beyond his resources and his empire was in decline by the time of his death in 565. Justinian is also remembered for his code of laws, which are the basis of civil law in many modern legal systems.

He defeated a larger Sasanian army at Dara in that year, but was beaten at Callinicum in 531 before being recalled to Constantinople during peace negotiations.

It was fortunate for Justinian that Belisarius was in the capital in 532, when rioters seized control of the city. While the emperor cowered in his palace, Belisarius led crack troops into the streets and subdued the rebellion through a ruthless massacre—as many as 30,000 citizens may have been slaughtered.

Belisarius was by then the obvious choice to spearhead Justinian's most treasured project, the reestablishment of control over what had been the western Roman Empire, now in the hands of "barbarians." Belisarius landed in north Africa in 533, defeating the Vandals at the battles of Ad Decimum and Tricamerum, and taking Carthage. In 535, it was the turn of Italy, ruled by the Ostrogoths. First taking Sicily, Belisarius moved north to seize Naples and then Rome itself. But throughout these campaigns, he had too few troops to occupy and control the territory he gained.

SURRENDER IN ITALY

Witiges, the Ostrogoth king, finally surrendered in 540. He may have done so after Belisarius promised to declare himself emperor of a re-formed western Roman Empire, with the Ostrogoths part of the imperial forces. Their surrender delivered their impregnable capital, Ravenna, to the Byzantines, after which Belisarius reneged on his promise for reasons that remain unclear. The reconquest did not hold, and in 544 Belisarius was back in Italy, battling a new Ostrogoth leader, Totila.

By this stage, he had lost Justinian's favor, and he withdrew into private life in 551. Belisarius emerged for one final battle in 559, when Constantinople was menaced by a band of Huns. He led a few hundred men out of the city, ambushed the Huns, and sent them running.

Legend claims that the ungrateful Justinian had his erstwhile general blinded and driven to beg on the streets in his final years. In reality, it would seem that Belisarius died in dignity and comfort.

Blind Belisarius
An 18th-century depiction of the Byzantine general reflects the legend that Belisarius was blinded and poor in old age.

NARSES

BYZANTINE GENERAL
BORN 478
DIED 573
KEY CONFLICTS Gothic War
KEY BATTLES Taginae 552, Vesuvius 553, Volturnus 554

Born in Armenia, Narses was a court eunuch in the Byzantine imperial palace in Constantinople. In 532, when riots threatened Emperor Justinian, he was commander of the imperial guard, but this was a court rather than a military appointment. In 538, Narses was chosen to lead an army to reinforce Belisarius fighting the Ostrogoths in Italy. He had no military experience, but the aging eunuch was intended to control Belisarius, whom Justinian distrusted, rather than to win battles.

Yet Narses was to turn into an outstanding battlefield leader. His first visit to Italy was short, his constant disagreements with Belisarius too disruptive of military operations. But in the 540s, he was given a real command, in charge of an army of Heruli—Germanic

“A FEEBLE DIMINUTIVE BODY CONCEALED THE SOUL OF A STATESMAN AND A WARRIOR”

EDWARD GIBBON ON NARSES, *THE DECLINE AND FALL OF THE ROMAN EMPIRE*, 18TH CENTURY

troops—whom he soon led to an important victory over raiding Slavs and Huns in Thrace.

In 552, Narses led another army to Italy to fight the Ostrogoths once more. Unlike Belisarius, he was given plenty of troops. Though a shriveled 74-year-old, he provided them with inspiration and organization. At Taginae he defeated the Ostrogoth leader, Totila, retook Rome, and finally crushed the Gothic army at a second battle in the foothills of Vesuvius. Narses had regained Italy in a single lightning campaign. In 554, he won another great victory, defeating the Franks and Alamanni tribes at Volturnus. He was still defending Italy against Goths and Franks in 562, when old age ended his unlikely military career.

Ivory warriors
A Byzantine army sets off on campaign in this 6th-century relief. Its foot soldiers carry spears and shields, its horsemen lances.

HERACLIUS

BYZANTINE EMPEROR
BORN c. 575
DIED February 11, 641
KEY CONFLICTS Byzantine-Persian Wars, Byzantine-Arab Wars
KEY BATTLES Nineveh 627, Yarmuk 636

Son of a Byzantine general, in 608, Heraclius began a revolt in north Africa against the tyrannous Emperor Phocas. Two years later, he executed Phocas and took the throne. As emperor, Heraclius began important reforms, which included creating a class of Byzantine soldier-farmers who held land in return for military service. However, Heraclius struggled to cope with attacks from Avars and Slavs in the Balkans and the Persian Sasanian Chosroes II in the East. When the Sasanians invaded Anatolia, threatening Constantinople, Heraclius at first thought of abandoning the capital and withdrawing to Carthage. Instead, in 622, he began to fight back. Of imposing physique and great personal courage, he led his armies on successful campaigns in Anatolia and Armenia. Beating off a siege of Constantinople in 626, the next year he struck deep into Mesopotamia. In December, the Byzantine and Sasanian armies clashed at Nineveh. The battle was a triumph for Heraclius, who allegedly killed the Sasanian commander, Rhahzadh, with a single blow of his sword. Chosroes was overthrown by his own people and his successor sued for peace.

Unfortunately for Heraclius, at this pinnacle of his success, Arab armies inspired by the new religion of Islam posed a sudden threat. No longer leading troops in the field, Heraclius sent armies to resist the Arabs in vain, suffering an especially severe defeat at Yarmuk in 636. By the time of his death in 641, the Byzantines had lost Egypt and the Levant to the rising Arab tide.

Battle of Nineveh
The cruelty and chaos of combat is underlined in this 13th-century depiction of Heraclius' victory over the Sasanians in 627. Heraclius fought in the thick of the 11-hour battle.

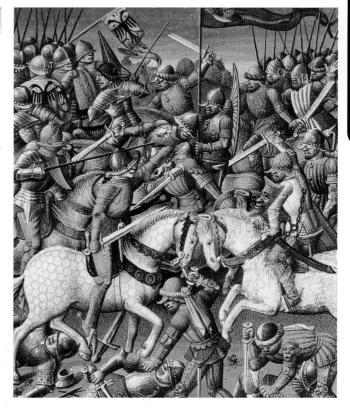

ARAB AND TURKISH COMMANDERS

IN THE 7TH CENTURY ARAB FORCES inspired by the new religion of Islam destroyed the Persian Sassanid empire and almost overran the Byzantine empire. In the next century Muslim rule extended from Spain to Afghanistan. The Arabs converted conquered peoples to Islam and integrated them into their armies.

Finding that the Turkish tribesmen of central Asia made outstanding fighters, they enrolled them as slave soldiers, or Mamelukes, a category known only in the Muslim world. Islamicized Turkish warriors developed ambitions of their own and by the 11th century were ruling most of Muslim Asia and threatening Christendom's eastern frontier.

KHALID IBN AL-WALID

ARAB GENERAL
BORN 592
DIED 642
KEY CONFLICTS Ridda Wars, Islamic Conquest of Persia, Byzantine-Arab Wars
KEY BATTLES Firaz 633, Damascus 634, Yarmuk 636

The most successful commander of the early period of Arab expansion, Khalid ibn al-Walid made an effortless transition from tribal warfare to fighting major armies. He originally opposed the Prophet Muhammad, but after converting to Islam, he became one of his trusted generals.

After the Prophet's death in 632, Khalid served under Caliph Abu Bakr, suppressing an Arab revolt in the Ridda Wars. He then fought in Mesopotamia, trouncing the Persian Sassanids in a lightning campaign that ended in a resounding victory at Firaz in December 633. Ordered to the aid of Abu Bakr, who was fighting the Byzantines in southern Syria, Khalid led his army across the Syrian Desert and, after more victories, captured Damascus in September 634.

FINAL TRIUMPH

During the siege of Damascus, Abu Bakr died and was replaced by Caliph Umar, who distrusted Khalid. Umar removed Khalid from high command, but he continued to play a leading role in Arab operations. In August 636, he achieved his greatest victory, routing a Byzantine army at the River Yarmuk. Umar finally dismissed Khalid in 638, after a religious dispute.

Deception at Yamama
This manuscript illumination shows an episode from the Ridda Wars of 632. Khalid's opponent, Musailima, convinced him that the fortress of Yamama was too well guarded to attack. In reality, his warriors were women in disguise.

MAHMUD OF GHAZNI

TURKISH SULTAN
BORN November 2, 971
DIED April 30, 1030
KEY CONFLICTS Campaigns in Central Asia and India
KEY BATTLES Peshawar 1001

Mahmud of Ghazni was the son of a Turkish slave soldier, Sebuktegin. After fighting in the service of the Persian Saminids, Sebuktegin rose to be ruler of the cities of Khorasan and Ghazni. Mahmud accompanied his father on his campaigns from the age of 14. In 996, Sebuktegin died and, after a short war with his brother, Ismail, Mahmud succeeded to his father's domains. The Abbasid Caliph confirmed his rule over Ghazni and Khorasan, and in return Mahmud vowed to campaign in Hindu India every year in the name of Islam. He did not quite fulfill this promise, but in

Turkish warriors
Mahmud of Ghazni and his followers were Turks, steppe nomads who had originated in central Asia and moved south into Afghanistan. Fighting on horseback with lance and bow, they were fast-moving and ruthless.

1001, he defeated Jayapala at Peshawar (now in Pakistan) and between 1000 and 1026 raided northern India at least 16 times. Although Muslim zeal justified these campaigns, plunder was the more obvious motive. Looting Hindu temples brought Mahmud untold riches, reflected in the splendor of his capital at Ghazni.

Mahmud's campaigns in India were usually timed to fit between the harvest and the monsoon rains, when his army could live off the land and move swiftly, without the hindrance of a supply train. He repeatedly defeated his main opponents, the Rajput princes, and in 1025 pushed as far south as Somnath, site of a famous temple on the coast of Gujarat. In his later years, however, Mahmud was challenged by the rising power of the Seljuk Turks, who by the time of his death in 1030 had seized the cities of Merv and Nishapur on the western edge of his empire.

> ## THE INDIANS MADE A DESPERATE RESISTANCE… SLAIN EXCEEDED 50,000.
> **ARAB HISTORIAN AL-KAZWINI,** ON MAHMUD'S DESTRUCTION OF SOMNATH

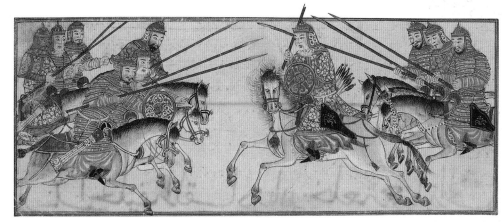

ALP ARSLAN

After the battle
Alp Arslan humiliates his prisoner, the Byzantine emperor, Romanus IV, after the battle of Manzikert in this 15th-century illustration from a French manuscript. In reality, Romanus was well treated by his captors and later released.

TURKISH SELJUK SULTAN
BORN 1029
DIED 1072
KEY CONFLICTS Byzantine-Seljuk Wars
KEY BATTLES Manzikert 1071

In the first half of the 11th century, Tugril Beg, a Turkish leader, created a tribal confederation known as the Seljuks and led them on campaigns of conquest. In 1040, he proclaimed the Great Seljuk Sultanate, which established its rule over Mesopotamia, Persia, and regions of central Asia. Tugril's nephew, Alp Arslan, won the succession after the sultan's death in 1063. Alp Arslan's name meant "valiant lion" and he was a brilliant military leader. In the first year of his reign he seized Armenia and Georgia and was soon

leading armies on incursions deep inside Anatolia, the heartland of the Byzantine empire.

At this stage, the Byzantines were still a major military power. Emperor Romanus IV mounted campaigns that initially forced the Seljuk Turks back into Mesopotamia. But Alp Arslan was a dauntless and subtle opponent. When Romanus led a force north of Lake Van in the summer of 1071, the Seljuk commander sensed the opportunity for a decisive victory. His defeat of the Byzantines at Manzikert was an epoch-making event. It led within a generation to the loss of virtually all Byzantine territory in Anatolia to Seljuk warlords who carved small states out of it. Alp Arslan was a superb military organizer as well as an outstanding commander. In the territories the Seljuks conquered, he instituted a system of military service in return for land, an arrangement that placed substantial armed forces at his disposal. However, he did not live long enough to exploit the potential of his military reforms. He died at age 42 while on campaign in central Asia.

KEY BATTLE
MANZIKERT

CAMPAIGN Byzantine-Seljuk Wars
DATE August 26, 1071
LOCATION Manzikert (Malazgirt), eastern Anatolia

Byzantine emperor Romanus IV marched eastward, seeking to confront Alp Arslan's Seljuks. The Turks withdrew in front of the advancing Byzantine forces, refusing battle, while their skirmishing horsemen harassed them from the flanks. When the Byzantines were weakened and exhausted, Alp Arslan's warriors fell upon them, surrounding the emperor in the vanguard of his army. The rest of the Byzantine troops fled, Romanus was captured, and most of those around him killed.

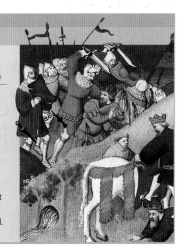

The battle of Lechfeld
Otto I's victory over the nomadic Magyars is shown in this 15th-century illustration. A chronicler remarked, "Never was so bloody a victory gained over so savage a people."

THE CHRISTIAN WEST

IN EARLY MEDIEVAL EUROPE, the kingdoms of the Franks and Anglo-Saxons were threatened by external rivals. Through defeating these enemies, a leader won the prestige to rule and might then take the offensive against pagan neighbors. The Franks were unified under the Carolingian dynasty after Charles Martel's victory over Arab intruders and went on to establish an expansive empire led by Charlemagne. In the 10th century, the Germanic Holy Roman Empire was created under Otto I after he defeated the Magyars. The kings of Wessex earned the right to lead the Anglo-Saxons through Alfred's resistance to Danish Vikings.

CHARLES MARTEL

FRANKISH MAYOR OF THE PALACE
BORN c. 688
DIED October 22, 741
KEY CONFLICTS Frankish civil wars, war against the Arabs
KEY BATTLES Amblève 716, Poitiers 732

By the 8th century, the Merovingian rulers of the Frankish kingdoms of Neustria and Austrasia had become figureheads, with real power exercized by their Mayors of the Palace. Charles Martel was the illegitimate son of a mayor, Pepin II. Pepin's death in 714 precipitated a violent power struggle. Charles defeated his rival Ragenfrid at the battle of Amblève in 716 and again at Vincy a year later. Ragenfrid fought on, forming an alliance with Duke Eudo of Aquitaine, but the struggle was finally decided with a victory for Charles over Eudo and Ragenfrid at Soissons in 718.

Over the following two decades Charles stamped his authority on the Franks and campaigned against the dynasties beyond the eastern Frankish borders, defeating Saxons, Frisians, and Bavarians. He built up a following of veteran warriors in these campaigns who served him well in the crucial test presented by the Arab incursion of 732. At the battle of Poitiers (also known as the battle of Tours), his steady fighters turned back Muslim cavalry that had conquered Spain and might well have overrun France. In 736-7, Charles extended his campaigns south to the Mediterranean, laid siege to the Muslim stronghold of Narbonne, and defeated another Arab army at the battle of the Berre River. By the time of his death in 741, he was ruling the Franks without the pretence of a puppet king and had laid the foundations for the future Carolingian Empire.

Charles the hammer
A 19th-century sculpture of Charles Martel shows him as a figure of power. His pulverizing victories earned him the nickname *Martel*, or "Hammer." He led the Franks like a king, while officially only holding the rank of Mayor of the Palace.

> ## THEY FORMED AS IT WERE A WALL OF ICE; AND WITH GREAT BLOWS OF THEIR SWORDS THEY HEWED DOWN THE ARABS.
>
> **ANONYMOUS,** *THE MOZARABIC CHRONICLE,* COMPILED BY A CHRISTIAN LIVING IN MUSLIM SPAIN, 754

KEY BATTLE
POITIERS

CAMPAIGN Frankish-Muslim War
DATE October 25, 732
LOCATION North of Poiters, France

Abd al-Rahman, governor of Muslim Spain, led an army of Arab and Berber horsemen into Frankish territory. Charles Martel took up a defensive position on a wooded hill, his men dismounted and formed a tight square. When the Muslim army attacked, the Franks stood firm behind their shield wall, hacking and stabbing with swords and spears. Distracted by an attack on their camp by Frankish scouts, the Muslims lost discipline. Abd al-Rahman was surrounded and killed, and the Muslim army withdrew.

ALFRED THE GREAT

ANGLO-SAXON KING OF WESSEX
BORN 849
DIED 899
KEY CONFLICTS Danish-Saxon wars
KEY BATTLES Edington 878

Alfred was the youngest son of Ethelwulf, king of Wessex. In 865, when Alfred was a youth, Wessex and the other Anglo-Saxon kingdoms in England—Northumbria, East Anglia, and Mercia—were threatened by invasion when a Danish Viking "Great Army" landed on the east coast. The Danes first conquered Northumbria and East Anglia and then turned to attack Mercia. Alfred first saw action with Wessex forces sent to aid the Mercians. In 870, Wessex itself was invaded. By that time Alfred's elder brother, Ethelred, was king. Ethelred and Alfred fought a series of battles against the Danes with varying success. They are credited with a victory at Ashingdon in Berkshire in 871, but Ethelred was routed at Basing soon after and was killed at Merton the following April. Alfred succeeded to the throne.

UNDER ATTACK

In the first years of Alfred's reign, the Danes tried to consolidate their other conquests, but in 876 they renewed their assault. Alfred had major weaknesses that made defending his realm

The Alfred Jewel
Found in Somerset, England, this beautiful ornament, only 2½ in (6 cm) long, has a Latin inscription that reads: "Alfred ordered me to be made."

difficult. He could not match Danish sea power, so the south coast was open to attack by their longships. On land his army, the *fyrd*, was a part-time force assembled by regional lords at the king's command. This meant the Danish army could advance deep into Wessex before Alfred's forces could gather. Even so, in 876, a Danish invasion was resisted. The Danes seized Wareham and Exeter, but each time were evicted after Alfred arrived and besieged them. Meanwhile, their navy was scattered by a storm. The respite proved brief, however. Striking in the dead of winter, in January 878, the Danish King Guthrum surprised Alfred at his royal camp at Chippenham. With only his personal followers to defend him, Alfred was lucky to escape with his

life. He sought refuge in the wild Sedgemoor marshes, where he soon established the fort of Athelney as a center for guerrilla warfare.

Perhaps surprisingly, Alfred's royal authority remained intact. In the spring, at his summons, three shires supplied soldiers for a *fyrd*. He led this army to confront the Danes on Salisbury Plain. In the battle of Edington, Alfred appears to have out-maneuvered his enemy, allowing his soldiers to rush down upon them from a hill and drive them from the field. Guthrum retreated with the remnants of his forces to Chippenham, where he was besieged by Alfred and starved into surrender.

MILITARY REFORMS

Although this victory did not end fighting with the Danes, Wessex was never again badly threatened during Alfred's reign. This was largely because of the king's military reforms. Alfred reorganized the *fyrd*, so that a part of the army was always assembled. He strengthened his navy with longships larger than any the Danes possessed and manned them with mercenaries. He built up to 30 fortified towns, or burghs, as strongholds to block an invader's path. Alfred's son, Edward the Elder, inherited a militarily and culturally revitalized kingdom.

> # BY DIVINE AID HE TRIUMPHED AND OVERTHREW THE PAGANS WITH A VERY GREAT SLAUGHTER.

BISHOP ASSER ON THE BATTLE OF EDINGTON, *LIFE OF KING ALFRED*, 893

OTTO I

FRANKISH KING AND EMPEROR
BORN November 23, 912
DIED May 7, 973
KEY CONFLICTS Magyar invasions
KEY BATTLE Lechfeld 955

In 843, the Carolingian Empire was divided, its easternmost part becoming the kingdom of East Francia. The father of the future emperor, Otto I, Saxon Duke Henry the Fowler, was elevated to the throne of East Francia in 919. Otto succeeded him in 936, but faced a tough fight to assert his authority. Powerful dukes rebelled against royal overlordship and even Otto's own brother and son campaigned against him. His authority might never have recovered but for a wave of raids by the Magyars, swift-moving nomadic horsemen from Asia who were pressing across Germany's eastern borders. To oppose Magyar incursions, the German nobles closed ranks

Imperial crown
This crown, shown with later embellishments, was made for the coronation of Otto I as emperor, a ceremony conducted by Pope John XII on February 2, 962.

behind Otto. The dukes led forces to support him in an attack on the invaders, who were besieging Augsburg. Otto placed his army, which consisted mostly of mounted armored troops, between Augsburg and the Magyars' home territory,

provoking them to give battle. The two sides eventually clashed at the battle of Lechfeld (pp. 60–61) on August 10, 955.

WINNING CHANCE

The Magyar horsemen, armed chiefly with bows, encircled Otto's troops and looked to be the likely victors until they were distracted by plundering the German baggage train. This gave Otto's men an opportunity to mount a series of cavalry charges, inflicting such heavy losses that the Magyars were driven from the field. The German nobles raised Otto on their shields, which was the traditional German manner of proclaiming an emperor. Otto's title was confirmed by the pope in 962, thereby establishing the tradition that the imperial crown would be worn by the king of the Eastern Franks.

Title of distinction
Otto I's suppression of his rebellious dukes, combined with his decisive victory over the Magyars at the battle of Lechfeld, earned him the nickname "the Great."

CHARLEMAGNE

FRANKISH KING AND EMPEROR
BORN April 2, 742
DIED January 28, 814
KEY CONFLICTS Campaigns against the Lombards, Saxons, Avars, and Saracens
KEY BATTLE Roncesvalles 778

Charlemagne, or Charles the Great, was the son of Pepin, the first king of the Carolingian dynasty. Pepin's domains at his death covered most of present-day France, in addition to Belgium and parts of Germany. The sole ruler of this extensive kingdom from 771, Charlemagne was above all a war leader, expecting to take his army on campaign every year. He is reckoned to have carried out 30 campaigns in person in the course of his reign—to assert his authority, expand his domains, and forcibly

Charlemagne at Pamplona
In 778, Charlemagne took the Spanish city of Pamplona by storm. A 14th-century artist has shown this event by portraying troops in the armor of his time, rather than Charlemagne's.

spread the Christian faith. Charlemagne had no standing army and no bureaucracy, yet he achieved a high level of organization in the assembly and supply of his forces. His chief nobles, the counts, were responsible for raising the various troops that he needed, with equipment for each man. The soldiers brought some food with them, while additional supplies were requisitioned from landowners. The

Talisman of Charlemagne
According to popular belief, this jewel was found in Charlemagne's tomb, opened c.1000.

army typically assembled in the spring and summer and fought in the fall. Charlemagne always gathered intelligence on the region where he intended to fight and prepared careful plans. He usually divided his forces in two or more columns when advancing into hostile territory, presumably because a smaller body of men would find it easier to cope with problems of movement and supply.

FRANKISH CAVALRY

Charlemagne's cavalry were his principal troops. Retainers of the Frankish nobles, the armored horsemen were obliged to show up ready for military service when required by the king. Equipped with a lance, sword, and shield, they fought mounted, relying on stirrups and a high-backed saddle to maintain a stable seat in combat.

> ## THE KING... EXCELLED ALL THE PRINCES OF HIS TIME IN WISDOM AND GREATNESS OF SOUL...

EINHARD, *LIFE OF CHARLEMAGNE*, C. 820

Pitched battles were rare, campaigns usually consisting of skirmishes, attacks on fortified settlements, resisting or avoiding ambushes, and much laying of waste to towns and countryside.

Although in the first quarter-century of his reign Charlemagne commanded his army in person, he was not a ruler known for prowess in face-to-face combat. His real

Emperor's relic
This reliquary bust of Charlemagne at Aachen Cathedral in Germany is said to contain his skull.

KNIGHTS AND NOMADS

qualities lay in his leadership, organization, willpower, and ruthless persistence.

Charlemagne fought his wars against mainly inferior opposition around his extensive borders, but even so success was not guaranteed. He faced tough resistance from insurgents and his resources were overstretched against multiple enemies.

ITALIAN CONTROL

The campaign in which Charlemagne triumphed over the Lombard kingdom of north Italy in 773–74 exemplified decisive military action. After marching across the Alpine passes in two columns, the Franks who emerged on the north Italian plain were too numerous for the enemy to take on. Charlemagne came to a halt at the Lombard capital, Pavia, and laid siege to the city until it capitulated. Although further campaigns in Italy against the Lombards and Byzantines were needed, the political settlement he imposed held firm, establishing Frankish control of the northern half of Italy. Campaigning in Iberia proved tougher. While most of Spain was under Muslim rule, divisions

Frankish weapon
The Carolingian Franks were renowned for the high quality of their swords. A double-edged longsword like this one would deliver a powerful blow.

between the Arabs and the few, small Christian states that did exist gave Charlemagne an opportunity to intervene. But the resulting expedition to northern Spain in 778 was the worst disaster of his career.

At the end of an unsuccessful foray to Zaragoza, he was leading his army back across the Pyrenees when the rearguard was ambushed and massacred at Roncesvalles. The death of prominent Frankish nobles in this attack provided material for a famous medieval epic poem, *The Song of Roland*. The incident was, in contrast, passed over in silence by Charlemagne's own chroniclers—it was embarrassing to have fallen into such a trap. Later in his reign, the Franks successfully occupied a defensive buffer zone south of the Pyrenees, including Barcelona.

SAXON REBELS

Most of Charlemagne's wars were directed across the open eastern frontier of his domains, above all against the Saxons. These independent, pagan people were repeatedly terrorized by Charlemagne's columns, but were always ready to rebel again when the Franks were distracted. Their resistance angered Charlemagne, who was guilty of an appalling massacre of 4,500 Saxons at Verden in 782. The submission of the inspired guerrilla leader Widukind in 785 did not end resistance, but marked the point at which it could no longer succeed.

By the 790s, Charlemagne had begun to delegate military operations to his sons or to nobles. He was not personally involved in destroying the Avar khanate (nomads who dominated the Danube Valley), but he did plan to build a canal linking the Maine and Danube to facilitate the movement of his troops—an engineering task well beyond the Franks' abilities.

By 800, when Charlemagne was crowned emperor by the pope, the era of annual campaigns was drawing to a close, as was his personal command of army operations. He had made his kingdom into an empire stretching as far south as central Italy and Barcelona, and as far east as the Elbe.

TIMELINE

■ **768** On the death of his father, Pepin the Short, Charlemagne becomes joint ruler of the Franks with his brother, Carloman.

■ **769** Charlemagne suppresses a revolt by Hunald, Duke of Aquitaine, forcing him to accept Carolingian authority.

■ **771** The death of Carloman allows Charlemagne to assert his rule as undisputed king of the Franks.

■ **772** Charlemagne invades Saxony, seeking to bring the Saxons under Frankish control.

■ **773–774** Charlemagne crosses the Alps and defeats the Lombards after a lengthy siege of Pavia; he is crowned king of Lombardy.

■ **775–777** Annual campaigns in Saxony lead to mass forced conversions to Christianity.

■ **776** Charlemagne returns to Italy to suppress a revolt by the dukes of Spoleto and Friuli.

■ **778** Returning across the Pyrenees from a fruitless campaign in Muslim Spain, Charlemagne's rearguard is cut off and destroyed by the Basques at Roncesvalles.

■ **782–785** Widukind leads a revolt in Saxony. After three years' fighting, Widukind surrenders and accepts baptism.

■ **788** Charlemagne deposes the Duke of Bavaria and integrates the region into his territory.

■ **792** Charlemagne faces renewed rebellion in Saxony; fighting continues until 803.

■ **796** The Franks capture the treasure of the Avars, precipitating the collapse of the Danubian Avar Empire.

CORONATION OF CHARLEMAGNE

■ **800** On Christmas Day, Charlemagne is crowned emperor by Pope Leo III in St. Peter's Basilica, Rome.

■ **801** Charlemagne's son, Louis the Pious, takes Barcelona from the Muslims; Charlemagne organizes the region as the Spanish Marches, a defensive outpost for his empire.

■ **813** To ensure the succession to his throne, Charlemagne crowns Louis the Pious as co-emperor. When Charlemagne dies the following year, Louis succeeds him.

Ambush at Roncesvalles
The attack on Charlemagne's rearguard in the Pyrenees in 778 became the stuff of legend from the 12th century and was depicted as such. The hero was Roland of Brittany, shown here in golden armor.

VIKINGS AND NORMANS

THE SCANDINAVIAN VIKINGS first appear in European history as raiding warbands, pillaging the coasts of the British Isles and western Europe from the late 8th century. Their longships carried them across seas and along rivers as far afield as the Black Sea and the Mediterranean. Speed of movement and surprise— as well as their ferocity as fighting men—made them formidable enemies. But the Vikings were settlers as well as warriors, and their pagan warband leaders mutated over time into Christian kings. Settling in northern France they became the Normans, French by culture, but nevertheless quarrelsome warriors impelled to invasion and conquest.

OLAV TRYGGVASON

VIKING KING
BORN c. 963
DIED 1000
KEY CONFLICTS Viking Invasions of England, Viking Civil Conflict
KEY BATTLES Maldon 991, Svold 1000

A Viking raider who rose to be king of Norway, Olav Tryggvason is a figure whose historical existence emerges obscurely from the pages of Norse sagas and Anglo-Saxon poetry. Allegedly a descendant of Harald Fairhair, the first king of Norway, as a young man he led the typical life of a Viking warrior. He served as a mercenary in Novgorod before leading his own warband on raids around the British Isles, ranging from the Hebrides to the Scilly Isles. He must have built up a substantial following for, in 991, he attacked the east coast of England from Kent to East Anglia with 93 longships and an army numbering in the thousands.

A CHRISTIAN DEAL
At Maldon in Essex a local earl and his thanes fought to the death in a vain attempt to repel the invasion. But the English king, Ethelred the Unready, thought it more prudent to do a deal with the Vikings, whose motives were purely mercenary. In 994, Olav allowed himself to be baptized a Christian and promised to stop raiding England in return for a hefty bribe in gold and other valuables. Bolstered with wealth and a prestigious faith, Olav now turned his attention to Norway. In 995, he overthrew the Norwegian ruler, Haaken, Jarl of Lade,

Olav the warrior
The king of Norway is depicted as a warrior in simple leather battle dress with wooden shield and iron helmet in this 19th-century statue by Hans Michelsen.

and embarked on the mass Christianization of the population, enforced by torture and massacre. But Olav's rise to power alienated other Scandinavian rulers. In 1000, he was ambushed at sea by the combined fleet of Sweyn Forkbeard of Denmark, Olav Eriksson of Sweden, and the new Jarl of Lade. The battle of Svold was hard fought, Olav performing heroics aboard his great ship the *Long Serpent*. Eventually, he was surrounded by his rivals and leapt into the sea to avoid being caught. His body was never found.

Godly Canute
King Canute was a friend to the Church and is said to have visited Pope John XIX in Rome in 1027.

CANUTE (CNUT)

VIKING KING
BORN c. 985
DIED November 12, 1035
KEY CONFLICT Invasion of England
KEY BATTLES Ashingdon 1016, Helgea 1026

> "MAY GOD PRESERVE US... AND BRING TO NOTHING THE POWER AND MIGHT OF ALL OUR ENEMIES!
>
> **KING CANUTE,** BY LETTER, 1027

In 1013, the young Canute joined his father, King Sweyn Forkbeard of Denmark, on an expedition across the North Sea. After decades of raiding, the Danes had decided upon the conquest of England. With his son acting as his main lieutenant, Sweyn drove King Ethelred into flight abroad and claimed the English throne. After reigning for five weeks, Sweyn died. Canute was acclaimed king by the Viking army in England, but Ethelred returned from exile to reclaim the crown. Canute sailed back to Denmark to assemble a new army and fleet drawn from all parts of Scandinavia and returned to England in 1015.

HARD-WON VICTORY
The conflict that followed was an arduous contest of fluctuating fortunes. Ethelred's son, Edmund Ironside, English king from April 1016, was a resourceful warrior. Canute led his army on destructive marches across swathes of English territory, exploiting the mobility provided by his fleet when necessary. But he failed to reduce London by siege and was several times bettered by Edmund in the field. At the battle of Ashingdon, however, the Scandinavian fighters triumphed, inflicting a defeat from which Edmund could not recover. In December 1016, Canute was crowned king of England. He also soon became king of Denmark and, in 1026, he decisively defeated the Norwegian king, Olav Haraldsson, and his Swedish allies in a Baltic battle at Helgea. This victory left Canute ruler of a North Sea empire, which he held until his death in 1035.

ROBERT GUISCARD

NORMAN WARRIOR
BORN c. 1015
DIED 1085
KEY CONFLICTS Byzantine-Norman Wars, Conquest of Sicily
KEY BATTLES Civitate 1053, Dyrrhachium 1087

In 1047, Robert Guiscard, youngest son of a minor Norman family, set out with a handful of followers to seek his fortune in southern Italy. Robert was cunning, fearless, and physically impressive, a promising combination for military success. In 1053, he proved his fighting skills in the defeat of a papal army at Civitate and, by 1061, he had made himself Duke of Apulia and Calabria. Robert's next step was to invade Sicily, then under Muslim rule. The Sicilian campaign sputtered on for years while he also fought to confirm and extend his domains in southern Italy. Robert's ambition, however, craved a larger stage and he dreamed of becoming master of the Byzantine empire.

In 1081, Robert defeated the Byzantine emperor, Alexius, at the battle of Dyrrhachium on the Adriatic. Although distracted by involvement in fighting between the Holy Roman Empire and the papacy in 1085, Robert returned to his attack on the empire, but died in an epidemic on the island of Cephalonia. His eldest son, Bohemond, continued the Norman drive eastward as a leader of the First Crusade in 1097–99.

Invested by the pope
Robert's relations with the papacy were unfriendly at first. But over time, he aided the pope against the Holy Roman Empire and was invested by him as Duke of Apulia and Calabria.

WILLIAM THE CONQUEROR

DUKE OF NORMANDY AND KING OF ENGLAND
BORN c. 1028
DIED September 9, 1087
KEY CONFLICT Conquest of England
KEY BATTLE Hastings 1066

An illegitimate son of Duke Robert of Normandy, William "the Bastard," as he was known, inherited the dukedom at the age of seven and his minority triggered the usual savage contests between rival contenders for power—three of his guardians were killed. William's first struggles after coming of age were against his own kinsmen and rebellious barons, who had to be beaten into acceptance of his authority. At Val-ès-Dunes in 1047, with the help of the French king, Henri I, William defeated the rebels in battle and by 1050 he was in possession of his rightful domains.

VYING FOR TERRITORY

Ruthless in the pursuit of his own interests, William practiced the medieval military arts of ravaging and laying waste with determination. He fought frequent wars with his neighbors, challenging Anjou for possession of the county of Maine and conducting a long feud with Duke Conan of Brittany. But he was also a crafty diplomatist, winning papal backing for his invasion of England in 1066. The famous cross-Channel venture was justified by two alleged promises—by Edward the Confessor to leave his throne to William and by Harold Godwinson to support William's claim. But when Harold was crowned king it provoked two invasions of England, by Norwegian King Harald Hardrada and by William. The latter invasion succeeded, mostly because Harald Hardrada's attack had already fatally weakened Harold's army. But William certainly showed himself a forceful leader in the organization of the invasion, the crucial battle at Hastings, and the subsequent brutal suppression of English resistance. William spent most of his final years in Normandy and died fighting the king of France during a siege of the city of Mantes.

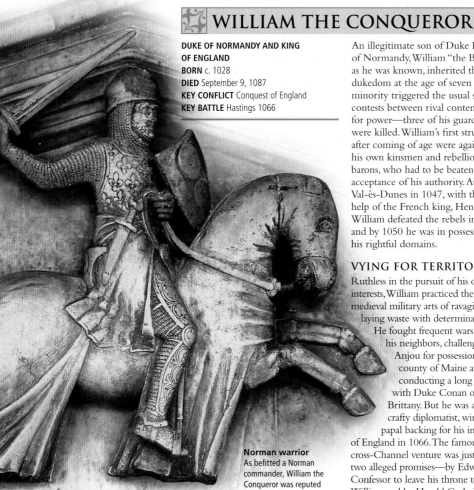

Norman warrior
As befitted a Norman commander, William the Conqueror was reputed to be a fine horseman and a dauntless fighter in face-to-face combat.

Channel crossing
A medieval artist depicts William's army crossing to England in 1066. A seaborne invasion was very much in the tradition of the Normans' Viking ancestors.

WILLIAM AT HASTINGS

LOCATION
North of Hastings, southeast England
CAMPAIGN Norman invasion of England
DATE October 14, 1066
FORCES Normans c. 7,000 infantry and cavalry; Anglo-Saxons c. 9,000 infantry
CASUALTIES (estimates) Normans 2,000 killed; Anglo-Saxons 4,000 killed

On September 27–28, 1066, William of Normandy led a fleet of around 700 ships across the Channel, with some 7,000 men and 2,000 horses aboard. William's opponent, Harold II, had waited and watched for this invasion all summer on England's south coast, while William was penned into port in Normandy by adverse winds. But now the English king had marched north to face another invader, Harald Hadrada of Norway. Thus, William landed at Pevensey unopposed.

DRAWN TO BATTLE

William may have been disconcerted by the absence of Harold's army, for he intended on bringing the Anglo-Saxons to battle while staying close to his ships. He moved along the coast to Hastings, where, on the evening of October 13, William's scouts informed him that Harold's army had at last arrived nearby.

The following morning William attended mass and then rode out to confront the enemy. He found the Anglo-Saxon army, consisting solely of armored infantry, drawn up in a tight defensive formation on Senlac Hill. William formed his own line with bowmen at the front, armored infantry behind them, and cavalry in three divisions to the rear. He positioned himself in the central division with the Norman elite. William's bowmen went forward first to open the fighting. They were supposed to soften up the enemy, but their arrows had little effect on the Anglo-Saxon shields and armor.

THE TIDE TURNS

Then William ordered a frontal charge, his armored infantry going in first with the cavalry following on. Charging uphill took the steam out of the Norman attack and the Anglo-Saxon shield wall held firm. As the Normans fell back in some disarray, William, in their midst, tore off his helmet to prove he was still alive and shouted for his men to rally.

Led by their duke, the horsemen turned and so did the tide of battle. The Anglo-Saxons had lost formation so the Norman cavalry got among them, isolating and destroying them. The rest of the battle was a grinding attrition, with Harold's men reduced to desperate defense until the survivors fled at dusk. William had taken great risks, flinging himself into the thick of the fighting and having several horses killed under him. But Harold himself had died.

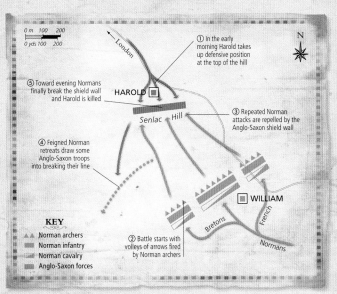

0 m 100 200
0 yds 100 200

① In the early morning Harold takes up defensive position at the top of the hill

N

⑤ Toward evening Normans finally break the shield wall and Harold is killed

HAROLD

Senlac Hill

③ Repeated Norman attacks are repelled by the Anglo-Saxon shield wall

④ Feigned Norman retreats draw some Anglo-Saxon troops into breaking their line

London

WILLIAM

Bretons

French

Normans

② Battle starts with volleys of arrows fired by Norman archers

KEY
▲▲ Norman archers
▬ Norman infantry
▬ Norman cavalry
▬ Anglo-Saxon forces

500—1450

Bayeux Tapestry
Depicting the Norman invasion and the
battle of Hastings, the Bayeux Tapestry
accurately represents the Anglo-Saxons
on foot behind their shield wall and the
charging Norman knights on horseback.

1095—1300

ERA OF THE CRUSADES

"HE IS TRULY A FEARLESS KNIGHT AND SECURE ON EVERY SIDE,
FOR HIS SOUL IS PROTECTED BY THE ARMOR OF FAITH JUST
AS HIS BODY IS PROTECTED BY ARMOR OF STEEL. HE IS THUS
DOUBLY ARMED AND NEED FEAR NEITHER DEMONS NOR MEN.
NOT THAT HE FEARS DEATH—NO, HE DESIRES IT."

BERNARD OF CLAIRVAUX WRITING OF THE KNIGHTS TEMPLAR, EARLY 12TH CENTURY

I N 1095 POPE URBAN II APPEALED for a crusade to rescue Christian Byzantium from the threat posed by the Seljuk Turks, and to free the Holy Land from Muslim control. A mix of religious enthusiasm, greed for land, and lust for adventure drove thousands of knights from western Europe to undertake the perilous journey to the eastern Mediterranean. In 1099 they captured the city of Jerusalem, and crusader states were established in Palestine and Syria. The Christian presence in the East was to endure for almost two centuries.

A Muslim counter-offensive was quick to develop, so that by 1147 a new Christian army was on its way from Europe to reinforce the crusader states. This Second Crusade, the first to be led by European kings, was a dismal failure. The impressive victory of the Kurdish warrior Saladin over the Christians at Hattin in 1187, followed by his capture of Jerusalem, precipitated the Third Crusade. Despite encompassing armies headed by the three most powerful European rulers—the kings of England and France, and the head of the Holy Roman Empire—this also achieved little. Holy war had become a feature of medieval European life, but the energies it released also found other targets. The Fourth Crusade in 1204 turned into an attack on the Byzantine empire—Constantinople was sacked —while other crusades were directed against heretics in Europe or pagans around the Baltic. After the abject failure of the Seventh Crusade, led to Egypt by the French king, Louis IX, in 1249, no further serious challenge was made to Muslim domination of the Middle East. The last of the crusader states fell in 1291.

TROOPS AND EQUIPMENT

The Christians brought to the East their own style of warfare, unmodified by the region's alien terrain and hot climate. Their elite fought as heavily armored mounted knights, despite the searing heat of summer that gave the advantage to the more lightly clad Muslim horsemen. Christian commanders led a mix of feudal troops, tied to their leader by an obligation of service, and mercenaries paid for out of limited financial resources. An important contribution to the crusader forces was made by the religious orders of knights, such as the Templars and the Hospitallers, first established in the Holy Land. These two orders developed superior training strategies, discipline, and leadership.

TACTICS AND TECHNIQUES

The crusaders were skilled at building castles and fortifying cities; they also showed great expertise in the conduct of sieges. On campaign, maintaining supplies, especially of water, was always a limiting factor. Crusader commanders, who developed a healthy respect for their Muslim opponents, used foot soldiers as a screen against skirmishers and attempted to restrain their headstrong knights from rash, premature charges and pursuits that too often ended in disaster. Commanders on both sides avoided pitched battle unless they felt at a clear advantage or were compelled to fight. In the long-drawn-out, subtle tactical game that resulted, the Muslims were always the likeliest long-term winners.

Christians against Muslims
The Christian knights wear the heavier armor in this medieval manuscript illumination of a violent clash between charging crusaders and Muslim horsemen.

Crusader armor
The pot helm, developed during the crusades, offered maximum protection to the head, neck, and face. However, the helmet restricted the knight's vision and was stifling in hot conditions.

ROYAL CRUSADERS

THE FIRST CRUSADE WAS LED by nobles and members of royal families, but not reigning monarchs. Its success, however, meant that some of the most powerful European rulers volunteered for later crusades. The Third Crusade, precipitated by the loss of Jerusalem to Saladin in 1187, attracted the participation of two kings—Richard I of England and Philip II of France—and the German emperor, Frederick Barbarossa. But this "dream team" brought only limited success, and the crusading spirit was waning by the time the French king Louis IX led the Seventh and Eighth Crusades to Egypt and Tunis, respectively.

RICHARD THE LIONHEART

ENGLISH KING
BORN September 8, 1157
DIED April 6, 1199
KEY CONFLICT Third Crusade
KEY BATTLES Siege of Acre 1191, Arsuf 1191, Jaffa 1192

Son of King Henry II and Eleanor of Aquitaine, Richard I was already leading troops at the age of 16. Tall, strong, and fearless, he had a natural aptitude for war. His courage earned him the nickname *Coeur de Lion*, or "Lionheart." He proved his skills against rebel barons, and also fought against his father. Inheriting the English throne in 1189, Richard saw England as a source of military funding and used the kingdom's wealth to equip a crusade in 1190. The journey was slow and eventful. In Sicily, Richard intervened in local politics and sacked the city of Messina. He was also delayed in Cyprus, which he seized from its Greek ruler. Finally reaching the Holy Land in June 1191, Richard joined the crusader army that was besieging Acre.

FRUITLESS VICTORY

Richard's arrival galvanized the Christian forces, weary from a long siege. Despite becoming seriously ill, he directed the siege operations that brought the city to surrender in July; he was also responsible for the massacre of the surrendered garrison. Marching south from Acre, Richard defeated the Muslim sultan, Saladin, in a battle at Arsuf, but stopped short of attempting the more difficult task of seizing the holy city of Jerusalem— the crusade's main objective. The fighting settled down to low-level skirmishing and sparring. In 1192, after Saladin seized Jaffa, Richard retook the city. It was a surprise assault and he held it against counterattack, leading his knights into the thick of the fight. But such heroics were of no

Crusader sword
A sword was part of the standard weaponry of a crusader knight, along with a lance, dagger, and mace. This heavy broad blade could hack through the light armor worn by most Muslim warriors.

Royal conflict
Richard's battle with Philip II Augustus (left) at Gisors, northern France, was depicted after the event as a symbolic duel between two knights.

consequence. Richard needed to go home and made a peace with Saladin that left Jerusalem in Muslim hands.

On his way back to England Richard was seized by his sworn enemies the Duke of Austria and the German emperor. His freedom was bought with a huge ransom collected in England. He spent the rest of his life defending his domains in France against Philip II Augustus, showing his usual reckless courage and tactical flair. Richard died after being hit by a crossbow bolt during a minor siege at Chalus in central France.

Tribute to a king
A 19th-century statue of Richard stands outside London's Houses of Parliament, a reminder of his reputation as a dauntless warrior king.

> " RICHARD HAD HIMSELF CARRIED OUT ON A SILKEN LITTER, SO THAT THE SARACENS MIGHT BE AWED BY HIS PRESENCE.
> **ROGER OF HOVEDEN DESCRIBING THE SIEGE OF ACRE,** *THE ACTS OF KING RICHARD,* c. 1200 "

PHILIP II AUGUSTUS

FRENCH KING
BORN August 21, 1165
DIED July 14, 1223
KEY CONFLICTS Third Crusade,
War of Bouvines
KEY BATTLES Siege of Acre 1291,
Bouvines 1214

Although lacking the dashing qualities of his contemporary Richard the Lionheart, Philip II Augustus became one of the most successful French monarchs of medieval times. Inheriting the throne in 1180, early in his reign he fought successfully against the English king Henry II, winning large territories in central France for the French crown. He felt obliged to participate in the Third Crusade with Richard I in the summer of 1190—the two set off together because neither trusted the other enough to remain behind. Philip reached the Holy Land first and contributed to the siege of Acre, but he was outshone when the more flamboyant Richard arrived.

Often ill and increasingly at odds with the English king, Philip left for home soon after the fall of Acre, eager to continue the consolidation and expansion of his realm. He made little progress until after Richard's death in 1199, succeeding then in taking most of Normandy from his successor, King John. In general, Philip excelled at making war while avoiding the hazardous business of fighting battles. But in July 1214 he was victorious in a desperately contested encounter with German and Flemish forces at Bouvines. Philip himself was nearly killed, unhorsed by a Flemish foot soldier— he was saved by his fine armor. But his knights had the best of a fierce melee and won the day. After these scares he did not risk his life again. His long reign left French royal territories greatly extended and the lands of the English kings in France much diminished.

The king's seal
Philip II is depicted holding the fleur de lys of France, encircled by the legend "Philip, by the grace of God, king of the French."

LOUIS IX

FRENCH KING
BORN April 25, 1214
DIED August 25, 1270
KEY CONFLICTS Seventh Crusade,
Eighth Crusade
KEY BATTLES Damietta 1249, Mansurah 1250,
Tunis 1270

Grandson of Philip II Augustus, the pious King Louis IX was an avid crusader, if an unsuccessful one. He embarked on the first and most important of his two crusades in 1248, sailing from Aigues-Mortes in southern France, initially to Cyprus. There he decided to attack Egypt, the heartland of the Muslim Ayyubid dynasty. In June 1249 Louis led a bold opposed landing on a beach at the mouth of the Nile and, defeating the Muslims on the sands, marched onward to occupy the port of Damietta.

This was a triumph, but Louis foolishly rejected an Ayyubid offer to trade Jerusalem for Damietta. Instead, after a prolonged delay waiting for reinforcements, he marched south toward Cairo. At Mansurah the crusaders encountered Egypt's slave soldiers, the Mamelukes. Louis' brother, Robert of Artois, led a surprise attack on the Mameluke camp. At first the raid swept away all before it, but Mameluke commander Rukn ad-Din Baibars lured the impetuous knights into a trap. The Christians were massacred, including Louis' brother. The king showed his mettle by rapidly organizing a defensive position with his remaining forces and then beating off fierce Mameluke counterattacks. But Louis' situation at Mansurah became untenable as the Egyptians cut his supply line down the Nile. When he attempted a withdrawal to Damietta, his army, weakened by disease, was surrounded and captured.

The king and his nobles were released in return for a huge ransom and the return of Damietta. Louis remained in the Holy Land for another four years before finally returning to France.

Louis did no further crusading until 1270, when he again set sail from Aigues-Mortes, this time bound for Tunis in north Africa. Landing in the summer heat, his army was soon decimated by disease. Louis was one of the first to die. His last words were reportedly "Jerusalem, Jerusalem!"

A king in captivity
After his defeat in Egypt in 1250, Louis was captured (on the left of the scene) and then held prisoner at Mansurah. The ransom paid to obtain his release was more than twice the total annual revenue of the French Crown.

TIMELINE

■ **May 1147** As Duke of Swabia, Frederick sets out with his uncle, King Conrad III of Germany, on the Second Crusade.

■ **October 25, 1147** Marching through Anatolia, the German crusader army is surprised and decimated by the Seljuk Turks at the battle of Dorylaeum.

SIEGE OF DAMASCUS

■ **July 1148** After arriving in Palestine, Frederick participates in the disastrous siege of Damascus. The Second Crusade is abandoned.

■ **March 9, 1152** Frederick is declared king of Germany at Aachen. He claims to have been named by Conrad III on his deathbed as his successor.

■ **June 18, 1155** Crowned emperor by Pope Adrian IV, Frederick restores papal control of Rome, hunting down Arnold of Brescia, a leading figure in the Commune of Rome.

■ **1158** Frederick invades Italy in the company of Henry the Lion of Saxony and forces the city of Milan to recognize his authority after a siege; the Milanese soon renege on the agreement.

■ **January 1160** The siege of the Italian town of Crema concludes with its destruction. Frederick is excommunicated by Pope Alexander III in March.

■ **March 1162** After a long and bitter siege, Milan surrenders and is destroyed by Frederick.

■ **1167** Victory against the army of the Commune of Rome at Monte Porzio in May is followed by the sack of Rome's Leonine City, on the west bank of the Tiber. But disease brings campaigning to a halt and forces Frederick to flee to Germany.

■ **May 29, 1176** The Lombard League defeats Frederick at the battle of Legnano. Afterward, the emperor is forced to make peace, recognizing Alexander III as pope.

■ **1181** Invading Saxony, Frederick drives out Henry the Lion, stripping him of his lands.

■ **March 1188** Frederick takes up the cross at Mainz Cathedral for the Third Crusade and begins to assemble a vast army.

■ **May 1189** He embarks on the crusade from Regensburg, marching to Constantinople months before the other crusading armies.

■ **1190** Entering Anatolia, Frederick captures Konya from the Muslims (May), before drowning in the Saleph River (June 10). His army loses confidence and returns to Germany.

FREDERICK BARBAROSSA

GERMAN KING AND EMPEROR
BORN 1122
DIED June 10, 1190
KEY CONFLICTS Second Crusade, Wars of the Guelphs and Ghibellines, Third Crusade
KEY BATTLES Siege of Milan 1162, Legnano 1176

Frederick I Hohenstauffen, known as Barbarossa, was the dominant European military and political figure of his time. He ruled as emperor for 35 years, stamping his authority on Germany and campaigning tirelessly to assert imperial power over Italy in the face of resistance from the papacy and Italian city-states.

Frederick's military career began, as it would end, with a crusade. In 1147, as Duke of Swabia, he left for the Holy Land with the German army assembled by his uncle, King Conrad III. Young Frederick was a far more dynamic, charismatic figure than Conrad and, although lacking experience, soon attained a prominent position among the German crusaders. When a flash flood inflicted heavy losses on the encamped army in Thrace, only Frederick's men were able to avoid damage, having set up their camp on high ground.

However, Frederick participated fully in the subsequent disasters of the campaign. When most of the German knights were massacred, ambushed by Seljuk Turks as they tried to march across central Anatolia,

Sleeping hero
Frederick drowned in 1190, but legend says he is not dead. Instead, he sleeps beneath Kyffhäuser Mountain in Germany and will awake one day to lead again.

KEY BATTLE

LEGNANO

CAMPAIGN War with the Lombard League
DATE May 29, 1176
LOCATION 18 miles (30 km) from Milan, northern Italy

Challenged to battle by the Italian Lombard League, Frederick was outnumbered and his forces unbalanced—his army consisted almost entirely of armored knights, without infantry support. However, he was not prepared to withdraw from confrontation with a citizen militia of foot soldiers armed with pikes. The imperial cavalry charged, with Frederick prominent in their midst. They might have carried the day, but the emperor was unhorsed by a pike and disappeared from view. Believing him dead, his knights wavered and allowed themselves to be driven from the battlefield.

he was one of the survivors. Then in Palestine he was party to the ill-fated decision to lay siege to Damascus, which ended in ignominious retreat.

EMPIRE AGAINST PAPACY

In 1152, Frederick succeeded Conrad to the German throne, not by hereditary right but as the approved choice of powerful German nobles. Unlike his predecessor, he also succeeded in having himself crowned emperor by the pope. This was in return for suppressing a rebellion against papal authority in Rome. For the next 20 years, however, the papacy and the empire were in conflict, and the politics of Italian city-states were polarized between Guelph supporters of the pope and the pro-imperial Ghibellines. From 1158 to 1162, Frederick campaigned in northern

Italy with the aim of reducing hostile cities to subjection, chief among them Milan. The style of warfare consisted almost exclusively of laying waste to the countryside and conducting long sieges. It so happened that Frederick had the patience and ruthlessness, as well as the heavy equipment, that successful siege warfare required.

Frederick's conquest of both Milan and its ally, Crema, were notable for ingenious siege techniques, making use of wheeled towers, battering rams, tunnels, and catapults. But they were also occasions of unspeakable cruelty, Frederick in his frustration having prisoners hacked to pieces or strung up in front of his siege engines and used as human shields. Starvation was the most effective weapon—and one that eventually brought both cities to surrender. Frederick razed Milan in

1162, yet he lacked the resources to impose his will permanently on Italy. His power base in Germany was too insecure, his presence constantly required to keep powerful nobles—particularly Henry the Lion of Saxony—under control. And cities such as Milan had the wealth to rebuild themselves and their citizen armies once Frederick had left.

THE LOMBARD LEAGUE

Frederick had been at odds with Pope Alexander III since a disputed papal election in 1159, in which he had intervened. He grew increasingly desperate to oust Alexander, but when he occupied Rome in the summer of 1167, the result was a catastrophe. The pope escaped and an epidemic killed most of Frederick's army. Boosted by this, Milan and other Italian cities formed an alliance against him: the Lombard League. The emperor had to slip back to Germany in disguise to evade his enemies. A proud man, Frederick was bound to seek revenge for this humiliation.

In 1174, Frederick returned to Italy in order to crush the Lombard League. But disagreements meant that Henry the Lion refused to come to his aid and Frederick's forces were too small for the task on their own. The imperial invasion stalled in a failed siege of Alessandria, and the Lombard League grew in confidence. In May 1176, its militia foot soldiers crushed and almost killed Frederick at Legnano. Although he narrowly survived the battle, turning up in

Pavia three days later to general astonishment, the disaster at Legnano effectively ended his ambitions to dominate Italy.

Frederick made his peace with the papacy, and later with Milan and the other city-states. Afterward, Henry the Lion felt the full weight of Frederick's fury for failing to aid him. The emperor invaded Saxony, exiled Henry, and stripped him of his lands.

THE THIRD CRUSADE

Frederick still had an overriding ambition: to lead a crusade. In 1189, he set out once more for the Holy Land. Like his uncle 40 years earlier, Frederick chose the overland route through the Byzantine Empire and Anatolia. After serious clashes with Byzantine forces, his crusaders entered the Anatolian territory of the Seljuk Turks in spring 1190. His men were in poor condition, exhausted by heat and thirst. Yet Frederick sustained morale and even succeeded in taking the Seljuk city of Konya. The hardest traveling appeared to be over when he was drowned while crossing the Saleph River. Exactly how this happened will never be known. Frederick's body was rescued and inadequately preserved in vinegar, and on their arrival at Antioch, the crusaders hurriedly buried his rotting remains.

Looted treasure
The gilded, jeweled Shrine of the Three Kings in Cologne Cathedral reputedly contains relics of the Magi, looted from Milan by Frederick in 1164.

> HIS GAIT IS FIRM AND STEADY, HIS VOICE CLEAR... HE IS A LOVER OF WARFARE, BUT ONLY THAT PEACE MAY BE SECURED THEREBY.

OTTO VON FREISING, *THE DEEDS OF EMPEROR FREDERICK*, C. 1158

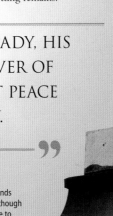

Restoring order
This 19th-century statue of Frederick stands in Goslar, in Lower Saxony, Germany. Although a ruthless campaigner, at home he strove to bring peace to the disparate German states with many concessions to influential and powerful nobles.

KNIGHTS AND NOMADS

MUSLIM WARRIORS

EUROPEAN CRUSADERS WERE able to carve out kingdoms in the eastern Mediterranean because of disunity and weakness among the region's Muslim states, more interested in fighting one another than the alien intruders. A counterattack was inevitable once strong leaders emerged capable of uniting Muslims in holy war against the infidels. Of the warriors who led the defeat of the crusades, the most famous in the West is Saladin, whose chivalrous relationship with Richard the Lionheart became legendary. But in the Islamic world, Baibars is the greater hero, revered for his victories over both Mongols and Christians.

SALADIN

AYYUBID SULTAN OF EGYPT AND SYRIA
BORN c. 1138
DIED March 4, 1193
KEY CONFLICTS Ayyubid-Crusader Wars, Ayyubid-Zengid Wars
KEY BATTLES Montgisard 1177, Jacob's Ford 1179, Hattin 1187, Arsuf 1191, Jaffa 1192

Correctly known as Salah ad-Din Yusuf ibn Ayyub, the warrior ruler familiar to Westerners as Saladin was a Kurd born in Tikrit in present-day Iraq. His family entered the service of the Zengid ruler, Nur ad-Din, in Syria and, from 1164, Saladin accompanied his uncle, Asad ad-Din Shirkuh, on a series of military expeditions to Egypt. There he was initiated into combat, distinguishing himself in a victory over the Egyptian Fatimids on the banks of the Nile and withstanding a lengthy siege in the ancient city of Alexandria.

The two Kurdish warriors developed their own ambitions in Egypt, Saladin inheriting the position his uncle had gained as vizier (high official) at the Fatimid court in 1169. Two years later he defeated the Fatimid caliph and took power for himself, founding the Ayyubid dynasty. After the death of Nur ad-Din in 1174, Saladin returned to Damascus, where he challenged the Zengids for control of Syria. The ensuing struggle continued for over a decade. While fighting his fellow Muslims in Syria, Saladin also undertook war against the crusader kingdoms of Palestine. Control of Jerusalem was the glittering prize he most sought.

In 1177, Saladin invaded Palestine, sacking strongholds along the coast. Underestimating the Christians and ill-informed of their movements, he allowed himself to be surprised at Montgisard with his forces dispersed. The result was a massacre that Saladin was fortunate to survive. He learned a lesson from this setback. For the rest of his career he would be prudent and patient, waiting for a chance to engage his enemy on his own terms. Saladin took his revenge two years later in a campaign that ended with the total destruction of a crusader fortress at Jacob's Ford.

Saladin coin
This Turkish copper dirham from 1190–91 shows Saladin seated and in his civic role as the dispenser of justice.

TO JERUSALEM

It was not until 1183 that the capture of Aleppo in Syria—a crucial breakthrough in his war with the Zengids— at last freed Saladin to focus on defeating the crusaders. He marched on Jerusalem, but was frustrated when the crusader army refused battle on unequal terms. No such judgment was exercised by King Guy, a French knight who ruled Jerusalem, when he faced Saladin at Hattin in 1187. The Christian army was slaughtered and Jerusalem exposed to a siege it could not withstand. Saladin entered the city on October 2, 1187, behaving with humanity and decency toward the defenders. This was policy as well as chivalry, for over the following years a number of crusader strongholds surrendered when assured of good treatment. However, his decision to release aristocratic prisoners allowed many to resume battle against him.

In failing health, and with limited control over the varied elements of his army, Saladin allowed the Christians to regain the initiative. King Guy, freed after his defeat at Hattin, led a siege of Acre from 1189. Saladin failed to relieve the city before Guy was joined by fresh crusaders from Europe in 1191,

Islamic hero
This monument to Saladin stands in front of the citadel in Damascus, Syria, a city that he ruled from 1174.

KEY BATTLE
HATTIN

CAMPAIGN Ayyubid-Crusader Wars
DATE July 4, 1187
LOCATION Near Lake Tiberias, Palestine

In the summer of 1187, Saladin threatened the Christian-held city of Tiberias, hoping to draw King Guy of Jerusalem into mounting a relief offensive. A crusader army advanced over bare hills in summer heat, harassed by Muslim skirmishers who prevented them from seeking water. Near hills known as the Horns of Hattin, they were surrounded by Saladin's far superior army. The thirsty crusader knights made repeated charges attempting to escape, but few broke through and the rest were killed or captured.

turning the balance of forces against him. He could only watch as Acre fell to the Christians, and he was defeated by Richard the Lionheart's army at Arsuf and the following year at Jaffa.

SUING FOR PEACE
Saladin's grasp of strategy was still good enough to deny the crusaders a chance to retake Jerusalem, but he sought a peace deal with Richard. His famous gesture of sending fruit and ice to the fever-struck English king formed part of a diplomatic offensive that secured the crusader king's departure in 1192. When Saladin died shortly after, he was still in possession of the Holy City.

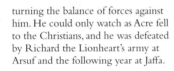

Krak des Chevaliers
The finest of all crusader castles, the Krak des Chevaliers in Syria belonged to the military order of the Hospitallers. Baibars captured it in April 1271, battering breaches in its thick walls and taking it by assault.

BAIBARS

MAMELUKE SULTAN OF EGYPT AND SYRIA
BORN c. 1223
DIED July 1, 1277
KEY CONFLICTS Mameluke-Crusader Wars, Mameluke-Mongol Wars
KEY BATTLES Al-Mansurah 1250, Ain Jalut 1260, Siege of Antioch 1268

The life of Baibars al-Bunduqdari was a triumph of talent and ruthless ambition over lowly origins. A Kipchak Turk enslaved at an early age, he became a Mameluke slave soldier in the service of the Ayyubid caliph of Egypt. After first attracting attention for his role in a victory over the crusaders outside Gaza in 1244, Baibars led the crushing defeat of the French King Louis IX's invading crusader army at al-Mansurah in February 1250.

The crisis of the crusader invasion led the Mamelukes to take power in Cairo, but Baibars was still no more than a trusted general. When the all-conquering Mongols threatened Syria and Egypt a decade later, Mameluke Sultan Qutuz ordered Baibars to lead the counteroffensive. At Ain Jalut, north of Jerusalem, in September 1260 the Mongols suffered their first defeat, sometimes seen as a decisive turning point in history. Baibars headed the Mameluke army, with Qutuz in overall command. The sultan did not live long to savor his triumph; on his way back to Cairo he was assassinated, probably on the orders of Baibars, who succeeded him.

MERCILESS OPPRESSOR
As sultan, Baibars imposed his rule effectively on Syria. He fought more campaigns against the Mongols and ground down the crusader states, reducing major strongholds one by one. He showed none of Saladin's chivalry toward those he defeated, indulging in pitiless massacre, despite promises of safety to those who surrendered. The capture of Antioch in 1268 was followed by a particularly shocking carnage, in which the entire Christian population was killed or enslaved. The crusader castle of the Krak des Chevaliers fell in 1271, but Baibars did not live to see the Christian presence in Palestine completely extinguished. He died either from poison or a fatal wound.

> ## THROUGH YOU GOD HAS PROTECTED THE RAMPARTS OF ISLAM AND PRESERVED THEM FROM THE PROFANATIONS OF THE ENEMY.
>
> **FAKHR AL-DIN IBN LUQMAN,** *EULOGY OF BAIBARS*, C. 1270

RICHARD VS. SALADIN

IN AUGUST 1191, RICHARD THE LIONHEART of England led a crusader army south along the Palestinian coast from Acre toward Jaffa, which he intended to use as a base for retaking Jerusalem from the Muslims. Aware of the dangers that heat and thirst posed to his armored knights, Richard proceeded by slow stages, stopping to allow the supply ships that accompanied his army offshore to keep up. The Muslim commander, Saladin, who had also been camped at Acre, followed the crusaders on higher ground inland, harassing them with skirmishing raids, all the while looking for the right opportunity to launch a decisive attack.

KNIGHTS AND NOMADS

RICHARD THE LIONHEART

Richard knew it was vital for his army to maintain discipline on the march. He placed a screen of foot soldiers, including crossbowmen, on the landward flank of his column, to shield the mounted knights, and gave strict orders that the knights were not to respond to provocation from skirmishing enemy horsemen.

On September 7, 1191, approaching the town of Arsuf, Richard suspected that Saladin intended to attack in force. He rearranged his column in preparation for battle, advancing with the elite Templars and Hospitallers in the van and the rear, respectively. When the Muslim onslaught began, Richard's response was to hold a tight formation, waiting for the right moment to signal a coordinated charge. This strategy required the knights to remain passive while arrows rained down on them, killing many of their horses.

INTO THE FRAY
Finally, discipline snapped and groups of Hospitallers began to break formation and charge the enemy, engaging in close-quarter combat. Finding himself unable to halt the knights, Richard joined them, in the words of a chronicler "cutting down the Saracens like a reaper with his sickle."

The Muslims fled the carnage, only to turn again and resume their harassing attacks. By plunging into the fray, Richard had lost overall control of his army, but his personal example was an inspiration to his knights in finally driving off the enemy. On the final balance of casualties, Richard justly celebrated a victory at Arsuf.

Fearless leader
Richard is shown in a heroic charge in this 19th-century illustration of the battle of Arsuf, trampling the enemy beneath the hooves of his horse.

> **THE FIERCE KING CUT DOWN THE TURKS IN EVERY DIRECTION.**
> A MEDIEVAL CHRONICLER, *THE ITINERARY OF RICHARD I*

TIMELINE

RICHARD	**Dawn** Expecting a Muslim onslaught during the day's march, Richard tightens and strengthens the formation of his column	The crusader army sets off from camp. Richard rides up and down the line to inspect and encourage the troops	Riding in the center of the column, Richard keeps his knights in disciplined formation, continuing the march	The Hospitallers at the rear come under intense pressure. Richard refuses to authorize a counterattack	Richard again refuses the Hospitallers permission to break formation, but the knights lose discipline and charge the enemy

1191: SEPT 7

SALADIN	Saladin draws up his forces on a plain north of Arsuf, between forested hills, and waits for the crusaders	**Around 9 a.m.** Saladin launches his skirmishers in a mass attack on the crusader column, hurling darts and shooting arrows	Saladin sends his cavalry forward, swarming around the rear of the crusader line	Saladin follows the progress of the battle from a hilltop, although the view is obscured by dust raised by the horses' hooves	Many Saracen bowmen are killed, surprised by the crusader knights' charge. Close-quarter combat becomes widespread

Mediterranean Sea

Arsuf

⑤ Richard orders a series of charges by his knights. These successfully drive off the Muslims

Templars

③ Attacks on the rear of the column force crossbowmen to face backward

① Muslim skirmishers launch constant attacks on crusaders as they march

RICHARD

Hospitallers

N

KEY

 Crusader cavalry
Crusader infantry/crossbowmen
Crusader fleet
Crusader baggage train
Muslim cavalry
Muslim infantry/skirmishers

SALADIN

② Mounted archers harass crusaders from a distance

④ Hospitaller knights break ranks and charge

| 0 km | 0.5 | 1 |
| 0 miles | 0.5 | 1 |

LOCATION Holy Land, near modern-day Tel Aviv, Israel

CAMPAIGN The Third Crusade
DATE September 7, 1191
FORCES Crusaders: under 50,000; Muslims: unknown
CASUALTIES According to Christian chroniclers, Crusaders: 700 killed; Muslims: 7,000 killed

SALADIN

Saladin had a clear tactical approach to defeating the Christian knights, well protected by their chain mail. He would provoke them into an attack on his forces during which they would lose formation, allowing his lighter horsemen to infiltrate, surround, and progressively destroy them. After harrying the progress of Richard's army with skirmishing attacks along their march from Jaffa, Saladin's forces waited on the plain at Arsuf. This plain had been chosen by Saladin as the location for battle because it provided a good open field for his cavalry, with the flanks secured by woods and hills.

BATTLE COMMENCES

Saladin's plan was to concentrate on the rear of the crusader column, sending in first his foot skirmishers—including both Numidians and Bedouin—to attack with darts and arrows. The mounted archers

would follow, swarming around the Christians to provoke them into an undisciplined charge.

Unlike Richard, Saladin had no intention of fighting in person, instead, observing the action from a good vantage point at the top of a nearby hill. The battle proceeded broadly as Saladin had planned, but not with the outcome he had intended. The Christians did eventually break formation and charge in a ragged fashion, and Saladin was able to respond with a vigorous counterattack. Further attacks and counterattacks followed, but the Christians ultimately had the better of the close-quarter fighting.

LOSS OF PRESTIGE

Saladin did not lose control of his army, but each time he returned his horsemen to the fight they were again driven off with heavy losses. The unsuccessful outcome of the battle was a serious blow to the Muslim commander's prestige.

The Christian victory was an indecisive one, however, and resulted in Saladin reverting to harassing tactics instead of engaging Richard again in open battle. Although Richard went on to take Jaffa, he was unable to capitalize on his gains and take Jerusalem—the ultimate goal of the crusade.

Unable to restrain his knights, who attack along the length of the line, Richard himself charges into the fray

The crusaders become disorganized in the melee. Richard temporarily loses effective control

The crusaders drive off the Muslims in a series of piecemeal countercharges; Richard himself fights in the thick of the action

Richard leads a small group of knights to the rear of the column and once more drives off the Muslims

The crusaders march on to Jaffa in celebratory mood and install themselves in the city

Saladin sees his men turn and flee in the face of the charge of the armored crusader knights

Saladin succeeds in rallying his fleeing troops and mounts a spirited counterattack

As the van of the crusader column reaches Arsuf, the Muslims again attack the straggling rear

Saladin withdraws in good order to Ramleh, where he takes up a blocking position on the road to Jerusalem

IBERIAN RECONQUISTA

IN THE 11TH CENTURY, the Iberian peninsula was unruly frontier country, where Muslim and Christian kingdoms sparred for advantage and any man with a horse could forge a reputation as a knight. Clear-cut religious wars developed as Christian kingdoms led crusades to reconquer Iberia for their faith, countered by militant Muslim dynasties from North Africa. In the 13th century, the Christians gained the upper hand. The kingdom of Portugal, founded by Afonso Henriques, evicted the last Muslim rulers from its territory in 1149. A Muslim emirate lingered in Granada until 1492, when Castile and Aragon founded the kingdom of Spain.

EL CID

CASTILIAN MILITARY LEADER
BORN c. 1040
DIED 1099
KEY CONFLICT Reconquista
KEY BATTLES Graus 1063, Morella 1084, Siege of Valencia 1093–94

Rodrigo Díaz de Vivar, known as El Cid ("the Lord"), was a Castilian warrior who fought on behalf of both Christian and Muslim rulers in 11th-century Spain, and later in life fought chiefly for his own interests. He has achieved near legendary status as a Castilian national hero, despite his ambivalent position as an honorable maverick during the Reconquista. Indeed, his life story shows the shifting complexity of relations between Spanish Christian and Muslim states at that time. Son of a minor official at the Castilian court in Burgos, El Cid served in wars fought by King Sancho II of Castile in the 1060s. In the most famous action of this period, the battle of Graus, Sancho was allied with the Muslim ruler of Zaragoza against the Christian army of Aragon. El Cid made a name for himself, reportedly killing one of the leading Aragonese knights in single combat. Besides his martial prowess, he proved an intelligent tactician and a natural leader of men. But, in 1072, Sancho was assassinated and succeeded by Alfonso VI. El Cid had a difficult relationship with the new king and was eventually exiled from Castile. He found employment at Muslim Zaragoza, which he defended ably against Christian attacks, again defeating the Aragonese at the battle of Morella in 1084.

Fearsome weapon
El Cid is supposed to have fought the Almoravids with this sword, which became associated with the dauntless nature of the man himself. It is currently a trophy of the Burgos Museum, Castile.

RETURN TO FAVOR
The situation changed radically in 1086 when the Almoravids— fervently Muslim Berber warriors from Morocco—invaded the Iberian peninsula, reigniting the holy war and defeating Alfonso VI at Sagrajas. Alfonso recalled El Cid to his court, but the general did not stay for long. Assembling an army of Christians and Muslims nominally in the service of Castile but actually owing personal loyalty to him, El Cid embarked on a complex series of campaigns against the crucial Muslim city of Valencia. After a long siege, the city fell to El Cid in June 1094. The ensuing ambush and defeat of a counterattack outside Valencia in December sealed El Cid's independent rule over the city. After his death in 1099, Valencia continued to be ruled by his widow Ximena for three more years, before falling to the Almoravids.

National hero
El Cid has been a legendary figure in Castilian culture, celebrated since the 12th century in epic poems and romances. This statue is housed in the Castilian fortress of Segovia.

AFONSO HENRIQUES

KING OF PORTUGAL
BORN July 25, 1109
DIED December 6, 1185
KEY CONFLICT Reconquista
KEY BATTLES Ourique 1139,
Siege of Lisbon 1147

In 1112, at the age of three, Afonso Henriques became titular monarch of Portugal, part of the kingdom of León. The regency was assumed by his mother, who sent Afonso into exile and ruled with her lover, the count of Galicia. At age 14, Afonso gave the first glimpse of his forceful nature by bestowing a knighthood upon himself, rather than receiving the title from a figure of authority. In 1128, he marched an army into Portugal and defeated the Galicians and his mother at the battle of Sao Mamede. Now in possession of the government, he took the title of king. Afonso aspired, above all, to independence from León.

This goal inspired him to campaign against his Muslim neighbors, hoping that victories over the infidel would raise his prestige and win him the support of the papacy. In July 1139, Afonso defeated five Muslim rulers at the battle of Ourique. Almost everything is obscure about this triumph, which legend attributes to the intervention of St. James. After the battle, Afonso's soldiers are said to have declared him king of Portugal, but the kingdom of León rejected this unilateral declaration of independence.

LISBON UNDER SIEGE

In 1147, Afonso exploited a stroke of fortune when a body of English, German, and Flemish knights, who had embarked by sea for the Second Crusade, took refuge from a storm at Porto. Afonso persuaded them to help him seize the Muslim city of Lisbon in return for plunder and land. A four-month siege ensued, after which the Muslim defenders of the city were starved into surrender and massacred.

The Tagus River marked the southern boundary of Afonso's realm for the rest of his life. In 1179, after many vicissitudes, Afonso at last gained the recognition of his independent kingdom by Pope Alexander III. A man of vigor, reputed to be a daunting opponent in face-to-face combat, he was still able to lead an army on campaign at the age of 75.

Family tree
This tapestry represents the line of descent of the Portuguese royal family from 1179, when it was founded by Afonso Henriques.

ALFONSO VIII

KING OF CASTILE AND TOLEDO
BORN November 11, 1155
DIED October 5, 1214
KEY CONFLICT Reconquista
KEY BATTLES Alarcos 1195,
Navas de Tolosa 1212

Alfonso VIII succeeded to the Castilian throne as an infant and was fortunate to survive as rival nobles battled over the regency. At the age of 15, he emerged from seclusion to reclaim his heritage, and was eager to lead Christian Spain in a religious war against the Muslims. Islamic radicals, the Almohads, had replaced the declining Almoravids as rulers of north Africa and Muslim southern Spain. In 1195, Alfonso encountered an Almohad army under Yakub al-Mansur at Alarcos. The battle was a catastrophe for Alfonso, his unsubtle tactics allowing his knights to be surrounded and massacred. The king escaped with his life and, in July 1212, had his revenge. The Almohad caliph, Muhammad III al-Nasir, led a powerful army from north Africa into Spain. Pope Innocent III declared a crusade to resist the Almohad host and knights flocked from northern Europe and the other Iberian kingdoms to join forces with Alfonso in Toledo. The Almohads waited for the Christian army in a strong defensive position on the plain of Las Navas de Tolosa.

IMPROVED TACTICS

Alfonso had learned from the defeat at Alarcos. Instead of making a frontal approach, he led his army across a mountain pass to arrive on the plain behind the Muslims. When battle was joined, he withheld a cavalry reserve to throw into the fray at the crucial moment and scatter the enemy with the force of its armored charge. The victory marked the beginning of the final decline of Muslim influence in Spain.

Cultured monarch
This bronze statue of Alfonso VIII stands in Soria, a city that supported him during the Reconquista. Married to Eleanor, daughter of Henry II of England, Alfonso presided over a cultured court and founded the first Spanish university, at Palencia.

IN THE MIDDLE AGES, BISHOPS ALSO LED TROOPS INTO BATTLE. AMONG THE CHRISTIAN FATALITIES AT ALARCOS, THREE WERE BISHOPS.

ASIAN CONFLICTS

" THOSE WHO WERE ADEPT AND BRAVE I HAVE MADE MILITARY COMMANDERS. THOSE WHO WERE QUICK AND NIMBLE I HAVE MADE HERDERS OF HORSES. THOSE WHO WERE NOT ADEPT I HAVE GIVEN A SMALL WHIP AND SENT TO BE SHEPHERDS. "

GENGHIS KHAN ON HIS ORGANIZATION OF DISPARATE NOMADIC TRIBESMEN, TRADITIONAL MONGOL SOURCES, c. 1206

LYING BETWEEN ANCIENT CENTERS of civilization in west Asia, China, and India, the vast expanses of central Asia were inhabited by nomadic or seminomadic peoples, given to raiding and banditry. Whether Mongols, Turks, or Tatars, under the right leadership these fierce and hardy warriors proved the most successful fighting men of medieval times. In the early 13th century, Genghis Khan laid the foundations for the world's largest land empire; almost two centuries later Timur the Lame was victorious from India to the Aegean.

The era of the Mongol conquests can be dated from 1206, when Genghis Khan established his leadership over the steppe tribes. This enabled him to form large armies for long-distance campaigns that continued under his successors. China was conquered in stages, the north coming under Mongol control by 1234, the south in the 1270s. The drive across Asia to the west brought Mongol armies as far as central Europe in 1241, where they defeated Christian forces at Liegnitz and Mohi. The Muslim world suffered worse, notably with the fall of Baghdad, capital of the Abbasid caliphate, in 1258.

But the golden era of the Mongol empire was brief. By 1300, its leadership was fragmented and had lost the desire for conquest. Yet the memory of Genghis's achievement remained potent, and in the late 14th century the Tatar Timur the Lame, claiming descent from the Mongol khan, revived his imperial ambitions. His military feats were truly awesome, as was the scale of his massacres. Those he defeated included the Mongol Golden Horde (the western division of the Mongol empire), the sultan of Delhi, the sultan of Egypt, and the previously invincible leader of the Ottoman Turks, Bayezid.

STRATEGIC ADVANTAGE

Mongol and Tatar successes owed much to the quality of their leadership. Their commanders did not lead from the front. Rather, they directed operations from a vantage point overlooking the battlefield, using flags, smoke, and other signals to transmit commands. Physical prowess was not at a premium—Mongol general Sübedei achieved some of his greatest victories when he was past the age of 60 and too fat to mount a horse, while Timur was both physically disabled and elderly at the time of his major triumphs. Instead, they possessed qualities of intellect and willpower. Exploiting the ability of their mounted armies to move fast over long distances, the Mongols often maneuvered opponents into a hopeless position without engaging in battle. They delighted in tricks and stratagems, such as the feigned retreat, and deliberately employed terror as psychological warfare.

SAMURAI RESISTANCE

The Mongols were not always victorious. In 1274, and again in 1281, Kublai Khan failed in attempted seaborne invasions of Japan. Although a typhoon played the major part in the defeat of the second and larger invasion, the defensive efforts of the Japanese themselves were certainly a significant factor in Kublai's failure to subdue them. The Japanese had developed a very different military system, honed entirely in civil wars. Their warfare was dominated by the samurai, a military caste in some ways similar to European knights, except that they were equipped with bows as well as swords. Although battle was partly ritualized—with a role for single combat between leading samurai and acceptance of a rigorous code of honor—fierce power struggles were fought out between noble clans. The most notable of these culminated in the Gempei Wars of the 12th century, which resulted in the rule of the Minamoto shogunate.

Mounted warriors
Mongol horsemen outclassed most of their diverse enemies, including some who deployed war elephants. The Mongols were always open to innovation and adopted military skills from other cultures.

Decorative sword mounting
Only members of the Japanese Imperial Court used the *kazari tachi* sword, a status symbol as well as a defensive weapon. This mounting has gold fittings and is inlaid with mother-of-pearl.

NOMADIC WARRIORS

THE TWO GREATEST LEADERS of the nomadic central Asian horsemen, the Mongol Genghis Khan and the Tatar Timur, both devoted much of their lives to subduing and unifying tribes under their leadership. Once united, the nomadic armies were unmatched as an instrument for military conquest. For the civilizations that they overran, the Mongol and Tatar commanders were notable above all for the atrocities they perpetrated. But men such as Sübedei and Timur were also sophisticated masters of strategy and tactics, and Kublai Khan could not have conquered Song China without the ability to organize warfare on an impressive scale.

KNIGHTS AND NOMADS

GHENGIS KHAN

MONGOL KHAN
BORN c. 1162
DIED 1227
KEY CONFLICTS Conquest of the Tangut Empire, Mongol-Jin War, Invasion of the Khwarezmian Empire
KEY BATTLES Beijing 1215, Samarkand 1220

The founder of the Mongol Empire was originally named Temujin, the son of the chieftain of one of the many nomadic tribes that inhabited what is now Mongolia. Temujin's father was murdered when he was a child and he grew up as a tough survivor in a hostile environment. Success in the raids and skirmishes of endemic tribal warfare made him the leader of a growing warrior band and allowed him to form valuable alliances with tribal leaders. By establishing his authority over his friends and defeating his enemies, he extended his control over the fragmented tribes until, in 1206, he was acknowledged as khan (ruler) of the united peoples of the steppe.

ALL-CONQUERING KHAN

As Genghis Khan he harnessed the energy of intertribal war to launch a campaign of conquest. His first target was the Tangut empire in western Xia (now northwestern China). First invaded in 1209, the Tanguts were absorbed into the Mongol empire in the last years of Genghis's reign. Farther south lay the territory of the Jin Dynasty, descendants of Jurchen steppe horsemen who ruled northern China from Zhongdu (now Beijing). Genghis attacked them in 1211, but was blocked by the defenses of their walled cities. He returned with a siege train in 1214 and captured Zhongdu the next year, although the Jin were only conquered under Genghis's successors.

The Mongols also struck westward into Muslim-ruled central Asia. The shah of the Khwarezmian empire—which stretched from Iran to Uzbekistan—had executed a Mongol ambassador, provoking an invasion that crushed the great cites of Samarkand and Bukhara. By the time Genghis died in 1227, his armies had swept as far west as the shores of the Black Sea.

Monument to power
A modern statue of Genghis Khan depicts the founder of the Mongol Empire as a truly imposing figure. As leader of the steppe tribes, he adopted his famous name, which means, appropriately, "supreme ruler."

KEY TROOPS

MONGOL HORSEMEN

Every Mongol tribesman was a horseman and a warrior. On their small, hardy mounts, these nomadic tent-dwellers sustained campaigns over thousands of miles without a supply train. Their weapon was the composite bow, which they used in disciplined maneuvers learned through collective hunting of game. The indifference of these warriors to the suffering or death of their enemies was absolute.

SÜBEDEI

MONGOL GENERAL
BORN c. 1176
DIED 1248
KEY CONFLICTS Invasion of Khwarezmian Empire, Mongol-Jin War, Kievan Rus, Poland, and Hungary
KEY BATTLES Kalka River 1223, Siege of Kaifeng 1232–33, Mohi 1241

Born into an insignificant Mongol tribal family, Sübedei joined Genghis Khan at the age of 17 and became a key figure in his early campaigns of conquest. After the Mongols attacked the Khwarezmian empire in 1219, Sübedei was unleashed to show what he could do with an independent command. Genghis ordered him to take 10,000 horsemen and track down the fleeing Khwarezmian shah.

The shah died before he could be caught, but Sübedei, finding himself in Azerbaijan, decided to explore farther. Pushing west of the Caspian Sea, he raided Georgia and then led his men north across the Caucasus, fighting local tribes, including the Cumans, as he went. In May 1223, he fought a Russian and Cuman army led by Mstislav of Kiev at the Kalka River. Drawing the enemy in with a feigned retreat, Sübedei turned and crushed them with a mixture of cavalry charges and volleys of arrows.

Over the following decade, first under Genghis and then under his successor, Ögedei Khan, Sübedei campaigned in the east. He led the final defeat of the Jin dynasty through the capture of Kaifeng, the Jin capital, following the loss of Zhongdu. This campaign showed his ability to deploy the full panoply of medieval siege-warfare techniques, employing experts recruited from China and conquered Muslim states.

MOVING WEST

In 1237, when Sübedei was over 60 years old, he embarked on another series of major campaigns in the west. He overran Russia, capturing the cities of Kiev and Vladimir. In 1241, he directed an invasion of central Europe on three lines of advance. As one army devastated Transylvania and another defeated the Christian knights at Liegnitz, Poland, Sübedei led an attack on Hungary. At Mohi on April 111,

Mongols versus Christians
During the invasion of central Europe, directed by Sübedei in 1241, Mongol horsemen proved superior to armoured Christian knights in both subtlety of manoeuvre and speed of movement.

> **I WILL WARD OFF YOUR ENEMIES LIKE CLOTH BLOCKS THE WIND.**
SÜBEDEI VOW TO GENGHIS KHAN, TRADITIONAL MONGOL SOURCES

he drove the army of the Hungarian king, Bela IV, into confused flight with a frontal attack across a river—supported by rock-throwing catapults used as field artillery—and a simultaneous flank attack delivered from a concealed position. Sübedei's

horsemen pursued and massacred the Christian troops as they fled. No army in Europe could have resisted the Mongols, but after their victories they went home to elect a new khan and never returned. Sübedei spent his last years campaigning against Song China.

KUBLAI KHAN

MONGOL KHAN AND CHINESE EMPEROR
BORN September 23, 1215
DIED February 18, 1294
KEY CONFLICTS Conquest of Song China, Invasions of Japan and Vietnam
KEY BATTLES Xiangyang 1268–73, Yamen 1279, Bach Dang 1288

A grandson of Genghis Khan, Kublai grew up as part of an elite ruling empire that stretched from Europe to China. Under Mongke, Great Khan from 1251, he was put in control of northern China, taken from the Jin two decades earlier. When Mongke died in 1259, Kublai fought a war against his brother, Ariq Böke, for the title of Great Khan. Kublai won, but the unity of the Mongol Empire was never fully restored. Indeed, Kublai mutated from a Mongol khan into a Chinese emperor. Throughout the 1260s, he campaigned on an expanding scale against the Song dynasty that still ruled prosperous,

Mongol emperor
Kublai Khan ruled China as the founding emperor of the Yuan Dynasty. The Mongol dynasty lasted for less than a century and was replaced by the Ming in 1368.

densely populated southern China. Showing the usual Mongol gift for bringing in foreign skills and adopting new forms of warfare, Kublai developed a river fleet to

contest control of the Yangtze and its tributaries, as well as deploying powerful catapults and primitive gunpowder weapons in sieges. The fall of the key city of Xiangyang in 1273 was soon followed by the collapse of the Song state. In 1279, the last remnants of the regime were destroyed at the naval battle of Yamen.

THE END OF AN ERA

Kublai became ruler of all China and founder of the Yuan Dynasty, but this did not sate his appetite for empire-building warfare. He sent invasion forces south into Vietnam, Burma, and Java, and twice attempted to invade Japan, in 1274 and 1281. These expeditions were far from successful, however. The Japanese ventures, involving the dispatch of large troop-carrying fleets, were beaten by a mix of vigorous samurai resistance and bad weather. In Vietnam Kublai's forces suffered a series of defeats, culminating in the battle of Bach Dang in 1288. In reality, with Kublai's takeover of Song China, the era of Mongol conquests had reached its limit.

TIMELINE

- **1362** Fighting at the head of a small band of followers in tribal warfare, Timur is wounded in a skirmish and made lame for life.

- **1366** Timur takes control of the city of Samarkand as a subordinate ally of Husayn, emir of Balkh.

- **1370** Timur defeats Husayn and captures Balkh in northern Afghanistan, establishing himself in Husayn's place as a significant regional ruler.

- **1386** Provoked by the incursions of Tokhtamysh and his Golden Horde into Persia, Timur begins a three-year campaign to the west, overrunning Georgia.

- **1387** Timur campaigns in Persia and Armenia. The Persian city of Isfahan is sacked and 70,000 of its citizens killed.

- **1391** War breaks out between Timur and Tokhtamysh. Timur wins an inconclusive victory at the battle of the Kandurcha River.

- **1393** Timur occupies Baghdad. Two of Timur's envoys are killed by the Mameluke sultan of Egypt.

OTTOMAN SULTAN, BAYEZID I

- **1395** Timur destroys Tokhtamysh's forces at the battle of Terek and subsequently crushes the Golden Horde.

- **1398** Timur invades northern India, captures Multan in the Punjab after a six-month siege, and sacks Delhi, leaving the city in ruins.

- **1399** Timur begins a campaign of extermination in Georgia, which is devastated over the following four years.

- **1400** Timur invades Syria, then ruled by the Egyptian Mamelukes. He takes and destroys the Syrian city of Aleppo.

- **1401** Timur moves on to the Syrian capital, Damascus, which he pillages and burns to the ground. He meets the scholar Ibn Khaldun and gleans information from him about Egypt.

- **1402** At the battle of Angora (Ankara) Timur defeats and captures the Ottoman sultan, Bayezid I. He advances as far west as Smyrna (Izmir) on the Aegean coast.

- **1404** After returning to Samarkand, Timur heads eastward for a campaign against Ming China. He dies the following year.

TIMUR

TURCO-MONGOL CONQUEROR
BORN April 8, 1336
DIED February 18, 1405
KEY CONFLICTS Tokhtamysh-Timur War, Ottoman-Timurid War
KEY BATTLES Kandurcha 1391, Terek River 1395, Delhi 1398, Aleppo 1400, Ankara 1402

Timur was born into a tribe of Turco-Mongol horsemen in Transoxiana, an area of central Asia roughly equivalent to present-day Uzbekistan and Tajikistan. As a young man, he was the leader of a lawless band of fighters engaged in endemic skirmishing between rival tribes and preying upon traveling merchants. He became known as Timur Lenk (Timur the Lame) because of an arrow wound that left his right arm and leg partially paralyzed.

Timur rose to prominence through an ambitious emir (Muslim ruler), Husayn of Balkh, who used the muscle provided by Timur's band to rise to power. Husayn was then supplanted by his erstwhile supporter. As ruler of Balkh and Samarkand, Timur continued to campaign, but by the age of 50, there was nothing to suggest he was destined for a major role on the world stage.

ASIAN CONQUEST

Timur's wider career of military aggression was triggered by rivalry with his fellow nomadic warrior, Tokhtamysh, who had reconstituted the Mongol Golden Horde. After

> ## THE MOST GREAT WARRIOR... LORD TIMUR, CONQUEROR OF THE EARTH.
>
> **INSCRIPTION ON TIMUR'S TOMB, SAMARKAND**, C. 1405

Tokhtamysh plundered northern Persia in 1385, Timur responded with his own destructive campaigns, destroying Shiraz and eventually taking Baghdad. The two warrior leaders soon engaged in an epic struggle for control of central Asia. The outcome was decided at the Terek River in 1395. Timur defeated Tokhtamysh in battle and then laid waste his former territory with such efficiency that the Golden Horde ceased to exist. Far from satisfying Timur's thirst for warfare and conquest, total

Sophisticated ruler
Timur is here depicted in 1774 with the spear, sword, bow, and shield of the steppe warrior. He had an astute, chess-player's mind and kept written records of his campaigns.

victory in central Asia was followed by a series of breathtaking campaigns that ranged from Delhi to Ankara in less than a decade.

TIMUR'S HORDE

The instrument of these campaigns, Timur's army, was at heart the traditional steppe nomad force, or horde, of tough mounted bowmen. Within this highly organized force, each *tuman* (ten thousand men) was subdivided into thousands, hundreds, and tens. Timur controlled every detail of his army's operations, from the method of constructing a temporary camp on the march to the technique for building pontoon bridges. He was always on the lookout for intelligence about his enemies and distant lands he might later invade. When he met the Arab historian Ibn Khaldun at Damascus in 1401, for example, he obtained a detailed description of Egypt, a likely future victim state. As well as the steppe warfare style of rapid movement and tactical trickery, Timur mastered siege warfare, using experts from settled populations to make and man battering rams and catapults, or provide incendiary and gunpowder devices. He was adept at psychological warfare, cunningly playing on his enemies' hopes and fears to weaken their resolve and divide them. To those peoples he defeated, he was no less than a nightmare of terror.

OPPORTUNIST

Timur did not plan a grand strategy for his campaigns, but was a raider, striking in whichever direction a challenge or an opening appeared. In 1398, he invaded northern India, where the death of a long-ruling sultan of Delhi had left a temporary weakness of political leadership. The forces of the new sultan were destroyed, as was the city. His next target was the Mameluke state of Egypt, where another young, weak ruler had recently come to power. Devastating Georgia en route, Timur marched into Syria, a territory owing allegiance to the Mamelukes. Defeating an army of Syrian emirs at Aleppo, he reduced the city to ruins. Damascus fared no better. The Mameluke sultan led an army to defend the city, but fled precipitately, unnerved by the size and ferocity of Timur's forces. The city surrendered, amid scenes of looting and massacre. Instead of pursuing the Mamelukes down to their capital at Cairo, Timur now took on the only rival worthy of his own military prestige. The

Ornate quiver
All central Asian warriors were first and foremost bowmen, carrying their arrows on their horses in a quiver.

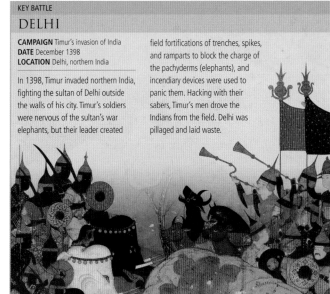

DELHI

CAMPAIGN Timur's invasion of India
DATE December 1398
LOCATION Delhi, northern India

In 1398, Timur invaded northern India, fighting the sultan of Delhi outside the walls of his city. Timur's soldiers were nervous of the sultan's war elephants, but their leader created field fortifications of trenches, spikes, and ramparts to block the charge of the pachyderms (elephants), and incendiary devices were used to panic them. Hacking with their sabers, Timur's men drove the Indians from the field. Delhi was pillaged and laid waste.

aggressive campaigns of Bayezid I, sultan of the Ottoman Turks, had won him the nickname Thunderbolt. He had destroyed a powerful Christian army at Nicopolis in 1396 and besieged the Byzantine capital, Constantinople. In summer 1402, Timur advanced deep into Anatolia, evading Bayezid's army marching east to meet him. When Bayezid realized that the enemy was behind him, he had to turn back. By the time his soldiers found Timur's army near the fortress of Angora (Ankara), they were hot, thirsty, and exhausted. Timur controlled the scarce sources of water on the dry plain, forcing Bayezid to attack. The battle was hard fought, but many Ottomans changed sides or fled. Bayezid was imprisoned and died in captivity. Timur advanced to the Aegean, seizing a Christian crusader castle at Izmir, before returning to Samarkand in triumph. He died two years later, having never fulfilled his final ambition to invade China.

Conqueror's tomb
Timur had many fine buildings constructed in his capital, Samarkand, including the tiled mausoleum where he was buried. In life, however, he followed the nomadic tradition of his people and only made brief visits to the city.

TIMUR: WARRIOR AND TYRANT

"The scourge of god and terror of the world."

Tamburlaine the Great (1587) by Christopher Marlowe highlights Timur's ambition and achievements.

STATUE OF TIMUR IN SAMARKAND, UZBEKISTAN

DESPITE SUFFERING from a serious physical disability, Timur was one of the most successful military leaders in history. Paralyzed down his right side as a result of an early wound, he could ride a horse but was only able to stumble short distances on foot, otherwise needing to be carried. Equally surprising is that his most spectacular triumphs occurred when he was in his sixties.

Yet despite this, Timur campaigned in person at the head of his steppe horsemen, enduring the hardships of travel in all weathers across the vast expanses of Asia. His forays took him north into the Golden Horde and east to the Altai region (present-day Russia), sacking and laying waste the land as he went.

Of his mental strength there was never the slightest doubt. Timur's keen intellect and unshakeable willpower were attested by all those who met him. He was a first-rate chess player and brought to military strategy and tactics the sharp and calculating mind of a potential grand master. Astrologers formed part of his entourage, but Timur ignored them when his estimation of a situation contradicted their predictions. He was also implacably cruel and expected his soldiers to be the same.

He was firm in mind, strong and robust in body, brave and fearless, like a hard rock… He loved bold and brave soldiers, by whose aid he opened the locks of terror and tore in pieces men like lions…

From a manuscript (1436) by Ahmed Ibn Arabshah, recounting his experiences as Timur's servant. He was captured as a boy in Damascus and taken to Samarkand.

By cleverly feigning flight, the hordes of Timur opened up a path for the army of the sultan and permitted them to get well inside their lines. Then they closed in and bore down upon the sultan's troops as though they were enclosed within a wall.

TIMUR ALWAYS TOOK great trouble to bring his opponents to combat while they were at a material and psychological disadvantage. He exploited the mobility of his forces to achieve a greater chance of success in numbers, taking advantage of every possible means to divide or demoralize enemy armies. Timur's standard warrior was a mounted archer equipped with a composite bow, but his forces soon acquired many other elements through his conquests—from Indian elephants to primitive flame-throwers.

The central Asian tradition of warfare was one in which cunning and trickery were admired, especially the feigned flight designed to lure the opponent into a trap. Battle tactics often aimed to draw the enemy into an encirclement. The fast-moving and elusive horsemen would shower their terrified victims with arrows while staying out of reach of attempted counterattacks.

When the opponent had been fatally weakened, Timur's skilled warriors would close in for the final kill, seeking annihilation with saber, spear, mace, and ax. However, there was no expectation that Timur would risk his own life in the thick of the action. Observing the battle's progress from a safe distance, he employed a range of visual and sound signals to direct the maneuvers of his horsemen.

Vita Tamerlani (1416) by Bertrando de Mignanelli. An Italian merchant living in Syria at the time of Timur's conquests, Mignanelli recounted how Aleppo was won.

First they seized their possessions and then tortured them with whips, knives, and fire… Often red hot irons were set on the flesh and they caused the smoke to rise with an odor of roast meat… Then he set fire to the city of Damascus with all its buildings… Sorrowful to relate, the whole of so great and large a city was reduced to a mountain of ashes."

THE ATROCITIES for which Timur was renowned went far beyond the customary medieval practice of permitting soldiers to indulge their worst instincts at the expense of a city taken by assault. It was a deliberate policy of terror by Timur, designed to intimidate his enemies and dissolve their will to resist. He orchestrated dramatic gestures that he knew would be widely reported and have the fullest psychological impact. Such measures included raising pyramids of skulls outside sacked cities or, at Damascus, incinerating thousands of people inside the Great Mosque. There is little doubt that Timur also took personal pleasure in the terror that he inspired in others, once boasting that God had "filled both horizons with fear of me."

Vita Tamerlani (1416) by Bertrando de Mignanelli. *An appalled witness, Mignanelli describes the destruction of Damascus by Timur's army in 1401.*

Arab historian Ibn Khaldun met Timur during the siege of Damascus, later describing the conqueror's generous treatment of him.

"He is one who is favored by Allah…"

Loyal followers
This 17th-century Mogul painting shows Timur during celebrations at Kan-i-Gil, near Samarkand. Despite his fierce reputation, he inspired great admiration among his men.

500—1450

JAPANESE SAMURAI

MEDIEVAL SAMURAI were elite armored warriors theoretically obeying a code of chivalry—the *bushido*—and serving the Japanese emperor. In practice, by the 12th century, the samurai had evolved into warlord clans ruling provincial powerbases and competing for control of Japan itself. The Gempei Wars, fought between the Taira and Minamoto clans in 1180–85, ended in the foundation of the military dictatorship of the shogunate. The samurai generals of this period established idiosyncratic Japanese military traditions, including ritual suicide as the correct response to defeat.

MINAMOTO YOSHIIE

JAPANESE SAMURAI
BORN 1041
DIED 1108
KEY CONFLICTS Early Nine Years' War, Later Three Years' War
KEY BATTLES Kawasaki 1057, Siege of Kanezawa 1086–89

Among the founders of the samurai tradition, Minamoto Yoshiie stands on the cusp between history and legend. As a young man he served alongside his father, Minamoto Yoriyoshi, in the Early Nine Years' War, asserting imperial authority over the Sadato clan in the northern region of Honshu island.

His first battle, fought during a snowstorm at Kawasaki, was a defeat, but his brave performance in the fighting withdrawal earned him the name Hachimantaro—son of Hachiman, the god of war.

Twenty years later, as a leader in his own right, Yoshiie fought the Later Three Years' War against a northern clan, the Kiyowara. This conflict saw two incidents famous in samurai legend. Yoshiie showed his astuteness in spotting an ambush by observing a flight of birds scared by the hidden troops, and he displayed his aesthetic flair by engaging in an exchange of verse with the Kiyowara leader in mid-battle. Yoshiie won the war, taking the fortress of Kanezawa by assault after a long siege.

Expert swordsman
Minamoto Yoshiie displays the sharpness of his sword blade in a ferocious attack on a Go board. Samurai used two-handed swords and never carried a shield.

TAIRA TOMOMORI

JAPANESE SAMURAI
BORN 1152
DIED 1185
KEY CONFLICTS Gempei Wars
KEY BATTLES Uji 1180, Mizushima 1183, Dan no Ura 1185

Tomomori was the outstanding Taira commander in the Gempei Wars. He was the son of the clan leader, Taira Kiyomori, who had established the first samurai government in Japan in 1160 and massacred or banished the leaders of the Minamoto clan.

In 1180 the Minamoto attempted a comeback, supporting another candidate to the imperial throne, Prince Mochihito. Taira Tomomori hunted down Mochihito and his Minamoto bodyguard, defeating them at the first battle of Uji and killing the prince shortly afterward.

Tomomori had further successes in 1181, beating off a night attack by Minamoto Yukiie at Sunomata and pursuing him to Yahagigawa, where the Taira forces again came off best. When the tide of war turned against the Taira from 1183, Tomomori remained successful, making a skillful defense of fortresses around Japan's Inland Sea. At Mizushima, in 1183, he intercepted a Minamoto army being ferried across, his samurai fighting on the decks of oared galleys. When the vanquished Minamoto soldiers fled to shore, Tomomori's samurai caught them on horses they had carried on board.

The last battle of the war at Dan no Ura, in 1185, was also at sea. Forced to fight a larger Minamoto fleet, Tomomori nearly triumphed by his knowledge of local tides. But in the end, he was defeated and, like many of his warriors, committed suicide.

Suicide of Tomomori
Defeated at the naval battle of Dan no Ura, Taira Tomomori ties himself to an anchor and plunges to his death, flanked by a retainer and his mistress. Honorable suicide became one of the salient features of the samurai tradition.

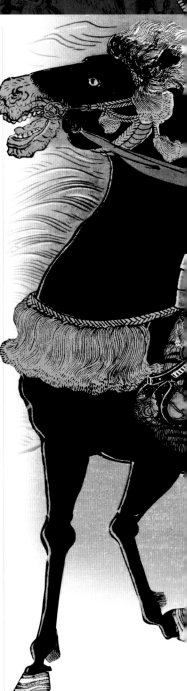

Exemplary warrior
The outstanding general Minamoto Yoshitsune embodied the samurai spirit. Like all samurai of the Gempei Wars era his main weapon was a bow and his armor was as much for display as protection.

MINAMOTO YOSHITSUNE

JAPANESE SAMURAI
BORN 1159
DIED 1189
KEY CONFLICTS Gempei Wars
KEY BATTLES Ichinotani 1184, Yashima 1184, Dan no Ura 1185, Koromogawa 1189

Minamoto Yoshitsune, a superb swordsman always accompanied by his faithful warrior-monk Benkei, is one of the most popular samurai figures in Japanese literary and cultural tradition. He was born in troubled circumstances. His father, Minamoto Yoshitomo, had made himself head of his clan by parricide in 1156, fighting in alliance with the Taira family against his own father. In 1159, the year Yoshitsune was born, Yoshitomo turned against the Taira in the Heiji Rebellion, but was defeated and killed, along with his two eldest sons. The baby Yoshitsune and his brothers, Yoritomo and Noriyori, were spared and exiled to different parts of Japan.

DEFEATING THE TAIRA
Yoshitsune was reunited with his brothers at the start of the Gempei Wars in 1180. When Yoritomo, the eldest, led an army against the Taira, Yoshitsune and Noriyori came to his support. There is no definite record of Yoshitsune's life until 1184, when he routed his cousin, Yoshinaka, in a Minamoto civil war. Yoritomo then authorized Yoshitsune to invade the Taira heartland around Japan's Inland Sea. Fast-moving and decisive, Yoshitsune took as his first objective the coastal fortress of Ichinotani. He divided his army, sending his brother Noriyori to attack the fortress from the front while he led a smaller force down a supposedly impassable cliff to the rear. The fortress was raided and the Taira defenders fled to their boats to escape by water. After a pause to consolidate his gains and build up his naval forces, Yoshitsune followed the Taira to the fortress fronting the beach at Yashima. While the enemy waited for him to close in by sea, Yoshitsune landed his army on the coast some 30 miles (50 km) distant and advanced on Yashima overland. The demoralized Taira once more fled to their boats.

In April 1185, Yoshitsune caught up with them at Dan no Ura. Although they had a far superior fleet, the Minamoto were wrong-footed as the Taira held the advantage of the tide in their favor. But the tide turned, the Taira were beaten, and the battle and the war ended in a mass suicide of the defeated.

Yoshitsune had little chance to enjoy his victory. Yoritomo, no doubt jealous and fearful of his militarily successful younger brother, became his mortal enemy. Yoshitsune fled into the hills and lived like a bandit with a small group of followers until he was hunted down at Koromogawa and, cornered, committed suicide.

500—1450

> BIOGRAPHY
> ## MINAMOTO YORITOMO
>
> Minamoto Yoritomo, the elder brother of Minamoto Yoshitsune, lacked military talent but was cunning and ruthless. Defeated by the Taira at the battle of Ishibashiyama in 1180, he left the rest of the fighting to his brothers. Once Yoshitsune had destroyed his rivals—both Taira and Minamoto—Yoritomo took power himself. And to secure his position, Yoritomo had his younger brother hounded to his death. Yoritomo became Japan's first shogun in 1192, ruling until his death seven years later.

IN BRAVERY, BENEVOLENCE, AND JUSTICE, HE IS BOUND TO LEAVE A GREAT NAME TO POSTERITY.

SAMURAI FUJIWARA KANEZANE, WRITING OF MINAMOTO YOSHITSUNE IN HIS DIARY, 1185

1300—1456

LATE MEDIEVAL EUROPE

"THE KING WENT ALONG THE RANKS... EXHORTING AND BEGGING THEM TO FIGHT VIGOROUSLY AGAINST THE FRENCH... AND THAT THEY SHOULD REMEMBER THAT THEY WERE BORN OF THE REALM OF ENGLAND."

JEHAN DE WAVRIN, A FRENCH KNIGHT, RECORDING HENRY V'S ADDRESS TO HIS MEN AT AGINCOURT, 1415

The beginning of a problematic period in European warfare was signaled at Courtrai, in Flanders, on July 11, 1302, when an army of Flemish weavers and tradesmen equipped with staves, pikes, and bows defeated a mounted charge by French armored knights, killing a thousand noblemen. A shock to accepted notions of social hierarchy and battle tactics, the upset at Courtrai indicated that military commanders needed to rethink the way they fought wars if they were going to keep abreast of a changing world.

The armored knight was still the dominant high-status figure in European armies throughout the 14th and 15th centuries. But no army could be effective without making intelligent use of plentiful lower-class infantry—whether armed with bows or pikes—and knights themselves chose increasingly to fight on foot. Thus, for much of the Hundred Years' War, fought by the French and English kings between 1337 and 1453, the English were dominant in pitched battles because they had discovered a winning formula for the deployment of densely massed longbowmen and dismounted knights.

This led to famous victories at Crécy (1346), Poitiers (1356), and Agincourt (1415). The French survived by adopting the strategic defensive. Protected by the walls of their fortified towns, they could avoid battle and wear the English down, limiting them to laying waste the surrounding countryside.

ADVANCED ARTILLERY

The evolution of cannon during this period, from a peripheral novelty into an essential weapon, gave commanders another element of change to absorb into their strategy and tactics. By speeding up siege warfare, cannon opened up the prospect of an end to strategic deadlock in the Hundred Years' War. They were used intelligently by the English king Henry V,

who bequeathed to his successors a policy of systematic reduction of French fortresses that, in the 1420s, seemed to offer a prospect of final victory. But the French king Charles VII was even more vigorous at adopting cannon, creating a superior artillery train that reduced the duration of sieges to days instead of months. Charles's cannon not only destroyed medieval stone walls but, deployed in the field, allowed the French to turn the tables in pitched battles and drive the English from their territory.

NEW MILITARY AGENDAS

Warfare in the 14th and 15th centuries required mental flexibility and freedom from prejudice. Charles VII had his cannon both built and commanded in action by the brothers Jean and Gaspard Bureau, specialists without the noble blood usually considered essential for military command. Tactical innovation often came from unexpected directions, such as the aggressive use of massed pikemen by the Swiss citizen militia, or the deployment of gunpowder weapons by the maverick Czech Hussite general, Jan Zizka. The new importance of infantry meant that the common people had to be motivated and organized by leaders who knew how to appeal to their incipient nationalism. Nobles brought up to view war as a chance for the high-born to earn glory had to be disciplined into accepting a less flamboyant place on the battlefield. Mercenary commanders leading bands of hardened, full-time soldiers played a growing role in this increasingly professionalized European warfare.

Clash of knights
The battle fought at Auray in Brittany in 1364, an episode in the Hundred Years' War, was a brutal clash between English and French armored knights supporting rival Breton factions.

500—1450

Lethal weapon
The poleax was a formidable weapon, wielded two-handed by a soldier on foot. It had a spike for stabbing, an ax edge for cutting, and a hammer for crushing blows.

THE HUNDRED YEARS' WAR

FOR MUCH OF THE PERIOD from 1337 to 1453, the kings of England and France were at war. The campaigns were fought predominantly on French soil, the English shipping troops across the Channel or launching raids from their base in Aquitaine. They were successful in the early phase of the war, culminating in their victory at Poitiers in 1356, but then were frustrated by a tougher French defensive strategy. King Henry V resumed English successes in 1415 against an enemy weakened by factional warfare. However, the inspiration of Joan of Arc and the crafty practicality of King Charles VII gave final victory to the French.

EDWARD III

KING OF ENGLAND
BORN November 13, 1312
DIED June 21, 1377
KEY CONFLICTS Scottish Independence Wars, Hundred Years' War
KEY BATTLES Halidon Hill 1333, Sluys 1340, Crécy 1346

Edward III was a powerful ruler who stamped his authority on England. The support of the nobility allowed him to campaign abroad in security and provided reliable lieutenants to lead armies on his behalf. His first military campaigns were against the Scots, who had humiliated his father, Edward II, at Bannockburn. He scored a great victory at Halidon Hill in 1333 using innovative tactics. His knights fought defensively on foot while the Scots were felled by his longbowmen.

CROSSING THE CHANNEL

From 1337, Edward began to stake his claim to the French throne, thus sparking the series of conflicts that became known as the Hundred Years' War. His aggressive campaigns across the Channel brought a naval victory at Sluys in 1340, when he destroyed a large French and Genoese fleet. Six years later he led an army of 15,000 men to Normandy, sacking Caen and ravaging northern France, forcing the French king, Philip VI, to fight a pitched battle at Crécy. For Edward it was a triumph, since the charging French knights were brought down by his archers, then beaten in a melee. He took Calais after a year's siege, a huge effort that involved shipping supplies to his army across the Channel.

Edward himself did not return to campaign in France until 1359, after the victory of his son, Edward the Black Prince, at Poitiers. Devastating areas of northern France, he induced the French to agree to onerous peace terms at Brétigny in 1360. Among other conditions, they ceded one-third of their country to Edward. However, he lived to see most of these gains lost by his sons in his old age.

Attack on Caen
Edward III's invasion of France in 1346 began with the taking of the city of Caen by assault. For five days, the victors sacked the city, burning and plundering as they went.

KEY TROOPS

ENGLISH LONGBOWMEN

The longbow was a simple weapon made from a single piece of wood, but in the hands of massed English and Welsh archers it became a battle-winning technology. An experienced bowman could shoot between six and 12 arrows a minute. With several thousand archers deployed, the effect was similar to a machine gun. During Edward III's reign, thousands of bows were stored in armories ready to equip the army on campaign. The archer himself was an even more precious resource, for the skill had to be learned from childhood. The reign of the longbow on the battlefield lasted from Halidon Hill in 1333 to Agincourt in 1415.

EDWARD THE BLACK PRINCE

ENGLISH PRINCE
BORN June 15, 1330
DIED June 8, 1376
KEY CONFLICTS Hundred Years' War, Castilian Civil War
KEY BATTLES Poitiers 1356, Najera 1367

Edward, Prince of Wales, was the eldest son of Edward III. Known as the Black Prince because of his distinctive armor, he was described by the chronicler Jean Froissart as "the Flower of Chivalry of all the world" and was undoubtedly an outstanding battlefield commander.

In 1346, Edward led a division at Crécy, where he fought alongside his father. He went on to replicate Edward III's tactics from that battle—dismounted troops arranged defensively—with his own army at Poitiers 10 years later (pp. 100–01). There Edward achieved an even greater victory.

Prince of Wales feathers
At Crécy, the Black Prince purportedly took his foe's ostrich-feather emblem and German motto, *Ich Dien* (I Serve).

Aquitaine's new ruler
The Black Prince kneels before his father, Edward III, to receive the grant of the duchy of Aquitaine. The king outlived his son by a year.

The reputation he earned at Poitiers was confirmed by his defeat of the Castilians and French in a pitched battle at Najera in Spain during 1367.

Edward was prepared to listen to advice, but firm in his own decisions. His battlefield style was tough and ruthless rather than glory-seeking. These were qualities he also brought to the *chevauchée*, a destructive ride through enemy territory, pillaging and burning on the way. He also presided over the massacre of Limoges in 1370, where thousands were killed for having switched allegiance to the king of France. By then Edward was already suffering from a disease that would kill him before he acceded to the throne.

JEAN II

KING OF FRANCE
BORN April 16, 1319
DIED April 8, 1364
KEY CONFLICTS Hundred Years' War
KEY BATTLES Poitiers 1356

The son of Philip VI, French king Jean II first experienced war against the English as Duke of Normandy in the 1340s. Acceding to the throne in 1350, he attempted to reform the French forces. His Royal Ordinance of 1351 set rates of pay for knights and soldiers and denied nobles the right to withdraw their troops from the battlefield on their own orders.

However, the king's authority was weak and contested. Jean assembled a large army to face the English at Poitiers in 1356, but his decision to attack with most of his knights on foot proved disastrous—as did his lack of control over his noble subordinates. He fought bravely in the latter stages of the battle, but fell into English hands and was imprisoned. Jean's treatment in captivity was an example of perfect chivalry, however. He was allowed to roam freely and given royal privileges. But the failure of France to raise the vast ransom demanded for his release meant that he died in captivity.

Jean the chivalrous
A prisoner of the English, Jean II was allowed to travel to France to help raise his own ransom, afterward returning honorably to captivity in England.

JOHN OF GAUNT

ENGLISH DUKE
BORN March 6, 1340
DIED February 3, 1399
KEY CONFLICTS Hundred Years' War, Castilian Civil War
KEY BATTLES Najera 1367, Lancaster's Raid 1373

The third son of Edward III, John of Gaunt inherited the title Duke of Lancaster through marriage. He had the misfortune to become the leading English commander as the tide of war was turning in favor of France. Having fought under his brother, the Black Prince, at Najera in 1367, John succeeded to the dukedom of Aquitaine in 1371.

King Edward was desperate to reanimate his flagging war with France but neither he nor the Black Prince was fit to fight, so in summer 1373, John crossed the Channel to Calais at the head of a large army. In what is known as Lancaster's Raid, he led an extraordinary five-month march to Aquitaine through eastern and central France. It was not a success. The French king, Charles V, and his constable, Bertrand du Guesclin, strictly avoided battle and the fortified towns along the route proved impregnable. Attempting to live off the country, John lost half his men to starvation and disease. His other major military venture was an invasion of Castile in 1386, where he claimed the throne in the right of his second wife. This was also a failure.

Father of a king
During the reign of Richard II, John of Gaunt was a dominant influence in English political struggles. His son became king as Henry IV seven months after John's death.

THE BLACK PRINCE AT POITIERS

LOCATION
East of Poitiers, central France
CAMPAIGN Hundred Years' War

DATE September 19, 1356
FORCES French c. 15,000–20,000; English c. 8,000
CASUALTIES French c. 2,000 killed, c. 2,500 prisoners; English unknown

In the summer of 1356, Edward the Black Prince led an army from English-ruled Aquitaine through central France, laying waste and looting French territory. At the Loire River he learned that the French king, Jean II, supported by his son, the Dauphin, and the Duc d'Orléans, had

assembled an army and sought to bring him to battle. Edward turned back toward Aquitaine, hoping to avoid an encounter. However, on September 17, outside Poitiers, a clash between English and French cavalry announced that the enemy was near.

The next day, knowing that he was heavily outnumbered, Edward found a defensive position on a wooded slope, with hedges, vines, and marshy ground that would inhibit a French cavalry charge. He ordered his men to dig ditches and construct palisades.

BATTLE LINES

On the morning of September 19, Edward drew up his army for battle, his knights on foot, divided into

three battalions, with longbowmen on the flanks. The prince himself took up position on high ground at the rear, with a clear view of the battlefield and at his disposal a cavalry reserve commanded by a trusted knight, the Captal de Buch.

The sight of the French army was daunting. Not only did it outnumber the English by two to one, but it also consisted almost entirely of armored knights, whereas many of the English were lightly armed foot soldiers. But Edward had chosen a field that limited the number of troops the French could feed into battle at any one time, reducing the impact of cavalry. The French knights were organized in three battalions on foot,

one behind the other, with a cavalry spearhead of 300 men. As the French prepared to attack, Edward called on his troops to have faith in God and obey their orders.

HAND-TO-HAND COMBAT

The initial French cavalry charge was a disaster. Funneled between the flanking archers, the French knights were brought down by arrows shot at their horses and then butchered by English men-at-arms with sword and dagger. From his vantage point the prince saw the first French battalion come up on foot, but fall back after prolonged hand-to-hand fighting. He then saw the inexplicable flight of the second battalion, apparently panicked

by events in front of them into quitting the field. The third French battalion, under Jean's command, was still an overwhelming mass of shining armor and banners.

A TIGHTENING CIRCLE

Weary English hearts wavered as the French advanced to renew combat. The archers were short of arrows, so many threw down their bows and took out their daggers. But Edward, advised by his experienced friend Sir John Chandos, dispatched the Captal de Buch with his horsemen to circle behind the advancing French knights. Then he mounted his own charger and led his entourage into battle with a flourish of trumpets. Attacked simultaneously by the Captal de Buch from the rear, the French were driven back on themselves in an ever-tightening circle. Amid scenes of massacre, Jean II surrendered and was taken prisoner along with most of the surviving French nobility.

> ## THE PRINCE, WHO WAS COURAGEOUS AND CRUEL AS A LION, TOOK THAT DAY GREAT PLEASURE.
>
> **JEAN FROISSART**, *CHRONICLES*, 14TH CENTURY.

① Majority of the French knights dismount before start of the battle

② English form up in defensive position behind a thick hedge

③ Initial French cavalry charge halted by English longbowmen

④ Successive French attacks fail

⑤ Cavalry charge, led by the Captal de Buch, outflanks the French left

KEY

- English cavalry
- English infantry
- English longbowmen
- French cavalry
- French infantry
- Hedge

Poitiers • *JEAN II* • *ORLÉANS* • *DAUPHIN* • *Maupertuis* • *Beauvoir* • *BLACK PRINCE* • *Wood of Nouaillé* • *Nouaillé* • *Moisson*

The battle of Poitiers
This medieval portrayal tries to show the effectiveness of the English longbowmen— although in reality, they would have been far more numerous and shot at longer range.

500–1450

BERTRAND DU GUESCLIN

**BRETON KNIGHT AND CONSTABLE
OF FRANCE**
BORN c. 1320
DIED July 13, 1380
KEY CONFLICTS Breton Civil War, Castillian
Civil War, Hundred Years' War
KEY BATTLES Siege of Rennes 1356–57,
Cocherel 1364, Auray 1364, Najera 1367,
Pontvallain 1370

Born into an obscure Breton family,
Du Guesclin made a famous military
career through sheer fighting skill. He
was blooded in the succession war
that tore Brittany apart in the 1340s
and 1350s, France and England
supporting opposing claimants to
the dukedom. Impressed with his
resistance to the English in the siege
of Rennes, Dauphin Charles, later
King Charles V, took Du Guesclin into
royal service. His battle record was
mixed. He was victorious against the
Captal de Buch at Cocherel, but
defeated by Sir John Chandos at

Auray and by the Black Prince at
Najera. In both defeats Du Guesclin
was captured, but on both occasions
thought worthy of a royal ransom.

Tough and ugly, once described
as "a hog in armor," Du Guesclin
was appointed constable of France
in 1370. He immediately justified
his position by routing the English
in a small-scale but significant
engagement at Pontvallain. From
then onward, he dominated the
English using Fabian tactics—
avoiding battle, disrupting supplies,
and harassing the enemy in a war of
attrition. His professionalism turned
the tide of the war back in France's
favor, justly earning him burial in the
royal abbey of St. Denis.

Badge of office
Du Guesclin is presented with the sword of
office by Charles V, on his appointment as
constable of France in 1370. This was the
highest military office in the country.

HENRY V

KING OF ENGLAND
BORN Born September 16, 1386
DIED August 31, 1422
KEY CONFLICTS Hundred Years' War
KEY BATTLES Agincourt 1415, Siege of Rouen
1418–19

Medieval ruthlessness
Henry V was a charismatic war leader and a
subtle politician. He could be ruthless even
by medieval standards, as in the infamous
massacre of French prisoners at Agincourt.

As heir to the English throne, the
future Henry V first commanded an
army at the age of 16 during Owain
Glyndwr's uprising in Wales. He
fought the rebellious Sir Henry
"Hotspur" Percy at Shrewsbury
in 1403 and had to have an arrow
removed from his face. It was
therefore as an expert fighter,
scarred by battle, that Henry
succeeded to the crown in 1413.

POLITICAL GOALS

Reviving the English monarchy's
claim to the French throne, in August
1415, Henry led an army across the
English Channel. After taking the
port town of Harfleur in a six-week
siege, he was outmaneuvered by the
French and forced to give battle, only
to win an unexpected victory at
Agincourt. This triumph
encouraged the English king's
military and political ambitions.
Showing a firm
grasp of strategy,
he ensured naval
superiority
by devoting
resources to

shipbuilding and equipping himself
with bombards—heavy cannon that
were becoming key to siege warfare.

Henry returned to northern France
in 1417. The defeat of the French at
Agincourt left the English largely free
from the risk of pitched battle. Henry
embarked on two lengthy sieges, at
Caen and Rouen. Both were
successful, and the fall of Rouen in
1419 left Paris exposed to an English
advance along the Seine. In 1420,
through military pressure and subtle
negotiations, Henry induced one
faction of the divided French elite
to recognize him as regent and
heir to the French throne. He
campaigned in alliance with
the Burgundians, reducing
one by one the fortresses
of the faction loyal to the
French Dauphin. His
sudden death from
dysentery in 1422 was
a severe setback for
England, and the
French gradually
gained the upper
hand over the
ensuing decades.

> ## EITHER BY FAMOUS DEATH OR GLORIOUS VICTORY WOULD HE BY GOD'S GRACE WIN HONOR.
>
> **HENRY V'S SPEECH AT AGINCOURT,** ACCORDING TO *HOLINSHED'S CHRONICLES,* 1587

KEY BATTLE

AGINCOURT

CAMPAIGN Hundred Years' War
DATE October 25, 1415
LOCATION Pas-de-Calais, northeast France

Henry V was marching toward Calais, with
men depleted by exhaustion and disease,
when he was intercepted by a much larger
French army. The English took up a solid
defensive position between dense woods.
Advancing over mud, the French knights were
overwhelmed by the English longbows, then
set upon by men-at-arms and archers wielding
swords and axes. When his baggage train was
attacked, Henry massacred his prisoners in
defense. The French defeat was total.

JOAN OF ARC

FRENCH COMMANDER
BORN c. 1412
DIED May 30, 1431
KEY CONFLICTS Hundred Years' War
KEY BATTLES Siege of Orléans 1429, Patay 1429

In 1429, French fortunes were at a low ebb. The English Duke of Bedford was claiming to rule France as regent for the child king, Henry VI; the English and their Burgundian allies controlled northern France and were besieging Orléans. In these dire circumstances the French Dauphin, Charles, cowering at Chinon, was ready to listen to a peasant girl from Lorraine claiming a holy mission to save France.

Joan of Arc, known in her lifetime as Joan the Maid, joined a small army sent to relieve Orléans. Her confidence in her mission was total. She dictated arrogant letters to the English demanding that they "return to the Maiden … the keys to all the good towns [they] took and violated in France." With no military experience, Joan showed an instinctive grasp of the psychology of warfare.

FIGHTING THE CAUSE

Joan's arrival in Orléans inspired the French soldiers with religious and patriotic enthusiasm, which she channeled into bold attacks that reversed the moral balance of the siege. Senior French commanders who had learned caution through bitter experience tried to exclude her from decision-making, but her ideas prevailed to spectacular effect. In a series of sorties from Orléans, the French seized English strongpoints by frontal assault. The demoralized enemy withdrew, ending in days a siege that had lasted months.

Given command of an army with the Duc d'Alençon, Joan then began clearing the Loire Valley. Encountering an English army at Patay, she broke it up with a lightning attack before the English could finish their defensive plans. Success brought volunteers flocking to the French ranks; towns and cities opened their gates to Joan's army and pledged allegiance to the Dauphin. She marched north through Burgundian-held territory to Reims,

where Charles was crowned king in July 1429. But her plan for an immediate attack on Paris was blocked by cautious courtiers. By September, when she did assault the city, the English and Burgundians were prepared and her attack failed. Joan was captured by the Burgundians at Compiègne in May 1430 and sold to the English. Tried for heresy, she was burned at the stake in Rouen. A rehabilitation trial in 1455–56 reversed the verdict; she was canonized in 1920.

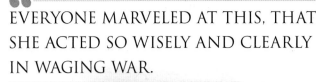

> ## EVERYONE MARVELED AT THIS, THAT SHE ACTED SO WISELY AND CLEARLY IN WAGING WAR.
>
> **TESTIMONY OF JEAN II, DUC D'ALENÇON,** AT THE RETRIAL OF JOAN OF ARC, 1455

Maiden commander
In 1429, Joan of Arc, an illiterate village girl inspired by religious visions, was provided with armor, a horse, banner, and other knightly equipment so that she could lead a French army to the relief of the siege of Orléans.

500—1450

NATIONAL HEROES

EUROPEAN CONFLICTS in the later medieval period saw more involvement of the common people in warfare and a new role for outstanding commanders who embodied ethnic identities forged in struggles against foreign invaders or alien overlords. Although by birth these leaders were members of the international aristocracy of knights, they learned to mobilize popular enthusiasm and make effective tactical use of lowborn foot soldiers. The reality of the lives of men such as Alexander Nevski or Robert Bruce was more complex than the myths later built around their exploits suggest, yet their struggles contributed to the building of nations.

ALEXANDER NEVSKI

GRAND PRINCE OF NOVGOROD
BORN May 30, 1220
DIED November 14, 1263
KEY CONFLICTS Sweden-Novgorod War, Northern Crusades
KEY BATTLES The Neva 1240, Lake Peipus 1242

The Russian national hero Alexander Nevski was a younger son of Yaroslav, prince of Vladimir. In 1236, Alexander was invited to rule the prosperous city-state of Novgorod, near the Baltic Sea, which had long been a major center of trade. At first, it was Alexander's diplomatic rather than tribute. As a result, Novgorod and its lands were never occupied by Mongol forces, and Alexander was free to combat another threat from the west.

In 1240, the Swedes, competitors of Novgorodians in the trapping and trading of fur, sailed up the Neva River to crush their rivals. Alexander's defeat of their army brought him the honorary title of Nevski.

He faced a sterner test two years later. The Roman Catholic Teutonic Knights were campaigning annually to the east of Germany against pagans and Orthodox Christians. They targeted Orthodox Novgorod, and

> ## ALEXANDER USED TO DEFEAT, BUT WAS NEVER DEFEATED...
> **SECOND CHRONICLE OF PSKOV**, 1270

military skills that were called on to protect Novgorod, as the Mongols swept westward to extend their vast empire in 1238–40. Alexander obtained the city's right to self-rule in exchange for paying a handsome

by 1241 much of its territory was in the hands of the Livonian branch of the Teutonic Knights. Despite his victory on the Neva, Alexander had been exiled from Novgorod because of political disputes, but was recalled to face the crisis.

Sainted Alexander
Alexander Nevski was venerated by Orthodox Christians from his death in 1263 and achieved official sainthood in 1547. His victory over German knights was invoked as propaganda during Soviet resistance to the German invasion in World War II.

BATTLE ON THE ICE
Alexander led an army to frozen Lake Peipus, where he fought the Livonian Knights on the ice on April 5, 1242. Alexander's army was larger but mostly consisted of foot soldiers with bows or pikes. The armored Germanic knights charged into their midst, but were soon worn down in prolonged hand-to-hand combat. Alexander's victory ensured that Orthodox Russia was never again seriously threatened by German crusader zeal.

Still collaborating with the Mongols in the interests of peace, Alexander was rewarded by them with the title of Grand Prince of Vladimir.

ROBERT BRUCE

KING OF SCOTLAND
BORN July 11, 1274
DIED June 7, 1329
KEY CONFLICTS War of Scottish Independence
KEY BATTLES Loudoun Hill 1307, Bannockburn 1314

Symbol of the heart of Bruce
Robert gave instructions that after his death that his heart be taken on crusade to expiate the crimes of his lifetime. It never reached Jerusalem and was finally buried in Scotland.

As Earl of Carrick, the young Robert Bruce was a waverer in the Scottish independence struggle. However, virtually forced to declare himself king in March 1306 after murdering a rival, Robert became leader of resistance to the English.

At first a fugitive with a handful of followers, he began an increasingly ambitious guerrilla war, ambushing patrols, destroying isolated fortresses, raiding northern England, and laying waste the lands of his Scots enemies. A victory over a small English army at Loudoun Hill in 1307 showed the potential of his spearmen, fighting in the close formation known as a *schiltron*. Confronted by the English king, Edward II, at Bannockburn in 1314, Robert opened the fighting by killing an English knight in personal combat. He chose boggy ground for the battle to disadvantage the English mounted knights and—deploying his spearmen aggressively in a mass push—drove the enemy from the field with heavy losses. Bannockburn established Scottish independence, recognized by the English in 1328.

Robert the knight
Depicted here in the Bannockburn memorial, Robert I of Scotland was a feudal knight who became a guerrilla leader out of necessity.

JÁNOS HUNYADI

REGENT OF HUNGARY
BORN c. 1400
DIED August 11, 1456
KEY CONFLICTS Ottoman-Hungarian War
KEY BATTLES Varna 1444, Belgrade 1456

Hero of two nations
Born in Wallachia, Hunyadi is claimed as a national hero by the Romanians as well as Hungarians.

The son of a minor nobleman, János Hunyadi rose on merit in the service of the kingdom of Hungary. Fighting Ottoman Sultan Murad II, he proved a flexible and imaginative general, inflicting defeats on the Turks at Smederevo in 1441 and the Iron Gates in 1442.

On the back of these victories he won papal support for a crusade to drive the Ottomans out of Europe. The only ruler to back Hunyadi was Władisław III, king of Poland and Hungary. The Long Campaign, as it is known, was at first very successful, but divisions in the Christian ranks left Hunyadi with inadequate forces to face Murad at Varna on the Black Sea in November 1444. The crusaders were defeated and Władisław killed. Hunyadi became regent of Hungary and continued to resist the Ottomans for the rest of his life, dying of disease after the valiant defense of Belgrade against a Turkish siege in 1456.

JAN ŽIŽKA

HUSSITE GENERAL
BORN c. 1376
DIED 1424
KEY CONFLICTS Hussite Wars
KEY BATTLES Kutna Horá 1421, Malešov 1424

When Catholic forces set out to crush Czech Hussite religious reformers in the 1420s, the Hussite resistance was led by Jan Žižka, a veteran of many wars. With a mainly peasant army at his disposal, Žižka invented superbly effective tactics for countering mounted knights. He deployed cannon, and soldiers armed with crossbows and primitive handguns, on crudely armored wagons. These could be used offensively, charging the enemy like tanks, or chained together in an impregnable defensive circle, known as a *Wagenburg*. Inspired by their faith—the troops entered battle singing hymns—Žižka's army repeatedly won battles, most notably at Kutna Horá. Even after losing his other eye in 1421, Žižka fought on to further victories, dying of the plague after his final win at Malesov.

One-eyed commander
Jan Žižka fought in Poland, Russia, and Lithuania, losing an eye along the way, before joining the Hussites around 1415. He was involved in the defeat of the Teutonic Knights at Grunwald in 1410.

3

MASTERS OF INNOVATION

FROM AROUND 1450 TO THE LATE 17TH CENTURY, the task facing military commanders grew in complexity. They had to respond to the increasing size of armies, a battlefield dominated by low-born foot soldiers, and a step change in the effectiveness of gunpowder weapons. In Europe, new technology made warfare more costly. It may have also made it more destructive, but it certainly did not render it more decisive, many conflicts extending over decades until sheer exhaustion ended hostilities.

The end of the medieval period in warfare is often dated to the fall of Constantinople in 1453. It was there that the Ottoman Turks deployed giant cannon to demolish stone fortifications—structures that had resisted aggressors for almost a thousand years. However, more effective gunpowder weapons did not in themselves revolutionize warfare. Innovative military commanders had to discover ways of exploiting the potential of the new technology in battle and siege—and find ways of negating its effect when used against them. But it soon became clear that cannon would not permanently dominate fortifications or bring an end to siege warfare—on the contrary.

BATTLEPLANS

In the 16th century, the construction of low-lying star fortresses—with walls immune to shot and themselves defended by artillery—forced besieging armies to resort to lengthy blockades and elaborate engineering works such as the digging of trenches and mines. The conduct of sieges became a supreme test of generalship and

some European wars consisted of little else. In pitched battles the key issue was how, and in what proportions, to combine the different strategies and weaponry available to the commander.

While fighting the Burgundians in the 1470s, Swiss infantry demonstrated the potential of massed pikemen, fighting in a disciplined tight formation. Other foot soldiers with firearms would later join the fray, their arquebuses evolving into matchlock muskets

16th-century flanged mace
This mace may have been used by an armored cavalryman, the ornate design showing the high status of its owner. The flanges, or protruding edges, could damage or penetrate even thick armor.

as the crossbow slowly faded from military use. Wherever firearms were introduced, in Japan and Turkey as in Christian Europe, commanders found they were only truly effective fired in volleys by groups of men. Thus, infantrymen had to be trained and drilled, whether using musket or pike.

Over time, the proportion of musket-armed soldiers grew and the ranks of pikemen

thinned. At first, medieval-style armored cavalry with lances still fought on European battlefields. However, faith in the cavalry charge gradually dwindled in the face of muskets, pikes, and cannon.

TAKING UP ARMS

Rearming horsemen with wheel-lock pistols from the mid-16th century led briefly to the abandonment of the charge in favor of the *caracole*, in which a tight row of cavalrymen rode up to the enemy and discharged pistols, then withdrew to make way for the next row.

This maneuver was abandoned in the 17th century, as commanders such as Sweden's Gustavus Adolphus sought to restore the shock effect of charging cavalry as part of an all-arms approach to battle.

The impact of cannon in pitched battles was initially limited by their poor mobility and low rate of fire. Technical advances in both these aspects made them an integral, though not dominant, part of battlefield forces by the early 17th century.

The traditional leadership and military skills of a hereditary ruling class, trained as mounted

1450–1700

Inglorious warfare
Albrecht von Wallenstein (center), a commander of the Thirty Years' War (1618–48), raised troops at his own expense, recouping the cost with profit in campaigns that devastated Germany.

warriors in pursuit of personal glory, proved evermore inadequate to the demands of this fast-evolving warfare. However, most commanders were inevitably still drawn from that class. In 17th-century Europe, the study of warfare became more systematic and the first academies for training officers appeared. Specialists in areas such as engineering, artillery, and transportation provided commanders with the beginnings of an expert staff. The real need was for permanent regular armies, but the countries of Christian Europe struggled to finance such forces and often chose to use troops raised and led by mercenary entrepreneurs. These were military businessmen who became some of the leading generals of the age. Better organized states such as the Ottoman Empire and Manchu China had fewer problems financing armies.

Naval warfare was more readily transformed by the introduction of cannon because ships made excellent gun platforms. This was demonstrated in the galley warfare of the Mediterranean at the great battle of Lepanto in 1571 and in Korean sea battles with Japan in the 1590s. But seaborne cannon were most effective when combined with newly developed ocean-going sailing ships that could circumnavigate the globe. Naval commanders—some of whom were sailors born and bred, others generals drafted to sea—evolved tactics for fighting ship-to-ship actions. They fired cannon in broadsides (firing all the cannons from one side of a ship simultaneously), as well as mastering techniques of command and control during battles at sea. By the mid-17th century this was one area in which Europe led the world.

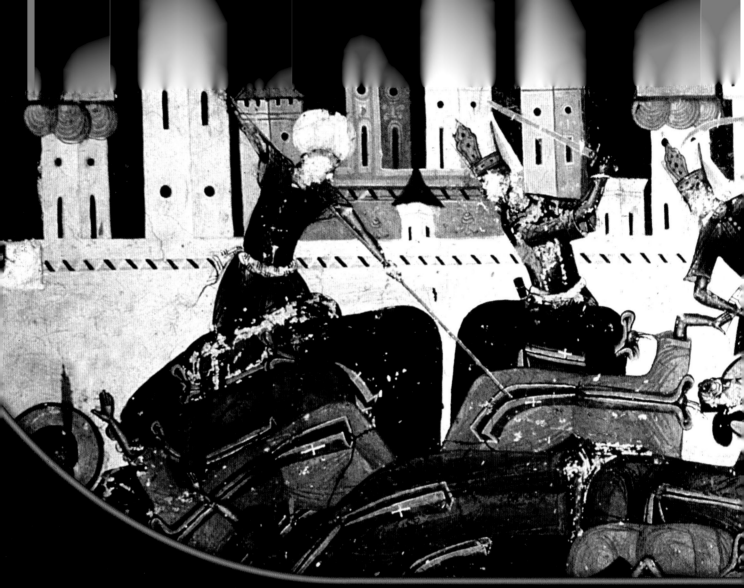

1450—1660

THE MUSLIM WORLD

❧

"ALL THROUGH THE DAY THE TURKS MADE A GREAT SLAUGHTER OF CHRISTIANS. BLOOD FLOWED LIKE RAINWATER IN THE GUTTERS AFTER A SUDDEN STORM, AND CORPSES FLOATED OUT TO SEA LIKE MELONS ALONG A CANAL."

NICOLO BARBARO, SURGEON, WRITING ON THE FALL OF CONSTANTINOPLE, 1453

URING THE 15TH AND 16TH CENTURIES, three great empires were founded in the Muslim world: the Mogul in India, the Safavid in Iran, and the Ottoman extending from the Balkans through the Middle East and north Africa. Under renowned rulers such as Suleiman the Magnificent and Akbar the Great, the Ottomans' armed forces were far larger than those of any contemporary Christian state. At their best, they combined the Asian nomadic warrior tradition with the use of gunpowder weapons and efficient organization of men and resources.

Originally no more than a band of Turkish warriors settled in Anatolia, the Ottomans began their rise to power in the late 13th century under Osman, the founder of their ruling dynasty. Exploiting the weakness of the Byzantine Empire, their forces crossed into Europe in the 14th century, occupying the Balkans and encircling the Byzantine capital, Constantinople. Christian armies fell before the warrior sultans. Bayezid I, known as the Thunderbolt, crushed a body of Christian knights at Nicopolis in 1396, and Murad II defeated Janos Hunyadi's crusaders at the battle of Varna in 1444. The fall of Constantinople to Mehmed II in 1453 completed the first phase of Ottoman expansion.

WIDENING AMBITIONS

From the early 16th century the scope of the Ottomans' ambitions widened. Aspiring to the leadership of the Muslim world, they conquered Syria and Egypt, beating the Egyptian Mamelukes with their superior weapons— they had cannon and firearms, the Egyptians did not. In Europe they advanced as far as Vienna in 1529.

Remarkably, with no seagoing tradition, the Ottomans also became a major naval power, their fleet dominating the eastern Mediterranean. Their activities soon spread into the western Mediterranean through the raids of the Barbary corsairs (pirates from the Barbary Coast) and access in and out of the north African ports that acknowledged Ottoman dominion. Despite setbacks at the failed siege of Malta in 1565 and the naval battle of Lepanto in 1571, the Ottoman Empire remained an expansionist power into the 17th century. Its army's combination of musket-armed infantry—the janissaries—feudal *sipahi* cavalry, and state-of-the-art artillery, all serving with high morale and good discipline, made the Ottoman army probably the most effective fighting force of the time.

INDIA AND IRAN

The founding of the Mogul Empire in India in the 16th century was the work of invaders from central Asia, descendants of the dreaded Timur, who rode into India to settle rather than to raid. Most of their campaigning was against inferior forces as they gradually extended their rule across an ever-greater area of the Indian subcontinent, a process that took almost two centuries. The Moguls are generally credited with introducing cannon and muskets into India, but they never trained their foot soldiers to the level of disciplined, coordinated fire found in Ottoman or European armies.

The Safavids for a long time suffered from similar weaknesses. Established as rulers of Iran from 1501, they constituted a Shi'ite opposition to the Sunni Ottomans, whom they fought repeatedly for control of Iraq and other contested territory between the empires. The Ottomans largely triumphed until Shah Abbas I came to power in 1587. He radically reformed the Safavid army with the help of European advisers, to make full use of firearms and cannon.

Despite such openness to innovative European ideas, by the late 17th century all three empires were falling into relative decline, confronted with the long-term rise of the European powers.

Massacre at Constantinople
Mehmed II and the Ottoman Turks took Constantinople in 1453 after a siege. The massacre that followed is depicted on a 16th-century fresco, partially defaced, at Moldovita Monastery in Romania.

Mogul weapon
This steel *khanjar* dagger, with its recurved double-edged blade, shows the influence of Arab styles on the Moguls. High-status Mogul warriors delighted in finely crafted weaponry.

OTTOMAN LEADERS

 THE SULTANS OF THE OTTOMAN Turkish Empire were first and foremost war leaders who legitimized their rule by conquest. A young and active sultan might expect to lead his army on campaign every year, setting out from his capital in the spring and returning in winter. Theirs was a harsh world, in which the accession of a new sultan, up to the mid-16th century, would be followed by the execution of all his brothers. And yet this ruthlessness was accompanied by a notable efficiency of administration, enabling the Ottomans to support an imposing army and navy that terrorized Christian Europe in the 15th and 16th centuries.

Italian portrait
More interested in Europe than Asia, Mehmed II aspired to be the successor to the Roman emperors and had his portrait painted by the Venetian artist Gentile Bellini.

MEHMED II

OTTOMAN SULTAN
BORN March 30, 1432
DIED May 3, 1481
KEY CONFLICTS Ottoman Wars in Europe
KEY BATTLE Siege of Constantinople 1453

Sultan Mehmed II is known as "the Conqueror" because of his role in the final destruction of the thousand-year-old Byzantine Empire. He first briefly occupied the Ottoman throne at the age of 12, in 1444. His father, Murad II, had abdicated but rapidly returned to face a threat from Christian forces under Janos Hunyadi, which he defeated at Varna. Mehmed was still young when his father died in 1451. He brought a youthful vigor to a project that had preoccupied Ottoman sultans since the previous century: the capture of Constantinople. The Byzantine capital had survived numerous sieges—the most recent in 1422—but its walls had always proved impregnable. Mehmed first prepared a complete blockade of the city. He built Rumeli Castle on the European shore of the Bosphorus to cut off the water route to the Black Sea. He also assembled a fleet of warships in the Sea of Marmara, isolating Constantinople from the Mediterranean.

Exploiting the skills of a mercenary Hungarian, Mehmed constructed an immense siege gun that had to be drawn into position by a team of a hundred oxen. He even had a wooden track built to move ships overland so they could be floated in the Golden Horn inlet under the walls of the city. The reward for all this preparation was a successful assault on May 29, 1453, in which the last Byzantine emperor was killed.

Mehmed's subsequent military career was not uniformly successful. He notably failed to take the island of Rhodes from the Knights of St. John, but his ambition remained far from sated. His obsession was to complete the triumph at Constantinople with the conquest of Rome. Mehmed's troops invaded southern Italy but his sudden death in 1481 terminated this project prematurely.

KHEIR ED-DIN (BARBAROSSA)

TURKISH PRIVATEER AND OTTOMAN ADMIRAL
BORN c. 1478
DIED July 4, 1546
KEY CONFLICTS Ottoman Wars in the Mediterranean
KEY BATTLE Preveza 1538

Born on the Aegean island of Lesbos, Kheir ed-Din was the younger of two brothers both known to the Christian world as Barbarossa (Redbeard). Based at Djerba, off the coast of Tunisia, they earned a fearsome reputation as corsairs (pirates) preying on Christian shipping. But their ambitions went beyond mere piracy. They seized the port of Algiers and, after his brother's death in 1518, Kheir ed-Din gave the city to the Ottoman Empire. He was appointed its official ruler, or *beylerbey,* in return. From this north African base he terrorized the western Mediterranean, raiding the coasts of Spain and Italy at will and enslaving thousands of Christians.

In 1533, Sultan Suleiman summoned Kheir ed-Din to Constantinople to take command of the Ottoman navy. He masterminded a major expansion of the fleet, which he then used to capture the north African port of Tunis. The emperor, Charles V, fought back energetically, leading an expedition to retake Tunis in 1535. Unfazed, Kheir ed-Din recovered quickly from this defeat. His attacks continued at such a level that the Christian states formed a Holy League to combat him.

UNBEATABLE FORCE
When the Holy League brought Kheir ed-Din to battle at Preveza in 1538, his skillfully handled galleys were victorious against odds of three to one. In his last great raids of 1543–44, he ravaged the Italian west coast, operating in alliance with the French king. François I let him use Toulon as a base, to the scandal of Christendom. Kheir ed-Din's tradition continued with his sons, two of them serving at the battle of Lepanto in 1571.

Ottoman corsair
Barbarossa is depicted by an Italian artist with a trident, symbol of the sea god Neptune. The Ottoman admiral was regarded with both admiration and terror in Christian Europe.

SULEIMAN THE MAGNIFICENT

OTTOMAN SULTAN

BORN November 6, 1494

DIED September 7, 1566

KEY CONFLICTS Ottoman Wars in Europe, Ottoman-Safavid Wars

KEY BATTLES Siege of Rhodes 1522, Mohacs 1526, Siege of Vienna 1529, Baghdad 1534, Siege of Malta 1565

The greatest of the Ottoman sultans, Suleiman I inherited from his father, Selim, rule of the Muslim Middle East, which included the recently conquered countries of Syria and Egypt. The new sultan

Potent image
In his younger years Suleiman I was an imposing figure. He was tall and his physical presence was deliberately exaggerated by the wearing of outsize turbans and fine kaftans.

focused on war with the Christian West. He took the Balkan city of Belgrade—the gateway to central Europe—in his first campaign in 1521. The next year he mounted a siege of Rhodes, the island fortress of the Knights of St. John that had defied his great-grandfather, Mehmed the Conqueror. Suleiman's willpower and resources accomplished the task, although Rhodes did not fall until midwinter. The surrender of the knights was accepted by the sultan in chivalrous fashion.

GRADUAL DECLINE

Having secured the eastern Mediterranean, Suleiman concentrated on further land campaigns in Europe. In 1526, the crushing defeat of a Hungarian army at Mohacs brought him to the border of Austria, the heart of the Christian Holy Roman Empire. Three years later he put the empire's capital, Vienna, under siege, but the city's defenses held. Facing critical supply problems as the weather worsened into

fall, Suleiman was forced to withdraw to Constantinople. In the 1530s, the struggle with the Christian world continued at sea as Suleiman's admiral Kheir ed-Din carried the war to Italy and the western Mediterranean. Suleiman was distracted by the challenge of Safavid Iran, leading his army on campaigns to the east and capturing Baghdad in 1534. With the passage of time his health deteriorated. He became reclusive and had two of his sons executed for allegedly plotting against him. Suleiman had long ceased campaigning in person when his forces suffered a humiliating defeat at the siege of Malta in 1565. In response to this catastrophe, the aged sultan, for a last time, accompanied his army into the field. He died in his tent during the siege of Szigeth in Hungary in 1566.

Sultan's weapon
Dating from 1533–34, Suleiman's sword has a curved blade that reflects its Ottoman origins and is decorated with gold from Damascus.

> " I WHO AM THE SULTAN OF SULTANS, THE SOVEREIGN OF SOVEREIGNS... THE SHADOW OF GOD UPON EARTH. "
>
> **SULEIMAN THE MAGNIFICENT**, IN A LETTER TO FRANÇOIS I OF FRANCE

KEY BATTLE

MOHACS

CAMPAIGN Ottoman Conquest of Hungary
DATE August 29, 1526
LOCATION Southern Hungary

Suleiman led an army 100,000 strong to invade Hungary, where he faced a smaller force under King Louis, in which armored knights predominated. He drew up his cannon and musket-armed janissaries in an unbreakable defensive formation screened by horsemen. As the Hungarian knights charged, Suleiman's horsemen gave way, exposing them to the guns. Skirmishers simultaneously harassed the knights from the flanks. At the critical moment, Suleiman ordered his cavalry forward, driving the Hungarians to flight. Louis was killed and half of Hungary reduced to a tributary state.

MOGUL LEADERS

THE MOGUL EMPERORS were Muslim conquerors from central Asia who imposed their rule on the subcontinent through two centuries of warfare. After the initial campaigns of their founder, Babur, the Moguls built up an army far superior to any they fought. They learned to use gunpowder from the Europeans and the Ottomans and, by the late 16th century, Indian craftsmen were producing excellent matchlock firearms. Mogul engineers were skilled at road-building and conducting sieges. By the 18th century, however, signs of military decadence were already apparent, with a bloated army failing to update its tactics, weaponry, or command system.

The emperor at rest
Founder of the Mogul Empire, Babur is here shown at rest during a hunt. He left perceptive memoirs, the *Baburnama*, recording his early struggles and later conquests.

BABUR

MOGUL CONQUEROR
BORN February 23, 1483
DIED January 5, 1531
KEY CONFLICT Mogul Invasion of India
KEY BATTLES First Battle of Panipat 1526, Khanwa 1527, Ghaghra 1529

A direct descendant of the great Turco-Mongol conqueror Timur, Babur was originally the ruler of the small kingdom of Ferghana, lying to the east of Samarkand. Early in life he was driven into exile and became the leader of a rootless warrior band in search of a territory to rule. In 1504, he captured Kabul, but for a long time the focus of his ambitions remained the reconquest of Ferghana and possession of Samarkand.

It was not until 1519 that, frustrated in his campaigns in central Asia, Babur turned south to invade India.

Exploratory raids soon revealed that Ibrahim Lodi, the sultan of Delhi, was likely to prove a vulnerable opponent. In 1526, aided by his son, Hamayun, Babur defeated Ibrahim at the first battle of Panipat and took over his sultanate. He used this as a base for extending his rule farther across northern India.

OPPOSING FORCES

At the time, the army of the Rajput confederacy, under the command of Rana Sanga, was the most formidable enemy in Babur's path. In March 1527, Babur defeated Rana's cavalry and war elephants in a pitched battle at Khanwa. He then took the Rajput fortress of Malwa after a siege, the defenders choosing to commit mass suicide rather than surrender. Babur's final victory was over a Bengali army in May 1529, whom he prevented from crossing the Ghaghra River. All his victories in India were achieved against superior numbers through rapid maneuver, discipline, and the intelligent use of artillery.

KEY BATTLE
PANIPAT

CAMPAIGN Mogul invasion of India
DATE April 21, 1526
LOCATION Panipat, north of Delhi

Babur was confident he could defeat the much larger army of Ibrahim Lodi, sultan of Delhi, by exploiting the weakness of its commander. He placed his cannon and matchlock-armed infantry in a defensive line behind wagons and raised earthworks. On the wings he stationed light horsemen with composite bows. Ibrahim allowed himself to be provoked into making a frontal attack. His vast mob of soldiers and elephants were stopped in their tracks by the gunfire, then enveloped by Babur's fast-moving horsemen whirling around their flanks. With no decisive leadership, Ibrahim's troops fell into disorder and were massacred by the main body of Babur's cavalry.

AKBAR THE GREAT

MOGUL EMPEROR
BORN November 23, 1542
DIED October 27, 1605
KEY CONFLICTS Wars of Mogul Expansion
KEY BATTLES Chitor 1567, Ahmedabad 1573, Patna 1574

When Akbar, grandson of Babur, succeeded to the Mogul throne as a 14-year-old in 1556, it was not clear whether the Mogul Empire had a glorious future—a lot of the territory won by Babur had been lost by Akbar's father, Hamayun. By creating a powerful, well-organized army and through tireless military campaigning, Akbar transformed this diminished inheritance into a great empire.

At first, Akbar was under the guardianship of Bairam Khan, but from 1560 took government and military command into his own hands. One of his earliest challenges was presented by the Hindu Rajputs at the hill fortress of Chitor in 1567. The fort was valiantly defended by the youthful Jaimal Rathore and Prince

Akbar and the Ganges
Akbar's conquest of India brought him into contact with the Ganges. The emperor revered the river's "water of immortality" and refused to drink from any other source.

Patta, but was finally taken by assault after a six-month siege amid scenes of massacre—by some estimates the death toll was 30,000. Akbar was, however, acutely aware of the need to integrate Hindus into his Muslim empire. He had statues of Jaimal and Patta erected at Agra as a gesture of respect, and many Rajput princes did eventually take service with their followers in the Mogul army.

A DIVERSE ARMY

Akbar's attitude was typical of the manner in which he built his army into a vast force, integrating separate bodies of men. Mounted archers from central Asia were recruited under their chiefs, as were the forces of Mogul warlords owing a form of feudal service to the emperor. Akbar's own troops provided a core of artillery, musketeers, and war elephants.

The campaigns Akbar conducted with this army, possibly numbering 200,000 men, ranged from the defeat of the sultan of Ahmedabad in 1573 and the capture of Patna in Bengal in 1574, to the conquest of Kabul in 1581 and Kandahar in 1594. By the time of his death in 1605, Akbar's empire extended over the whole of the north of the Indian subcontinent.

1450—1700

AURANGZEB

MOGUL EMPEROR
BORN November 4, 1618
DIED March 3, 1707
KEY CONFLICTS War of Succession, Deccan Wars
KEY BATTLE Samugarh 1658

The last of the great Mogul emperors, Aurangzeb had to fight for his throne and continued fighting for most of his long reign. His career as a military commander began under his father, Shah Jahan, who gave him the task of resisting pressure from the Iranian Safavid Empire—by then forcing its way into Afghanistan. Although his campaigns there were not a success, they did prepare Aurangzeb for the power struggle that broke out between

himself and his three brothers when Jahan became ill in 1657. Aurangzeb's defeat of his father's favorite son, Dara, at Samugarh in May 1658, was the triumph of an experienced general over a novice. Outmaneuvered and outfought, Aurangzeb's siblings were destroyed one by one, leaving him to inherit the throne unopposed on Jahan's death in 1666.

TERRITORIAL EXPANSION

With the full resources of the empire at his disposal, Aurangzeb campaigned tirelessly to extend its borders and to suppress internal revolts, of which there were many. These were in part provoked by his Muslim zeal, which led to a policy of intolerance toward

Pious emperor
Aurangzeb was a strict Muslim who, late in life, regretted many of his acts. On his deathbed he reportedly said: "I have sinned terribly and I do not know what punishment awaits me."

the Hindu population. In 1670, the Hindu Marathas of the Deccan went to war with Aurangzeb under their leader, Shivaji. After two decades of fighting, the Moguls reestablished a measure of control over the region, but it was never complete.

At the close of the 17th century, Aurangzeb could point to the extent of his empire as a measure of success. No previous ruler had come so close to ruling the entire subcontinent. But constant war left a trail of destruction and exhausted the emperor's finances, without winning the allegiance of many of his subjects.

> ## ENDOWED WITH A VERSATILE AND RARE GENIUS... HE IS A CONSUMMATE STATESMAN, AND A GREAT KING.
> **FRANÇOIS BERNIER DESCRIBING AURANGZEB**, FROM *TRAVELS IN THE MOGUL EMPIRE*, 1670

EAST ASIAN WARFARE

" I MEAN TO DO GLORIOUS DEEDS AND I AM READY FOR A
LONG SIEGE, WITH PROVISIONS AND GOLD AND SILVER IN
PLENTY, SO AS TO RETURN IN TRIUMPH AND LEAVE A GREAT
NAME BEHIND ME. I DESIRE YOU TO UNDERSTAND THIS AND
TO TELL IT TO EVERYBODY. "

JAPANESE DAIMYO TOYOTOMI HIDEYOSHI IN A LETTER TO HIS WIFE c. 1592

THE GREATEST DEMANDS ARE PLACED on military commanders in periods when changing technological or social circumstances demand rapid innovation in warfare, rendering traditional tactics obsolete. In China and Japan in the 16th and 17th centuries, large-scale conflicts brought the dynamic deployment of mass armies and the decisive use of gunpowder weapons. Leaders who could exploit the new style of warfare, such as Japanese daimyo (warlord) Toyotomi Hideyoshi and Chinese Emperor Kangxi, held the key to conquest.

The East Asian wars of this period fall into three groups. One is the series of conflicts between powerful daimyo (warlords) in Japan that ended in the unification of the country under the Tokugawa shogunate in the early 17th century. Another is the long sequence of wars through which the Manchu steppe nomads replaced the Ming Dynasty as rulers of China, roughly between the 1620s and 1680s. Finally, there are the wars fought in Korea, first in the 1590s, when Japanese invaders were fought off by the Koreans with the aid of the Ming Chinese army, and then in the 1620s and 1630s, when the Manchu overran Korea as a prelude to their conquest of China.

TACTICAL SUPERIORITY

The key to success in these wars lay in the mobilization and organization of large-scale forces and in the reshaping of tactics that made the best use of innovative technology. The Manchu might simply have remained marginal raiders, like other nomads and pirates by land and sea who gnawed at the edges of the weakening Ming Empire. But the system of "banners," or companies, into which their army was organized under the inspired leadership of Nurhaci around 1620, proved capable of integrating vast numbers of Chinese peasant conscripts under commanders drawn from an elite of steppe horsemen. Similarly, in Japan, successful warlords needed to sustain armies in which *ashigaru* (peasant foot soldiers) formed the majority and were properly trained,

disciplined, and officered. It was more important that a commander show professionalism in the organization of supplies and in the movement of large bodies of troops than skill with the bow or the sword. By this time, it had even become unnecessary for a Japanese commander to be a samurai—the great Toyotomi Hideyoshi was himself of peasant origins.

RECENT INNOVATIONS

The advantage gained by a commander capable of deploying new technologies effectively is a constant theme of East Asian warfare in this period. Famous examples of this include Oda Nobunaga's training of soldiers to fire arquebus in volleys—displayed at Nagashino (pp. 120–21)—and Korean Admiral Yi Sun-sin's supremely effective use of large, cannon-armed, armored warships against the Japanese. The Manchu became expert in the deployment of cannon on land, having learned the effectiveness of this technique from their Ming enemies. The key commanders of the period, in short, were open-minded realists who achieved superiority of forces by any means available to them.

1450—1700

Siege of Osaka
Samurai Honda Tadatomo, sporting a fine antler headdress, leads a Tokugawa onslaught during the 1615 siege of Osaka. This was the last episode in the pacification of Japan under the Tokugawa shogunate.

Multiple rocket launcher
Deployed by the Koreans in the defense of their country against Japanese invasion in the 1590s, this *hwacha*, or multiple rocket launcher, is typical of the ingenious weapons used in East Asian warfare during this period.

JAPANESE DAIMYO

 BY THE 16TH CENTURY, central authority in Japan had collapsed, allowing the leaders of samurai clans to build local power bases. These daimyo (warlords) jostled for advantage. The relative formality of earlier samurai combat, which emphasized the individual prowess of samurai swordsmen, was supplanted by a more ruthless style of warfare with larger armies. Oda Nobunaga was the first daimyo to attempt to unify Japan through military campaigns. His example inspired Toyotomi Hideyoshi—whose ambition extended to an attempted conquest of China—and Tokugawa Ieyasu, founder of the shogunate that ended the civil wars.

MASTERS OF INNOVATION

 ## ODA NOBUNAGA

JAPANESE DAIMYO
BORN June 23, 1534
DIED June 21, 1582
KEY CONFLICT Japanese Feudal Wars
KEY BATTLES Okehazama 1560, Anegawa 1570, Siege of Mount Hiei 1571, Sieges of Nagashima 1571–74, Nagashino 1575

A commander of exceptional tactical skill and political ambition, Oda Nobunaga had an inauspicious start in life. The son of the head of the Oda clan in Owari province, he earned a reputation for unruliness in his youth that cost him automatic succession to his father, who died when he was 15. Nobunaga awoke to his sense of duty when his retainer, Hirade Kiyohide, committed ritual suicide in protest at his young master's irresponsible behavior. Duly sobered, Nobunaga wrested control of the clan from his uncle. In 1560, he launched his military career in earnest with the stunning defeat of the far larger army of rival daimyo Imagawa Yoshimoto at Okehazama, making a daring night attack on his enemy under cover of a rainstorm.

ENEMIES AND RIVALS

In 1568, Nobunaga seized control of the Japanese capital, Kyoto. His rising power was opposed by rival samurai clans and by militant Buddhist sects: the warrior monks of Mount Hiei, crushed by Nobunaga in 1571, and the Ikko-ikki fundamentalist league, reduced to subjection in 1580.

Nobunaga used maximum force to achieve success, particularly in his victories over the Asai and Asakura clans at Anegawa in 1570 and the Takeda at Nagashino in 1575. Unsentimental about samurai values, Nobunaga allotted his peasant foot soldiers (*ashigaru*) the front line role, and maximized use of the arquebus as a weapon for trained infantry firing in volleys. He also made unsparing use of terror, incinerating the 20,000 inhabitants of Nagashima fortress in 1574. He promoted subordinates on merit regardless of their origins, and so ensured the efficiency of his generals but not necessarily their loyalty. At the height of his power, Nobunaga was cornered by a rebel general, Akeche Mitsuhide, and committed suicide.

Battle of Anegawa
Nobunaga's victory over the Azai and Asakura clans at Anegawa in 1570 was achieved with the aid of future shogun Tokugawa Ieyasu. It was here that he made his first systematic use of musket fire.

> 66
> ## DO YOU REALLY WANT TO SPEND YOUR ENTIRE LIVES PRAYING FOR LONGEVITY? WE WERE BORN IN ORDER TO DIE!
> **ATTRIBUTED TO ODA NOBUNAGA**, SPEAKING BEFORE THE BATTLE OF OKEHAZAMA IN 1560
> 99

TOYOTOMI HIDEYOSHI

**JAPANESE DAIMYO AND KAMPAKU
(REGENT)**
BORN February 2, 1536
DIED September 18, 1598
KEY CONFLICTS Japanese Feudal Wars,
Korean Campaigns
KEY BATTLES Yamazaki 1582, Shizugatake
1583, Nagakute 1584, Siege of Odawara 1590

Toyotomi Hideyoshi was born a peasant on the lands of the Oda clan in Owari province. Of unprepossessing appearance—he was nicknamed Monkey because of his shriveled looks—Hideyoshi nonetheless attracted the attention of Oda Nobunaga, who adopted him as his sandal-bearer. From this lowly rank, Hideyoshi rose to a position of authority by demonstrating competence in all tasks with which he was entrusted. As a reward for his performance as a general at the battle of Anegawa in 1570, he was made a daimyo in his own right.

THE ROAD TO POWER
Nobunaga's suicide in 1582 triggered a struggle for the succession that Hideyoshi won. His style of warfare was based on forced marches to bring his enemy to battle at a disadvantage, followed by a crushing application of superior force. He defeated Akechi Mitsuhide, who was responsible for Nobunaga's death, at the battle of Yamazaki, then destroyed Shibata Katsuie at Shizugatake the following

War trumpet
Toyotomi Hideyoshi is represented blowing his great war trumpet before the crucial victory at Shizugatake in 1583 over Shibata Katsuie. This success freed Hideyoshi to continue Oda Nobunaga's conquest of Japan.

year. Tokugawa Ieyasu succeeded in checking Hideyoshi at Nagakute in 1584, but subsequently agreed to accept his authority.

By 1590, Hideyoshi had overcome the last opposition to his rule in Japan with the successful siege of Odawara, stronghold of the rival Hojo clan. As regent of the empire, he initiated the pacification of Japanese society by banning peasants from bearing arms— in effect, a blow against his own origins. Hideyoshi now planned an audacious conquest of Ming China, sending an invasion force through Korea toward Beijing. The Korean campaigns of 1592 to 1598—which he did not lead in person— ended in disaster, with major defeats at sea and on land. Hideyoshi himself died peacefully.

> ## ODA NOBUNAGA POUNDS THE RICE CAKE, TOYOTOMI HIDEYOSHI KNEADS IT, AND IN THE END TOKUGAWA IEYASU SITS DOWN AND EATS IT.
> **TRADITIONAL JAPANESE SAYING**

TOKUGAWA IEYASU

**JAPANESE DAIMYO
AND SHOGUN**
BORN January 31, 1543
DIED June 1, 1616
KEY CONFLICTS Japanese Feudal Wars,
Osaka Campaign
KEY BATTLES Nagakute 1584, Sekigahara
1600, Tennoji 1615

The founder of the Tokugawa shogunate was the son of a minor daimyo. His clan, the Mikawa, was split between supporters of its two powerful neighbors, the Imagawa and Oda clans. As a child, Ieyasu was seized by the Oda and narrowly escaped execution when his father persisted in backing the Imagawa.

The child returned to his family with a fixed determination to survive in a dangerous world. He first proved himself a valiant samurai while still a youth, at the siege of Terabe in 1558, an action fought on behalf of the Imagawa. When Oda Nobunaga crushed the Imagawa at Okehazama two years later, however, Ieyasu's troops kept well away from the fighting. In the wake of the battle, he nimbly changed sides and fought as Nobunaga's ally at the battle of

Anegawa in 1570. Ieyasu did not lack physical courage, but his most salient characteristics were patience and cunning. In 1572, defeated in a conflict with the Takeda clan at Mikatagahara, he skillfully avoided further fighting until Nobunaga was lured into throwing his superior forces into battle against the Takeda at Nagashino in 1575.

SUBTLE DEALINGS
At the time of Nobunaga's death in 1582, Ieyasu reacted cautiously at first to Toyotomi Hideyoshi's swift seizure of power, before taking up arms on behalf of a rival claimant in 1584. When Hideyoshi and Ieyasu's forces met at Nagakute, Ieyasu had the better of the fighting, but he avoided a decisive showdown, stalling for time until a truce could be arranged. He then recognized Hideyoshi's authority, all the while building up a power base around Edo (modern-day Tokyo).

Ieyasu did not participate in Hideyoshi's disastrous campaigns in Korea, instead, husbanding his strength for the inevitable succession struggle. On Hideyoshi's death in 1598, he launched his bid for power, opposed by a faction led by Ishida Mitsunari. Ieyasu took pains to suborn various daimyo allied to Mitsunari. When battle was joined at Sekigahara in October 1600, many contingents switched sides to join Ieyasu, ensuring his victory.

BIRTH OF A DYNASTY
Ieyasu founded the Tokugawa shogunate in 1603, a date generally accepted as the end of Japan's civil wars. However, the fighting was not quite over. In 1614, supporters of Hideyoshi's son, Toyotomi Hideyori, rose in revolt. Ieyasu responded with an implacable marshaling of his forces to overwhelm the rebels. After a lengthy siege of Osaka castle, the revolt was ended with the battle of Tennoji in 1615. Ieyasu died the following year, but the shogunate he had founded was destined to rule Japan for two and a half centuries.

Shogun's armor
The armor worn by Ieyasu was crafted in the Japanese *tosei gusoko* style, adopted in the 16th century as more practical than the earlier elaborate samurai armor.

ODA NOBUNAGA AT NAGASHINO

LOCATION
Nagashino, Mikawa province, Japan
CAMPAIGN Wars of the Sengoku Era

DATE June 28, 1575
FORCES Nobunaga c. 38,000; Takeda c. 12,000
CASUALTIES Nobunaga unknown; Takeda c. 3,000

In the summer of 1575, the army of the Takeda clan, under Takeda Katsuyori, laid siege to Nagashino, the Tokugawa clan fortress. Tokugawa Ieyasu succeeded in winning the backing of powerful daimyo Oda Nobunaga for an operation to relieve the fortress. Combining their forces, Nobunaga and Ieyasu advanced toward Nagashino with an army two or three times as strong as Katsuyori's.

The Takeda enjoyed a formidable military reputation, however. They had introduced the cavalry charge into Japanese warfare, executed by their mounted samurai to crushing effect against the Tokugawa at the battle of Mikatagahara in 1573. Nobunaga, therefore, intended to ensure that his superior numbers, which consisted mostly of *ashigaru* (peasant foot soldiers), would translate into battlefield success.

ARQUEBUS VOLLEYS
Nobunaga took up a defensive position 165 ft (50 m) behind a steep-banked stream, an obstacle that would interrupt the momentum of the charging horsemen. The key to his battleplan was the use of the arquebus, a matchlock musket that had been present in Japanese armies since the 1540s without having had any dramatic impact. About 3,000 of Nobunaga's foot soldiers carried these primitive firearms. He arranged them in three ranks at the front of his army, behind protective wooden stockades. They had been trained to deliver disciplined fire in volleys by rank.

VICTORY FOR REALISM
On the morning of June 28, Katsuyori ordered his mounted samurai to attack. Followed by foot soldiers, they advanced from wooded hills down on to the plain and across the stream. The crossing of the stream was the signal for the arquebusiers to open fire. Many samurai were felled before their final headlong charge carried them to the stockades. There they were fended off by pike-wielding *ashigaru* and channeled through gaps in the fencing into killing grounds, where they were surrounded by Oda and Tokugawa samurai with short spears and swords. Eventually, the Takeda broke and fled, pursued and hunted down by their adversaries.

The battle exemplified Nobunaga's hard-headed realism. He was a commander who had no intention of fighting without superior forces, and who had no time for the noble traditions of samurai warfare, which would have given pride of place to the bow and sword.

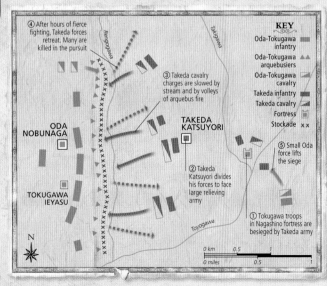

④ After hours of fierce fighting, Takeda forces retreat. Many are killed in the pursuit

ODA NOBUNAGA

TOKUGAWA IEYASU

N

③ Takeda cavalry charges are slowed by stream and by volleys of arquebus fire

TAKEDA KATSUYORI

② Takeda Katsuyori divides his forces to face large relieving army

⑤ Small Oda force lifts the siege

① Tokugawa troops in Nagashino fortress are besieged by Takeda army

Rengogawa
Takigawa
Toyogawa

KEY
▬ Oda-Tokugawa infantry
▲▲ Oda-Tokugawa arquebusiers
▬ Oda-Tokugawa cavalry
▬ Takeda infantry
▬ Takeda cavalry
▣ Fortress
x x Stockade

0 km   0.5   1
0 miles   0.5   1

Nobunaga's forces
A screen painted in the 17th century depicts the whole sweep of the battle. In this section, Oda and Tokugawa samurai are shown in position on the west bank of the stream that would deter Katsuyori's charging cavalry.

CHINA AND KOREA

THE FAILED JAPANESE INVASIONS of Korea between 1592 and 1598 have a special place in Korean history as epics of resistance. The genius of Admiral Yi Sun-sin doomed Japan to failure by winning Korea command of the sea. The ultimate objective of the Japanese had been to attack China, an ailing giant under the decaying Ming Dynasty. Instead, Manchu steppe nomads were the invaders who took over from the Ming, establishing the Qing Dynasty in 1644. Resistance to the Manchu by Ming loyalists lasted for decades, but by the 18th century a reunited China was extending its territories and influence in Asia.

YI SUN-SIN

KOREAN ADMIRAL
BORN April 28, 1545
DIED December 16, 1598
KEY CONFLICTS Japanese Invasions of Korea
KEY BATTLES Hansando 1592, Myeongnyang 1597, Noryang 1598

Yi-Sunsin was originally an army commander who earned a reputation fighting Manchu nomads on Korea's northern border. After a period out of favor, he was made commander of the Cholla naval district.

Faced with the looming threat of a Japanese invasion, Yi took vigorous measures to prepare his fleet for war, gathering supplies and improving manning and equipment. Alongside the cannon-armed warships, known as *panokseon*, which formed the core of his fleet, he built a number of *kobukson* (literally, turtle ships), whose upper decks were enclosed in iron plates. Yi's task as an admiral was to maneuver these gun platforms so that their cannon, firing solid shot and incendiary devices, destroyed the lighter Japanese warships, while avoiding being boarded by the well-armed Japanese soldiers. Yi achieved this by exploiting his superior knowledge of the sea currents and channels around the Korean coast.

NAVAL VICTORIES

Yi is credited with 23 victories against Japan. His greatest triumph during the first invasion was at Hansando, in August 1592, when Japanese ships were lured into an encirclement from which only a handful escaped. Success earned him jealousy at the Korean court, however. Yi was arrested, tortured, and relegated to common soldier.

A severe naval defeat during the second Japanese invasion brought Yi's reinstatement. He registered another victory at Myeongnyang in September 1597. During the final battle of the war, at Noryang in November 1598, Yi was shot by a Japanese arquebus and died on the deck of his ship.

Battle of Hansando
Japanese ships founder and burn as one of Yi's turtle ships, with a dragon figurehead, is rowed into action. Japan lost 47 ships in the battle, the Koreans none.

Korean hero
Admiral Yi Sun-sin led Korea's naval resistance to Japanese invasions in the 1590s. He is a national hero, celebrated by statues in a number of Korean cities, including Seoul.

KOXINGA

CHINESE MING LOYALIST
BORN 1624
DIED 1662
KEY CONFLICT Manchu Conquest of China
KEY BATTLES Nanjing 1659, Taiwan 1661

Zheng Chenggong, better known to Europeans as Koxinga, was the son of a Japanese mother and a Chinese father who had grown rich on trade and piracy. During the Manchu conquest of China in the mid-17th century, Koxinga established himself as a leader of Ming loyalist resistance, from his base in the southeastern coastal province of Fujian.

Koxinga was able to assemble naval forces far superior to any available to the Manchu, using armed merchant and pirate ships to raid at will along the coast and funding his war effort through trade. In 1659, he overreached himself, however, by attacking the major city of Nanjing. The city's troops would have been crushed had Koxinga not been overcautious, laying formal siege and taking smaller outposts rather than launching an immediate assault. The siege was a slipshod affair, so that morale in Nanjing remained high and the besiegers were eventually pursued back to Koxinga's base at the port of Amoy (Xiamen) by a Manchu fleet.

SAVED REPUTATION

Manchu military pressure on land became too much for Koxinga, and, in 1661, he took the bold decision to withdraw from the mainland to Taiwan—then a sparsely populated island dominated by Dutch traders.

After a nine-month siege, he captured the Dutch fort at Zeelandia in February 1662, effectively ending 38 years of Dutch rule.

Koxinga established Taiwan as a military base for continued resistance to the Manchu. But after his death his heirs negotiated with the enemy and the island fell under Manchu domination.

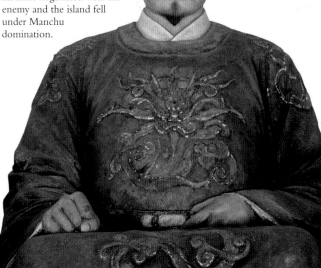

Venerated leader
Zheng Chenggong remains a hero among the people of Taiwan to this day, and is celebrated in many shrines and temples across the island.

> ## THE SAGE KING WHO OPENED UP TAIWAN…
>
> THE PEOPLE OF TAIWAN, ON THEIR DEIFICATION OF KOXINGA FOLLOWING HIS DEATH, 1662

THE EMPEROR KANGXI

CHINESE EMPEROR
BORN May 4, 1654
DIED December 20, 1722
KEY CONFLICTS Revolt of the Three Feudatories, Zunghar Wars
KEY BATTLE Battle of Jao Modo 1696

The Emperor Kangxi was just seven years old when he inherited the Chinese throne in 1661. Eight years later, he took control of the government and oversaw the large-scale operations that, at last, fully established Manchu control of China.

Three Chinese generals, who had collaborated in the Manchu conquest, had been allowed to rule southern China as their personal fiefdoms. In 1673, they rose up against Kangxi in an episode known as the Revolt of the Three Feudatories. Kangxi had already decided that they must be brought to heel, and although he did not lead his armies in person, he directed the strategy of campaigns that ground down the powerful forces of the three feudatories over eight years of fighting. Their defeat released the resources that Kangxi needed to end the other outstanding Chinese resistance to his rule,

maintained by the Zheng clan, descendants of Koxinga, on the island of Taiwan. Employing Shi Lang, an admiral who had once fought as Koxinga's ally, Kangxi assembled a fleet of 300 warships and defeated the Zheng forces at sea in 1683.

CHINESE EXPANSIONISM

Kangxi realized his ambition to command armies in the field through China's subsequent expansionist campaigns in central

Manchu emperor
Kangxi was sometimes represented with the armor and weapons of a steppe nomad, a reminder of the origins of his dynasty.

Asia. After confronting the Russians on the Amur River in the late 1680s, the Chinese went to war with the Zunghars, nomadic tribesmen from Mongolia who had found an inspired leader in Galdan. In 1696, Kangxi led three armies numbering 80,000 men across the Gobi Desert to defeat Galdan at Jao Modo, north of the Kerulen River. By the end of the Emperor Kangxi's long reign, his forces had penetrated as far as the Tibetan capital of Lhasa.

KEY TROOPS

MANCHU BANNERS

The Manchu armies that invaded China in the 1640s were organized into eight banners, or fighting units, each with its own flag and uniform armor. The bannermen became the elite troops of the Qing Dynasty until the 19th century and were especially entrusted with upholding Manchu traditions against native Han Chinese influence.

1490—1625

THE EARLY GUNPOWDER ERA

"

EXPERIENCE TEACHETH HOW SEA-FIGHTS IN THESE DAYS COME SELDOM TO BOARDING... BUT ARE CHIEFLY PERFORMED BY THE GREAT ARTILLERY BREAKING DOWN MASTS AND YARDS, TEARING, RAKING, AND BILGING THE SHIPS...

"

WARFARE WAS ENDEMIC IN EUROPE from the 1490s to the mid-17th century. Traditional power struggles were given a bitter ideological dimension by the Reformation, which split the Christian world into mutually hostile Catholic and Protestant factions. Constant warfare provided a test bed for new technology and tactics as commanders adjusted to the predominance of gunpowder weapons and disciplined infantry. Cannon-armed sailing ships became a major element in warfare between European states and in European global power projection.

The background to the European wars of the early gunpowder period lay in the conquest of parts of the Americas by adventurers acting in the name of the Spanish crown. The Aztec Empire in Mexico and the Inca Empire in Peru were expansionist warrior states, but they proved vulnerable to European diseases and fell victim to the aggressive self-confidence of the Spanish commanders. Whether the outcome would have been any different in the absence of gunpowder weapons is doubtful—in fact, cannon and arquebus played almost no part in the conquest of Peru. The possession of steel weapons and armor, horses, and crossbows was enough to place the European invaders on a different technological and military plane from the Aztecs and Incas. An immediate effect of these conquests in the 1520s and 1530s was to fill the coffers of the Habsburg rulers of Spain with silver, allowing them to pay for armies that fought to sustain their imperial domination of Europe.

RELIGIOUS CONFLICT

The central dynastic conflict in Europe in the 16th century was between the Habsburgs, whose domains included Spain, the Holy Roman Empire, and the Netherlands, and the French Valois kings, notably François I. Successive Habsburg rulers—especially Emperor Charles V and Philip II of Spain— regarded themselves as the champions of Catholicism. Consequently, they were also opposed by states that became committed to the Protestant side of the Christian divide, such as England under Queen Elizabeth I. Religious conflict split countries internally as well as externally, leading to revolts and civil wars. The main geographical focus of conflict between the 1490s and the 1550s was Italy. The Habsburgs were the ultimate winners in these Italian Wars, and the French the losers. Through the second half of the 16th century, France was racked by religious wars, while the Dutch revolted against Spanish Habsburg rule in the Netherlands, starting the Eighty Years' War in 1568. England was sucked into support for the Dutch and war with Habsburg Spain, leading to the famous failed invasion of England by the Spanish Armada in 1588.

A GROWING EXPENSE

The task of commanders in these wars was complicated by the need to establish effective roles for different elements of a fighting force—armored cavalry, pikemen, infantry with arquebus and crossbow, and cannon. The need for well-trained professional forces to implement new tactics that incorporated disciplined use of pikes and firearms made warfare more expensive. This was true whether payment went to regular troops such as the Spanish *tercios* or to mercenary forces such as the German *Landsknechte*. Even the silver of the Americas could not prevent the Habsburgs' finances from being exhausted by their constant military effort in Europe, which had to be sustained while also combating the Ottoman Muslims in the Mediterranean. Dutch and English sailors used their cannon-armed ships to prey upon Spanish treasure fleets and colonies in the Americas, as well as to maintain command of the sea in their own waters. The decline of Habsburg power, under way from the early 17th century, opened a new phase in the history of European warfare.

Dutch victory
The Spanish flagship explodes during the battle of Gibraltar in 1607, a conflict of the Eighty Years' War. The Dutch fleet destroyed 21 Spanish vessels, including 10 large galleons, anchored in the bay of Gibraltar.

Infantry weapon
Combining a pike, an ax, and a hook at the back for grappling with mounted combatants, the halberd was an effective weapon for foot soldiers. Extensively used by the Swiss, this example dates from 1500.

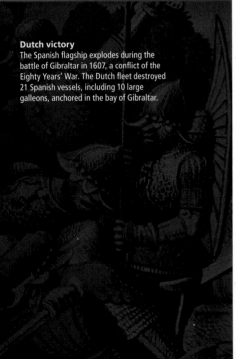

1450—1700

CONQUESTS OF THE AMERICAS

THE WARLIKE EMPIRES of the Aztecs in Mexico and the Incas in Peru proved startlingly vulnerable to attack by small bands of Spanish conquistadores. Hernán Cortés benefited from the combined arrogance and fatalism of Aztec Emperor Moctezuma II, which allowed him to establish himself in the heart of the empire. He was then able to defeat the Aztecs in 1521, fighting in alliance with their traditional allies, the Tlaxcalans. Francisco Pizarro's seizure of power in Inca Peru was an even more remarkable demonstration of the psychological element in war—sheer self-confidence and savage boldness triumphing over unlikely odds.

PEDRO DE ALVARADO

SPANISH CONQUISTADOR
BORN 1490
DIED July 4, 1541
KEY CONFLICTS Spanish Conquest of Mexico and Guatemala
KEY BATTLES Night of Sorrows 1520, Acajutla 1524

Pedro de Alvarado was from the Extremadura region of western Spain. Of a noble but impoverished family, he sought his fortune in the Americas, taking part in an expedition to the Mexican coast in 1518. He then joined Hernán Cortés in his famous venture to conquer Mexico in 1519.

Left in control of Tenochtitlán in 1520, Alvarado was responsible for the massacre of Aztec nobles that provoked a revolt. When the Spanish fought their way out of the city on the night of June 30, known as the Night of Sorrows, he commanded the rearguard, losing many of his men.

After the fall of the Aztec Empire, in 1523, Alvarado took an army into Guatemala to conquer the Maya who had settled there. This culminated in the battle of Acajutla in 1524. His campaigns over the next four years were brutal, but a number of further expeditions came to nothing.

Contempt for life
Pedro de Alvarado was noted for his good looks and love of fine clothes, but his contempt for human life was notorious. The war he waged against the Maya in 1523–27 was characterized by unremitting torture and massacre.

CUAUHTÉMOC

AZTEC EMPEROR
BORN 1502
DIED February 28, 1525
KEY CONFLICT Spanish Conquest of Mexico
KEY BATTLE Siege of Tenochtitlán 1521

Cuauhtémoc was the young Aztec emperor who led the final resistance to the conquistadores in the siege of Tenochtitlán. Nephew and son-in-law of Moctezuma II, he opposed his uncle's collaboration with the Spanish, which had allowed Cortés's army to install itself in the Aztec capital. He was also a leading participant in the Tenochtitlán revolt that broke out after the conquistadores' massacre of Aztec nobles on May 10, 1520. Some even suggest that Cuauhtémoc was one of a group who threw the stones, striking and mortally wounding Moctezuma. He certainly took part in the attacks on Cortés's men as they fled the city under cover of darkness on June 30.

Cuitlahuac succeeded Moctezuma as emperor, but he reigned for only four months before being struck down by smallpox. Cuauhtémoc was then elected emperor by a council of nobles despite his youth, presumably because of his vigorous commitment to resisting the invaders. The new emperor sensibly sought to find allies among neighboring peoples, but traditional hatred of the Aztec and fear of the Spanish blocked all his efforts. Standing alone, he roused his people to fight, rejecting peace negotiations and declaring the death penalty for Christian converts. He prepared Tenochtitlán to face attack, packing it with warriors, although he failed to amass enough food supplies to withstand a siege.

ATTEMPTED ESCAPE

During the battle for Tenochtitlán, Cuauhtémoc remained remote from the fighting. Most likely, direct involvement in the street fighting was not considered suitable for the emperor. When defeat loomed, he tried to escape by canoe across the lake, hoping to fight on elsewhere. Instead, he was captured by the Spanish and tortured in an effort to extract from him the location of treasure that probably did not exist. Cortés eventually had Cuauhtémoc hanged in 1525, accused of treachery against his Spanish masters.

Surrender of an empire
When Cuauhtémoc surrendered to Cortés, the conquistador was courteous, saying, "A Spaniard knows how to respect valor even in an enemy." He was not true to his word.

FRANCISCO PIZARRO

SPANISH CONQUISTADOR
BORN 1471
DIED June 26, 1541
KEY CONFLICT Spanish Conquest of Peru
KEY BATTLE Cajamarca 1532

The illegitimate son of a Spanish army officer, Francisco Pizarro was an early colonist in Panama. He led expeditions down the coast of South America in the 1520s, then won the backing of the Habsburg emperor, Charles V, for the conquest of Peru.

By chance, Pizarro attacked the Inca Empire just as it was recovering from a bitter civil war. With a force of fewer than 200 men he marched to confront Emperor Atawallpa at Cajamarca. Luring the emperor into meeting them, Pizarro's men opened fire on his unarmed entourage and took Atawallpa prisoner. Pizarro later executed him and occupied the Inca capital, Cuzco, unopposed. Motivated by the basest greed, Pizarro and the other conquerors of Peru constantly quarreled. When conquistador Diego de Almagro was killed by Pizarro's brother in 1538, Almagro's followers took revenge, murdering Pizarro in Lima in June 1541.

Bandit style
Pizarro acted more like a bandit than a conventional general, but showed great powers of leadership in the face of adversity.

> WHEN HAS IT EVER HAPPENED...
> THAT SUCH AMAZING EXPLOITS
> HAVE BEEN ACHIEVED?
>
> **FRANCISCO XERES**, *NARRATIVE OF THE CONQUEST OF PERU*, c. 1534

MANQO QAPAC II

INCA LEADER
BORN 1516
DIED 1544
KEY CONFLICTS Spanish Conquest of Peru
KEY BATTLES Cuzco 1536, Ollantaytambo 1537

When Francisco Pizarro had the Inca emperor Atawallpa executed in 1533, many Incas were prepared to rally to the Spanish. In 1534, an Inca noble, Manqo Inca Yupanqui, won the conquistadores' backing to become official ruler of the Inca Empire as Manqo Qapac II. But a year of humiliation at the hands of the Spanish revealed to Manqo that he was being used as a puppet and that Pizarro and his associates intended to control the empire themselves.

In April 1536, Manqo escaped from Cuzco, where he had in effect been a prisoner, and raised an army to fight the conquistadores. Returning to Cuzco he occupied most of the city, but the Spanish and their Inca auxiliaries retained control of strongpoints and fought back under siege. Manqo's forces were weakened by the ravages of smallpox and a diversionary attack on Lima failed.

In January 1537, the conquistadores in Cuzco launched an attack on Manqo's main base for the siege at nearby Ollantaytambo. Manqo had organized his defenses to negate the effect of Spanish cavalry, diverting streams to flood the approaches to his fortress. Exploiting the defensive potential of the high terraces cut into hillsides, he beat off the attack.

GUERRILLA ASSAULT

Without a supply system to sustain his troops indefinitely, Manqo was forced to abandon the siege of Cuzco and withdraw from Ollantaytambo. He retreated to the jungles and mountains of Vilcabamba, where he fought a guerrilla campaign with the aid of fugitive conquistadores. These fugitives were followers of Diego de Almagro, who was in conflict with Pizarro and his brothers. In 1544, one of these conquistadores murdered Manqo, but his successors maintained their resistance until 1572.

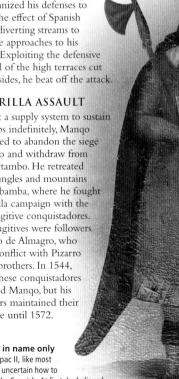

Emperor in name only
Manqo Qapac II, like most Incas, was uncertain how to deal with the Spanish. At first, he believed they would help him rule the empire, before becoming the leader of doomed resistance.

TIMELINE

- **1504** The son of a minor noble family, Cortés sails from Seville to Hispaniola in the West Indies as a colonist.

- **1511** Cortés joins an expedition to conquer Cuba, led by Diego Velázquez. He becomes a man of substance on the island.

- **October 1518** Velázquez appoints Cortés as leader of an expedition to the Mexican coast.

- **February 1519** Cortés sails from Cuba to Mexico with 11 ships, despite Velázquez having revoked his commission.

- **April 1519** Cortés defeats local forces in Tabasco, on the Mexican coast, and acquires the services of a native woman, Malinche, as a translator and adviser.

- **July 1519** Cortés founds the settlement of Veracruz and destroys his ships, committing himself to a campaign of conquest.

- **August–October 1519** Cortés marches toward the Aztec capital of Tenochtitlán, forming an alliance with the Tlaxcala and massacring nobles at the city of Cholula.

- **November 1519** Reaching Tenochtitlán with their Indian allies, the conquistadores alone are invited into the city by Emperor Moctezuma II, who becomes their prisoner.

- **April 1520** Cortés defeats Pánfilo de Narváez, sent by Velázquez to arrest and supersede him. In his absence, a massacre provokes an Aztec revolt in Tenochtitlán.

MOCTEZUMA II AND HIS AMBASSADORS

- **June–July 1520** After Moctezuma is killed, the conquistadores flee Tenochtitlán with heavy losses on the Night of Sorrows (June 30/July 1). Cortés defeats the pursuing Aztecs at Otumba (July 7).

- **May–August 1521** Cortés conducts the siege of Tenochtitlán, a long and costly mix of blockade and assaults. The capture of Emperor Cuauhtémoc finally leads to an Aztec surrender on August 13.

- **1524–26** Cortés leads an army into Honduras and defeats Spanish rebel Cristóbal de Olid. During the expedition he executes Cuauhtémoc.

- **1530–40** After a visit to Spain, Cortés returns to Mexico, but his efforts to organize further conquests and explorations are hindered by quarrels with other Spanish leaders.

- **1541** Finally back in Spain, Cortés joins a disastrous expedition against Barbary corsairs (pirates) in Algiers. It is his last military venture.

HERNÁN CORTÉS

SPANISH CONQUISTADOR
BORN 1485
DIED December 2, 1547
KEY CONFLICT Spanish Conquest of Mexico
KEY BATTLES Otumba 1520, Siege of Tenochtitlán 1521

Hernán Cortés was born in the small town of Medellín in Extremadura, a backwoods region of Castile. Seeking his fortune in the West Indies, where Spain had recently established its first colonies, he rose to the modest post of mayor of Santiago in Cuba. His appointment to lead an expedition to the American mainland in 1518 was his first military command and he seized upon it as an opportunity to pursue far grander ambitions. Cortés arrived on the coast of Mexico as a rebel, for he had not only flouted an order from Cuba's governor, Diego Velázquez, canceling his mission, but also planned on his own initiative to pursue a campaign of conquest in the Mexican interior. He imposed this project upon his followers by executing those who disagreed and destroying the boats that could have carried his men back to Cuba.

On the Mexican coast, Cortés learned of the existence of the Aztec Empire and of its fabled vast wealth. He devised a strategy that was simple yet bold. He would march on Tenochtitlán, the Aztec capital, with his 600 men and his handful of horses and cannon, and make the Aztec emperor, Moctezuma II, accept the Christian faith and the overlordship of the Spanish monarch, Emperor Charles V. Cortés hoped to succeed without a battle, by intimidation and manifest cultural superiority.

THE SPANISH ADVANCE

Advised by Malinche, a local woman whom he adopted as a translator and who became his chief intelligence officer, Cortés knew that the Aztecs were hated and feared by many other Mexican peoples. The alliance he formed with the Tlaxcalans en route to Tenochtitlán was vital, providing a large local army to back up his own.

The Aztecs, meanwhile, were fearful of the strangers' advance. Moctezuma ordered the city of Cholula, an Aztec ally, to give them hospitality. But once inside the city, Cortés, suspecting a trap, ordered a mass slaughter of the nobility—a move that turned up the psychological pressure on the Aztecs. Moctezuma's reaction when Cortés arrived in Tenochtitlán has never been fully explained. It is not known whether he really believed that Cortés was a god and that his arrival fulfilled a prophecy of doom for the Aztec people. He was certainly overawed by the Spaniard's

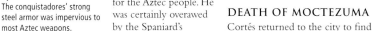

Spanish armor
The conquistadores' strong steel armor was impervious to most Aztec weapons.

CHARLES V

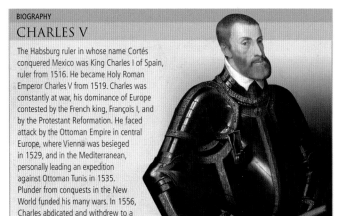

The Habsburg ruler in whose name Cortés conquered Mexico was King Charles I of Spain, ruler from 1516. He became Holy Roman Emperor Charles V from 1519. Charles was constantly at war, his dominance of Europe contested by the French king, François I, and by the Protestant Reformation. He faced attack by the Ottoman Empire in central Europe, where Vienna was besieged in 1529, and in the Mediterranean, personally leading an expedition against Ottoman Tunis in 1535. Plunder from conquests in the New World funded his many wars. In 1556, Charles abdicated and withdrew to a monastery, dying two years later.

Translator and counselor
A local woman named Malinche, known to the Spanish as Doña Marina, became Cortés's long-term mistress and bore him a child.

arrogant self-belief and lack of deference. By inviting the Spanish and not their native allies into his city, Moctezuma may have hoped to control them; instead, he found he had delivered himself into Cortés's hands.

Up to this point, Cortés had shown ruthless determination and fearless self-confidence. Far greater qualities of leadership were now required. In spring 1520, a substantial body of Spanish soldiers under Pánfilo de Narváez arrived in Mexico from Cuba with an order for Cortés's arrest. Cortés marched to meet Narváez and swiftly overcame his larger force with a surprise attack at night. He then persuaded most of the defeated men to join him, much enlarging his army in Mexico. This was timely, for in Cortés's absence an Aztec revolt broke out, provoked by the brutality of the conquistadores.

DEATH OF MOCTEZUMA

Cortés returned to the city to find his men under siege. The death of Moctezuma, killed by his own people, was the signal for Cortés to lead a retreat. The Spanish tried to slip away from Tenochtitlán under the cover of darkness, but were detected and had to fight their way across the causeways that linked the lake city to the shore. Spanish losses were heavy and in the aftermath demoralization could easily have taken hold. Cortés, with admirable calm and self-possession, assured his panicking men that they were merely engaged in a tactical withdrawal and the project to conquer the Aztec Empire remained firm.

The pursuing Aztec army caught up with the fleeing Spanish at Otumba. The conquistadores had many advantages—horses, steel weapons and armor, crossbows, arquebuses, cannon, and even fighting dogs—but they were almost overwhelmed by sheer numbers. Cortés, with five companions, mounted a cavalry charge with lances, putting the senior Aztec commanders to flight.

Having survived this crisis, Cortés began systematic preparations for a fighting return to Tenochtitlán. He isolated the lake city with campaigns that intimidated neighboring peoples into supporting the Spanish or at least denying aid to the Aztecs. The Spaniard imported supplies and new troops and constructed a fleet of boats to operate on the lake around Tenochtitlán. Cortés's conduct of the siege and capture of the city was equally thorough, energetic, and determined.

For Cortés, victory led, perhaps predictably, to anticlimax. He spent much of the rest of his life battling his political enemies and defending his reputation in Spain.

> WE CAME TO SERVE GOD AND HIS MAJESTY... AND ALSO TO ACQUIRE THAT WEALTH WHICH MOST MEN COVET.
>
> **BERNAL DIAZ**, *TRUE HISTORY OF THE CONQUEST OF NEW SPAIN*, C. 1568

Conquering hero
Cortés rides in triumph after his victory over the Aztecs at Otumba in 1520. He provided confident and decisive leadership when the conquistadores' fortunes were at a low ebb.

1450–1700

CORTÉS AT TENOCHTITLÁN

LOCATION Tenochtitlán, present-day Mexico City
CAMPAIGN Spanish Conquest of Mexico
DATE May 31–August 13, 1521
FORCES Spanish: c. 1,000; Tlaxcalans: c. 100,000; Aztecs c. 300,000
CASUALTIES Spanish: c. 400; allies of Spanish: c. 20,000; Aztecs: c. 100,000

Spanish commander Hernán Cortés prepared meticulously for the siege of the Aztec capital, Tenochtitlán, a vast city built on a lake and connected to the shore by causeways. One of his first acts was to cut off the city's main supply of fresh water. To achieve control of the lake he constructed 13 brigantines, vessels big enough to carry 25 soldiers and each with a cannon mounted in the bow. Cortés took personal command of this fleet, manned exclusively by Spanish troops, while Pedro de Alvarado and others were sent to seize control of the main causeways with the support of large numbers of Tlaxcalan allies.

TAKING THE CITY

On June 1, the brigantines carved a swathe through a swarming mass of Aztec canoes on the lake and took command of the water. They were able to support troops fighting on the causeways, eventually making them impossible for the Aztecs to defend. From June 10, Cortés began mounting a series of coordinated drives toward the center of the city from the different causeways. Once in the narrow streets, the advantage of Spanish horses and cannon was lost, with the Aztecs hurling missiles from the rooftops. The conquistadores had to fight their way in afresh each day, for Cortés believed it was too risky to station men in the city overnight, where they might be cut off.

SYSTEMATIC SLAUGHTER

On June 30, 69 Spanish who had been captured by the Aztecs were ritually sacrificed. This was a dangerous moment for Cortés, whose hold on his vital local allies and his own followers depended on maintaining an aura of invincibility. He suspended the assault on the city and sent troops to intimidate people in nearby settlements, ensuring there was no wave of support for the Aztecs.

From mid-July, the daily attacks on Tenochtitlán resumed. Weakened by hunger and the European diseases sweeping the populations, the Aztecs were far less able to defend the streets, now the site of systematic destruction and massacre. Cortés moved his headquarters to a tent on a rooftop inside the city. In a letter to Emperor Charles V, he described the horrors around him: "We expected them to sue for peace… but we could not induce them to do it." The flight and capture of Emperor Cuauhtémoc on August 14 mercifully brought the siege of Tenochtitlán to an end.

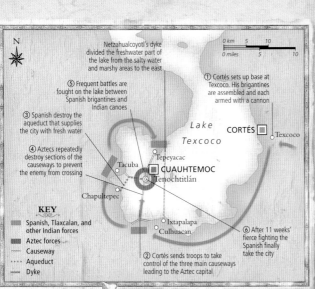

Netzahualcoyotl's dyke divided the freshwater part of the lake from the salty water and marshy areas to the east

① Cortés sets up base at Texcoco. His brigantines are assembled and each armed with a cannon

⑤ Frequent battles are fought on the lake between Spanish brigantines and Indian canoes

③ Spanish destroy the aqueduct that supplies the city with fresh water

④ Aztecs repeatedly destroy sections of the causeways to prevent the enemy from crossing

CORTÉS ▪ Texcoco

Lake Texcoco

Tepeyacac

Tacuba

CUAUHTEMOC ▪ Tenochtitlán

Chapultepec

⑥ After 11 weeks' fierce fighting the Spanish finally take the city

Ixtapalapa
Culhuacan

② Cortés sends troops to take control of the three main causeways leading to the Aztec capital

KEY
▪ Spanish, Tlaxcalan, and other Indian forces
▪ Aztec forces
— Causeway
···· Aqueduct
— Dyke

0 km 5 10
0 miles 5 10

1450—1700

Battle for Tenochtitlán
This 17th-century painting of Cortés's occupation of Tenochtitlán in 1521 shows one of the causeways into the city and a Spanish ship combating Aztec canoes.

THE ITALIAN WARS

IN 1494, CHARLES VIII OF FRANCE invaded Spain, sparking a series of wars that lasted into the mid-16th century and involved, at various times, most of the major powers of western Europe, as well as the Italian city-states and the papacy. These wars occurred during a period when military commanders were striving to exploit new technology and tactics—not only gunpowder weapons but also the integration of dense bodies of pike-armed infantry with traditional armored cavalry and crossbowmen. The broad result was the rise of the Spanish infantry as a dominant military force and of the Habsburgs as a commanding dynasty.

GONZALO DE CÓRDOBA

SPANISH GENERAL
BORN September 1, 1453
DIED December 2, 1515
KEY CONFLICTS Granada War, Italian Wars
KEY BATTLES Atella 1496, Cerignola 1503, Garigliano 1503

Gonzalo de Córdoba deserves much of the credit for turning the Spanish army into the dominant force in 16th-century European warfare. Distinguished in the 1492 defeat of the Muslim kingdom of Granada, his reputation largely rests on his Italian campaigns, which began in 1496 with a victory over the French at Atella.

BATTLEFIELD TACTICIAN
Gonzalo de Córdoba harnessed the discipline of the highly trained *tercios*—regular Spanish infantry combining a mass of pikemen with arquebusiers. With his military engineer, Pedro Navarro, he also developed expertise in siege warfare and the use of cannon. He was the first commander to see the importance of field fortifications in the warfare of the gunpowder age, positioning his infantry and artillery behind defensive earthworks. At Cerignola in April 1503, he scored a landmark victory over French knights and Swiss pikemen by blasting them with firepower from behind a ditch and palisade.

The following December, Gonzalo de Córdoba showed his offensive flair by defeating a larger French force at Garigliano through a bold maneuver that involved moving troops across a river unobserved on an improvised pontoon bridge. His military career ended with his return to Spain in 1507.

The great captain
Gonzalo de Córdoba lived at a time when commanders were still, in appearance and attitude, similar to medieval knights, while military tactics and technology were undergoing rapid change.

GASTON DE FOIX

FRENCH DUKE
BORN December 10, 1489
DIED April 11, 1512
KEY CONFLICT Italian Wars
KEY BATTLES Brescia 1512, Ravenna 1512

Gaston de Foix was appointed French army commander in Italy in 1511 at the age of 21. His enthusiasm had an immediate impact on the war. He relieved Bologna from a siege and then marched on Brescia, storming the city in a swift and bloody assault. Heading south toward Ravenna, he encountered a Spanish army dug into field fortifications. His aggressive use of artillery and infantry achieved an outstanding victory, but he was killed leading the pursuit of the fleeing foe.

Young hero
Gaston de Foix was a naturally gifted young commander, and his death after little more than a year in service a huge loss for France.

GEORG VON FRUNDSBERG

LANDSKNECHT MERCENARY LEADER
BORN September 24, 1473
DIED August 20, 1528
KEY CONFLICT Italian Wars
KEY BATTLES Bicocca 1522, Pavia 1525

A knight from southern Germany, Georg von Frundsberg was a faithful servant of the Holy Roman Emperor. He is famed for his leadership of the *Landsknecht* mercenary foot soldiers from 1508. The tough *Landsknechte*, first recruited in 1486, had been of limited use to the emperor, as many of their mercenary bands left to serve other rulers. When Frundsberg took command, he formed them into a highly effective imperial force.

FRUNDSBERG'S INFANTRY

In the battle of La Bicocca, near Milan, in 1522, the *Landsknechte* defeated the Swiss mercenary pikemen, an elite of European battlefields for half a century. At the great battle of Pavia in 1525 they again played a decisive role in the rout of the French, massacring the *Landsknechte* Black Band that had taken service with France against the empire. Frundsberg's career ended sadly, for, in 1527, he was unable to pay his mercenaries in Italy and lost control. The enraged *Landsknechte* brutally sacked Rome and Frundsberg suffered a stroke as a result. He died shortly after.

Mercenary knight
While commanding the *Landsknecht* mercenaries, Frundsberg fought as a man of honor in the service of his emperor.

FRANÇOIS I

FRENCH KING
BORN September 12, 1494
DIED March 31, 1547
KEY CONFLICT Italian Wars
KEY BATTLES Marignano 1515, Pavia 1525

Coming to the throne in January 1515 at the age of 20, French king François I sought instant military glory as a necessary attribute of a Renaissance prince. Forming an alliance with Venice, he assembled an army to invade northern Italy and attack the Swiss, who were in control of Milan. With great daring he led his forces across untried high Alpine passes, dragging heavy cannon along precarious tracks improvised by his engineers. This enabled him to debouch on to the north Italian plain

Renaissance ruler
François I was famous for his support of artists, such as Leonardo da Vinci, as well as for his continual military endeavors.

> ## THAT YOU MAY KNOW THE STATE OF THE REST OF MY MISFORTUNE, THERE IS NOTHING LEFT TO ME BUT HONOR AND MY LIFE, WHICH IS SAVED.
>
> **FRANÇOIS I**, LETTER WRITTEN AFTER PAVIA, 1525

from a wholly unexpected direction and catch the enemy cavalry unawares, taking the whole force prisoner. He then encamped outside Milan, offering liberal bribes to induce some of the Swiss mercenaries to go home. The remainder he defeated in a costly battle at Marignano. It was a prestigious beginning to the French king's reign.

A BITTER FEUD

François spent most of the rest of his life fighting the Habsburg Holy Roman Emperor Charles V. He and Charles developed a bitter enmity, standard dynastic rivalry sharpened by the French king's resentment at seeing his own candidature for the imperial throne rejected. In February 1525, François led his army into battle against imperial forces at Pavia. He fought with his usual impulsive courage, but failed to coordinate his cavalry, which he led in person, with his foot soldiers. He also allowed his horsemen to move in front of his cannon, blocking their line of fire.

These errors contributed to a catastrophe, with many French nobility killed and the king himself taken prisoner. Released after a period of captivity on terms that he did not honor, François resumed war with the Habsburgs, fighting intermittently for the next two decades with limited success. He even made an alliance with the Ottoman Empire, fighting with the Muslims against the Habsburgs in the 1540s. His campaigns broadly maintained France's frontiers but never shook Habsburg predominance in Europe.

Sword of François I
The sword used by François at Pavia bears the Latin inscription *In brachio suo* (In his arm), a scriptural quote that implies his role as a Christian warrior.

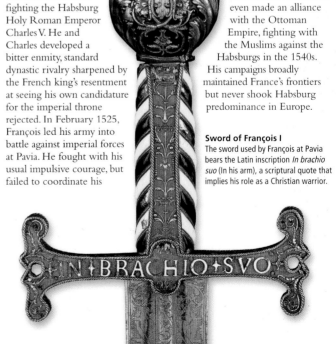

KEY BATTLE

MARIGNANO

CAMPAIGN Italian Wars
DATE September 13–15, 1515
LOCATION Marignano, 10 miles (16 km) from Milan

Around 21,000 Swiss infantry moved out of Milan to attack François I's army on the plain outside the city. The closest French contingent would have been overrun but for their tough Landsknecht mercenaries, who countered the Swiss pike to pike. François arrived at the head of his armored cavalry, charging with couched lance (held firmly under the arm for maximum impact). A vast melee ensued, the disorganized troops fighting a murderous piecemeal battle past nightfall. After sleeping on the field, the two sides re-formed to resume combat the next morning. The French looked close to defeat when mercenary cavalry, paid for by France's ally, Venice, arrived. With around 8,000 casualties, the Swiss were forced to withdraw.

The battle of Pavia
Georg von Frundsburg's *Landsknecht* troops were instrumental in the decisive Spanish-Imperial victory over the French forces of François I at Pavia in 1525.

THE DUTCH REVOLT

FOUGHT IN TWO PHASES, 1568–1609 and 1621–48, the struggle between the Protestants of the Netherlands and the Roman Catholic rulers of Spain is often known as the Eighty Years' War. The land warfare of this long conflict was dominated by protracted sieges, with few pitched battles. Commanders earned reputations for their ability to handle logistics and organize siege lines and engineering works, rather than for bold maneuvers or imaginative tactics. The Spanish infantry, or *tercios*, were the best troops for most of the war and Spain found some distinguished commanders, but Dutch tenacity in the end exhausted Spanish finances.

WILLIAM THE SILENT

DUTCH LEADER
BORN April 24, 1533
DIED July 10, 1584
KEY CONFLICT Eighty Years' War
KEY BATTLES Jemmingen 1568, Mons 1572

William I, Prince of Orange, is regarded by the Dutch as the father of their nation. Known as "the Silent," he was an unsuccessful army commander but a determined war leader. Originally a servant of the Habsburgs, he led the revolt in opposition to Philip II's harsh

Prudent ruler
William I is said to have been called "the Silent" because of his prudence and ability to keep his own counsel.

religious and political program in the Netherlands. Taking the field in 1568 against the Duke of Alba, he failed to bring the Spanish to battle, while his other rebel forces were crushed at Jemmingen. In 1572, William initially had greater success leading an army in an attempt to relieve Mons, where Alba was besieging his brother, Louis. Several cities fell to William along the way, but again Alba refused a pitched battle and the rebel army, lacking money and supplies, disintegrated. Despite these setbacks, William kept the revolt going until he was assassinated in Delft in 1584 by a Catholic, Balthasar Gérard.

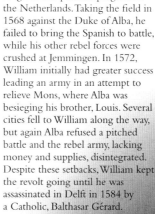

MAURICE OF NASSAU

DUTCH LEADER
BORN November 14, 1567
DIED April 23, 1625
KEY CONFLICT Eighty Years' War
KEY BATTLES Breda 1590, Steenwijk 1592, Nieuwpoort 1600

The son of William the Silent, Maurice of Nassau inherited the leadership of the Dutch revolt. In a bid to match the professionalism of the Spanish, he studied military theory and instituted major army reforms. His officers were properly trained and his infantry drilled in more flexible battlefield tactics. Improvements in organization ensured the soldiers were reliably fed, equipped, and paid.

None of this brought much success against superior Spanish forces, but Maurice was very competent at organizing sieges. He captured a series of fortified cities, including Breda in 1590, Steenwijk in 1592, and Groningen in 1594, bringing the northern Netherlands under Dutch control. His defeat of a small Spanish army at Nieuwpoort, achieved by a combined use of infantry and cavalry, assured his international reputation as an innovative commander.

Victor of Nieuwpoort
Maurice was later depicted on a white charger captured at Nieuwpoort from the commander of the Spanish army, Archduke Albert of Austria.

MORE THAN 29,000 ROUNDS WERE FIRED BY THE DUTCH ARTILLERY AT THE SIEGE OF STEENWIJK IN 1592.

DUKE OF PARMA

ITALIAN GENERAL SERVING SPAIN
BORN August 27, 1545
DIED December 3, 1592
KEY CONFLICTS Habsburg-Ottoman Wars, Eighty Years' War
KEY BATTLES Lepanto 1571, Gembloux 1578, Siege of Antwerp 1584–85

Alexander Farnese, Duke of Parma, a nephew of Philip II of Spain, learned the principles of command from Don John of Austria, whom he followed to Lepanto in 1571, and subsequently to the Netherlands. Parma was given credit for the rout of the rebels at Gembloux in 1578 and succeeded Don John as governor-general soon after. He was a thorough professional with a lucid grasp of strategy and showed his skill in siege warfare from the outset, taking Maastricht in 1579.

Stamped in gold
A gold ducat depicts Alexander Farnese and describes him as duke of the joint Farnese duchy of Parma and Piacenza.

From 1582, he embarked on a systematic campaign of reconquest, capturing a series of strategic towns, culminating with Antwerp.

THWARTED PLANS

Just as Parma was poised to reconquer all of the Netherlands, he was stopped. Philip II, frustrated by English piracy, resolved on an invasion of England. He ordered Parma to keep his Army of Flanders on standby at coastal ports, waiting for Spanish vessels to carry it to England. Parma opposed this plan, which ended in a debacle for Spain, and it deprived him of the chance of suppressing the Dutch revolt.

KEY BATTLE
THE SIEGE OF ANTWERP

CAMPAIGN Eighty Years' War
DATE September 1584–August 1585
LOCATION Antwerp, southern Netherlands

In September 1584, the Duke of Parma laid siege to the major port city of Antwerp. He knew that the answer to reducing the city lay in cutting it off from supplies arriving by sea, so he built a 2,500-ft (750-m) pontoon bridge blocking access to the port from the Scheldt estuary. On land, Parma surrounded the city with siege lines and forts. Antwerp's defenders responded by opening the dykes to flood the land around the city and attempting to destroy the bridge with fireships and floating explosives. Parma's thorough conduct of the siege resisted all such efforts to break it, however, and after almost a year, the starving city had no choice but to surrender.

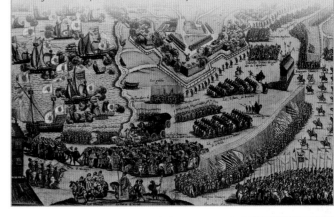

AMBROGIO SPINOLA

ITALIAN GENERAL SERVING SPAIN
BORN 1569
DIED September 25, 1630
KEY CONFLICTS Eighty Years' War, Thirty Years' War
KEY BATTLES Siege of Ostend 1604, Siege of Breda 1624–25

The eldest son of a powerful Genoese banking family, Ambrogio Spinola sought an outlet for his ambitions in the service of Spain. In 1602, he raised and paid for a force of 1,000 men and marched to the Netherlands. Here, he was welcomed by Archduke Albert and Infanta Isabella, joint rulers of the Spanish Netherlands, and set to work besieging Dutch-held Ostend. The siege was a major success and the capture of the ruined city in 1604 made his reputation.

RISKY INVESTMENT

Over the following years, Spinola was successful in a number of sieges, using his own credit and that of Genoese bankers to make up for dwindling Spanish finances. This involved him in increasing credit risks, and he pushed for the truce that halted the fighting

in the Netherlands in 1609. He resumed his military career 12 years later, early in the Thirty Years' War. Spinola occupied the Palatinate on the Rhine, which consolidated communications between Flanders and northern Italy—then ruled by Spain—and resumed war with the Dutch United Provinces. The siege of Breda (August 1624–June 1625), though costly in men and resources, was his masterpiece. It concluded with the humane treatment of its governor, Justin of Nassau, and the defeated garrison. Spinola now returned to Spain to persuade Philip IV to make a favorable peace with the Dutch. But he was instead sent to command the Spanish army in northern Italy, where he died of plague during the siege of Casale-Monferrato in 1630.

The keys of the city
The Spanish court artist, Diego Velázquez, painted his famous *Surrender of Breda* in 1635. Justin of Nassau hands the keys to Spinola, on the right, who accepts them graciously.

SPANISH SEA BATTLES

SPAIN WAS EUROPE'S LEADING naval power in the second half of the 16th century. Commanded by aristocrats, its oared galleys fought an epic struggle with the Ottoman Empire in the Mediterranean, while its fleet of ocean-going sailing ships sought domination over the Atlantic, the link with its valuable empire in the Americas. The reign of the Spanish galleons was challenged by buccaneering English sailors with lower status and fewer resources but plentiful skills and aggression. The attempt to use Spanish naval dominance to effect an invasion of England with the Armada of 1588 failed in the face of English resistance and atrocious weather.

MASTERS OF INNOVATION

MARQUÉS DE SANTA CRUZ

SPANISH ADMIRAL
BORN December 12, 1526
DIED February 9, 1588
KEY CONFLICTS Habsburg-Ottoman War, Portuguese Succession War
KEY BATTLES Lepanto 1571, Azores 1582

Álvaro de Bazán, the Marqués de Santa Cruz, followed in the footsteps of his father, who commanded the Spanish Mediterranean fleet. The future marqués saw his first naval combat at the age of 18 and, by the 1560s, had risen to command of the important Spanish galley fleet in Naples, which he worked up to a high standard of efficiency and discipline. When a Christian force headed for the eastern Mediterranean under Don John of Austria in 1571, Santa Cruz commanded the reserve squadron. He consistently advocated an aggressive approach, arguing in favor of seeking battle with the Ottoman fleet. In the great encounter at Lepanto his contribution was decisive. He fed his reserves into battle at crucial moments, first to

Versatile admiral
The Marqués de Santa Cruz was unique in performing outstandingly as a commander both of oared galleys and of sailing galleons. His family had served the Spanish crown since the 15th century.

prevent a collapse of the Venetians on the Christian left and then to support the center at the climax of the fight. These timely interventions allowed the Christian fleet to carry the day.

A SHIFT OF FOCUS

In 1582, Santa Cruz was entrusted with suppressing a French-backed multinational fleet gathering in the Azores to contest Spanish control of Portugal. He won a famous victory with a numerically inferior force, raising his prestige considerably. A fine administrator as well as a skilled tactician, Santa Cruz started to build and equip a fleet that he intended to lead in an invasion of England. After long delays, this Armada was almost ready when Santa Cruz died. His leadership was to be sorely missed.

DON JOHN OF AUSTRIA

HABSBURG ARMY AND NAVAL COMMANDER
BORN February 24, 1547
DIED October 1, 1578
KEY CONFLICTS Morisco Revolt 1569, Habsburg-Ottoman War, Eighty Years' War
KEY BATTLE Lepanto 1571

Don John of Austria was a bastard son of the Habsburg emperor, Charles V. Reckless and dashing, John was naturally inimical to his cautious, reclusive half-brother, King Philip II of Spain. When John was 21, Philip appointed him commander of the Spanish Mediterranean galley fleet, but surrounded him with advisers who were expected to keep him under control and report

Brief life
A contemporary portrait depicts Don John with confident demeanour. But he died young, just after the Namur campaign.

back to the king. In 1569, Moriscos—Moors forcibly converted to Christianity—rose in revolt in Granada. John led an army to suppress the rebellion, a mission accomplished in a campaign marked by savage combat and massacre.

A NATURAL LEADER

John proved an excellent choice as leader of the Holy League fleet sent to oppose the Ottomans in 1571, his charisma, innate aggression, and idealistic enthusiasm pulling the quarrelsome Christian allies together.

Victory at Lepanto made John one of Europe's most famed commanders. The aftermath was disappointing. He captured Tunis from the Ottomans in 1573, but it was soon lost again. In 1576, he was appointed to command Spanish forces in the Netherlands, a post he could only take up by crossing France in disguise. Arriving at a low point in Spain's fortunes, he first made peace with the Dutch rebels, before resuming the war on his own initiative with the seizure of Namur in 1577.

KEY BATTLE

LEPANTO

CAMPAIGN Habsburg-Ottoman Wars
DATE October 7, 1571
LOCATION Gulf of Patras, off Greece

An alliance of Christian states, the Holy League sailed more than 200 galleys to the eastern Mediterranean under Don John of Austria. It met a similar-sized Ottoman fleet at Lepanto. The Christians depended on the firepower of cannon and arquebus, while the Muslims sought to outmaneuver and board their enemy's ships. A close-fought contest ended with the capture of the Ottoman flagship. Lepanto was the last major battle between oared galleys.

SIR FRANCIS DRAKE

ENGLISH NAVAL COMMANDER
BORN 1540
DIED January 27, 1596
KEY CONFLICT Anglo-Spanish War
KEY BATTLES Cádiz 1587, Gravelines 1588

Son of a Devon lay preacher and farmer, Francis Drake went to sea from an early age. In the 1560s, he accompanied his cousin, John Hawkins, on illegal trading and privateering voyages to the Spanish-ruled Caribbean. Drake narrowly escaped with his life when Hawkins's ships were trapped between Spanish galleons and shore batteries at San Juan de Ulúa (in present-day Mexico) in 1569. He took revenge by further plunder of the Spanish colonies—the capture of a treasure-laden mule train in 1573 made him a wealthy man.

England's Queen Elizabeth I backed Drake's personal war against Spain, although the two countries were officially at peace. In 1577, she

Armada engagement
The English forced the galleons of the Spanish Armada to engage in a duel of cannons, exploiting the superior maneuverability of their smaller ships to avoid being grappled and boarded.

sent him to prey upon the Spanish in the Pacific, awarding him a knighthood when he returned, laden with plunder, from England's first circumnavigation of the globe.

DEFENDING THE REALM

Open war between England and Spain from 1585 widened the scope of Drake's activities. To disrupt preparations for the Armada, in spring 1587, he led a fleet of 21 ships in preemptive strikes on Spanish ports. The destruction he wreaked in his daring raid on Cádiz justified his claim to have "singed the king of Spain's beard." Feared in the enemy camp, Drake was too arrogant and quarrelsome to be popular on his own side. When England faced the Armada in 1588, he had to

accept, with bad grace, the role of second-in-command. During the running battle with the Spanish fleet along the Channel, he showed a total lack of discipline by abandoning his station to capture an individual galleon. But he played a full part in the fireship attack that drove the Armada from its anchorage off Calais and in the subsequent battle of cannonades at Gravelines.

Drake's career after the Armada was an anticlimax. A follow-up attack on Spain was a costly fiasco. He joined with Hawkins in a resumption of their earlier Caribbean privateering in 1595, but by this time Spanish defenses had strengthened. The voyage was already a failure before Drake died of dysentery.

Circumnavigator of the world
This statue of Sir Francis Drake stands on Plymouth Hoe, England, where legend asserts that he played lawn bowling as the Armada drew near.

> ❝ I DARE NOT ALMOST WRITE OF THE GREAT FORCES WE HEAR THE KING OF SPAIN HATH. PREPARE IN ENGLAND STRONGLY AND MOST BY SEA! ❞
>
> **SIR FRANCIS DRAKE**, FROM A LETTER TO FRANICS WALSINGHAM, MAY 1587

1450—1700

1620—1680

BIBLE, PIKE,
AND MUSKET

"
JOINING BATTALIONS TOGETHER, WE CAME TO PUSH OF PIKE
AND DISPUTED THE BUSINESS SO LONG, TILL IT PLEASED GOD
THAT WE ROUTED THEM, AND GAVE US THE VICTORY.
"

JOHN FORBES, A MAJOR IN THE SWEDISH ARMY, WRITING TO HIS FATHER AFTER THE BATTLE OF BREITENFELD, SEPTEMBER 10, 1631

THE 17TH CENTURY WAS A TURBULENT PERIOD in European history and conflicts within and between states were rife. Protestants and Catholics, with the embittered religious divide between them, fueled the situation, as did the traditional dynastic ambitions of kings and emperors. In military commanders such as the English Oliver Cromwell and Swedish monarch Gustavus Adolphus, religious, political, and economic motivations could hardly be separated. Faith gave a sharpened edge to European struggles for power.

The Thirty Years' War, fought in Germany between 1618 and 1648, dominated the first half of the 17th century. At once a struggle between the Protestant and Catholic subjects of the Holy Roman Emperor, it was also a continuation of the long-standing conflict between the French kings and the Habsburgs, with the Catholic French supporting the German Protestants against their Habsburg rivals. The war brought major interventions by Denmark and Sweden on the Protestant side and was accompanied by a renewal of the conflict, begun in the previous century, between the Dutch and Habsburg Spain. The outcome of the Thirty Years' War was hardly commensurate with the appalling devastation and loss of life it caused: the Habsburgs were weakened, Dutch independence was secured, and a compromise on religion left Germany split between Protestant and Catholic states.

After 1648, there was certainly no general peace in Europe. The French and the Spanish Habsburgs continued to fight throughout the 1650s, as France also stumbled into its own civil conflict—the *Fronde* (literally, sling)—which took its name from the weapons used by rioters. In Britain, a civil war that had broken out in 1642 between Royalists and Parliamentarians was eventually resolved in the early 1650s by the victories of Cromwell's New Model Army. There followed the first of three naval wars between the English and the Dutch. Motivated by commercial rivalry, the Anglo-Dutch Wars achieved nothing for the two participating Protestant states.

EFFICIENT FIREPOWER
In the absence of dramatic technological innovations in this period, commanders sought more effective tactics to gain the edge in battle. As in the previous century, the pike and the matchlock musket remained the infantry weapons of choice, but over time their ratio of use changed radically. In 1600, there was one musket to every five pikes; in 1680, five muskets to every one pike.

Artillery weapons were interspersed with the foot soldiers to increase firepower. Cavalry, now armed with pistol and sword, could no longer carry off a frontal charge against well-organized infantry. Instead, they charged the enemy horse on the wings, attempting to drive them off before picking off the foot soldiers from the flank or rear.

To a modern eye, the armies of the early 17th century were ramshackle bodies of men. Mostly mercenaries or hastily drafted conscripts, they had no uniforms, no regular supply system, and no reliable pay. By the end of this period, uniforms had come into general use and most European states were managing to sustain regular armies—a feat achieved only by Spain and France in the 16th century. By the 1680s, these cumulative changes left Europe on the verge of a new era.

1450—1700

Massed pikemen
The battlefields of the Thirty Years' War—like this one at Thionville in 1639—were dominated by clumps of long pikes, although muskets were proving more effective as an infantry weapon. Light cavalry wore little or no armor and had abandoned the medieval lance altogether.

Effective weapon
The falconet was a light, mobile gun of the 16th–17th centuries. In the 1620s, Swedish king Gustavus Adolphus sought to combine such maneuverability with a heavier weight of shot.

COMMANDERS OF THE THIRTY YEARS' WAR

THE THIRTY YEARS' WAR began in 1618 with a revolt by Protestant Bohemia against the Catholic Holy Roman Empire. Although the revolt was repressed, fighting spread to Germany. The power of the German Catholic League and the Habsburg forces of the empire and Spain was balanced by the intervention of the Danes from 1625, the Swedes from 1630, and the French from 1635. The quality of leadership in this destructive, ultimately indecisive conflict was mixed. Many commanders were mercenaries, some with little talent but for plunder. But others, notably Swedish King Gustavus Adolphus, provided bold examples of inventive generalship.

ALBRECHT VON WALLENSTEIN

COMMANDER OF IMPERIAL FORCES
BORN September 24, 1583
DIED February 25, 1634
KEY CONFLICT Thirty Years' War
KEY BATTLES Dessau 1626, Lützen 1632

Raised a Calvinist (Protestant), Wallenstein was a Catholic convert and one of the few nobles in Bohemia to choose the imperial side against a Protestant revolt in 1618. Enriched by the new political order in conquered Bohemia, in 1625, he raised an army for Emperor Ferdinand II, equipping almost 50,000 men and extorting "contributions" from occupied areas to recoup the costs.

Wallenstein proved an able commander, crushing Mansfeld at Dessau in 1626 and leading the defeat of the Danish king, Christian IV, over the following three years. The depredations of his army were much resented, however, and, in 1630, pressure from German princes forced the emperor to fire him.

Recalled two years later to defend the empire against Gustavus Adolphus, he won a defensive victory at the Alte Veste in August 1632. In November 1632, he was on the losing side at the battle of Lützen, but imposed heavy losses on the Swedes, which included their king. The emperor was led to believe that Wallenstein was plotting against him and may have ordered his assassination at Eger in 1634.

Seeds of mistrust
Ambitious and arrogant, Wallenstein was a skillful military commander but did not inspire trust. He was assassinated by three of his own officers.

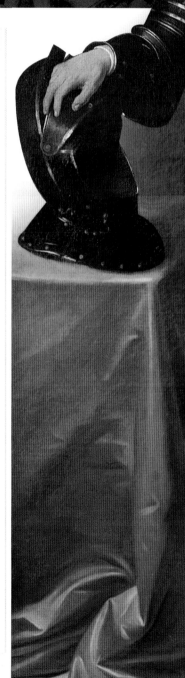

ERNST VON MANSFELD

MERCENARY COMMANDER
BORN c. 1580
DIED November 29, 1626
KEY CONFLICT Thirty Years' War
KEY BATTLES Fleurus 1622, Dessau 1626

The illegitimate son of a Saxon general who had prospered in the service of Spain, Mansfeld was a military adventurer by birth. As a Catholic, he gained his early military experience fighting for the Holy Roman Empire, but, in 1618, was recruited to defend the rebellious Protestants in Bohemia. Mansfeld's interest in the conflict was purely financial and he abandoned the Bohemians as soon as they ran out of cash. Yet prospective employers continued to find his ability to raise an army at low cost and short notice irresistible. He was once more employed by the German Protestants when the war shifted northward in 1622, before being invited to fight for the Dutch, then hard-pressed by Habsburg Spain. On his way to the Netherlands he was intercepted by a Spanish army at Fleurus, but broke through with heavy losses. The Dutch soon discovered how costly it was being helped by Mansfeld's rapacious and unruly army. His contract was terminated and, in 1624, he shifted to England. Regarded as a Protestant hero, Mansfeld received £55,000 to raise an army with which to regain the Palatinate (a major German state).

True mercenary
Mansfeld regarded the Thirty Years' War as a career opportunity for a professional commander, profiteering unscrupulously.

MOVING ON

Mansfeld assembled a large rabble that, on landing in Europe, mostly disintegrated through desertion and disease. However, he did enter the fray in 1626, but was defeated by Wallenstein at Dessau. Later that same year, Mansfeld abandoned the remnants of his army in Silesia and died en route to a new job in the service of Venice.

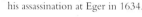

COUNT TILLY

COMMANDER OF CATHOLIC FORCES
BORN 1559
DIED April 30, 1632
KEY CONFLICTS Eighty Years' War,
Thirty Years' War
KEY BATTLES White Mountain 1620,
Lutter 1626, Magdeburg 1631, First
Breitenfeld 1631, Rain am Lech 1632

Jean Tserclaes, Count Tilly, was a
Flemish Catholic who learned the
art of military command under the
Duke of Parma and Ambrogio

Fighting monk
Count Tilly was a devout
Catholic who once thought
of becoming a Jesuit. He was
nicknamed "the monk
in armor."

Spinola in the Dutch independence
war. A devout and professional man,
he was commended for the tight
discipline of his foot soldiers.

THE CATHOLIC CAUSE

At the outbreak of the Thirty Years'
War, Tilly commanded the army of
the Catholic League. After his victory
at White Mountain ended the
Bohemian revolt, he turned to
Germany, campaigning successfully
against Mansfeld, among others, in

1622–23. When Christian IV entered
the war, Tilly defeated the Danish
king at Lutter in August 1626. But, in
1631, he had the misfortune to face
the Swedish king, Gustavus Adolphus.

In May, Tilly took the key Protestant
city of Magdeburg by storm. The city
was burned and the massive loss of
life was used by his enemies to blacken
his reputation. Four months later, he
was defeated by the Swedes under
Gustavus Adolphus at Breitenfeld
(pp. 146–47). He withdrew and fought
on, but was struck by a cannonball at
an encounter near Rain am Lech in
April 1632, dying two weeks later.

KEY BATTLE

WHITE MOUNTAIN

CAMPAIGN Thirty Years' War
DATE November 8, 1620
LOCATION Near Prague, now Czech Republic

The forces of the Holy Roman Empire and
the Catholic League under Tilly were
pursuing a smaller force of Protestant
Bohemians (Czechs) under Christian of

Anhalt as it withdrew toward Prague. The
Bohemians, established on a hilltop, did not
expect to be attacked up a steep slope. But
Tilly ordered a charge while his heavy guns
softened up the enemy position. As the
Bohemians broke and ran, the battle was
concluded in an hour.

THE DUC D'ENGHIEN

FRENCH COMMANDER
BORN September 8, 1621
DIED November 11, 1686
KEY CONFLICTS Thirty Years' War, Franco-
Spanish War, Wars of Louis XIV
KEY BATTLES Rocroi 1643, The Dunes 1658

Bourbon prince
Proud and impulsive,
le grand Condé (the
great Condé), as he
was known, was
a prince of the
Bourbon line.

At age 22, the duc d'Enghien led the
French army to victory at Rocroi
in May 1643, using his cavalry to
outflank and defeat the redoubtable
Spanish infantry *tercios*. He served
with distinction during the rest of
the Thirty Years' War alongside the
Vicomte de Turenne. He
became Prince de Condé
on his father's death, and, in
1652, fled to Spain after action in the
Fronde revolt against Louis XIV. In
command of the Spanish forces, he
was defeated at the Dunes in 1658.
Condé later returned to France as one
of Louis XIV's senior commanders,
fighting his last campaign in 1675.

GUSTAVUS ADOLPHUS

KING OF SWEDEN
BORN December 19, 1594
DIED November 16, 1632
KEY CONFLICTS Polish-Swedish War, Thirty Years' War
KEY BATTLES Dirschau 1627, First Breitenfeld 1631, Lützen 1632

King Gustav II Adolf of Sweden, known as Gustavus Adolphus, is best remembered for his dramatic intervention in the Thirty Years' War between 1630 and his death in 1632. But this was only the culminating phase of a lifetime of military struggle. Gustavus had inherited a contested throne. His Protestant father, Charles IX, usurped the crown from Sigismund, the Catholic king of Poland. As a consequence, Gustavus was at war with the Poles, with intermittent truces, throughout his reign.

Christian IV of Denmark was another enemy. A Danish army was invading Sweden when Gustavus acceded to the throne, and there was bitter fighting before a peace, most unfavorable to the Swedes, was brokered in 1613. Building up his armed forces and learning how to win battles was, for Gustavus, essential to survival. However, he had inherited a decrepit navy and a weak army.

MILITARY STRENGTH

Gustavus was not a sailor. He had a fleet built, but the embarrassing sinking of his largest warship, the *Vasa*, on its maiden voyage in 1628 gave an indication of his weakness in maritime matters. His skills as a soldier were far greater. Sweden had an army of poorly

Cavalry sword
Gustavus Adolphus insisted that the cavalryman's decisive weapon was to be the sword, not the pistol. He liked to lead a cavalry charge in person.

trained conscript infantry and dilatory feudal cavalry, but in the early years of his reign he turned this into the finest battle-winning force in Europe.

Gustavus learned the skills of military command on the job. His training ground was the war against Poland in the 1620s. He was a general who sought personal experience of every aspect of operations. He handled a shovel to learn about earthworks and taught himself to fire a cannon to understand artillery. He enjoyed plunging into the thick of battle, at grave risk to his life.

TACTICAL EDGE

Personal experience also allowed Gustavus to modify the latest tactical theories—mostly devised by the much-admired Maurice of Nassau—into an effective practice of aggressive combined-arms warfare. Influenced by his Polish opponents, he emphasized charging cavalry as a shock force on the battlefield. He also saw his drilled, disciplined infantry as an offensive force, the musketeers firing massed salvoes to break open the enemy line for the pikemen to penetrate. He initiated the deployment of lightweight mobile artillery in the front line. The key to his tactical concept was that the arms must support one another, the shock of firepower from cannon and musket preparing the way for the push of pike and cavalry charge.

Gustavus had as his strategic focus control of the Baltic. Through the 1620s, he kept out of the conflict in Germany, refusing to support the Protestant cause despite his genuine Lutheran faith.

Instead, the Thirty Years' War came to him, when the defeat of Christian of Denmark in 1628 brought the forces of the Catholic empire under Wallenstein north to the Baltic coast. This posed a direct threat to Sweden's independence. In summer 1630, Gustavus responded with a seaborne invasion of Germany, landing an army in Pomerania. The core of his force consisted of Swedish conscripts and volunteer cavalry, a much improved version of the army he had inherited. But he also recruited large numbers of mercenaries—they constituted half of his men at the start of his

Swedish lion
King Gustavus Adolphus was nicknamed the Lion of the North. His intervention in Germany during the Thirty Years' War transformed Sweden into a major military power.

> **I AM THE KING OF SWEDEN AND THIS DAY I SEAL WITH MY BLOOD THE LIBERTY AND THE RELIGION OF THE GERMAN PEOPLE.**
>
> **GUSTAVUS ADOLPHUS**, BEFORE THE BATTLE OF LÜTZEN, 1632

Battle of Dirschau
Gustavus Adolphus, on the dark brown horse, joins in a melee at Dirschau in August 1627. He suffered a serious neck wound in the battle.

campaign, rising to nine-tenths by its end. Swedish officers had to train these multinational professionals in Gustavus's novel tactics.

The Swedish campaign in Germany began hesitantly. Gustavus tightened his hold on Pomerania while seeking allies among the Protestant Germans. However, his failure to come to the aid of the city of Magdeburg, sacked by the imperial army, did nothing to help his cause. Pressing south across the Elbe in summer 1631, Gustavus found a major ally in Saxony and, thus reinforced, sought battle. The victory at Breitenfeld (pp. 146–47) transformed him overnight into the most admired general in Europe. Instead of pursuing Tilly, the defeated Catholic commander, Gustavus went on a triumphal progress through Germany and across the Rhine.

IMPERIAL DESIGNS

At the pinnacle of his power, Gustavus's ambitions grew. He may even have thought of deposing the Habsburg emperor and establishing Swedish leadership of the empire—

but his army was no match for this task. In spring 1632, after crossing the Lech in the face of enemy forces, he eliminated Tilly at the battle of Rain. But Wallenstein had returned to the fray and begun a game of maneuver and countermaneuver in which Gustavus lost the strategic initiative. Forced into an attack on Wallenstein's entrenched position at the Alte Veste in August 1632, he suffered the first defeat of his German campaign. As supply problems hit, men began to drift away. Gustavus desperately sought to bring the enemy to battle.

In November, with the rival forces shadowing one another at Lützen, bad weather set in. Assuming that campaigning was over for the year, Wallenstein began dispersing his army to winter quarters. Seeing the possibility of a snap victory, Gustavus attacked. Wallenstein was quick to reorganize his defenses and a grim battle was joined, with heavy losses on both sides. At the end of the day, the Swedes held the field, but Gustavus was dead, probably killed involving himself in a cavalry melee.

BIOGRAPHY

LENNART TORSTENSSON

Gustavus Adolphus gave Lennart Torstensson complete command of the Swedish artillery in 1629. Torstensson led the first modern artillery force, with standardized sizes of cannon and an emphasis on battlefield mobility. He played a major role at Breitenfeld in 1631, but was taken prisoner at the Alte Veste the next year. Returning to service in 1635, he fought in the later stages of the Thirty Years' War, first as Swedish artillery commander, then from 1641 as overall commander of the Swedish army. He won a notable victory against the imperialists at Jankow in 1645, and his campaigning finally persuaded the emperor he had no choice but to sue for peace.

TIMELINE

■ **1611** At age 16, Gustavus Adolphus inherits the throne on the death of his father. Sweden is at war with Denmark, Poland, and Russia.

■ **1613** Gustavus extricates Sweden from a failing war with Denmark by agreeing to pay a large indemnity.

■ **1614** The Swedish king campaigns in person for the first time against Russia. The war concludes in 1617 with a settlement that strengthens Sweden's position in the Baltic.

■ **1621** Gustavus seizes the major Baltic port of Riga from Poland after a short siege, starting a new round of warfare with the Poles.

■ **January 1626** In a defeat of the Poles at Wallhof, Gustavus uses a new tactic of dispersing musketeers among his cavalry.

■ **August 1627** In a battle against the Poles at Dirschau, Gustavus is wounded in the neck and nearly killed.

■ **1628** Sweden becomes involved in combat with the forces of the Holy Roman Empire at Stralsund and in Poland.

■ **1629** Gustavus concludes a treaty with Poland—the Truce of Altmark—on terms highly advantageous to Sweden, leaving him free to lead a military expedition to Germany.

■ **July 1630** Carried by a fleet of transport ships, the Swedish army lands at Peenemunde in Pomerania.

■ **May 1631** Gustavus fails to save his ally, the German city of Magdeburg, from destruction by the imperial army.

■ **September 1631** In alliance with the Saxons, Gustavus defeats the imperial army under Count Tilly at Breitenfeld.

■ **April 1632** Gustavus is again victorious at Rain am Lech, where Count Tilly is killed. He goes on to occupy Munich.

SILVER MEDALLION DEPICTING THE DEATH OF GUSTAVUS ADOLPHUS

■ **August 1632** Outmaneuvered by Wallenstein, Gustavus is rebuffed attacking the imperial army's strong defensive position at the Alte Veste near Nürnberg.

■ **November 1632** The Swedish army is victorious at the battle of Lützen, but Gustavus is killed, paying the price for his charismatic but risky style of leadership from the front.

1450–1700

GUSTAVUS VS. TILLY

IN THE SUMMER OF 1631, Saxony, ruled by Elector John George I, lay between the Catholic Imperial army of Count Tilly to the south and the Protestant Swedish army of King Gustavus Adolphus to the north. Saxony was so far largely unharmed by the war and John George was attempting to remain neutral, but when Tilly invaded his territory he hastily formed an alliance with Gustavus. On September 15, the Saxon and Swedish rulers agreed to march together to come to the aid of Leipzig, besieged by Tilly. They were too late, for Leipzig fell to the Imperial army that same day. Battle was joined, nonetheless, on a plain outside the city.

MASTERS OF INNOVATION

GUSTAVUS ADOLPHUS

Gustavus Adolphus found Tilly's Imperial troops drawn up on a low ridge, with the sun and wind behind them. There had been no chance for Gustavus and the Saxon Elector to coordinate the allied armies, so they formed up separately side by side, the Saxons on the left and the Swedish on the right. Gustavus's infantry was in battalions six ranks deep, each battalion supported by four three-pounder cannon. His cavalry formed flexible small units interspersed with musketeers, and behind his relatively thin line he kept substantial reserves. Before battle was joined, Gustavus called on his troops to believe that God would give them victory.

As the artillery of both sides began to come into action, Gustavus was happy for the Imperial forces to lose patience under the bombardment first and take the offensive. He could not have anticipated that the Saxon army would perform so poorly, swept from the field by the first enemy onslaught. As Elector John George disappeared in headlong flight, Gustavus had to continue the battle outnumbered and with the left of his line open to a flanking attack. Thanks to the good discipline and flexibility of his infantry formations, he was able to swiftly reposition his troops to cover the left flank. His artillery commander Torstensson directed cannon fire on the slow-moving Imperial infantry.

DRIVING FORWARD

Switching to the right, where his cavalry and musketeers had survived a fearful battering, Gustavus mustered his reserves and drove a body of cavalry forward in a charge that broke through to the top of the ridge where Tilly was positioned. Riding to wherever the fighting was hardest and exposed without armor to enemy fire, Gustavus remorselessly urged his men forward. Pike, musket, cannon, and cavalry saber all took their toll on the weakening Imperial army. By the time night fell, Gustavus was in possession of the battlefield.

Observing his troops
An engraving of the time shows Gustavus Adolphus (third from left) with his commanders watching the advance and disposition of his forces on the plain at Breitenfeld.

GOD IS WITH US. MAY THESE WORDS BE OUR RALLYING CRY...

GUSTAVUS ADOLPHUS, ADDRESSING HIS TROOPS BEFORE BREITENFELD

GUSTAVUS

Dawn Gustavus, breaking camp at Wolkau, musters his forces in battle order and begins a march in the direction of Leipzig

9 a.m. Gustavus's forces advance toward the Imperial position, driving off a screen of cavalry commanded by Pappenheim

Gustavus marshals his marching files into line of battle, with the Saxon army on the left and the Swedish army on the right

12 noon Gustavus kneels and prays in front of the army, then orders his artillery to begin returning fire

Cavalry and musketeers on the Swedish right beat off repeated charges by Pappenheim's cavalry

1631: SEPT 17

TILLY

Early morning Tilly deploys his army on a ridge between Seehausen and Breitenfeld and rides slowly down the line to show himself to the troops

Tilly orders the Imperial artillery to open a bombardment of the enemy forces as they form up

Tilly maintains a defensive posture through a lengthy artillery duel, hoping that Gustavus will attack

2:30 p.m. Pappenheim, commanding the Imperial left, orders a cavalry charge on his own initiative, trying to envelop the Swedish right with a sweeping encirclement

Tilly orders Fürstenberg to launch a cavalry attack against the Saxons on the left of Gustavus's line

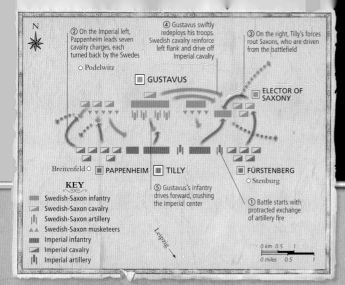

② On the Imperial left, Pappenheim leads seven cavalry charges, each turned back by the Swedes

④ Gustavus swiftly redeploys his troops. Swedish cavalry reinforce left flank and drive off Imperial cavalry

③ On the right, Tilly's forces rout Saxons, who are driven from the battlefield

○ Podelwitz

■ GUSTAVUS

■ ELECTOR OF SAXONY

Breitenfeld ○ ■ PAPPENHEIM ■ TILLY ■ FÜRSTENBERG

○ Stenburg

⑤ Gustavus's infantry drives forward, crushing the Imperial center

① Battle starts with protracted exchange of artillery fire

Leipzig →

KEY
- Swedish-Saxon infantry
- Swedish-Saxon cavalry
- Swedish-Saxon artillery
- Swedish-Saxon musketeers
- Imperial infantry
- Imperial cavalry
- Imperial artillery

0 km 0.5 1
0 miles 0.5 1

LOCATION
North of Leipzig, present-day Germany
CAMPAIGN
Thirty Years' War
DATE September 17, 1631
FORCES Imperial forces: 36,000; Swedes: 26,000; Saxons: 16,000
CASUALTIES Imperial forces: 7,000 killed, 6,000 prisoners, plus many more deserters; Swedes and Saxons: 4,500 killed

COUNT TILLY

Informed of the enemy's approach, Tilly led his army out of Leipzig on September 16. His destination was a ridge that reconnaissance had previously identified as a suitable defensive position. An aging and prudent commander, he planned to induce Gustavus into a frontal attack uphill against his dense formations of pikemen, each *tercio* 1,500-strong. He also hoped that height would give him the advantage in an artillery duel. His second-in-command, the aggressive cavalry commander Pappenheim, had no respect for Tilly's cautious approach.

ARTILLERY DUEL

As soon as the Swedish and Saxon armies came within range on the morning of September 17, Tilly ordered his cannon to begin their bombardment. Their fire was slow and largely ineffectual at long range, failing to disrupt the formation of

Gustavus's battle line. When the Swedish cannon returned fire in the afternoon, they had considerably greater impact. Tilly still clung to the advantage of his defensive position on the ridge, but Pappenheim's patience gave way. Launching an attack with his elite cavalry—the feared black cuirassiers—he swept around the Swedish right. This insubordinate initiative threw Tilly into despair, yet he had no choice but to join in with a cavalry attack against the Saxons on the left wing of Gustavus's positions. When the Saxons unexpectedly collapsed, Tilly found himself about to achieve an unintended double envelopment of Gustavus's army.

POWERLESS TO REACT

Unfortunately for Tilly and his army, Pappenheim's cuirassier attacks were repulsed time after time by Gustavus's resolute horse-and-musket formations. Meanwhile, Tilly's attempt to advance his *tercios* against the maimed Swedish left only revealed how vulnerable these densely packed columns of pikemen were to the fire of mobile, well-handled artillery. With no reserves, Tilly was helpless to respond. His attacks were thrown back and his position crumbled. The battle was lost well before he was carried off the field, too badly wounded to continue.

1450—1700

The Saxon army falls apart, mostly fleeing in disorder as the Imperial cavalry strikes home

Gustavus orders Count Horn to withdraw the left of the Swedish army to form a defensive line protecting the flank denuded by the disappearance of the Saxons

With his left flank holding, Gustavus organizes a cavalry charge on the right that breaks into Tilly's line and captures his heavy cannon on the ridge

Late afternoon Attacking with all arms, the Swedish forces inflict heavy losses on the Imperial army

Morning Gustavus holds a solemn thanksgiving service in his camp before marching after the defeated enemy

SEPT 18

Tilly orders his infantry to advance from the right, wheeling to attack the Swedish left. In their slow maneuver, they are exposed to Swedish artillery fire

Fürstenberg's cavalry returns from the pursuit but fails to break Horn's defensive line

Evening Wounded in the neck, chest, and arm, Tilly is carried from the field as his army disintegrates around him

Late evening Under cover of falling darkness, Pappenheim stages a fighting retreat to Leipzig with the surviving Imperial cavalry

THE BRITISH CIVIL WARS

 IN 1642, A CIVIL WAR BROKE OUT between King Charles I and the English parliament over the extent of royal powers and religious differences. The war, fought mostly under commanders with experience in European warfare, spread across the British Isles, with Scottish forces in particular making important interventions on both sides. The first round of fighting ended in 1646, with the Parliamentarian armies soundly beating the Royalists. The second was ignited in 1647 by an alliance between Royalists and Scots. The king was executed in 1649, and by 1651 Parliament's best general, Oliver Cromwell, had defeated Royalists, Scots, and rebel Irish.

MASTERS OF INNOVATION

THOMAS FAIRFAX

PARLIAMENTARY COMMANDER-IN-CHIEF
BORN January 17, 1612
DIED November 12, 1671
KEY CONFLICTS British Civil Wars
KEY BATTLES Marston Moor 1644, Naseby 1645

Yorkshire-born Thomas Fairfax gained his first military experience in the Netherlands, volunteering to fight on the side of the Protestant Dutch against the Spanish in the 1630s. He served Charles I in his campaigns against the Scots in 1639–40, leading a troop of dragoons, but followed his father, Lord Fairfax, in backing parliament when the Civil War broke out. The Fairfaxes suffered major reverses in fighting against Yorkshire's more numerous Royalists and were pinned inside Hull by the summer of 1643. Thomas Fairfax moved to East Anglia, where he had more success fighting alongside Oliver Cromwell, but in spring 1644 he rejoined his father in Yorkshire.

VICTORY AT MARSTON

Combined with an invading Scottish army and Cromwell's East Anglians, Fairfax's Parliamentarian cavalry fought Prince Rupert in a crucial battle at Marston Moor in July. Fairfax led the cavalry, which suffered heavy losses. Despite taking a saber cut to the face, he nonetheless succeeded in joining Cromwell's horse on the left. Together, they carried the day.

In January 1645, Fairfax reluctantly took control of the New Model Army. He shaped the force with honesty and efficiency and led it to victory at Naseby in June (pp.152–53). The following year his mopping up of western Royalist strongholds was accomplished with skill and humane restraint. But he was less at home with the political intrigues that followed—he opposed the king's execution. His influence in the New Model Army waned as Cromwell's fame rose and he resigned in 1650. Fairfax later played an important role in the restoration of the monarchy.

Fairfax and the Levellers
Fairfax resisted and eventually suppressed the Levellers (a Parliamentarian faction) within the New Model Army. He was more comfortable with military command than with politics.

PRINCE RUPERT OF THE RHINE

ROYALIST CAVALRY COMMANDER AND ADMIRAL
BORN December 17, 1619
DIED November 29, 1682
KEY CONFLICTS British Civil Wars, Anglo-Dutch Wars
KEY BATTLES Edgehill 1642, Marston Moor 1644, Naseby 1645

Youthful commander
Young and arrogant, Rupert was a charismatic leader and popular with his men, but his conceit alienated senior members of King Charles I's entourage.

A nephew of King Charles I, Prince Rupert was born in Prague but brought up in the Netherlands, after his Protestant father, Frederick V, was ousted from the Bohemian throne. Aged 18, Rupert was taken prisoner fighting against imperial forces in the Thirty Years' War. Released on parole, in August 1642, he traveled to England to fight for his uncle.

Rupert was given command of the Royalist cavalry and in October 1642 led a dashing charge at Edgehill that routed the enemy horse. He lost the chance of a decisive victory by a headlong pursuit off the battlefield. Yet, he proved efficient and energetic as well as bold, becoming commander-in-chief of the Royalist army in 1644. Major defeats at Marston Moor and Naseby harmed Rupert's reputation, however, and he was dismissed, then exiled from England in 1646. For six years, he commanded a Royalist fleet, and after the Restoration, naval affairs remained his main interest. Rupert was one of England's most effective admirals in the Anglo-Dutch Wars of 1665–67 and 1672–74.

OLIVER CROMWELL

PARLIAMENTARY COMMANDER
BORN April 25, 1599
DIED September 3, 1658
KEY CONFLICTS British Civil Wars
KEY BATTLES Marston Moor 1644, Naseby 1645, Preston 1648, Dunbar 1650

Born into the minor gentry, Cromwell was an active member of parliament during the buildup to the Civil War. Totally without military experience, when the war began he raised a troop of horse. He proved so effective as a leader of cavalry that by January 1644 he was a lieutenant-general in the Eastern Association army.

The discipline of Cromwell's troopers, nicknamed the Ironsides, was decisive in the Parliamentary victories at Marston Moor in July 1644 and at Naseby the following June (pp. 152–53). By 1648, when he defeated a Scottish army at Preston, Cromwell was recognized as England's foremost general.

Cromwell took an army to Ireland in 1649, where massacres at Drogheda and Wexford made him much hated. In 1650, he took over supreme command of the New Model Army. The subsequent Scottish campaign culminated in his most brilliant victory, achieved at Dunbar when he was cornered and outnumbered.

Cromwell was never slow to engage in politics, quelling Leveller mutinies but supporting the execution of the king. In 1653, he lost patience with parliament and led an army against it, emerging as Lord Protector. He ruled England until his death in 1658.

Puritan general
Cromwell was a devout Puritan and believed his military victories reflected God's approval of his army's moral conduct and mission.

KEY TROOPS

NEW MODEL ARMY

Parliament formed the New Model Army in 1645 to centralize its forces—previously raised and organized on a regional basis. It was to be a disciplined army with uniforms, regular pay, and a reliable supply system. Its first commander, Thomas Fairfax, ensured that its officers were appointed on merit, and he assembled an effective staff. Cromwell, appointed second-in-command, had responsibility for the cavalry, while other competent officers were in charge of supply, intelligence, military justice, and artillery and engineering. Although many of the infantry were reluctant conscripts, a core of dedicated veterans made sure the New Model Army became an ideologically motivated force. In 1647, soldier representatives asserted that they were "not a mere mercenary army," but fighting for "the defense of our own and the people's just rights and liberties." Successful in battle and siege, the army gained a decisive political influence, forcing the execution of King Charles I in 1649 and permitting Cromwell's assumption of power as Lord Protector in 1653.

> ❝ I HAD RATHER HAVE A PLAIN RUSSET-COATED CAPTAIN THAT KNOWS WHAT HE FIGHTS FOR, AND LOVES WHAT HE KNOWS, THAN THAT WHICH YOU CALL A GENTLEMAN. ❞
>
> **OLIVER CROMWELL**, IN A LETTER TO SIR WILLIAM SPRING, 1643

Forced capitulation
In 1648, Cromwell took Pembroke Castle in Wales after a lengthy siege. Unable to breach the walls, he forced a surrender by cutting off the castle's water supply.

1450—1700

FAIRFAX VS. RUPERT

NASEBY WAS A CRUCIAL VICTORY for the Parliamentary side in the British Civil War. In May 1645, Thomas Fairfax, leading Parliament's recently formed New Model Army, besieged Royalist Oxford. To induce him to lift the siege, Royalist general, Prince Rupert, sacked the Parliamentary stronghold of Leicester. Parliament ordered Fairfax to engage the Royalist army before it could make further depredations. To respond, the Royalists needed to concentrate their dispersed forces, but on June 12, Fairfax located them near Daventry. At first, the Royalists withdrew northward, but then decided to make a stand near the village of Naseby.

THOMAS FAIRFAX

Joined on June 13 by his newly appointed second-in-command, Oliver Cromwell, Fairfax had superior forces and therefore good reason to seek battle. On the misty morning of June 14, however, he was unsure how or where to bring about an engagement. At Cromwell's suggestion, Fairfax directed his army toward a low ridge that might invite a Royalist attack. The deployment was hasty, since the Royalists had indeed decided to advance and appeared on a hill across the moor. Fairfax chose to position himself with his infantry in the center. The cavalry were commanded by Cromwell on the right and Henry Ireton on the left.

The Royalist onslaught was swift and effective. Fairfax had little chance to use his artillery because a close-quarters melee was quickly joined. Relying on his cavalry commanders to exercise their own judgment, Fairfax flung himself into the infantry struggle, stiffening the second Parliamentary line when the first had been broken. His infantry were pushed back but did not break, giving the cavalry the chance to envelop the Royalist foot soldiers. Attacked by cavalry from both sides, these soon gave way. Fairfax was then able to organize and lead an annihilating assault on the stubborn Royalist Bluecoat infantry, fighting through, sword in hand, to their banner. He made no attempt to control the aftermath of the battle, in which his troops ran amok, causing severe casualties among the Royalists.

Parliamentary triumph
An engraving shows the English king, Charles I, being restrained from joining the fray. His army's defeat at Naseby was followed by a series of Parliamentary victories throughout England. Charles surrendered in May 1646.

> ❝ I SAW THE FIELD SO BESTREWED WITH CARCASSES OF MEN AND HORSES AS WAS MOST SAD TO BEHOLD. ❞
> **FAIRFAX'S CHAPLAIN, JOSHUA SPRIGGE,** EYEWITNESS ACCOUNT OF THE BATTLE OF NASEBY

TIMELINE

FAIRFAX

Cromwell arrives from East Anglia with his cavalry to join Fairfax. At a council of war they resolve to pursue and engage the Royalists	**Dawn** Fairfax's army breaks camp and starts moving toward Naseby, but halts in the mist, unsure exactly where the enemy is	After a sharp debate, Fairfax accepts Cromwell's suggestion to form up on a nearby hilltop in a position that invites attack	Fairfax deploys his army in a hastily chosen position between Sulby Hedges on the left and rough ground on the right	Cromwell sends dragoons under Colonel John Okey to line Sulby Hedges on the flank of the Royalist advance	The Parliamentary infantry step forward from the reverse slope to meet Royalist foot soldiers. After a single volley of musket fire, there is hand-to-hand fighting

1645: JUNE 13 — **JUNE 14**

RUPERT

Night After clashes with Parliamentary cavalry, the king holds a council of war and accepts Rupert's argument that they should stand and fight	**Early morning** Rupert deploys his army in a strong defensive position on a commanding ridge south of Market Harborough	Rupert rides forward to locate the enemy army hidden by mist. Spotting them on the move, he decides to take the offensive	The Royalists form up on Dust Hill, facing the Parliamentary army across Broad Moor. Rupert positions himself with the cavalry on the right	**10 a.m.** The Royalists attack, their infantry advancing in the center and Rupert's cavalry trotting forward on the right, exchanging fire with Okey's dismounted dragoons

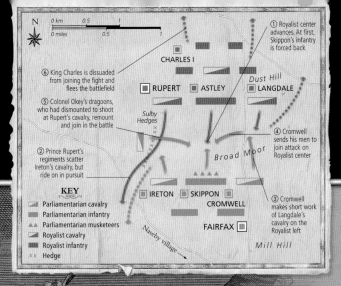

① Royalist center advances. At first, Skippon's infantry is forced back

⑥ King Charles is dissuaded from joining the fight and flees the battlefield

CHARLES I

⑤ Colonel Okey's dragoons, who had dismounted to shoot at Rupert's cavalry, remount and join in the battle

RUPERT   ASTLEY   Dust Hill   LANGDALE

Sulby Hedges

② Prince Rupert's regiments scatter Ireton's cavalry, but ride on in pursuit

Broad Moor

④ Cromwell sends his men to join attack on Royalist center

KEY
- Parliamentarian cavalry
- Parliamentarian infantry
- Parliamentarian musketeers
- Royalist cavalry
- Royalist infantry
- × × Hedge

IRETON   SKIPPON
CROMWELL

③ Cromwell makes short work of Langdale's cavalry on the Royalist left

FAIRFAX

Naseby village

Mill Hill

LOCATION Northern Northamptonshire in the English Midlands
CAMPAIGN British Civil War

DATE June 14, 1645
FORCES Royalists: 7,500, including 4,000 cavalry; Parliamentarians: 13,500, including 4,500 cavalry
CASUALTIES Royalists: at least 5,500, including 1,000 dead and 4,500 captured; Parliamentarians: 500 killed and wounded

PRINCE RUPERT

Although the English king, Charles I, was with the Royalist army, he had devolved field command to Prince Rupert. Influenced by the example of the much respected Swedish king, Gustavus Adolphus, in the Thirty Years' War, Rupert espoused aggressive battlefield tactics and an offensive strategy. He was well aware of the inferiority of the Royalist forces at Naseby, however, and on the morning of June 14 sensibly chose the best defensive position he could find to face Fairfax. Had he held his army ready on this ridge, the Parliamentary army would either have had to attack up a steep slope or march past, opening its flank to the Royalists. As the armies moved into position, Rupert rode forward to reconnoitre in person, since his scouts had failed to locate the enemy precisely. He observed movement through the mist that made him believe Fairfax

was vulnerable to a snap attack. Galloping quickly back to his line, he led the Royalists down from their ridge to advance on the enemy.

As his troops deployed opposite the Parliamentary army, Rupert gave instructions for the cavalry to ride in tight formation and not fire their pistols until they had reached close quarters. Ordering the attack to begin without waiting for his artillery to arrive, he himself rode with the cavalry on the right, which performed splendidly in shattering Ireton's cavalry.

RECKLESS PURSUIT

Rupert had failed to keep any cavalry reserves on his wing, and when he continued the pursuit of fleeing enemy cavalry to the rear, he lost any further influence on the battle. By the time, he had gathered some of his cavalry who were attacking the Parliamentary baggage train and led them back to the Royalist lines, his infantry and the Northern Horse regiment on the left were in hopeless disarray. Rupert's attempts to organize a counterattack by infantry and cavalry reserves came to nothing.

In the end, the king and the Royalist commanders abandoned the field, leaving behind most of their foot soldiers dead or taken prisoner and all their cannon captured.

Fairfax stiffens the resolve of the Parliamentary infantry as the Royalist foot soldiers break through the front line

Ireton leads some cavalry from the Parliamentary left to attack the Royalist infantry from the flank, but he is wounded and taken prisoner

Cromwell countercharges and his first line drives Langdale into retreat. His second line turns and attacks the Royalist infantry from the flank

12 noon Fairfax leads infantry and horse in an encircling attack on the stubborn Royalist Bluecoat infantry, finally himself killing the ensign holding their colors

Midafternoon Parliamentary forces pursue and kill fleeing Royalists, overcoming pockets of resistance

---

Rupert's cavalry smashes through the Parliamentary left and gallops on uncontrollably to the rear

Rupert and his cavalry reach the Parliamentary baggage train, where they are fiercely resisted by its guards

10:30 a.m. On the Royalist left, the Northern Horse under Sir Marmaduke Langdale rides forward to engage Cromwell's Ironsides (cavalry)

Attacked by Okey's dragoons, now mounted, from one side and Cromwell's Ironsides from the other, the Royalist foot soldiers fall back in disorder or surrender

Rupert returns to the Royalist lines, but the cavalry reserve has disappeared. The king is restrained from leading a final suicidal charge and led away

ADMIRALS OF THE ANGLO-DUTCH WARS

THE THREE ANGLO-DUTCH WARS took place in 1652–54, 1665–67, and 1672–74, the latter fought by the English in alliance with the French. They were intensive, if inconclusive, naval wars involving full-scale battles for control of trade routes. Initially chaotic, these battles were increasingly fought by ships in line astern (following the flagship) firing broadsides. This approach maximized the use of cannon and allowed admirals to maintain some control over their fleets in combat. English admirals were army generals drafted to fight at sea, whereas Dutch commanders, such as Maarten Tromp and Michiel de Ruyter, were born seamen.

ROBERT BLAKE

ENGLISH ADMIRAL
BORN 1599
DIED August 17, 1657
KEY CONFLICTS British Civil Wars, First Anglo-Dutch War, Anglo-Spanish War
KEY BATTLES Kentish Knock 1652, Portland 1653, Gabbard 1653, Tenerife 1657

Robert Blake was committed to the Parliamentary side in the British Civil Wars, serving with distinction in sieges on land before being appointed a General-at-Sea in 1649. He proved an outstanding sea commander from the outset, ensuring Parliamentary dominance at sea in the Civil War. Blake was involved in the outbreak of the First Anglo-Dutch War in 1652 and fought in most of the major battles of that fierce naval contest. He suffered a serious defeat at Dungeness, but was the victor at the battle of the Kentish Knock, Portland, and the Gabbard. Peace with the Dutch in 1654 brought no rest for Blake, who led a fleet to the Mediterranean and destroyed the Tunisian Barbary pirate base at Porto Farina. England then went to war with Spain, allowing Blake to show his prowess in a winter blockade of Cádiz and the destruction of a Spanish treasure fleet at Tenerife. At both Porto Farino and Tenerife he used naval guns to suppress land batteries, a major tactical innovation.

Father of the navy
Blake improved the organization and tactics of the Royal Navy. He was mostly responsible for the Fighting Instructions of 1653, which ordered naval captains to fight in a disciplined line of battle.

JAMES, DUKE OF YORK

ENGLISH ADMIRAL AND MONARCH
BORN October 14, 1633
DIED September 16, 1701
KEY CONFLICTS Second and Third Anglo-Dutch Wars, War of the League of Augsburg
KEY BATTLES Lowestoft 1665, Solebay 1672, The Boyne 1690

James, Duke of York, brother of the English king, Charles II, was Lord High Admiral during the Second and Third Anglo-Dutch Wars. He led the English fleet to victory at Lowestoft in 1665—although almost killed by Dutch chainshot on the deck of his flagship the *Royal Charles*—but was defeated at Solebay in 1672. Despite his physical courage, in neither battle did James succeed in keeping effective command of his forces. He became James II of England in 1685, but was deposed by William of Orange in 1688. His defeat by William at the battle of the Boyne in Ireland ended his hopes of regaining the throne.

Weak in command
Despite his personal bravery and military experience—he fought in Europe as an exile from England during the Civil War—James, Duke of York, lacked firmness as a commander and was liable to panic under pressure.

MAARTEN TROMP

DUTCH ADMIRAL
BORN April 23, 1598
DIED August 10, 1653
KEY CONFLICTS Eighty Years' War, First Anglo-Dutch War
KEY BATTLES The Downs 1639, Dungeness 1652, Portland 1653, Scheveningen 1653

Born in the Dutch port of Brill, Maarten Tromp went to sea at the age of nine. He was twice captured by pirates and sold as a slave, the first time at the age of 12. Surviving these spells of servitude, he became a Dutch naval officer, serving with distinction as a captain under the famous privateer-turned-admiral Piet Heyn in 1629. Amid the politicking that

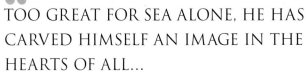

Commemoration
This medal was struck in honor of Maarten Tromp's death in action against the English. Tromp was a superb sailor as well as a fighting commander.

plagued Dutch naval administration, Tromp fell from favor until, in 1637, he was elevated to the rank of lieutenant-admiral and took effective command of the Dutch fleet. His victory over the Spanish at the Downs in 1639 made him a national hero.

A FIGHTING MAN

Tromp's combative spirit helped spark the First Anglo-Dutch War. On May 29, 1652, he was escorting a merchant convoy through the Straits of Dover when he encountered English General-at-Sea Robert Blake. Blake demanded that the Dutch dip their flag in salute, Tromp refused, shots were fired, and a five-hour battle followed. Three months into the ensuing war, Tromp was relieved of command by his political enemies, but the Dutch defeat in his absence at the

> ## TOO GREAT FOR SEA ALONE, HE HAS CARVED HIMSELF AN IMAGE IN THE HEARTS OF ALL…
>
> **JOOST VAN DEN VONDEL**, DUTCH POET, ON MAARTEN TROMP, C. 1653

CORNELIS TROMP

DUTCH ADMIRAL
BORN September 9, 1629
DIED May 29, 1691
KEY CONFLICTS Anglo-Dutch Wars, Scanian War
KEY BATTLES Lowestoft 1665, Texel 1673, Oland 1676

The son of Maarten Tromp, Cornelis Tromp came to prominence in his own right in the Second Anglo-Dutch War. As a vice-admiral commanding a squadron at the battle of Lowestoft, he kept his head amid the chaos of a Dutch disaster, supervising a fighting withdrawal. This success inflated his ego and his reputation, but he still had to serve under Michiel de Ruyter, who found him a difficult subordinate.

Commanding the Dutch rear squadron at the Four Days Battle in June 1666, Tromp failed to see a signal flag deployed by de Ruyter.

Failing to move with the fleet, he had to be rescued from encirclement. At the St. James's Day Battle six weeks later, he led his squadron in a savage attack on the English rear, commanded by Sir Edward Spragge. His efforts were shatteringly effective, but carried him out of sight of the rest of the fleet. De Ruyter had his revenge for Tromp's disappearance, when his squadron commander was afterward fired from the navy.

RECALLED FOR DUTY

The vagaries of Dutch politics brought Tromp back to command in the Third Anglo-Dutch War. At the battle of Texel, he engaged in a ship-to-ship duel with Spragge, who vowed to kill him but was drowned himself. Tromp ended his career in the service of Denmark, leading a Dutch-Danish fleet to victory over the Swedes at Oland in 1676.

KEY BATTLE

THE DOWNS

CAMPAIGN Eighty Years War
DATE September–October 1639
LOCATION English Channel

In 1639, Spain sent a fleet of warships and transports to reinforce their army fighting the Dutch. Maarten Tromp, with a far inferior force, boldly attacked the Spanish in the Channel on September 25. Firing broadsides in line of battle, he drove them to take refuge in the Downs, an anchorage on the English coast. Tromp received reinforcements and blockaded the Spanish with over 100 ships. A tense standoff developed, as the English threatened to intervene on the Spanish side. On October 31 Tromp ended the stalemate by sailing into the crowded bay. Some Spanish ships were burned by fireships, some ran aground, and many were captured. Only a dozen escaped.

Kentish Knock brought a rapid return. Tromp had a difficult task combining convoy escort with fighting the English fleet, but he had the better of Blake at Dungeness in December 1652 and showed outstanding skill in holding off the English at the three-day running battle of Portland in February–March 1653. At the Gabbard, however, he suffered heavy losses to the English, who had bigger ships and heavier guns. In August 1653, he attempted to break the English blockade of the Dutch coast at Scheveningen. In the course of the battle he showed all his usual brilliance of maneuver, but was killed by a sharpshooter hidden in the rigging of an English ship. The engagement cost the Dutch 15 ships, while the English fleet survived intact. However, the actions of the Dutch had persuaded the English to end their blockade.

Vain admiral
Cornelis Tromp was hard-drinking, irascible, untrustworthy, and vain, but a fearsome fighting commander.

MICHIEL DE RUYTER

DUTCH ADMIRAL
BORN March 24, 1607
DIED April 29, 1676
KEY CONFLICTS Anglo-Dutch Wars,
Franco-Dutch War
KEY BATTLES Four Days' Battle 1666, Raid
on the Medway 1667, Solebay 1672,
Schooneveld 1673, Texel 1673, Agosta 1676

Michiel de Ruyter came to warfare late in life. The son of a laborer in the port of Vlissingen, he went to sea as a boy and worked his way up to solid prosperity. By the age of 30, he was captain of his own ship and, by 40, a successful merchant in the colonial trade. During this time, he was occasionally involved in naval action, because armed merchant vessels were pressed into service as fighting ships when required. The experience did not impress him. Taking part in an action off Cape

Unassuming hero
A modest and humane man of impeccable physical courage, capable of bold aggression and yet prudent when occasion required, Michiel de Ruyter is one of the Netherlands' most respected national heroes.

St. Vincent in 1641, he was so infuriated by the lack of discipline among fellow Dutch captains that he vowed never to serve in battle again.

A CHANGE OF HEART
The outbreak of the First Anglo-Dutch War in 1652 transformed his life. An experienced and respected sailor, he was persuaded to enter naval service as a vice-commodore. His first tour of duty made his reputation. Escorting a merchant convoy into the Atlantic, he was intercepted by an English naval force under George Ayscue that outnumbered his warships two to

one. De Ruyter rounded on the English and attacked them with such spirit that they were driven back into Plymouth. On the way home, he was involved in a Dutch defeat at the Kentish Knock, but emerged with credit by managing a prudent withdrawal when the battle was lost.

Following the death of Admiral Maarten Tromp in the last encounter of the war in August 1653, the Dutch leader, Johan de Witt, invited de Ruyter to take overall command of the navy. The offer was firmly declined, however, as de Ruyter rightly feared the personal jealousies and political intrigues that such a meteoric rise would cause. Instead, he continued to perform more modest but distinguished service from the Mediterranean to the Baltic.

The crisis of the Second Anglo-Dutch War in 1665 finally overcame de Ruyter's reluctance to assume supreme command. He was engaged in colonial warfare with the English on the coast of Africa in the last year of peace and moved seamlessly into attacks on English colonies in the Caribbean and North America once war was declared. Returning home

Fierce engagement
The battle at Solebay in 1672 showed de Ruyter's command of all aspects of naval warfare, from disciplined maneuver in line of battle to savage close-quarters combat that brought the admiral himself under intense fire.

from this successful marauding at a low point in Dutch fortunes, he was hailed as a potential savior. But his appointment as navy commander was not welcomed by the de Witts' political enemies, the Orange faction, or by their favored admiral, Cornelis Tromp, who had assumed he would get the job. In the series of epic battles of the summer of 1666, the failure of Tromp, commanding a squadron, to follow orders and coordinate his movements with the rest of the Dutch fleet was almost disastrous for de Ruyter, whose tactics depended on disciplined maneuver. After the St. James's Day Battle in August—the closest to a total defeat de Ruyter ever suffered—Tromp was dismissed for negligence. It is a measure of the bitterness at the heart of these disputes

TIMELINE

- **1637–40** A merchant sea captain, Michiel de Ruyter is employed fighting pro-Spanish privateers operating out of Dunkirk.

- **November 4, 1641** On board his armed merchant ship, de Ruyter commands a squadron in an action against the Spanish off Cape St. Vincent.

- **August 26, 1652** At the beginning of the First Anglo-Dutch War, de Ruyter, now vice-commodore, defeats a larger English force at the battle of Plymouth.

- **1654** At the end of the war, de Ruyter turns down Johan de Witt's offer of supreme command.

- **1664–65** As the Second Anglo-Dutch War begins, de Ruyter raids English outposts and colonies around the Atlantic.

- **August 11, 1665** Johan de Witt appoints de Ruyter commander of the Dutch fleet with the rank of lieutenant-admiral.

- **June 11–14, 1666** At the Four Days' Battle, de Ruyter inflicts a severe defeat on the English in a hard-fought, costly fleet action.

- **June 12, 1667** The Dutch lay waste the English dockyard in a raid on the Medway River. De Ruyter is unwell, so Cornelis de Witt exercises effective command.

- **June 7, 1672** De Ruyter carries off a daring surprise attack on the English and French at Solebay at the start of the Third Anglo-Dutch War.

COMMEMORATIVE MEDAL SHOWING THE RAID ON THE MEDWAY, 1667

- **June–August 1673** Exploiting the protection of shoals off the Dutch coast, de Ruyter mounts sallies against an allied blockade fleet, winning victories at the battles of Schooneveld and Texel.

- **July 1674** De Ruyter leads a fleet to the West Indies, where it makes unsuccessful attacks on French colonies, returning after disease breaks out on his ships.

- **1675** The Spanish, on naval campaign in Sicily to suppress a revolt, call on their former foes, the Dutch, for help. De Ruyter is dispatched with a small squadron to their aid.

- **1676** De Ruyter engages with the French fleet in an inconclusive battle at Alicudi (January 8). He is mortally wounded aboard his flagship the *Eendracht* at the battle of Agosta, off the east coast of Sicily (April 22).

that one of Tromp's supporters tried to assassinate de Ruyter at his home three years later.

The Second Anglo-Dutch War ended in triumph for de Ruyter after his bold and successful raid on the English naval dockyard at Chatham on the Medway River. The resulting Treaty of Breda brought a spell of peace, and the aging de Ruyter, still precious to the Dutch state and people, was ordered to stay ashore.

RENEWED AGGRESSION

De Ruyter was therefore safeguarded for the climactic challenge of his career in 1672. England allied itself with Louis XIV's France against the Dutch and they looked certain of victory. De Ruyter's impulse was to attack the two enemy fleets separately before they could join up, but he was frustrated by administrative delays.

He took the offensive regardless, surprising the allied fleets in Solebay, eastern England. He inflicted heavy losses on the numerically superior enemy, and extricated his fleet in a skillful withdrawal. The downfall of his political allies, the de Witts, brought the Orange party to power, and could have ended de Ruyter's career. But he was too valuable to fire and continued in command, at the price of accepting Tromp's return as his subordinate. He fought defensive battles at Schooneveld and Texel in 1673, masterpieces of deft maneuver and brilliant exercises in strategic calculation, denying the allies the chance of mounting a seaborne invasion or sustaining a blockade without risking the loss of his fleet.

The English made peace in 1674 and de Ruyter ought to have retired. Instead, in 1676, he led an inadequate fleet to the Mediterranean to join the Spanish who were fighting the French around the coast of Sicily. At the battle of Agosta on April 22, in the thick of the action, de Ruyter's leg was severed by a cannonball. He died of gangrene a week later.

BIOGRAPHY
DE WITT BROTHERS

Johan de Witt (above right) became Grand Pensionary, or leader, of the Dutch Republic in 1653, during the First Anglo-Dutch War. He befriended Michiel de Ruyter, while his elder brother, Cornelis, accompanied de Ruyter in the Raid on the Medway and at the battle of Solebay. In summer 1672, after the French invasion of a virtually unprepared Dutch Republic, the de Witts' political enemies, the Orangists, took power and the two brothers were brutally lynched by a mob in the Hague.

>
> ## THE DUTCH FLEET UNDER DE RUYTER CAN ENTER A MOONLESS NIGHT IN HEAVY WIND AND FOG AND EMERGE THE NEXT DAY IN PERFECT LINE AHEAD.
>
> **FRENCH ADMIRAL ABRAHAM DUQUESNE**, REPORT TO LOUIS XIV, 1676

1660—1850

4 RULERS AND REVOLUTIONARIES

THIS WAS AN ERA IN WHICH COMMANDERS with exceptional qualities—from the Duke of Marlborough and Frederick the Great to George Washington and Napoleon Bonaparte—played decisive roles in wars and revolutions that shaped the course of history. Amid the political and social upheaval, the actual weapons of war changed hardly at all. The flintlock musket and bayonet, adopted in the dynastic wars of the late 1600s, were still in use when the Texans fought the Mexicans at the Alamo in 1836.

From the late 17th century, European states with increasingly powerful centralized governments created standing armies organized into permanent regiments. Their uniformed troops were subjected to strict discipline and drill, while their officers were distinguished by clear gradations of rank. Armies were also much larger than in earlier centuries—half a million troops fought at the battle of Leipzig in 1813.

The increase in numbers was accompanied by greater firepower. Replacing the pike with the bayonet allowed every foot soldier to be equipped with a firearm. The flintlock was more reliable than earlier infantry arms and capable of a higher rate of fire. Field guns became more mobile and effective, with greater range and a heavier weight of shot.

ARMY MANAGEMENT

Commanders aspired to move formations like chess pieces to outwit and outfight the enemy. The formal training of officers at military schools and colleges was still in its infancy—the US Military Academy at West Point was established in 1802—but of growing significance as military theorists flourished. Communications came to be conducted in writing. Army staff evolved to support the commander in his task, initially in the form of personal aides, but developing under Napoleon into a sophisticated staff organization for gathering intelligence and distributing orders. Improvements in surveying furnished generals with better maps, while accurate portable timepieces increased the potential for coordination between different sections of an army.

Despite these advances, commanders for the most part had to manage with technology that would have been familiar to Alexander the Great. Messages still traveled at the pace of a horse and supplies went even slower, at the speed of a cart. Intelligence depended on reconnaissance by mounted scouts and the interrogation of local people or captured enemy soldiers. Commanders often had only a vague notion of where their enemy was and could be sure of the position of their own army only by traveling

Borrowing from the past
French regiments in Napoleon's standing army carried eagle emblems that would not have looked out of place in ancient Rome.

with it. Meanwhile, the increasing size of armies multiplied the problems of logistics, coordination, and control—most of an army's efforts on campaign were focused on keeping the mass of men and animals fed.

ON THE BATTLEFIELD

To a large degree, command remained direct, hands-on, and instinctive. Napoleon interrogated prisoners himself and surveyed the terrain in person before a battle. Commanders no longer led from the front, but they were expected to be a visible presence on the battlefield and were often exposed to enemy fire—Wellington was lucky to survive Waterloo unscathed.

With the increased size of armies, battle lines sprawled over miles of terrain. A commander would select a high point for the best view, but even with a spyglass could rarely keep the whole field under observation. His view was in any case obscured by smoke once battle was joined and he had to rely on messengers. If it

Signing the dispatch
John Churchill, the 1st Duke of Marlborough, makes a field report from the battle of Blenheim in 1704. Written orders and letters became the standard method of military communication during this era.

appeared that a critical action was under way, he might ride across to see what was happening. Skillful commanders kept reserves to be thrown in to reinforce a breakthrough or block an enemy thrust. But the degree of control that could be exercised in the course of a battle was necessarily limited.

LEADERSHIP STYLES
Although there were exceptions—Frederick the Great of Prussia, Charles XII of Sweden, and Britain's George II among them—it became rare for monarchs to take personal command of their armies in the field. But

kings still liked to observe sieges and battles and sometimes overruled their commanders, as Russian Emperor Alexander did at Austerlitz in 1805, to disastrous effect. Napoleon was both head of state and field commander, so was able to make decisions with reference to no one but himself.

Until well into the second half of the 18th century, commanders projected a cool, rational persona and aspired to order and formality in their operations. Frederick the Great of Prussia planned his battles in fine detail and expected his army to carry out the plans like clockwork soldiers. However, the self-dramatizing style of the most famous

commanders of the Napoleonic Wars— Napoleon on land and Horatio Nelson at sea—was quite different. They sought the swift and total defeat of their enemies, an ambition that required the abandonment of formality in favor of speed of movement and decisiveness in combat. Meticulous preparation and training remained essential to their military success, but in the last resort they rode to victory on the back of chaos— what Nelson called a "pell-mell" battle.

Spyglass of the 1st Duke of Wellington
Innovations such as the spyglass made it much easier for commanders to get a good overview of the situation while staying away from the thick of battle.

1660—1720

EUROPE IN THE AGE OF LOUIS XIV

" BATTLES DO NOT NOW DECIDE NATIONAL QUARRELS, AND
EXPOSE COUNTRIES TO THE PILLAGE OF THE CONQUERORS AS
FORMERLY. FOR WE MAKE WAR MORE LIKE FOXES THAN LIONS
AND YOU WILL HAVE 20 SIEGES FOR ONE BATTLE. "

ROGER BOYLE, EARL OF ORRERY, BRITISH SOLDIER AND STATESMAN, 1677

LOUIS XIV, KNOWN AS THE SUN KING, came to power in France in 1661 and ruled until his death in 1715. Although he never commanded an army in battle, his military ambitions dominated an era in European warfare. The size and efficiency of French armed forces obliged other powers to mobilize resources and improve military organization. Larger armies with increased firepower were formidable instruments of war, but they needed skilled generals with the intelligence and professionalism to control them.

The European conflicts during Louis XIV's reign have been called dynastic wars, as they expressed the personal ambitions of monarchs, rather than broader ideological or nationalistic goals. But religious differences were also at the forefront, the Protestant Dutch and English reacting to Louis' aggressive Catholicism with fear and disgust.

The period began with France on the offensive in the Spanish and Dutch Netherlands (present-day Belgium and Holland) in the War of Devolution (1667–68), the Dutch War (1672–78), and the War of the Reunions (1683–84). Louis' very strength propelled other states to ally against him. In the later wars of the League of Augsburg (1688–97) and the War of the Spanish Succession (1701–14), he fought a largely defensive struggle against a Grand Alliance in which the English, Dutch, and Austrians were the main players. Elsewhere in Europe, there was a prolonged fight for domination around the Baltic, and the Great Northern War (1700–21) saw Russia, under Peter the Great, emerge victorious. The centuries-old struggle with the Ottoman Empire continued to the south, running entirely in favor of Christian Europe after the failed Ottoman siege of Vienna in 1683 marked a turning point.

MILITARY REORGANIZATION

European armies were transformed during this period. Regular forces were organized into permanent regiments with a clear hierarchy of officers. The men wore uniforms and increasingly traded their pikes and matchlock muskets for flintlocks with bayonets. France set the pace

for improvements in administration and finance, allowing far greater resources to be devoted to warfare. By the end of the 17th century, the French had between 300,000 and 400,000 men under arms. The supply and movement of forces on this scale imposed severe technical demands on commanders. A general was supported by only a minimal staff, whose key figures were his personal secretary and the quartermaster-general, an individual whose responsibilities ranged from logistics through writing and distributing orders to reconnaissance and intelligence.

SIEGE SPECIALISTS

Fortresses were the main prizes of European territorial warfare and so operations centered on sieges, with field battles mostly occurring when a relief force was sent to counter a besieging army. Fortifications themselves had to become more sophisticated to withstand more powerful artillery. Experts in both the building and destruction of fortifications, such as France's Marquis de Vauban and the Dutch engineer Menno van Coehoorn, were highly prized specialists whose knowledge gave them the right to command.

Those few bold commanders who sought to engage and destroy enemy forces on the battlefield—such as Britain's Duke of Marlborough and Sweden's King Charles XII—were less typical of their age, but, nevertheless, were generally much admired. But even the greatest master of maneuver and tactics could no longer hope to campaign successfully without first ensuring that his men were properly drilled, his supply system was efficient, and his artillery train moved in good order.

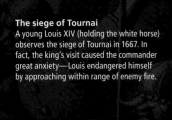

The siege of Tournai
A young Louis XIV (holding the white horse) observes the siege of Tournai in 1667. In fact, the king's visit caused the commander great anxiety—Louis endangered himself by approaching within range of enemy fire.

Siege weapon
Mortars were designed to propel explosive devices over the walls of a besieged fortress. This type of mortar was introduced by Dutch engineer Menno van Coehoorn in 1674.

GENERALS OF LOUIS XIV'S WARS

BETWEEN 1667 AND 1717 Louis XIV's France fought a series of wars that produced remarkably little change to the borders of Europe. Yet at times, these were desperately hard-fought contests, only stalemated by the balance of forces maintained between France and opposing coalitions. If the French produced the period's foremost military engineer in the Marquis de Vauban, France's enemies had the fortune to find the era's outstanding field commanders in Prince Eugène of Savoy and the Duke of Marlborough—under whose command an English army played a crucial role in Europe for the first time since the Hundred Years' War.

PRINCE EUGÈNE OF SAVOY

HABSBURG GENERAL
BORN October 18, 1663
DIED April 21, 1736
KEY CONFLICTS Ottoman-Habsburg Wars, War of the League of Augsburg, War of the Spanish Succession
KEY BATTLES Zenta 1697, Blenheim 1704, Oudenarde 1708, Malplaquet 1709, Belgrade 1717

Raised at the French court, Prince Eugène of Savoy was refused the chance to serve in Louis XIV's army because of the king's personal animosity. Instead, he shifted to Vienna, defending the city under Ottoman siege in 1683.

EARLY DISTINCTION
Eugène so distinguished himself in subsequent Austrian campaigns against the Turks and the French that he had risen to field-marshal by the age of 30. A bold and decisive commander, in September 1697

Eugène surprised a large Turkish army crossing the Tisza River at Zenta in Serbia, inflicting a crushing defeat on numerically superior forces. The battle made Eugène one of the most celebrated generals in Europe.

During the War of the Spanish Succession, Eugène met the Duke of Marlborough and, after the victory at Blenheim (pp. 168–69), cooperated with him at Oudenarde in 1708 and Malplaquet in 1709. He also drove the French out of northern Italy in campaigns of his own. His later years were less brilliant, although seizing Belgrade from the Ottomans in 1717 was another major step in the repulse of the Turks in southeast Europe. Much of Eugène's life outside combat was devoted to improving the organization of the Austrian army.

Eugène in the field
Prince Eugène (center with baton) was noted for his plain features and—by the standards of his time—sober dress. He was a disciplinarian who placed heavy demands on his officers.

WILLIAM III

Irish victor
William III's victory over James II at the Boyne in 1690 made him a hero to Irish Protestants.

DUTCH LEADER AND KING OF ENGLAND
BORN November 14, 1650
DIED March 8, 1702
KEY CONFLICTS Franco-Dutch War, War of the League of Augsburg
KEY BATTLES The Boyne 1690, Steenkirk 1692, Neerwinden 1693

William of Orange was born hereditary stadtholder (head of state) of the Dutch Republic but, until 1672, was excluded from power by political opponents. In that year, Louis XIV invaded the Netherlands, threatening to overrun the entire country. At age 22, William was appointed captain-general of the Dutch armed forces, fighting France to a compromise peace. However, the survival of his Protestant country remained precarious in the face of Louis' aggressive Catholicism.

THE NEW KING
William could not allow England to become a Catholic country allied to France. In 1688, he secured a formal invitation from some English grandees to take the throne from the Catholic James II. When William invaded England with an army of 15,000 Dutch troops, James was abandoned by his chief military commanders, including the future Duke of Marlborough. William was thus able to assume the English throne jointly with his wife, Mary, without a fight.

From 1689, William was again at war with Louis. The French backed the deposed James in an invasion of Ireland. William crossed the Irish Sea with a substantial army and defeated the French and Jacobites (supporters of James) at the Boyne River in July 1690. But he continued to campaign in the Netherlands.

Driven from the field at Steenkirk in 1692 and again at Neerwinden in 1693, William still held the war effort together. In 1695, he regained the key fortress of Namur, a major blow to Louis' prestige. In his goal of maintaining Dutch independence, William was wholly successful.

MARQUIS DE VAUBAN

FRENCH MILITARY ENGINEER
BORN May 15, 1633
DIED March 30, 1707
KEY CONFLICT Wars of Louis XIV
KEY BATTLES Siege of Lille 1667, Siege of Maastricht 1673, Siege of Namur 1692

Sébastien Le Prestre, Marquis de Vauban, was born into a poverty-stricken family of minor nobility in Burgundy and orphaned, fortuitously receiving a basic education in math and science. At age 17, he joined the rebel forces in the *Fronde* revolt of certain French nobles against Louis XIV. Captured by the royalists he

1672, in which there were six major sieges but no land battles. His conduct of the siege of Maastricht, taken in only 13 days, was so successful that it established a new method for attacking fortifications. It had long been the custom to dig saps (zigzag trenches) toward the fortress walls until close enough to effect a breach and attempt an assault. Vauban added the digging of three parallels—trenches aligned with the wall under attack—connected by the saps. The third parallel nearest the wall was the base from which siege

The siege of Namur in 1692 seems, in retrospect, the beginning of the end of Vauban's style of fortress. The Namur citadel was defended by the great Dutch engineer Menno van Coehoorn, but Vauban's siege batteries reduced it after 36 days. Only three years later, Namur was retaken by the Dutch. Vauban's new fortresses were proving embarrassingly easy to seize, although possession of such strongpoints remained a focal point of war in the early 18th century. Vauban directed the last of his 48 sieges in 1703, the year in which he was honored with the rank of marshal of France.

Military reformer
In addition to his achievements in military engineering, Vauban was partly responsible for the adoption of the socket bayonet and other military reforms.

> ## CITY BESIEGED BY VAUBAN, CITY TAKEN; CITY DEFENDED BY VAUBAN, CITY UNTAKEABLE.
>
> **POPULAR SAYING IN FRANCE** ON VAUBAN'S MILITARY PROWESS, LATE 17TH CENTURY

changed sides, becoming a devoted servant of the king. Vauban showed an aptitude for military engineering and siege warfare from a young age. By 1657, aged 24, he was considered sufficiently experienced to direct the sieges of Gravelines and Ypres. During the brief, successful War of Devolution

cannon, grenadiers, and miners would attempt to force an entry. Under constant fire from the fortress bastions, these approach works were hazardous. Vauban was often at the forefront, directing operations, inspecting progress, or examining a breech in a wall. He bore a scar from a wound received at Douai.

END OF AN ERA
Vauban's prestige was all the greater because Louis and his courtiers took such an avid interest in sieges, which they treated as a form of spectacle. He was thus able to push through his policy for a large-scale program of fortress-building to render France's northern and eastern borders secure.

Vauban oversaw construction of some 30 fortresses and the rebuilding of hundreds of others. He was not a strikingly innovative fortress designer, producing variations on the currently standard star-shaped bastion design originally invented in Italy. Indeed, his own improvements in offensive siege warfare, which included the ricochet firing of cannon to bounce solid shot over obstacles, rendered fortresses increasingly difficult to defend.

Star fortress
Vauban's forts were star-shaped, the points providing bastions for artillery and musketeers to direct crossfire at an approaching enemy.

in 1667–68, he impressed Louis XIV by the speed with which he overcame the fortified towns of Douai, Tournai, and Lille. At the request of the Marquis de Louvois, French Secretary of State for War, Vauban wrote a treatise on the conduct of sieges. He was also entrusted with building new fortifications for captured towns.

Vauban's ascendancy was confirmed in the war initiated by France's attack on the Dutch United Provinces in

1660—1850

TIMELINE

■ **1668** After being commissioned as an ensign in the Guards, John Churchill serves in the English garrison of Tangiers in north Africa.

■ **June 7, 1672** In the Third Anglo-Dutch War, Churchill takes part in the naval battle of Solebay on board the Duke of York's flagship.

■ **July 6, 1685** As a major-general, Churchill plays a leading role in the defeat of the rebel Duke of Monmouth at Sedgemoor.

■ **November 1688** Churchill deserts the king, James II, and welcomes William of Orange's invasion force advancing on London.

■ **1690** Now Earl of Marlborough, he leads an expedition to Ireland, which retakes Cork and Kinsale from the Jacobites.

■ **1692** Marlborough is accused of treason and locked up in the Tower of London; soon released, he remains in disfavor.

■ **1702** Queen Anne accedes to the throne as the War of the Spanish Succession begins. Marlborough is appointed captain-general and elevated to a dukedom.

■ **1704** Marlborough defeats France and Bavaria in the Blenheim campaign; the queen promises him a great mansion (Blenheim Palace) to be built at Woodstock in Oxfordshire.

■ **May 23, 1706** Marlborough routs a French army under Marshal Villeroi at Ramillies and overruns the Spanish Netherlands.

■ **1707** By the Convention of Altranstaedt, Marlborough persuades Charles XII of Sweden not to advance farther into Germany, so that he can remain focused on the war with France.

■ **1708** Marlborough defeats the French again at Oudenarde (July 11) and takes Lille after a lengthy siege conducted with Eugène of Savoy (August 12–December 10).

■ **September 9, 1709** A fourth field victory over the French at Malplaquet is so costly it leads to criticism of Marlborough's generalship.

■ **1711** Despite overcoming the French defensive lines, Marlborough is dismissed as captain-general.

■ **1714** Marlborough is restored as captain-general when Britain's first Hanoverian monarch, George I, comes to the throne.

BLENHEIM PALACE

■ **1719** Crippled by the effects of a stroke, Marlborough moves into the east wing of the still unfinished Blenheim Palace, where he spends his final years. He dies three years later.

DUKE OF MARLBOROUGH

ENGLISH MILITARY COMMANDER
BORN May 26, 1650
DIED June 16, 1722
KEY CONFLICT War of the Spanish Succession
KEY BATTLES Blenheim 1704, Ramillies 1706, Oudenarde 1708, Malplaquet 1709

The future Duke of Marlborough was born John Churchill, son of an impoverished rural gentleman. Ambitious and handsome, he forged a position for himself at the court of Charles II through luck and charm. His sister, Arabella, became the mistress of the king's Catholic brother, James, Duke of York. In 1677, Churchill married Sarah Jennings, a close friend of James's daughter, Princess Anne. When James came to the throne in 1685, Churchill was elevated to the House of Lords.

SHIFTING LOYALTIES

Churchill had picked up a measure of military experience during this period and he soon proved his ability. Leading the king's troops, he crushed an invasion by James's nephew, the Duke of Monmouth, making a bid for the throne. But barely three years later, when William of Orange landed in England to claim the throne, Churchill shamelessly deserted James to serve the new king. William rewarded him with the title of Earl of Marlborough, yet trust was not so easily gained. In 1692, he was dismissed for alleged treasonable contacts with James.

It was a trick of fate that Sarah's friend Anne became queen in 1702, the year the War of the Spanish Succession began. Suddenly enjoying strong royal support, Marlborough

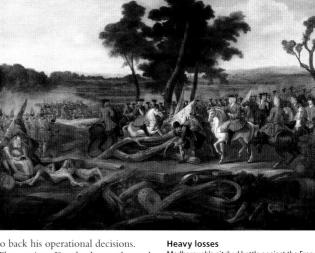

took overall command of the allied forces fighting France. It was a task that would have crushed a man of lesser ability. He had to lead armies on a scale far surpassing his previous experience, as well as deal with the commanders and governments of the Grand Alliance: primarily the Netherlands, Austria, and Britain itself. They also had to be persuaded

to back his operational decisions. The cautious Dutch, always obsessed with national defense, were especially suspicious of his offensive instincts.

It is a tribute to Marlborough's personal charm that, in 1704, he persuaded his allies to back bold action to save the Austrian Empire from defeat by France and Bavaria. Seizing the strategic initiative, Marlborough marched his main forces from Cologne to the Danube River, a movement conducted with exemplary efficiency. It denuded the defenses of the Netherlands, but he rightly gambled that the French would follow him southward. Finding a fellow spirit in Austria's Prince Eugène of Savoy,

English weapon
The flintlock firing mechanism introduced at this time made firearms far more reliable and effective.

Heavy losses
Marlborough's pitched battle against the French at Malplaquet in 1709 ended as a Pyrrhic victory. The high casualty figures—even more on the allied than the French side—shocked Europe.

the opportunity to bring his enemy to battle. In May 1706, he led an Anglo-Dutch army against the French at Ramillies. The forces were roughly equal in number and the French had an apparently solid defensive position. Marlborough was often in the thick of the fighting—he was even unhorsed in a cavalry melee—but once more carried the day with his tactical genius. He tricked the French Marshal Villeroi into reinforcing his left wing, while covertly shifting his

> **"BY HIS INVINCIBLE GENIUS IN WAR...**
> **HE HAD COMPLETED THAT GLORIOUS**
> **PROCESS THAT CARRIED ENGLAND...**
> **TO TEN YEARS' LEADERSHIP OF EUROPE."**
>
> WINSTON S. CHURCHILL, *MARLBOROUGH: HIS LIFE AND TIMES*, 1933

Marlborough inflicted a shattering defeat on the Franco-Bavarian army at Blenheim (pp. 168–69).

In contrast to the prudent warfare of sieges and fortified lines favored by most of his contemporaries, Marlborough was always seeking

own men to the center, where they powered a breakthrough. The crushing French defeat was followed by the fall of a string of fortresses to his army.

Marlborough's last outright victory was at Oudenarde in July 1708. At Malplaquet the following year, the

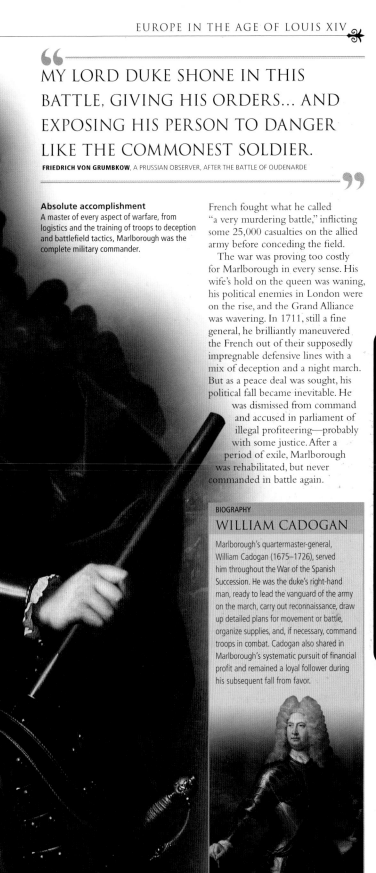

> ## MY LORD DUKE SHONE IN THIS BATTLE, GIVING HIS ORDERS... AND EXPOSING HIS PERSON TO DANGER LIKE THE COMMONEST SOLDIER.
>
> **FRIEDRICH VON GRUMBKOW**, A PRUSSIAN OBSERVER, AFTER THE BATTLE OF OUDENARDE

Absolute accomplishment
A master of every aspect of warfare, from logistics and the training of troops to deception and battlefield tactics, Marlborough was the complete military commander.

French fought what he called "a very murdering battle," inflicting some 25,000 casualties on the allied army before conceding the field.

The war was proving too costly for Marlborough in every sense. His wife's hold on the queen was waning, his political enemies in London were on the rise, and the Grand Alliance was wavering. In 1711, still a fine general, he brilliantly maneuvered the French out of their supposedly impregnable defensive lines with a mix of deception and a night march. But as a peace deal was sought, his political fall became inevitable. He was dismissed from command and accused in parliament of illegal profiteering—probably with some justice. After a period of exile, Marlborough was rehabilitated, but never commanded in battle again.

BIOGRAPHY
WILLIAM CADOGAN

Marlborough's quartermaster-general, William Cadogan (1675–1726), served him throughout the War of the Spanish Succession. He was the duke's right-hand man, ready to lead the vanguard of the army on the march, carry out reconnaissance, draw up detailed plans for movement or battle, organize supplies, and, if necessary, command troops in combat. Cadogan also shared in Marlborough's systematic pursuit of financial profit and remained a loyal follower during his subsequent fall from favor.

1660—1850

MARLBOROUGH AT BLENHEIM

LOCATION
By the Danube, Bavaria
CAMPAIGN The
War of the Spanish
Succession

DATE August 13, 1704
FORCES Grand Alliance: 52,000; French and
Bavarian: 56,000
CASUALTIES Grand Alliance: 14,000 killed or
wounded; French and Bavarian: 20,000 killed
or wounded, 14,000 taken prisoner

In the summer of 1704, the Duke
of Marlborough led an army from
Cologne on a 250-mile (400-km)
march south to attack Bavaria, whose
Elector had sided with France against
the Grand Alliance. The force reached
the Danube River in good order and,

after a swift but costly storming of
defenses at Donauwörth, rampaged
around Bavaria. In the first week of
August, a French army commanded
by Marshal Tallard arrived to support
the Elector's forces. Marlborough was
joined by the Austrian army of Prince
Eugène of Savoy, a commander who
shared his militant spirit. The two
men agreed to seek out and engage
the Franco-Bavarian forces.

BATTLE PREPARATION
On August 12, Marlborough and
Eugène advanced along the north
bank of the Danube and located
the enemy. Climbing a church tower
in the village of Tapfheim, they
observed the French and Bavarian

armies in the distance. Their
opponents were drawn up in a
defensive position between a forest
and the Nebel, a tributary of the
Danube. Very few commanders
would have chosen to take the
offensive against such a position with
inferior numbers, yet the decision to
attack was taken without hesitation.

Eugène was assigned to distract the
Bavarians on the left of the enemy
line, while Marlborough smashed the
French in their center and right. The
duke had spotted that the French
were too far back from the Nebel to
defend it properly. He ordered his
infantry to cross the stream and hold
the opposite bank until they were

> ## GIVE MY DUTY TO THE QUEEN, AND LET HER KNOW HER ARMY HAS HAD A GLORIOUS VICTORY.
>
> **MARLBOROUGH** IN A MESSAGE TO HIS WIFE, FROM THE BATTLEFIELD AT BLENHEIM, AUGUST 13, 1704

In possession of the field
The French are put to flight at Blenheim,
with a red-coated Marlborough on the right
astride the prancing horse. The contested
village of Blenheim is in the center.

joined by his cavalry, which he was confident would sweep away the French horse. His infantry on his left were to attack the village of Blenheim.

SURPRISING THE ENEMY

The French were ignorant of their enemy's location, strength, and goals. They woke on August 13 to the unexpected sight of Marlborough's infantry columns marching across the plain toward them. There was a delay while Eugène got into position on the far right, during which Marlborough's troops had to wait under cannon fire—the duke was covered in dust from a near miss. Then the message came that Eugène was ready and the plan went into action, broadly unfolding as conceived. Marlborough's infantry forded the Nebel and its firepower halted French countercharges. The French allowed

their foot soldiers to be sucked into a desperate defense of Blenheim village, leaving their cavalry exposed without infantry support when Marlborough's horse charged them on the plain. Eugène kept up constant pressure on the enemy left, which became detached from the rest of the battle.

The duke rode around the field throughout the day, dispatching messengers or giving orders. At critical moments, he intervened and was on hand to call up reserves from Eugène's forces when his own Dutch infantry almost gave in to French cavalry counterattack. After a day's fighting, Tallard was captured and pleaded with Marlborough for terms, but the duke insisted on total surrender. Pinned against the river, virtually the entire French center and right were killed either fighting or fleeing, or were taken prisoner.

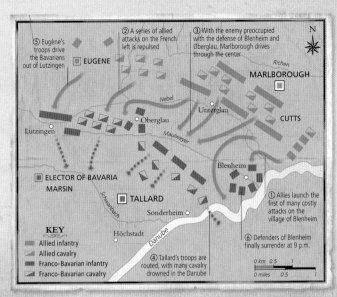

⑤ Eugène's troops drive the Bavarians out of Lutzingen

EUGENE

② A series of allied attacks on the French left is repulsed

③ With the enemy preoccupied with the defense of Blenheim and Oberglau, Marlborough drives through the center

Richen

MARLBOROUGH

Nebel

Oberglau

Unterglau

CUTTS

Lutzingen

Maulweyer

Blenheim

ELECTOR OF BAVARIA

MARSIN

Schwarzbach

TALLARD

Sonderheim

① Allies launch the first of many costly attacks on the village of Blenheim

⑥ Defenders of Blenheim finally surrender at 9 p.m.

KEY

Höchstadt

Danube

④ Tallard's troops are routed, with many cavalry drowned in the Danube

- Allied infantry
- Allied cavalry
- Franco-Bavarian infantry
- Franco-Bavarian cavalry

0 km   0.5   1
0 miles   0.5   1

ROYAL COMMANDERS

MONARCHS FROM COUNTRIES in northern Europe—Sweden, Poland, and Russia—provided some of the most exceptional examples of military command in the late 17th and early 18th centuries. The Poles were among the major losers in the wars of this period, yet the flamboyant career of Jan Sobieski shines through the gloom of longer-term decline. The Great Northern War of 1700–20 centered on the confrontation between Charles XII of Sweden and Russia's Peter the Great. Charles's inspired but reckless flair for the offensive led to disaster in the face of Peter's long-term planning and mobilization of resources.

JAN SOBIESKI

KING OF POLAND-LITHUANIA
BORN August 17, 1629
DIED June 17, 1696
KEY CONFLICTS Polish-Ottoman War, Ottoman-Habsburg War
KEY BATTLES Khotyn 1673, Vienna 1683

Jan Sobieski was the son of a noble Polish family in Lwów and, at the time of his birth, the Polish-Lithuanian Commonwealth was a major power in Europe. But the beginning of his military career coincided with a disastrous period for his nation, which was attacked by Swedes, Russians, and Ukrainian Cossacks. In 1655–60, Sobieski first distinguished himself in the desperate conflict against Swedish invaders.

By 1666, he was fighting in a border war against Cossacks and Tatars in Ukraine, where a victory at Podhajce saw him being appointed Grand Hetman of the Crown (commander-in-chief of the Polish army).

The Ottoman Empire invaded Poland in 1672. Weakened by internal dissent and lack of money, the Poles alternated attempts at resistance with humiliating peace deals. Even so, Sobieski's leadership—in particular, his victory at Khotyn—won admiration in Europe and earned him election to the Polish throne in 1674 as King Jan III.

His finest hour came in 1683 when an Ottoman army invaded the Holy Roman Empire and besieged Vienna. Committed to fight in an alliance for the defense of Christendom, Sobieski raced from Poland with a relief army. Joining up with German forces led by Charles of Lorraine, the Poles reached Vienna just in time to prevent a Turkish assault on the city. On September 12, Sobieski's armored lancers charged into the Ottoman camp in an irresistible tide, breaking their battle lines and driving the Turks into retreat. The Polish king was hailed as the savior of Christian civilization. Sobieski could not, however, save Poland, which continued its inexorable decline through the latter part of his reign.

> ## ALL THE COMMON PEOPLE KISSED MY HANDS, MY FEET, MY CLOTHES; OTHERS ONLY TOUCHED ME...
>
> **JAN SOBIESKI**, IN A LETTER TO HIS WIFE AFTER THE SIEGE OF VIENNA, 1683

Savior of Vienna
Sobieski is greeted as a hero in Vienna after saving the city from the Ottomans. The joyful occasion is one of the highlights of Polish history, here depicted by Jan Matejko.

Aggressive monarch
Charles XII was limited as a military commander by his single-minded commitment to the offensive, both in strategy and tactics. The end result of his campaigns was to weaken and impoverish his country.

CHARLES XII OF SWEDEN

KING OF SWEDEN
BORN June 17, 1682
DIED November 30, 1718
KEY CONFLICT Great Northern War
KEY BATTLES Narva 1700, Kliszów 1702, Holowczyn 1708, Poltava 1709

Acceding to the Swedish throne in 1697 at age 14, Charles XII ran a headlong course from triumph to disaster. His early military campaigns were a brilliant success. Faced with a hostile alliance of Russia, Poland, Saxony, and Denmark, he attacked and defeated the Danes. Then, in November 1700, he trounced a Russian army besieging the Estonian city of Narva with a surprise attack in a blizzard. The Russian army was at least three times as large as Charles's force but was split apart and completely routed. Next it was the turn of the Poles and Saxons, invaded and crushed by Charles at Kliszów in July 1702. But he had no taste for ending wars short of total victory. After prolonged campaigning to subdue the Poles, in 1708 Charles embarked on the conquest of Russia.

DEFEAT AT POLTAVA
In the summer of 1708, Charles beat the Russians at Holowczyn. However, after a freezing winter without sufficient food, his forces met disaster at Poltava. Wounded, the king escaped on a stretcher to find refuge with Russia's enemies, the Ottomans.

For five years, Charles remained as an increasingly unwelcome guest of the Turks before returning to Sweden in 1714. In an attempt to rebuild his power, he invaded Norway in 1716 and again two years later, but was killed besieging Fredriksten in 1718.

> ## STUDY CHARLES XII... TO BE CURED OF THE MADNESS OF CONQUERING.
> **VOLTAIRE**, *HISTORY OF CHARLES XII*, 1731

1660—1850

KEY BATTLE

POLTAVA

CAMPAIGN Swedish Invasion of Russia
DATE July 8, 1709
LOCATION Poltava, Ukraine

Swedish king Charles XII besieged the fortress of Poltava hoping to seize much-needed supplies. Peter the Great met the Swedes with a relief army twice as large. Although wounded and unable to command in person, Charles ordered a frontal attack on Russian field fortifications. But the Russians fought a resolute defensive action, their firepower inflicting massive casualties on the Swedes. Most of the Swedish survivors were taken prisoner after the battle.

PETER THE GREAT

CZAR OF RUSSIA
BORN June 9, 1672
DIED February 8, 1725
KEY CONFLICTS Russo-Turkish War, Great Northern War
KEY BATTLE Poltava 1709

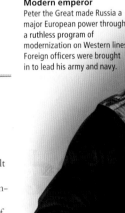

Modern emperor
Peter the Great made Russia a major European power through a ruthless program of modernization on Western lines. Foreign officers were brought in to lead his army and navy.

Czar of Russia from 1682, Peter I was a relentless modernizer. He imported the expertise of foreign advisers but also traveled to the West incognito in the 1690s to study shipbuilding and military organization. He suppressed a revolt by the *streltsy*, Russia's traditional military elite, and created a Western-style regular army and navy.

The defeat suffered at the hands of the Swedes at Narva in 1700 showed how much work was required to make the Russian army an efficient fighting force. The victory at Poltava nine years later gave the measure of Peter's achievement—and a rare example of his ability as a field commander.

Peter achieved his strategic objective of turning Russia into a maritime power. At his death, navies were operating on the Baltic and the Black Sea.

18TH-CENTURY WARFARE

" WHEN THE TWO ARMIES ARRIVE WITHIN A CERTAIN
DISTANCE FROM EACH OTHER, THEY BOTH BEGIN TO FIRE
AND CONTINUE THEIR APPROACHES, TILL… EITHER THE ONE
OR OTHER TAKES TO FLIGHT. "

MAURICE DE SAXE, MARSHAL OF FRANCE, FROM *REVERIES ON THE ART OF WAR*, PUBLISHED 1756–57

THE EUROPEAN COMMANDERS of the period between the death of Louis XIV in 1715 and the French Revolutionary Wars of the 1790s have often been criticized as unimaginative in their approach to warfare, valuing inflexible discipline over initiative and formal rules over innovation. This, for example, is the popular American view of the British generals who fought to prevent the independence of the United States. Yet, this was, in fact, the time when European armies first established a clear superiority over those of other civilizations.

There were long periods of peace in Europe between 1715 and 1792, broken only by marginal warfare against the Turks or small-scale fighting in Poland. The chief source of conflicts between major states was the disturbance caused by the rising military power of Prussia under the leadership of Frederick the Great. The War of the Austrian Succession (1740–48) and the Seven Years' War (1756–63) both originated in Frederick's expansionist ambitions and provided him with opportunities to establish a reputation as an outstanding military leader.

During this time, the focus of warfare shifted. The sieges and fixed fortifications so prevalent in Louis XIV's era were on the wane. Instead, thoughtful commanders worked on combining infantry, cavalry, field artillery, and light skirmishing troops. This aggressive style of fighting was marked by sweeping maneuvers and bold battle tactics. But such tough military principles were shackled by limited political objectives. Combatant states were always ready to do a deal rather than fight to a finish, so, ultimately, even spectacular campaigns produced little result.

COLONIAL RIVALRY

Arguably more decisive and more important in their outcome were the wars fought by European armies on other continents. Britain and France in particular had emerged as colonial powers and their rivalry gave European conflicts global scope. Engaged on opposing sides in the Seven Years' War in Europe, the British and French also fought one another in India, the West Indies, and North America. The result was a resounding defeat for

France, but the French had their revenge when Britain's North American colonies rebelled, precipitating the American Revolutionary War in 1775. France's entry into the conflict as an ally of the colonists virtually guaranteed the success of a rebellion. And it was one that Britain showed no sign of being able to repress.

ADAPTING TO THE TERRAIN

Military officers educated in the European tradition, such as the American commander-in-chief George Washington, adapted the principles of European warfare to the challenges of fighting in alien environments. Good discipline combined with efficient firepower meant those armies campaigning in the North American wilderness or the Indian subcontinent were more than adequately equipped for the job. Flintlock muskets and field cannon repelled the enemy sufficiently, although rifle-armed skirmishers and Native Americans scored some notable successes in North American conflicts. The results, however, were never decisive.

In India, local rulers intelligently adopted European methods to counter the expanding influence of Britain, but those in power consistently lost to Europeans in crucial engagements. In Iran, Nadir Shah, a ruler whose reign overlapped with that of Frederick the Great, achieved substantial conquests with his rigidly drilled infantry and effective mobile artillery. But he depended heavily on bought-in expertise from Europe. The effectiveness of the uniformed European army and its rational-minded officers could not ultimately be denied.

Prussian formation
At the battle of Hohenfriedberg in 1745 Frederick the Great's Prussian grenadiers advance in a tight line into enemy fire—the standard method of attack for infantry in the mid-18th century.

1660—1850

Socket bayonet
Mounted on a ring slipped over the barrel of a musket, the socket bayonet allowed a single infantryman to combine the functions of a musketeer and a pikeman.

EUROPEAN ARMY COMMANDERS

ALTHOUGH THE WARS between European states in the mid-18th century were fought for limited objectives, they generated battles and campaigns contested with ferocity and determination by some outstandingly skillful commanders. The causes and consequences of the War of the Austrian Succession and the Seven Years' War may be lost byways of diplomatic history, but battles such as Fontenoy or Leuthen remain vivid examples of the art of warfare. Frederick the Great of Prussia dominated the period, dramatic in his defeats as well as his victories. However, it was the Russian General Suvorov who is often considered the most gifted.

MAURICE DE SAXE

FRENCH ARMY COMMANDER
BORN October 28, 1696
DIED November 20, 1750
KEY CONFLICTS War of the Polish Succession, War of the Austrian Succession
KEY BATTLES Prague 1741, Fontenoy 1745, Rocoux 1746, Maastricht 1748

Maurice, Comte de Saxe, is reputed to be one of the most distinguished military commanders in Europe, alongside the Duke of Marlborough and Frederick the Great. His successful career demonstrates the feeble hold national identity had on aristocrats of the period. As the illegitimate son of the Elector of Saxony, Maurice served a military apprenticeship with the Austrian army of Eugène of Savoy and the Russian forces of Peter the Great, before opting to enter the service of France. He was made a lieutenant-general in 1734 for his part in the siege of Philippsburg during the War of the Polish Succession.

In the opening stages of the subsequent War of the Austrian Succession, Maurice's coup in seizing Prague through a surprise night attack was much admired. He would have led an invasion of Britain in 1744 if the French navy had been able to transport his troops across the Channel. In 1745, he gained control of the Austrian Netherlands (present-day Belgium) with his victory at Fontenoy and remained in command there until the end of the war. He also won at Rocoux in 1746, and at the end of the war took Maastricht. Maurice's treatise, *Reveries on the Art of War*, was published after his death. It contributed much to modern military theory, although his ideas range from the sensible (recruitment by conscription for a five-year term) to the eccentric (lambskin wigs as standard issue for all troops).

Military thinker
The intelligence of Maurice de Saxe shines through this portrait by court artist Quentin de la Tour. He was made Marshal General of France—a rare honor—in 1747.

KEY BATTLE

FONTENOY

CAMPAIGN War of the Austrian Succession
DATE May 11, 1745
LOCATION Near Tournai, Belgium

The Duke of Cumberland marched to relieve Tournai, under siege by Maurice de Saxe. The French commander took up a strong defensive position. He repulsed Cumberland's resolute infantry advance with a series of spirited counterattacks that resulted in savage close combat. After taking heavy casualties, Cumberland withdrew; Tournai fell to Maurice.

DUKE OF CUMBERLAND

Merciless leader
Prince William Augustus, Duke of Cumberland, was known in Scotland as "the Butcher" for his brutal suppression of the Jacobite rebellion led by Bonnie Prince Charlie in 1745–46.

BRITISH ARMY COMMANDER
BORN April 26, 1721
DIED October 31, 1765
KEY CONFLICTS War of the Austrian Succession, Jacobite Uprising, Seven Years' War
KEY BATTLES Fontenoy 1745, Culloden 1746, Hastenbeck 1757

The Duke of Cumberland was the younger son of King George II. His first active service was under his father at Dettingen in 1743, where he was wounded in the leg. His reputation survived defeat by Maurice de Saxe at Fontenoy in 1745. The next year he crushed the Scottish Jacobite uprising with the ruthless use of his superior artillery at Culloden. His promising military career came to an abrupt end when he was dismissed after signing an ill-judged treaty with France in the wake of defeat at Hastenbeck.

GRAF VON DAUN

AUSTRIAN ARMY COMMANDER
BORN September 24, 1705
DIED February 5, 1766
KEY CONFLICTS War of the Austrian Succession, Seven Years' War
KEY BATTLES Kolín 1757, Leuthen 1757, Hochkirch 1758, Torgau 1760

Leopold Graf von Daun was the only Austrian commander able to take on Frederick the Great, his patience and steadiness successful against Frederick's rash aggression. Daun defeated the Prussian king at Kolín in June 1757, only to cede supreme command for reasons of social precedence before opposing Frederick at the disastrous battle of Leuthen six months later. He escaped responsibility for this defeat and secured overall command for the rest of the Seven Years' War. Daun defeated the Prussians at Hochkirch in 1758 and imposed heavy casualties on Frederick at Torgau in 1760.

Academy founder
Daun possessed excellent organizational skills and supported various army reforms, setting up the Theresian Military Academy in 1751.

ALEXANDER SUVOROV

RUSSIAN ARMY COMMMANDER
BORN November 24, 1730
DIED May 18, 1800
KEY CONFLICTS Bar Confederation War, Russo-Turkish Wars, Kosciuszko Uprising, French Revolutionary Wars
KEY BATTLES Ochakov 1788, Focsani 1789, Izmail 1790, Novi 1799

One of Russia's greatest generals, Alexander Suvorov was born into a military family and chose an army career from an early age, despite his slight physique and sickly constitution. He soon overcame his physical weaknesses, however, and proved a tough leader, performing well in the Seven Years' War. He was appointed colonel in 1762.

Suvorov fought against the Ottoman Turks and the Poles in his subsequent campaigns as a senior commander under Catherine the Great. Although neither offered first-rate opposition, he found opportunities to flaunt his tactical commitment to speed of movement and violence of attack. In the Russo-Turkish war of 1787–92, his decisive defeat of an Ottoman army encamped at Focsani, together with his storming of the fortresses of Ochakov and Izmail, contrasted starkly with the inertia of other Russian commanders. He was widely criticized for massacres committed by his army in Warsaw during the suppression of the Polish Kosciuszko Uprising in 1794. His stated view was that it was better to kill 7,000 and end a war than prolong it and kill 100,000.

ROUTING THE FRENCH

Suvorov trained his men rigorously but still won their affection. Despite this, he fell out of favor with the new czar, Paul I, who wanted more formal discipline. In February 1799, however, he was recalled to lead an army in northern Italy against the forces of the French Revolution. He won a series of whirlwind victories, culminating at Novi in August with a French retreat. But failures elsewhere left his army exposed, and he had to lead a fighting withdrawal across the Alps in winter, returning his men to the Rhine. He died soon after.

> ## ONE MINUTE DECIDES THE OUTCOME OF A BATTLE, ONE HOUR THE SUCCESS OF A CAMPAIGN...
>
> **ONE OF ALEXANDER SUVOROV'S MANY OBSERVATIONS ON STRATEGY AND TACTICS**

Alpine ordeal
Suvorov was 70 years old when he led his ragged army across the Alps in 1799–1800. An epic of endurance and valor, the escape earned him the nickname the Russian Hannibal.

1660—1850

RULERS AND REVOLUTIONARIES

FREDERICK THE GREAT

KING OF PRUSSIA
BORN January 24, 1712
DIED August 17, 1786
KEY CONFLICTS War of the Austrian Succession, Seven Years' War
KEY BATTLES Hohenfriedberg 1745, Rossbach 1757, Leuthen 1757, Zorndorf 1758, Kunersdorf 1759, Torgau 1760

Frederick II of Prussia, or Frederick the Great, was the most lauded military commander of the mid-18th century. His early life was dominated by his father, Frederick William I, who trained him for a spartan military life with the harshest discipline. In 1732, he was made colonel of an infantry regiment to learn his military trade. Two years later, he had the privilege of accompanying the aged Prince Eugène of Savoy on campaign in the War of the Polish Succession. This was his only experience of warfare before inheriting the Prussian throne in June 1740.

INVASION OF SILESIA

Within six months of becoming king, Frederick determined to lead his army in person in an invasion of Silesia that provoked war with Austria. At Mollwitz in April 1741, fighting on snow-covered ground, he was almost routed by Austrian cavalry and, in effect, relieved of command by the experienced General Kurt Schwerin, who took

over and turned the battle around. Frederick performed somewhat better at the battle of Chotusitz the following year, but it was not until 1745 that he showed his ability as an outstanding military leader. At Hohenfriedberg he faced an army of Austrians and Saxons roughly equal

Victor of Rossbach
During his famous victory over French and imperial troops at Rossbach in November 1757, Frederick was in direct command on the battlefield.

in strength to his own forces. He achieved an overwhelming victory through the disciplined maneuvers of his infantry—which was initially thrown in force against the weakest point in the enemy position—and the aggression of his cavalry commanders, who were licensed to charge on their own initiative.

SEVEN YEARS' WAR

Frederick emerged from war with Austria basking in military glory. His seizure of Silesia, however, made Austria and Saxony his sworn enemies. In 1756, he faced an alliance between these two states and France, with Russia likely to join them. Seeing attack as a means of defence, Frederick invaded Saxony, precipitating the Seven Years' War.

1660—1850

BIOGRAPHY
FREDERICK WILLIAM I

Ruling Prussia from 1713 to 1740, Frederick the Great's father, Frederick William I, is sometimes called the "Soldier-King" owing to his obsessive concern with military affairs. A bluff and boorish man, he was frugal to the point of meanness and treated his son with great brutality. He was universally mocked for his eccentric attachment to very tall soldiers, whom he collected from all over Europe for his Grenadier Guards regiment. Yet Frederick William was a formidably talented administrator. Believing a ruler should "always put his trust in a good army and in hard cash," he doubled the strength of the Prussian armed forces to over 80,000 men. He introduced a number of important innovations, including the use of iron ramrods that allowed muskets to be loaded more quickly than previous wooden ramrods. He began the practice of soldiers marching in step, which served not only for parades but also for efficient movement in formation on the battlefield. Despite his interest in the army, Frederick William avoided warfare, only briefly joining in the Great Northern War against Sweden, 1715–20. He left his son a well-stocked treasury, well-organized armed forces, and an efficient system of civil administration.

move. He crushed the enemy with the combined use of cavalry, infantry, and field artillery. The Prussians suffered 500 casualties, whereas the French and Austrians lost 10,000 men.

A month later at Leuthen in Silesia, Frederick again took on an army twice his strength: the Austrians under Prince Charles of Lorraine. Again Frederick attacked, bringing his disciplined infantry down on the weaker left wing of the Austrian line, while his cavalry distracted the Austrian right. Marching in column and deploying into line as if on parade, the Prussian infantry smashed the Austrian left and pushed into their centre from the flank, supported by field artillery, while Prussian cavalry put to flight the Austrian horse.

FIGHTING TO SURVIVE

Frederick's victories did not bring his enemies to terms and the war grew into a long attritional struggle. The brutal battles of Zorndorf and Hochkirch in 1758 cost the Prussian army dearly. As new recruits were brought in to make up for losses, the

> ## THE ENEMY STANDS... ARMED TO THE TEETH. WE MUST ATTACK HIM AND WIN, OR PERISH.
>
> **FREDERICK THE GREAT,** ADDRESS TO HIS TROOPS BEFORE LEUTHEN, DECEMBER 5, 1757

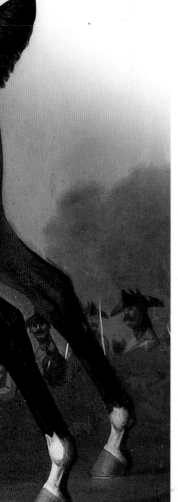

Prussia fought this conflict against heavy odds—a splendid opportunity for Frederick to demonstrate military prowess, but nearly disastrous for his country. In the spring of 1757, a bold Prussian advance into Bohemia had to be abandoned after Frederick was defeated at Kolin. In dire straits, as Prussia was threatened by armies from three sides, Frederick won his two greatest victories. At Rossbach in November, he was outnumbered two to one by French and Austrian forces, and decided to attack while they attempted an outflanking

Royal Coat
Frederick the Great's coat and staff are preserved in the German Historical Museum in Berlin.

quality of the infantry in particular deteriorated. Prussian troops were slaughtered attacking well-prepared Russians and Austrians at Kunersdorf in August 1759. With just 3,000 from an original army of 50,000 surviving to regroup in Berlin, Frederick contemplated suicide.

In 1762, Peter III, who was pro-Prussia, acceded to the Russian throne, and this saved Frederick from catastrophe. Frederick had proved himself an outstanding master of battlefield tactics, but not of strategy or diplomacy. He had needed his victories against the odds to rescue him from those perilous situations that marked his career. In fact, Frederick's reign narrowly survived the war that gave him a reputation as one of the greatest commanders of all time.

TIMELINE

■ **June 1740** At age 28, Frederick II accedes to the Prussian throne after the death of his father, Frederick William I, on May 31.

■ **December 1740–July 1742** Frederick fights Austria for control of Silesia; he commands in battle for the first time at Mollwitz (April 10, 1741).

■ **August 1744–December 1745** Frederick resumes war with Austria, defeating the Austrians and Saxons at Hohenfriedberg (June 4, 1745); he begins to be known as "Frederick the Great."

■ **1748** Frederick reflects upon his experience of battle in his book of military theory, *The General Principles of War.*

■ **August 1756** Frederick invades Saxony, precipitating the Seven Years' War. In this conflict he is opposed by Austria, France, Russia, and Sweden.

■ **1757** Invading Bohemia, Frederick is defeated at Kolin (June 18); he then scores remarkable victories over the French and Austrians at Rossbach (November 5) and the Austrians at Leuthen (December 5).

■ **1758** Frederick suffers heavy losses fighting the Russians at Zorndorf (August 25) and is defeated by the Austrians at Hochkirch (October 14).

FREDERICK PURSUED BY COSSACKS AT THE BATTLE OF KUNERSDORF, 1759

■ **1759** The Prussians experience many setbacks. The worst is Frederick's catastrophic defeat at the hands of the Russians and Austrians at Kunersdorf (August 12).

■ **1760** Frederick momentarily loses Berlin to his enemies (October) but staves off disaster with victories at Liegnitz (August 14–15) and Torgau (November 3).

■ **1761–62** With the collapse of Prussia imminent, Frederick is saved by the death of Empress Elizabeth of Russia early in 1762, after which Russia withdraws from the war.

■ **February 15, 1763** The Treaty of Hubertusburg ends the Seven Years' War, leaving Prussia in possession of Silesia.

■ **1772** Frederick participates with Austria and Russia in the First Partition of Poland, taking a swathe of Polish territory.

■ **1778** Frederick opposes Austria for a last time in the War of the Bavarian Succession, known as the Potato War, because the armies search for food instead of fighting.

FREDERICK AT ZORNDORF

LOCATION
Zorndorf, 6 miles (10 km) from Küstrin (Kostrzyn) on the present-day Polish-German border

CAMPAIGN Seven Years' War
DATE August 25, 1758
FORCES Prussian 36,000; Russian 43,000
CASUALTIES Prussian 13,000 dead and wounded; Russian 19,000 dead and wounded

In August 1758, a Russian army under Count William Fermor was besieging Küstrin on the Oder River, within 50 miles (80 km) of Berlin. Frederick's army arrived by forced marches from Silesia and crossed the Oder undetected north of Küstrin. At dawn on August 25, he embarked on a flanking march to approach the Russian rear from the south. His plan was for his usual attack in "oblique order," thrusting the best of his infantry on the left forward against the Russian right, which consisted mostly of inexperienced conscripts, while his own right was "refused" (held back from contact).

Frederick's plan failed. The Russian infantry stood firm against the Prussian vanguard, which was then cut to pieces by a Russian cavalry charge into its exposed flank. The main body of Prussian infantry, meant to come up behind the vanguard, lost direction and marched instead into the densely packed center of the Russian line. Torn apart by musket fire and grapeshot, the Prussians were in danger of being routed. Frederick was distraught at the disaster occurring on his left. Leaping from his horse, he grabbed a banner and ran around among the soldiers, trying to rally them for the fight. The situation was saved by Prussian cavalry commander, Friedrich von Seydlitz, who chose the right moment to fling his horsemen into the fray, forcing the Russians back with the impact of the charge.

CHAOS REIGNS

Throughout the afternoon, the battle disintegrated into a series of savage melees fought with bayonets, swords, and musket butts. In the heat and dust confusion reigned, cavalry and artillery on both sides at times attacking their own infantry.

Frederick rode back and forth in the thick of the action, a fearless but impotent observer of a battle beyond control. Sheer exhaustion brought the fighting to an end in the evening, the armies retiring from contact but otherwise holding their positions.

When Frederick rode across the corpse-strewn battlefield the following morning, he was fired on, but neither side had the heart to renew the battle after suffering around 30 percent casualties. Finally, on September 1, the Russians withdrew, allowing Frederick to claim a strategic victory, commenting, "It is easier to kill these Russians to the last man than to defeat them."

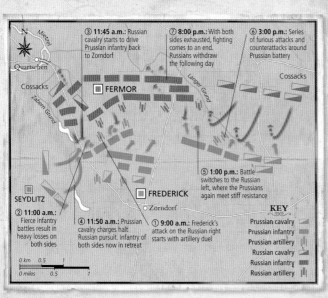

③ **11:45 a.m.:** Russian cavalry starts to drive Prussian infantry back to Zorndorf

⑦ **8:00 p.m.:** With both sides exhausted, fighting comes to an end. Russians withdraw the following day

⑥ **3:00 p.m.:** Series of furious attacks and counterattacks around Prussian battery

⑤ **1:00 p.m.:** Battle switches to the Russian left, where the Prussians again meet stiff resistance

② **11:00 a.m.:** Fierce infantry battles result in heavy losses on both sides

④ **11:50 a.m.:** Prussian cavalry charges halt Russian pursuit. Infantry of both sides now in retreat

① **9:00 a.m.:** Frederick's attack on the Russian right starts with artillery duel

KEY
Prussian cavalry
Prussian infantry
Prussian artillery
Russian cavalry
Russian infantry
Russian artillery

0 km   0.5   1
0 miles   0.5   1

RULERS AND REVOLUTIONARIES

1660—1850

Rallying the infantry
Fredrick the Great of Prussia seizes a
banner to rally his troops at Zorndorf,
urging them to fight on against the
Russians after his initial plan of attack
has gone awry.

COLONIAL WARS

IN THE MID-18TH CENTURY, Britain and France were engaged in a struggle for control of commercially valuable colonies in North America, the West Indies, and India. These conflicts, involving local forces, demanded both the skills of contemporary European warfare and adaptation to an alien cultural and geographical environment. The battles fought were mostly on a small scale, but some had lasting consequences for history. Robert Clive's victory at Plassey in 1757 ensured Britain would become the dominant power in Bengal, and eventually India, while James Wolfe's success at Quebec in 1759 gave the British control of Canada.

ROBERT CLIVE

BRITISH MILITARY COMMANDER
BORN September 29, 1725
DIED November 22, 1774
KEY CONFLICTS Wars in India
KEY BATTLES Arcot 1751, Plassey 1757

The son of minor gentry, Robert Clive was an unruly child of no obvious talent. At age 18, he was sent to work as a clerk in Madras, a trading outpost of the British East India Company. Clive was rescued from the tedium of bookkeeping by war. After Madras was attacked by the French in 1746, Clive performed courageously in a series of skirmishes and minor battles, winning promotion

Clive of India
Though he became governor-general of Bengal, Clive's later years were plagued by accusations of corruption.

to captain in the Company forces. In 1751, a British-backed local ruler, Muhammad Ali, was in conflict with French-backed Chanda Sahib. Sent from Madras with a force of 800 men, Clive seized Chanda Sahib's fort at Arcot and held it for 53 days under siege by French and Indian troops until relief arrived. He returned to Britain in 1753 a minor celebrity.

BATTLE FOR BENGAL
In 1755, Clive went back to India with the rank of lieutenant-colonel. Attention soon focused on Bengal, where the accession of the pro-French Siraj ud-Daulah as nawab (ruler) menaced British interests. The nawab overran British posts, including Calcutta, where British prisoners were grossly maltreated. Clive sailed from Madras and reoccupied Calcutta in January 1757. A risky foray against the nawab's army then procured a breathing space during which Clive plotted the ruler's overthrow, secretly promising the throne to one of the nawab's generals, Mir Jafar. Clive then advanced inland toward the Bengali capital, Murshidabad, confronting the nawab's horde by the Bhaghirathi River. The battle of Plassey (Palashi) was a strange encounter. Clive had 2,000 sepoys and 950 Europeans against 50,000 Bengali troops supported by French artillery.

Allied with a traitor
After the battle of Plassey, Clive greets Mir Jafar, the general who betrayed the nawab of Bengal in return for a promise of the Bengali throne.

Some 15,000 of the Bengalis, however, were commanded by the disloyal Mir Jafar, and few others showed any great resolve. An artillery duel that should have favored the French went against them when a downpour dampened their powder. Late in the afternoon, Clive ordered an advance and Siraj ud-Daulah quit the field on a camel, leaving the victor to install Mir Jafar as nawab. Clive had lost only 22 men, achieving a momentous step toward Britain's takeover of India.

KEY TROOPS
EAST INDIA COMPANY SEPOYS

The East India Company, which represented British power in India up to 1858, depended heavily upon sepoys, local Indian soldiers serving mostly under British officers. The sepoys were drilled and equipped to fight in the style of European troops, with a similar regimental organization. The British learned to trust, and to believe that they understood, these soldiers who served so well under Clive at Plassey and under Wellington at Assaye. Consequently, the mutiny of sepoys in 1857 (known as the Indian Mutiny) was a profound shock to Britain. It resulted in the replacement of the East India Company by direct British rule.

> " WITH 22 SOLDIERS KILLED AND 50 WOUNDED, CLIVE... SUBDUED AN EMPIRE LARGER AND MORE POPULOUS THAN GREAT BRITAIN. "
>
> **THOMAS MACAULAY,** *LORD CLIVE,* 1840

MARQUIS DE MONTCALM

FRENCH ARMY OFFICER
BORN February 28, 1712
DIED September 14, 1759
KEY CONFLICTS War of the Austrian Succession, French and Indian War
KEY BATTLES Fort Oswego 1756, Fort William Henry 1757, Fort Carillon 1758, Quebec 1759

Sent to defend Canada against the British in May 1756, Louis-Joseph, Marquis de Montcalm, was a professional soldier who had proved his courage and competence in the War of the Austrian Succession. Accustomed to the honorable formalities of European warfare, he was not impressed by the Canadian colonial troops and militia that formed a large part of his new command, and he was appalled at the need to use Native American auxiliaries who behaved, in his view, with unpardonable savagery. Montcalm's initial successes in the capture of Fort Oswego and Fort William Henry were marred by Indian massacres of prisoners and the wounded that he could not prevent. At Fort Carillon in July 1758, he routed a poorly led British force that outnumbered his troops by four to one.

Brave soldier
The death of the steadfast Montcalm at Quebec was a serious blow to French morale.

DEATH IN BATTLE

Montcalm's insistence on conducting the war on European lines, however, held out little long-term prospect of success against the growing strength of British forces. Rejecting the possibility of a guerrilla war and unleashing Indian raids, in 1759, he concentrated his forces around Quebec and Montreal. From June to September he defended Quebec skillfully against British attack. He died honorably, as he would have wished, cut down by grapeshot facing the enemy in open battle outside the city on the Plains of Abraham.

> ## I AM HAPPY THAT I SHALL NOT LIVE TO SEE THE SURRENDER OF QUEBEC.
> **MARQUIS DE MONTCALM**, ON HIS DEATHBED, SEPTEMBER 14, 1759

JAMES WOLFE

BRITISH ARMY OFFICER
BORN January 2, 1727
DIED September 13, 1759
KEY CONFLICTS Jacobite Rising, French and Indian War
KEY BATTLES Siege of Louisbourg 1758, Quebec 1759

The son of a general, James Wolfe was an army officer at the age of 14. In 1746, he took part in the battle of Culloden, allegedly refusing an order to shoot a wounded Jacobite rebel. In 1758, Wolfe served as a brigadier under General Jeffery Amherst, in an expedition by land and sea that seized the key French North American fortress of Louisbourg on Cape Breton Island. He distinguished himself by his boldness and energy in this operation, and obtained command of an expedition to sail up the St. Lawrence River and attack Quebec.

Precocious brilliance
The frail-looking Wolfe possessed extraordinary energy and drive, but because of his youth, the battle for Quebec was called "a boy's campaign."

MISGUIDED PLAN

In late June 1759, Wolfe's forces reached Quebec. Fortified by Montcalm, the city appeared impregnable. On quarrelsome terms with his brigadiers and unsure how to proceed, on July 31, Wolfe launched an ill-conceived, badly executed frontal assault on the French defenses that failed dismally. His health broke under the strain and for much of August he was bedridden. In early September, accepting his brigadiers' suggestion to attack Montcalm from the rear, Wolfe made a reconnaissance that identified a path up the cliffs behind Quebec. On the night of September 12–13, he landed troops at the foot of the cliffs and by morning they had climbed to the Plains of Abraham. A French counterattack was defeated, leaving the British in control of Quebec. Wolfe was shot dead early in the battle. His death in victory ensured his place in the pantheon of British imperial heroes.

The taking of Quebec
Wolfe's red-coated forces sailed upstream of Quebec along the St. Lawrence River and scaled cliffs to reach the Plains of Abraham, where they defeated Montcalm's army.

1660—1850

The Death of General Wolfe
Wolfe received a fatal chest wound at the battle of Quebec, but he died knowing that the city had fallen to the British. His death was famously depicted by Benjamin West.

THE AMERICAN REVOLUTIONARY WAR

IN 1775, THIRTEEN AMERICAN colonies rebelled against British rule and declared their independence. Establishing a Continental Army under the command of George Washington to fight the British forces sent to suppress their revolt, they also won the support of France. The British commanders were neither inflexible nor unintelligent, but they lacked the resources to achieve the decisive victory they needed. Faced with American resolve and Washington's well-judged strategy, they focused on keeping the army going. A humiliating defeat at the siege of Yorktown in 1781 broke Britain's will to continue the war.

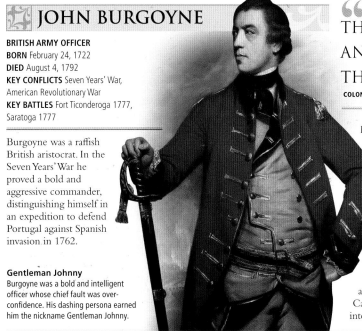

JOHN BURGOYNE

BRITISH ARMY OFFICER
BORN February 24, 1722
DIED August 4, 1792
KEY CONFLICTS Seven Years' War, American Revolutionary War
KEY BATTLES Fort Ticonderoga 1777, Saratoga 1777

Burgoyne was a raffish British aristocrat. In the Seven Years' War he proved a bold and aggressive commander, distinguishing himself in an expedition to defend Portugal against Spanish invasion in 1762.

Gentleman Johnny
Burgoyne was a bold and intelligent officer whose chief fault was over-confidence. His dashing persona earned him the nickname Gentleman Johnny.

> ## THE COUNTRY ENGENDERS REBELS, AND AS WE PURSUE THEM IN FRONT THEY EMERGE AFRESH IN THE REAR...
> **COLONEL WILLIAM PHILLIPS**, SERVING UNDER BURGOYNE, JULY 10, 1777

In May 1775, he was one of three major-generals—with William Howe and Henry Clinton—sent to revive operations in America.

MOVING SOUTH

Burgoyne believed the American forces would collapse under energetic attack, but was frustrated in his desire for decisive action until 1777, when he obtained authorization to lead troops from Canada down the Hudson River into New York. Dragging his artillery up a mountain to a dominant vantage point, Burgoyne took Fort Ticonderoga with startling ease in July. However, his subsequent advance southward through wild territory ran into mounting logistical difficulties. Trapped at Saratoga, he negotiated a controversial surrender that permitted his return to Britain. He never commanded an army again.

HORATIO GATES

AMERICAN GENERAL
BORN 1727
DIED April 10, 1806
KEY CONFLICTS French and Indian War, American Revolutionary War
KEY BATTLES Saratoga 1777, Camden 1780

Horatio Gates was born in England, the son of a servant. Through noble patronage, he obtained a commission in the British army, but his promotion was hampered by lack of money. He was in the American colonies when the French and Indian War broke out in 1754 and was badly wounded in a British defeat at Monongahela a year later—the battle in which George Washington first won renown. Gates saw further action in the West Indies, but his British army career went nowhere. In 1772, Gates settled in Virginia as a plantation owner. Siding with the American patriots in 1775, he was seen as a valuable asset because of his regular army experience and was appointed adjutant-general of the Continental Army.

THWARTED AMBITION

Through political maneuver, Gates gained command of the forces in the northern theater (roughly, the states north of Virginia), allowing him to mastermind the defeat of Burgoyne at Saratoga. Briefly in the ascendant, he was named president of the Board of War, but failed in his aspiration to replace Washington as commander-in-chief. Appointed to command the southern theater in 1780, Gates unwisely led a scratch force of Continental Army troops and untried militia into battle against the British general, Charles Cornwallis, at Camden, South Carolina. In the resulting disaster, Gates is alleged to have fled the field more rapidly than any of his men. This effectively ended his military career.

Delusions of grandeur
Gates had solid qualities, but was an unscrupulous political operator. His vanity led him to desire the post of commander-in-chief, for which he was unsuited.

Capitol Hill statue
At the start of the Revolutionary War, Greene joined his local militia as a private, a rank from which he rose straight to general. His statue stands near the heart of American government, on Capitol Hill, Washington, D.C.

NATHANAEL GREENE

AMERICAN GENERAL
BORN August 7, 1742
DIED June 19, 1786
KEY CONFLICT American Revolutionary War
KEY BATTLES Springfield 1780, Guilford Court House 1781

Born into a Rhode Island Quaker family and brought up to manual labor, Nathanael Greene was self-taught in military science. He offered his services to the rebel cause at the outset of the war and soon attracted the attention of Washington, proving an essential contributor to his victories at Trenton and Brandywine in 1777–78 and a companion through the winter encampment at Valley Forge.

GATES'S SUCCESSOR

For two years, Greene performed the role of quartermaster-general, while yearning after field command. In June 1780, at Springfield, he repulsed a raid into New Jersey by British Hessian mercenaries and was then chosen by Washington to succeed Horatio Gates in command of the southern theater. Making the best of inadequate forces, he harassed Cornwallis and led him on an exhausting chase across the south, before successfully concentrating his forces for a pitched battle at Guilford Court House in March 1781. The British held the field, but Cornwallis was fatally weakened, paving the way for his defeat at Yorktown.

1660—1850

MARQUIS DE LAFAYETTE

FRENCH ARMY OFFICER
BORN September 6, 1757
DIED May 20, 1834
KEY CONFLICTS American Revolutionary War, French Revolutionary Wars
KEY BATTLES Brandywine 1777, Yorktown 1781

Gilbert du Motier, Marquis de Lafayette, was a young, wealthy, well-connected French aristocrat who sailed to America in 1777 to offer his services to the revolution. The American Congress, which was desperately seeking to draw France into the war, accorded him the rank of major-general, despite his minimal military experience.

EARNING RESPECT

Sent to join Washington, Lafayette was initially expected to be an observer. Grudgingly allowed to take part in the fighting at Brandywine in

September 1777, he acquitted himself well, sustaining a wound to the leg. His enthusiasm, courage, and loyalty won him Washington's respect, and he was soon an active, trusted subordinate commander. In 1779,

Lafayette visited France, where he was instrumental in dispatching a French army under Rochambeau to support the American patriots. He returned to America to play a vital role at Yorktown in 1781, leading the troops that pinned Cornwallis until Washington arrived with the main army. He also took part in the attack

on a British redoubt during the final stages of the siege. Returning to France, Lafayette was involved in the revolution of 1789. A commander on France's eastern frontier when the French Revolutionary Wars began in 1792, he became increasingly at odds with the revolutionary regime and defected to the Austrians.

Close confidant
Lafayette (left) was Washington's constant companion during the harsh winter encampment at Valley Forge in 1777–78. The two men established a father-son relationship.

TIMELINE

■ **1754–58** Washington serves with distinction as a Virginian officer in the French and Indian War, finishing as brigadier-general.

■ **August 1774** A landowner living on his estate at Mount Vernon, Washington is elected as a Virginian delegate to the rebel First Continental Congress.

■ **June 15, 1775** The Second Continental Congress appoints Washington as commander-in-chief of the newly created Continental Army.

■ **March 1776** Washington forces the British to leave Boston after an 11-month siege.

■ **August 1776** Washington is defeated at the battle of Long Island but rescues his army and subsequently withdraws into Pennsylvania.

■ **December 25–26, 1776** Crossing the Delaware River, Washington successfully raids the Hessian garrison at Trenton, New Jersey. He goes on to defeat other British forces at Princeton (January 3, 1777).

■ **September 11, 1777** Washington is defeated at the battle of Brandywine, allowing the British to occupy Philadelphia.

WASHINGTON'S ESTATE, MOUNT VERNON

■ **December 1777–June 1778** Encamped at Valley Forge, Pennsylvania, Washington's army endures great hardship, while its commander survives political plots to remove him from his post.

■ **June 28, 1778** At the battle of Monmouth, Washington attacks British forces withdrawing from Philadelphia under Sir Henry Clinton, but is repulsed.

■ **January 1781** Washington suppresses mutinies in the Pennsylvania and New Jersey regiments of the Continental Army.

■ **August–September 1781** Washington's Continental Army joins forces with the Comte de Rochambeau's French expeditionary force and they march south from New York to Virginia.

■ **September 28–October 19, 1781** Washington besieges a British army under Lord Cornwallis at Yorktown, bringing it to surrender after three weeks.

■ **December 23, 1783** Washington resigns his commission as army commander-in-chief at the end of the Revolutionary War.

■ **April 30, 1789** Washington is sworn in as the first president of the United States under the Constitution.

GEORGE WASHINGTON

AMERICAN COMMANDER-IN-CHIEF AND PRESIDENT
BORN February 22, 1732
DIED December 14, 1799
KEY CONFLICTS French and Indian War, American Revolutionary War
KEY BATTLES Monongahela 1755, Boston 1775–76, Long Island 1776, Trenton 1776, Princeton 1777, Brandywine 1777, Monmouth 1778, Yorktown 1781

George Washington made his mark on American history with his first entry into combat. On May 28, 1754, as a young lieutenant-colonel in the Virginia militia, he clashed with French troops in the backwoods of the Ohio Valley, firing the first shots of what became the French and Indian War. In July 1755, returning to the Ohio country as aide to the British general Edward Braddock, he distinguished himself by his calm and courageous conduct amid the mayhem of a defeat at Monongahela. When the war ended in 1758, he married and settled down as a Virginia landowner. The American Revolution tore him from a peaceful life, however. He was elected as a Virginia delegate to the rebel Congress, and his experience of command in the French and Indian War made him an obvious choice to lead the Continental Army.

ORDER AND HUMANITY

Washington was a conservative man, who believed in hierarchy and order. Although aware of the value of irregular troops in the American wilderness, he set out to make the Continental Army a European-style force built around disciplined, drilled infantry—a struggle, given the rag-tag group of militiamen, backwoods riflemen, and recruits from the lowest levels of society that he had to work with. The colonies could never be induced to provide enough men for his needs, nor enough money to pay and supply such troops as there were. Washington also had to cope with political machinations in Congress and stave off ambitious opponents who aspired to replace him.

Within the army, Washington imposed discipline with necessary severity, yet always showed proper concern for the welfare of his men. This approach carried him through

Crossing the Delaware
The most famous image of the American Revolutionary War, Emanuel Leutze's *Washington Crossing the Delaware* shows the resolute American commander on his way to victory at Trenton in 1776.

KEY TROOPS

CONTINENTAL ARMY

The Continental Army was founded on June 14, 1775, as a joint force for the 13 colonies rebelling against British rule. The army suffered a host of problems, ranging from desertion and indiscipline to lack of pay, food, and clothing. It became nonetheless, in Washington's words, "a patriotic band of brothers" capable of resisting and ultimately beating the well-trained British regulars.

the worst of crises, from near-starvation in the winter encampment at Valley Forge in 1777–78 to widespread mutinies in early 1781.

Washington realized that keeping his army going was his essential task—the British needed to win the war; he needed not to lose it. He used tricks and stratagems suitable to inferior forces, avoiding pitched battle where possible. His famous victory over British Hessian mercenaries at Trenton over Christmas 1776 was, in effect, a guerrilla raid. But political considerations often obliged him to stand and fight when it was unwise

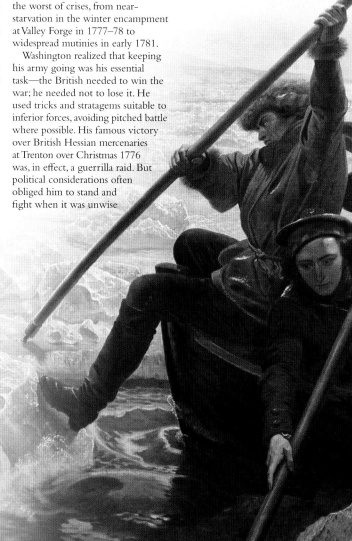

> ## TO THE MEMORY OF THE MAN, FIRST IN WAR, FIRST IN PEACE, AND FIRST IN THE HEARTS OF HIS COUNTRYMEN…

CONGRESSMAN HENRY LEE, EULOGY OF WASHINGTON, 1799

to do so. In August 1776, he was forced to defend New York City, leading to a defeat on Long Island from which he extricated his surviving troops with consummate skill. In September 1777, it was Philadelphia that had to be defended from a British offensive. The resulting defeat at Brandywine gave him another unwanted chance to show how well he could handle a beaten army in retreat. He was unable to interrupt a British withdrawal to the coast at the battle of Monmouth in June 1778, which caused a violent argument between the usually even-tempered Washington and his subordinate, Charles Lee. After this,

the commander-in-chief could only exercise patience with his army in the north, while the south became the main active theater of war.

MARCH TO VIRGINIA

The arrival of a French expeditionary force in 1780 shifted the balance of the conflict. The French commander Rochambeau agreed to place his army at Washington's disposal. They planned to trap the British forces under Lord Cornwallis at Yorktown. Leading the British to expect an attack on New York City, Washington marched an army 450 miles (700 km) south to Virginia, where he forced Cornwallis to surrender.

Washington took off his uniform as soon as duty allowed, having once said that the post of commander-in-chief was one he had "used every endeavor in his power to avoid." No historic victory was ever achieved by a more reluctant hero.

Purple Heart
Washington introduced a Badge of Military Merit in 1782 in the form of a purple heart. The current Purple Heart decoration was revived on the 200th anniversary of the commander's birth and bears his profile.

1660—1850

The surrender at Yorktown
General Benjamin Lincoln, on the white horse, receives the sword of General Charles O'Hara, delegated by Lord Cornwallis to make the formal surrender. Washington, to the right on the brown horse, looks on.

GATES VS. BURGOYNE

IN SUMMER 1777, THE BRITISH had taken the offensive in the American Revolutionary War. General John Burgoyne marched down the Hudson Valley from Canada, intending to join up with an army advancing northward from New York. After his capture of Fort Ticonderoga, the Americans fell back in some disarray, but the British found progress down the Hudson hard going and suffered significant losses in a clash at Bennington. Meanwhile, the American forces in the sector were assigned a new commander, Horatio Gates, and were much strengthened, notably with a corps of riflemen under Daniel Morgan and a brigade led by Benedict Arnold.

HORATIO GATES

Gates established a fortified defensive line at the Bemis Heights, where the road alongside the Hudson River passed through a narrow defile between wooded hills. He reasoned that Burgoyne, if unable to resupply his troops, would be forced either to attempt a breakthrough or stage a difficult and humiliating retreat.

DEFENSIVE GAME
The American commander intended, at all costs, to avoid being tempted out of his fortified position, fearing his troops might be outfought on open ground. This defensive stance was anathema to Benedict Arnold, who favored taking the offensive at all times, and an already strained relationship between the two commanders soon worsened.

On September 19, Gates received reports of enemy activity to the left of his line around Freeman's Farm. He accepted Arnold's argument that Daniel Morgan's riflemen and other light troops should be sent into the woods to investigate. To Morgan's surprise, he found himself in the path of a full-scale British advance.

LEADERSHIP CLASH
Arnold took the initiative in throwing reinforcements into a fierce, fluctuating battle around the farm. At nightfall, the Americans pulled back to their fortified line, but Gates knew that the repulse of a British attack with heavy losses was a major success. He rejected Arnold's call for the Americans to move on to the offensive. A full-blown argument between the two commanders ended absurdly, with uncertainty over whether Arnold still held a command and, if so, over what forces.

Gates's waiting game paid off on October 7 when, as he had hoped, Burgoyne was again tempted into a risky attack (see map). While Gates organized a systematic and controlled response, Arnold flung himself into the forefront of a death-or-glory counterattack that managed to breach the British defenses. Burgoyne's withdrawal the following day began the endgame. Advancing as ever with caution, Gates was able to encircle the British troops and induce a historic surrender with the minimum of casualties on his own side.

> ## "THE ENEMY MUST ENDEAVOR BY ONE STROKE TO REGAIN ALL THEY HAVE LOST [OR] THEIR RUIN IS INEVITABLE.

HORATIO GATES, GENERAL ORDERS, OCTOBER 4, 1777

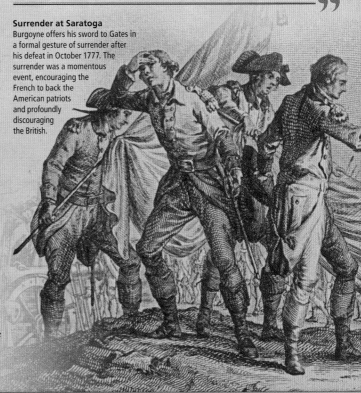

Surrender at Saratoga
Burgoyne offers his sword to Gates in a formal gesture of surrender after his defeat in October 1777. The surrender was a momentous event, encouraging the French to back the American patriots and profoundly discouraging the British.

GATES

- Gates leads his American forces north to the Bemis Heights, where he establishes a fortified defensive line
- **12:30 p.m.** Sent by Gates to investigate British activity on his left, Morgan's riflemen decimate a British advanced party at Freeman's Farm
- **Afternoon** Fighting around Freeman's Farm intensifies as both sides channel in more troops. Gates remains convinced the main thrust will come on his right
- **Sunset** Gates recalls his troops to their defensive line as nightfall ends the fighting, leaving the British in possession of the ground
- A fierce agrument between Benedict Arnold and Gates results in Arnold tendering his resignation, although he remains in place

| 1777: SEPT 12 | SEPT 18 | SEPT 19 | | SEPT 20 | SEPT 22 |

BURGOYNE

- Advancing south along the Hudson Valley from Saratoga, Burgoyne arrives in front of the Bemis Heights
- **Morning** British columns leave camp and march into the wooded hills to take Gates's line in its left flank
- British light infantry under General Fraser counterattack on Morgan's left, revealing the scope of the British attack
- **4:30 p.m.** Burgoyne calls on his Hessians, stationed near the Hudson, to join the fighting around Freeman's Farm
- Burgoyne begins construction of field fortifications and calls urgently for assistance from British forces in New York

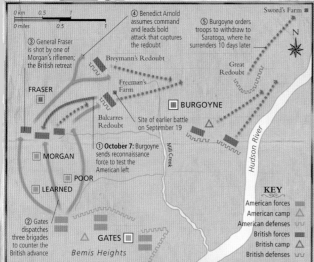

0 km 0.5 1
0 miles 0.5 1

④ Benedict Arnold assumes command and leads bold attack that captures the redoubt

⑤ Burgoyne orders troops to withdraw to Saratoga, where he surrenders 10 days later

③ General Fraser is shot by one of Morgan's riflemen; the British retreat

Sword's Farm

Breymann's Redoubt

Great Redoubt

Freeman's Farm

FRASER

■ **BURGOYNE**

Balcarres Redoubt

Site of earlier battle on September 19

① **October 7:** Burgoyne sends reconnaissance force to test the American left

■ **MORGAN**

Mill Creek

Hudson River

■ **POOR**

■ **LEARNED**

② Gates dispatches three brigades to counter the British advance

△ **GATES** ■

Bemis Heights

KEY
American forces
American camp
American defenses
British forces
British camp
British defenses

LOCATION Saratoga County, New York State

CAMPAIGN American Revolutionary War

DATE September 19–October 17, 1777

FORCES: American: 15,000; British: 10,000

CASUALTIES: American: 1,600; British: 800, plus 6,000 taken prisoner

JOHN BURGOYNE

Burgoyne was an adventurous gambler who would always take the riskier of two options. Aware that support from other British forces was not materializing and that his supply situation was precarious, the major-general nonetheless opted to press on south for Albany in New York State. He counted on his British regulars and Hessian mercenaries to outfight any American troops that might block his path.

DIVIDING FORCES

Encountering Gates's position at the Bemis Heights, Burgoyne decided to climb the hills obliquely and attack the fortified line from its left flank. He divided his forces into three. The Hessians under General Riedesel stayed by the river to pin Gates's right, while two columns mounted the hills. This bold plan came to grief against the strong resolve of American troops

faced with musket, bayonet, and cannon. Morgan's rifle sharpshooters took a heavy toll on Burgoyne's officers, nearly killing the commander himself. Burgoyne avoided a disaster by calling the Hessians into the fray at the crucial moment, but his attack failed and his losses were grievous.

DESPERATION SETS IN

Over the following days, Burgoyne dug into a defensive position and vainly placed his hopes in help arriving from New York. As supplies ran dangerously low, debate raged among the British and Hessian commanders about their course of action. Burgoyne remained committed to a breakthrough to Albany, although he knew how desperate such an attempt would be.

Burgoyne's waning confidence showed in the strangely half-baked operation that he led on October 7. His flanking move into the hills, with only part of his forces, was more a probing reconnaissance than a full offensive. It was repulsed by the Americans with disastrous loss of men and material. By the time Burgoyne attempted to withdraw north with the demoralized remnants of his army, it was too late and there was simply nowhere to go. Under bombardment and out of supplies, he had no choice but to surrender.

1 p.m. Gates and Arnold agree to send Morgan and support regiments out of their line to counter the British movement on their left

Late afternoon Arnold leads a counterattack in person. He is shot in the leg and fallen on by his horse, but takes a key British strongpoint

As Burgoyne withdraws north to Saratoga, Gates sends detachments to the far bank of the Hudson to prevent the British from escaping across the river

Gates accepts Burgoyne's formal surrender at his headquarters

OCT 4 — OCT 7 — OCT 7–8 — OCT 9–10 — OCT 13 — OCT 17

Burgoyne holds a council of war in which his colleagues argue for a withdrawal. He decides to attempt another flanking attack on Gates's line

12 noon Burgoyne leads part of his forces, including field artillery, around the American left flank, triggering the battle of Bemis Heights

Afternoon As fierce fighting develops, Burgoyne risks his life riding around encouraging his troops. Fraser is killed by an American sharpshooter

Night Burgoyne disengages, pulling his shattered forces back to the Hudson

Surrounded, outnumbered, and out of supplies, Burgoyne takes a poll of his officers, who vote unanimously for surrender

WARFARE IN ASIA

DURING THE 18TH CENTURY, Asian rulers sustained armies of immense size and fought wars on a large scale. The Chinese emperors probably had the world's most formidable forces in numerical terms. Commanders such as Nader Shah and Tipu Sultan were unsurpassed in their day in terms of military skills and personal courage. It was a sign of the times, however, that such Asian rulers often turned to European expertise for progress in the technology of gunpowder weapons and improvements in the drilling of infantry and battlefield tactics. Occasions when even the most gifted Asian commanders defeated European-led armies were few.

NADER SHAH

TURCOMAN WARRIOR AND SHAH OF IRAN
BORN October 22, 1688
DIED June 19, 1747
KEY CONFLICTS Persian-Ottoman Wars, Conquest of Afghanistan, Invasion of India
KEY BATTLES Kandahar 1736, Karnal 1739

An obscure bandit in Khorasan (an area including northeastern Iran), Nader Shah emerged as a major war leader in the anarchy that enveloped Iran in the 1720s. Driving out

Dynastic founder
Raised as a shepherd boy, Nader Shah rose to found a dynasty, the Afsharids, that ruled Iran for 60 years. He made plentiful use of European military expertise in developing his armed forces.

Afghan and Ottoman invaders, he was in a position to declare himself shah by 1736. His powerful forces combined the swift movement of traditional Asiatic horsemen with field artillery overseen by imported European specialists. Nader also appreciated the importance of disciplined infantry firepower.

INVASION OF INDIA

Having conquered Kandahar, the leading city in Afghanistan, Nader invaded India, routing the forces of the Mogul Empire at Karnal in February 1739. This enabled him to enter Delhi and loot its finest treasures, including the fabled Koh-i-Noor diamond and the Peacock Throne, which became the symbolic seat of the Persian Empire. The wealth from Nader's Indian campaign helped finance the construction of a navy, with which he carried out the conquest of the Gulf state of Oman in 1743. His military performance deteriorated with age, however, and his acts of cruelty multiplied. He was assassinated while on campaign in Khorasan by his own bodyguards, who feared they might be next on his list of executions.

EMPEROR QIANLONG

CHINESE EMPEROR
BORN September 25, 1711
DIED February 7, 1799
KEY CONFLICTS The Ten Great Campaigns
KEY BATTLE Altishar 1757

Born Hongli, the Emperor Qianlong enjoyed the longest ever Chinese imperial reign, effectively holding power from 1735 to his death in 1799. During that time he doubled the territorial extent of China with wide-ranging campaigns of conquest, although his conservatism stopped his country from imitating the military innovations being introduced by the European powers of his day.

Qianlong's forces retained the "banner" structure invented by the Manchu in the early 17th century. They were large permanent armies whose upkeep imposed great expense on the Chinese treasury, but were considered worthwhile as a means of underlining imperial power. The most impressive of Qianlong's military achievements was the crushing of the Dzunghars, steppe warriors in remote Xinjiang in northwestern China. Direct control of the campaign was in the hands of General Zhaohui, who defeated the Dzunghars in battle at Altishar in 1757 and took the key cities of Kashgar and Yarkand two years later.

SUPREMACY CHALLENGED

Not all Qianlong's campaigns were so successful, however. An invasion of Burma (Myanmar) in the 1760s led to four years of costly campaigning from which the Chinese withdrew without gain. An intervention in Vietnam in the 1780s was also a failure in the face of determined resistance by Tay Son peasant rebels.

Late in his reign, Qianlong was still able to send troops into Tibet to fight the warlike Gurkhas and drive them back into Nepal, a notable feat of logistics, given the distances involved and the hostile Himalayan terrain. But his forces never came into conflict with an 18th-century European army, and so their absolute efficiency must remain uncertain.

Long-lived emperor
Qianlong ruled China through most of the 18th century. This portrait of him was based on sketches by William Alexander, who was part of an English embassy to China, from 1792 to 1794.

TIPU SULTAN

RULER OF MYSORE
BORN 1750
DIED May 4, 1799
KEY CONFLICT Anglo-Mysore Wars
KEY BATTLES Pollilur 1780, Srirangapatna 1799

Known as the Tiger of Mysore, Tipu Sultan inherited his kingdom in southern India, his army, and his ambitions from his father, Hyder Ali. Hyder had made himself ruler of Mysore through his military prowess. As European colonial powers jostled for control of coastal India, Hyder aligned himself with the French, who provided training and equipment for his army. He fought against the British and the East India Company, as well as against his Indian neighbors to the north: the Nizam of Hyderabad and the Maratha Confederacy.

Tipu accompanied his father on campaign from the age of 15, and by the time the Second Anglo-Mysore War broke out in 1780, was an experienced field commander. In September of that year, he attacked a British force under Colonel William Baille at Pollilur and broke up its defensive formation with his cannon and cavalry, forcing Baille to surrender.

This striking victory was followed by other impressive performances in a war that neither side could win. In the midst of the conflict in 1782, Hyder died and Tipu took the throne. Two years later, he negotiated peace with the British on equal terms by the Treaty of Mangalore.

AVID MODERNIZER

Tipu expressed a great interest in technological innovation. In addition to his ground-breaking rocket forces and French-supplied cannon, he deployed a well-drilled infantry armed with flintlock muskets and bayonets. The quality of his light cavalry was also much admired. He hated the British and even owned

Commemorative fresco
Tipu Sultan had this mural painted in one of his palaces to record his victory over the British at Pollilur in September 1780. It gives pride of place to the dashing Mysorean cavalry.

an automaton representing a tiger savaging a British soldier. Yet, his connection with France was ultimately his undoing, since it inspired Britain to devote substantial resources to campaigns against him.

In the Third Anglo-Mysore War of 1789–92, Tipu suffered a series of defeats by the British East India Company and had to cede territory to obtain peace. In 1799, with the French Revolutionary Wars raging, Britain decided that the independence of Mysore was a threat to their interests. Tipu's kingdom faced an invasion by an overwhelming force,

including East India Company sepoys, British regular infantry under the future Duke of Wellington, and the army of the Nizam of Hyderabad. They took the capital, Srirangapatna, after a swift but hard-fought campaign. Tipu was a conspicuous presence in the final defense of the fortress and died fighting, gun in hand.

KEY TROOPS

ROCKET FORCES

Tipu Sultan's Mysorean army deployed some 20 rocket brigades of around 200 men each. Their rockets consisted of gunpowder-filled metal cylinders attached to bamboo sticks. These were usually mounted on frames on a cart as wheeled artillery. Smaller versions were carried by infantry in quivers. Fired in salvos, they were effective at ranges up to 3,300ft(1,000m). The British were so impressed by the metal rockets that they made their own version, the Congreve rocket, in the early 19th century.

> " BY WHAT RIGHT DO I COMMEND MY MEN TO DIE FOR MY CAUSE IF I [AM] AFRAID TO LAY DOWN MY OWN LIFE… WOULD YOU ADVISE A TIGER TO FOLLOW THE LIFE-STYLE OF A JACKAL? "
>
> **TIPU SULTAN**, IN A SPEECH TO HIS MEN FOLLOWING THE TREATY OF MANGALORE, 1784

FRENCH REVOLUTIONARY AND NAPOLEONIC WARS

> "THE YOUNG MEN SHALL FIGHT; THE MARRIED MEN SHALL FORGE ARMS AND TRANSPORT PROVISIONS… THE OLD MEN SHALL BETAKE THEMSELVES TO THE PUBLIC SQUARES IN ORDER TO AROUSE THE COURAGE OF THE WARRIORS."

THE FRENCH REVOLUTION of 1789 triggered war in Europe on a scale not to be surpassed until the 20th century. Between 1792 and 1815, France was only at peace for two brief periods. The Revolutionary Wars, which set the French Republic against Britain, Austria, and other European monarchies, blended seamlessly into the Napoleonic Wars after Bonaparte's seizure of power in 1799. These dramatic conflicts changed the face of war, as a new generation of ambitious young commanders brought a fresh dynamism to military operations.

The social and political upheavals of the early years of the revolution drove much of the French aristocracy, including a large percentage of senior officers, into exile. When France was invaded by Austria and Prussia in 1792, the defense of the country still lay in the hands of generals of the old royal army who had embraced the revolution. Never in military history was promotion to high rank swifter than over the following two years; by 1794, the average age of a French general was 33. The road to command was opened to men of lowly origins, typically noncommissioned officers in the pre-revolutionary army, who could never have attained high rank under the old regime.

A NEW REVOLUTION

In August 1793, the French revolutionary government proclaimed a *levée en masse*—total mobilization for the war effort, including universal conscription for men of fighting age. Although often poorly supplied, the new revolutionary armies were superior to their enemies in numbers and patriotic enthusiasm. As the radical impetus of the revolution waned after 1794, the armies' ambitious young commanders emerged as arbiters of political power. Outstripping his rivals in both military skill and political ambition, the Corsican soldier Napoleon Bonaparte rose irresistibly on the back of victories in the field. He played the leading role in imposing a peace treaty on Austria in 1797 and two years later returned from an expedition to Egypt to head a coup in Paris.

Victory over Austria in 1801 confirmed France as the dominant power in Europe and Napoleon as absolute ruler of France—he assumed the title of emperor in 1804. But Britain, as dominant at sea as France was on land, refused to accept Napoleonic ascendancy. The country remained in almost constant war with France, periodically joined in its struggle by allies on mainland Europe. In an astonishing sequence of victories over Austria, Prussia, and Russia from 1805 to 1807, Napoleon demonstrated the superiority of new forms of army organization, military strategy, and tactics. His army corps, each commanded by a marshal of the empire, were all-arms formations capable of independent maneuver. Living off the land, they moved faster than their opponents, boldly seeking the destruction of the enemy's forces.

THE EMPIRE DEFEATED

France's enemies learned from their defeats. Prussia and Austria reformed their armies on partially Napoleonic lines, but it was the unreformed forces that performed the best against Napoleon. Britain's Duke of Wellington and Russia's Kutuzov adopted defensive strategies to deny the French the swift victories their warfare system required. For Napoleon, weakened by embroilment in the Peninsular War in Spain and Portugal and a campaign against Austria in 1809, the invasion of Russia in 1812 was a fatal error from which he never recovered. Even then, complex campaigns by massive allied armies were required to bring about his abdication in 1814. He still returned the year after, before a final defeat at Waterloo.

The battle of Somosierra
A key battle early in the Peninsular War (1808–14), Napoleon's defeat of Spanish militia and artillery batteries at the Somosierra Pass on November 30, 1808, led to the capture of the Spanish capital, Madrid, a few days later.

Model *an XIII* sword
Named after the 13th year (*an XIII*) of the French Republican calendar (equivalent to 1804–05), this single-edged blade was issued to French dragoons and heavy cavalry later in the Napoleonic Wars.

GENERALS OF THE FRENCH REVOLUTION

MEN OF NOBLE LINEAGE commanded beside sons of peasants in the French revolutionary armies. While some had been generals in the old royal army, others had been noncommissioned officers or common soldiers. The revolutionary authorities viewed military commanders with suspicion—often justifiably,

since some deserted to or conspired with the revolution's royalist enemies. During 1793–94, no fewer than 84 generals were executed, and many spent time in prison. However, the greatest commander to emerge in the Revolutionary Wars, Napoleon Bonaparte, eventually took power; many revolutionary generals served as marshals in his empire.

CHARLES-FRANÇOIS DUMOURIEZ

FRENCH GENERAL
BORN January 25, 1739
DIED March 14, 1823
KEY CONFLICTS War of the Bar Confederation, French Revolutionary Wars
KEY BATTLES Lanckorona 1771, Jemappes 1792, Neerwinden 1793

Dumouriez served Louis XV in various sensitive foreign missions, notably, in organizing the rebel army of the Polish Bar Confederation. Unfortunately, his Poles were trounced by Russian General Suvorov at Lanckorona in 1771. The French Revolution rescued him from a dull post as commandant of a provincial

city. Plunging into revolutionary politics, he showed a talent for intrigue and was appointed foreign minister in March 1792. In August, he took command of the armies in northeast France. In November, he marched into the Austrian Netherlands (Belgium), where he crushed a much smaller Austrian army at Jemappes.

Victory made Dumouriez a popular hero, but he opposed the execution of Louis XVI in January 1793 and criticized the oppressive behavior of French revolutionary commissaires in occupied territories. His head was already on the line when he lost to the Austrians at

Neerwinden in March, his barely trained troops no match for the Austrian regulars. Facing almost certain execution for military failure and political deviance, Dumouriez tried to persuade his troops to march on Paris and restore the monarchy. When they refused, he defected to the Austrian camp. During the Napoleonic Wars, he acted as a military adviser to the British.

Dumouriez at Jemappes
On horseback, General Dumouriez urges his infantry forward to attack the entrenched Austrians at the battle of Jemappes. The French were victorious, but at a heavy cost.

FRANÇOIS-CHRISTOPHE KELLERMANN

FRENCH GENERAL AND MARSHAL
BORN May 28, 1735
DIED September 23, 1820
KEY CONFLICTS French Revolutionary Wars, Napoleonic Wars
KEY BATTLE Valmy

Kellermann—a brigadier general in 1789—put his military experience at the disposal of the revolutionary cause. At Valmy, on September 20, 1792, his

Army of the Rhine faced an invasion force led by the Prussian Duke of Brunswick. Kellermann inspired his troops with the cry *"Vive la nation!"* ("Long live the nation!"). His steady infantry and effective artillery persuaded Brunswick to call off his march on Paris and withdraw.

The battle at Valmy was a boost to morale, but after a period of renown, Kellermann was wrong-footed by

shifts in political power, serving 13 months in prison. He reemerged as an army commander in 1795, but had to make way for the young rising star, Napoleon. Under the empire, he was rewarded with a dukedom and the rank of marshal. His son, François-Étienne, was one of Napoleon's most admired cavalry commanders.

Battle of Valmy
Kellermann turns to consult his staff during the cannonade at Valmy. White-uniformed French regulars are backed up by new volunteers in blue.

JEAN-BAPTISTE JOURDAN

FRENCH GENERAL AND MARSHAL
BORN April 29, 1762
DIED November 23, 1833
KEY CONFLICTS French Revolutionary Wars, Peninsular War
KEY BATTLES Wattignies 1793, Fleurus 1794, Talavera 1809, Vitoria 1813

As a young apprentice in the silk trade, Jourdan enlisted with the French forces sent to fight in the American Revolutionary War. On his return, he settled into the life of a provincial tradesman in his native Limoges, until the Revolution opened new opportunities. Volunteering a second time for the army, he became a junior officer by 1792 and, with startling rapidity, was promoted to general the following year. Jourdan owed his appointment to Lazare Carnot, a member of the revolutionary Committee of Public Safety, who saw Jourdan as a handy propaganda tool—a general of lowly social origins to lead the revolutionary war effort. When the Army of the North defeated the Austrians at Wattignies in October 1793, Jourdan was officially in command, but Carnot was on the spot pulling the strings.

VICTORY AND DISASTER

In the winter of 1793, Jourdan narrowly escaped the guillotine and returned to civilian life in Limoges. Restored to command in 1794, he had his finest hour in June, when he defeated a combined Austrian and Dutch army at Fleurus. From this peak, Jourdan's military career waned. A string of defeats earned him the nickname "the anvil"—because he was hammered so often. Nonetheless, Napoleon made him a marshal in 1804 and he won the confidence of the emperor's brother, Joseph. When Joseph was placed on the Spanish throne in 1808, Jourdan became his chief-of-staff. He achieved little in this role because none of Napoleon's other marshals accepted his authority. He fought Wellington twice, at Talavera in 1809 and Vitoria in 1813.

Revolutionary colors
The victor at the battle of Fleurus, General Jourdan, accompanied by an aide, sports the revolutionary tricolor cockade on his bicorne hat.

KEY BATTLE
FLEURUS

CAMPAIGN French Revolutionary Wars
DATE June 26, 1794
LOCATION Belgium, north of Charleroi

At Fleurus, Austrian and Dutch forces under the Prince of Saxe-Coburg boldly attacked Jourdan's numerically superior French troops, who had their backs to the Sambre River. In command of 75,000 men along an 18-mile (30-km) front, Jourdan used a hydrogen balloon to keep informed of the battle's progress. Skillfully feeding in reserves where needed to counter the thrusts of Saxe-Coburg's columns, he beat off the attack and drove the enemy from the field.

JEAN-VICTOR-MARIE MOREAU

FRENCH GENERAL
BORN February 14, 1763
DIED September 2, 1813
KEY CONFLICT French Revolutionary Wars
KEY BATTLES Tourcoing 1794, Hohenlinden 1800

An unwilling law student in Brittany, Moreau had always wanted to be a soldier. The Revolution transformed his life. In 1792, a regiment of local army volunteers elected him as their colonel and he led them off to fight in the early battles of the Revolutionary Wars. He distinguished himself in the defeat of Austrian and British forces at Tourcoing in May 1794 and subsequently campaigned with great skill in the war against Austria on the Rhine front. In 1796, he advanced into Bavaria, but when Jourdan's army on his left suffered a series of defeats, he was forced to retreat across Germany. Conducting a fighting withdrawal with consummate skill, he brought his army back intact to the west bank of the Rhine.

In April 1797, Moreau once more took the offensive, with a successful crossing of the Rhine at Diersheim. This victory, however, was upstaged by Napoleon's successes in Italy, which forced Austria to make peace. In one of the reversals of fortune so common at the time, Moreau was implicated in a plot to restore the monarchy and dismissed from the army.

In 1799, with France once more facing a military crisis, Moreau was recalled. He supported the coup that brought Napoleon to power as First Consul and was rewarded in 1800 with leadership of the Army of the Rhine. His brilliant victory against superior Austrian forces at Hohenlinden in December was achieved through a Napoleon-like use of divisions maneuvering independently to outflank and envelop enemy forces. His downfall followed directly from this triumph. The First Consul had him arrested on trumped-up charges and banished from France. He lived in the United States until 1812, when he returned to Europe to assist in the defeat of Napoleon. He was killed while acting as adviser to Czar Alexander at the battle of Dresden in 1813.

Medallion of Moreau
This medallion commemorates Moreau's death in 1813 and gives his name in Latin—appropriately, "Victorius."

> REST EASY, GENTLEMEN, IT IS MY DESTINY.
>
> **MOREAU'S LAST WORDS**, SEPTEMBER 2, 1813

NAPOLEON BONAPARTE

FRENCH GENERAL AND EMPEROR
BORN August 15, 1769
DIED May 5, 1821
KEY CONFLICTS French Revolutionary Wars, Napoleonic Wars
KEY BATTLES Rivoli 1797, Pyramids 1798, Marengo 1800, Ulm 1805, Austerlitz 1805, Jena-Auerstedt 1806, Eylau 1807, Friedland 1807, Wagram 1809, Borodino 1812, Leipzig 1813, Waterloo 1815

Born into an impoverished Corsican family of noble descent, Napoleon Bonaparte was commissioned as an officer in the French artillery in 1785. He decamped with his family to France at the height of the Revolution in 1793. Proving himself to be an able military officer, he achieved rapid promotion. He also proved an accomplished politician. In 1794, he survived the downfall of the ruling Jacobin clan, with whom he had been closely linked, and in 1796 married Josephine de Beauharnais, who was well-connected to the Directorate—the French governing body that succeeded the Jacobins.

Napoleon was aged 26 when he first took command in the field. The Army of Italy was a semimutinous body of men short of equipment, food, and pay. Understanding his soldiers' mix of grumbling self-pity,

Empress Josephine
Napoleon's first wife could no longer have children, so he divorced her to make a dynastic marriage to Marie-Louise, Archduchess of Austria.

collective pride, and base rapacity, he won their support with the promise of glory and plunder. He also had exceptional luck, for early victories could easily have ended in disaster.

EMPIRE BUILDING

Fearing the political ambitions of a successful general, the Directorate was relieved when Napoleon's search for glory took him to Egypt. Though his victories over the Egyptian Mamelukes and Ottoman Turks were negated by Nelson's destruction of the French fleet at Aboukir Bay in 1798, the Middle East expedition provided an exotic boost to the evolving Napoleonic legend. Slipping back to France in 1799, Napoleon ratified his claim to power with a crushing victory over the Austrians at Marengo in 1800, and he took control of the French state. From that point on, Napoleon had the advantage of being both ruler and supreme commander of France and was able to transform the French forces into the tool he required to fulfill his extensive military ambitions.

Napoleon's defeat of Austria (twice), Prussia, and Russia in campaigns between 1805 and 1809 ensured his reputation as one of the greatest military commanders of all time. The basis for his victories was the rapid maneuver of large bodies of troops living off the land. He used

Napoleon's sword
Dating from 1780, this sword was presented to the young Napoleon when he became an artillery officer in the French army.

speed of movement to achieve "a superiority of force at the point at which one attacks," in his own words. His army appeared unexpectedly behind the enemy or struck at enemy armies in quick succession, before they could concentrate in overwhelming numbers. On the battlefield, Napoleon liked to throw the enemy off balance by drawing the fighting to one wing, then punching with the maximum force of artillery, heavy cavalry, and infantry columns at a point where the enemy line had weakened.

OVERREACHER

Napoleon's drive to impose a continent-wide boycott of British imports led to widening war. The placing of his relatives or marshals on European thrones aroused resentment and, in Spain, a full-scale revolt. His marriage to Josephine was annulled in 1810 and

The Battle of the Pyramids
After the resounding defeat of the Egyptian army outside Cairo in 1798, Napoleon incorporated a body of Egyptian Mameluke cavalry into his Imperial Guard.

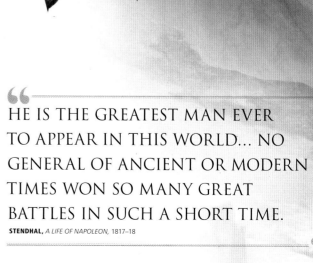

> HE IS THE GREATEST MAN EVER TO APPEAR IN THIS WORLD... NO GENERAL OF ANCIENT OR MODERN TIMES WON SO MANY GREAT BATTLES IN SUCH A SHORT TIME.
>
> **STENDHAL,** *A LIFE OF NAPOLEON,* 1817–18

Crossing the Alps
Napoleon commissioned the neoclassical artist Jacques-Louis David to paint this heroic portrayal of his crossing of the St. Bernard Pass in 1800. He actually made the journey more prosaically: on the back of a mule.

KEY TROOPS
THE IMPERIAL ARMY

Napoleon's Grande Armée was divided into a number of all-arms corps, each capable of functioning as an independent army in its own right. The corps were commanded by talented French revolutionary generals who had become marshals of the Napoleonic empire. The whole force was directed through Napoleon's headquarters, headed by his chief-of-staff, Marshal Berthier. The ranks of the Grande Armée were fed by annual drafts of French conscripts, but it was also a multinational force that exploited the expansion of the country's borders, as conquered states were required to provide troops.

FRENCH CORPORAL'S INFANTRY UNIFORM

> " I HAVE OFTEN SAID THAT I CONSIDERED NAPOLEON'S PRESENCE ON THE FIELD TO BE EQUAL TO 40,000 MEN. "
>
> **DUKE OF WELLINGTON,** IN CONVERSATION, 1836

he married into the Austrian royal family but never achieved acceptance Europe-wide as a legitimate ruler. His campaigns became increasingly costly—French casualties were around 8,000 at Austerlitz in 1805, but almost 40,000 at Wagram four years later. Losses in the Russian invasion in 1812 may have been over half a million.

A FINAL FLOURISH

As war dragged on, a megalomaniac streak began to undermine Napoleon's reasoning, and his health deteriorated due to his constant campaigning. The brilliance of his battlefield tactics waned; at Borodino, in 1812, he merely flung his forces forward in a frontal assault against Russian defensive positions, achieving no more than a Pyrrhic victory at crippling cost.

Yet, he never lost his hold over his troops. He understood that citizen soldiers required heroic leadership and he tirelessly cultivated his personal image and mythology. His skills in the large-scale defensive campaigns of 1813–14 have been much admired. His ability to stage a comeback in 1815, a year after abdication, with Frenchmen flocking to serve him, speaks volumes for his undimmed charisma. But from defeat at Waterloo (pp. 210–11) there was no return.

(pp. 210–11)

TIMELINE

■ **September 1785** Napoleon graduates from the Royal Military School in Paris. He joins the French artillery as a sub-lieutenant.

■ **December 22, 1793** After commanding artillery at the siege of Toulon, Napoleon is promoted to brigadier-general.

■ **October 5, 1795** Napoleon suppresses an uprising in Paris by turning his cannon on the crowd. He is rewarded with command of the Army of the Interior.

■ **March 1, 1796** Napoleon is given command of the Army of Italy. Ensuing victories over Austria and Piedmont, including Rivoli (1797), make his reputation as a general.

■ **May 19, 1798** Napoleon embarks with the Army of the Orient on an expedition to Egypt. He defeats the Egyptian Mamelukes at the battle of the Pyramids (July 21).

■ **November 9, 1799** Napoleon takes part in a coup that establishes the Consulate, which he leads as First Consul from December 25.

■ **June 14, 1800** After crossing the Alps, Napoleon defeats the Austrians in a close-fought battle at Marengo in Italy.

■ **May 18, 1804** Napoleon is proclaimed Emperor of the French. He crowns himself in Notre-Dame Cathedral, Paris, on December 2.

■ **October 20, 1805** Napoleon defeats the Austrians at Ulm. He defeats the Austrians and their Russian allies at Austerlitz on December 2.

■ **October 14, 1806** Napoleon defeats the Prussians at Jena and Auerstedt. After a draw at Eylau (February 8, 1807), he triumphs over the Russians at Friedland (June 13, 1807).

■ **May 20–23, 1809** In his first failure in battle, Napoleon is checked by the Austrians at Aspern-Essling. The Austrians are overcome at the costly battle of Wagram (July 5–6).

THE RETREAT FROM MOSCOW, 1812

■ **September 7, 1812** Napoleon invades Russia, but fails to secure victory at Borodino. The subsequent retreat is a military catastrophe.

■ **October 16–19, 1813** Prussia, Sweden, and Austria defeat Napoleon at Leipzig.

■ **April 6, 1814** Napoleon abdicates as enemy forces occupy Paris. He is exiled to the island of Elba, off the coast of Italy, but escapes back to France (March 1, 1815).

■ **June 18, 1815** The British and Prussians defeat Napoleon at Waterloo. He is imprisoned on St. Helena in the south Atlantic until his death.

1660—1850

NAPOLEON: MASTER OF EUROPE

> "A giant surrounded by pygmies"

Waterloo—The Hundred Days, *David Chandler*, 1980. *British military historian Chandler has written admiringly of Napoleon's skill as a general.*

ANTONIO CANOVA'S BUST
OF NAPOLEON, c. 1806

NAPOLEON INSPIRED an impressive degree of personal loyalty in his troops. This was partly achieved through showmanship. He created the impression that he knew his men personally, taking care to greet some veterans by name as he rode up and down the lines. He also made the soldiers feel that he shared their hardships on campaign and faced the same dangers in battle, even if this was only partially true. But Napoleon's charisma is not entirely open to rational explanation. British Field Marshal Sir Archibald Wavell wrote of his performance with the Army of Italy in 1796: "If you discover how... [he] inspired a ragged, mutinous, half-starved army and made it fight as it did… then you will have learned something." Napoleon's soldiers remained loyal to the bitter end.

> "At night he wished to visit on foot and incognito all the posts; but he had not gone many steps when he was recognized. It would be impossible to depict the enthusiasm of the soldiers upon seeing him. Lighted straw was placed in an instant upon the tops of thousands of poles, and eighty thousand men appeared before the emperor, saluting him with acclamations…"

30th Bulletin of the Grand Army, (December 3, 1805). *This official report describes an incident on the night before the battle of Austerlitz.*

> There are in Europe many good generals, but they see too many things at once. I see only one thing, namely the enemy's main body. I try to crush it, confident that secondary matters will then settle themselves."

Napoleon, statement of his strategic principles (1797). *At this time the young Napoleon Bonaparte had won spectacular victories in the Italian campaign of 1796–97.*

NAPOLEON'S APPROACH to strategy disregarded the occupation of territory or fortresses. His goal was, by rapid maneuver, to bring the enemy's forces to battle at a disadvantage and destroy them. His army corps marched separately, making fast progress living off the land, and joined up to fight. Napoleon's specialities included maneuvering around the enemy's flank to take up a position to his rear, forcing him to give battle. Or he might adopt a central position from which to strike at different enemy armies, delivering a series of punches to defeat them one by one. On the battlefield, his victories depended on the shock effect of artillery, infantry columns, and heavy cavalry. In his early battles, shock attacks were subtly delivered against weak points opened up in the enemy position; later, they degenerated into bludgeoning frontal assaults.

It is clear that luck is leaving Bonaparte and that his frightful career has reached its zenith. Europe can be saved through Spain, if Europe still has the courage and determination to save itself. "

NAPOLEON'S CAREER was mostly a triumphal progress until around 1808. He had defeated all the major land powers in Europe. Yet he was unable to create a stable new order to sustain a peaceful domination of the continent—neither by placing his relatives and marshals on thrones, nor by allying himself by marriage to Austrian royalty. The revolt against the French in Spain in 1808 was the beginning of waves of resistance that eventually saw Napoleon fighting simultaneously against Russia, Prussia, Austria, Sweden, Britain, Spain, and Portugal. Traditional ruling classes were able to mobilize nationalist sentiment against France. Napoleon could no longer achieve quick victories, and in Russia and Spain attempts to have troops live off the land failed disastrously.

Friedrich von Gentz, Prussian statesman, in a letter (September 1808). Gentz was a spokesman for German resistance to French domination.

"The curse of all the human race."

Czar Alexander I, in a letter to his sister Catherine (January 5, 1812). To his enemies, Napoleon was a uniquely evil figure.

Napoleon facing defeat
Jean-Louis-Ernest Meissonier's painting shows Napoleon on campaign with his generals in 1814, when he was fighting a defensive war against overwhelming odds.

NAPOLEON AT AUSTERLITZ

LOCATION Moravia, modern-day Czech Republic
CAMPAIGN War of the Third Coalition
DATE December 2, 1805
FORCES French: 73,000; Allies: 70,000 Russians, 15,000 Austrians
CASUALTIES French: 1,300 killed, 7,000 wounded; Allies: 16,000 killed or wounded, 11,500 taken prisoner

During Napoleon's 1805 campaign, he was drawn into a strategically perilous situation. In October, French troops forced an Austrian army under General Mack to surrender near Ulm in Württemberg. But the onset of winter would find Napoleon's army at the end of extended lines of supply and communication. The forces of the Russian and Austrian allies were strengthening in Moravia, and there was a possibility that Prussia might join the anti-French coalition.

PLANNING THE BATTLE

Napoleon's instinct was to pursue the annihilation of his enemy's forces, despite his marshals' arguments for a prudent withdrawal. By various stratagems, he sought to persuade his enemies that he was weak and fearful. The cautious veteran Russian General Kutuzov was unmoved, favoring a waiting game. But he was overruled by the young Russian and Austrian emperors, Alexander and Francis.

As Napoleon had intended, the allies began preparations for an immediate offensive to crush the French Army. After a careful survey of the terrain, Napoleon selected a stretch of land near the village of Austerlitz as his battlefield, positioning his forces with clever calculation. By leaving his right wing weak, he invited the allies to concentrate their attack on that flank. Instead of garrisoning the Pratzen Heights, the dominant feature in the area, he left a tempting path open for the enemy to advance along. His headquarters and the bulk of his forces were reserved on the left of his line. When the Russians and Austrians advanced to attack his right, he

> ## SOLDIERS, I AM SATISFIED WITH YOU… YOU HAVE COVERED YOURSELVES WITH ETERNAL GLORY.
>
> **EMPEROR NAPOLEON**, PROCLAMATION TO THE ARMY AFTER THE BATTLE OF AUSTERLITZ, DECEMBER 3, 1805

Capturing the enemy
After the battle, French general Jean Rapp presented the defeated Russian Prince Repnin to Napoleon, along with other enemy prisoners, flags, and cannon.

intended to sweep from the left, envelop, and crush them. The allied chief-of-staff, General Weyrother, duly obliged Napoleon by planning a mass attack against the French right.

THE ENGAGEMENT

Through the early morning mist on December 2, Russian and Austrian columns crossed the Pratzen Heights and descended on Napoleon's right flank, which barely held its ground. At 8:30 a.m. Napoleon ordered Soult's infantry, in the center of his line, to move forward and occupy the supposedly deserted Pratzen Heights. Through sheer incompetence, the allies still had a column of troops belatedly crossing the Heights, and a desperate fight developed when they collided with Soult's troops emerging from the mist. At this point, Napoleon shifted his headquarters to the

Heights for a clearer view of the battle. Both sides threw in heavy cavalry and the French ended in possession of the ground after much slaughter.

The bulk of the allied army was still stalled in an attempt to break through on the French right. But Napoleon's plan for an enveloping movement from the left of his line had aborted, because of unexpected resistance by forces on the allied right, commanded by the Russian General Bagration. As an improvised substitute for the planned left hook, Napoleon ordered Soult's men on the Pratzen to turn and attack the main body of the allied forces from the flank and rear. The result was a rout. Fleeing Russian and Austrian troops suffered heavy losses. The remnants of the Russian Army withdrew to continue the war, but Austrian Emperor Francis made peace on humiliating terms.

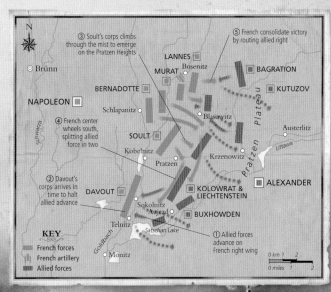

NAPOLEON'S MARSHALS

NAPOLEON ESTABLISHED the rank of Marshal of the Empire in 1804, conferring it immediately on 18 of his generals, a select group to which only eight more were added during his reign. The marshals included Louis Berthier, Napoleon's chief-of-staff, and some honorary appointees, but most were expected to be capable of commanding army corps or even independent armies in the field. Drawn from a range of social backgrounds, the marshals experienced equally diverse fates after Napoleon's fall—from the unfortunate Ney and Murat, shot by firing squad, to the lucky Bernadotte, who improbably founded a royal dynasty in Sweden.

LOUIS-NICOLAS DAVOUT

FRENCH MARSHAL
BORN May 10, 1770
DIED June 1, 1823
KEY CONFLICTS French Revolutionary Wars, Napoleonic Wars
KEY BATTLES Austerlitz 1805, Auerstedt 1806, Eylau 1807, Wagram 1809, Eckmühl 1809, Hamburg 1814

The son of an aristocratic cavalry officer in Louis XVI's army, Louis-Nicolas Davout joined his father's regiment when he came

Plain looks
Davout was balding and myopic and his external appearance gave no hint of his exceptional qualities as a general.

of age. He was rapidly promoted to brigadier-general in the early stages of the French Revolutionary Wars, but his career was interrupted because his noble origins aroused suspicion. Napoleon had no such prejudices, taking Davout with him on his expedition to Egypt in 1798. Here he performed impressively as commander of a cavalry brigade.

SUCCESS AT AUSTERLITZ

At age 34, Davout was the youngest of the marshals appointed in 1804. At Austerlitz the following year, he brought a corps by forced marches from Vienna to reach the battlefield as the fighting began, and held the French right against the main thrust of the Austro-Russian attack. In October 1806, he defeated the main body of the Prussian army at Auerstedt with a

single corps, while Napoleon was engaged with lesser forces at Jena. Davout continued to serve with distinction through the campaign against Russia in 1807, including the winter battle of Eylau, and in the 1809 Wagram campaign against Austria. Napoleon accorded him the title Prince of Eckmühl after his victory there in April 1809.

Davout's part in the disastrous invasion of Russia in 1812 did not enhance his reputation, but he stood firm amid failing French fortunes, holding Hamburg under siege in 1813–14. He rejoined Napoleon for the Hundred Days as his minister of war, but was later reconciled to the French monarchy. Though Davout lacked the appeal of some marshals—he was a severe disciplinarian—his military skill, dependability, and tactical judgment were the qualities of a truly outstanding commander.

NICOLAS SOULT

FRENCH MARSHAL
BORN March 29, 1769
DIED November 26, 1851
KEY CONFLICTS French Revolutionary Wars, Napoleonic Wars
KEY BATTLES Zurich 1799, Austerlitz 1805, Ocana 1809, Toulouse 1814

Nicolas-Jean-de-Dieu Soult came from a provincial middle-class family. Thrown into poverty on the death of his father, he enlisted as a private in 1785. Benefiting from exceptional opportunities for promotion in the Revolutionary Wars, he gained much combat experience, notably taking part in the defeat of Austrian and Russian forces at Zurich in 1799.

Tough general
Marshal Soult was disliked by many of his fellow officers, who considered him devious and self-seeking, but he was a resolute commander under tough conditions.

As a marshal, he commanded a corps in the center of the line at Austerlitz, leading the crucial assault on the Pratzen Heights. After campaigns against the Prussians and Russians in 1806-07, he was sent to Spain.

SPORADIC SUCCESS

Soult fumbled the pursuit of the British army to Coruña in January 1809, allowing it to escape, but the following November crushed the Spanish army at Ocana.

His reputation then suffered during the Peninsular War, where he became involved in destructive disputes with other French commanders and found the mobile warfare demanded by Napoleon impossible in war-ravaged,

guerrilla-ridden countryside. When he did go to battle, as at Albuera in May 1811, he failed to defeat his enemy. Nonetheless, he fought brilliantly with inadequate forces against Wellington, pressing up from the Pyrenees to Toulouse in 1814. His role as Napoleon's chief-of-staff during the Hundred Days was less impressive. After a period in exile, he returned to France and lived his final years as a respected political and military dignitary.

> ❝
> ## THE DAY WAS MINE, BUT THEY DID NOT KNOW IT AND WOULD NOT RUN.
> **MARSHAL SOULT**, REPORTING HIS FAILURE TO DEFEAT THE BRITISH AT ALBUERA, 1811
> ❞

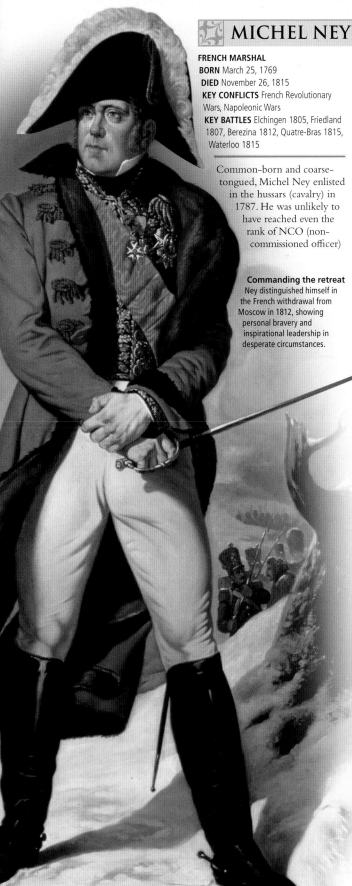

MICHEL NEY

FRENCH MARSHAL
BORN March 25, 1769
DIED November 26, 1815
KEY CONFLICTS French Revolutionary Wars, Napoleonic Wars
KEY BATTLES Elchingen 1805, Friedland 1807, Berezina 1812, Quatre-Bras 1815, Waterloo 1815

Common-born and coarse-tongued, Michel Ney enlisted in the hussars (cavalry) in 1787. He was unlikely to have reached even the rank of NCO (non-commissioned officer)

Commanding the retreat
Ney distinguished himself in the French withdrawal from Moscow in 1812, showing personal bravery and inspirational leadership in desperate circumstances.

under the old regime, but in the Revolutionary Wars promotion was rapid. A commander who led from the front, he impressed Napoleon, who made him a marshal in 1804. Ney distinguished himself as a corps commander in the Ulm campaign of 1805—blocking the escape of the Austrian army at Elchingen—and against Prussia and Russia, which culminated in victory at Friedland.

After a difficult spell in Spain and Portugal, he took part in the invasion of Russia in 1812. Commanding the rearguard in the retreat from Moscow, he fought in the desperate crossing

of the Berezina River and allegedly was the last French soldier to leave Russian soil. The emperor hailed him as "the bravest of the brave."

WAVERING SUPPORT

Ney's allegiance to Napoleon was far from unwavering. He led the pressure on the emperor to abdicate and volunteered to arrest him after his escape from Elba, only to rejoin his old master on impulse. During the Hundred Days Ney's performance was marred by poor judgment. His failed attack at Quatre-Bras lost vital French forces, and he made reckless cavalry charges at Waterloo. Arrested and charged with treason, Ney was executed by firing squad in Paris.

> ## I HAVE FOUGHT 100 BATTLES FOR FRANCE AND NOT ONE AGAINST HER…
>
> **MARSHAL NEY**, IN HIS SPEECH TO THE FIRING SQUAD, 1815

JOACHIM MURAT

FRENCH MARSHAL AND KING OF NAPLES
BORN March 25, 1767
DIED October 13, 1815
KEY CONFLICTS French Revolutionary Wars, Napoleonic Wars
KEY BATTLES Aboukir 1799, Austerlitz 1805, Eylau 1807, Tolentino 1815

The son of an innkeeper, Joachim Murat profited from the revolution to become a cavalry officer. He attached himself to Napoleon from 1795, serving in his early campaigns in Italy and Egypt. After becoming a marshal in 1804, Murat performed well at Austerlitz, but his outstanding moment of glory was leading a mass

charge of around 10,000 cavalry against the Russians at Eylau in February 1807. Napoleon then made him king of Naples, and the rest of his life was uncomfortably torn between the roles of monarch and marshal.

In 1815, Murat's focus was on saving his throne, but he lost to the Austrians at the battle of Tolentino in May and was executed by a Neapolitan firing squad five months later.

Murat the flamboyant
Always dressed in flamboyant uniform, Murat's forte was leading cavalry charges, as depicted here against the Ottomans at Aboukir, Egypt, in 1799.

RULERS AND REVOLUTIONARIES

NAPOLEON'S ADVERSARIES

DESPITE HIS MILITARY GENIUS, Napoleon was ultimately beaten not only by superior forces, but also by commanders who outthought and outfought him. Austrian, Prussian, and Russian armies trounced by the French emperor between 1805 and 1807 revived their fighting spirit to impose heavy losses on him at Wagram in 1809 and Borodino in 1812. The patient strategies of Mikhail Kutuzov in Russia in 1812 and the Duke of Wellington in the Peninsular War exhausted the French by attrition. At the climactic battle of Waterloo in 1815, Wellington and the Prussian marshal, Gebhard von Blücher, defeated Napoleon outright.

ARCHDUKE CHARLES

AUSTRIAN COMMANDER
BORN September 5, 1771
DIED April 30, 1847
KEY CONFLICTS French Revolutionary Wars, Napoleonic Wars
KEY BATTLES Stockach 1799, Aspern-Essling 1809, Wagram 1809

The son of the Austrian emperor, Leopold II, Archduke Charles held command by right of birth but justified his position by outstanding merit. He served from the outset of the French Revolutionary Wars, learning his trade in battles in the Netherlands. Charles showed how much he had learned when commanding Austrian forces on the Rhine front in 1796. Faced with two French armies under Jourdan and Moreau, he skillfully brought them to battle on his own terms, defeating them and driving them out of Germany. His success culminated in the battle at Stockach in 1799, when he defeated Jourdan again, leading reserves into the fight in person at the crucial moment. Charles was commanding forces in Italy in 1805 and therefore missed the Austerlitz campaign, but after that debacle he was entrusted with the reform of the Austrian military system. He imitated the organization of the Napoleonic army and tried to encourage German nationalism as a means of combating Napoleon in 1809. But his doctrine was relatively cautious, stressing the need to defend key strategic points rather than destroy the enemy's forces in the Napoleonic manner.

PUT TO THE TEST
At Aspern-Essling, Charles had the chance to try out his reforms, achieving a defensive victory and the first serious reverse suffered by Napoleon. The French emperor was too much for Charles at the follow-up battle of Wagram in July, but the French paid heavily for victory and Charles avoided a rout. After Wagram he retired from military command.

Lured to battle
Charles defeated Napoleon at Aspern-Essling on May 21–22, 1809, tempting him to cross a river and then repulsing his half-formed forces. He made no attempt to move on to the offensive.

GEBHARD VON BLÜCHER

PRUSSIAN COMMANDER
BORN December 16, 1742
DIED September 12, 1819
KEY CONFLICTS French Revolutionary Wars, Napoleonic Wars
KEY BATTLES Auerstedt 1806, Katzbach 1813, Leipzig 1813, Ligny 1815, Waterloo 1815

As a young man, Blücher joined the Swedish army, then switched to the Prussian side after they took him prisoner in 1760. For a long spell he retired from military life but, by the outbreak of the French Revolutionary Wars, he was back in the saddle as a cavalry commander. A prominent figure in Prussia's disastrous war against Napoleon in 1806, he led spirited but vain cavalry charges in the defeat at Auerstedt. In the following years, he became a symbol of Prussian patriotism and, when war with France resumed in 1813, he commanded the powerful Russo-Prussian Army of Silesia.

TOWER OF STRENGTH
Blücher defeated the French at Katzbach in August and contributed to the coalition victory at Leipzig in October. In 1814, his army fought across France to Paris, taking much of the credit for forcing Napoleon's abdication. Blücher then retired with the title Prince of Wahlstatt, only to be called back precipitately when Napoleon escaped from Elba in 1815. Facing the French commander at Ligny, the 72-year-old Blücher had his horse shot from underneath him and was trapped beneath its corpse for two hours. After recovering, he overruled his chief-of-staff, Gneisenau, and marched to join Wellington at Waterloo, arriving in time to turn the battle decisively against Napoleon and end his career with a glorious victory.

Respect and remembrance
Blücher was an honorary citizen of the cities of Berlin—celebrated here in this commemorative coin—Hamburg, and Rostock.

PRINCE PYOTR BAGRATION

RUSSIAN COMMANDER
BORN 1765
DIED September 24, 1812
KEY CONFLICTS Russo-Turkish Wars, French Revolutionary Wars, Russo-Swedish Wars, Napoleonic Wars
KEY BATTLES Austerlitz 1805, Borodino 1812

Descended from a line of Georgian princes, Pyotr Bagration cut his teeth as a Russian army officer under Alexander Suvorov. He displayed precocious talents in wars against the Ottoman

Georgian prince
A warm and chivalrous spirit, Prince Bagration was much loved by the troops serving under him.

Turks and the Poles and was a major-general by the time he accompanied Suvorov on his campaigns against the French in Italy and Switzerland in 1799.

FACING DISASTER

An impulsive, instinctive fighter endowed with great physical courage, Bagration shone amid the disasters of the Austerlitz campaign in 1805. After a much-admired rearguard action against far superior French forces at Schongrabern, he commanded the Russo-Austrian right wing at Austerlitz, blocking Napoleon's attempted envelopment and covering the withdrawal of the surviving allied forces.

After 1807, when the czar made peace with France, Bagration fought Sweden in Finland and Ottoman Turkey on the Danube, before being appointed to command the Second West Army confronting Napoleon's invasion of Russia in 1812. However, he failed to cooperate with the commander of the First West Army, Barclay de Tolly, during a series of withdrawals as the French rolled towards Moscow.

When the Russians chose to stand and fight at Borodino in September, Bagration commanded the center and left. A ferocious defense of his field fortifications elicited heroic efforts from his troops. But Bagration was struck by a bullet that lodged in his leg and he died two weeks later.

MIKHAIL KUTUZOV

RUSSIAN COMMANDER
BORN September 16, 1745
DIED April 28, 1813
KEY CONFLICTS Russo-Turkish Wars, Napoleonic Wars
KEY BATTLES Austerlitz 1805, Borodino 1812, Maloyaroslavets 1812, Berezina 1812

Russian aristocrat Mikhail Kutuzov was fortunate to survive his early military career—twice shot through the head, he lost only an eye. He was recalled from retirement in 1805 to command an army against Napoleon, although his caution before Austerlitz was ignored by Czar Alexander. He

thus avoided blame for this defeat. In August 1812, with Russian armies falling back in the face of Napoleon's invasion, he was again called upon to take command. Although aging and somnolent, Kutuzov was welcomed as embodying Russian patriotism. He withdrew to the gates of Moscow before making a stand at Borodino. During this epic battle, he issued few orders but allowed carnage to ensue.

The decision to withdraw beyond Moscow, yet refuse to make peace, was his masterstroke. He shadowed the French retreat and, through a clash at Maloyaroslavets, forced

> ## THE ONE AND ONLY AIM OF ALL OUR OPERATIONS IS TO DO EVERYTHING WE POSSIBLY CAN TO ANNIHILATE THE ENEMY.
>
> **MARSHAL MIKHAIL KUTUZOV**, ON TAKING COMMAND AFTER NAPOLEON'S INVASION, 1812

Napoleon to march through already devastated land. Harassing the French while refusing to seek battle, he allowed hunger, cold, and distance to ravage them before the crossing of the freezing Berezina River claimed many thousands more casualties.

Conference at Fili
After Borodino, Kutuzov held a conference with his generals at the village of Fili. He decided to withdraw beyond Moscow, sacrificing the city to keep his army intact.

DUKE OF WELLINGTON

BRITISH COMMANDER
BORN May 1, 1769
DIED September 14, 1852
KEY CONFLICTS Anglo-Mysore Wars, Anglo-Maratha Wars, Napoleonic Wars
KEY BATTLES Assaye 1803, Vimeiro 1808, Talavera 1809, Badajoz 1812, Salamanca 1812, Vitoria 1813, Waterloo 1815

A younger son from an impoverished Anglo-Irish aristocratic family, Arthur Wellesley, later Duke of Wellington, entered the army to earn a living. His first active experience of war was serving in the Duke of York's disastrous expedition to the Netherlands in 1794 where, he later said, he "learned what not to do."

His career breakthrough owed much to the appointment of his brother as governor-general in India, which maximized his chances of advancement in wars against Indian states. But his exceptional abilities shone through for the first time in tricky conflicts with Mysore and the Maratha Confederacy. Wellington later judged his victory over the Marathas at Assaye in 1803 as "the best thing I ever did in the way of fighting." It was certainly one of the riskiest, for he had two horses killed under him during the battle.

DEFENDING PORTUGAL

Wellesley was still no more than an officer of acknowledged competence when the Napoleonic Wars took him to Portugal, invaded by France, in summer 1808. His first battle in command against the French, at Vimeiro in August, was an indication of much to come. With skillful deployment of his steady, disciplined infantry in line, backed by cannon firing rounds of shrapnel (a recent introduction), he drove

> ## I ALWAYS SAY THAT NEXT TO A BATTLE LOST, THE GREATEST MISERY IS A BATTLE GAINED.
>
> **DUKE OF WELLINGTON**, AS RECORDED BY DIARIST LADY SHELLEY, 1815

KEY BATTLE

BADAJOZ

At Badajoz, a fortress city on the Portuguese-Spanish border, the French resisted a British siege in 1811, but in March 1812 Wellington returned for a second attempt. A three-week siege gained breaches in the fortifications. He ordered an assault on the night of April 6, aware that this was a desperate venture but in a hurry to move on. Repeated attacks on the breaches were repulsed with heavy losses, but Wellington held firm, urging his men to scale the walls on ladders. After savage fighting, the city was penetrated and the French surrendered. Over the following days, British troops, who had shown outstanding courage in the assault, engaged in a drunken orgy of rape and pillage at the expense of the city's population.

■ **1785–86** In preparation for a career in the army, Wellesley attends a military academy in Angers, France.

■ **1787** Wellesley joins an infantry regiment as an ensign and is promoted to lieutenant by the year's end.

■ **1794** Wellesley has his first combat experience commanding a brigade in the Duke of York's expedition against the French in the Netherlands.

■ **1799** Sent to India, Wellesley commands British infantry in the Fourth Anglo-Mysore War against Tipu Sultan.

■ **September 23, 1803** Now a major-general, Wellesley defeats the army of the Maratha Confederacy in a hard-fought battle at Assaye in western India.

■ **August–September 1807** After returning to Britain, Wellesley leads British troops in a successful attack on Copenhagen and is promoted to lieutenant-general.

■ **1808** Sent to Portugal, Wellesley defeats Marshal Junot at Vimeiro (August 21), but is recalled to Britain to face an inquiry after French troops are allowed free passage home.

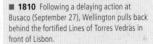

WATERLOO MEDAL

■ **1809** Returning to the Iberian Peninsula, Wellesley drives the French out of Porto and fights them at Talavera (July 27). After this battle, he is created Viscount Wellington of Talavera.

■ **1810** Following a delaying action at Busaco (September 27), Wellington pulls back behind the fortified Lines of Torres Vedràs in front of Lisbon.

■ **1811** The French are forced to withdraw from Portugal and fighting shifts to the Portuguese-Spanish border, where Wellington wins the battle of Fuentes de Oñoro (May 3–5).

■ **1812** After seizing the fortresses of Ciudad Rodrigo (January 20) and Badajoz (April 6), Wellington routs the French at the battle of Salamanca (July 22).

■ **1813** Defeating the French at the major battle of Vitoria (21 June), Wellington is promoted to field-marshal.

■ **1814** Pursuing the French across the Pyrenees, Wellington takes Toulouse in April as Napoleon abdicates; he is created Duke of Wellington.

■ **1815** After Napoleon's return from Elba, Wellington fights Marshal Ney at Quatre-Bras (June 16) and then, with Prussian Marshal Blücher, defeats Napoleon at Waterloo (June 18).

off the attack of French columns inflicting heavy losses. However, the outcome of this victory looked set to ruin his career. By the Convention of Cintra, his superiors agreed to ship the defeated French back to France with their weapons and booty. In the resulting uproar in Britain, Wellesley had to defend himself as not being responsible for this extraordinary decision. He was not only exonerated, but also persuaded the government to send him back to Portugal with command of a considerable army.

The Peninsular campaign fought by Wellington—as he then became known—between 1809 and 1814 is a classic of military history. Its success was based on an exact assessment of the broad strategic situation. He correctly judged that it would be impossible for the French to concentrate sufficient troops to crush his Anglo-Portuguese forces, while simultaneously coping with pressure from Spanish guerrillas and regulars. He turned Lisbon into an unassailable base where he could sit, amply supplied by sea, while the French starved in the impoverished countryside outside his fortified lines.

DRIVING BACK THE FRENCH

A harsh disciplinarian, Wellington worked his troops up into a fine fighting force. On the offensive, his marches were meticulously organized, with the fullest consideration given to maintaining supplies. He was cautious out of necessity, because until 1813 the French forces in the peninsula greatly outnumbered his own. He was always ready to concede ground to keep his army intact. But Wellington could be bold and aggressive at the right moment, as he demonstrated in his striking victory at Salamanca in July 1812. This was an improvised opportunist attack on a French army that was momentarily overextended, maneuvering around

Quatre-Bras 1815
Wellington once described his soldiers as "the scum of the earth," yet he placed his faith in the steady fire of British line infantry, as here in the clash at Quatre-Bras, two days before Waterloo.

the British flank. With a superior army in the campaigns of 1813–14, he kept up a relentless forward momentum until the French surrender.

Wellington was already a national hero when he faced Napoleon in person as commander-in-chief of British and Netherlands forces in Belgium in June 1815. Victory at Waterloo (pp. 210–11) ensured him a place among the greatest of generals.

Royal Fusiliers uniform
This uniform belonged to a Waterloo-era officer in the Royal Fusiliers. The bright red jackets worn by British soldiers of this period helped them to distinguish friend from foe on a battlefield filled with gunpowder smoke.

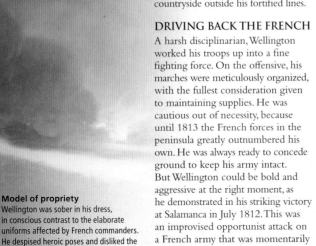

Model of propriety
Wellington was sober in his dress, in conscious contrast to the elaborate uniforms affected by French commanders. He despised heroic poses and disliked the vulgarity of popular acclaim.

WELLINGTON VS. NAPOLEON

IN JUNE 1815, A PRUSSIAN ARMY under General Blücher and a coalition force of British, Dutch, Belgian, and German soldiers under the Duke of Wellington were in Belgium, preparing for a joint invasion of France. Napoleon wrong-footed them by invading Belgium on June 15. Unsure of his opponent's plans, Wellington failed to join up with the Prussians and the two fought separate battles on June 16. Blücher was defeated by Napoleon at Ligny; Wellington fought Ney to a draw at Quatre-Bras. With the French rather tardily in pursuit, the Prussians fell back to Wavre, and Wellington retreated to the ridge of Mont St. Jean.

DUKE OF WELLINGTON

The Duke of Wellington planned to fight a defensive battle, reacting to Napoleon's moves. Only the arrival of General Blücher's Prussian forces would enable him to win.

Concealed from Napoleon's cannon, Wellington positioned the bulk of his troops on the reverse slope of the ridge of Mont St. Jean. He garrisoned the château of Hougoumont and the farm of La Haye Sainte, directly in front of his line. Another substantial division of 18,000 men was stationed at Halle, far to the right of the battlefield, to rebuff a possible French flanking move that, in the event, never came. At first, Wellington took up a vantage point by an elm tree, from where he issued a stream of scribbled orders, concentrating initially on the desperate defense of Hougoumont.

AN OBSCURED VIEW

As the French dispatched troops forward throughout the afternoon, Wellington had limited control of events on the smoke-obscured battlefield—a crucial charge by Scottish cavalry happened without his orders. He rode to wherever the fighting was heaviest, observing his infantry squares and steadying nerves with his presence. As his position threatened to crumble, he directed reserves to shore up weak points. Wellington did not take the offensive until the late evening, when the French had been broken by his troops' sturdy resistance and persistent musket fire.

> **I NEVER TOOK SO MUCH TROUBLE ABOUT ANY BATTLE, AND WAS NEVER SO NEAR BEING BEAT.**
> **DUKE OF WELLINGTON**, IN A LETTER TO HIS BROTHER RICHARD AFTER WATERLOO, JUNE 1815

Charge of the Scots Greys
The Scots Greys were among the British cavalry that repulsed the French attack in the early afternoon. They took part in a charge that Wellington had not ordered, leading to heavy casualties. The duke was not impressed.

TIMELINE

WELLINGTON

7 a.m. Wellington leaves for the battlefield and tours his army's positions throughout the morning. Blücher begins marching troops from Wavre toward Wellington

12 noon Wellington reinforces Hougoumont with artillery support and fresh troops. The château is held throughout the day without the diversion of major resources

British cavalry commander, the Earl of Uxbridge, leads a cavalry counterattack that routs the French infantry and cuirassiers

In a lull in the fighting, Wellington reinforces the farm at La Haye Sainte, in the center of his position

1815: JUNE 18

NAPOLEON

6 a.m. Napoleon holds a council of war with his generals over breakfast, rejecting the warning that the Prussians might march from Wavre to join Wellington

11:30 a.m. After a long delay waiting for rain-sodden ground to dry, Napoleon opens the battle. The French attack Hougoumont on Wellington's right

1 p.m. Napoleon sees the vanguard of the Prussians in the distance advancing from his right. He later orders a reserve corps to move to face them

1:30 p.m. Napoleon orders d'Erlon's corps to attack in the center. The French infantry almost break through but are checked by musket fire and field artillery

Napoleon orders a coun025charge by his cavalry reserves as Uxbridge's horsemen plunge forward into the French line. The British cavalry are driven back with heavy losses

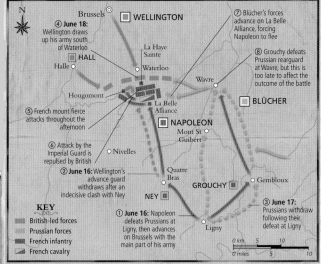

LOCATION
Outside Waterloo village, south of Brussels

DATE 18 June 1815

CAMPAIGN Napoleonic Wars

FORCES Anglo-Dutch: 67,000; Prussians: 53,000; French: 74,000

CASUALTIES Anglo-Dutch: 15,000 killed or wounded; Prussians: 7,000 killed or wounded; French: 25,000 killed or wounded

Map labels:
- ④ **June 18:** Wellington draws up his army south of Waterloo
- ⑦ Blücher's forces advance on La Belle Alliance, forcing Napoleon to flee
- ⑧ Grouchy defeats Prussian rearguard at Wavre, but this is too late to affect the outcome of the battle
- ⑤ French mount fierce attacks throughout the afternoon
- ⑥ Attack by the Imperial Guard is repulsed by British
- ② **June 16:** Wellington's advance guard withdraws after an indecisive clash with Ney
- ③ **June 17:** Prussians withdraw following their defeat at Ligny
- ① **June 16:** Napoleon defeats Prussians at Ligny, then advances on Brussels with the main part of his army

Place names: Brussels, WELLINGTON, La Haye Sainte, HALL, Halle, Waterloo, Wavre, Hougomont, La Belle Alliance, BLÜCHER, NAPOLEON, Mont St Guibert, Nivelles, Quatre Bras, GROUCHY, Gembloux, NEY, Ligny

KEY
- British-led forces
- Prussian forces
- French infantry
- French cavalry

0 km 5 10
0 miles 5 10

NAPOLEON BONAPARTE

Napoleon faced the battle with two misconceptions. He underestimated the fighting spirit of Wellington's army, and he believed that the Prussians would not march to join Wellington following their defeat two days earlier at the battle of Ligny. Marshal Grouchy, facing the Prussian forces at Wavre with 30,000 men, was given confusing orders that kept him immobile as Blücher sent three Prussian corps to attack Napoleon.

FRENCH TACTICS

Napoleon planned to open with a diversionary attack on the strongpoint of Hougoumont on Wellington's right, followed by a straightforward frontal assault on the allied center. This strategy would force Wellington's army west and Blücher's troops eastward. When Marshal Soult queried the wisdom of these tactics, Napoleon snapped that Wellington was "a bad general" and the British,

"bad troops," and that the battle would be "nothing more than eating one's breakfast."

The initial attack on Hougoumont did not go as planned. Ever increasing numbers of French troops were drawn in during the day in vain attempts to seize the stronghold. The frontal attack on Wellington's center was repulsed by infantry fire, as was a cavalry charge, though Napoleon was able to savage the British cavalry when they continued their charge too far.

CAVALRY ASSAULT

Throughout the afternoon, tactical control devolved from Napoleon at the inn of La Belle Alliance to Marshal Ney on the front line. Ney led a series of costly cavalry attacks that were unaided by infantry. Meanwhile, Napoleon had to divert forces to face the Prussians arriving to his right rear. Ney focused on capturing La Haye Sainte, which allowed him to move cannon forward to decimate British infantry squares at close range. Pressure from Blücher was mounting and Napoleon needed to finish off Wellington quickly. He sent his Imperial Guard into battle. When they were put to the flight by the duke's infantry, Napoleon had lost the day. He failed to organize a fighting withdrawal and his army was routed.

4:30 p.m. Wellington hears the sound of Prussian cannon fire as Blücher's troops fight the French for the village of Plancenoit, to the right rear of Napoleon's position

7 p.m. Wellington intervenes to steady his center as infantry come under raking fire from French cannon advanced in front of La Haye Sainte

Wellington orders the British guards to their feet to attack the Imperial Guard, already faltering in the face of concentrated fire

Wellington gives the signal for a general advance with a wave of his hat as the French abandon the field

9 p.m. Wellington meets Blücher at La Belle Alliance. They agree that the Prussians will mount the pursuit

4 p.m. Marshal Ney launches the first of a series of mass cavalry charges. Unsupported by infantry, they are repulsed by British infantry squares with heavy losses

6:30 p.m. Having at last abandoned his cavalry onslaught, Ney belatedly fulfills an order from Napoleon to capture La Haye Sainte from its courageous defenders

7:30 p.m. Napoleon leads his Imperial Guard to the front in a final bid to win the battle. Ney takes over to lead them into combat

Attacked by Wellington's troops and a Prussian corps that has joined Wellington's left, the Imperial Guard falls back and a rout begins

Napoleon flees to France, escaping capture at Genappe but failing to regain control of his troops for a fighting withdrawal

1680—1830

NAVAL WARFARE

"EVERY PERSON IN THE FLEET, WHO THROUGH COWARDICE, NEGLIGENCE, OR DISAFFECTION, SHALL, IN TIME OF ACTION, WITHDRAW OR KEEP BACK... OR SHALL NOT DO HIS UTMOST TO TAKE OR DESTROY EVERY SHIP WHICH IT SHALL BE HIS DUTY TO ENGAGE... SHALL SUFFER DEATH."

AMENDMENT TO THE ROYAL NAVY'S ARTICLES OF WAR GOVERNING THE CONDUCT OF OFFICERS, 1779

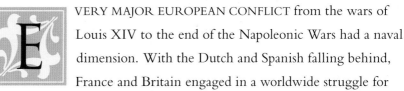

EVERY MAJOR EUROPEAN CONFLICT from the wars of Louis XIV to the end of the Napoleonic Wars had a naval dimension. With the Dutch and Spanish falling behind, France and Britain engaged in a worldwide struggle for control of the seas. The quality of naval commanders was crucial to the outcome of this contest, which was ultimately and decisively won by Britain's Royal Navy. Although their ships were not the biggest or the best, British seamanship and aggression were unmatched.

Britain's naval officers traditionally started their seagoing careers as midshipmen (probationary officers) aged 12 to 14 years old. As a result, they were poorly educated in all matters not relating to the sea, but developed an excellent practical knowledge of sailing, gunnery, winds, and tides. Although promotion depended largely on patronage and seniority, men of real talent were able to rise to the top on merit. British commanders were under orders to fight aggressively at all times—Admiral John Byng was shot for failing to do so in 1757.

In France, the system was quite different. Senior naval commanders were often army officers who had exchanged fighting on land for a life at sea. Those who sought a naval officer's career from youth received a formal education far superior to their British counterparts, but gained much less practical experience.

SHIPS OF THE LINE

Large, robust sailing ships, known as ships of the line, were constructed to carry heavy cannon and fire broadsides of solid shot. Sometimes, they would also close in to grapple and board: a grappling iron was thrown across to secure a ship for the attacking side to board safely. Fleets entered combat in line, in three squadrons, with the senior admiral commanding the middle squadron and subordinate admirals in command of the van (the leading ships) and rear. This arrangement was intended to allow a degree of coherent instruction and control. Orders were transmitted by flag signals, for which elaborate codes were developed, or by sending messengers from ship to ship in small boats. Senior commanders, standing on deck, inevitably found themselves in the thick of fierce fighting. There was no equivalent to a distant hilltop from which a general might direct a land battle.

THWARTING INVASION

In successive wars, one of the British navy's most important tasks was to ensure that the French could not ship an army across the Channel. Edward Hawke's victory over a French fleet at Quiberon Bay in 1759 and Horatio Nelson's defeat of the French and Spanish at Trafalgar in 1805 were both responses to invasion threats.

The Royal Navy was also tasked with protecting Britain's trade routes and capturing or defending colonies. France's single decisive naval victory of this period was at Chesapeake Bay in 1781, when the Comte de Grasse determined the outcome of the American Revolutionary War. His defeat of the British at sea enabled Washington to beat them on land at Yorktown. Despite losing its North American colonies, by 1815 Britain had gained a naval supremacy that made it the world's dominant imperial and trading power.

Britain victorious
A ship of the line, *Santo Domingo*, blows up as British admiral George Rodney savages a Spanish squadron off Cape St. Vincent in 1780. Spain had a poor record in naval combat in this period.

1660—1850

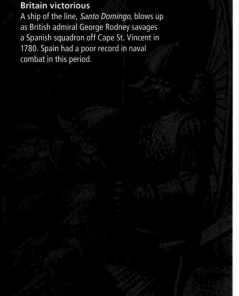

18th-century sextant
Naval commanders benefited from new navigational instruments, such as this English-made sextant. It was a major improvement on the astrolabe as an instrument for measuring the angle of the Sun.

18TH-CENTURY ADMIRALS

ALTHOUGH 18TH-CENTURY naval warfare evolved around ships fighting in formal lines of battle, many admirals practiced bolder tactics, prefiguring the aggressive style of the British admiral, Horatio Nelson. Edward Hawke's victory at Quiberon Bay in 1759 was an extraordinary example of risk-taking unorthodoxy, and Nelson's favorite tactic of breaking the line—cutting through the enemy line of battle instead of sailing parallel to it—was pioneered in George Rodney's victory at the Saints in 1782. French admirals were less likely to fight fleet engagements with attacking flair, but Pierre André de Suffren proved a notable exception.

KEY BATTLE
QUIBERON BAY

CAMPAIGN Seven Years War
DATE November 20, 1759
LOCATION Brittany, France

Edward Hawke was blockading the French fleet in Brest. Driven off station by bad weather he allowed the French to slip out, but then pursued them to Quiberon Bay. In a howling gale and treacherous seas, Hawke mounted a general chase into the bay and brought his enemy to battle, destroying those that failed to flee.

EDWARD HAWKE

BRITISH ADMIRAL
BORN February 21, 1705
DIED October 16, 1781
KEY CONFLICTS War of the Austrian Succession, Seven Years' War
KEY BATTLES Cape Finisterre 1747, Quiberon Bay 1759

The son of a lawyer, Edward Hawke joined the Royal Navy at the age of 15 in 1720. He saw his first action in 1744, distinguishing himself by his aggression in an otherwise timid British performance against the French and Spanish at Toulon.

THE GENERAL CHASE
Given command of the Western Squadron blockading France's Atlantic coast, in October 1747, he ambushed a French convoy in the mid-Atlantic, 300 miles (500 km) west of Cape Finisterre, capturing six ships of the line serving as escorts.

This bold action displayed Hawke's favorite method of operation, the "general chase," in which his ships pursued the enemy as fast as they could without reference to their position in the fleet's line of battle.

Hawke also insisted that his captains engage the enemy at close quarters, firing only once within pistol shot. These tactics proved devastating in the battle of Quiberon Bay, making Hawke a national hero. He had risen to be First Lord of the Admiralty by his retirement in 1771.

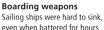

Boarding weapons
Sailing ships were hard to sink, even when battered for hours by cannon fire, so engagements frequently ended with an assault by a boarding party armed with cutlasses and axes.

GEORGE RODNEY

BRITISH ADMIRAL
BORN February 13, 1719
DIED May 24, 1792
KEY CONFLICTS Seven Years' War, American Revolutionary War
KEY BATTLES Cape St. Vincent 1780, The Saints 1782

George Rodney joined the navy at the age of 13 and first saw action as a captain in Hawke's famous attack on the French convoy off Cape Finisterre in 1747. For three decades, his career followed a path that was distinguished but unspectacular, its high point being the capture of the French colony Martinique in 1762. In the 1770s, he went bankrupt and moved to Paris to escape his creditors. When France and then Spain went to war with the British in 1778, he returned to command, paying his debts with money provided by a French aristocrat. In January 1780, Rodney came upon a weak Spanish squadron off Cape St. Vincent and launched a general chase that he carried through to the destruction of the Spanish ships.

BATTLE OF THE SAINTS
Rodney's greatest triumph followed in the West Indies in April 1782, when he met a French fleet commanded by the Comte de Grasse, victor over the British at Chesapeake Bay. Five French ships were taken and de Grasse made prisoner. It is not clear if Rodney intended the breaking of the French line for which the battle is famous, and he was criticized for his failure to pursue the defeated enemy, but it was a striking victory and he retired heaped with honors.

Senior admiral
Rodney was aging and in poor health by the 1780s, when he achieved his famous victories at Cape St. Vincent and the Saints.

> " WITHIN TWO LITTLE YEARS I HAVE TAKEN TWO SPANISH, ONE FRENCH, AND ONE DUTCH ADMIRALS. "

ADMIRAL GEORGE RODNEY, WRITING IN 1782

JOHN JERVIS

BRITISH ADMIRAL
BORN January 9, 1735
DIED March 14, 1823
KEY CONFLICTS American Revolutionary War, French Revolutionary Wars
KEY BATTLE Cape St. Vincent 1797

Intended by his family for the law, 13-year-old John Jervis ran away to sea. He saw action in the American Revolutionary War, but did not exercise high command until the French Revolutionary Wars. After leading an expedition to the West Indies, in 1795, he assumed command of the Mediterranean fleet, whose captains included Horatio Nelson.

On February 14, 1797, patrolling off Cape St. Vincent with 15 ships of the line, Jervis sighted a fleet of 27 Spanish ships. Undaunted by the disparity of numbers, he attacked.

A complex set of maneuvers broke up the Spanish formation and it was savaged as the battle turned into a melee. Occurring at a low point in Britain's fortunes, the victory was greeted with enthusiasm and Jervis was ennobled as Earl of St. Vincent.

THE CHANNEL FLEET

At a time of widespread mutiny in the Royal Navy, Jervis maintained order in his fleet through strict discipline, and was as tough with his officers as his men. In 1799, he took command of the Channel fleet, which he reformed with the same bracing discipline, instituting a close blockade of the French coast that was a remarkable feat of seamanship and logistical organization. He was a vigorous but controversial First Lord of the Admiralty from 1801 to 1804.

Harsh measures
Determined to improve the morale and efficiency of the British navy, Jervis did not hesitate to hand out severe punishments. His insistence on hanging two mutineers on a Sunday caused protests.

PIERRE ANDRÉ DE SUFFREN

FRENCH ADMIRAL
BORN July 17, 1729
DIED December 8, 1788
KEY CONFLICTS War of the Austrian Succession, Seven Years' War, American Revolutionary War
KEY BATTLES Providien 1782, Trincomalee 1782, Cuddalore 1783

The son of a Provençal nobleman, Pierre André de Suffren joined the French naval officer corps as a cadet in 1743. He was captured by the British at Cape Finisterre in 1747 and subsequently served with the Maltese galleys of the Knights of St. John—a common peacetime occupation for French naval officers. The Seven Years' War brought him back to fighting the British, and he was again taken prisoner, this time at the battle of Lagos in 1759. These experiences left

Lone tactician
Probably France's most gifted admiral, de Suffren never had a chance to show his abilities to the full. His belief in aggressive tactics was not shared by most French officers.

him with a conviction that French commanders needed to match the aggression of British naval tactics. Independent command came in 1781, when he led a squadron from Brest to the Indian Ocean during the American Revolutionary War.

TROOP ESCORT

In February 1782, he took command of a fleet escorting troops to French colonial outposts in India. There he encountered a British fleet under Sir Edward Hughes, against whom he fought several sharp actions. These included the battles of Providien, Trincomalee, and Cuddalore, before peace was declared in April 1783.

In these battles, de Suffren showed consistent daring and aggression, but many of his captains lacked the desire to engage in a close-quarters exchange of broadsides with enemy ships. As a result, the battles were all indecisive, but they sufficed to make de Suffren's reputation. He had been appointed Vice-Admiral of France when sudden death cut short his career.

TIMELINE

■ **1771** Nelson joins the Royal Navy at the age of 12, serving as a midshipman on the warship HMS *Raisonnable*, commanded by his uncle, Maurice Suckling.

■ **June 1779** At the age of 20, Nelson is promoted to the rank of post-captain. Reporting for active service, he becomes the youngest captain in the Royal Navy.

■ **1780** After taking part in a military expedition up the San Juan River in central America, Nelson becomes seriously ill and almost dies of fever.

■ **January 1793** After five years on shore, Nelson is given command of a ship of the line in time for the outbreak of war with Revolutionary France in February.

■ **July 12, 1794** On land, while organizing the siege of Calvi in Corsica, Nelson is wounded. He suffers irreparable damage to his right eye, losing the sight in it.

■ **April 1796** Sir John Jervis, commander-in-chief of the Mediterranean fleet, gives Nelson independent command of a squadron as a commodore.

■ **February 14, 1797** Nelson's bold performance under Jervis while fighting the Spanish at the battle of Cape St. Vincent wins him public renown. He is made Rear Admiral.

■ **July 24, 1797** Leading a night attack on the Spanish port of Santa Cruz de Tenerife, Nelson loses his right arm after being struck by a musket ball.

■ **August 1–2, 1798** At the battle of the Nile (Aboukir Bay), Nelson's squadron captures or destroys 13 French ships. He becomes Britain's most celebrated naval hero.

■ **September 1798–July 1800** Nelson spends most of his time at Naples and Palermo with Lady Emma Hamilton, and backs the savage suppression of a revolutionary movement.

■ **April 2, 1801** After returning to Britain, Nelson carries through a successful attack on the Danish capital, Copenhagen.

CANNONBALL FIRED FROM A SPANISH SHIP INTO THE *VICTORY* AT TRAFALGAR

■ **July 1803** On board his flagship HMS *Victory*, Nelson arrives off the coast of Toulon to take command of the Royal Navy's fleet in the Mediterranean.

■ **October 21, 1805** At the battle of Trafalgar, Nelson trounces the combined French and Spanish fleets, but dies after being shot by a sniper from the *Redoutable*.

HORATIO NELSON

BRITISH ADMIRAL
BORN September 29, 1758
DIED October 21, 1805
KEY CONFLICTS French Revolutionary Wars, Napoleonic Wars
KEY BATTLES Cape St. Vincent 1797, Nile 1798, Copenhagen 1801, Trafalgar 1805

The son of a Norfolk clergyman, Horatio Nelson joined the Royal Navy as a boy and had sailed to the West Indies, America, India, and the Arctic by the time he was 18. He had a stroke of fortune when his uncle, Maurice Suckling, was appointed controller of the navy in 1776. With this influence behind him, plus an evident competence at his job, Nelson was able to progress rapidly to the coveted rank of post-captain, beyond which level promotion in the Royal Navy was conferred inexorably by seniority. His career up to the outbreak of war with Revolutionary France in 1793 was respectable but average. The war presented a chance for advancement and glory.

Serving with the Mediterranean fleet, Nelson's aggression and eagerness for action won him favorable notice from his commanders-in-chief, first Lord Hood and then John Jervis. His spectacular rise to public celebrity, however, only began with the battle of Cape St. Vincent in February 1797.

SPANISH SURRENDER

Nelson was a late addition to Jervis's squadron of 15 ships of the line that intercepted 27 Spanish ships of the line off the coast of Portugal. Despite their superior numbers, the Spanish were eager to escape engagement and run for port. Commanding the 74-gun HMS *Captain* near the rear of Jervis's line of battle, Nelson broke away from the formation and engaged the enemy on his own, preventing their flight. Even though *Captain* was badly damaged before other British ships came to its support, Nelson succeeded in boarding and accepting the surrender of two large Spanish vessels, *San Nicolas* and *San José*, which had collided in the confusion.

Although leaving position in the line of battle was most unusual, the initiative that Nelson had shown was fully within the Royal Navy tradition and certainly approved by Jervis. But

Indomitable spirit
Nelson was a physically frail individual by 1801, when this portrait was painted. Although a vain man, he was not haughty—his warmth, courage, and generosity of spirit won the affection of his officers and men.

KEY BATTLE

COPENHAGEN

CAMPAIGN Napoleonic Wars
DATE April 2, 1801
LOCATION Copenhagen, Denmark

A fleet under Admiral Sir Hyde Parker, with Nelson as second-in-command, was sent to pressure Denmark into abandoning an anti-British stance. With 12 ships of the line, Nelson sailed into treacherous shallow waters off Copenhagen under the fire of shore guns and engaged a Danish fleet at anchor. As the British were bombarded, Parker signaled for Nelson to withdraw. But Nelson ignored him, crushing the Danish fleet and forcing the Danes to negotiate by threatening to bombard the city.

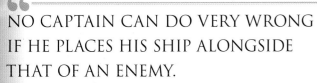

> ## NO CAPTAIN CAN DO VERY WRONG IF HE PLACES HIS SHIP ALONGSIDE THAT OF AN ENEMY.
>
> **HORATIO NELSON**, IN HIS INSTRUCTIONS TO HIS CAPTAINS, OCTOBER 9, 1805

Nelson's subsequent behavior in publicizing his own role in the battle and claiming more credit than was his due did not endear him to others. Self-advertisement was one of several failings that began to feature as a counterpoint to the heroic virtues he so amply exhibited.

ATTACKING POSTURE

Nelson's triumph over the French at the battle of the Nile in Aboukir Bay in 1798 (pp. 218–19) made him the most celebrated man in Britain. It exemplified the distinctive character of his leadership and tactics. As the commander of a squadron he had made the captains of the ships serving under him into a "band of brothers." Bonded with their leader and fully versed in his way of fighting, they could be trusted to use their initiative in implementing his broad tactical concepts. Nelson's preference was always for attack, seeking to create a "pell-mell" battle—a great scrimmage in which enemy ships would lose formation and be destroyed by superior British gunnery at close range. He sought local superiority in numbers through concentrating all his force on one part of the enemy line while the rest was left out of the fight, to be dealt with later. His goal was simple: the complete destruction of the enemy fleet. He achieved this so successfully at Aboukir Bay that his reputation largely survived the subsequent scandals: his affair with Lady Hamilton and his commitment to the royal court of Naples, which led him to be complicit in the massacre of opponents of that repressive regime and to disobey orders to rejoin the Mediterranean fleet, instead returning to England by land with Lady Hamilton.

CONFIDENCE IN BATTLE

Nelson's readiness to take risks, as shown at Aboukir Bay, was repeated at Copenhagen in 1801. These were operations that could easily have gone badly awry. The same was true of his climactic battle at Trafalgar in 1805. Nelson was determined to engage and destroy the combined French and Spanish fleet when it sailed out of Cádiz, even though he had inferior strength—27 ships of the line to 33—and knew that a defeat would be disastrous for Britain. Nelson's plan was for an attack in two squadrons, each to approach at right angles to the Franco-Spanish line and cross it at different points, engaging the enemy center and rear and leaving the vanguard initially cut out of the battle. He led one squadron from HMS *Victory*, hoisting the famous signal "England expects that every man will do his duty." Nelson seems to have entered the fray with a death wish, exposing himself so blatantly to fire that his survival would have been surprising. It was a tribute to his delegating style of leadership that the battle continued to a successful conclusion after his death. He was deservedly accorded a magnificent state funeral.

Adulterous liaison
Emma Hamilton, painted here by George Romney, was the wife of the British ambassador to Naples when she became Nelson's mistress.

Death at Trafalgar
Standing on the quarter deck of HMS *Victory*, Nelson was shot by a soldier in the rigging of the French ship *Redoutable*. He was carried below, where he died three hours later.

1660—1850

NELSON AT THE NILE

LOCATION
Aboukir Bay, near
Alexandria, Egypt
CAMPAIGN French
Revolutionary Wars

DATE August 1–2, 1798
FORCES British: 14 ships of the line; French:
13 ships of the line, four frigates
CASUALTIES British: 900 killed or wounded,
no ships lost; French: 2,000–5,000 killed
or wounded, 11 ships of the line and two
frigates lost

Rear Admiral Horatio Nelson, commanding a squadron of 14 ships, had been searching for the Egypt-bound French fleet since May 1798. But Napoleon's army had eluded him and landed at Aboukir Bay in July. It was here, on the afternoon of August 1, that Nelson discovered Napoleon's naval escort anchored in line. Although outgunned by the French ships and unsure of the sailing channels in the sandy bay, Nelson ordered an immediate attack.

Nelson's intention was known: to attack the van and center of the enemy line, which he had planned to defeat while an adverse wind kept the ships of the enemy rear from joining the battle. Beyond this, he trusted his captains to use their initiative, in accord with his preference for engaging the enemy at close quarters with unsparing aggression. He ordered his ships to fit lights that would identify them after nightfall.

They also prepared anchors to hold them for broadside fire against the stationary enemy. As Nelson's captains raced one another for the privilege of entering the bay first, his chief concerns were to keep the squadron in reasonably tight formation and avoid ships running aground. Soundings were taken to measure the water's depth, thus identifying a safe channel into the bay.

CAUGHT UNAWARES

The French admiral, François-Paul Brueys, was fatally surprised by Nelson's decision to attack so late in the day. His decks were still not cleared for battle when the first British ship, Captain Thomas Foley's

Goliath, arrived. On his own initiative, Foley sailed around the French van and anchored in the shallow waters between the port side of Brueys' line and the shore. He was followed in this wholly unexpected, hazardous maneuver by four of his colleagues. The five 74-gun ships of the French van found themselves under fire from opposite sides as other British ships, including Nelson's *Vanguard*, drew up to starboard. The fighting was savage, but as darkness fell the French van was blasted into submission.

Nelson himself was a casualty in this phase of the fighting, struck on the forehead by a projectile and temporarily blinded. Examined by

a surgeon, he was found to have only a superficial wound. Ignoring advice to remain below, he went on deck to witness the climax of the battle.

BATTLE IN THE DARK

In the French center, the vast 120-gun flagship *L'Orient* had dueled with the British 74-gun *Bellerophon* under Captain Henry Darby. Badly damaged, *Bellerophon* withdrew, but only after inflicting heavy casualties—including Brueys, blasted in half by a cannonball.

The rearmost British ships belatedly joined the fight, guiding themselves toward the action by the gun flashes in the darkness, and attacked *L'Orient*. At around 10 p.m. the French flagship caught fire, its powder magazine exploding. The remainder of the battle was in effect a mopping-up operation. The next morning, Villeneuve, in charge of the passive French rear, slipped away with two ships of the line and two frigates, the only French vessels to escape the debacle.

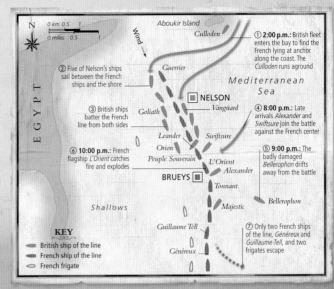

0 km 0.5   1
0 miles 0.5   1

N

Wind

EGYPT

Aboukir Island

Culloden

Mediterranean Sea

① **2:00 p.m.:** British fleet enters the bay to find the French lying at anchor along the coast. The *Culloden* runs aground

② Five of Nelson's ships sail between the French ships and the shore

Guerrier

③ British ships batter the French line from both sides

■ NELSON

Goliath

Vanguard

④ **8:00 p.m.:** Late arrivals *Alexander* and *Swiftsure* join the battle against the French center

Leander

Swiftsure

Orion

⑥ **10:00 p.m.:** French flagship *L'Orient* catches fire and explodes

Peuple Souverain

L'Orient

Alexander

⑤ **9:00 p.m.:** The badly damaged *Bellerophon* drifts away from the battle

BRUEYS ■

Tonnant

Bellerophon

Majestic

Shallows

KEY

Guillaume Tell

⑦ Only two French ships of the line, *Généreux* and *Guillaume Tell*, and two frigates escape

━ British ship of the line
━ French ship of the line
◦ French frigate

Généreux

Fire at night
In the confusion of a swiftly initiated battle fought partly at night, Nelson relied on the initiative of subordinates who had absorbed his tactical doctrine.

1790—1850

WAR IN THE AMERICAS

―❧

" WITHIN THE NARROW COMPASS OF A FEW HUNDRED YARDS,
WERE GATHERED TOGETHER NEARLY A THOUSAND BODIES, ALL
OF THEM ARRAYED IN BRITISH UNIFORMS... AN AMERICAN
OFFICER STOOD BY SMOKING A CIGAR, AND APPARENTLY
COUNTING THE SLAIN WITH A LOOK OF SAVAGE EXULTATION... "

BRITISH INFANTRY CAPTAIN GEORGE GLEIG, ON THE AFTERMATH OF THE BATTLE OF NEW ORLEANS, 1815

URING THE FIRST HALF of the 19th century, a rash of wars occurred in the Americas that had important, long-term historical significance in shaping the future of the continent. The irregular nature of the warfare gave individuals of a bold temperament, such as Simón Bolívar and Andrew Jackson, plenty of opportunities to carve out reputations as military commanders at the head of ad hoc forces. Although conflicts were small-scale by European or Asian standards, they were, nonetheless, hotly contested.

The leaders of armed struggles in the Caribbean and Latin America were inspired by principles of freedom enunciated in the American and French Revolutions. In Haiti, former slave Toussaint l'Ouverture mounted guerrilla campaigns against the French and the British, creating the first black-ruled state. In South America, a series of campaigns for independence from Spanish rule were fought between 1810 and 1824. These complex, many-sided conflicts gave direction and purpose to inspired commanders such as Simón Bolívar and the Argentinian José de San Martín. However, the establishment of statehood under the leadership of strong military personalities was, in the long run, unfortunate. Throughout the 19th century, Latin American countries proved vulnerable to seizures of power by warlords and prone to costly territorial wars over disputed borders.

CONFLICT WITH BRITAIN
In the early 19th century, the United States was torn between an instinctive antimilitarism—hostile even to the maintenance of a standing army—and the aggressive tendencies of a dynamic, proud, expansionist young country. In 1812, President James Madison declared war on Britain, partly in reaction to high-handed British conduct toward American shipping, but also with designs on seizing control of Canada. Lasting until 1815, the War of 1812 was seen by many Americans as "a second war of independence" and provided them with many episodes of heroism to celebrate: from the triumphs of American frigates over British warships to the renowned defense of New Orleans at the conflict's end. This period was known as the Era of

Good Feelings for its prevailing sense of political unity. Americans were reluctant to acknowledge how often the war, a mere sideshow to the British people, had gone against them.

Two of the heroes of the War of 1812, Andrew Jackson and William Harrison, went on to be United States presidents. And Winfield Scott, another general who had established his reputation during the conflict, was still exercising his command at the advent of the Civil War in 1861.

WINNING REPUTATIONS
In truth, 19th-century America neither needed nor wanted to sustain armed forces on the scale of the European powers. Wars with Native Americans and Mexicans provided an outlet for belligerence that required no great investment of money or manpower. From Harrison's victory over the Indian leader Tecumseh at Tippecanoe in 1811 to Zachary Taylor's defeat of the Seminole at Lake Okeechobee in 1837, American generals won nationwide reputations in backwoods clashes. These engagements with Native Americans were comparatively small—involving hundreds, rather than thousands, of troops.

The Texas War of Independence (1835–36), including the famous siege of the Alamo, was fought on a similar scale, but the Mexican-American War of 1846–48 demanded much larger forces. By now, senior officers' posts had come to be dominated by graduates from the military academy set up at West Point in 1802, bringing a new professionalism to the US Army. The campaigns in Mexico provided combat experience for a generation of American officers who would later win fame in the Civil War.

British raiders
The American frigate *Chesapeake* was boarded by the crew of HMS *Shannon* outside the port of Boston in a fierce naval encounter during the War of 1812. Here, British Captain Philip Broke takes on four American sailors.

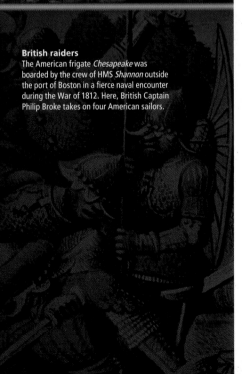

Congreve rocket
The British used Congreve rockets to bombard Baltimore in 1814 and they are immortalized in the US national anthem: "the rockets' red glare…"

1660—1850

REBELS IN THE AMERICAS

EVENTS IN EUROPE from the French Revolution of 1789 to the end of the Napoleonic Wars in 1815 destabilized European colonies in the New World, both by spreading ideas of freedom and equality and by temporarily weakening the colonial powers. Saint-Domingue, a French possession in the West Indies, won its independence as Haiti in 1804 after prolonged warfare. Spain lost effective control of its South American colonies while occupied with the Peninsular War from 1808 to 1815, but a series of complex and dramatic military campaigns had to be fought before the shape of a post-colonial, independent South America emerged.

TOUSSAINT L'OUVERTURE

HAITIAN REVOLUTIONARY
BORN May 20, 1743
DIED April 8, 1803
KEY CONFLICT Haitian Revolution
KEY BATTLES Guerrilla warfare

Born on Saint-Domingue (now Haiti), Toussaint L'ouverture was a freed plantation slave who emerged as a skilled leader of guerrilla forces amid the chaos that descended on the colony after the French Revolution. He created a well-trained force consisting chiefly of black slaves fighting for their freedom. In a fast-changing political and military arena, he fought for the Spanish, invading the colony from neighboring Santo-Domingo (the Dominican Republic), and then for the French revolutionary government, which made him a brigadier-general in 1794. He opposed various rival rebel groups in Saint-Domingue, as well as the French, Spanish, and British armies. Britain sent some 10,000 men to invade Saint-Domingue

Distinguished leader
A well-read and intelligent man, Toussaint organized and disciplined his forces in the formal European style, while also employing guerrilla tactics.

but, largely owing to Toussaint's grasp of strategy and tactics, they were restricted to ever-narrower zones of occupation and driven out in 1798.

THE FRENCH RETURN
Toussaint had effective control of Saint-Domingue by 1800, and of Santo-Domingo in 1801. Sadly, this high point of his fortunes was brief. Napoleon had taken power in France and sent General Charles Leclerc with a substantial army to regain control of the colony. In 1802, Leclerc seized Toussaint and deported him to France, where he died in prison.

JOSÉ DE SAN MARTÍN

SOUTH AMERICAN INDEPENDENCE LEADER
BORN February 25, 1778
DIED August 17, 1850
KEY CONFLICT South American Wars of Liberation
KEY BATTLES San Lorenzo 1813, Chacabuco 1817, Maipú 1818

Born in Argentina, San Martín was raised in Spain and served as an army officer, fighting the French in the Peninsular War. Returning to South America in 1812, he aided Argentinian officers asserting independence against Spanish royalists. He founded a regiment of mounted grenadiers that won a skirmish at San Lorenzo in 1813 and repulsed a royalist invasion in northern Argentina the following year. In January 1817, with exiled Chilean rebel Bernardo O'Higgins, he marched a 5,000-strong army over the high Andes into Chile to defeat the royalists at Chacabuco. Chilean independence was confirmed by a subsequent victory at Maipú. San Martín went on to take control of Peru in 1821, but had withdrawn to private life within a year.

Leading the charge
The gallant San Martín leads a decisive charge by his mounted grenadiers to win a victory at Chacabuco in Chile on February 12, 1817.

 ANTONIO JOSÉ DE SUCRE

SOUTH AMERICAN INDEPENDENCE LEADER
BORN February 3, 1795
DIED June 4, 1830
KEY CONFLICT South American Wars of Liberation
KEY BATTLES Boyacá 1819, Pichincha 1822, Ayacucho 1824

Antonio José de Sucre was born in Venezuela and joined the struggle for independence at the age of 19. After the battle of Boyacá, he was made Bolívar's chief-of-staff and, in 1821, received his first independent command, leading the army in a campaign to liberate Quito.

A close-run victory over the royalists on the slopes of the Pichincha volcano in May 1822 confirmed his growing military reputation and gave Bolívar control of Ecuador. To achieve independence required the defeat of the Spanish Viceroy, José de la Serna, who still controlled part of Peru. In 1824, Sucre confronted de la Serna in the Andean mountains at Ayacucho. The viceroy had command of some 10,000 troops and substantial artillery, but Sucre, with 6,000 lightly armed volunteers, attacked with spirit and carried the day. De la Serna was imprisoned and the surrender terms ended the Spanish presence in South America.

BRUTAL END
President of newly independent Bolivia, Sucre was never comfortable amid the savage power struggles that followed the liberation wars. He had probably decided to withdraw from politics when he was assassinated in June 1830.

Exemplary leader
Sucre inspired his subordinates by his integrity and selflessness. His murder in 1830 has never been fully explained.

KEY BATTLE

BOYACÁ

CAMPAIGN Independence War in New Granada
DATE August 7, 1819
LOCATION Boyacá, Colombia

In 1819, Simón Bolívar invaded Spanish-held New Granada from Venezuela. He achieved strategic surprise by attacking in the rainy season, leading a 3,000-strong army through malarial swamps and across Andean passes to emerge in front of the capital, Bogotá, in July. His forces won a number of minor clashes before encountering the main Spanish and royalist army under José Maria Barreiro at the Boyacá River. Bolívar attacked with his British Legion in the vanguard, veterans of the Napoleonic Wars. While these experienced infantrymen bore the brunt of the fighting, light cavalry harassed the Spanish rear. With just 66 casualties, Bolívar captured 1,600 enemy soldiers, including their commander, and entered Bogotá in triumph.

SIMÓN BOLÍVAR

SOUTH AMERICAN INDEPENDENCE LEADER
BORN July 24, 1783
DIED December 17, 1830
KEY CONFLICT South American Wars of Liberation
KEY BATTLES Boyacá 1819, Carabobo 1821, Junin 1824

Simón Bolívar was born into a wealthy Venezuelan family in Caracas. In 1811, he fought in defense of a newly declared Venezuelan republic, but was forced into exile by a pro-Spanish royalist reaction. Based in neighboring New Granada, he launched an invasion of Venezuela in February 1813, sweeping aside the royalist forces to enter Caracas in August and install himself at the head of a military government. Lacking popular support, however, he was driven out again the following year by an army of pro-royalist *llaneros*, mounted bandits of the Venezuelan plains. The arrival of a powerful expeditionary force from Spain completed his discomfiture by occupying New Granada. Bolívar

> ## I HAVE BEEN CHOSEN BY FATE TO BREAK YOUR CHAINS... FIGHT AND YOU SHALL WIN.
>
> **SIMÓN BOLÍVAR**, IN A LETTER FROM JAMAICA, 1815

had to rebuild from scratch. Based in the Venezuelan outback, he allied with the previously hostile *llaneros*. He also recruited a legion of battle-hardened British and Irish volunteers.

RETURN TO VENEZUELA

In 1819, Bolívar led his army on a march across reputedly impassable terrain into New Granada, routing the Spanish at Boyacá. In 1821, he returned to Venezuela at the head of an army of 7,000, scoring a decisive victory at Carabobo in June. Now in possession of Colombia and Venezuela, Bolívar moved on to campaigns in Ecuador and Peru.

His second-in-command, Sucre, was responsible for most of the fighting, although Bolívar commanded in person at the cavalry battle of Junin in August 1824. Bolívar aspired to unite a large area of South America under his personal rule, but the continent was already disintegrating into warring states when he died, at the age of 47.

Victory at Carabobo
Bolívar (on the white horse) hands a captured Spanish flag to one of his victorious commanders after the battle of Carabobo in June 1821. This hard-fought success owed much to the fighting skills of British and Irish volunteers.

US COMMANDERS 1800–1850

IN WARS AGAINST the British in 1812–15, against various Native American groups, and against the Mexicans in 1846–47, a number of US generals achieved the status of national hero. Some were identified with the frontier style of irregular warfare, disdaining formal military training and hierarchies; others studied the tactics and organization of European armies, aspiring to imitate their standards of drill, discipline, and staff work. On the whole, the American people preferred the idea of the victory of backwoodsmen over uniformed regulars, which was exemplified at New Orleans in 1815. But they would applaud any general who brought them victories.

ANDREW JACKSON

AMERICAN MILITARY LEADER, POLITICIAN, AND PRESIDENT
BORN March 15, 1767
DIED June 8, 1845
KEY CONFLICTS Creek War, War of 1812, Seminole War
KEY BATTLES Horseshoe Bend 1814, New Orleans 1815

Andrew Jackson was born in the Carolinas to a Presbyterian family who had emigrated from Ulster, in Ireland. A tall, thin, hot-tempered individual with deep reserves of anger, Jackson was a fighter from childhood. At the age of 13, he joined the militia in the Revolutionary War against Britain. Taken prisoner, he suffered indignities and hardships that bred an undying hatred of the British.

After the war ended, Jackson headed west to Tennessee, where he made a fortune in land speculation and earned a fearsome reputation as a man who fought duels to the death. Appointed major-general in command of the Tennessee militia, in 1812, he was sent to fight Creek warriors who were attacking frontier settlements while

America was distracted by the war with Britain. Jackson brought a manic energy and fierce determination to the task, holding together his motley army of short-term volunteers and militiamen by threatening to kill any man who tried to go home. The climax came in March 1814, when Jackson attacked Creeks holding a fortified camp at Horseshoe Bend in Alabama. After a stiff fight, the majority of the 1,000 Creeks were killed. Jackson then moved on to organize the successful defense of New Orleans, threatened by a British landing from the sea.

JACKSON FOR PRESIDENT

Jackson's victory at New Orleans, in January 1815, made him the most popular man in the United States. He went on to become US president, serving from 1829 to 1837.

KEY BATTLE

NEW ORLEANS

CAMPAIGN War of 1812
DATE January 8, 1815
LOCATION New Orleans, Louisiana

To defend New Orleans against a British attack, Andrew Jackson built a breastwork behind a ditch between the Mississippi River and a swamp. He defended this with around 4,000 men—assorted militia, volunteers, Native Americans, free blacks, and pirates—armed with muskets, rifles, and cannon. About 9,000 British troops under Edward Pakenham advanced at dawn. A flanking movement on the opposite bank of the river was delayed, so the frontal assault on Jackson's defensive line went in unsupported. Pakenham was killed and 2,000 of his men left dead or wounded as American fire drove them into flight.

Old Hickory
Jackson, who was nicknamed after the tough hickory tree, had no military training, but was a natural fighter and leader. He was one of those rare commanders who frightened his own men more than the enemy did.

ZACHARY TAYLOR

AMERICAN GENERAL AND PRESIDENT
BORN November 24, 1784
DIED July 9, 1850
KEY CONFLICTS War of 1812, Black Hawk War, Seminole War, Mexican-American War
KEY BATTLES Fort Harrison 1812, Palo Alto 1846, Monterrey 1846, Buena Vista 1847

Born into a prominent Virginia family but raised in Kentucky, Zachary Taylor joined the US Army in 1807. A career soldier, he first distinguished himself as a captain in the defense of Fort Harrison against Shawnee leader Tecumseh in 1812. In later conflicts with Native Americans—the Black Hawk War in 1832 and the Seminole War later in the 1830s—he proved a decisive military commander, but also humane and honorable in his dealings with defeated Indians. His victory over the Seminole at Lake Okeechobee in 1837 brought him promotion to brigadier-general.

> ## IT WOULD BE JUDICIOUS TO ACT WITH MAGNANIMITY TOWARD A PROSTRATE FOE.
>
> **ZACHARY TAYLOR**

Taylor became a well-known officer with a distinctive style—his disdain for formality and "spit and polish" earned him the nickname "Rough and Ready." But it was the outbreak of war with Mexico that made him famous. In January 1846, President James Polk ordered him to lead troops south to the Rio Grande, an act of provocation to which Mexico reacted with force. Fighting against heavy odds, Taylor defeated the Mexicans at Palo Alto in May, principally through aggressive use of mobile field artillery.

DEFYING THE PRESIDENT

In September, Taylor took Monterrey by assault, agreeing to an armistice with the defenders to limit the bloodshed. This agreement outraged Polk, who took the best of Taylor's troops away for an invasion of Veracruz. But Taylor refused to be relegated to the backstage and continued his campaign. In February 1847, he defeated an army led by the Mexican general Santa Anna at Buena Vista, even though he was outnumbered five to one. The popularity he gained in these victories provided a springboard for Taylor's election as president in 1848. He died in office.

Decisive in command
Zachary Taylor issues orders during the battle of Buena Vista against the Mexicans in 1847. Field artillery played a large part in his victories.

WINFIELD SCOTT

AMERICAN GENERAL
BORN June 13, 1786
DIED May 29, 1866
KEY CONFLICTS War of 1812, Black Hawk War, Seminole War, Mexican-American War, American Civil War
KEY BATTLES Chippewa 1814, Lundy's Lane 1814, Veracruz 1847, Cerro Gordo 1847, Chapultepec 1847

A privileged Virginian, Winfield Scott joined the army in 1808 as a captain and entered the War of 1812 as a lieutenant-colonel. Captured by the British early in his first campaign, he was released in a prisoner exchange and resumed his meteoric rise, making brigadier-general by spring 1814.

Scott was an impressive character in terms of stature, organizational ability, and combat performance. He stormed Fort St. George on Lake Ontario in May 1813 and beat off an attack by British troops at Chippewa in July 1814, a victory that reflected his relentless work drilling his soldiers in disciplined fire and charge with the bayonet. At Lundy's Lane two months later, an attack on a British-held knoll ended in confused carnage, with Scott among the 800 American casualties.

Scott participated in campaigns against Native Americans, supervising the infamous eviction of the Cherokee to Oklahoma in 1838, known as the "Trail of Tears." Within the army, he strove for improvements in staff work, medical care, sanitation, and tactical training. Ambitious and arrogant, he also spent much time on disputes over seniority, promotion, and presumed insults.

WELL-EARNED PRAISE

In 1841, Scott was appointed the army's commanding general, a post he held for 20 years. The war against Mexico provided an opportunity to demonstrate his skills on a larger battlefield. He conceived and led an amphibious operation that captured the Mexican port of Veracruz in March 1847 and then marched on Mexico City, gambling on defeating numerically superior Mexican forces wherever he encountered them. From Cerro Gordo in mid-April to the storming of Fort Chapultepec in mid-September, Scott scored an unbroken series of victories praised by the aged Duke of Wellington.

After a failed presidential bid in 1852, Scott was still in command of the army when the Civil War broke out in 1861. His sensible advocacy of the Anaconda Plan—a patient, long-term strategy for encircling and strangling the Confederacy—was rejected and he resigned soon afterward.

Parade-ground perfect
Scott's preoccupation with formal dress and discipline earned him the nickname Old Fuss and Feathers.

5

AGENTS OF
EMPIRE

ETWEEN 1850 AND 1914, MILITARY LEADERS of widely varying styles and standing won fame and glory. They ranged from mustachioed imperialists, such as Lord Kitchener, to the Italian freedom fighter, Giuseppe Garibaldi, and from hard-fighting generals of the American Civil War, such as Ulysses S. Grant and William T. Sherman, to the Prussian war manager, Helmuth von Moltke. Their exploits took place at a time of sweeping technological changes that had a profound impact on the conduct of war.

On the battlefield, technological innovation brought above all an increase in firepower. Infantry weapons were transformed in terms of rate of fire, accuracy, and range, progressing from the muzzle-loaded musket to the rapid-fire rifle and the machine-gun. The replacement of cannon firing solid shot with steel rifled guns loaded with high-explosive shells not only made artillery more powerful, but eventually increased its range beyond the line of sight. From the early stages of this firepower revolution, which was still in its infancy at the time of the Crimean War (1854–56) and the American Civil War (1861–65), generals struggled to respond with appropriate tactics. Most continued to hope that, with the right fighting spirit, through frontal assault or charge, infantry or cavalry could overcome the firepower of troops in a prepared defensive position. On the whole, they could not.

TELEGRAPH AND RAILROADS

Commanders also had to learn to use new means of communication and transportation—the telegraph and the railroads. The invention of the electric telegraph, first used militarily during the Crimean War, allowed the movement of large armies to be coordinated over a wide geographical area. It also placed a general in the field within reach of orders from superiors in distant headquarters. The Prussian field marshal, Helmuth von Moltke, said, "No commander is less fortunate than he who operates with a telegraph wire stuck in his back." The first large-scale movement of troops by rail was carried out by the French army in 1859, and the railroads played an essential role in the American Civil War that broke out two years later. In Europe, railroads were especially critical for the rapid movement of armies to the battle zone at the start of a conflict.

GROWING PROFESSIONALISM

In any war, once armies had alighted at the railhead they returned to marching on foot and used horse-drawn carts to carry supplies. Similarly, the telegraph in principle allowed command at a distance, but generals still liked to see the battlefield for themselves and were rarely far from the front line when combat was joined. There was a widespread acceptance of the need for greater professionalism in the command and control of armed forces. Armies were growing in size and

Gatling Gun
Introduced in the mid-1860s, the Gatling gun was one of the new rapid-fire weapons that transformed warfare.

could easily fall into chaos if their movements were not properly planned and executed—especially if railroads were used. Commanders needed an efficient staff specializing in such areas as intelligence, movement of troops, and supply. The success of the highly professional Prussian general staff in mobilizing and directing hundreds of thousands of men efficiently in wars with Austria in 1866 and France in 1870–71 made an indelible impression. Other countries slowly and reluctantly accepted the need for a well-trained staff and, to a

degree, a managerial approach to war. It was a sign of the times that Britain felt compelled to abolish the time-honored practice of the purchase of commissions in the army.

TESTING NEW TECHNOLOGY

After 1871, only the Russo-Japanese War (1904–05) provided a thorough test-bed for rapidly evolving new technologies, which by then included field telephones, radio, and steel battleships. This war involved two major powers, but otherwise, commanders usually led relatively small armies in imperial

Battle of the Wilderness, 1864
American Civil War battles, although fought mostly with muzzle-loading weapons, showed the dominance of defensive firepower over infantry and cavalry.

conflicts in distant locations, or fought one-sided wars against clearly inferior states, such as America's war with Spain over its colonies in 1898. These small wars provided plenty of drama and excitement, and made generals and admirals into national heroes, but on the whole they were poor preparation for the world war that was to come in 1914.

1849—1880

EUROPEAN WARS

> THE AIR WAS LITERALLY FILLED WITH SHELLS, SHRAPNEL, AND CANISTER... IT WAS AS IF THE WORLD WAS COMING TO AN END. BUT NOTHING COULD MAKE THE BRAVE FUSILIERS QUAIL; THEY FELL IN ROWS, BUT THEY WERE WORTHY OF THE OLD BREED... THEY DIDN'T WAVER A FOOT'S BREADTH.

AN AUSTRIAN OFFICER, ON THE BATTLE OF KÖNIGGRÄTZ (SADOWA), 1866

THE WARS BETWEEN THE EUROPEAN powers in the mid-19th century saw the deployment of new and more devastating forms of weaponry. At Königgrätz, for example, the Prussian infantry's quick-firing needle guns wreaked havoc on the Austrians, whose muzzle-loading rifles fired only a fifth as fast. The lessons generals had learned by studying or taking part in the battles of Napoleon and Wellington were still relevant, but the cavalry charge or advance of infantry over open ground were fast becoming excessively costly tactics.

The first major conflict of the European wars of this period was the Crimean War of 1854–56, in which France, Britain, and Ottoman Turkey fought the Russian Empire. For the French and British this was a "war in peace": one that was fought without mass mobilization for objectives that were apparent to diplomats and strategists, but less than obvious to the general public. The new phenomenon of the war correspondent put commanders under critical scrutiny in the press, and any combat involving heavy casualties brought accusations that, in the words of British poet laureate Alfred Tennyson, "someone had blunder'd." The Crimean War—a conflict of grim siege warfare in which far more men died of disease than in combat—did not enhance many generals' reputations.

PRUSSIAN DOMINANCE

In the other major wars of this period—France's campaign against Austria in Italy in 1859, the Austro-Prussian War of 1866, and the Franco-Prussian War of 1871—commanders set out to fight decisive battles that would settle the issue as swiftly as possible, and in this they largely succeeded. These wars were short conflicts fought with definite and limited objectives, and undertaken in line with the dictum of the Prussian theorist, Carl von Clausewitz, that war was "the continuation of politics by other means." The French intervention in Italy evicted Austria from Lombardy, and Prussia's wars with Austria and France were part of a grand plan orchestrated by Chancellor Otto von Bismarck to assert Prussian dominance

over Germany. The overall result was a large-scale shift in European borders and in the balance of power on the continent. By 1871, new nation-states had been created. Italy had been united under King Victor Emmanuel II and Germany was unified under William I of Prussia. France and Austria were humiliated and lost heavily in territory and status, while Prussian-led Germany emerged as the single dominant power within the European mainland.

NEW HEROES

The European public subscribed to a glamorous, romanticized view of warfare. Because of this, they were eager to find heroic commanders to admire. One such was the freedom fighter Giuseppe Garibaldi. Involved in the struggle for Italian independence, he was idolized far beyond the borders of Italy as a courageous war leader who put his life on the line.

Despite the rose-tinted public image of conflict, the need to coordinate the movement of large bodies of troops meant that major wars called for a high level of professionalism in military command. The battle of Solferino in 1859 was the last in the history of Europe to feature monarchs commanding on both sides—Emperor Napoleon III of France and Emperor Franz Joseph I of Austria. The success of the Prussian Army was largely due to the efficiency of its general staff under Helmuth von Moltke, who appreciated that the unglamorous essentials of warfare in his time were the rapid mobilization of mass forces, their deployment to the theater of war by railroad, and subsequent large-scale maneuvers to bring the enemy to battle at a disadvantage.

Von Bredow's death ride
Prussian General von Bredow's cavalry brigade charges French artillery during the battle of Mars-la-Tour in the Franco-Prussian War. Von Bredow's brigade suffered 50 percent casualties but achieved its objective.

Prussian officer's helmet
The *pickelhaube* (spiked helmet) was adopted by the Prussian army in 1842. Most were made of leather, but high-ranking officers wore metal ones.

THE CRIMEAN WAR

IN APRIL 1854, BRITAIN AND FRANCE sent expeditionary forces to the Black Sea to support Turkey in a war with Russia. The campaign focused on the Russian naval base at Sevastopol. The allies besieged Sevastopol until September 1855; after its surrender, peace soon ensued. The conflict revealed grave deficiencies of command and organization, especially in Britain and Russia—the French Army performed best. But the extent of blunders committed was exaggerated. Generals inevitably struggled to adjust to increases in infantry and artillery firepower, but there were intelligent innovations, especially in the design of field fortifications.

FRANÇOIS CANROBERT

FRENCH MARSHAL
BORN June 27, 1809
DIED January 28, 1895
KEY CONFLICTS Crimean War, Italian Independence Wars, Franco-Prussian War
KEY BATTLES Alma 1854, Inkerman 1854, Solferino 1859, Gravelotte 1870

François Certain Canrobert was educated at the prestigious military academy of St.-Cyr in Brittany and blooded in the French conquest of Algeria in the 1830s. He became a colonel in the Zouaves, who were establishing themselves in this period as an elite of volunteers within the French Army. Energetic and courageous, Canrobert continued to see lively action against rebels in North Africa up to 1850, by which time he was a brigadier-general. He returned to France to take an active part in the coup that brought Napoleon III to power in 1851.

Canrobert was sent to the Crimea in 1854 as a divisional commander. He participated in the attack at the Alma River and immediately after became commander-in-chief on the death of Marshal St. Arnaud. As an army commander, Canrobert proved less assured and more cautious than at a lower level. The British unkindly nicknamed him "Robert Can't" because of his insistence on slow preparations before any attempt to take Sevastopol. He played a notable part in the repulse of a Russian attack at Inkerman in November, having a horse killed under him, but resisted British urgings to pursue the Russians as they fell back on their fortifications. In May 1855, a failed attempt to capture the port of Kerch brought inter-allied relations to their nadir and Canrobert resigned to resume command of his division.

His unhappy Crimean experience made Canrobert refuse command above corps level in France's subsequent wars against Austria in Italy in 1859, in which he fought at Magenta and Solferino, and against Prussia in 1870–71. In both conflicts, he served with great distinction as a fighting general in the thick of the action. His finest moment was the defense of St. Privat against a desperate onslaught by the Prussians during the battle of Gravelotte in August 1870, although in its aftermath he was involved in the French surrender at Metz.

Old warrior
Elevated to marshal of France in 1856, Canrobert was at his best involving himself in combat rather than considering larger strategic issues. He lived to a ripe old age, entering politics and serving as a senator.

FRANZ TOTLEBEN

RUSSIAN MILITARY ENGINEER
BORN May 20, 1818
DIED July 1, 1884
KEY CONFLICTS Crimean War, Russo-Turkish War.
KEY BATTLES Siege of Sevastopol 1854–55, Siege of Plevna 1877

Franz Eduard Totleben (or Todleben) was born in Latvia, then part of the Russian Empire, to a middle-class ethnic German family. He joined the Russian Army at the age of 18 and rose to be an officer in the engineers, the branch of the army in which advancement was least dependent on aristocratic status. His first active service was in the 1840s in campaigns against Muslim tribes in the Caucasus.

After Russia went to war with Turkey in 1853, he served at the siege of the Danubian fort of Silistria in the spring of 1854, before moving to Sevastopol later in the year. Although he was only a 37-year-old lieutenant-colonel, his energy and intelligence made him the driving force behind the defense of Sevastopol under siege. He built an extensive system of earthworks thrown out from the fortress, with formidable artillery and infantry redoubts linked by trenches. In front of the main defenses he had rows of rifle pits dug, from where marksmen could snipe at the enemy lines. The fortifications in effect ceased to be static, changing constantly as the conditions of the siege altered and keeping the besieging forces under continuous pressure. In June 1855, Totleben's trenches and redoubts comfortably withstood a general assault by the allied armies, but he was wounded. By the time he recovered, the city had surrendered.

Totleben emerged from the Crimean War with an immense reputation. He became chief of the Russian Department of Engineers, but saw no further combat until the Russo-Turkish War of 1877–78. His intervention brought Russia eventual success in the initially disastrous siege of Plevna and saw the war through to a victorious conclusion.

Courage of conviction
Totleben possessed immense self-confidence, which allowed him to criticize the senior officers misdirecting the defense of Sevastopol.

> ## IT IS NOT A FORTRESS... BUT AN ARMY DEEPLY ENTRENCHED.
>
> **GENERAL SIR JOHN FOX BURGOYNE**, ON THE DEFENSES OF SEVASTOPOL

LORD RAGLAN

BRITISH GENERAL
BORN September 30, 1788
DIED June 29, 1855
KEY CONFLICTS Crimean War
KEY BATTLES Siege of Sevastopol 1854–55, Balaclava 1854, Inkerman 1854

Fitzroy Somerset, 1st Baron Raglan, commander of the British forces sent to the Crimea in 1854, had a long career of faithful military service behind him but had never led an army in the field. An impeccably aristocratic infantry captain, he had been taken on by Wellington as an aide-de-camp from the start of the Peninsular War in 1808. The close working relationship between the two men lasted over 40 years. Somerset was with Wellington at Waterloo in 1815 when a musket ball struck his right arm, which had to be amputated. Through the long peace that followed, he continued to serve Wellington in his various high offices and was disappointed not to succeed him as commander-in-chief of the British Army in 1852.

The choice of the 65-year-old Raglan to lead the expedition to the Crimea initially appeared justified with a victory at the Alma River in September 1854. His tactics in this battle were simple: British infantry would be thrown forward in a frontal assault on Russian positions. Raglan displayed notable personal courage, taking his staff to an exposed forward position to observe the fighting, and from there directing artillery against enemy infantry at a crucial moment in the battle.

Expectations of a swift allied capture of Sevastopol after this victory were soon disappointed, however. By the last week of October, the Russians had taken the initiative and

Bugle call
This bugle was used in the charge of the Light Brigade. In battle, bugle notes conveyed simple instructions.

One-armed veteran
Lord Raglan was a fine staff officer who lost an arm at Waterloo. His conduct of battles in the Crimea, based on what he had learned serving under Wellington, was mostly competent.

Raglan had to defend his supply port at Balaclava against an attack. He did this successfully, but the repulse of the Russians was overshadowed by the blunder of the charge of the Light Brigade.

DISASTROUS CHARGE

Because of confused orders, for which Raglan was largely responsible, and poor judgment by his subordinates, the British light cavalry charged the wrong Russian gun battery, resulting in casualties of over 30 percent. Despite a hard-fought defensive victory at Inkerman in November, Raglan came under mounting press criticism for his conduct of the war. He was also blamed for the hardship his troops suffered in their winter encampment, due to supply failings over which he had no control.

Vigorously defending his conduct, Raglan was still in command when allied general assaults on the defenses of Sevastopol were mounted in June 1855. On June 18, Raglan ordered his infantry to mount a frontal attack on the heavily fortified Redan as a gesture of support to the French, aware it had little chance of success. The men were mown down by concentrated infantry and artillery fire in front of the Russian trenches. The debacle was too much for Raglan, who died 10 days later, a victim as much of depression and overwork as of cholera.

The charge of the Light Brigade
British light cavalry led by Lord Cardigan charge a Russian battery on October 25, 1854. This was a fatal misunderstanding of orders that exposed them to enemy fire on both sides.

1850—1914

NATION-BUILDING WARS

BETWEEN 1848 AND 1871, a series of wars created the nation-states of Italy and Germany out of territory previously fragmented or under foreign rule. The Italian Independence Wars of 1848–49, 1859–61, and 1866 made the former king of Sardinia ruler of a united Italy, with the aid of guerrilla fighter Giuseppe Garibaldi. Prussia unified Germany under its leadership through wars manufactured by Chancellor Otto von Bismarck and executed by Chief-of-Staff Helmuth von Moltke. The largest conflict was the Franco-Prussian War of 1870–71, which ended France's long reign as the leading European military power.

NAPOLEON III

FRENCH EMPEROR
BORN April 20, 1808
DIED January 9, 1873
KEY CONFLICTS Crimean War, Italian Independence Wars, Franco-Prussian War
KEY BATTLES Solferino 1859, Sedan 1870

Founder and ruler of the French Second Empire, from 1851 to 1870, the French emperor, Napoleon III, was a nephew of the great Napoleon Bonaparte. As a young man, he was known as Louis Napoleon and served as an artillery captain in Switzerland, before devoting his life to the restoration of Bonapartist rule in France. Elected president of the Second Republic in 1848, he established his empire through a military coup.

DYNASTIC LEGACY

The Bonapartist tradition required Louis Napoleon to demonstrate a talent for war that he did not, in fact, possess. During the Crimean War, he sent orders by telegraph from Paris to the French expeditionary force, which his generals on the spot found unhelpful. In a war against Austria in support of the Kingdom of Sardinia in 1859, he led his army in person at the battles of Magenta and Solferino in northern Italy. Tactically, his performance as a field commander was undistinguished, and he was so horrified by the bloodshed that he agreed to a premature peace. His health was in decline when he blundered into war with Prussia in 1870. Although he was expected to lead his armies into war himself, he was little more than an observer in the catastrophic campaign that ended at Sedan in 1870. Forced to abdicate, he lived his final years in exile in Britain.

The emperor at Solferino
Napoleon III is shown observing the battle between French and Piemontese troops against the Austrian armies. The toll amounted to almost 40,000 casualties in a single day.

PATRICE DE MACMAHON

FRENCH MARSHAL
BORN July 13, 1808
DIED October 17, 1893
KEY CONFLICTS Crimean War, Italian Independence Wars, Franco-Prussian War
KEY BATTLES Malakoff 1855, Magenta 1859, Sedan 1870

Born into a family of Irish origin long established in France, MacMahon saw extensive service in the French occupation of Algeria from 1830, rising to be commander of the Foreign Legion in 1843 and a general in 1848. During the Crimean War, he commanded a division in the siege of Sebastopol, winning renown for the storming of the Malakoff redoubt, the key to the Russian defenses, in September 1855. The Malakoff was fiercely defended and its capture cost 7,500 French casualties. At the height of the battle, MacMahon replied to a messenger sent from high command to inquire whether he could hold the redoubt: "Tell your general that here I am and here I stay."

ARMY OF AFRICA

In Napoleon III's campaign against the Austrians in Italy in 1859, MacMahon commanded a corps composed of elements of the Army of Africa, including *zouaves* from Algeria and foreign legionaries. On June 4, he drove the Austrians back into the town of Magenta, leading his troops in person up to the first buildings. The town fell to the French after bitter fighting, and the following day a grateful Napoleon III made MacMahon a marshal and Duke of Magenta. Later in the campaign, his corps was also in the thick of the bloody battle of Solferino. MacMahon saw no further combat until the Franco-Prussian War. Again leading his trusted troops from Africa, at the start of the war he was defeated by Prussian forces at Froeschwiller. Made commander of the Army of Châlons, he was ordered to relieve General Bazaine, under siege in Metz, but MacMahon himself ended up besieged in Sedan (pp. 240–41). He recovered from the wound received during this disaster to lead the troops that crushed the revolutionary Paris Commune uprising in May 1871, restoring the authority of the French Republican government by executing up to 30,000 rebels.

Mixed army record
MacMahon showed exceptional personal bravery in the thick of a fight, but he was out of his depth commanding an army against the Prussians in 1870.

GIUSEPPE GARIBALDI

ITALIAN FREEDOM FIGHTER
BORN July 4, 1807
DIED June 2, 1882
KEY CONFLICTS Uruguayan Civil War, Italian Independence Wars, Franco-Prussian War
KEY BATTLES Rome 1849, Volturno 1860, Aspromonte 1862

Giuseppe Garibaldi was born into a seafaring family in Nice, a city disputed between France and the Italian Kingdom of Sardinia. In the 1830s, he became involved with Italian revolutionaries seeking to create a united Italy under a republican government. After a failed uprising in Genoa in 1834, he fled to South America. There he became a guerrilla fighter among the gauchos of Rio Grande del Sol in Brazil, before joining in the defense of Uruguay's independence against Argentina from 1842. He led a band of followers known as the Italian Legion, as well as commanding the Uruguayan navy.

In 1848, when revolutionary uprisings spread through the Italian peninsula, Garibaldi returned to take part in the struggle. His presence attracted a large number of volunteers, whom he commanded first in support of King Victor Emmanuel II of Piedmont–Sardinia, fighting for the Italian cause against Austria. He then aided the revolutionary Roman republic that had seized Rome from the pope.

ITALIAN UNIFICATION

When the French intervened to restore papal authority in June 1849, Garibaldi held their army at bay for several weeks before returning to exile. He was an international celebrity, lauded as a noble fighter for freedom, but he pragmatically accepted that Italian unification could only be achieved under Victor Emmanuel II. He fought alongside the royal army against the Austrians in 1859 and 1866,

Personal weapon
Garibaldi's pistol was part of his personal weaponry, along with a saber and dagger. Depictions of him as a fearless freedom fighter often show him saber in hand.

leading a volunteer force known as the Hunters of the Alps. His most famous exploit, however, was his invasion of Sicily with his Redshirts in May 1860 (see box below). The largest battle of his career was fought against the army of the Kingdom of the Two Sicilies at Volturno in October 1860, opening the way for Sardinian forces to take over southern

Italy. The creation of the Kingdom of Italy left Garibaldi unsatisfied because the papal states and Venice were excluded. In 1862, he attempted to repeat his success of 1860, landing volunteers in southern Italy and marching on Rome, but the Italian monarchy blocked this initiative. In an encounter with royal forces at Aspromonte in August, Garibaldi was wounded, but stopped the clash from escalating, thus preventing civil war.

Garibaldi despised French Emperor Napoleon III, who had sent troops to protect papal rule in Rome. When Napoleon fell from power in 1870, Garibaldi welcomed the founding of the French Third Republic by leading international volunteers, dubbed the Army of the Vosges, to fight on its behalf against Prussian troops occupying eastern France.

First freedom fighter
Garibaldi was admired by liberals who saw him as a noble figure and lauded his use of force in the cause of freedom. This photograph shows him as a dignified veteran around 70 years old.

> # LET HIM WHO LOVES HIS COUNTRY WITH HIS HEART, AND NOT MERELY WITH HIS LIPS, FOLLOW ME.
> **GARIBALDI**, ADDRESSING VOLUNTEERS IN ROME, 1849

KEY TROOPS
REDSHIRTS

In May 1860, Garibaldi landed on the coast of Sicily with around 1,000 red-shirted volunteers, mostly recruited from northern Italy. Although the Redshirts had naval backing from Britain, they were heavily outnumbered by the troops of the Kingdom of the Two Sicilies. However, the volunteers were better motivated and led than the forces of the decrepit monarchy, and after sharp fighting at Calatafimi and Milazzo they took control of Sicily. Garibaldi continued his campaign into southern Italy, eventually leading some 25,000 men, but the achievement of the original 1,000 Redshirts became an Italian national legend.

The liberation of Sicily
Garibaldi and his volunteer army broke into Palermo on May 27, 1860, but heavy fighting with Neapolitan forces ensued before they gained full control of the city.

HELMUTH VON MOLTKE THE ELDER

PRUSSIAN CHIEF OF GENERAL STAFF
BORN October 26, 1800
DIED April 24, 1891
KEY CONFLICTS Second Schleswig War, Austro-Prussian War, Franco-Prussian War.
KEY BATTLES Königgrätz (Sadowa) 1866, Sedan 1870, Siege of Paris 1870–71

Known as "the Elder" to distinguish him from his nephew, a World War I commander, Helmuth von Moltke was the architect of Prussian military supremacy in mid-19th-century Europe. The son of an impoverished, aristocratic army officer, he was brought up in Denmark. Notably different from the traditional, boorish type of Prussian officer, Moltke was an intellectual with quiet manners and considerable literary talent. He progressed within the Prussian Army because Prussia had recognized the need for intelligent and professionally capable staff officers, and because his cultured manner made him an able courtier, attracting the favor of the royal family. During the first four decades of Moltke's career, Prussia was at peace and his only experience of combat occurred in 1839 when, sent to serve the Ottoman Empire, he commanded the Turkish artillery in a battle against Egypt.

ROYAL FAVOR

As chief of the Prussian general staff from 1857, Moltke showed impressive energy in driving through a radical improvement in organization, planning, and training. However, his personal status, and that of the general staff, was at first uncertain. In 1864, when Prussia went to war with Denmark, command was entrusted to an 80-year-old general who ignored Moltke's plans for the conduct of operations. When Moltke was allowed to take charge, he brought the war to a swift, successful conclusion, in the process winning the confidence of King Wilhelm I.

In 1866, when a major war broke out with Austria, Moltke was free to behave like a commander-in-chief, using royal authority to issue orders to army and divisional commanders who outranked him in terms of formal social and military hierarchy.

Chief of general staff
Calm, firm, and astute, Moltke habitually dressed with the simplicity of a professional soldier, though he proudly displayed the Iron Cross at his throat. He was a master of planning and large-scale maneuver.

> " NO PLAN OF OPERATIONS SURVIVES BEYOND CONTACT WITH THE ENEMY'S MAIN STRENGTH. "
>
> **HELMUTH VON MOLTKE**

BIOGRAPHY
OTTO VON BISMARCK

Prince Otto von Bismarck was the political mastermind behind the wars that Moltke won. A Prussian *junker* (landowner) of aggressive, energetic temperament, he became Prussia's chief minister in 1862. His goal was to unify the states of Germany under Prussian leadership and he saw war as a practical means to this end. His diplomatic skills succeeded in isolating Denmark, Austria, and France, in turn, so that they could be beaten in isolation without a general European war. The victory over Austria in 1866 allowed Prussia to form a North German Federation, and the war against France in 1870 brought southern Germany into the Prussian fold. The German Empire was founded in 1871, with Bismarck as its chancellor until 1890. Having achieved his goal, he sought peace and stability, regretting the annexation of Alsace and Lorraine from France that left the French with a burning grievance.

AGENTS OF EMPIRE

> ## THE GERMAN ARMIES ARE IN THE HIGHEST STATE OF EFFICIENCY THAT CAN BE REACHED, BY SCIENTIFIC PREPARATION FOR WAR, BY CONCENTRATION, BY COMPACT DISCIPLINE, AND BY FORETHOUGHT.
>
> **COLONEL CHESNEY AND H. REEVE**, *THE MILITARY RESOURCES OF PRUSSIA AND FRANCE*, 1870

Dreyse needle gun
The breech-loading Dreyse needle gun was the Prussian infantry rifle used in the wars against France and Austria. It was far superior to Austrian rifle-muskets, but was outclassed by the French Chassepot rifle.

Despite his success, some officers still resented receiving commands from a man whom they regarded as an obscure military bureaucrat.

VICTORY OVER AUSTRIA

The rapid defeat of Austria made Moltke a celebrity and his authority unquestionable. The war showed his ability to combine forward planning with a keen appreciation of the chaotic reality of conflict. The key to Prussia's victory lay in the efficient mobilization of almost 300,000 men and their equipment by train, in line with precise timetables drawn up by the railroads section of the general staff. This enabled the Prussians to seize the initiative from the outset.

Moltke planned for three armies to maneuver separately, then come together to destroy the Austrian forces in a decisive battle. But he understood the need for flexibility and did not try to control the campaign in detail.

His crisp, clear-written instructions—early on in the war sent by telegram from Berlin—always allowed commanders on the spot plenty of freedom to exercise their initiative. Similarly, he trusted the inner circle of his general staff, a bonded band of brothers, to make independent judgments in line with his strategy. The climactic battle of Königgrätz (Sadowa) on July 3, 1866, was almost a disaster, as the last of Moltke's three armies failed to arrive until halfway through the day, but victory was finally achieved, after which Austria sued for peace.

When Prussia went to war with France in 1870, Moltke ensured that its army was the best trained in Europe, and that its officers and NCOs were imbued with a shared ethos and tactical doctrine. France's mobilization was a shambles, while Prussian mobilization was faultless. Overcoming momentary confusion and errors as his armies advanced into eastern France, Moltke issued constantly changing orders to meet a rapidly evolving situation.

ENTRAPMENT

By remaining flexible, Moltke was able to lure the courageous but disorganized French field armies into traps at both Metz and Sedan (pp. 240–41), from which they could not escape. With the surrender of Paris after a lengthy siege in January 1871, Moltke was recognized as the architect of a military victory that had made a Prussian-led Germany the dominant power in Europe.

Battle of Königgrätz
King Wilhelm I rides through the field of victory at Königgrätz on July 3, 1866, with Helmuth von Moltke on his right. The battle resulted in 44,000 Austrian casualties, compared with only 9,000 on the Prussian side.

TIMELINE

■ **1819–21** After attending a cadet academy in Copenhagen, Moltke serves as a junior officer in the Danish Army.

■ **1822–26** Moltke is commissioned as an officer in the Prussian Army and studies at the Berlin War Academy, graduating at the top of his class.

■ **1832** Moltke is appointed to the Prussian general staff. He uses his literary talents to supplement his low income, writing novels and translating English texts.

■ **1835–39** Serving Ottoman Sultan Mahmud II as a military adviser, Moltke is present at the battle of Nezib, in which the Ottomans are defeated by the Egyptians (June 24, 1839).

SULTAN MAHMUD II

■ **1848** Progressing steadily through staff positions in the peacetime Prussian Army, Moltke is appointed chief-of-staff of an army corps.

■ **1855** Appointed personal adjutant to the Prussian king's son, Prince Frederick William, Moltke becomes a familiar figure in court circles.

■ **October 1857** Moltke becomes chief of the Prussian general staff and begins a general reorganization of staff work and war planning.

■ **February–October 1864** In a war with Denmark over Schleswig-Holstein, Moltke's plans prove superior to those of traditional commanders, winning him the confidence of King Wilhelm I.

■ **June–August 1866** Moltke masterminds a Prussian victory over Austria in a war lasting seven weeks, decided by the battle of Königgrätz on July 3.

■ **1868** Moltke finalizes detailed plans for a war with France, taking into account the experience of the Austro-Prussian War.

■ **1870–71** Victory in the Franco-Prussian War is the crowning triumph of Moltke's career. He is made a field-marshal and *Graf* (count) and serves as German chief of general staff until 1888.

MOLTKE VS. MACMAHON

AT THE OUTBREAK OF THE Franco-Prussian War in July 1870, the Prussians mobilized so quickly and efficiently that they were able to invade France and split the French forces. One army under Marshal Bazaine was trapped in Metz, while Marshal MacMahon fell back on Châlons. Prussian Chief-of-Staff Helmuth von Moltke, in overall command of the armies of Prussia and allied German states, sought to locate MacMahon's Army of Châlons and destroy it in a decisive war-winning battle. In the last week of August, Moltke and MacMahon engaged in a chase across eastern France, which ended at Sedan.

HELMUTH VON MOLTKE

Moltke and his staff traveled with the royal headquarters of the Prussian king, Wilhelm I, keeping up with the movements of the Third Army under Crown Prince Friedrich Wilhelm of Prussia and the Army of the Meuse under Crown Prince Albert of Saxony. Both crown princes acted according to Moltke's orders, although he allowed them broad scope to decide how those orders were carried out.

PURSUING THE ENEMY

Moltke was unclear about the intentions of the French. At first, he assumed that MacMahon would fall back toward Paris and so prepared to march westward. On August 25, however, studying reports in French newspapers and evidence from his own cavalry patrols, Moltke decided MacMahon must have embarked upon a march north and east to join up with Bazaine. Seeing an unmissable opportunity for a decisive victory, he ordered his armies to wheel northward. Using his cavalry assertively to keep in contact with the enemy, he was able to catch up with MacMahon crossing the Meuse River near Sedan on August 30.

The following day, in order to stop the French from escaping, as he assumed they would try to do, Moltke rushed troops across the river east and west of the French Army—the path northward was blocked by the Belgian border. As the French remained passively inside Sedan, Moltke held them in a trap.

OBSERVING THE BATTLE

At dawn on September 1, Moltke's armies, outnumbering the French with 200,000 men to 120,000, were in position to attack. By early afternoon they had completed the encirclement of Sedan and begun driving in the French defenses. Although fighting was fierce and casualties high, Moltke had no doubt the outcome would be favorable.

Watching proceedings from a hilltop alongside King Wilhelm, Bismarck, and other dignitaries, Moltke did not issue a single written order that day until the battle was over, leaving his army and corps commanders to do their jobs and force a French surrender.

> ## OUR SUPERIORITY OVER THE ENEMY WAS SO OVERWHELMING THAT WE SUFFERED NO LOSS AT ALL.
>
> **A GERMAN OFFICER**, DESCRIBING THE SUPERIORITY OF THE PRUSSIAN ARTILLERY, 1870

French cavalry charge
Launched in furious charges against the encircling Prussian armies, French cavalry were cut down by infantry and artillery fire. Formations such as the Chasseurs d'Afrique lost half their men.

AGENTS OF EMPIRE

TIMELINE

MOLTKE

- Moltke orders the Army of the Meuse and the Third Army to wheel northward and attempt to bring the French to battle
- The capture of a French staff officer, the Marquis de Grouchy, carrying written orders, tells Moltke that MacMahon intends to cross the Meuse River
- **Night** Moltke issues an order for the advance to continue the next day and for the enemy to be trapped between the Meuse and the Belgian frontier
- Elements of the Prussian Third Army cross the Meuse to the west of Sedan at Donchery, and Bavarian troops cross to the east of the city

| 1870: AUG 22 | AUG 25 | AUG 27 | AUG 29 | AUG 30 | AUG 31 |

MACMAHON

- MacMahon orders the Army of Châlons to march around the northern flank of the Prussian armies to link up with Bazaine's Army of the Rhine at Metz
- Worried by contact with Prussian cavalry, MacMahon orders his army to turn away to the northwest. This order is countermanded the following morning
- The Prussian vanguard surprises a French corps at Beaumont and heavy fighting takes place. MacMahon hurries his army across the Meuse
- MacMahon concentrates all his forces in and around the fortress of Sedan. He rejects suggestions of attempting a breakout to the west

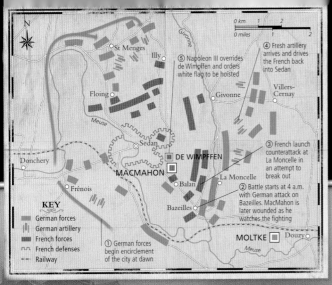

KEY
- German forces
- German artillery
- French forces
- French defenses
- Railway

① German forces begin encirclement of the city at dawn

② Battle starts at 4 a.m. with German attack on Bazeilles. MacMahon is later wounded as he watches the fighting

③ French launch counterattack at La Moncelle in an attempt to break out

④ Fresh artillery arrives and drives the French back into Sedan

⑤ Napoleon III overrides de Wimpffen and orders white flag to be hoisted

0 km 1 2
0 miles 1 2

LOCATION Sedan on the Meuse river
DATE September 1, 1870
FORCES Prussians: 200,000; French: 120,000
CASUALTIES Prussians: 9,000 casualties; French: 200,000 killed, wounded, or taken prisoner

PATRICE DE MACMAHON

MacMahon's dilemma was whether to attempt to link up with Bazaine's army or to fall back toward Paris. The French emperor, Napoleon III, who had joined MacMahon at Châlons, urged withdrawal westward, but MacMahon opted for a long march around the Prussian flank to meet Bazaine, optimistically presumed to be breaking out of Metz.

MacMahon's army was ill-prepared to execute a maneuver on such a grand scale—it had no maps of France, having expected to fight in Germany. Slowed by logistical difficulties, they were also confused by their commander's hesitations. On the evening of August 27, MacMahon issued orders to turn toward Paris, only to cancel this command the following morning.

Inexplicably failing to send his cavalry patrol in the direction of the Prussian armies, MacMahon was ignorant of their strength and their position. The unexpected clash with the Prussians on August 30 led the French to complete a hasty, panic-stricken crossing of the Meuse.

To rest and regroup his harassed forces, MacMahon ordered them to concentrate in Sedan, a fortress town where much-needed food and ammunition were to be found. He could still have made a fighting escape to the west on August 31, but did nothing, while Moltke's armies crossed the Meuse unopposed.

CRUSHING DEFEAT

MacMahon designated September 1 as a rest day, but at 4 a.m. the Prussians launched an attack. MacMahon was wounded early on by an artillery shell. In a sequel typical of the confusion in the French camp, he was succeeded first by General Auguste Ducrot and then by General Emmanuel de Wimpffen, who had authorization from the government in Paris. In practice, it made little difference who gave the orders, for the French position was untenable.

Prussian artillery dominated the battlefield. Attempts at breakouts by cavalry and infantry showed immense bravery but could not succeed. Napoleon III humanely insisted on a surrender to save lives. More than 100,000 French soldiers were taken prisoner.

1850–1914

4 a.m. Fighting begins to the east of Sedan as Bavarians advance into the suburb village of Bazeilles

7:30 a.m. Moltke arrives at his position on a hill near Frénois, from which he will observe the battle

12 noon The encirclement of Sedan is completed by the Prussian Third Army pressing around the north of the city

3 p.m. Prussian shelling of the Bois de la Garenne, north of Sedan, crushes French infantry resistance in a key defensive position

7:15 p.m. After a letter from Napoleon III is delivered to the Prussian king, Wilhelm I, Moltke orders a ceasefire while negotiations take place for a French surrender

SEPT 1

5 p.m. MacMahon declares that September 1 will be a rest day for his exhausted army

6 a.m. MacMahon is wounded by an artillery shell. He is succeeded first by Ducrot and then by de Wimpffen

9 a.m. The French mount a vigorous defense, under attack at a series of points around Sedan

1 p.m. French General Margueritte, shot in the face, waves the cavalry forward at Floing. A series of French cavalry charges are a glorious failure

4 p.m. Napoleon III insists on raising the white flag as Sedan comes under artillery bombardment, but Wimpffen orders the fighting to continue

1861—1865

THE AMERICAN CIVIL WAR

"OUR MEN ADVANCED WITH ENTHUSIASM. A FEARFUL FIRE OF ARTILLERY AND MUSKETRY GREETED THEM. NOW THEY WOULD STOP A MOMENT, THEN PLUNGE FORWARD AGAIN. THROUGH OUR GLASSES WE SAW THEM FALL BY HUNDREDS... LIKE TALL GRASS SWEPT DOWN WITH A SCYTHE."

BRIGADIER-GENERAL CARL SCHURZ, DESCRIBING THE BATTLE OF FREDERICKSBURG, DECEMBER 1862

Pickett's Charge
The battle of Gettysburg, July 1–3, 1863, was a major defeat for Confederate commander Robert E. Lee. One of its disastrous episodes was a hopeless charge into Union fire by infantry under General George Pickett.

HE AMERICAN CIVIL WAR was a large-scale conflict that involved some four million soldiers engaged in around 40 major campaigns and battles. Fought over a vast geographical area, from the Mississippi to Maryland, it posed daunting problems of command and control. This challenge was taken up by men who had little or no previous combat experience and, in most cases, had not advanced beyond junior officer rank. Catapulted into command of armies, though many failed the test, a few deservedly earned enduring renown.

In April 1861, the US government of President Abraham Lincoln went to war with the 11 Southern, slave-owning states that had seceded from the Union to form the Confederate States of America. The preexisting US Army numbered only 16,000 men, and, therefore, mass armies had to be improvised on both sides, initially from militia and volunteers. Serving army officers and former officers who had retired into civilian life were in great demand. In the spring of 1861, 313 officers resigned from the US Army to serve with the Confederacy. The Union decided to keep the prewar US Army stationed in frontier posts in the event of Native American raids, and turned mainly to retired officers to lead its volunteers. Among these were Ulysses S. Grant, who quit the clerk's counter of a shop, and George B. McClellan, who left the presidency of a railroad company.

A CHAOTIC START

Fought with inexperienced troops unused to discipline, serving under officers often unsuited to command, the early stages of the war were chaotic. The Prussian chief of general staff, Helmuth von Moltke, was an observer who reputedly described the war as "two armed mobs chasing each other around the country." Most senior commanders had been through the West Point military academy, where the stress was placed more on engineering and fortifications than on tactics and drill. As a consequence, they coped relatively well with using new technologies such as railroads, steam ships, and the electric telegraph, but had more difficulty fighting coherent battles. The tactical impact of the increased firepower of rifle-muskets and improved artillery surprised everyone. Throughout the war, even the best generals attempted frontal infantry assaults on prepared defenses, resulting in the fruitless loss of many lives.

THE UNION TRIUMPHS

The war was fought broadly in two theaters. In the eastern theater, the Confederate capital of Richmond, Virginia, was within striking range of Washington, D.C. Meanwhile, the western theater was focused on the control of the Mississippi. The Union had by far the greater resources of manpower and industry, but despite this, the Confederates had the best of the early fighting, boasting Robert E. Lee and Thomas Stonewall Jackson as their star generals. The nearly simultaneous Union victories in the east at Gettysburg and in the west at Vicksburg in July 1863 proved to be the turning point. The Confederates persevered grimly as the war descended into attrition, masterminded by Grant and his subordinate, William T. Sherman. Over 600,000 soldiers had died by the time the Confederacy surrendered in 1865.

Captured Stars and Bars
This Confederate battle flag was captured at the battle of Gettysburg in 1863. The 13 stars represent the 11 secessionist states, along with Kentucky and Missouri, both of which initially had pro-Confederacy governments but later opted for the Union.

CONFEDERATE COMMANDERS

MANY OF THE FINEST serving US Army officers opted for the Confederacy at the start of the war. Men like Robert E. Lee and Jeb Stuart brought a professionalism and flair to high command that the Union generals initially could not match. Yet the Confederate commanders labored at all times under a severe deficiency of numbers and material. Whereas some individuals, such as Joseph Johnston, demanded caution to conserve forces, others, including Lee and Stonewall Jackson, believed that only striking offensive victories could give the Confederates a chance, since they were fighting against the odds.

AGENTS OF EMPIRE

JEB STUART

CONFEDERATE CAVALRY GENERAL
BORN February 6, 1833
DIED May 12, 1864
KEY CONFLICT American Civil War
KEY BATTLES First Bull Run 1861, Chancellorsville 1863, Brandy Station 1863, Yellow Tavern 1864

The son of a Virginian politician, James E. B. "Jeb" Stuart was recognized as an outstanding horseman while at West Point and served as a cavalry lieutenant on the western frontier in the 1850s. He notably aided Colonel Robert

Intelligence gatherer
Jeb Stuart was a dashing cavalry officer whose reconnaissance skills ensured the Confederates superior intelligence in the early years of the Civil War.

E. Lee in the capture of antislavery rebel John Brown in 1859. Having joined the Confederate Army at the outbreak of the Civil War, he led the First Virginia Cavalry flamboyantly into battle at the first battle of Bull Run in July 1861. Here, he executed the first—and only—cavalry charge of the Civil War with drawn sabers. Stuart's exploits were soon legendary, as he raided deep into Union territory and rode a complete circuit around Union forces during the Peninsula campaign in June 1862. Lee promoted Stuart to major-general and made him commander of the Army of Northern Virginia's 15,000-strong cavalry. He proved to be disciplined and effective, dutifully fulfilling the cavalry's reconnaissance role and accepting the need for his troopers at times to fight as ancillary infantry. At Chancellorsville, in May 1863, Stuart distinguished himself by taking over command of the infantry after Stonewall Jackson was wounded.

STUART UNSETTLED
In June 1863, Stuart's troopers were surprised by Union cavalry at Brandy Station and badly mauled. Perhaps shaken by this, Stuart subsequently failed to provide the reconnaissance Lee needed prior to the battle of Gettysburg in July. The rising strength of Union cavalry also placed Stuart under intolerable pressure. In May 1864, mounting a hastily improvised defense of Richmond against a mass cavalry raid led by Sheridan, Stuart was mortally wounded at the battle of Yellow Tavern. His loss was a grave blow to Confederate morale.

JOSEPH E. JOHNSTON

CONFEDERATE GENERAL
BORN February 3, 1807
DIED March 21, 1891
KEY CONFLICTS Seminole Wars, Mexican-American War, American Civil War
KEY BATTLES First Bull Run 1861, Seven Pines 1862, Atlanta 1864, Bentonville 1865

A classmate of Robert E. Lee at West Point, Joseph Johnston served in the Seminole Wars in the 1830s and the Mexican War in the 1840s, standing out as a commander at the storming of the fortress of Chapultepec in September 1847. He was newly appointed quartermaster-general of the army when the Civil War broke out. Resigning to join the Confederates, he led troops from Harpers Ferry to join the forces at Bull Run in July 1861, a move that contributed greatly to Confederate victory there. Commanding the Army of Northern Virginia in the Yorktown Peninsula in spring 1862, Johnston fought a series of holding actions while withdrawing toward the

Seasoned professional
Always the professional, Johnston resisted pressure from Confederate President Jefferson Davis to attack when facing superior forces.

Southern capital, Richmond. He was wounded counterattacking at Seven Pines in May and ceded command to Lee. On his recovery, he was given command of Confederate forces in the west. Failing to relieve Vicksburg with inadequate forces, he was sidelined after the fortress fell in July 1863.

FACING SHERMAN
Recalled to lead the demoralized Army of Tennessee in December, Johnston fought yet another skillful defensive campaign, falling back toward Atlanta in the face of William T. Sherman's superior forces. He was fired by President Jefferson Davis in July 1864, but was reappointed one last time in February 1865, fighting at Bentonville before surrendering to Sherman in April.

First Bull Run
The battle of Bull Run on July 21, 1861, was a Confederate victory, thanks in no small part to Johnston's forces, which arrived the day before.

STONEWALL JACKSON

CONFEDERATE GENERAL
BORN January 21, 1824
DIED May 10, 1863
KEY CONFLICT American Civil War
KEY BATTLES First Bull Run 1861, Second Bull Run 1862, Antietam 1862, Fredericksburg 1862, Chancellorsville 1863

Born in Clarksburg, Virginia, Thomas Jackson was orphaned at the age of six and grew up clumsy, introverted, eccentric, and prone to psychosomatic illnesses. He did not shine at West Point, but after graduating in 1846, proved his worth as a fighting officer in the Mexican War. In 1851, he quit the army to teach at the Virginia Military Institute, and at the same time he became a devout Calvinist, so that he believed his life was directed by divine predestination. The institute's cadets unkindly dubbed him "fool Tom."

A LEGEND IS BORN

Jackson entered the Civil War with his home state in April 1861, and his evident professionalism saw him promoted in just two months from colonel to brigadier-general. Leading a Virginia brigade at the first Bull Run on July 21, his infantry stood firm against a Union onslaught. Confederate General Barnard E. Bee cried, "There stands Jackson like a stone wall!" Although it is not certain this was meant as a compliment, Jackson was known as "Stonewall" ever after. Jackson's reputation as a brilliant general was earned in the Shenandoah Valley campaign of spring 1862. Outnumbered four to one, his small force goaded and defied the Union Army. Unforgiving of weakness and a harsh disciplinarian, Jackson was a tough man to serve under, but by driving his troops pitilessly on forced marches he ran circles around the enemy and repeatedly brought them to battle at times of his own choosing.

Sheer exhaustion may account for Jackson's uncharacteristically lethargic performance under Robert E. Lee in the Seven Days' Battles in June 1862. This did not prevent him from becoming Lee's most trusted colleague. In August, his seizure of Manassas rail junction by a hard-driven flanking march led to a Confederate victory at the second Bull Run. He fought alongside Lee in the desperate defensive battle at Antietam in September, and in the crushing repulse of a Union offensive at Fredericksburg in December.

Chancellorsville in May 1863 was both Jackson's triumph and his downfall. Wounded by "friendly fire" from one of his own infantrymen, he died of complications after surgery. Lee felt his loss deeply and it was a severe setback for the Confederacy.

> ## TO MOVE SWIFTLY, STRIKE VIGOROUSLY, AND SECURE ALL THE FRUITS OF VICTORY IS THE SECRET OF SUCCESS...
>
> **STONEWALL JACKSON**, ON ACHIEVING SUCCESS IN WAR, 1863

God's general
Jackson had the assurance of a man convinced his every act was fulfilling God's plan for the world. He sought to "mystify, mislead, and surprise the enemy" to compensate for the heavy odds against the Confederates.

KEY BATTLE
CHANCELLORSVILLE

CAMPAIGN American Civil War
DATE May 1–6, 1863
LOCATION Spotsylvania County, Virginia

From his headquarters at Chancellorsville Mansion, the Union general, Joseph Hooker, with 130,000 men to Robert E. Lee's 60,000, launched an offensive against the Confederates. Learning that Hooker's right flank was exposed, Lee sent Jackson on a circuitous 12-mile (20-km) march to attack it, while himself engaging the Union Army frontally at Chancellorsville. Jackson's maneuver did not go unnoticed, but was taken by most of the Union commanders as a sign of retreat. When Jackson burst on Hooker's right flank on May 2, his assault was devastating and the Union corps was routed. Fighting continued into the evening, in the course of which Jackson was shot in the arm by one of his own pickets. Command of his corps fell to Jeb Stuart. With Lee hammering his eastern flank, Hooker was at last forced to withdraw, leaving Lee victorious. But when he heard that Jackson's arm had been amputated, Lee commented, "He has lost his left arm, but I have lost my right." His words were prophetic, for Jackson died of pneumonia on May 10.

TIMELINE

- **1825–29** Robert E. Lee attends West Point, the US military academy, graduating to enter the Corps of Engineers as a lieutenant.

- **1847** In the Mexican War, Lee fights with distinction under General Winfield Scott in the advance from Vera Cruz to Mexico City.

US INVASION OF MEXICO, 1847

- **1852–55** Lee is superintendent of West Point, leaving to serve as a lieutenant-colonel in the 2nd US Cavalry.

- **October 1859** Aided by Jeb Stuart, Lee commands the force that arrests abolitionist John Brown at Harper's Ferry.

- **April 1861** Lee is offered field command of the Union Army by Abraham Lincoln but instead resigns from the US Army and takes command of Virginia rebel forces.

- **November 1861** A general in the Confederate Army, Lee fails to prevent Union forces from dominating the South Carolina coast.

- **June 1862** Lee takes command of the Army of Northern Virginia after General Joseph Johnston is wounded and drives back the Union Army of the Potomac in the Seven Days' Battles (June 25–July 1).

- **August 28–30, 1862** The long and bloody second battle of Bull Run (Manassas) ends in victory for the Confederates.

- **September 14–17, 1862** Lee launches a bold invasion of Maryland on September 14, narrowly escaping destruction at Antietam.

- **December 11–15, 1862** Lee blocks a Union offensive at Fredericksburg, inflicting more than 12,000 casualties.

- **May 1–6, 1863** Victory over Union forces at Chancellorsville is marred by the fatal wounding of Stonewall Jackson.

- **June–July 1863** Lee launches a second invasion of the North, marching into Pennsylvania, but the invasion ends in defeat at Gettysburg (July 1–3).

- **May–June 1864** In a fighting withdrawal, Lee resists Ulysses S. Grant at the battles of the Wilderness (May 5–7), Spotsylvania (May 8–21), and Cold Harbor (May 31–June 12).

- **June 1864–March 1865** Lee boosts Confederate forces at the Siege of Petersburg, during which he is promoted to commander-in-chief of the Confederate armies.

- **April 9, 1865** Cornered by Union forces, Lee surrenders to Grant at Appomattox Court House, Virginia.

ROBERT E. LEE

CONFEDERATE GENERAL
BORN January 19, 1807
DIED October 12, 1870
KEY CONFLICTS Mexican-American War, American Civil War
KEY BATTLES Seven Days' Battles 1862, Second Bull Run 1862, Antietam 1862, Fredericksburg 1862, Chancellorsville 1863, Gettysburg 1863, Spotsylvania 1864, Siege of Petersburg 1864–65

Robert E. Lee, the quintessential Virginia gentleman, was the son of the American Revolutionary War hero and former state governor Major-General Henry Lee. Second in his class at West Point, he entered the elite Corps of Engineers and spent almost two decades supervising both civil and military engineering projects. His evident ability earned him a place on General Winfield Scott's staff for the invasion of Mexico in 1847.

Entrusted with reconnaissance missions, he twice led troops on routes he had discovered around the flanks of Mexican forces, thereby contributing to American victories at Cerro Gordo and Churubusco. These excitements were soon over, though, as Lee returned to a quiet career in

Victory at Fredericksburg
In December 1862, Lee organized a strong defensive position on a ridge behind Fredericksburg, Virginia. The Union assault on Lee's determined infantry and artillery was repulsed with heavy losses.

the peacetime army and by the late 1850s was a lieutenant-colonel commanding cavalry in Texas. By chance, he had returned to Virginia in 1859 when antislavery activists led by John Brown attacked the US Arsenal at Harper's Ferry. Lee was ordered to the scene and directed the assault that captured Brown.

The Harper's Ferry raid was a sign of increasing division on the slavery issue. Although Lee owned slaves himself, he considered slavery a bad thing. He did not want the breakup of the Union, but was loyal first and

Appointed to succeed the wounded Joseph Johnston in charge of the army in the Peninsula, Lee quickly launched the offensive known as the Seven Days' Battles.

INITIAL ERRORS
Commanding in battle for the first time, not surprisingly, Lee made plenty of mistakes. It was his good fortune that his opponent, George B. McClellan, was so easily unnerved and so willing to withdraw when attacked. Lee's other great stroke of luck was to discover an ideal partner

> ## HIS NAME MIGHT BE AUDACITY. HE WILL TAKE MORE DESPERATE CHANCES... THAN ANY OTHER GENERAL IN THIS COUNTRY.
>
> **CONFEDERATE COLONEL JOSEPH IVES**, SPEAKING OF ROBERT E. LEE, JUNE 1862

foremost to Virginia. Turning down an offer of senior command in the Union Army, in April 1861, he sided with the Confederacy. President Jefferson Davis made him a general and took him as his closest military adviser. As Lee set men to digging fortifications in front of Richmond, no one suspected this courteous professional soldier would turn out to be an aggressive field commander.

in Stonewall Jackson. Lee and Jackson had contrasting temperaments—Lee cool and poised, Jackson driven and intense—but they shared the view that only aggressive tactics and an offensive strategy offered the South any hope against the Union's much larger, better-equipped armies. Lee was prepared to risk dividing his forces, giving Jackson free rein to strike at the enemy's weak points

Image of a gentleman
Consistently calm and dignified, Lee held the trust and admiration of his troops even in defeat. The South's desperate strategic situation made him adopt a high-risk approach, despite his naturally sober temperament.

KEY TROOPS

CONFEDERATE ARMY

Created out of nothing at the start of the Civil War, the Confederate Army was initially a volunteer force, with conscription introduced in 1862. It was an all-white army—only at the very end was any attempt made to enlist black slaves. The Confederate troops, convinced that they were fighting in defense of their homes and families, on average showed greater

commitment than the Union soldiers. Often ragged, underfed, and short of every necessity of war, they fought with a tremendous courage that Lee said "entitles them to rank with the soldiers of any army and of any time." Out of a total of one million men who served in the Confederate forces, a quarter died through combat or as a result of disease.

through swift and unexpected maneuvers. This was the secret of their joint victories at the second battle of Bull Run (known as the second battle of Manassas to the Confederates) and Chancellorsville. This commitment to the strategic offensive overstretched Confederate resources. Lee's September 1862 invasion of Maryland nearly ended in disaster at Antietam (pp. 248–49), and at Gettysburg the next year, his invasion of Pennsylvania came to grief. In fact, it was when the Union side took the offensive that Lee and his troops performed best.

At Fredericksburg in December 1862, Union troops were slaughtered in an ill-advised assault on Lee's well-prepared defensive position, and his subsequent fine victory at Chancellorsville was a decisive counterpunch against an advancing Union army, brilliant in conception and execution.

Minié balls
The muzzle-loaded rifle-muskets used by Civil War infantry fired grooved lead Minié balls.

The loss of Jackson in the aftermath of Chancellorsville was a serious blow to Lee. He had no other subordinate with an independent capacity for aggressive maneuver. In the absence of Jackson, Lee saw no alternative at Gettysburg to frontal assaults that climaxed in the infamous Pickett's Charge, repulsed with grievous losses. For the rest of the war, the Confederates were forced on to the defensive. Lee offered to resign, but no one could be found to replace him. Facing Ulysses S. Grant in 1864, Lee fought a skillful series of defensive actions and imposed heavy casualties on advancing Union forces that outnumbered his troops by two to one. His dwindling army was then pinned down in trenches outside Petersburg—it was sheer loyalty to Lee as their commander that held the men at their posts. Eventually cornered at Appomattox, Lee opted for a dignified surrender.

> IT IS I WHO HAVE LOST THIS FIGHT, AND YOU MUST HELP ME OUT OF IT THE BEST WAY YOU CAN.
>
> **ROBERT E. LEE**, ADDRESSING HIS TROOPS AFTER GETTYSBURG, 1863

1850—1914

LEE VS. McCLELLAN

IN SEPTEMBER 1862, Robert E. Lee's Army of Northern Virginia invaded Maryland. George B. McClellan was given command of the Army of the Potomac to oppose him. Lee riskily scattered his forces, the largest contingent under Thomas Stonewall Jackson attacking Harpers Ferry. By sheer chance, McClellan came into possession of Lee's Special Order 191, describing this dispersal. He saw the opportunity to keep Lee's forces divided and defeat them systematically, but was too slow to take it. After a holding action in the passes of the South Mountain, Lee fell back on Sharpsburg between Antietam Creek and the Potomac River.

ROBERT E. LEE

On September 15, encouraged by the news that Jackson had taken Harpers Ferry, Lee decided to stand and fight at Sharpsburg. Ordering Jackson's men and other scattered forces to join him, he established a defensive line exploiting existing features—hills, fences, and a sunken road. His strength increasing as dispersed contingents arrived, Lee faced McClellan across Antietam Creek. Skirmishes on the evening of September 16 revealed Union troops had crossed the Creek and were assembling on Lee's left. The next morning he was well prepared to face an onslaught from that direction. As the battle unfolded, Lee stayed in close touch with the fighting, shifting troops rapidly to places where collapse threatened. Divisions were first thrown into the desperate battle in the Cornfield and West Wood on his left, then switched back to the center and the right as the focus of the Union attacks altered.

DIGNIFIED RETREAT

Lee's aggressive use of artillery compensated for his inferior numbers of infantry, but he was greatly relieved when the last division from Harpers Ferry under A. P. Hill was sighted marching toward the battlefield. His arrival in mid-afternoon saved Lee's right flank from being overwhelmed, forcing Union troops back to the creek. Holding his position the following day, Lee was then allowed to stage a nighttime withdrawal unmolested across the Potomac.

> **[McCLELLAN] IS AN ABLE GENERAL BUT A VERY CAUTIOUS ONE. HIS ARMY IS IN A VERY... CHAOTIC CONDITION.**
>
> **ROBERT E. LEE**, SEPTEMBER 9, 1862

TIMELINE

LEE

Evening Confederate troops clash with Hooker's Union troops in East Wood, indicating to Lee the direction from which he would be attacked

7 a.m. John Bell Hood's division counterattacks in the Cornfield and West Wood, halting Hooker's advance but suffering up to 80 percent casualties

8:30 a.m. As Hooker's advance has run out of steam, Lee shifts Confederate forces from that sector to drive back the attack on Dunker Church. Mansfield is fatally wounded

9:30 a.m. Lee sends troops from his center to the left, catching Sumner's lead division in the flank and rear. The fighting on the Confederate left then subsides

1862: SEPT 16 — **SEPT 17**

McCLELLAN

Late afternoon McClellan sends Union troops under Joseph Hooker to take up position on the Confederate left, exploiting undefended crossings of Antietam Creek

Dawn Hooker's corps begins advance along Hagerstown Pike. Both sides take heavy casualties from artillery and infantry fire

7:30 a.m. A second Union corps under Joseph Mansfield joins the attack on the Confederate left, advancing toward Dunker Church

9 a.m. McClellan belatedly orders a third Union corps under Edwin Sumner to cross Antietam Creek and attack the Confederates in West Wood

10 a.m. McClellan orders Burnside's corps to attack across Antietam Creek on the Confederate right. Other Union forces attack in the center

KEY

■ Union forces
■ Confederate forces

N

① 6:00 a.m.: Hooker launches powerful attack against the Confederate left

③ Attack in the center leads to fierce fighting around the sunken road. McClellan fails to commit his reserves

④ 12:30 p.m.: After more than three hours' fighting, Burnside's men succeed in crossing Lower Bridge

⑥ Burnside withdraws to the bridge and fighting comes to an end. The next day, both sides gather their dead and wounded

⑤ 3:30 p.m.: A. P. Hill's division arrives just in time to bolster the Confederate right

② Union artillery mows down Confederate troops in the Cornfield. Lee moves troops from center to prevent breakthrough

McCLELLAN · Upper Bridge · Antietam Creek · BURNSIDE · Middle Bridge · Lower Bridge · HOOKER · SUMNER · MANSFIELD · East Woods · North Woods · cornfield · West Woods · Dunker Church · Sharpsburg · LONGSTREET · A.P. HILL · Harpers Ferry Road · JACKSON · LEE · STUART · Potomac · Potomac

0 km 0.5 1
0 miles 0.5 1

LOCATION Near Sharpsburg, Maryland
CAMPAIGN American Civil War
DATE September 17, 1862
FORCES Union: c. 75,000; Confederate: c. 40,000
CASUALTIES Union: c. 12,000; Confederate: c. 10,000

GEORGE B. McCLELLAN

On September 15, President Lincoln wired McClellan: "Destroy the rebel army, if possible." It seemed possible, for he had some 75,000 soldiers, twice Lee's strength, and the Union troops were well equipped and in excellent morale. McClellan devised a neat plan to crush Lee. Three corps would attack the Confederate left in overwhelming force, while Ambrose Burnside's corps on the other flank would cut off Lee's only line of retreat. Two corps were kept in reserve, along with all McClellan's cavalry, for a final annihilating attack on the trapped and weakened enemy.

The execution of this plan on September 17 was thwarted by two factors. One was McClellan's distance from the battle: he established his headquarters at a house about a mile from the fighting and never left it. This meant he could not successfully coordinate his corps commanders, who made their attacks sequentially.

By the time Burnside was ordered to attempt crossing Antietam Creek, the fighting on the Confederate left had subsided. McClellan also grossly overestimated Lee's forces and clung on to his reserves rather than commit them to the battle. When the bravery of Union infantry at last overcame stubborn resistance at the sunken road (later, Bloody Lane) and the Confederate center was exposed, McClellan refused a request from a reserve corps commander to attack. As a result, 20,000 Union soldiers never fired a shot.

HEAVY CASUALTIES

McClellan was especially criticized for his failure to renew the battle on September 18. Both sides had sustained heavy losses: 12,000 Union casualties to 10,000 Confederate made it the costliest day's fighting in US history. McClellan's unused reserves alone were almost equal in number to Lee's remaining fit troops, yet the Confederates were allowed to slip away. While it may be questionable who won the battle, it is clear who showed better generalship: Lincoln fired McClellan three weeks later.

Burnside's bridge
Union troops flood over Lower Bridge on the Antietam, overcoming resistance by Confederate sharpshooters and artillery.

1850–1914

10:30 a.m. Lee throws his final reserve division into the fight to hold the sunken road, later known as Bloody Lane, in the center of his line

12:30 p.m. After a long and hard fight at Lower Bridge, Georgia sharpshooters finally fail to prevent Union troops from crossing to establish a bridgehead

1:30 p.m. Confederate troops on the right fall back before a Union division that has crossed Antietam Creek at Snavely's Ford, south of Lower Bridge

3:30 p.m. Lee sees a Confederate division under A. P. Hill arriving along the road from Harpers Ferry. It marches straight into battle, smashing into Burnside's flank

6 p.m. Fighting ends as the light begins to fail. Lee's army is shaken and battered, but unbroken

Night Lee stages an uncontested withdrawal to a ford over the Potomac, crossing into Virginia

SEPT 18

12 noon Burnside still fails to cross Lower Bridge over Antietam Creek. Frustrated, McClellan sends him a message saying, "If it costs 10,000 men he must go now"

1 p.m. Union infantry take Bloody Lane, but McClellan refuses to commit reserves to exploit the opening, saying, "It would not be prudent to make the attack"

3 p.m. After a long delay to bring up ammunition, Burnside resumes his attack and pushes back the Confederate right toward Sharpsburg

4:30 p.m. Burnside falls back to Lower Bridge and requests reinforcements, but McClellan cautiously declines to commit one of his reserve corps

Evening McClellan decides that it is too risky to resume the battle, saying there is "no absolute assurance of success"

UNION COMMANDERS

THE MAJORITY OF SUCCESSFUL Union commanders in the Civil War were graduates of the US Military Academy at West Point. Many of them were returning from civilian life after previously less than glorious military careers. Political influence was essential for a fast track to high command at the start of the war, whether a man was competent or not, although merit displayed in battle became more important to promotion as the war went on. It was in the nature of the conflict that George McClellan, full of high-flown European notions, should fail, while the hard-bitten fighter, Ulysses S. Grant, emerged as the hero of the Union.

AGENTS OF EMPIRE

GEORGE B. McCLELLAN

UNION GENERAL
BORN December 3, 1826
DIED October 29, 1885
KEY CONFLICT American Civil War
KEY BATTLES Williamsburg 1862, Seven Days' Battles 1862, Antietam 1862

A graduate of West Point, George McClellan fought as a lieutenant in the Corps of Engineers in the Mexican War of 1846–48. In 1855, after transferring to the cavalry, he served as official US observer of the Crimean War. Proud of his knowledge of European military theory, he came home convinced of his expertise in the latest practice of warfare.

McClellan had resigned by the time the Civil War broke out. Aided by his social contacts and a reputation for military wisdom, in May 1861, he rejoined the army as a major-general. In the panic that followed the Union defeat at the first Bull Run in July, he was called upon to save Washington, D.C., and by November had replaced Winfield Scott as general-in-chief. McClellan, an outstanding organizer and motivator, turned the capital into a fortified camp, where he equipped and trained the 150,000-strong Army of the Potomac. In principle, he advocated a single swift campaign to win the war. In practice, he sat cautiously on the defensive, overrating Confederate strength.

A POOR FIGHTER

Pushed by Lincoln, he finally launched an offensive in March 1862. A plan to land the Army of the Potomac on the Virginia coast and march down the Yorktown Peninsula to Richmond was thwarted by hesitant execution.

McClellan the cautious
Though he was an imposing figure and popular with his troops, McClellan was also vain, overcautious, and secretive.

McClellan's logistics were perfect but his movement was slow. He advanced on Richmond after a victory at Williamsburg, but was unnerved by Confederate counterattacks. On the battlefield McClellan positioned himself too far from the action and held too many troops in reserve. Outfought by Robert E. Lee in the Seven Days' Battles, he carried out a typically well-organized withdrawal.

No longer general-in-chief, in September 1862, McClellan was once more given command of the defense of the capital by Lincoln, who recognized that "if he can't fight himself, he excels in making others ready to fight." Lee's offensive in Maryland offered McClellan a golden opportunity for a crushing victory. When he failed to deliver, allowing Lee to escape destruction at Antietam (pp. 248–49), Lincoln dismissed him. McClellan never held command again.

PHILIP SHERIDAN

UNION CAVALRY GENERAL
BORN March 6, 1831
DIED August 5, 1888
KEY CONFLICTS American Civil War, Plains Indian Wars
KEY BATTLES Chickamauga 1863, Chattanooga 1863, Shenandoah Valley Campaign 1864, Appomattox Campaign 1865

The son of poor Irish immigrants, Philip Sheridan obtained a place at West Point by lucky chance. An undistinguished officer until the Civil War, his outstanding performance in the western theater in 1862 earned him promotion from captain to major-general. He showed aggression and resolve leading infantry at Chickamauga and Chattanooga in the fall of 1863, and in spring 1864 was brought east by Grant to lead the cavalry of the Army of the Potomac.

His cavalry adopted a mass-raiding role, which led to Confederate Jeb Stuart's death at the battle of Yellow Tavern. In August 1864, Sheridan was ordered to clear the Shenandoah Valley of Confederates. His scorched-earth campaign devastated the area and was accompanied by hard-fought combat in which he proved an excellent commander. In the final campaign of the war, he cornered Lee at Appomattox, forcing his surrender.

Sheridan's ride
In a famous episode of the Shenandoah Valley Campaign in October 1864, Sheridan galloped to rejoin his army engaged in battle at Cedar Creek and was cheered as he rode down the line.

> **THE PEOPLE MUST BE LEFT NOTHING BUT THEIR EYES TO WEEP WITH.**
>
> **GENERAL PHILIP SHERIDAN**, ON THE PROPER CONDUCT OF WAR, 1870

WILLIAM T. SHERMAN

UNION GENERAL
BORN February 8, 1820
DIED February 14, 1891
KEY CONFLICTS American Civil War, Plains Indian Wars
KEY BATTLES Shiloh 1862, Chattanooga 1863, Atlanta Campaign 1864, March to the Sea 1864, Bentonville 1865

When Sherman was nine years old, his father died and his family became poverty-stricken. He was adopted by a leading Ohio politician, Thomas Ewing, and grew up asthmatic and depressive. Ewing found him a place at West Point and after graduation Sherman took part in the war against the Seminole Indians in Florida. He missed the Mexican War, however,

supported Grant ably enough during the siege of Vicksburg and afterward at the battle of Chattanooga. When Grant left for Washington in March 1864, Sherman was given command of the western theater. Skillfully forcing the Confederates back through maneuver rather than assault, he reached Atlanta in September.

Sherman had long believed that waging economic and psychological war on the Southern population would best win the conflict. This motivated his March to the Sea through Georgia to the port of Savannah, laying waste to the land as he went. The Confederates only halted him temporarily

en route at such battles as Bentonville. He continued the policy into South Carolina the next year.

After the Civil War, Sherman took over from Grant as commander of the army and led a pitiless campaign to break Native American resistance. He retired from the army in 1884.

Advocate of total war
Sherman was a depressive and conflicted character who hesitated to take on the responsibility of command. He is remembered for his harsh commitment to total war against the civilian population of the South, although he argued that this would save lives by ending the war more quickly.

> ❝ WAR IS CRUELTY. THERE IS NO USE TRYING TO REFORM IT. THE CRUELER IT IS, THE SOONER IT WILL BE OVER. ❞
> **GENERAL WILLIAM T. SHERMAN**

1850—1914

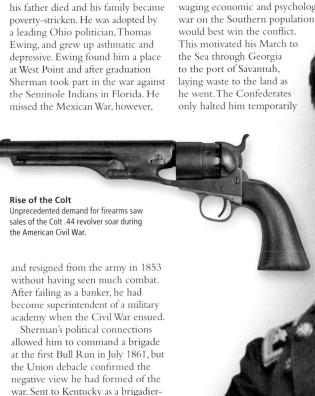

Rise of the Colt
Unprecedented demand for firearms saw sales of the Colt .44 revolver soar during the American Civil War.

and resigned from the army in 1853 without having seen much combat. After failing as a banker, he had become superintendent of a military academy when the Civil War ensued.

Sherman's political connections allowed him to command a brigade at the first Bull Run in July 1861, but the Union debacle confirmed the negative view he had formed of the war. Sent to Kentucky as a brigadier-general, he asked to be relieved of his post when the resignation of his superior officer made him senior commander. Newspaper reports appeared questioning his sanity.

A CHANGE OF STANCE

The turning point in Sherman's life came when he was serving under Ulysses S. Grant at Shiloh in April 1862. Nearly routed by an unexpected Confederate attack, Sherman performed with courage and competence in the heat of battle, helping Grant save the day. In the aftermath, he encouraged Grant to weather criticism, so creating a lasting bond between the two men. As Sherman put it, "Grant stood by me when I was crazy, and I stood by him when he was drunk." After a costly failure attacking the Chickasaw Bluffs in December 1862, Sherman

ULYSSES S. GRANT

UNION GENERAL AND US PRESIDENT
BORN April 27, 1822
DIED July 23, 1885
KEY CONFLICTS Mexican-American War, American Civil War
KEY BATTLES Fort Donelson 1862, Shiloh 1862, Vicksburg 1863, Chattanooga 1863, Siege of Petersburg 1864–65

The son of a tanner and small-town mayor in Ohio, Ulysses Grant entered the US Military Academy at West Point hoping to be "safe for life"—that is, ensured a career and an income. By mistake, he was registered

first full-scale battle at Shiloh, he got a different kind of press. His camp was surprised by Confederate forces in his absence and his army nearly routed. Grant returned to take control and managed to achieve an unlikely victory on the second day's fighting, but heavy Union losses shocked the Northern public. Tales of Grant's heavy drinking circulated, but Lincoln kept faith in him, saying, "I can't spare this man: he fights."

Sidelined after Shiloh by his theater commander, General Henry Halleck, Grant contemplated quitting the

> ## WHAT I WANT IS GENERALS WHO WILL FIGHT BATTLES AND WIN VICTORIES. GRANT HAS DONE THIS...
> **PRESIDENT ABRAHAM LINCOLN**, 1863

AGENTS OF EMPIRE

with the middle initial S, which he kept for life. He distinguished himself only in horsemanship—but on graduating, was sent to the infantry.

Serving in the Mexican War as a regimental quartermaster, he saw a good deal of action, proving he had the gift of physical courage—a Union soldier would later say of him, "Ulysses don't scare worth a damn." His military talent was noticed, but this did him no good in the subsequent peace. In 1854, posted to California far from his family, he suddenly resigned from the army. Rumor said he had been forced to quit or be dismissed for heavy drinking.

In civilian life he failed to prosper, but the Civil War rescued him from obscurity. Throwing himself with immense energy into the raising and training of volunteers, by August 1861 he was a brigadier-general assigned to the western theater.

Grant first attracted the attention of President Lincoln and the press with the capture of Fort Donelson in Tennessee in February 1862. At a time of low morale in the Union camp, Grant's widely reported insistence on the "unconditional surrender" of the fort's defenders was lauded. Two months later, fighting his

army but held on with moral support from General William T. Sherman. By fall 1862, he was back in command and seeking a means to take the fortress of Vicksburg, the key to the Mississippi. Grant was a master of logistics, using river steamers and railroads to move troops and supplies. But in swampy terrain crawling with Confederate raiders, conventional maneuvers broke down. Following months of frustration, in April 1863, Grant abandoned links with a supply base and marched across country. Seizing Jackson, Mississippi, he cut the communications of the Confederate forces who had been driven back into Vicksburg. After a six-week siege, Vicksburg surrendered and the Union had control of the Mississippi.

Grant's successes continued when he was transferred to Chatanooga in October, where a Union army was under virtual siege after defeat at Chickamauga. Grant moved in reinforcements, and then took the offensive, opening the way for an advance into Georgia.

In March 1864, Grant had the satisfaction of replacing Halleck as Union general-in-chief. Lincoln had

Grant's field glasses
Binoculars were in use on the battlefield by the 1860s and gave commanders an improved view of the action.

Unassuming commander
Grant's portrait, taken by the celebrated Civil War photographer Matthew Brady, reveals the commander-in-chief's casual style. He is pictured outside his tent headquarters after the battle of Cold Harbor in June 1864.

The siege of Vicksburg, *1863*
Known as the Gibraltar of the West, Vicksburg was a formidable fortress dominating the vital Mississippi transport route. Grant took it by marching south to cross the river, then moving inland to besiege the town on its east side.

recognized in him the man who would apply the Union's superior force unflinchingly to grind down rebel resistance. Grant moved to the eastern theater, leaving the trusted Sherman to run the campaign in Georgia and Tennessee.

Grant was in many ways a surprising person to mastermind the Union victory. He had surrounded himself with a personal staff of acquaintances from Illinois, men of no military training or distinction in civilian life, but whom he trusted and with whom he felt at ease. He hardly ever consulted his subordinate commanders, running operations through a stream of clear, succinct orders written in his own hand. There was, in the words of one observer, "no glitter or parade about him." He made no flowery speeches—indeed, he never addressed his troops at all—and usually wore a private's coat, going around with a cigar clenched between his teeth.

TOTAL WARFARE

Grant's way of fighting was equally sober and gritty. Convinced of the need for the "complete subjugation of the South" through the destruction of its economic life, he fully backed Sherman's scorched-earth campaign for devastating the land in Georgia. He later ordered General Philip

Sheridan to pursue the same policy in the Shenandoah Valley. His own Overland Campaign in Virginia in May and June 1864 was a relentless series of attacks on Robert E. Lee's Army of Northern Virginia, kept up regardless of cost and giving Lee no time to catch his breath.

The slaughter at the bludgeoning battles of the Wilderness, Spotsylvania, and especially Cold Harbor earned Grant a reputation as a "butcher," but in his view there was no easier way to win the war. The Overland Campaign cost 55,000 Union casualties and failed to annihilate the Confederate Army, thanks to Lee's defensive skill. But it did impose losses on the Confederates that they could not afford and forced Lee to entrench around Petersburg. Grant played out the endgame implacably, yet showed generosity in the terms allowed to Lee on his surrender.

> # FIND OUT WHERE YOUR ENEMY IS. GET AT HIM AS SOON AS YOU CAN. STRIKE HIM AS HARD AS YOU CAN...
>
> **ULYSSES S. GRANT**, ON HIS PRINCIPLES OF WARFARE

BIOGRAPHY
ABRAHAM LINCOLN

President Lincoln had no experience of military command when he led the United States into war in 1861 and he had difficulty handling generals such as McClellan, who did not respect him and resented his "meddling." Yet Lincoln's instinctive grasp of the principles of warfare was superior to theirs. He knew that a war was only won by bringing the enemy to battle and striking hard, at any cost. The Union's success depended largely on Lincoln's ability to choose good generals. In Grant and Sherman he at last found leaders with the bulldog tenacity he required. Lincoln was a man of exceptional qualities, and his assassination in the hour of victory was a disaster for the United States.

1850–1914

TIMELINE

■ **1839–43** Grant studies at West Point Military Academy, emerging 21st in a class of 39. He is assigned to the infantry.

■ **1846–47** Fighting in the Mexican War, Grant performs coolly under fire at Monterrey (September 1846) and in the attack on Chapultepec (September 1847).

■ **April 1854** Grant resigns from the US Army while serving as a captain in California. Some allege heavy drinking is the cause of his resignation.

■ **April 1861** At the outbreak of the Civil War, Grant is working as a clerk in Galena, Illinois. He raises a volunteer company and is swiftly promoted to colonel (June) and brigadier-general (August).

■ **February 1862** His successful attacks on Fort Henry and Fort Donelson in Tennessee, with the capture of over 12,000 Confederate soldiers, win him praise and promotion to major-general.

■ **April 6–7, 1862** Grant is almost routed at Shiloh but retrieves the situation. His reputation is harmed by the high casualties suffered.

BATTLE OF CHAPULTEPEC, 1847

■ **May–July 1863** Grant traps 30,000 Confederate soldiers at Vicksburg and forces them to surrender after a six-week siege.

■ **October–November 1863** Taking command of the besieged Army of the Cumberland at Chattanooga, he wins a notable victory at Missionary Ridge (November 25).

■ **March 1864** Promoted to general-in-chief of all Union armies with the rank of lieutenant-general, Grant moves to the eastern theater to lead the fight against the main Confederate force, Lee's Army of Northern Virginia.

■ **May–June 1864** Grant leads a Union advance through Virginia in the Overland Campaign, fighting Lee at the Wilderness and Spotsylvania (May 5–21), and Cold Harbor (May 31–June 12).

■ **June 1864–March 1865** Grant fights trench warfare around Petersburg and Richmond, Virginia, eventually wearing down the Confederate defenders.

■ **April 9, 1865** Grant accepts Lee's surrender at Appomattox Court House, effectively bringing the war to an end; the terms allow Confederate soldiers and officers to return to their homes.

■ **1869–77** Grant serves two terms as Republican President of the United States.

The battle of Chattanooga
The clash at Chattanooga on November 25, 1863, ended in victory for Ulysses S. Grant, as Union troops broke through Confederate lines, taking Lookout Mountain.

1865—1905

FRONTIERS
AND COLONIES

"IT IS FOOLISH NOT TO RECOGNIZE THAT WE ARE FIGHTING A FORMIDABLE AND TERRIBLE ADVERSARY... WE MUST FACE THE FACTS. THE INDIVIDUAL BOER MOUNTED IN SUITABLE COUNTRY IS WORTH THREE TO FIVE REGULAR SOLDIERS."

WINSTON CHURCHILL, *MY EARLY LIFE: A ROVING COMMISSION,* 1930

Battle of Isandhlwana
On January 22, 1879, Zulu warriors attacked a British camp at Isandhlwana, slaughtering the British troops to the last man. It was a harsh lesson in the fate that could befall imperial forces under inadequate command.

UCH WARFARE BETWEEN 1850 and 1914 was fought by European and American armies in imperialist campaigns in Africa and Asia, or on the expanding borders of the United States and Russia. Pitting relatively small numbers of western troops against traditional warriors with inferior weaponry, these wars made a colorful spectacle for the patriotic public of industrialized countries. Commanders were as likely to earn fame with dramatic deaths—like George Custer and Gordon of Khartoum—as with victories through superior strength.

In this period, there were many outbreaks of colonial and frontier warfare as non-European peoples resisted subjection to European or American domination. These campaigns ranged from Indochina and Afghanistan to New Zealand and Namibia. They included the conflict between the US Army and Native American tribes, such as the Sioux and Apache, from the 1860s to the 1880s; the British conquests of the warlike Zulu in the 1870s and the Sudanese Mahdists in the 1890s; and France's long struggle to subject countries in North Africa to its rule. There was also a unique contest between the British and the Boers in South Africa, a war in which farmers of European origin adopted guerrilla tactics against an imperial power.

NEW THEATERS OF WAR

In retrospect, frontier and colonial wars may appear one-sided, but for the European or American commanders entrusted with defeating either tribal forces or the armies of ancient and far-flung kingdoms, the task was not necessarily straightforward. The lessons of European warfare were unlikely to apply easily to unfamiliar conditions. An overconfident general from a more technologically advanced state could easily blunder into disaster against a skilled enemy able to achieve short-term, local superiority. This was the

fate of Britain's Lord Chelmsford in South Africa, whose careless division of his forces allowed the Zulu to massacre a detachment at Isandhlwana in 1879. It is equally true of US Cavalry commander George Custer, who advanced into a trap set by the Lakota Chief Crazy Horse at Little Bighorn in 1876. Successful approaches ranged from subtle pacification strategies based on an understanding of the enemy, to the more frequently used ruthless and persistent application of superior force.

CLASH OF TECHNOLOGIES

Less technologically advanced societies had their own fighting methods and conventions of leadership. In the case of the tribes of the American West, intelligent and charismatic commanders conducted guerrilla warfare against the US Army. In Africa, too, there were leaders capable of organizing warfare on a substantial scale just as there were ideologies to sustain resistance, especially where Islam had been established. But traditional warrior groups needed to adapt their tactics to combat powerful new enemies. Generally, they did not do so adequately. For example, some modern weapons were quite easy to obtain and use since basic firearms were by now mass-produced. However, integrating these weapons usefully into familiar fighting methods proved difficult. In consequence, while Plains Indians and Zulu both used western firearms, neither group employed them as effectively as their traditional bows or spears.

Feathered headdress
Made from the immature tail feathers of a golden eagle, this headdress belonged to the Arapaho chief Yellow Calf. The feathers represented achievements in war.

NATIVE AMERICAN WARRIORS

FROM THE 1860s through to the 1880s, a series of conflicts was triggered by the encroachment of white Americans upon the territory of Native American tribes on the Great Plains west of the Mississippi River and in areas of the southwest taken over by the United States from Mexico. Peoples such as the Lakota and the Apache were skilled warriors and inflicted some notable defeats on the US Army. Although they had no real chance of resisting the eventual destruction of their way of life and their people, some of their war leaders provided outstanding examples of skill in guerrilla warfare and of dignified courage in adversity.

RED CLOUD

LAKOTA CHIEF
BORN c. 1822
DIED December 10, 1909
KEY CONFLICT Plains Indian Wars
KEY BATTLES Fetterman Massacre 1866, Wagon Box Fight 1867

Red Cloud was a member of the Oglala branch of the Lakota Sioux. As a young man, he fought the Pawnees and the Crows and was an Oglala war leader by the 1860s.

In spring 1866, he opposed a proposal by the United States to extend the Bozeman Trail through the Lakota Powder River hunting grounds to the Montana gold fields. Red Cloud became one of the principal leaders of Lakota warbands dedicated to keeping the Americans out of the Powder River region. Newly built Fort Phil Kearny and Fort C. F. Smith were placed under virtual siege by harassing attacks. The total annihilation of a cavalry force led by Captain William J. Fetterman by a Lakota ambush outside Fort Phil Kearny in December 1866 shook US opinion. But Red Cloud's attempts to overrun the forts in summer 1867

failed. At the Wagon Box Fight in August, he saw 3,000 of his warriors held off by a handful of US soldiers armed with breech-loading rifles.

With neither side capable of securing a clear victory, a peace deal was agreed to in 1868 and the forts were dismantled. For the rest of his life, Red Cloud defended the rights of the Lakota by peaceful means.

Respected leader
Red Cloud was an imposing figure who won the respect of many white Americans for his dignified defense of Native American rights. This photograph was taken in 1904, by which time he was living on the Pine Ridge Reservation in South Dakota.

GERONIMO

APACHE WAR LEADER
BORN June 16, 1829
DIED February 17, 1909
KEY CONFLICT Apache Wars

The Apache warrior Goyathlay is better known by the name Geronimo, attributed to him by the Mexicans. In his youth, he joined fighting against Mexican settlers and soldiers orchestrated by the Apache chief, Cochise. Geronimo's success in battle earned him a reputation as a medicine man, with the power to protect against bullets, and as a war leader. In the 1850s, his mother, wife, and children were killed in a Mexican raid, a tragedy that could only have fueled his implacable will to fight.

The Mexicans were at this time being supplanted by Americans as the United States expanded westward. Soon it was the US Army that Geronimo was fighting. Precise details of his participation in raids against settlers and clashes with US troops are hard to pin down.

Old fighter
This posed photograph of Geronimo was taken after his surrender in 1886. Such images were popular with white Americans, who made Geronimo into a celebrity as part of their myth of the Wild West.

> ❝ I WAS BORN ON THE PRAIRIES WHERE THE WIND BLEW FREE... WHERE THERE WERE NO ENCLOSURES ❞
> **GERONIMO**

He probably took part in an attack led by Cochise against a regiment marching through Apache Pass, Arizona, in July 1862, and he almost certainly led an ambush of US cavalry in the Whetstone Mountains in May 1871.

By the 1870s, Apache resistance was failing. Under the intelligent leadership of General George Crook, the US Army had adapted to countering guerrilla warfare, employing Apache scouts and traveling light to track down the warbands. Gradually the Apache warriors gave in and reluctantly moved into reservations—Cochise

died in a reservation in 1874. But Geronimo remained stubbornly opposed. Three times he was forced to surrender—in 1877, 1879, and 1883—but each time he managed to escape and resume the leadership of a fugitive warband.

As the last leader of Native American resistance, Geronimo's exploits attracted the attention of the American press. By 1885, some 5,000 US soldiers were engaged in hunting him down, although his followers consisted of a mere 16 warriors and their families. In August 1886, he was persuaded to surrender for good.

At first exiled to Florida with other Apaches, he ended his days at Fort Sill, Oklahoma. As a celebrated survivor from the days of the Wild West, he took part in the St. Louis World's Fair of 1904 and the next year rode in President Theodore Roosevelt's inaugural procession.

CRAZY HORSE

LAKOTA WAR LEADER
BORN c. 1840
DIED September 5, 1877
KEY CONFLICT Plains Indian Wars
KEY BATTLES Fetterman Massacre 1866,
The Rosebud 1876, Little Bighorn 1876,
Wolf Mountain 1877

As a young Lakota warrior from the Oglala branch, Crazy Horse proved himself a fierce fighter against rival tribes. He was known for his visions and magical powers, which were attributes expected of a war leader.

In the mid-1860s, he fought with great skill in Red Cloud's war against the US Army and American settlers.

Sioux knife
Plains Indians used knives in war for finishing off the wounded and scalping the dead. Metal blades were mostly of European manufacture.

In December 1866, he lured troops under Captain William J. Fetterman into an ambush outside Fort Phil Kearny, where they were massacred.

When Red Cloud made peace in 1868, Crazy Horse was among those who continued resistance. He joined Sitting Bull in opposing American encroachment on the sacred Lakota territory of the Black Hills in the 1870s. In June 1876, Crazy Horse ambushed 1,300 US soldiers and Indian scouts led by General George Crook at Rosebud Creek, Montana,

forcing them to withdraw. He then defeated General George Custer at Little Bighorn (pp. 260–61).

In the wake of this triumph, however, the victors were soon reduced to fugitives, facing hardship and starvation as they evaded US forces through the fall and winter. In January 1877, Crazy Horse again attacked US forces at Wolf Mountain, but this time was beaten off by superior firepower. In May, he led his surviving followers to Camp Robinson, Nebraska, and finally surrendered. Crazy Horse died four months later, bayoneted in a confused scuffle with US soldiers.

BIOGRAPHY

SITTING BULL

A chief of the Hunkpapa Sioux, Sitting Bull was a fierce opponent of American expansion. In the 1870s, he attracted to his camp thousands of warriors who wanted to fight white settlers and the US Army. His moral authority and prophetic visions inspired them to victory at Little Bighorn. Continuing persecution led him to seek refuge in Canada with his tribe, but in 1881, Sitting Bull was starved into surrendering to the authorities. In 1890, he was about to join a Ghost Dance, a ceremony believed to restore the Sioux way of life and sweep away the whites', when he was shot dead by a Lakota policeman.

> ## I WAS NOT HOSTILE TO THE WHITE MEN... ALL WE WANTED WAS PEACE.
>
> **CRAZY HORSE**, REPORTED DYING SPEECH, SEPTEMBER 5, 1877

Rosebud ambush
A newspaper illustration of August 1876 shows Crazy Horse leading the attack on General Crook at Rosebud Creek. In reality, both Lakota and US cavalry would have dismounted to fight.

1850—1914

CRAZY HORSE AT LITTLE BIGHORN

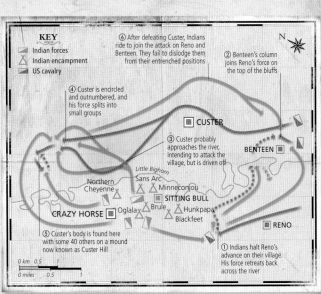

LOCATION
Little Bighorn River, Montana
CAMPAIGN Great Sioux War

DATE June 25, 1876
FORCES Native American c. 1,800; US Army c. 600
CASUALTIES Native American c. 300; US Army 258 killed, 52 wounded

In June 1876, Sioux, Cheyenne, and other warriors, including Lakota Sioux war leader, Crazy Horse, and chief of the Hunkpapa Sioux, Sitting Bull, were encamped near the Little Bighorn River. In a bid to force the tribes back on to their reservations, the US Army sent three columns of troops to attack their encampment. Crazy Horse disrupted the offensive by ambushing one of the US columns at Rosebud Creek on June 17. The remaining US forces split up, hoping to achieve a combined attack on the Indian encampment. General George Custer, commanding the 7th US Cavalry, reached the encampment first on June 25. Underestimating the number of warriors he was facing, he decided on an immediate surprise attack, without waiting for the rest of the US forces to arrive.

CUSTER'S OFFENSIVE

Dividing his force of 600 men into three, Custer tried to encircle the encampment. Major Marcus Reno attacked first at around 3:00 p.m. with about 150 men. Crazy Horse and the other Indian war leaders responded swiftly. Counterattacking in strength, they forced Reno to take refuge on a ridge, where he was joined by a second detachment under Captain Frederick Benteen and pinned down. Custer's own body of around 210 men, delayed by crossing difficult terrain, reached the encampment after Reno had been driven off. Faced by Indian warriors in overwhelming numbers, he too pulled back to high ground, but found it hard to stabilize a defensive position. His men were weakened by volleys of arrows and by individual warriors boldly penetrating their skirmish line.

INDIAN VICTORY

Crazy Horse led a body of warriors on horseback circling around the flank of Custer's position, and charged into the midst of the demoralized American soldiers. Indian eyewitnesses described it as a "buffalo run." Under the shock of this unexpected attack, discipline collapsed and soldiers fled, now easy targets for Indian warriors. Custer and his detachment were massacred. The US soldiers on Reno's hill held out until the following day, when the Indians withdrew on news of the approach of the main body of US troops. Crazy Horse's degree of command over warriors at Little Bighorn remains uncertain, but a Sioux warrior described him as "the greatest fighter in the whole battle."

AGENTS OF EMPIRE

KEY
▢ Indian forces
△ Indian encampment
▢ US cavalry

⑥ After defeating Custer, Indians ride to join the attack on Reno and Benteen. They fail to dislodge them from their entrenched positions

② Benteen's column joins Reno's force on the top of the bluffs

④ Custer is encircled and outnumbered, and his force splits into small groups

▢ CUSTER

③ Custer probably approaches the river, intending to attack the village, but is driven off

BENTEEN ▢

Little Bighorn

Northern Cheyenne
Sans Arc
△ Minneconjou
△ **SITTING BULL**
CRAZY HORSE ▢ Oglala △ Brule △ Hunkpapa
Blackfeet

▢ RENO

⑤ Custer's body is found here with some 40 others on a mound now known as Custer Hill

① Indians halt Reno's advance on their village. His force retreats back across the river

0 km 0.5   1
0 miles 0.5   1

1850–1914

Custer's last stand
An imaginary depiction shows Crazy Horse
charging Custer's hilltop position at Little
Bighorn. The Indians had modern repeating
rifles to the cavalry's single-shot carbines.

AFRICAN LEADERS

FROM THE FRENCH invasion of Algeria in 1830 to the Italian campaign in Ethiopia in 1896, the European takeover of Africa in the 19th century met with determined opposition. African military resistance was led by the existing rulers of peoples with a warlike tradition, such as the Zulu and the Ethiopians, or by self-appointed leaders of insurgent movements. Their best hope of success lay in combining local knowledge and traditional fighting skills with some modern European weaponry. There were many occasions on which intelligent African commanders inflicted defeats on European colonial forces, but only Ethiopia successfully upheld full independence.

AGENTS OF EMPIRE

MUHAMMAD AHMED AL-MAHDI

SUDANESE ISLAMIC LEADER
BORN August 12, 1844
DIED June 22, 1885
KEY CONFLICT Mahdist War
KEY BATTLES El Obeid 1883, Abu Klea 1885, Khartoum 1885

Leader of the jihad
The self-proclaimed Mahdi established an Islamic state in Sudan that survived until 1898, when the British overthrew his successors and desecrated his tomb.

In 1881, Muhammad Ahmed, a Sudanese Muslim, proclaimed himself the Mahdi (a successor of the prophet Muhammad) and declared a religious war on the Egyptians who ruled Sudan. Britain, largely in control of Egypt, was drawn into the conflict.

DERVISH DEFIANCE
The Mahdi had no modern weaponry, but he inspired his followers—known to the British as "Dervishes"—with a death-defying enthusiasm. At El Obeid in November 1883, an 8,000-strong British-led Egyptian force was surrounded and wiped out. General Gordon, sent to organize a withdrawal of Egyptian officials, was trapped in Khartoum by the Mahdist army. The Mahdists were at first repulsed by a British column sent to relieve Khartoum at Abu Klea in January 1885, but they successfully stormed the city before British reinforcements arrived and held it against recapture. Muhammad Ahmed died shortly after.

MENELIK II

ETHIOPIAN EMPEROR
BORN August 17, 1844
DIED December 12, 1913
KEY CONFLICT First Italo-Ethiopian War
KEY BATTLE Adowa 1896

Menelik II was born Prince Sahle Maryam into the ruling family of the kingdom of Shoa. This region of southern Ethiopia enjoyed a degree of independence, relative to the strength of the Ethiopian imperial regime. Menelik became *negus* (king) of Shoa in 1865 and was obliged to pay tribute to the Ethiopian emperor, Yohannis IV. He built up his army by importing modern weapons from Italy and France and expanded his realm through campaigns against peoples around Shoa's borders.

EMPEROR MENELIK
In 1889, Emperor Yohannis was killed in a battle with the Sudanese Mahdists. Menelik made a successful bid for the imperial throne with the backing of Italy, to whom he gave the territory of Eritrea as a colony. But, unsated by this gain, Italy saw its treaty with Menelik as establishing an Italian protectorate over Ethiopia—a pretension that was scotched at the battle of Adowa. Menelik won diplomatic recognition from European states, who excluded Ethiopia from their imperial claims on Africa. In his later years, Menelik achieved a limited modernization of Ethiopia and strengthened central government.

Historic victory
Menelik II's defeat of the Italians at Adowa was hailed as the greatest victory by an African army over a European one since Hannibal.

KEY BATTLE
ADOWA

CAMPAIGN First Italo-Ethiopian War
DATE March 1, 1896
LOCATION Adowa, northern Ethiopia

In 1895, Emperor Menelik led a vast army to the Tigre region of Ethiopia to contest Italian encroachment across the border from Eritrea. An Italian colonial detachment was annihilated at Amba Alagi in December 1895, after which General Oreste Baratiere took up a strong defensive position near Adowa. Menelik had around 100,000 to Baratiere's 18,000 troops, but doubted an attack could succeed. He had resigned himself to withdrawal when, on the night of February 29, 1896, Baratiere unwisely decided to take the offensive himself. Advancing in darkness across unmapped broken terrain, the Italian colonial troops became hopelessly disorganized. Daylight found them split up into isolated brigades, exposed to envelopment by swarming masses of Ethiopian warriors armed with rifles, swords, and spears. Systematically defeated, by midafternoon the Italians were utterly routed, losing around 7,000 men.

CETSHWAYO

ZULU PARAMOUNT CHIEF
BORN c. 1826
DIED February 8, 1884
KEY CONFLICT Anglo-Zulu War.
KEY BATTLES Isandhlwana 1879,
Ulundi 1879

Military chief
Cetshwayo was an energetic ruler who worked to revive the Zulu military system established by Shaka in the early 19th century. This photograph of him was taken around 1870.

Eldest son of the Zulu leader, Mpande, Cetshwayo took effective control of the Zulu nation in 1856 on defeating his brother, Mbuyazi, in battle. But he did not inherit the title, Paramount Chief, until Mpande's death in 1872.

Cetshwayo expanded the Zulu army to around 50,000 warriors and bought firearms to supplement the traditional stabbing spear and shield. In January 1879, the British authorities in South Africa invaded Zululand on a flimsy pretext. Cetshwayo's army destroyed a 1,700-strong British force encamped at Isandhlwana but failed to overcome a small garrison at Rorke's Drift. Heavy losses left the Zulu exposed when the British returned in greater force four months later. The Zulu capital, Ulundi, was captured and burned and, in August, the chief himself was taken prisoner. In 1882, he was brought to England, where he was patronized by London society. His return to Zululand in 1883 was opposed by rivals for power and he died soon after, possibly assassinated.

ABD AL-QADIR

ALGERIAN GUERRILLA LEADER
BORN September 6, 1808
DIED May 26, 1883
KEY CONFLICT Algerian resistance struggle
KEY BATTLES Macta 1835, Sidi Brahim 1845

Retired guerrilla
By the time this portrait was painted by a European artist in the 1860s, Abd al-Qadir had become a respected friend of the French, who even awarded him the Légion d'Honneur.

> " THESE ARE UNFORTUNATE NECESSITIES THAT ANY PEOPLE WISHING TO MAKE WAR ON THE ARABS MUST ACCEPT. "
>
> **ALEXIS DE TOCQUEVILLE, FRENCH POLITICIAN**, ON BUGEAUD'S COUNTERINSURGENCY CAMPAIGN, 1841

A devout and well-educated Muslim, Abd al-Qadir was the son of a sheikh in the Algerian town of Mascara. In 1830, the French seized control of Algiers and began extending their rule into the interior. Leading the tribes around Mascara, Abd al-Qadir declared a holy war against the infidel invaders in 1832. He showed an instinctive grasp of the principles of guerrilla warfare, evading and harassing French columns sent to attack him. In June 1835, he inflicted an especially costly defeat on General Camille Trézel in the marshes alongside the Macta River. The scale of losses induced General Thomas Bugeaud to sign the Treaty of Tafna in 1837, by which France recognized Abd al-Qadir's rule in most of Algeria beyond their zone of occupation.

THE FRENCH RETURN

In 1839, Abd al-Qadir resumed his guerrilla campaign after French troops trespassed on to his territory. Bugeaud responded with a vicious counterinsurgency campaign, launching punitive raids on villages with his "flying columns," and destroying crops and poisoning wells to deny the Algerian fighters the food and water they needed to survive.

Abd al-Qadir managed to rout a body of French troops at Sidi Brahim in September 1845, but by then his star was waning. When Morocco gave way to French pressure and withdrew its support for the Algerian insurgents, Abd al-Qadir surrendered. He was held prisoner in France from 1848 to 1852, when he was released by Napoleon III. He spent most of the remainder of his life in Damascus.

IMPERIAL COMMANDERS

FRANCE AND BRITAIN were the leading imperial powers of the 19th and early 20th centuries. As they extended their direct rule or "protectorates" over swathes of Africa and Asia, a host of small wars were fought against inferior enemies in exotic lands. The generals who engaged in these conflicts were self-styled representatives of Christian civilization, expected to defeat the empire's enemies while upholding the values of allegedly superior societies. Yet colonial service attracted officers too eccentric to fit in easily at home. The troops they commanded were often locals but their style of fighting was always distinctively European.

AGENTS OF EMPIRE

HUBERT LYAUTEY

FRENCH ARMY OFFICER
BORN November 17, 1854
DIED July 21, 1934
KEY CONFLICTS Pacification of Madagascar, Conquest of Morocco

Hubert Lyautey was France's most idealistic practitioner of colonial counterinsurgency warfare. From an upper-class family in Nancy, he became a cavalry officer under the Third Republic (1870–1940). In 1891, he attracted attention with a provocative article in the political journal, *Revue des Deux Mondes*, which criticized the conservative French officer corps for commanding a national army that was not based on universal conscription.

In 1894, Lyautey was posted to French Indochina, where he met General Joseph Gallieni. He adopted and developed Gallieni's ideas on pacification, linking the military defeat of anticolonial insurgents to the promotion of social and economic progress in pacified zones.

Lyautey played a leading role in the Madagascar occupation from 1897, before moving to Algeria in 1903. He advocated respect for local cultures and cooperation with their elites, but his attempts to follow this line when France took over Morocco in 1912 were only partially successful. There was always the requirement for extreme force to suppress those in opposition and Lyautey's career ended in the 1920s fighting a rebellion led by Berber leader Abd el-Krim.

Distinguished figure
Lyautey was awarded the title of Marshal of France in 1921, one of only eight men to receive this military distinction in the 70 years of the French Third Republic.

HERBERT KITCHENER

BRITISH ARMY OFFICER
BORN June 24, 1850
DIED June 5, 1916
KEY CONFLICTS Mahdist War, Second Boer War
KEY BATTLES Atbara 1898, Omdurman 1898, Paardeberg 1900

An officer in the Royal Engineers, in 1883, Herbert Kitchener was loaned out to the British-led Egyptian Army. He was a member of the military expedition to the Sudan in 1885 that failed to rescue General Gordon from the Mahdists. Appointed Egyptian *sirdar* (commander-in-chief) in 1892, he showed meticulous organizational skills in preparing a second campaign to regain control of the Sudan.

Kitchener's one-sided victories over the Mahdists at Atbara and Omdurman in 1898 (pp. 266–67) made him a British national hero. He was sent to fight the Boers in South Africa in December 1899, but was criticized for wasting soldiers' lives in a frontal assault at Paardeberg. Overall commander from November 1900, he instigated a brutal counterinsurgency campaign to suppress Boer guerrillas, while favoring a conciliatory peace.

After senior postings to India and Egypt, in 1914, Kitchener joined the British government as war minister at the outset of World War I. Correctly predicting a long war, he initiated the recruitment of a mass volunteer army. He drowned in 1916, his warship torpedoed on its journey to Russia.

African lord
Kitchener wears the fez of an officer in the Egyptian Army. He was elevated to the peerage as Lord Kitchener of Khartoum after his victory at the battle of Omdurman in 1898.

> **WITH MACHINELIKE PRECISION HE CARRIED OUT HIS PLANS; NEVER IN A HURRY... NEVER WASTING A MOMENT.**
> **HENRY S. L. ALFORD AND W. DENNISTOUN SWORD**, *THE EGYPTIAN SOUDAN, ITS LOSS AND RECOVERY*, 1898

CHARLES GEORGE GORDON

BRITISH ARMY OFFICER
BORN January 28, 1833
DIED January 26, 1885
KEY CONFLICTS Taiping Rebellion, Mahdist War
KEY BATTLES Peking 1860, Changzhou 1864, Siege of Khartoum 1884–85

The son of a general, Charles George Gordon was commissioned to the Royal Engineers in 1852. He first saw action in the Crimean War, where he discovered a taste for the excitement of combat and an indifference to death springing from his idiosyncratic brand of evangelical Christianity. In 1860, Gordon took part in the occupation of Peking (Beijing), joining the Franco–British forces engaged in punitive action against China during the Second Opium War.

EVER VICTORIOUS

Gordon stayed in China, which was under threat of takeover by the Taiping rebel movement, and in 1862, he was invited to command the Ever Victorious Army, a force of Chinese soldiers operating around Shanghai under European and American mercenary officers. Enforcing strict discipline and outwitting the Taiping with rapid maneuvers, Gordon led this force to a series of victories against the odds, culminating in the storming of Changzhou in May 1864.

Victory over the Taiping rebels made Gordon famous. Henceforth known as "Chinese" Gordon, he returned to Britain but found it difficult to readapt to life in the British Army. In 1873, he gladly accepted an invitation from the ruler of Egypt to govern the southern Sudan. In six years, Gordon largely suppressed the Sudanese slave trade and the local wars associated with it. Despite this impressive work, even his most admiring acquaintances found him increasingly odd. He returned to England, and, in the 1880s, became obsessed by such issues as the quest for the true site of the Garden of Eden.

BESIEGED IN KHARTOUM

In 1884, Gordon was dispatched to Khartoum, where Egyptian soldiers and civilians were under threat from the Mahdi. The British government reluctantly agreed to send the hero popularly seen as the only man to retrieve the situation.

Gordon reached Khartoum and evacuated most of those at risk, but in March allowed himself to be trapped there by the Mahdists. For 317 days he held out under siege while a relief expedition—belatedly sent by a government that privately regarded Gordon as an insubordinate nuisance—drew slowly closer. In January 1885, the waters of the Nile River were shallow enough to allow the Mahdists to penetrate Khartoum. Gordon was killed and his head severed as a trophy.

An officer's death
Gordon was stabbed by Mahdists on the steps of the governor's palace in Khartoum. Soon after the event, George William Joy's painting, *Gordon's Last Stand*, was exhibited to the delight of the Victorian public.

KEY BATTLE

THE TAKING OF PEKING

CAMPAIGN Second Opium War
DATE October 6, 1860
LOCATION Peking, China

In 1860, the British and French sent an invasion force to China after the Chinese government renounced a treaty opening its ports to western trade. The Anglo-French army marched on Peking (present-day Beijing), brushing aside Chinese resistance. The exquisite imperial Summer Palace on the outskirts of the city was first looted by allied troops and then burned down in revenge for the Chinese murder and torture of British diplomatic envoys. Gordon, then a captain in the Royal Engineers stationed in Britain, had volunteered to join the expedition and arrived in time to be present at the sacking of the palace.

KITCHENER AT OMDURMAN

LOCATION
5 miles (8 km) north of Omdurman, Sudan
CAMPAIGN The Mahdist War
DATE September 2, 1898
FORCES British and allies: c. 26,000; Mahdists: c. 50,000
CASUALTIES British and allies: 430 killed and injured; Mahdists: 30,000 killed and injured

As *sirdar* (commander-in-chief) of the British-officered Egyptian Army, General Herbert Kitchener was tasked with regaining control of the Sudan, lost in 1885 to the Islamic Mahdists (known to the British as "Dervishes"). Kitchener mounted an expedition down the Nile with meticulous attention to logistics, building a railroad and using riverboats to carry troops and supplies. Approaching Omdurman—the capital of the Mahdist leader Khalifa al-Taashi—at the end of August 1898, Kitchener's army of about 8,000 British regulars and 17,000 Sudanese and Egyptian troops was accompanied by gunboats to augment the already impressive firepower of its field artillery and Maxim guns.

On September 1, Kitchener camped by the Nile at El Egeiga, within 6 miles (10 km) of Omdurman. He sent out a screen of cavalry to keep watch for the enemy while the gunboats began shelling the town. Around noon, Kitchener received a message from his scouts announcing the approach of a large army. Riding out to a hilltop, Kitchener saw for himself the Mahdists approaching across the plain. He rapidly drew up his infantry in a defensive perimeter, but that day the Mahdists did not come. There followed a nerve-racking night, with soldiers sleeping alongside their rifles and gunboats playing searchlights over the ground in front of the perimeter. Soon after sunrise, British cavalry reported seeing the enemy once more on the advance. Dressed in a white uniform on a white horse, Kitchener observed the enemy's approach through his field glasses.

> ❝ I THANK THE LORD OF HOSTS FOR GIVING US VICTORY AT SO SMALL A COST IN OUR DEAD AND WOUNDED. ❞
>
> **GENERAL HERBERT KITCHENER**, AFTER THE BATTLE OF OMDURMAN, 1898

AGENTS OF EMPIRE

Charge of the 21st Lancers
The Lancers' headlong charge through the Mahdist infantry is the most famous incident of the battle of Omdurman, partly because the young Winston Churchill was involved.

At 10,000 ft (3,000 m), he ordered his gunboats and heavy guns to open fire. The Mahdists came forward in a wide arc, white-clad under bright banners, armed with spears and rifles. As they charged in two waves of 8,000 men, artillery, Maxim guns, and rapid-fire rifles cut them down in swathes. Not a single warrior reached the defensive perimeter alive; only one British soldier was killed.

ENTERING OMDURMAN

Kitchener's priority was to take Omdurman before the enemy could reorganize to defend it. At around 9:00 a.m., he ordered a general advance on Omdurman in columns. Sent ahead to reconnoitre, the 21st Lancers charged into the middle of several thousand Mahdists concealed in a dried-up watercourse, suffering 61 casualties. Meanwhile, the brigade on Kitchener's

far right—Sudanese troops commanded by General Hector MacDonald—was unexpectedly attacked by a horde of over 15,000 enemy warriors. As MacDonald vigorously defended himself, Kitchener at first irritably rejected his appeals for help, but when the scale of the threat became apparent, he issued a flow of orders to lower-level commanders who were already moving to support MacDonald on their own initiative. Again firepower worked and the Mahdists were driven off with heavy losses.

In the afternoon, Kitchener entered Omdurman unopposed. He narrowly escaped being killed by a shrapnel round fired by a gunboat. But the fighting was over. Kitchener had lost 48 men killed and 382 wounded. The Mahdist dead numbered around 10,000.

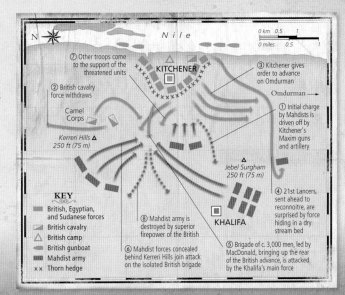

KEY

- British, Egyptian, and Sudanese forces
- British cavalry
- British camp
- British gunboat
- Mahdist army
- ×× Thorn hedge

① Initial charge by Mahdists is driven off by Kitchener's Maxim guns and artillery

② British cavalry force withdraws

③ Kitchener gives order to advance on Omdurman

④ 21st Lancers, sent ahead to reconnoitre, are surprised by force hiding in a dry stream bed

⑤ Brigade of c. 3,000 men, led by MacDonald, bringing up the rear of the British advance, is attacked by the Khalifa's main force

⑥ Mahdist forces concealed behind Kerreri Hills join attack on the isolated British brigade

⑦ Other troops come to the support of the threatened units

⑧ Mahdist army is destroyed by superior firepower of the British

Nile · KITCHENER · Omdurman · Camel Corps · Kerreri Hills 250 ft (75 m) · Jebel Surgham 250 ft (75 m) · KHALIFA

THE BOER WAR

BRITAIN'S IMPERIAL AMBITIONS in southern Africa brought it into conflict with the Boers, the descendants of Dutch settlers, in the republics of Transvaal and the Orange Free State. Transvaal successfully asserted its independence in the First Boer War of 1880–81. During the Second Boer War (1899–1902), the Boer commandos (militia) initially took the offensive, inflicting humiliating defeats on the British Army. In response, Britain sent large-scale forces to southern Africa, occupying the Boer republics. But it would face a two-year long guerrilla campaign—an offensive that was only suppressed after the internment of Boer families and the devastation of the land.

CHRISTIAAN DE WET

BOER COMMANDER
BORN October 7, 1854
DIED February 3, 1922
KEY CONFLICTS First Boer War, Second Boer War, Maritz Rebellion
KEY BATTLES Sanna's Post 1900, Reddersburg 1900, Groenkop 1901

A Boer farmer, Christiaan De Wet presented himself for commando service as an ordinary burgher (citizen of the Boer republics) in October 1899, rising rapidly to the rank of general. In March 1900, he initiated the transition to guerrilla warfare, his mounted commandos taking more than 400 British soldiers prisoner in a raid on a garrison at Sanna's Post, near Bloemfontein.

De Wet dealt the British another blow at Reddersburg, attacking an enemy column on April 3.

In a sustained campaign, De Wet repeatedly eluded thousands of troops sent to trap him, but his attempts to take the war into the British Cape Colony failed. In winter 1901, De Wet scored a last victory at Groenkop, but laid down his arms the year after. He joined the failed Maritz rebellion in 1914 against his country's decision to back Britain against Germany.

Commander of the veldt
De Wet was an inspired leader of mounted guerrillas, exploiting speed of movement and familiarity with the flat, open landscape of the veldt.

LOUIS BOTHA

BOER COMMANDER-IN-CHIEF
BORN September 27, 1862
DIED August 27, 1919
KEY CONFLICTS Second Boer War, Southwest African Campaign (World War I)
KEY BATTLES Colenso 1899, Spion Kop 1900

Serving in the siege of Ladysmith early in the war, Louis Botha so distinguished himself that he was made a general in November 1899. He inflicted a costly reverse on the British at Colenso in December, showing superior tactical sense and knowledge of terrain. His victory at Spion Kop the following month was even more striking, but he was then driven into a series of retreats by the weight of British forces.

RECONCILIATION

By September 1900, Botha had turned to guerrilla tactics in order to maintain resistance. In 1902, he became reconciled with Britain, fighting the Germans in southwest Africa during World War I on behalf of the British Empire.

Clever tactician
Botha was an impressive commander in the conventional battles of the war. He excelled at exploiting the terrain to conceal his men and guns, trapping the British in exposed positions.

AGENTS OF EMPIRE

REDVERS BULLER

BRITISH ARMY OFFICER
BORN December 7, 1839
DIED June 2, 1908
KEY CONFLICTS Anglo-Zulu War, Second
Boer War
KEY BATTLES Hlobane 1879, Colenso 1899,
Spion Kop 1900, Relief of Ladysmith 1900

Medal for bravery
Buller was a popular officer
who had won a Victoria
Cross for bravery at Hlobane
during the Zulu War.
His dismissal from
the army in 1901
was widely seen
as unfair.

Redvers Buller was a British veteran
of wars in China, Egypt, Zululand,
Sudan, and west Africa. Despite being
commended for his leadership at
Hlobane in 1879, his dispatch to
South Africa as British commander-
in-chief in November 1899 was
fraught with problems. Lacking
resources, he was outfought by
Boer commanders. After several
defeats, ending with his retreat at
Colenso during the "Black Week"
of December 1899, he was
replaced by Frederick Roberts.

Buller retained command
in Natal, compensating for
past mistakes by lifting
the Ladysmith siege
in February 1900.
Returning to
Britain as a hero,
he was later made
a scapegoat for
British failures.

KEY BATTLE
SPION KOP

CAMPAIGN Second Boer War
DATE January 23–24, 1900
LOCATION Near Ladysmith, Natal

In January 1900, General Buller faced Louis
Botha's entrenched troops as he attempted to
cross the Tugela River to relieve the besieged
British garrison at Ladysmith. Buller ordered
General Charles Warren and 13,000 soldiers to
cross the Tugela at Trikhardt's Drift. On the night
of January 23, as this attack bogged down,
Warren sent men to occupy Spion Kop, a high
point from which he hoped to dominate the
Boer defenses. In darkness and mist, the
soldiers took up a position that in daylight
would turn out to be exposed to fire from the

Boers' Mauser rifles and artillery. Entrenchment
was barely possible on the rocky height and
the British were soon taking heavy casualties.
Command devolved to Colonel Alexander
Thorneycroft. But Buller and Warren neglected
to give him orders or information about the
reinforcements they were bringing up.
Meanwhile, Botha, desperate to regain the hill,
mounted costly infantry assaults that were
repulsed. When night fell, his commando militia
abandoned the Kop. But Thorneycroft, lacking
orders from his superiors and short of supplies,
insisted on withdrawal just as reinforcements
arrived. The next day the Boers reclaimed the
Kop, finding the trenches filled with British dead.

FREDERICK ROBERTS

BRITISH ARMY OFFICER
BORN September 30, 1832
DIED November 14, 1914
KEY CONFLICTS Second Afghan War,
Second Boer War
KEY BATTLES Kandahar 1880, Paardeberg
1900, Kimberley 1900, Mafeking 1900

The son of an officer in the British
East India Company army, Frederick
Roberts won a Victoria Cross during
the suppression of the Indian Mutiny
in 1857–58. In the Anglo-Afghan

War of 1878–80, his capture of the
Afghan capital, Kabul, followed by
a 300-mile (480-km) march to defeat
Afghan forces besieging the British at
Kandahar, made him a national hero.

British defeats at the hands of
the Boers in 1899 saw the veteran
Roberts, after two decades of peaceful
senior command, sent back into the
field to repeat the magic of Kandahar.
His only son was killed at the battle
of Colenso shortly before he arrived
in South Africa. Taking over from

Buller as commander-in-chief in
January 1900, Roberts benefited from
large-scale reinforcements that made
his task considerably easier. He was
also lucky in his subordinates, with
the experienced Herbert Kitchener

Afghan Earl
General Roberts (standing)
went on from his South
African role to become
commander-in-chief of
the British Army and was
ennobled to Earl Roberts
of Kandahar. The troops
called him "Bobs."

as his chief-of-staff and John French
as cavalry commander. Between
them, they were mainly responsible
for a key defeat of the Boers at
Paardeberg in February.

In just 10 months, Roberts
presided over a total victory in the
conventional war, from the relief of
the sieges of Ladysmith, Mafeking,
and Kimberley to the capture of the
Boer capitals Bloemfontein and
Pretoria. He handed over to Kitchener
in November 1900, leaving his
successor the unenviable task
of suppressing the tenacious
Boer guerrilla campaign.

> " THE COUNTRY CANNOT AFFORD
> TO RUN ANY UNAVOIDABLE
> RISK OF FAILURE. A
> SERIOUS REVERSE IN
> SOUTH AFRICA WOULD
> ENDANGER THE EMPIRE. "
>
> **FREDERICK ROBERTS**, IN A LETTER TO THE SECRETARY OF STATE FOR WAR, 1899

1850—1914

NAVAL WARFARE
IN THE AGE OF STEAM

> IT SEEMED IMPOSSIBLE EVEN TO COUNT THE NUMBER OF
> PROJECTILES STRIKING US. I HAD NOT ONLY NEVER WITNESSED
> SUCH A FIRE BEFORE, BUT I HAD NEVER IMAGINED ANYTHING
> LIKE IT. SHELLS SEEMED TO BE POURING UPON US INCESSANTLY.

AVAL WARFARE WAS TRANSFORMED between 1815 and 1914 through the introduction of a host of new technologies. Steam replaced wind power, metal hulls replaced wood, and high-explosive shells replaced cannonballs. The best admirals attempted to adapt Nelson's bold, aggressive approach to naval warfare to the new technological situation. There were few major occasions of naval combat, but commanders such as Japan's Admiral Togo Heihachiro and America's Commodore George Dewey were celebrated as national heroes.

The first battle between steam-powered ironclad warships occurred during the American Civil War, when the USS *Monitor* and the CSS *Virginia* clashed in the Hampton Roads on March 9, 1862. Steamships went on to play an important part throughout the Civil War, especially on the Mississippi, but the new naval warfare was then still in its infancy. The real transformation came later in the 19th century, with the construction of fleets of steel-built battleships and cruisers deploying huge, breech-loading rifled guns that were mounted on turrets.

SYMBOLS OF POWER

Steam fleets became an essential symbol of great power status, no doubt partly because they were so hugely expensive to build and maintain. Britain, still the world's leading maritime power, found itself challenged by Japanese, American, and German naval expansion. Ever larger warships with ever more powerful guns were built, but generations of vessels succeeded one another without seeing significant use in combat. The American fleet enjoyed a chance to show what destruction its guns could wreak in an unequal war with Spain in 1898, but it was not until the Russo-Japanese War of 1904–05 that a full-scale contest between naval powers equipped with the new types of ship took place. It was necessary for commanders to devise new tactical maneuvers for fighting naval battles with ships that were

more powerfully armed and much faster than before. Whereas sailing ships had exchanged broadsides within musket shot, the new warships engaged at ranges of over 3 miles (5 km). The tactical picture was complicated further by the introduction of torpedoes and mines, which proved devastatingly effective even against the largest warships. The transmission of orders to the fleet was improved when signal lamps were brought in to supplement flags, and later with the introduction of radio—although this threatened the naval commander's traditional autonomy by putting him within range of orders from his Admiralty on shore.

CLINGING TO TRADITION

The officers of the new navies had the benefit of more formal training than their predecessors and achieved higher social status. The United States established its Naval Academy at Annapolis in 1850 and even the ultra-conservative British Royal Navy felt it necessary to establish a Naval College at Dartmouth. Traditions were maintained as far as possible. Although the use of explosive shells eventually made it impossible for admirals or captains to stand on the open deck during battles, they still adopted the most exposed position practicable on the bridge. Despite all the changes to naval warfare in this period, Japanese Admiral Togo consciously modeled his great victory at Tsushima in 1905 on Nelson's triumph at Trafalgar.

Forcing the Mississippi forts
On April 24, 1862 a squadron of Union ships, commanded by David Farragut, forced a passage up the Mississippi past Confederate forts to take New Orleans. Most steamships at that time also had masts and sails.

Signal lamp
Aldis lamps are used to send visual signals between ships, typically in Morse code. This British example dates from 1913.

NAVAL COMMANDERS

BETWEEN THE NAPOLEONIC WARS and World War I, major naval actions were very rare, yet there was a fund of popular admiration for naval heroes and daring exploits. Commanders could therefore achieve a status out of proportion to their achievements, as in the case of George Dewey, victor in a one-sided contest with the Spanish. Some of the hardest fighting of the period, although on a relatively small scale, was in the American Civil War, but only the Russo-Japanese War of 1904–05 constituted a full-scale conflict between major naval powers, making Togo Heihachiro the first great admiral of the era of steam.

DAVID FARRAGUT

AMERICAN ADMIRAL
BORN July 5, 1801
DIED August 14, 1870
KEY CONFLICTS American Civil War
KEY BATTLES Mississippi Forts 1862, Mobile Bay 1864

David G. Farragut was a traditional leader, entering the US Navy at age nine and seeing action in the War of 1812 while still a child. A Southerner from Tennessee, he nonetheless opted for the Union side in the Civil War and was given charge of a blockading squadron operating in the Gulf of Mexico. In April 1862, he broke through the defenses in front of New Orleans in a daring night attack, his wooden ships defying the guns of two Confederate forts.

The popular acclaim gained by his victory was confirmed at Mobile Bay in August 1864. To enter the bay he had to pass through a minefield under the guns of a fort. When one of his ships was sunk by a mine (then confusingly known as a "torpedo"), Farragut pressed on with the attack, shouting "Damn the torpedoes! Full speed ahead!" Once in the bay, his ships captured the ironclad *Tennessee* and three other vessels after a stiff fight.

First admiral
Farragut was promoted to admiral in 1866, the first officer to hold that rank in the US Navy.

GEORGE DEWEY

AMERICAN ADMIRAL
BORN December 26, 1837
DIED January 16, 1917
KEY CONFLICTS Spanish-American War
KEY BATTLES Manila Bay 1898

George Dewey was among the earliest graduates of the US Naval Academy. His baptism of fire came with the Civil War. As a lieutenant on the steam sloop *Mississippi*, he participated in the capture of New Orleans as part of David Farragut's squadron in April 1862. Ending the war as a lieutenant-commander, he settled into a comfortable peacetime career, rising eventually to the rank of commodore.

In 1897, Dewey was appointed to command the US Asiatic Squadron based at Hong Kong. The following year, America went to war with Spain, and Dewey was ordered to destroy the enemy fleet in the Philippines, which at that time was a Spanish colony. On board the cruiser *Olympia*, he took his squadron into Manila Bay under cover of darkness and early on May 1, 1898, pummeled the anchored Spanish warships into surrender with a storm of shellfire. Dewey's laconic style in this one-sided battle enchanted the American public and he returned home to a hero's welcome. A special rank, "Admiral of the US Navy," was created for him.

Dewey at Manila Bay
This heroic image of Dewey (with the white mustache) was painted soon after the battle. Naval leaders were traditionally required to expose themselves to shot and shell.

TOGO HEIHACHIRO

JAPANESE ADMIRAL
BORN January 27, 1848
DIED May 30, 1934
KEY CONFLICTS Russo-Japanese War
KEY BATTLES Port Arthur 1904, Yellow Sea 1904, Tsushima 1905

Togo Heihachiro was born into the Satsuma samurai clan in the port city of Kagoshima. As a youth, he saw the bombardment of Kagoshima by British ships in 1863. The next year, the Satsuma set out to create a modern navy and Togo was among its first volunteers. In 1868, he saw action in the Boshin War, a civil war in which the Satsuma fleet fought for Emperor Meiji against the Tokugawa shogunate. After their victory, the Satsuma force became the nucleus of the new Imperial Japanese Navy.

In the 1870s, Togo was among a number of officers sent to naval college in Britain. He developed a lifelong admiration for the traditions of the Royal Navy and modeled himself on its hero, Nelson. When Japan went to war with China in 1894, he was captain of a cruiser. His sinking of a British-registered transport ship carrying Chinese troops caused a diplomatic furore.

Togo's appointment to command the Japanese Combined Fleet in 1903 was unexpected, but his leadership in the Russo-Japanese War fully justified the choice. After the initial surprise attack on Port Arthur (before Japan's formal declaration of war), Togo blockaded the Russian First Pacific Squadron for six months. When the Russians attempted a breakout in August 1904, he inflicted heavy losses on them in the battle of the Yellow Sea. His defeat of the Russian Baltic Feet at Tsushima the following year (pp. 274–75) won him worldwide renown.

> ## GENTLEMEN, WE ARE AT WAR, AND ONLY HE WHO ACTS FEARLESSLY CAN HOPE FOR SUCCESS.
>
> **TOGO HEIHACHIRO**, ADDRESS TO HIS OFFICERS BEFORE PORT ARTHUR ATTACK, 1904

Honored admiral
Japan's greatest national hero after his victories in the Russo-Japanese War, Admiral Togo lived to an advanced age. When he died in 1934, warships from Britain, the United States, and many other countries took part in a naval parade in his honor.

KEY BATTLE
PORT ARTHUR

CAMPAIGN Russo-Japanese War
DATE February 8–9, 1904
LOCATION Liaodong Peninsula, Manchuria

Admiral Togo planned a surprise attack on Port Arthur to neutralize the First Russian Pacific Squadron before a declaration of war. He ordered a squadron of destroyers to approach the port under cover of darkness and sink Russian warships in the harbor with torpedoes. The attack was not as effective as Togo intended. The destroyers' formation became disrupted and only four took part in the first torpedo run, with others straggling behind. The brightly lit ships at anchor were an easy target, but they were protected by torpedo nets. Three Russian warships were badly damaged, including their largest battleship. The following morning, believing the Russian defenses crippled, Togo steamed his battle fleet in line toward Port Arthur, only to come under heavy fire from shore batteries and ships in the harbor. Togo's flagship *Mikasa* was hit and the Japanese withdrew, settling down to a lengthy blockade of the port.

TOGO AT TSUSHIMA

LOCATION
Tsushima Strait, between Japan and Korea

CAMPAIGN
Russo-Japanese War

DATE May 27–28, 1905

FORCES Japanese: 4 battleships, 24 cruisers, 36 other ships; Russians: 8 battleships, 8 cruisers, 12 other ships

CASUALTIES Japanese: 117 killed, 3 torpedo boats sunk; Russians: 4,380 killed, 7 battleships, 4 cruisers, and 10 other ships sunk

On the night of May 26, 1905, Admiral Togo Heihachiro, commanding the Japanese Combined Fleet, had patrol ships strung out across the Tsushima Strait, anxiously seeking Russian warships bound for Vladivostok. Commanded by Admiral Zinovi Rozhdestvenski, the Russian fleet had sailed 18,000 miles (33,000 km) from the Baltic to join the war against Japan in the Pacific. Togo had traced their progress and was now awaiting their arrival in his home waters with all his ships on full alert. He had guessed that, being short of coal, they would try to slip through between Japan and Korea, rather than take the longer route to the east of Japan.

SURVEILLANCE BY RADIO

At 4:55 a.m. on May 27, Togo received the message he wanted. By the novel medium of wireless telegraphy (radio), the cruiser *Shinano Maru* informed him it had made contact with the Russians. Informing Tokyo of the sighting, he said, "Our fleet will proceed forthwith to sea to attack the enemy and destroy him."

Throughout the next morning, Japanese cruisers kept contact with the Russian fleet, radioing updates to Togo as he raced to give battle on board his flagship *Mikasa*. Togo was amazed at the way radio made the movements and dispositions of the enemy "as clear to us, who were 30 or 40 miles [50 or 65 km] distant, as though they had been under our very eyes." Later, at around 1:40 p.m., he established visual contact with the Russians. In conscious imitation of

> ❝ THE EMPIRE'S FATE DEPENDS ON THE RESULT OF THIS BATTLE, LET EVERY MAN DO HIS UTMOST DUTY. ❞
>
> **ADMIRAL TOGO'S** "Z FLAG" MESSAGE TO HIS FLEET, MAY 14, 1905

his hero, Admiral Nelson, before the battle of Trafalgar, Togo hoisted the Z Flag on *Mikasa*, a signal calling on every man to do his duty.

AN AUDACIOUS ATTACK

The Russian fleet was in poor shape after its long journey and steaming at 6 knots. With ships capable of around 15 knots, Togo had complete freedom to engage as and when he wished. His initial choice of maneuver was recklessly daring. To attack the Russian line with his flagship in the lead, he performed a U-turn within range of the Russian guns. The Russians hit *Mikasa*, but their armor-piercing shells had limited effect. It was very different when the Japanese rounds, designed to explode on contact, rained on the Russian ships. The Japanese gunners were better trained and had up-to-date range-finders. Fired at

3.6 miles (5.8 km), their salvoes were devastating. Rozhdestvenski's flagship *Knyaz Suvorov* was an early victim, the admiral himself badly wounded.

Swirling mist offered the Russians protection, but each time they were forced to exchange fire the result was the same. The sinking of their battleship *Borodino* at around 7:00 p.m. was an apt conclusion to a daylight battle that had decimated the Russian fleet. Togo withdrew his battleships, unleashing his destroyers and torpedo boats to harass the Russians with attacks through the night. The next morning, Admiral Nikolai Nebogatov surrendered six warships surrounded by Togo's battle fleet. Only three Russian ships reached Vladivostok. Togo claimed the scale of the victory had been so great that his own officers and men "found no language to express their astonishment."

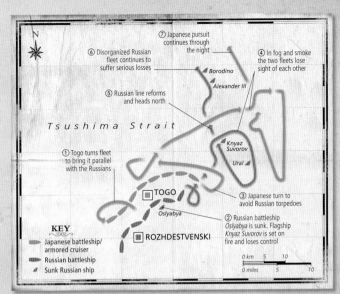

⑦ Japanese pursuit continues through the night

⑥ Disorganized Russian fleet continues to suffer serious losses

④ In fog and smoke the two fleets lose sight of each other

Borodino

Alexander III

⑤ Russian line reforms and heads north

Tsushima Strait

① Togo turns fleet to bring it parallel with the Russians

Knyaz Suvorov

Ural

③ Japanese turn to avoid Russian torpedoes

TOGO

Oslyabya

② Russian battleship *Oslyabya* is sunk. Flagship *Knyaz Suvorov* is set on fire and loses control

ROZHDESTVENSKI

KEY

▬ Japanese battleship/ armored cruiser

▬ Russian battleship

◢ Sunk Russian ship

0 km   5   10
0 miles   5   10

Russian disaster
The Russian battleship *Oslyabya* sinks after a shell strikes its magazine. More than 500 sailors died as the ship went down, one of seven Russian battleships lost in the battle.

1850—1914

6
1914—PRESENT

MODERN
COMMANDERS

MARKED BY THE TWO COSTLIEST WARS in history, the 20th century saw the development of weapons vastly more destructive than any known before. In an age of global conflicts, military leaders became major actors on the world stage, with their successes and failures at times determining the course of history. Rapid developments in the nature of warfare, as well as its extraordinary scale, placed severe strain on men who carried the burden of command.

Since 1914, command and control have undergone a series of transformations, driven largely by technological innovation, but also influenced by the social and political context of war. In World War I (1914–18), generals took charge of citizen armies of unprecedented size endowed with massive firepower. However, once battle was joined, they lacked the technological means to exercise command effectively. Relatively primitive radios and field telephones were not sufficiently effective and, despite new sources of intelligence—such as observation by aircraft—commanders easily lost touch with developments on the battlefield.

LEADING FROM THE REAR

The headquarters of high command was necessarily stationed well to the rear, in order to maintain contact with forces spread over a vast front. Lower-level army or corps commanders were closer to the action but still remote by the standards of Wellington or Napoleon. Fearing that operations would descend into chaos, generals too often resorted to rigid plans that denied initiative to officers on the ground and were unresponsive to changes on the battlefield. Denunciation of the incompetence of

World War I generals has been overdone, however. Wrestling with intractable problems, over time, they found effective tactical solutions that by 1918 had ended the stalemate of the trenches.

After World War I, military experts sought ways of restoring the supremacy of attack over defense, using tanks and aircraft to avoid tactical and strategic deadlock. The gasoline engine offered the possibility of rapid movement, and improvements in radios presented a potential solution to the problem of exercising command on a large-scale, mobile battlefield. Tank commanders, such as the German General Heinz Guderian, saw that radio might even allow generals to return to the thick of the battle. A radio-equipped general could theoretically command from anywhere.

German Blitzkrieg in the early phase of World War II combined the use of tanks and motorized infantry with air power, enabling

WWII field telephone
Widely used in World War II, this American EE-8 field telephone had a range of 10–15 miles (16–24 km).

generals to execute rapid maneuvers—military genius in a bad cause. The fightback by the Allies (chiefly the Soviet Union, the United States, and Britain) used the same technology but a different strategy. Allied commanders sought to overcome the enemy by decisively deploying superior material forces. Radio had its drawbacks as a command tool, since messages were open to interception and decoding—a major source of intelligence for both sides in the war. Modern communications also gave political leaders the means to interfere directly in the exercise of military command. German generals in particular found Adolf Hitler usurping their functions.

THE COLD WAR ERA

After World War II, in the context of the Cold War nuclear confrontation between the United States and the Soviet Union, command systems were developed that far surpassed in sophistication any previously seen. A vast increase in the

Control center
Operators at work in the air traffic control center on board the American nuclear-powered aircraft carrier USS *Abraham Lincoln*.

quantity of information available, facilitated by the introduction of satellites—both for communication and observation—required banks of computers to process input and generate appropriate solutions. The role of military commander looked close to being sidelined by automated weapons systems. However, despite technological advances, most actual warfare was fought at a very different level.

Rather like imperialist commanders of the 19th century, American and European generals of this period had to fight relatively small-scale wars under diverse and challenging geographical conditions in countries such as Vietnam, Algeria, and Afghanistan. The guerrilla and terrorist warfare practiced by their opponents evolved its own theory and practice, which focused

on ways of achieving the political defeat of a militarily superior enemy. By the 21st century, an American commander could personally direct an attack on an individual vehicle or building from his headquarters in another continent. Finding ways of using the impressive technology available to some real tactical and strategic purpose, however, has remained a serious challenge.

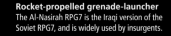

Rocket-propelled grenade-launcher
The Al-Nasirah RPG7 is the Iraqi version of the Soviet RPG7, and is widely used by insurgents.

1914–PRESENT

1914—1918

WORLD WAR I

THERE IS NO COURSE OPEN TO US BUT TO FIGHT IT OUT. EVERY POSITION MUST BE HELD TO THE LAST MAN; THERE MUST BE NO RETIREMENT. WITH OUR BACKS TO THE WALL AND BELIEVING IN THE JUSTICE OF OUR CAUSE EACH ONE OF US MUST FIGHT ON TO THE END.

FIELD MARSHAL SIR DOUGLAS HAIG ORDER OF THE DAY, APRIL 11, 1918

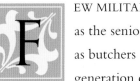

EW MILITARY MEN IN history have been so widely reviled as the senior commanders of World War I, condemned as butchers and bunglers who threw away the lives of a generation of young men in pointless slaughter. Yet generals such as Douglas Haig, Alexei Brusilov, Erich Ludendorff, and Ferdinand Foch deserve more serious consideration for the vast and intractable problems they faced and the determined—and not always unimaginative—efforts they made to fight and win a war under almost impossible conditions.

World War I was a conflict for which European military commanders ought to have been thoroughly prepared, since they had been creating detailed plans for it for years. Germany and Austria-Hungary expected to fight France and Russia, although the decision of Britain to stand alongside the French was less predictable.

In August 1914, armies of millions were efficiently mobilized and rushed into combat. The Germans planned to impose a rapid defeat on France and then concentrate on fighting Russia. Instead, the war on the Western Front became bogged down in stalemated trench warfare, while Germany recorded a series of victories in the east. The war in the trenches, breathtaking in its apparently pointless consumption of human lives, remained virtually immobilized between December 1914 and March 1918.

GRINDING STALEMATE

Commanders of the period tended to believe that highly motivated troops on the offensive would win battles. But the mass firepower of high-explosive artillery shells and machine-guns gave a strong advantage to defenders in prepared positions. As the war spread to Germany's ally, Ottoman Turkey—with British and French landings at Gallipoli—and to Italy, the result

was the same: immobility and stalemate. Generals such as Haig and Petain came to the fore. These were men who, above all, were temperamentally capable of taking the strain of this grinding style of warfare. Even at sea, commanders trained in the naval tradition of gun duels between fleets were held in check, since sailing boldly into action meant exposure to mines or torpedoes that could sink a battleship in minutes.

THE END DRAWS NEAR

Despite appearances, however, the war was not static and unchanging. Not only were there major shifts among the participants, with Russia withdrawing defeated in the grip of revolution and the United States entering the war alongside Britain and France, but also new battlefield tactics made successful offensives possible. The use of tanks and aircraft was important, but even more vital were subtle new infantry tactics supported by an intelligent use of artillery. Both the German offensive of March 1918, which almost won the war, and the Allied offensives from August 1918 that finally secured victory, showed a high level of competence at all levels of command.

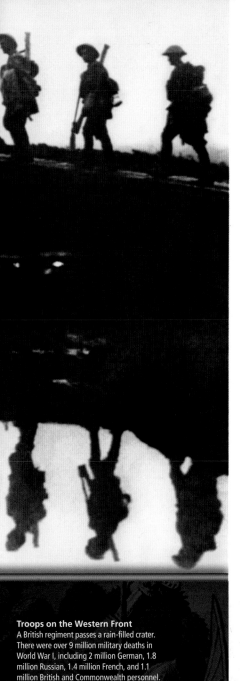

Troops on the Western Front
A British regiment passes a rain-filled crater. There were over 9 million military deaths in World War I, including 2 million German, 1.8 million Russian, 1.4 million French, and 1.1 million British and Commonwealth personnel.

1914—PRESENT

Hotchkiss machine-gun
The Hotchkiss was the standard French heavy machine-gun in World War I. The rate of fire of such weapons made frontal assaults by infantry immensely costly.

BRITISH COMMANDERS

THE HIGHLY TRAINED British Expeditionary Force (BEF) sent to France in August 1914 was almost wiped out in early battles, before the fighting settled into trenches. Meanwhile, volunteer "New Armies" recruited by the war secretary, Lord Kitchener, were being trained and equipped, giving Britain a mass army later augmented by conscription. Sustaining vast casualties for little gain during 1916 and 1917, the British gradually improved their fighting skills, introducing tanks and refining coordination between artillery and infantry. They played a major role in the defeat of Germany in the final offensives of 1918, known as the Hundred Days.

MODERN COMMANDERS

JOHN FRENCH

BRITISH FIELD MARSHAL
BORN September 28, 1852
DIED May 22, 1925
KEY CONFLICTS Boer War, World War I
KEY BATTLES Mons 1914, First Marne 1914, Neuve Chapelle 1915, Loos 1915

A distinguished cavalry officer during the Boer War, Sir John French became commander of the BEF in August 1914. Initially overly optimistic, after the battle of Mons, he despaired over heavy losses and enforced retreat.

OUT OF DEPTH

French failed to cooperate effectively with the French generals or with his own subordinates. Heavy pressure from the war secretary, Kitchener, made him commit British troops to the crucial first battle of the Marne in September, when he would rather have withdrawn for recuperation. During the trench warfare of spring 1915, French publicly blamed failure at Neuve Chapelle on a shortage of shells, precipitating a political crisis in Britain. He could not, however, avoid responsibility at Loos in September, when his failure to commit reserves quickly after a successful initial attack led to disaster. Replaced by Haig in December, French was relegated to the home front, overseeing the suppression of the Irish Nationalist Easter Rising in Dublin in 1916.

Inspecting the damage
With two other officers, John French looks over the wreckage of a German Zeppelin shot down in France returning from a raid on England.

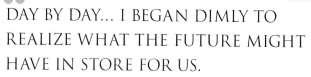

> **DAY BY DAY... I BEGAN DIMLY TO REALIZE WHAT THE FUTURE MIGHT HAVE IN STORE FOR US.**
>
> SIR JOHN FRENCH, ON HIS EXPERIENCE OF TRENCH WARFARE IN *1914*, PUBLISHED 1919

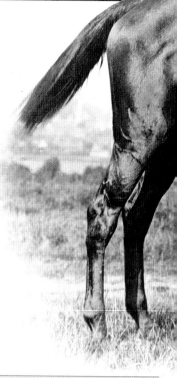

Triumphal entry
Edmund Allenby enters Jerusalem on foot on December 11, 1917, having taken the city from the Turks. This triumph was a huge morale-booster for Britain at a low point in the war.

EDMUND ALLENBY

BRITISH GENERAL
BORN April 23, 1861
DIED May 14, 1936
KEY CONFLICTS Boer War, World War I
KEY BATTLES Second Ypres 1915, Arras 1917, Jerusalem 1917, Megiddo 1918

A successful leader of cavalry during the Boer War, Edmund Allenby was given command of the BEF's cavalry in August 1914 and performed well in the early mobile battles. In 1915, he became an infantry commander in the trench warfare at the second battle of Ypres and Loos, and was later promoted to head the Third Army.

Known as "the Bull," Allenby was a brusque and irascible officer, disliked by his men and by Haig, his commander-in-chief. After the Third Army failed to make an impression at Arras in April 1917, he was transferred to Palestine.

Allenby reinvigorated the British and Commonwealth forces fighting the German-supported Turks around Gaza. Using mounted troops on horse and camel in outflanking maneuvers, he forced the Turks to abandon their defensive line without a frontal assault and took Jerusalem in December. His greatest victory was at Megiddo in September 1918. Using a lightning artillery barrage and aircraft in a ground-attack role, he punched a hole in Turkish defenses north of Jerusalem through which infantry and cavalry poured. The routed Turks surrendered at the end of October.

Reticent character
Haig had a taciturn and aloof personality. His manner distanced subordinate officers, who were deterred from questioning plans or drawing attention to inconvenient facts.

DOUGLAS HAIG

BRITISH FIELD MARSHAL
BORN June 19, 1861
DIED January 29, 1928
KEY CONFLICTS Boer War, World War I
KEY BATTLES First Ypres 1914, Neuve Chapelle 1915, Somme 1916, Third Ypres 1917, Spring Offensive 1918, Hundred Days' 1918

Before World War I, Douglas Haig was a socially well-connected cavalry officer with campaign experience in the Sudan and the Boer War. Given command of a corps in August 1914, he acquitted himself well in the BEF's early battles. At the crisis point in the first battle of Ypres in November 1914, Haig held his corps firm in the face of a powerful German onslaught. His reward was command of the First Army for the trench battles of Neuve Chapelle and Loos.

Increasingly discontented with French as commander-in-chief, Haig conspired to replace him, a goal that he achieved in December 1915. Over the course of the following two years, he carried out appallingly costly offensives, especially at the Somme and the third battle of Ypres (Passchendaele). Sustained by the belief that he was "a tool in the hands of the Divine Power," he was able to keep going under immense strain.

A MAN OF VIRTUE

Haig believed, against all evidence, that a war-winning breakthrough was always within reach. He continued offensives for far too long, paid too little attention to inhibiting factors such as bad weather—crucial in the mud of Passchendaele—and allowed too little initiative to lower-level commanders. Yet, he had positive virtues. He was a consistently loyal ally to France, resisted political pressure to divert resources away from the Western Front, and was eager to adopt technological innovations, such as the use of tanks.

In the Spring Offensive of 1918, when the Germans drove the British army into retreat, Haig rallied his men. From August 1918, he presided over possibly the greatest string of victories ever achieved by the British army in the Hundred Days.

> ## TO THROW AWAY MEN'S LIVES WHEN THERE IS NO REASONABLE CHANCE OF ADVANTAGE IS CRIMINAL.
>
> **B. H. LIDDELL HART**, *HISTORY OF THE FIRST WORLD WAR*, 1970

HENRY RAWLINSON

BRITISH GENERAL
BORN February 20, 1864
DIED March 28, 1925
KEY CONFLICTS Boer War, World War I
KEY BATTLES Antwerp 1914, First Ypres 1914, Somme 1916, Amiens 1918

Reassessing tactics
A thinker, Rawlinson at last found the tactical combination that would succeed in the trench warfare of the Western Front.

An infantry officer, Henry Rawlinson saw action in the Sudan and the Boer War. Early in World War I, he was involved in the defense of Antwerp and the first battle of Ypres, doing well enough to be made a corps commander in 1915. He was then given command of the Fourth Army, a force of New Army volunteers and Territorials chosen to spearhead the Somme Offensive in July 1916.

The slaughter on the Somme did not ruin his reputation entirely, but he was sidelined for over a year. Called back in the summer of 1918, he developed tactics based on coordination between artillery, infantry, tanks, and aircraft that allowed his army to launch a successful attack at Amiens in August, devastating German morale. He overran the Hindenburg Line using the same formula during the final victorious advance of the Hundred Days.

KEY BATTLE
THE SOMME

CAMPAIGN World War I
DATE July 1–November 13, 1916
LOCATION Eastern France

The opening of the Somme Offensive on July 1, 1916, was the costliest day in British military history, with total casualties of around 58,000. The Anglo-French operation was planned by Haig and the Fourth Army commander, Henry Rawlinson. Facing German troops in impressive defensive positions, they hoped a week-long preparatory artillery bombardment would destroy barbed wire and concrete bunkers, after which infantry would cross no-man's-land to occupy the enemy trenches. Much of the infantry was ordered to advance in line at walking pace, owing to overoptimism about the impact of artillery. They were mowed down by machine-gun fire. After the slaughter on the first day, the offensive continued for five months. Some attacks were more imaginative—for example, night operations and the first use of tanks—but none was strikingly successful.

FRENCH COMMANDERS

FRANCE MOBILIZED AROUND 2.5 million men in August 1914, but was at first driven into retreat. The French Army fought fiercely to reverse the tide, with victory at the Marne in September the turning point. The troops were ill-prepared, both mentally and in equipment, for the trench warfare that followed, attacking flair proving of little use against heavy artillery and machine-guns. After a bloodbath at Verdun, French morale slumped in spring 1917. The army had to be nursed through to 1918 when, with assistance from British and American forces, it revived to resist a final German offensive and counterattacked to win the war.

JOSEPH JOFFRE

FRENCH MARSHAL
BORN January 12, 1852
DIED January 3, 1931
KEY CONFLICT World War I
KEY BATTLES Frontiers 1914, First Marne 1914, Champagne 1915, Artois 1915, Verdun 1916

"Papa" Joffre
Projecting an assured image, Joffre was a popular figure despite failed offensives.

A career officer in the engineers, Joseph Joffre was chosen as French chief of general staff in 1911. He believed in the virtue of the offensive, adopting Plan XVII, which, in the event of war, committed France "to advance with all forces united to attack the German armies." Applied in August 1914, the French suffered catastrophic casualties against German defenses in Alsace and Lorraine (the battle of the Frontiers), while the bulk of German forces marched into France through Belgium. Joffre kept a cool head, redeployed his armies and counterattacked at the Marne. The German armies were forced into retreat and France was saved.

ON THE ATTACK

As commander-in-chief, Joffre ruled the "zone of the armies" in France like a dictator, still certain that *élan* (attacking spirit) would triumph over defensive firepower. In the Champagne and Artois offensives of 1915, his theory failed at the cost of hundreds of thousands of lives. Joffre lost his command in December 1916 after Verdun.

KEY TROOPS
FRENCH POILUS

The French infantryman, popularly known as a *poilu* (hairy one), went to war in August 1914 in a bright blue uniform and kepi. A product of universal conscription, he was trained to attack at all costs. Despite support from the excellent quick-firing 75mm field gun, French infantry were cut down by German firepower, suffering a million casualties in the first three months of the war. By 1918, the French infantryman was a soberly clad, steel-helmeted warrior, tenacious but thoroughly disillusioned.

STANDARD POILU UNIFORM IN 1914

PHILIPPE PÉTAIN

FRENCH MARSHAL AND VICHY PRESIDENT
BORN April 24, 1856
DIED July 23, 1951
KEY CONFLICT World War I
KEY BATTLES First Marne 1914, Artois 1915, Champagne 1915, Verdun 1916

After 38 years' service, Philippe Pétain was only a colonel when the war began, but his evident competence brought rapid advancement. He took command of a division during the battle of the Marne, of a corps in October 1914, and of the Second Army in July 1915. Engaged in the costly Artois and Champagne offensives, Pétain disagreed with Joffre's commitment to a breakthrough and belief in *élan*. Instead, he advocated a war of attrition, based on minimizing French infantry losses while killing as many Germans as possible with artillery bombardment. Appointed to lead the defense of Verdun in February 1916, he showed resolution and good sense, but his caution did not win favor with Joffre or French political leaders, who preferred to trust the optimism of Robert Nivelle.

AN IGNOMINIOUS END

After the disaster of the Nivelle offensive in spring 1917, Pétain was recalled to restore the morale of the disintegrating French armies. He remained commander-in-chief, but was in effect superseded by Foch and played little part in the final victories of 1918. He became head of the pro-German Vichy government in 1940 and died in prison, convicted of treason after the liberation.

"SUCCESS WILL COME... TO THE SIDE THAT HAS THE LAST MAN STANDING.

PHILIPPE PÉTAIN, MEMORANDUM, JUNE 29, 1915

Pétain decorates troops
As commander-in-chief in 1917, Pétain restored the morale of the mutinous French Army by halting offensive operations, improving living conditions, and liberally distributing medals.

MODERN COMMANDERS

Aggressive marshal
Ferdinand Foch was an instinctively aggressive commander who performed best when on the counterattack. He regarded the peace terms imposed on Germany at Versailles in 1919 as criminally lenient.

FERDINAND FOCH

FRENCH MARSHAL AND ALLIED SUPREME COMMANDER
BORN October 2, 1851
DIED March 20, 1929
KEY CONFLICT World War I
KEY BATTLES First Marne 1914, First Ypres 1914, Artois 1915, Somme 1916, Spring Offensive 1918, Second Marne 1918

Before World War I, Ferdinand Foch had a reputation as a military theorist. His *Principles of War* (1903) advocated all-out offensives by massed infantry as the answer to increasing firepower. A corps commander in August 1914, he performed well amid the slaughter that resulted from such offensives, earning promotion to command an army at the first battle of the Marne in September. True to his principles, he mounted counterattacks when under pressure, and took much of the credit for the Marne victory and for stopping a German breakthrough at the first battle of Ypres in November. Following the failure of the Artois offensive and the French element of the Somme Offensive, he was fired in December 1916, only to return as Pétain's chief-of-staff in May 1917.

COOPERATIVE CHARM
In the crisis precipitated by Germany's Spring Offensive in March 1918, Foch became Allied Supreme Commander. Without formal control over British and American armies, he succeeded by force of personality in coordinating their operations. Halting the Germans at the Marne in June 1918, he launched a counterattack that shifted the initiative in favor of the Allies. He was the ideal man to preside over the great offensives that ended the war. The Armistice was signed in a car of his command train.

> **I AM HARD PRESSED ON MY RIGHT; MY CENTER IS GIVING WAY; SITUATION EXCELLENT; I ATTACK.**
> FERDINAND FOCH, MESSAGE TO HIGH COMMAND, SEPTEMBER 1914

ROBERT NIVELLE

FRENCH GENERAL
BORN October 15, 1856
DIED March 22, 1924
KEY CONFLICT World War I
KEY BATTLES Verdun 1916, Nivelle Offensive 1917

A talented artillery officer, Nivelle entered World War I as a colonel. His skilled handling of artillery attracted the attention of Joffre, who liked his aggressive style and promoted him rapidly. In April 1916, he was chosen to inject offensive spirit at Verdun. Taking over command of the Second Army from Pétain, he was successful in driving back German forces. In December 1916, he replaced Joffre as French commander-in-chief.

Man of charm
Nivelle charmed politicians, including the British prime minister, David Lloyd George, into supporting his offensive.

FALSE HOPE OF VICTORY
Nivelle had made innovative use of artillery at Verdun, experimenting with a "lightning" bombardment followed by a creeping barrage advancing ahead of the infantry. He promoted his new techniques as a recipe for a quick and decisive victory, to end the war in 48 hours. Launched in April 1917, in northeast France, the offensive failed to surprise the enemy, coordination between artillery and infantry faltered, casualties were heavy and gains limited. As morale collapsed, Nivelle became discredited. He was fired and sent to North Africa for the rest of the war.

1914—PRESENT

The Taking of Vimy Ridge
As part of the battle of Arras in northern France, the 5-mile (8-km) Vimy Ridge—on the German front line—was captured by the Canadian Corps on April 9–12, 1917. It was a strategic point of great value to the Allies.

OTHER ALLIED COMMANDERS

 THE BRITISH DOMINIONS provided some of the war's most inventive generals. Both Canadian Arthur Currie and Australian John Monash proved that the well-planned use of offensive firepower to destroy enemy defenses could avoid a waste of infantrymen's lives, while achieving limited but cumulatively decisive gains.

Russia's Alexei Brusilov demonstrated that well-executed coordination of artillery and infantry could unblock the trench stalemate. The American commander, John Pershing, entered battle in 1918. He valued the rifle above the machine-gun, and his failure to work out how to use artillery effectively cost the Allies dearly.

ARTHUR CURRIE

CANADIAN GENERAL
BORN December 5, 1875
DIED November 30, 1933
KEY CONFLICT World War I
KEY BATTLES Vimy Ridge 1917, Third Ypres 1917, Amiens 1918, Canal du Nord 1918

A part-time officer in the Canadian militia, Arthur Currie was sent to France as a brigade commander in the Canadian Corps. He faced the first German poison gas attack at Ypres in April 1915.

A divisional commander at the Somme in 1916, Currie earned a reputation for being careful of his men's lives and forceful in questioning orders from superior officers. He deserved much of the credit for the taking of Vimy Ridge in April 1917, a famous Canadian victory based on detailed planning and coordination of artillery and infantry. Currie took command of the Canadian Corps before the capture of Passchendaele at the third battle of Ypres in the fall of 1917, a costly operation that he carried out under protest.

THE HUNDRED DAYS

In August 1918, the Corps moved in secrecy from Arras to Amiens to join the offensive that began the victorious Hundred Days. The Canadians continued to attack up to the last day of the war, Currie attracting praise for his imaginative tactics in the assault on the Canal du Nord in September.

Astute planner
Currie excelled at finding tactical solutions to attacking defensive positions, using his imagination and careful planning to avoid excessive casualties.

ALEXEI BRUSILOV

RUSSIAN GENERAL
BORN August 19, 1853
DIED March 17, 1926
KEY CONFLICT World War I
KEY BATTLES Brusilov Offensive 1916, Kerensky Offensive 1917

An aristocratic Russian cavalry officer and a professional in military affairs, Alexei Brusilov despaired of the czarist regime's disorganization and incompetence. As commander of the Russian Eighth Army fighting in Galicia in 1914–15, he proved the most talented of czarist generals even when defeated.

ON THE OFFENSIVE

Appointed to command South-Western Front army group in 1916, he launched a well-prepared offensive against Austro-Hungarian forces in June, achieving surprise attacks at a number of points along a broad front, supported by precise artillery. In two months, his troops advanced up to 90 miles (150 km) and took 400,000 prisoners, before being halted by the arrival of German troops.

In 1917, Brusilov was among those who encouraged Czar Nicholas to abdicate. As commander-in-chief for Aleksander Kerensky's Provisional Government in summer 1917, he failed to repeat the success of his 1916 offensive, for by now the Russian Army was in a desperate, mutinous state. In 1920, Brusilov supported the Bolsheviks in Russia's Civil War, acting as adviser to Trotsky.

Patriotic general
Brusilov was above all a patriot, who wanted the Russian Army to be properly led and supplied for the defense of the homeland. His offensive in 1916 was one of the most successful operations of the whole war.

> THE HEART OF THE COUNTRY WAS BEATING IN SYMPATHY WITH THE... SOLDIERS OF MY VICTORIOUS ARMIES.

ALEXEI BRUSILOV, *A SOLDIER'S NOTEBOOK 1914–18,* PUBLISHED IN THE UK IN 1930

JOHN MONASH

AUSTRALIAN GENERAL
BORN June 27, 1865
DIED October 8, 1935
KEY CONFLICT World War I
KEY BATTLES Gallipoli 1915, Messines 1917, Le Hamel 1918, Amiens 1918, Hindenburg Line 1918

John Monash was a militia officer before 1914 and led a brigade in the Anzac forces at Gallipoli in 1915. Raised to command of a division, he trained his troops to a high standard in England before taking them to the Western Front. Haig was impressed by Monash's performance in Flanders in 1917, especially at Messines Ridge, and in May 1918, he was made commander of the Australian Corps.

At Le Hamel in July 1918, Monash used massed machine-guns, tanks, artillery, and aircraft in a devastating lightning attack on a sector of the enemy line. It was then occupied by his infantry at little cost. On a much larger scale, he employed the same tactics when his Australian forces spearheaded the Amiens Offensive in August. Overcoming the Hindenburg Line defenses at the St. Quentin Canal in September was his final major action.

Corps commander
An Australian engineer of Prussian-Jewish origin, Monash proved an outstanding general on the Western Front. He planned and organized combined-arms offensives that gave maximum fire support to the advancing infantry.

JOHN J. PERSHING

AMERICAN GENERAL
BORN September 13, 1860
DIED July 15, 1948
KEY CONFLICTS Philippine-American War, Mexican Expedition, World War I
KEY BATTLES Château-Thierry 1918, Belleau Wood 1918, St. Mihiel 1918, Meuse-Argonne Offensive 1918

When the United States entered World War I in 1917, Pershing was its most experienced officer. He had seen action from the Plains Indian Wars through the Spanish-American War and the Philippine insurrection to a recent punitive expedition against Pancho Villa's Mexicans. However, this was not necessarily useful preparation for leading a mass army on the Western Front as commander of the American Expeditionary Force.

COSTLY STRATEGY

Pershing's first division arrived in France in June 1917. Determined to lead an independent American army, he would not allow his men to be assigned to the front under British or French command. He relaxed this policy when the German Spring Offensive of 1918 threatened to win the war, American troops supporting the French at Chateau-Thierry and Belleau Wood in early June.

Pershing's chance to lead a US army into battle came at St. Mihiel in September 1918, followed rapidly by the larger-scale Meuse-Argonne Offensive. He flung his men forward into machine-gun fire and failed to coordinate artillery with infantry, just as Allied generals had done earlier in the war, with the same result. After six weeks of fighting, the Americans eventually achieved victory in the Meuse-Argonne operation, but at a cost of over 120,000 casualties. Pershing disagreed with the granting of an armistice to Germany, believing the war should have been continued until military victory was complete.

1914—PRESENT

KEY BATTLE
ST. MIHIEL

CAMPAIGN World War I
DATE September 12–16, 1918
LOCATION Eastern France, near Metz

Over half a million troops of Pershing's American First Army, supported by 100,000 French soldiers, carried out a carefully planned attack on the St. Mihiel salient south of Verdun. The Germans considered the position untenable and were in the process of withdrawing to a more defensible line when the Americans attacked. The salient was taken in four days at a cost of fewer than 9,000 casualties. Pershing believed the victory proved that the American was "a superior soldier to that existing abroad."

"Black Jack"
As his nickname suggests, Pershing was not popular with his troops, appearing distant and reserved. He was emotionally numbed by the death of his wife and three children in a house fire in 1915.

GERMAN COMMANDERS

GERMANY HAD THE MOST powerful army in Europe, led by a general staff with a proud reputation for efficiency. Despite some notable failures—especially in the mishandled initial invasion of France in August 1914—German commanders proved tactically superior to their enemies through most of the war.

However, they failed to find effective solutions to Germany's strategic problems. From the violation of Belgian neutrality in 1914, which brought Britain into the war, to the adoption of unlimited submarine warfare in 1917 that brought in the United States, they took aggressive military decisions that eventually stacked the odds against their own side.

MODERN COMMANDERS

HELMUTH VON MOLTKE THE YOUNGER

CHIEF OF GERMAN GENERAL STAFF
BORN May 25, 1848
DIED June 18, 1916
KEY CONFLICTS World War I
KEY BATTLES Frontiers 1914, First Marne 1914

Known as "the Younger" to distinguish him from his uncle, a celebrated Prussian commander, Helmuth von Moltke was a close friend of Kaiser Wilhelm II and thus appointed head

of the general staff in 1906. From his predecessor, Alfred von Schlieffen, he inherited a plan for a war against France and Russia, involving a powerful "right hook" through Belgium into northern France.

In August 1914, Moltke set this plan in motion, invading France in the battle of the Frontiers. Slowed by resistance in Belgium, Moltke then weakened his right wing by diverting troops to face advancing Russian

forces on the Eastern Front. He lost contact with his armies from his headquarters in Luxembourg, so commanders on the ground made crucial decisions: to turn east of Paris instead of west, and to retreat when counterattacked at the Marne.

Overwhelmed by the pressure, Moltke was fired in mid-September, although the news was initially suppressed to avoid giving encouragement to the Allies. His last order was for German armies to dig in to fortified lines, in effect, initiating trench warfare.

The younger Moltke
Moltke never escaped from the shadow of his more famous uncle, victor of the Franco-Prussian War.

> ## OUR ADVANCE IN BELGIUM IS BRUTAL BUT... ALL WHO GET IN THE WAY MUST TAKE THE CONSEQUENCES.
>
> **HELMUTH VON MOLTKE**, FROM A LETTER, AUGUST 5, 1914

ERICH VON FALKENHAYN

CHIEF OF GERMAN GENERAL STAFF
BORN September 11, 1861
DIED April 8, 1922
KEY CONFLICTS World War I
KEY BATTLES First Ypres 1914, Verdun 1916, Romanian Campaign 1916, Jerusalem 1917

A Prussian *Junker* (a member of the noble, landowning class), Falkenhayn was a career soldier who rose to the top before World War I largely on merit. He was Prussian war minister in August 1914 and succeeded Moltke as chief of general staff in mid-September. On the Western Front he ordered the series of outflanking moves

Realistic view
Falkenhayn was an intelligent officer whose clear grasp of the strategic situation made him pessimistic about German chances of an outright victory.

known as the "Race to the Sea," which definitively failed at the first battle of Ypres in November 1914. After this costly experience, Falkenhayn abandoned the notion of achieving victory through a decisive breakthrough. He believed Germany's best hope lay in inflicting such dispiriting losses upon its enemies that they would sue for peace.

Falkenhayn supported the offensives of Paul von Hindenburg and Erich Ludendorff in the east, but earned their enmity by removing troops for an eventually successful

attack on Serbia. The perceived failure of his offensive at Verdun (pp. 292–93) gave Hindenburg and Ludendorff the opportunity to have him fired in August 1916.

FALL FROM POWER
Demoted to command of German Ninth Army campaigning against Romania, Falkenhayn captured the capital, Bucharest, in four months. In 1917, he took command of the Yilderim Force, a mostly Turkish army with German officers in the Middle East, but was removed after failing to stop the British from taking Jerusalem. By the end of the war he was leading German Tenth Army in Lithuania.

Gas mask
At Second Ypres in April 1915, Falkenhayn authorized the first use of poison gas.

PAUL EMILE VON LETTOW-VORBECK

GERMAN GENERAL
BORN March 20, 1870
DIED March 9, 1964
KEY CONFLICTS World War I
KEY BATTLES Tanga 1914, Jassin 1915,
Mahiwa 1917

An officer with experience of colonial
wars in China and German South-
West Africa, Lettow-Vorbeck was
sent to command the *Schutztruppe*

Guerrilla poster
Lettow-Vorbeck's exploits in east Africa had a
romance entirely lacking in trench warfare. He
made excellent material for propaganda posters.

(defense force) in German East Africa
in April 1914. When the British
landed troops at Tanga in November,
Lettow-Vorbeck defeated them
despite being heavily outnumbered,
capturing a large haul of weaponry.

After another battle at Jassin in
January 1915, he realized such clashes
were rapidly exhausting his limited
supplies of men and ammunition.
From then on, he used guerrilla
tactics. Hunted by expanding British
forces, Lettow-Vorbeck led his band
of around 3,000 whites and 11,000
Africans in a campaign of raids and
ambushes, living off the land and

sidestepping all attempts to pin him
down. Although the guerrillas suffered
mounting hardship, discipline and
loyalty remained high.

A HERO'S RETURN
In October 1917, Lettow-Vorbeck
was forced to fight at Mahiwa,
losing 500 men but inflicting five
times as many casualties on his
opponents and escaping into
Portuguese Mozambique. He was
still unbeaten when the war ended.
Returning as a hero to Berlin in
1919, he was involved in a failed
coup and dismissed from the army.

ERICH LUDENDORFF

GERMAN ARMY QUARTERMASTER
BORN April 9, 1865
DIED December 20, 1937
KEY CONFLICTS World War I
KEY BATTLES Liège 1914, Tannenberg 1914,
Masurian Lakes 1914, Gorlice-Tarnow 1915,
Spring Offensive 1918

Ludendorff sprang to fame in the
early days of the war when he led
an attack on the Belgian fortress city
of Liège. Hastily transferred to the
Eastern Front as chief-of-staff to Paul
von Hindenburg, he participated in
the defeat of two Russian armies in
a single month, at Tannenberg and

the Masurian Lakes, demonstrating
his skill in organizing the rapid
maneuver of large-scale forces.
Further successes, notably the
Gorlice-Tarnow Offensive in Poland
in 1915, contrasted starkly with the
stalemate on the Western Front.

RUNNING THE WAR
Hindenburg was appointed German
chief of general staff in August 1916,
with Ludendorff as his quartermaster.
In practice, Ludendorff took control
of the German war effort, mobilizing
the German economy to maximize
war production and implementing

unrestricted submarine warfare
in a failed effort to defeat Britain
that instead provoked the United
States into declaring war. After
imposing punitive peace
terms on a defeated Russia,
in spring 1918, he gambled
on winning the war through
a swift offensive in France
before the Americans arrived.
Despite initial breakthroughs,
the gamble failed. As his
exhausted armies fell back
in the face of counterattacks
from July 1918, Ludendorff's
nerve broke. By September, he
was insisting that Germany must
make peace immediately. He was
forced to resign in October 1918.

Agressive tactics
Ludendorff was an aggressive
militarist who coined the
term *totale krieg*
(total war).

> ## LUDENDORFF… IS ONLY GREAT AT A TIME OF SUCCESS. IF THINGS GO BADLY HE LOSES HIS NERVE.
> **GERMAN CHANCELLOR THEOBALD VON BETHMANN-HOLLWEG**, 1916

PAUL VON HINDENBURG

Hindenburg retired from the German Army in
1911 as a corps commander with a respectable
career behind him. He was recalled in August
1914 to resist the Russian advance on the
Eastern Front and the spectacular victory
at Tannenberg made him a national hero.
Appointed chief of general staff in August
1916, he supplanted the kaiser as a focus for
German patriotism, but allowed Ludendorff to
run the war. When Ludendorff resigned in
October 1918, Hindenburg remained in place,
overseeing the Armistice and the abdication of
the kaiser. Elected president of the Weimar
Republic in 1925, he gave in to pressure to
appoint Adolf Hitler chancellor in 1933.

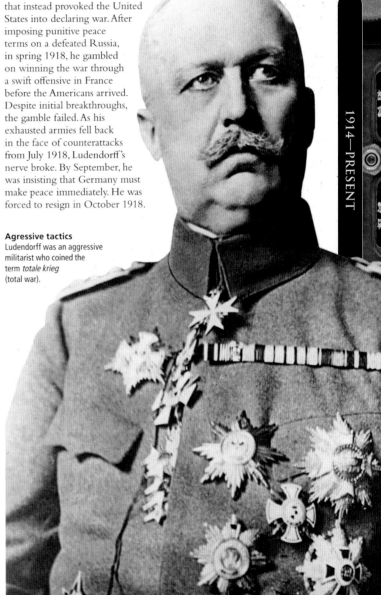

PÉTAIN VS. FALKENHAYN

IN DECEMBER 1915, German chief of general staff, Erich von Falkenhayn, decided that a major offensive on the Western Front might break France's will to fight. The chosen target was Verdun, a city on the Meuse River protected by a perfunctory trench system and a ring of undermanned forts. Joseph Joffre, the French commander-in-chief, had withdrawn many guns from the forts, believing such strongpoints were outdated, and had dismissed calls to reinforce the Verdun trenches, which even lacked barbed wire. In early 1916, the Germans moved 1,200 guns and more than 2 million artillery shells to the Verdun sector in preparation for their offensive.

PHILIPPE PÉTAIN

On February 24, 1916, three days after the Germans launched their offensive, the French high command took the fateful decision to attempt to hold Verdun, rather than withdrawing west of the Meuse River. General Philippe Pétain, commanding the French Second Army, was ordered to take over the defense of the city. He arrived at Verdun on February 25, only to find the French forces in disarray and to learn of the fall of the key fortress at nearby Douaumont.

DEFENSIVE TACTICS

Pétain instantly made his presence felt, despite suffering a bout of pneumonia. He ordered subordinate officers to stop mounting futile and costly infantry counterattacks. Instead, they were to concentrate their efforts on grinding down the enemy with artillery fire. Exploiting the fact that the Germans had advanced only on the east bank of the Meuse, he arrayed guns on the west bank that raked their advancing infantry. A supreme effort was made to bring up men and supplies on the small road linking Verdun to the rest of France—which became known as *La Voie Sacrée* (The Sacred Way). To avoid morale cracking on the hellish battlefield, Pétain instituted a system of troop rotation, which meant that in principle no soldier should spend more than eight days at the front.

NIVELLE TAKES OVER

Pétain's determinedly defensive posture did not satisfy Joffre, who resented constant demands for more troops and artillery from a general who offered nothing but the prospect of holding his ground. Popular with his troops and the public, Pétain could not be dismissed, but in April a decision was made to promote him away from the front, replacing him with Robert Nivelle, a commander who favored more offensive tactics. Pétain remained in overall command of the Verdun sector through the summer of 1916, as the German offensive finally ground to a halt. But Nivelle took the credit for later French counterattacks, successful against much reduced German forces.

PÉTAIN

Afternoon French battalions led by Colonel Émile Driant are overcome at the Bois des Caures after holding up the German advance

Pétain takes over as commander at Verdun. He stabilizes the front over the following three days, using artillery to stop advancing German infantry

Pétain has to rush troops to the extreme left of his line as the Germans threaten to break through at Malancourt, near *Côte 304*, a key French artillery position

Pétain encourages his desperate troops with the famous order of the day: *Courage, on les aura!* (Be brave, we will beat them!)

Pétain assumes command of Center Army Group, his responsibilities including the Verdun sector. Nivelle replaces him in field command at Verdun

| 1916: FEB 21 | FEB 22 | FEB 25 | MAR 6 | MAR 20 | APR 9 | APR 16 | MAY 2 |

FALKENHAYN

7:15 a.m. The battle of Verdun opens with a massive German artillery bombardment. After 10 hours' shelling, German infantry attack

4:30 p.m. German infantry enter Fort Douaumont, the central strongpoint of the French Verdun defenses, almost unopposed

The Germans expand their offensive to the west bank of the Meuse, after Falkenhayn releases a reserve corps to enter the battle

Reinforced with fresh troops and material, the Germans launch major attacks simultaneously east and west of the Meuse

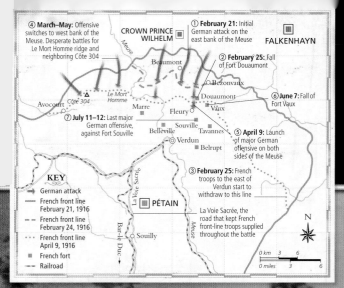

CROWN PRINCE WILHELM

FALKENHAYN

④ **March–May:** Offensive switches to west bank of the Meuse. Desperate battles for Le Mort Homme ridge and neighboring Côte 304

① **February 21:** Initial German attack on the east bank of the Meuse

② **February 25:** Fall of Fort Douaumont

⑥ **June 7:** Fall of Fort Vaux

⑦ **July 11–12:** Last major German offensive, against Fort Souville

⑤ **April 9:** Launch of major German offensive on both sides of the Meuse

③ **February 25:** French troops to the east of Verdun start to withdraw to this line

La Voie Sacrée, the road that kept French front-line troops supplied throughout the battle

PÉTAIN

Beaumont · Bezonvaux · Douaumont · Vaux · Marre · Fleury · Belleville · Souville · Tavannes · Verdun · Belrupt · Avocourt · Côte 304 · Le Mort Homme · Souilly · Meuse · Bar-le-Duc

KEY
- German attack
- French front line February 21, 1916
- French front line February 24, 1916
- French front line April 9, 1916
- French fort
- Railroad

N

0 km 3 6
0 miles 3 6

LOCATION 120 miles (195 km) east of Paris, France
DATE February 21– December 18, 1916
FORCES Germans: 140,000 at start of battle—overall, about half the German Army in France fought at Verdun; French: 50,000 at start of battle—overall, three-quarters of the French Army fought at Verdun at some time
CASUALTIES Germans: at least 355,000; French: at least 400,000

ERICH VON FALKENHAYN

Falkenhayn entrusted the offensive to Crown Prince Wilhelm's German Fifth Army. The tactical plan was for an intensive bombardment by massed artillery, followed by a rapid infantry advance spearheaded by assault troops armed with grenades and flame-throwers. Progress was at first impressive, and the Germans might have taken Verdun had it not been for Falkenhayn's cautious decision to hold back reserves.

Once French resistance stiffened and prospects of a swift victory evaporated, Falkenhayn could see no better option than to commit his infantry to renewed attacks month after month for minimal gains— the usual pattern for Western Front offensives. Falkenhayn had accepted from the outset that Verdun might turn into a battle of attrition, which he assumed would drain French manpower and break French morale. However, by the spring, his own troops' morale was collapsing in the face of numerous casualties.

GROUND DOWN
In April, the Crown Prince called for further attacks to be halted, but Falkenhayn insisted the operation must continue. It was not until the launch of the Allied offensive on the Somme on July 1 that he accepted the need to switch resources away from Verdun. A final push was attempted, but by mid-July the German offensive had failed. Falkenhayn's reign as chief of general staff ended soon after.

> **THE FORCES OF FRANCE WILL BLEED TO DEATH... WHETHER WE OURSELVES REACH OUR GOAL OR NOT.**
> **ERICH VON FALKENHAYN**, MEMORANDUM TO KAISER WILHELM II, DECEMBER 25, 1915

La Voie Sacrée
The French relied on a single minor road, with a narrow-gauge railroad track alongside, to move their men and supplies into beleaguered Verdun. Motor trucks, horse-drawn carts, and marching soldiers filed along this route day and night.

MAY 3–4
After a 36-hour artillery bombardment with 500 guns, the Germans take the French artillery position of *Côte 304*, west of the Meuse

MAY 22–26
Nivelle launches an attack aimed at retaking Fort Douaumont, but despite a heavy concentration of artillery, it fails with heavy casualties

MAY 29
In some of the fiercest fighting of the battle, the Germans take Le Mort Homme ridge, under attack since March 6

The strongpoint of Fort Vaux falls to the Germans after an assault by Stormtroopers and prolonged fighting within the fortress

JUN 1–7

JUN 23
The greatest crisis of the battle, according to Pétain: he wrings reinforcements from a reluctant Joffre to stem further German advances

JULY 2
Falkenhayn visits the Somme, where an Allied offensive has begun the previous day. He orders artillery transferred to the Somme from Verdun

JULY 12
The French succeed in defending Fort Souville against a furious German onslaught, marking the end of German offensives at Verdun

AUG 29
Falkenhayn is replaced as chief of German general staff by Hindenburg, partly because of his failure at Verdun, which ceases to be a German priority

OCT 24
The French recapture Fort Douaumont. They go on to retake Fort Vaux (November 2), and then most other lost ground in a final counterattack (December 15–18)

NAVAL COMMANDERS OF WWI

WORLD WAR I BROKE OUT at the end of an intense period of naval expansion that raised expectations of a dramatic all-guns-blazing contest for control of the seas between Britain and Germany. The strategic situation, however, made both sides adopt an essentially defensive posture. Britain's Grand Fleet and the German High Seas Fleet faced each other across the North Sea, but the Germans were too weak to challenge British dominance, and the British did not need a victory to keep the Germans under blockade. German submarines in the end came closest to a decisive impact on the war through large-scale sinking of Allied merchant shipping in 1917.

MODERN COMMANDERS

DAVID BEATTY

BRITISH ADMIRAL
BORN January 17, 1871
DIED March 11, 1936
KEY CONFLICTS World War I
KEY BATTLES Heligoland Bight 1914, Dogger Bank 1915, Jutland 1916

David Beatty first showed promise in 1898 commanding gunboats on the Nile during Kitchener's Omdurman campaign. By 1910, he was a rear admiral, at 39 the youngest British sailor to achieve that rank since the 18th century. In 1913, he took command of the Battlecruiser Squadron. The fast and powerful battlecruisers were expected to provide the best opportunity for dash and daring in the Nelson tradition.

When war broke out, expectations at first looked likely to be fulfilled. At the Heligoland Bight in August 1914, Beattie's squadron sank three German cruisers and a destroyer. An engagement with Franz Hipper's battlecruisers at Dogger Bank in January 1915 was less successful. Beatty won applause for impeccable courage as his flagship *Lion* suffered heavy punishment leading the charge, but failure of communication with the rest of his squadron meant the Germans were allowed to escape with the loss of a single obsolete cruiser. At Jutland Beatty's battlecruisers proved tragically vulnerable to accurate enemy gunnery—three were sunk along with almost their entire crews. Beatty was appointed to command the Grand Fleet in December 1916. Despite a theoretical commitment to aggression, however, he was unable in practice to abandon the cautious policy of his predecessor, John Jellicoe. Beatty's first and last major action as commander-in-chief was to accept the surrender of the German fleet in November 1918.

Dash and charisma
With his cap at a jaunty angle as depicted on this French journal, Beatty fulfilled the image of a dashing British naval commander that was cherished by the public at home and abroad.

> **BEATTY... SAID, 'THERE SEEMS TO BE SOMETHING WRONG WITH OUR BLOODY SHIPS TO-DAY.'**
> **CAPTAIN ERNIE CHATFIELD**, RECALLING AN INCIDENT AT THE BATTLE OF JUTLAND

FRANZ HIPPER

GERMAN ADMIRAL
BORN September 13, 1863
DIED May 25, 1932
KEY CONFLICTS World War I
KEY BATTLES Scarborough Raid 1914, Dogger Bank 1915, Jutland 1916

As commander of the German fleet's battlecruiser scouting group in December 1914, Hipper bombarded British coastal towns, including Scarborough, causing significant civilian casualties. The Royal Navy succeeded in engaging Hipper's group at the Dogger Bank in January 1915, but he escaped with the loss of only one ship. At Jutland Hipper's battlecruisers again performed impressively, and in August 1918 he took over command of the German High Seas Fleet. While armistice negotiations were in progress in

Hipper medal
This medal commemorates Hipper at the battle of Jutland. He was much honored and received a knighthood from the king of his native Bavaria.

October, he gave orders for a final sortie to engage the British Grand Fleet, but this suicide mission was aborted when his sailors mutinied.

REINHARD SCHEER

GERMAN ADMIRAL
BORN September 30, 1863
DIED November 26, 1928
KEY CONFLICTS World War I
KEY BATTLE Jutland 1916

Leading a battleship squadron in 1914–15, Reinhard Scheer became commander-in-chief of the High Seas Fleet in January 1916. Pursuing an aggressive strategy, in May he attempted to lure the British battlecruiser squadron into an engagement with his battleships. The plan backfired when Scheer found himself unexpectedly facing the might of Britain's Grand Fleet off Jutland. He handled the race back to port well and claimed a victory on the basis of the losses suffered by the two fleets. But after Jutland Scheer made only a few tentative sorties before his promotion from fleet to higher command in August 1918.

Commander-in-chief 1916
An aggressive naval commander, Scheer resented the German fleet being confined to port. Yet, after the battle of Jutland in 1916, he found almost no opportunity for offensive action.

JOHN JELLICOE

BRITISH ADMIRAL
BORN December 5, 1859
DIED November 20, 1935
KEY CONFLICTS World War I
KEY BATTLES Jutland 1916

Of more modest social origins than most naval officers of his time, John Jellicoe rose to prominence in the peacetime Royal Navy through hard work and technical expertise. He saw some action in colonial conflicts, but the bulk of his career was spent not at sea but at the Admiralty. Appointed to command the Grand Fleet at the outbreak of war in August 1914, he accepted the job with reluctance and approached it in a spirit of caution. He believed that he was, in Winston Churchill's words, "the only man on either side who could lose the war in an afternoon." His overriding concern was to maintain the Royal Navy's superiority over the German navy by not losing ships.

A CAUTIOUS APPROACH

Acutely aware of the threat to his battleships posed by German submarines, mines, and torpedo boats, Jellicoe instigated a distant blockade of Germany, sealing the exits from the North Sea, rather than a close blockade that would have pinned the German High Seas Fleet in its ports. A patient cat-and-mouse game ensued in the North Sea, with Jellicoe waiting to react to occasional sorties by German warships. In May 1916, he caught the High Seas Fleet at Jutland, but the engagement did not go as planned. Commanding on board the battleship *Iron Duke*, he found it impossible to form any clear picture of the battle as it evolved. Jellicoe had instituted a centralized command system in which captains were discouraged from taking initiatives, but was badly placed to dictate the maneuvers of a fleet of over 150 ships. His overwhelming concern remained not to destroy the Germans but to keep his ships safe, and in this he largely succeeded.

Frustration with the indecisive outcome at Jutland contributed to Jellicoe's replacement in December 1916 by the more flamboyant Beatty. Jellicoe was moved to the Admiralty as First Sea Lord, where his main problem was to find a response to the expanding German U-boat campaign against merchant shipping. He eventually adopted the right solution— forming escorted merchant convoys—but introduced it only slowly and hesitantly. No politician, he was defenseless in the snakepit of Whitehall war management and was forced out of office in December 1917.

Risk averse
Jellicoe was an intelligent officer with an aversion to risk—far from the swashbuckling tradition of the navy of Nelson's day.

> ## THERE IS ONE TEST, AND ONLY ONE, OF VICTORY. WHO HELD THE FIELD OF BATTLE AT THE END OF THE FIGHT?
>
> **THE GLOBE, A BRITISH NEWSPAPER**, FOUR DAYS AFTER THE BATTLE OF JUTLAND, 1916

KEY BATTLE

JUTLAND

CAMPAIGN World War I
DATE May 31–June 1, 1916
LOCATION North Sea, off Denmark

On the night of May 30–31, 1916, Admiral Jellicoe led his Grand Fleet out of Scapa Flow, off northern Scotland. He knew from Admiralty signals intelligence that Scheer's High Seas Fleet was making a sortie into the North Sea. He hoped to engage and destroy it with his far superior forces—28 battleships to Scheer's 16. On the afternoon of May 31, in poor visibility, the two fleets made contact off Jutland. The opposing battlecruiser squadrons, under Beatty and Hipper, were first to engage, and the Germans had by far the better of the exchange. Scheer was shocked when the rest of the Grand Fleet loomed out of the mist, for he had no idea Jellicoe was at sea. The Germans bolted for home and running engagements developed through the rest of the day and the following night. Scheer slowed the British pursuit with counterattacks, especially by torpedo-armed destroyers, while Jellicoe was hampered by a lack of night-fighting equipment. By morning Scheer had reached safety. The British had lost 14 ships, the Germans 11.

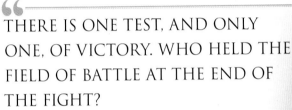

A WORLD IN TURMOIL

> "MEANWHILE WOMEN, CHILDREN AND OLD MEN WERE FALLING IN HEAPS, LIKE FLIES... I SAW AN OLD PEASANT STANDING ALONE IN A FIELD: A MACHINE-GUN BULLET KILLED HIM. FOR MORE THAN AN HOUR THESE EIGHTEEN PLANES... DROPPED BOMB AFTER BOMB ON GUERNICA."

FATHER ALBERTO DE ONAINDIA, RECALLING THE RAID BY GERMAN AIRCRAFT ON APRIL 26, 1937, DURING THE SPANISH CIVIL WAR

I N THE SECOND DECADE of the 20th century, the world entered turbulent times, marked by social upheavals, political and economic collapse, and widespread warfare. In many countries, military command became inextricably entwined with politics—rebels and revolutionaries led military campaigns while prominent generals plunged into political life as nation builders or dictators. Differing tactics were employed, from guerrilla warfare to the use of aircraft and armored vehicles in shock attacks that presaged World War II.

Although overshadowed by World War I, the other conflicts of the period from the 1910s to the 1930s were numerous and, in some cases, of very considerable size and duration. In Mexico, for example, the overthrow of dictator Porfirio Díaz in 1910 was followed by a decade of civil war that involved at least 200,000 combat deaths. In China, the fall of the last emperor in 1912 initiated an era of civil strife and foreign invasion that lasted almost 40 years.

The overthrow of czarist rule in the Russian Revolution of 1917—precipitated by Russia's involvement in World War I—led to a civil war of terrible destructiveness. In the course of this, the Bolshevik (Communist) regime sought first to survive against the attacks of its political enemies, and then to extend its control over the former Russian Empire, creating the Union of Soviet Socialist Republics, or Soviet Union. In Poland, Turkey, and Ireland, armed force determined the shape of new states formed in the chaotic aftermath of World War I.

THE GROWTH OF NATIONALISM

Hopes for a more peaceful world briefly surged when the Briand-Kellogg Pact, solemnly renouncing war, was signed in August 1928 by 15 countries, including the United States, Japan, Britain, Germany, Italy, and France. The 1930s brought a complete reversal of this pacifist tendency, with the establishment of aggressively nationalist regimes by the Nazi movement in Germany, and by army and navy officers in Japan.

The uniformed leaders of militarist regimes were not necessarily themselves military commanders. The Nazi leader Adolf Hitler and the Italian Fascist leader Benito Mussolini had both served in World War I, but neither had been a commissioned officer. However, they pursued a policy of rearmament and sought every opportunity for conquest.

In retrospect, the armed conflicts of the 1930s may be seen as an irresistible slide toward World War II. Japan's occupation of Manchuria in 1931 was followed by the Italian conquest of Ethiopia in 1935–36. In the Spanish Civil War of 1936–39, Germany and Italy intervened on one side and the Soviet Union on the other, while—again in the Far East—Japan invaded China in 1937.

A CHANGE OF DIRECTION

The main concern of reflective military commanders throughout the 1920s and 30s was to avoid a repeat of the static trench warfare of World War I. Strategy focused on uses for tanks and of advances in aircraft design that enabled the bombing of cities and other key targets. There were advocates of mobile armored warfare in most countries, such as Charles de Gaulle in France and Mikhail Tukhachevsky in the Soviet Union. But the Germans gained a clear lead in developing the combined use of tanks and aircraft, and they tried out such tactics when they sent their Condor Legion to intervene in the Spanish Civil War. The Japanese also experimented with air power in their war with China.

While many commanders espoused aggressive tactics, some had drawn defensive conclusions from World War I. For example, the French constructed their Maginot Line fortifications along their border with Germany. But these proved of little value when a second global conflict erupted in 1939.

1914—PRESENT

Spanish Civil War
General Francisco Franco's Nationalist soldiers give the fascist salute. Around half a million people died in the Spanish Civil War, which started with a military uprising against a left-wing government.

Mosin-Nagant rifle
Designed in 1891, the Mosin-Nagant rifle was widely used by both sides in the Russian Civil War. Mosin-Nagants were also supplied to the Republican side in the Spanish Civil War.

REBELS AND REVOLUTIONARIES

IN A WORLD RACKED WITH civil war and revolution in the 1910s and 20s, gifted individuals with no formal military experience organized and led armed campaigns, sometimes on a large scale. The Berber rebellion of Abd el-Krim in North Africa presaged the colonial wars of the second half of the 20th century. In Ireland, the independence war, and the subsequent civil war, were fought at the small-scale level of terrorism, reprisals, and ambushes. In Russia, by contrast, the civil war that followed the Bolshevik Revolution involved armies of millions. Mexico had its own style of military hero in semi-bandit warlords, such as Pancho Villa.

ABD EL-KRIM

BERBER REBEL LEADER
BORN c. 1880
DIED February 6, 1963
KEY CONFLICT Rif Rebellion
KEY BATTLES Annual 1921

Abd el-Krim al-Khattabi was born into an educated Berber family in Ajdir, in the mountainous region of Morocco known as the Rif. In the early 20th century, Morocco was divided between France and Spain, most of the Rif falling within the Spanish sphere of influence. During World War I Abd el-Krim fell afoul of the Spanish authorities and served time in prison. He returned to Ajdir determined to fight for independence.

In 1921, an army of poorly led, ill-trained Spanish troops marched into the Rif from their base at Melilla. Abd el-Krim's irregulars overran isolated Spanish outposts and threatened to encircle the main body of troops at Annual in July. Thousands of Spanish soldiers were killed by harassing Riffians in a panic-stricken retreat to Melilla. Abd el-Krim

declared a Republic of the Rif, equipping a small regular army with captured artillery, machine-guns, and modern rifles. It was a force that found the support of tens of thousands of Berber villagers.

CHALLENGING FRANCE

Abd el-Krim overreached himself by extending his operations into French Morocco in April 1925. The French World War I hero Philippe Pétain was given the task of crushing the revolt using Spanish aid. He treated the war like a conventional European conflict, massing heavily armed troops with artillery and air support in a 10-month campaign. Abd el-Krim surrendered in May 1926 and spent the rest of his life in exile.

Respected leader
Abd el-Krim was much admired in Europe and North America. He lived to see Morocco and Algeria gain independence from European rule.

> **ABD EL-KRIM IS ENCIRCLED. HE IS NO LONGER TO BE FEARED.**
>
> **MARSHAL PHILIPPE PÉTAIN,** QUOTED IN *THE NEW YORK TIMES*, NOVEMBER 8, 1925

 ## MICHAEL COLLINS

IRISH NATIONALIST LEADER
BORN October 16, 1890
DIED August 22, 1922
KEY CONFLICTS Irish Independence War, Irish Civil War
KEY BATTLES Easter Rising 1916, Dublin 1922

Born in County Cork, Michael Collins became a member of the revolutionary Irish Republican Brotherhood while living in England. He returned to Ireland in 1916 to take part in the Easter uprising against British rule. Arrested when the rebels surrendered, he was soon released.

Displaying great charisma, Collins became both a political and military leader of the Irish Republican

Leader of the Irish Free State
Collins addresses a crowd in Dublin on March 18, 1922, as he attempts to overcome opposition to the treaty that divided Ireland.

Irish conflicts
Rebels fight in the streets of Dublin during the Irish Civil War of 1922, a conflict that was triggered by the treaty that gave self-governance to southern Ireland.

independence movement. In the guerrilla warfare waged against the British authorities from 1919, he helped to found the Irish Republican Army (IRA) and ran an intelligence operation. He also led a terrorist hit squad, which assassinated 13 people, including 11 British intelligence officers, on November 21, 1920, that became known as Bloody Sunday.

THE ROAD TO CIVIL WAR

When a truce was declared in July 1921, Collins led negotiations with the British government, agreeing to the treaty that gave southern Ireland its own government, but which left six counties in the north under British rule. After the IRA rejected the treaty, in June 1922, Collins attacked their headquarters in Dublin with artillery borrowed from the British, precipitating civil war. While acting as commander-in-chief of the government forces Collins still hoped for a compromise, but on August 22 he was ambushed and shot dead.

LEON TROTSKY

BOLSHEVIK REVOLUTIONARY LEADER
BORN November 7, 1879
DIED August 21, 1940
KEY CONFLICTS Russian Civil War,
Russo-Polish War
KEY BATTLES Petrograd 1919, Warsaw 1920

Leon Trotsky, born Lev Davidovich
Bronstein, was a Marxist revolutionary
who came to prominence during the
failed Russian popular uprising of
1905. He fled into exile, returning
to Russia after the overthrow of the
czarist regime in March 1917. He
joined Lenin's Bolshevik (later
Communist) Party in time for its
seizure of power in November 1918.
    Commissar for foreign affairs in
Lenin's revolutionary government,
Trotsky negotiated peace with
Germany at Brest-Litovsk in March

War commissar
Trotsky was an inspiring orator, a talent he put
to good use in motivating the Red Army during
the Russian Civil War of 1918 to 1920.

1918. He became commissar for war,
facing large-scale civil war in which
the Bolshevik regime was threatened
by White (counterrevolutionary)
armies and foreign forces.

A NEW RED ARMY
Trotsky transformed the small
Red Army—evolved from
revolutionary workers' Red
Guard units—into a mass
regular army. Employing
former czarist officers to
take command as "military
specialists," he reimposed
formal discipline and hierarchy
of ranks. Between 1918 and 1920,
conscription swelled the ranks of the
Red Army to five million troops, far
more than could be adequately
supplied or equipped. Nonetheless,
the Red Army won the civil war,
thanks in no small measure to
Trotsky, who toured the fronts
delivering fiery speeches and
ordering the execution of deserters.

In October 1919, he organized
the last-ditch defense of Petrograd
(St. Petersburg) against the White
general, Nikolai Yudenich, at one
point mounting a horse to round up
retreating troops and turn them back
to face enemy tanks. He was sceptical
about the invasion of Poland in 1920,

Red Guard armband
This armband identified a member of the
Red Guards—armed workers who defended
factories during the 1917 Russian Revolution.

which led to defeat, but by then faced
opposition within the Communist
leadership. After a long struggle
against Joseph Stalin, Trotsky was
expelled from the Soviet Union in
1929 and assassinated by one of
Stalin's agents in Mexico in 1940.

PANCHO VILLA

MEXICAN REVOLUTIONARY GENERAL
BORN June 5, 1878
DIED July 20, 1923
KEY CONFLICT Mexican Revolution
KEY BATTLES Tierra Blanca 1913,
Columbus 1916

Hero of the people
Pancho Villa's exploits made him a folk hero
in the United States as well as in Mexico. His
assassination in 1923 remains a mystery.

Born Doroteo Arango, Francisco
"Pancho" Villa lived as a bandit in
northern Mexico. He led his outlaws
in support of the overthrow of
dictator Porfirio Díaz in 1910 and
participated in the many-sided
conflicts that followed. Villa was a
charismatic leader whose División
del Norte attracted adventurous

volunteers from the United States.
He fought the brutal General
Victoriano Huerta, winning a series
of victories, notably at Tierra Blanca
in November 1913, and riding into
Mexico City in December 1914.

TAKING ON THE US
The following year, Villa clashed with
former allies Venustiano Carranza and
Álvaro Obregón. He turned his ire
upon the United States, which had

backed Carranza and Obregón. In
March 1916, he sent 500 men across
the border to raid Columbus, New
Mexico, fighting a sharp engagement
with US cavalry. The United States
responded with a punitive expedition,
in which General Jack Pershing led
10,000 troops into Mexico to search
for Villa. They failed to find him, and
Pershing complained that he had
been "outwitted and out bluffed."
Villa was assassinated in 1923.

1914–PRESENT

Bolshevik, 1920
A giant figure, symbolic of Bolshevism, waves the red flag of Communism as he strides among the masses. The picture, by painter and set designer Boris Kustodiev, captures the revolutionary spirit of the time.

INTERWAR MILITARY STRONGMEN

MILITARISTIC NATIONALIST governments flourished in the unsettled atmosphere of the 1920s and 30s. Modern-day Poland and Turkey were states that came into existence through wars, and the military commanders who led in these conflicts—Jozef Pilsudski and Mustafa Kemal—also dominated the states' early political life. In post-imperial China, civil war and foreign invasion made it impossible for any government to control all of the country, although Jiang Jieshi came close to establishing national leadership. Spain's civil war was bitterly contested and the victor, Francisco Franco, could make no claim to represent the whole Spanish nation.

JOZEF PILSUDSKI

POLISH MILITARY AND POLITICAL LEADER
BORN December 5, 1867
DIED May 12, 1935
KEY CONFLICTS World War I,
Polish-Soviet War
KEY BATTLES Kostiuchnowka 1916,
Warsaw 1920

Before World War I, Jozef Pilsudski ran an underground paramilitary organization opposing Russian rule in Poland. When war broke out, he led volunteer Polish Legions to fight with Austria against Russia. The Poles performed well at Kostiuchnowka in July 1916, but cooperation with the Austrians broke down. Pilsudski was arrested and his Legions disbanded.

FRAGILE INDEPENDENCE
Pilsudski became head of state of an independent Poland after World War I. He then fought a series of wars to establish Poland's borders, the most important against Bolshevik Russia. In April 1920, he invaded Ukraine.

The Bolsheviks counterattacked, driving the Poles back to Warsaw. Pilsudski executed an inspired counter-blow, cutting across the Bolshevik lines of communication with a thrust from the south. Some Russian forces were destroyed, the rest withdrew. Pilsudski resigned as head of state in 1922, but returned to power four years later in a military coup. He remained the effective dictator of Poland until he died.

Polish hero
A militarist who rejected democracy, Pilsudski nonetheless remains a hero for most Poles for his role in creating an independent Poland.

> ## HE GAVE POLAND FREEDOM, BOUNDARIES, POWER, AND RESPECT.
> **GENERAL MOSCICKI,** FUNERAL ORATION FOR PILSUDSKI, 1935

MUSTAFA KEMAL ATATURK

TURKISH GENERAL AND PRESIDENT
BORN c. 1881
DIED November 10, 1938
KEY CONFLICTS World War I,
Greco-Turkish War
KEY BATTLES Gallipoli 1915, Sakarya 1921,
Dumlupinar 1922

The founder of modern Turkey, Mustafa Kemal was originally a career officer in the army of the Ottoman Empire. He saw action in Libya and the Balkans before Turkey's entry into World War I as an ally of Germany in October 1914. Commanding Turkish 19th Division, Kemal led resistance to the Allied landings at Gallipoli from April 1915. His determination to hold ground regardless of cost turned Kemal into a national hero.

The remaining years of the war gave him few chances to shine, but he emerged from defeats in both the Caucasus and Palestine with more credit than other Turkish generals.

In 1919, Kemal emerged as the leader of nationalist opposition to punitive peace terms and the occupation of parts of Turkey by Greek and

Father of the Turks
As leader of the Turkish Republic from 1924 to 1938, Mustafa Kemal Ataturk was a radical modernizer, creating a secular Westernized state.

other foreign armies. Heading a revolutionary government based in Ankara, in the summer of 1921, he successfully resisted a Greek offensive at the line of the Sakarya River.

A NEW REPUBLIC
The following year, advancing on Greek-occupied Smyrna (now Izmir), he routed the Greek armies at the battle of Dumlupinar, driving them out of Anatolia. The Ottoman sultan was deposed and Kemal became the first president of the Turkish Republic. He took the title Ataturk (father of the Turks) in 1934 and remained in office until his death in 1938.

Nationalist army
Mustafa Kemal inspects his troops in Anatolia in 1922 during the war of Turkish Nationalists against Greece.

JIANG JIESHI

CHINESE NATIONALIST LEADER
BORN October 31, 1887
DIED April 5, 1975
KEY CONFLICTS Chinese Civil Wars, Sino-Japanese War, World War II
KEY BATTLES Shanghai 1937, Wuhan 1938

Dynamic leader
In the 1930s Jiang Jieshi impressed many foreign observers as a Chinese political and military leader with energy and dynamism.

Chinese military commander Jiang Jieshi emerged as leader of the Nationalist movement in the 1920s. Fighting campaigns against regional warlords and the Communists, he extended his rule over most of China. In 1937 war broke out with Japan. Jiang led resistance to Japan's invasion forces at Shanghai and then, retreating inland, fought a complex series of engagements around Wuhan. Defeated, he withdrew to remote Chongqing. From 1941, as the Sino-Japanese War was absorbed into World War II, Jiang received financial and military support from the United States, but frustrated America by preferring to conserve his forces rather than fight Japan.

After the surrender of Japan in 1945, Jiang attempted to restore his rule over China but was defeated in a civil war by Mao Zedong's Communists. In 1949, he took refuge with the remnants of his Nationalist army on Taiwan, ruling as dictator of the Republic of China to his death.

FRANCISCO FRANCO

SPANISH GENERAL AND DICTATOR
BORN December 4, 1892
DIED November 20, 1975
KEY CONFLICTS Rif War, Spanish Civil War
KEY BATTLES Madrid 1936, Brunete 1937, Teruel 1938, Ebro 1938

Francisco Franco Bahamonde made his reputation fighting rebels in the Spanish protectorate of Morocco in the Rif War up to the 1920s. Courageous and able, he was made

Victory medal
This medal was awarded to Nationalist soldiers and records the military uprising of July 18, 1936.

commander of the Spanish Legion in 1923 and, in 1926, became the youngest general in the Spanish Army.

After the election of a left-wing Popular Front government in February 1936, Franco was relegated to the Canary Islands. Five months later, other generals staged a military uprising, and Franco flew to Morocco to take command of the Army of Africa, which had declared for the Nationalist rebels. Carried to mainland Spain in aircraft supplied by Nazi Germany and Fascist Italy, Franco's African troops marched on Madrid, and raised the siege of Toledo in September. The victory established Franco as military and political head of the Nationalists.

Franco was ruthless in the ensuing civil war. After an assault on Madrid failed in December, he settled for attrition, leaving the Republicans to exhaust themselves in costly offensives while he targeted major centers of resistance, such as Brunete, Teruel, and Ebro. The Condor Legion of the German army and air force and Italian troops contributed greatly to the Nationalist victory of March 1939, but Franco joined neither of those countries in World War II. He ruled Spain as dictator until his death.

Franco in Morocco
A young Franco directs Spanish legionaries in the harsh terrain of the Moroccan mountains during the Rif War in the early 1920s.

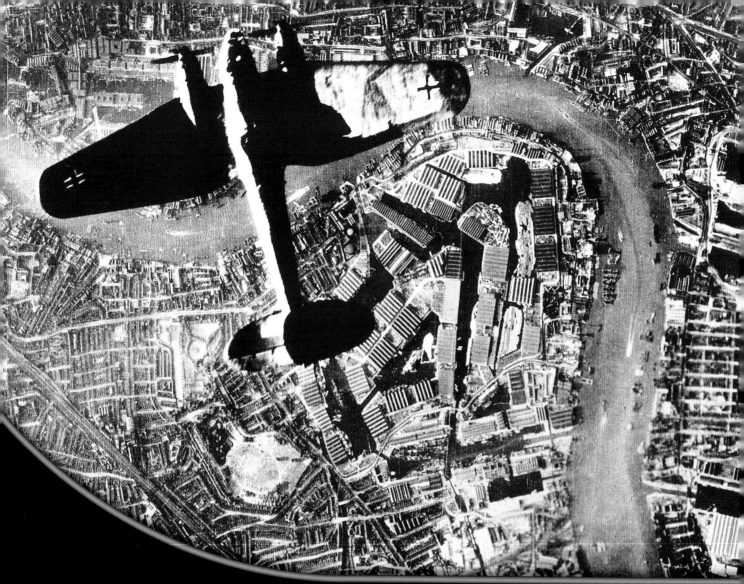

1939—1945

WORLD WAR II

T HE LARGEST CONFLICT IN HISTORY, World War II was really two separate wars. One was fought against Nazi Germany and its Axis allies (mainly Italy) in Europe and North Africa, the other against Japan in the Pacific, Southeast Asia, and China. On land, at sea, and in the air, aggressive commanders came to the fore as technology and tactics swung in favor of the offensive. Germany's Erwin Rommel, the US's George Patton, and the Soviet Union's Georgi Zhukov won heroic reputations, inflated by the propagandists of a publicity-conscious war.

Early in the war, Germany and Japan repeatedly outperformed their enemies. German commanders had worked out how to mount mobile lightning campaigns, deploying tanks, aircraft, and motorized and airborne infantry, coordinated by radio. The French, who had resisted Germany for four years in World War I, were defeated in a six-week campaign. When the Germans, with Hungarian, Romanian, and Finnish forces, invaded the Soviet Union by launching Operation Barbarossa in June 1941, a similar result at first appeared likely. Soviet commanders took orders from the dictator, Josef Stalin, and threw away their men's lives in futile frontal counterattacks and fight-to-the-death struggles to hold untenable positions.

German successes in Europe were matched by Japanese victories in the first stages of the Pacific War from December 1941 to spring 1942, achieved through the decisive use of naval air power and fast-moving army offensives. Despite astonishing territorial gains, however, by 1942 Germany and Japan confronted an alliance that far exceeded them in potential resources.

The long fight back by the Allies—chiefly Britain, the United States, and the Soviet Union—required commanders who could make superiority of numbers and equipment translate into military success. Allied generals achieved exceptional feats of planning, logistics, and all-arms coordination in mounting large-scale amphibious operations and conducting land campaigns with armies sometimes totaling over a million men. The Pacific War involved possibly the largest naval battles in history, without loss of coherent central command. Allied determination to achieve total victory ensured that the end game was lengthy and desperately hard fought. In the war against Germany, the Soviet Union always bore the greater burden of fighting: after the D-day landings in the summer of 1944, there were 58 German divisions stationed in Western Europe, but 228 on the Eastern Front.

CHAINS OF COMMAND

The enormous scale of the war and improved communications meant that complex chains of command stretched upward, well away from the battlefield. To a considerable degree, the conduct of the war was dominated by political leaders: US President Franklin D. Roosevelt, British Prime Minister Winston Churchill, Soviet General Secretary and Prime Minister Stalin, and the German Führer (leader) Adolf Hitler. Roosevelt left purely military matters to his chiefs of staff, while Churchill had difficult relationships with some of his generals and could barely be restrained from interfering with decisions at field command level. Stalin tried to act as Soviet supreme military commander until late 1942, but eventually found generals who spoke their minds and won his precarious trust. Hitler, however, lost faith in his generals as the war progressed, and increasingly tried to manage military operations himself, to disastrous effect.

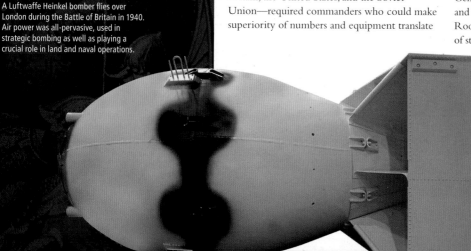

Air power
A Luftwaffe Heinkel bomber flies over London during the Battle of Britain in 1940. Air power was all-pervasive, used in strategic bombing as well as playing a crucial role in land and naval operations.

Fat Man replica
The plutonium bomb codenamed Fat Man was dropped on the Japanese city of Nagasaki on August 9, 1945, killing at least 40,000 people. Japan surrendered six days later.

GERMAN GENERALS

GERMANY HAD THE MOST GIFTED generals of World War II. Their doctrine of mobile warfare welded bold operational plans to flexible tactics and allowed initiative at all levels. Politically, however, they served a fascist regime that embroiled the German Army in dishonor and defeat. After the invasion of the Soviet Union and the American entry into the war in December 1941, German commanders were fighting against mounting odds under a dictator whose constant interventions in military decision-making grew ever more irrational. But most could not bring themselves to seek the overthrow of their Führer, however disillusioned they became.

MODERN COMMANDERS

HEINZ GUDERIAN

GERMAN GENERAL
BORN June 17, 1888
DIED May 14, 1954
KEY CONFLICT World War II
KEY BATTLES Poland 1939, France 1940, Operation Barbarossa 1941, Advance to Moscow 1941

A career officer, Heinz Guderian served in World War I, originally as a signals officer. After the war, he specialized in planning for armored warfare and—when the Nazis expanded the German forces— was given command of a panzer (armored) division. Published in 1937, his book *Achtung—Panzer!* stressed the need for motorized infantry to support the tank spearhead and for radio to facilitate command and control. He put his theories into

Guderian at Langres, June 1940
In command of 19th Panzer Corps in France, Guderian conducted a swift and devastating campaign across the country.

practice in the invasion of Poland in September 1939 and, above all, in the invasion of France in May 1940. His panzer corps advanced through the Ardennes to cross the Meuse River at Sedan, punching a hole in the French defenses. Leading from the front, Guderian raced toward the Channel coast, refusing to stop until ordered to by Hitler himself.

INVASION HALTED

Guderian was prominent in Operation Barbarossa but, when forced to pull back from Moscow in the winter of 1941, he was dismissed, alleged to have ignored Hitler's "stand fast" order. Sidelined until 1943, he returned as inspector-general of armored troops. After refusing to join the plot to assassinate Hitler in July 1944, he was appointed chief of the army general staff. Irascible as ever, he argued bitterly with Hitler until sent on permanent leave in March 1945.

ERICH VON MANSTEIN

GERMAN GENERAL
BORN November 24, 1887
DIED June 9, 1973
KEY CONFLICT World War II
KEY BATTLES Poland 1939, France 1940, Sevastopol 1941–42, Stalingrad 1942–43, Kharkov 1943, Kursk 1943

Born into the Prussian military aristocracy, Erich von Manstein regarded Hitler and the Nazi Party with disdain, yet was seduced by their revitalization of the German Army and nation.

Manstein was a staff officer in Germany in World War I and during most of the interwar era. In 1940, as chief-of-staff of Army Group A, he persuaded Hitler to adopt a plan for

Manstein in the Soviet Union
Seen here on the Eastern Front in 1943, Manstein is widely considered to have been the most able of German generals in World War II.

attacking France that—rather than the more traditional ideas of the high command—gave the major role to an armored thrust in the Ardennes. Manstein's plan was a startling success.

In the campaigns in the Soviet Union from 1941, he demonstrated his skill as a field commander, climbing rapidly to command an army group. A hard-fought victory at Sevastopol was followed by frustration at Stalingrad, where his attempt to break the Soviet encirclement of the city failed.

In early 1943, Manstein inflicted another defeat on the Soviets at Kharkov, but a failed attack at Kursk (pp. 312–13) brought major German offensive action in the East to an end. Increasingly at odds with Hitler, Manstein was dismissed in March 1944 and held no other posts. He was later imprisoned for war crimes committed on the Eastern Front.

WALTER MODEL

GERMAN GENERAL
BORN January 24, 1891
DIED April 21, 1945
KEY CONFLICT World War II
KEY BATTLES Operation Barbarossa 1941, Kursk 1943, Operation Market Garden 1944, The Bulge 1944–45

Figure of hate
Tactless, demanding, and foul-tempered, Model was almost universally hated by officers on his staff. Hitler once remarked, "I trust that man to do the job, but I wouldn't want to serve under him."

Walter Model came from a non-military, middle-class family and carved out a career in the aristocratic German officer corps through talent and hard work. He made slow progress until Hitler came to power, however. Currying favor with the Nazi regime, he reached general's rank in 1939. Operation Barbarossa brought Model rapid promotion. He led a panzer division in the initial invasion of the USSR, but seven months later was in command of the Ninth Army, resisting a Soviet counteroffensive at Rzhev. Hitler came to trust him as no other of his generals. Known as the "Führer's fireman," Model specialized in defensive warfare. In 1944, he halted the advancing Soviet armies east of Prussia and was then switched to France. He failed to halt the Allied breakout from Normandy, but repulsed their airborne offensive at Arnhem during Operation Market Garden. Against his better judgment, he executed Hitler's order for the attack that became the battle of the Bulge (pp. 326–27), which proved a disaster for the German Army. In 1945, his forces now encircled in the Ruhr, Model committed suicide.

ERWIN ROMMEL

GERMAN GENERAL
BORN November 15, 1891
DIED October 14, 1944
KEY CONFLICT World War II
KEY BATTLES France 1940, Gazala 1942, El Alamein 1942, Kasserine Pass 1943, Normandy 1944

The son of a school principal, Erwin Rommel served as an infantry officer in World War I, earning the coveted *Pour le Mérite* decoration for gallantry. He followed a dull path in infantry training and administration until his aggressive tactical ideas, detailed in his 1937 book *Infantry Attacks*, caught Hitler's attention. He was drawn into the Führer's circle, taking command of his personal security battalion.

Rommel had no experience with tanks, but his connection with Hitler got him command of the 7th Armored Division for the invasion of France. It was an inspired appointment, for Rommel spearheaded the breakneck advance from the Ardennes to the Channel, emerging as one of the heroes of the triumphant campaign.

In February 1941, he was given command of the Afrika Korps, a force sent to North Africa to prevent the Italians from losing Libya. He was soon given command of all Axis forces in the desert. Though starved of resources, Rommel outfought his

Rommel's cap
The standard German general officer's headwear of World War II.

> ## A VERY DARING AND SKILLFUL OPPONENT... A GREAT GENERAL
> **WINSTON CHURCHILL** ON ROMMEL, SPEECH IN PARLIAMENT, JULY 1942

British opponents, coordinating tank maneuvers that constantly wrong-footed his sluggish enemies. At Gazala in May–June 1942, he destroyed more than 500 British tanks. But Rommel's grasp of strategy did not equal his tactical gifts. Ignoring insuperable supply problems, he plunged forward into Egypt. Halted and then forced to retreat at El Alamein (pp. 318–19), he continued to display great skills in a long fighting withdrawal. His inspired counterpunch against the Americans at the Kasserine Pass in February 1943, however, could not prevent eventual defeat in Tunisia.

RETURN TO EUROPE
Rommel was recalled from North Africa before the final Axis surrender. He supervised the defense of the French coast against Allied invasion, but was away on leave on D-Day. In July 1944, he was wounded in an air attack. Although not a participant in the Hitler assassination plot, Rommel fell under suspicion and committed suicide to avoid a trial and execution.

The Führer and the field marshal
Hitler gives Rommel his field marshal's baton in 1942. Rommel had a starry-eyed admiration for Hitler at first, describing him as a "military genius," but later became more critical.

Victory parade
A small boy approaches German soldiers taking part in a victory procession through the Brandenburg Gate in Berlin on July 18, 1940. The parade was held to celebrate the capitulation of France during World War II.

SOVIET COMMANDERS

THE GENERALS WHO SERVED under Soviet dictator Josef Stalin in what was called "the Great Patriotic War" were survivors of the purges of the 1930s. These led to the execution or dismissal of 720 out of 837 Soviet officers above the rank of colonel, for supposed disloyalty to the regime. From June 1941,

Soviet commanders had to cope not only with a massive invasion by the armies of Germany and its Axis allies, but also with Stalin's constant interference in decision-making and the severe risks involved in contradicting him. Yet Stalin finally had the sense to back generals who stood up to him, and by 1943, he was allowing them more autonomy.

Victorious allies
Rokossovsky (right) and Zhukov flank Montgomery during the Allied victory celebrations in Berlin in 1945.

KONSTANTIN ROKOSSOVSKY

SOVIET MARSHAL
BORN December 21, 1896
DIED August 3, 1968
KEY CONFLICTS World War II
KEY BATTLES Moscow 1941, Stalingrad 1942–43, Kursk 1943, Operation Bagration 1944

Son of a Polish father and a Russian mother, Konstantin Rokossovsky fought for the Bolsheviks in the Russian Civil War and was a senior Soviet commander in the 1930s. When Stalin purged the officer corps, he was tortured and imprisoned.

Rehabilitated in time for the Nazi invasion, he performed brilliantly in the defense of Moscow in 1941–42. He commanded the Don Front army group that encircled German Sixth Army at Stalingrad, and then Central Front at the battle of Kursk. In these battles and in Operation Bagration to liberate Byelorussia and eastern Poland, Rokossovky frequently and fearlessly resisted orders he thought mistaken, whether from Georgi Zhukov or Stalin himself. In August 1944, he led the Soviet forces that were halted on the Vistula, not intervening as the Germans suppressed the Warsaw uprising. His army group ended the war in north Germany. Afterward, he became a member of the Communist Polish government.

VASILII CHUIKOV

SOVIET GENERAL
BORN February 12, 1900
DIED March 18, 1982
KEY CONFLICTS World War II
KEY BATTLES Stalingrad 1942–43, Berlin 1945

Born into a Russian peasant family, Vasilii Chuikov fought on the Bolshevik side in the Russian Civil War and became an officer in the Soviet Army. Passing unscathed through Stalin's purges, he served as an army commander in the invasion of eastern Poland in 1939 and the subsequent Winter War with Finland. Chuikov was fortunate to be abroad during the Nazi invasion of 1941, working as a military adviser to the Chinese Nationalists, and thus avoided being implicated in the early Soviet disasters. He did not enter combat against the Germans until 1942. On September 12, Chuikov was placed in command of the forces inside Stalingrad, with orders to

defend the city or die in the attempt. Robust and ruthless, he stamped his personality on the battle. Soldiers were commanded to "hug" the Germans amid the ruins—staying so close to them the Germans could not use air strikes or artillery without hitting their own men. Anyone who showed the slightest reluctance to fight was shot. Contesting every inch of ground, Chuikov held Stalingrad and became a Soviet hero.

Chuikov subsequently led the Eighth Guards Army through the campaigns that brought the Soviet forces into Germany in 1945 and was entrusted with the capture of Berlin, accepting the surrender of the city's garrison after some of the fiercest fighting of the war on May 2.

The taking of Berlin, 1945
Chuikov (center, at an observation point) directs the grueling battle for Berlin. He later said that every stone and brick of the city was stained with his men's blood.

> **THERE IS ONLY ONE WAY TO HOLD THE CITY [STALINGRAD], WE MUST PAY IN LIVES. TIME IS BLOOD!**
> **VASILII CHUIKOV**, SEPTEMBER 1942

GEORGI ZHUKOV

SOVIET MARSHAL
BORN December 1, 1896
DIED June 18, 1974
KEY CONFLICTS Sino-Japanese War,
World War II
KEY BATTLES Khalkhin Gol 1939, Leningrad
1941, Moscow 1941, Stalingrad 1942–43,
Kursk 1943, Operation Bagration 1944,
Berlin 1945

Born into poverty, Georgi Zhukov was conscripted into the Russian imperial army in World War I. He fought for the Bolsheviks in the Russian Civil War and made a successful career as a Soviet officer, avoiding death or dismissal in Stalin's purges. In 1938, he commanded Soviet troops fighting a border war against the Japanese in Mongolia. In 1939, at Khalkhin Gol, he crushed the Japanese forces with aggressive use of tanks and motorized infantry. The prestige gained in this war earned Zhukov the position of chief of the general staff in January 1941. He did not welcome the job, seeing himself as a field commander rather than a staff officer. He openly disagreed with Stalin's response to the German invasion and his insistence on "no retreat." Zhukov was dismissed in July 1941, but remained one of the inner circle running the war. In September, he was sent to hold Leningrad (St. Petersburg), which looked close to falling to the enemy. In fact, the Germans did not try to take the city, but Zhukov appeared to have saved it. The next month, Stalin asked him to repeat the miracle at Moscow. German forces advancing on the capital were first halted and then, in December, driven back with a well-handled counteroffensive.

SAVING STALINGRAD

In October 1942, Stalin made Zukhov deputy supreme commander and ordered him to save Stalingrad. Operation Uranus, the offensive that cut off the German army in the city, was methodically planned and rapidly and ruthlessly executed, showing Zhukov's skills at their best.

In 1943, he masterminded the great Soviet victory at Kursk (pp. 312–13). Operation Bagration, the massive

Side arm
The Tokarev TT-33 self-loading pistol was a popular Soviet weapon during World War II and was often used as a general's side arm.

Byelorussian offensive of the summer of 1944, showed how Zhukov and other Soviet generals had by now mastered combining all arms to smash through enemy defenses, maintaining momentum across difficult terrain and crushing resistance, whatever the cost in lives and material.

Zhukov supervised the capture of Berlin in spring 1945 and ended the war as the most celebrated of Soviet commanders. Soon demoted by a jealous Stalin, he returned for a time as defense minister in the 1950s.

Soviet hero
This poster shows Zhukov on the white horse he rode at the Moscow victory parade in June 1945. The ruins of Berlin provide the backdrop and Nazi banners lie trampled beneath his horse's hooves.

KEY BATTLE

STALINGRAD

CAMPAIGN Eastern Front, World War II
DATE September 1942–February 1943
LOCATION Stalingrad (now Volgograd)

In mid-September 1942, Friedrich Paulus's German Sixth Army advanced into the city of Stalingrad. Soviet troops under Chuikov, fighting with their backs to the Volga River, defended every street, factory, and apartment building. As Chuikov held on, in November, Zhukov launched an offensive outside the city. Attacking in a pincer movement from the north and south, his forces trapped the Sixth Army in Stalingrad. Hitler refused Paulus permission to attempt a breakout, but relief operations failed. Caught in a tightening Soviet noose in bitter winter weather, Paulus surrendered at the end of January 1943 and the last troops soon after, on February 3.

ZHUKOV VS. MANSTEIN

IN SPRING 1943, GERMAN AND Soviet armies faced one another on a line stretching from Leningrad to the Sea of Azov. Seeking their next move, both sides focused on the Kursk salient, a Soviet-controlled area 125 miles (200 km) wide, thrusting 95 miles (150 km) into German-held territory. In April, after visiting Kursk, Soviet deputy supreme commander, Georgi Zhukov, guessed the Germans would attack from the north and south of the salient in a pincer movement to cut off and destroy the forces inside. In the same month, German Führer Adolf Hitler was persuaded to authorize precisely such an offensive, codenamed Operation Citadel.

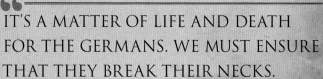

MODERN COMMANDERS

GEORGI ZHUKOV

Zhukov resisted Soviet dictator Joseph Stalin's idea for counterattacks that would have preempted the expected German offensive. Instead, Zhukov constructed formidable fortified lines, defended by minefields, entrenched infantry, antitank guns, and other artillery. He would let the German tanks exhaust themselves against these defenses before unleashing his armored reserves in a counterattack. Inside the salient were Konstantin Rokossovsky's Central Front army group and Nikolai Vatutin's Voronezh Front.

Thanks to Soviet spies, Zhukov was informed of the place and timing of the German offensive. He was present at Rokossovsky's headquarters on the early morning of July 5, when Soviet artillery delivered a massive bombardment on German forces assembling for the attack. Over the following two days, Rokossovsky's defenses in the north held firm, but in the south German armored forces threatened to break through.

COUNTERATTACK

On July 6, Zhukov ordered the Fifth Guards Tank Army to advance from its reserve position 220 miles (350 km) to the east. The T-34 tanks reached Prokhorovka on July 12 and plunged into battle with the panzers, fighting them to a standstill in the largest armored encounter in history. Much hard fighting was still needed, but the German offensive had failed, and Zhukov was able to go on the offensive on a broader front.

> ## IT'S A MATTER OF LIFE AND DEATH FOR THE GERMANS. WE MUST ENSURE THAT THEY BREAK THEIR NECKS.
>
> **NIKITA KHRUSHCHEV**, AT VORONEZH FRONT HEADQUARTERS KURSK, JULY 5, 1943

TIMELINE

ZHUKOV

2–3 a.m. A Soviet artillery bombardment aims to disrupt enemy preparations. An attempted preemptive air strike on German airfields fails, with heavy losses of Soviet aircraft	Rokossovsky, commanding Soviet Central Front on the northern side of the salient, commits his tanks to counterattacks, but these fail	Pavel Rotmistrov's Fifth Guards Tank Army, in strategic reserve, begins a 220-mile (350-km) drive from the east to join the battle in the southern sector	

1943: JULY 4	JULY 5	JULY 6	JULY 7–9	JULY 10

MANSTEIN

2:45 p.m. Manstein begins Operation Citadel with preliminary air and artillery attacks to seize advanced Soviet positions on the southern shoulder of the Kursk salient	**5 a.m.** The Fourth Panzer Army advances from the south and Model's Ninth Army from the north. They fight their way about 5 miles (8 km) into the Soviet defensive lines	The Ninth Army engages in an intense fight for Ponyri, a strongpoint the Germans need to gain. It is eventually taken, but at heavy cost	Model renews his attacks in the north of the salient, but achieves only limited gains and calls off further frontal assaults. The Ninth Army's progress is stopped

③ **July 7–8:** German advance is halted at Ponyri

MODEL ■

Orel ○

KLUGE ■

Ponyri

④ **July 8–11:** German breakthrough makes faster progress in the south

UKRAINE

Kursk ○

① **July 5:** Hoth's Fourth Panzer Army makes preliminary attack

Tomarovka ○   ○ Belgorod

HOTH ■

■ **MANSTEIN**

Kharkov ○

⑥ **July 12:** Soviet counteroffensive toward Orel fails to encircle German forces

■ **ROKOSSOVSKY**

ZHUKOV ■

② **July 5–6:** Massive air battles over northern and southern sectors of Operation Citadel

■ **VATUTIN**

⑤ **July 12:** Vast tank battle around small town of Prokhorovka halts German advance

⑦ Soviet offensive in the south leads to recapture of Kharkov on August 23

KEY

— German front line July 4, 1943

— Farthest extent of German advance

··· Soviet defensive lines

km 30 60
0 miles 30 60

LOCATION
Around Kursk, Ukraine
DATE July 5–15, 1943
FORCES Soviets:
1.3 million men,
3,500 tanks; Axis: 900,000 men, 2,700 tanks
CASUALTIES Soviet: 178,000; Axis: 210,000

Tank battle
Kursk is famous as history's largest tank battle, with more than 5,000 armored vehicles taking part. Antitank guns and tank-busting aircraft inflicted heavy damage on the panzers and T-34s involved.

ERICH VON MANSTEIN

Erich von Manstein, commander of Army Group South, was responsible for the southern half of Operation Citadel. The attack from the north was entrusted to Walter Model's Ninth Army, part of Army Group Center. The two men disagreed over the operation and although Manstein was the most prestigious German general on the Eastern Front, he had no authority over Model.

DIFFERENCE OF OPINION

Aware from aerial reconnaissance that the Soviets were constructing impressive defenses, Model concluded that an attack would play into the enemy's hands. Manstein—although he would have liked a subtler offensive—believed Citadel offered a chance to inflict a crushing defeat on Soviet forces through a classic double envelopment. He knew, however, that it needed to be executed quickly. It was not: after

various delays, the operation was put back from an initial planned date of May 3 to July 5.

Manstein and Model adopted different tactics. While Model tried to clear a path through the minefields and trenches with his infantry before pushing his tanks forward, Manstein committed the concentrated armor of the Fourth Panzer Army in punching through the Soviet lines.

RESISTANCE AND DEFEAT

Winning air superiority at the start of the battle gave the Germans an inestimable advantage, but Soviet resistance was tougher than expected. By July 10, Model had reached the limits of his advance. Manstein did better, his panzers grinding through the Soviet defensive lines and swatting off counterattacks. Victory looked within his grasp when, on July 12, the wholly unexpected arrival of Soviet armored reserves precipitated the vast tank melee at Prokhorovka.

On July 13, Manstein was summoned to Hitler's headquarters, where he argued against terminating the offensive. Model, however, was soon in full retreat, eager to avoid encirclement as the Soviets opened a new offensive behind him at Orel. Manstein persisted, but by July 23, the Fourth Panzer Army had been driven back to its start lines.

Zhukov commits reserves to Operation Kutuzov, an offensive aimed at Orel, to the rear of Model's Ninth Army. Model is forced to transfer forces away from the Kursk salient

Zhukov orders Soviet Fifth Guards Tank Army counterattacks against II SS Panzer Corps at Prokhorovka. Soviet T-34s are lost in large numbers, but German progress is halted

Soviet forces advancing on Orel in Operation Kutuzov make rapid progress, forcing Model to begin a withdrawal to avoid encirclement

Soviet counterattacks to the south of the salient force Manstein on to the defensive. Hitler cancels Citadel and begins moving tanks to the Italian front

The Soviets launch Operation Rumyantsev, a large-scale counteroffensive against Manstein's Army Group South. They retake Kharkov on August 23

| JULY 11 | JULY 12 | JULY 13 | JULY 14 | JULY 15 | JULY 17 | JULY 23 | AUG 3 |

Manstein believes that he is on the verge of the desired armored breakout in the southern sector of the salient as his tanks advance on Prokhorovka

Manstein meets Hitler at his headquarters at Rastenburg. Hitler says Citadel must end, especially in the light of the Allied invasion of Sicily (July 10), but Manstein argues for going on

Manstein announces a continued push northward, despite the failure of Ninth Army's side of Operation Citadel

Fourth Panzer Army is back at its starting point. The German offensive at the Kursk salient is over

ALLIED COMMANDERS

 THE SPECTER OF WORLD WAR I haunted British, Commonwealth, and French leaders in World War II, for they dreaded a repeat of the huge losses of 1914–18. Bernard Montgomery, the most successful of the British generals, had a reputation for being careful with his men's lives. Australian and New Zealand generals had orders from their governments to avoid excessive casualties. Few commanders from Britain or its Commonwealth showed great attacking flair, although organizational ability and determination were in plentiful supply. For the French, after the initial defeat in June 1940, fighting was about restoring honor and national pride.

ARCHIBALD WAVELL

BRITISH FIELD MARSHAL
BORN May 5, 1883
DIED May 24, 1950
KEY CONFLICT World War II
KEY BATTLES Operation Compass 1940–41, Operation Battleaxe 1941

The son of a general, Wavell was a career officer who lost an eye in World War I. Between the wars, he rose to senior command, and, in summer 1939, he was sent to organize British forces in the Middle East. When Italy entered the war in June 1940, Wavell faced numerically superior armies in North and East Africa. Even though the Italian forces were generally of poor quality, his success was still extraordinary. In Operation Compass, his desert forces seized Cyrenaica, taking more than 100,000 prisoners. The Italians were also defeated in Ethiopia and Somaliland. Wavell's popularity with the British public ran high, but he offended Churchill with his blunt manner and pessimistic air. In February 1941, he agreed, against his better judgment, to divert troops

Commander-in-chief's flag
This Union flag was flown on Wavell's car when he commanded in the Middle East from 1939–41.

from North Africa to Greece. There followed a string of disasters. Greece and Crete were lost, and so was Cyrenaica, overrun by Rommel's Afrika Korps. Overstretched by simultaneous operations in Syria and Iraq, in June, Wavell mounted a new desert offensive, Operation Battleaxe. It was a costly failure, and Churchill transferred Wavell to a backwater as commander-in-chief in India.

WAR IN ASIA
The Japanese entry into the war thrust Wavell once more into the front line, again with inadequate resources. Briefly supreme commander of Allied forces in Southeast Asia, he presided over the loss of Singapore and Indonesia, and then had to retreat from Burma. In 1943, he became viceroy of India.

Against the odds
Wavell was a thoughtful and humane commander who was never given the chance to conduct military operations with forces that were truly adequate to the task.

BIOGRAPHY
WINSTON CHURCHILL

The British prime minister from May 1940, Churchill provided energetic direction to the war effort and a resolute focus for national resistance. An avid amateur strategist, he was behind the decisions to invade Italy in 1943 and hold back the invasion of France until summer 1944. He regarded his generals as unimaginative and disinclined to fight and prodded them to take offensive action, but, ultimately, he let them do their jobs.

BERNARD FREYBERG

NEW ZEALAND GENERAL
BORN March 21, 1889
DIED July 4, 1963
KEY CONFLICT World War II
KEY BATTLES Crete 1941, Second El Alamein 1942, Monte Cassino 1944

Raised in New Zealand, Bernard Freyberg served as a British officer in World War I. Displaying conspicuous bravery, he was wounded nine times and won the Victoria Cross at the Somme in 1916. Freyberg stayed in the British Army after the war, but at the outbreak of World War II was appointed to command the New Zealand Expeditionary Force. Ordered to defend Crete in May 1941, he failed to stem a German airborne assault and was driven from the island.

FIERCE FIGHTER

Freyburg thoroughly redeemed his reputation in subsequent fighting in the North African desert, where his New Zealanders were the opponents Rommel most feared. In 1944–45, he fought in the liberation of Italy, at Monte Cassino, and at the very end racing his division to Trieste. He arrived on May 2, the very day that German forces in Italy surrendered.

Leading by example
Fearless and pugnacious, Freyberg always led from the front. He disliked formal discipline, exercising authority through the respect he inspired.

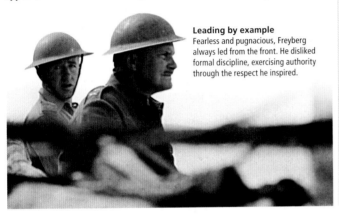

LESLIE MORSHEAD

AUSTRALIAN GENERAL
BORN September 18, 1889
DIED September 26, 1959
KEY CONFLICT World War II
KEY BATTLES Siege of Tobruk 1941, Second El Alamein 1942

Effective leader
A highly distinguished commander, Morshead was a tough disciplinarian, which earned him the nickname Ming the Merciless.

When World War I broke out, Leslie Morshead was a schoolteacher in Melbourne. Enlisting with the Australian Imperial Force, he took part in the Gallipoli landings in 1915 as a junior officer. Rapidly promoted, he led a battalion in the great battles of 1917–18 on the Western Front, from Messines and Passchendaele to the final Hundred Days' offensives.

Returning to civilian life, Morshead remained active in the militia, and he was given command of a brigade when war broke out in 1939. In spring 1941, as commander of the Ninth Australian Division, he was tasked with holding the North African port of Tobruk, placed under siege by Erwin Rommel's desert forces. His vigorous handling of the defense through eight grueling months earned him a knighthood.

At the second battle of El Alamein, in 1942, still leading Ninth Division, Morshead once more performed outstandingly, playing a crucial role in reviving Bernard Montgomery's offensive in the last days of October. For the rest of the war, Morshead fought in the Southwest Pacific, taking command of First Australian Corps and notably directing the recapture of Borneo by a series of amphibious landings in 1945.

PHILIPPE LECLERC

FRENCH GENERAL
BORN November 22, 1902
DIED November 28, 1947
KEY CONFLICT World War II
KEY BATTLES France 1940, Kufra 1941, Normandy 1944, Paris 1944, Strasbourg 1944

Hero of France
Leclerc is most famous for his role in the liberation of Paris in August 1944. He died at the age of 45 and was posthumously made a marshal of France.

Vicomte Philippe Leclerc de Hautecloque came from a family with a military history stretching back to the Crusades. He graduated from St.-Cyr military academy in 1924, and was a captain at the start of World War II. Wounded in June 1940 during the battle of France, Leclerc escaped via Spain to London, where he joined General de Gaulle's Free French movement. De Gaulle sent him to French Equatorial Africa, where he led a small mobile force from Chad to capture an Italian base at the Kufra oasis in Libya in March 1941.

After fighting in Tunisia in August 1943 as part of Montgomery's Eighth Army, Leclerc formed the Second Armored Division from his Kufra veterans and a mixed bag of other available troops. By the time Leclerc's division joined George Patton's Third Army in Normandy in August 1944, he had transformed his division into a superb fighting force.

LIBERATION OF PARIS

Taking part in the destruction of German tanks at the Falaise Pocket, Leclerc then fought his way into Paris on August 23, accepting the surrender of the city's German garrison two days later. Leclerc's division also liberated Strasbourg in November 1944, after a dash through the Vosges at the Saverne Gap, and at the war's end captured Berchtesgaden, Hitler's Alpine retreat.

After the war, Leclerc was sent to reimpose French rule in Indochina, where he failed to negotiate a peaceful settlement with the Viet Minh. He died in an air accident in Algeria.

BIOGRAPHY

CHARLES DE GAULLE

An infantry officer in World War I, de Gaulle was wounded three times and captured at Verdun. Between the wars, he made a reputation as a military theorist, arguing for the primacy of mobile armored warfare. In the battle of France, commanding the Fourth Armored Division, he inflicted a few tactical reverses on the German Army. In June 1940, he established the Free French forces from his base in London to continue the fight after the fall of France. He linked up with the Resistance inside France to ensure his army a leading role when liberation came in 1944. De Gaulle was briefly president of a provisional French government, but returned in 1958 to found the Fifth Republic.

TIMELINE

- **1908** Montgomery graduates from Sandhurst Military Academy and is commissioned as an infantry officer in the Royal Warwickshire Regiment.

- **October 1914** Fighting in France with the British Expeditionary Force, Montgomery is shot in the lung. He survives to serve as a staff officer through the rest of World War I.

- **May–June 1940** In World War II, commanding British 3rd Division, Montgomery distinguishes himself by handling the retreat to Dunkirk and evacuation competently and with minimal casualties.

- **August 1942** Montgomery takes command of Eighth Army in North Africa (August 13) and defeats an attack by Erwin Rommel's Panzerarmee Afrika at Alam Halfa.

- **October 23–November 5, 1942** Mounting a large-scale offensive at El Alamein, Montgomery drives Rommel's forces into headlong retreat.

- **July 9, 1943** After the defeat of the Axis forces in North Africa, Montgomery leads Eighth Army in the seaborne invasion of Sicily, later moving on to the Italian mainland.

- **December 1943** Montgomery leaves Eighth Army in Italy, returning to Britain to take part in planning for the invasion of Normandy.

- **June–August 1943** Montgomery is commander of Allied ground forces at the D-day landings (June 6) and in the subsequent battle to break out of Normandy.

GERMAN SURRENDER AT LUNEBURG HEATH

- **September 17, 1944** Montgomery launches a bold and imaginative airborne operation called Market Garden. The goal is to capture bridges in the Netherlands and advance into Germany, but the operation fails at Arnhem.

- **December 1944–January 1945** Montgomery plays a controversial role in the repulse of the German Ardennes offensive in the battle of the Bulge.

- **March 24, 1945** Montgomery's 21st Army Group crosses the Rhine in a meticulously planned operation that opens up the Ruhr to attack.

- **May 4, 1945** At Luneburg Heath Montgomery accepts the unconditional surrender of the German forces in northern Germany, Denmark, and the Netherlands.

- **1951** Montgomery becomes NATO's Deputy Supreme Allied Commander in Europe, a position he holds until his retirement in 1958.

BERNARD MONTGOMERY

BRITISH FIELD MARSHAL
BORN November 17, 1887
DIED March 24, 1976
KEY CONFLICT World War II
KEY BATTLES El Alamein 1942, Mareth Line 1943, Sicily 1943, Normandy 1944, Operation Market Garden 1944, The Bulge 1944–45, The Rhine Crossing 1945

Bernard Law Montgomery was the son of the Anglican bishop of Tasmania. Serving as a staff officer on the Western Front during World War I was a formative experience for him. Faced with the slaughter in the trenches, he became convinced that "the whole art of war is to gain your objective with as little loss as possible." This was to be achieved through meticulously planned combined arms operations executed by thoroughly trained troops that enjoyed superiority of numbers and equipment. After 1918, Montgomery saw some active service in Ireland and in Palestine, but most of his energies were focused on tactical training and military exercises.

WORLD WAR II

Although Montgomery's quarrelsome, opinionated nature frequently set him at odds with colleagues and superiors, he entered World War II as a divisional commander. Sent to Europe, Montgomery ensured his division was the best trained in the British Expeditionary Force (BEF). Scornful of the BEF's commanders, he was well prepared for

Command tank
This Grant M3A3 tank was used by Montgomery as a command vehicle in the desert war in North Africa.

a rapid retreat from Belgium and got his men home from Dunkirk without heavy losses. After holding important positions in Britain, he was appointed to lead the Eighth Army in North Africa when the first choice, William Gott, died in an air crash.

Montgomery restored army morale, making his presence known to the men through his natural showmanship. His long-held tactical views were vindicated at El Alamein (pp. 318–19), which was a victory that made him a national hero. However, the aftermath revealed

Approachable leader
Montgomery addresses part of the Eighth Army in Tunisia in 1943. He strongly believed that a commander should be visible to his troops and explain the operations they were engaged in.

Montgomery to be no master of mobile warfare, his sluggish maneuvers missing a chance to cut off Rommel's retreat.

THE ROAD TO VICTORY

The continuation of the desert war into Tunisia brought Montgomery another hard-fought victory in the taking of the Mareth Line. He began dealing with the Americans, with whom relations were soon strained. In summer 1943, Allied amphibious landings in Sicily showcased Montgomery's skill at planning complex

KEY BATTLE

OPERATION MARKET GARDEN

CAMPAIGN World War II
DATE September 17–24, 1944
LOCATION The Netherlands

Montgomery conceived Operation Market Garden to maintain the momentum of the Allied advance across France and Belgium. Airborne troops were to seize bridges at Grave, Nijmegen, and Arnhem, while British armored forces dashed through the Netherlands, crossing the bridges and threatening northern Germany. US Airborne did take the first two bridges, but at Arnhem, British parachute troops were trapped by SS panzer divisions. The armored advance was too slow to relieve the British troops, most of whom were killed or taken prisoner.

> # DISCIPLINE STRENGTHENS THE MIND SO THAT IT BECOMES IMPERVIOUS TO THE CORRODING INFLUENCE OF FEAR.
>
> **BERNARD MONTGOMERY**, IN A SPEECH ON MORALE IN BATTLE, 1946

operations, yet American General George Patton then took delight in upstaging the British commander with his speed of movement in the conquest of the island.

Montgomery's prestige remained high and he was given command of all Allied land forces for the invasion of Normandy in June 1944. Again, his tactical judgment was vital in preparing for the landings, but once

Complex character
Montgomery had personality flaws—he was argumentative, arrogant, and vain—but he understood soldiers well and had a firm grasp of operations.

Montgomery's medals
This impressive collection of awards includes the Order of the Bath, the Distinguished Service Order, the Italy Star, and the Africa Star.

ashore his painfully slow struggle to take Caen drew American criticism. In September, the failure of Market Garden, an operation of uncharacteristic riskiness, was the worst setback of his career.

Bad relations with American generals came to a head in the battle of the Bulge in the winter of 1944. There were complaints at US forces being placed under Montgomery's command, and resentment at his excessive claims of credit for the repulse of the German offensive. His methodical approach to crossing the Rhine in March 1945 further annoyed his allies, but kept casualties low. While occupying northern Germany, he accepted one of the German surrenders at Luneburg Heath.

MONTGOMERY VS. ROMMEL

BERNARD MONTGOMERY took command of the British Eighth Army in the Western Desert on August 13, 1942. His task was to defeat Erwin Rommel's Panzerarmee Afrika, a German and Italian force that had repeatedly proved its mastery of desert fighting. Montgomery's predecessor, Claude Auchinleck, had stopped Rommel's advance by taking a stand at El Alamein. After blocking a further Axis attack on August 31, Montgomery began preparations for a major offensive. Rommel— outnumbered two-to-one and with long, vulnerable supply lines—established a formidable defensive position fronted by minefields and waited for Montgomery to move.

MODERN COMMANDERS

BERNARD MONTGOMERY

Montgomery intended to win a decisive victory by making superior force count against a more skillful enemy. He would attack the Axis forces where they were strongest and "crumble" their defenses until they broke. Resisting pressure from Prime Minister Winston Churchill for swift action, Montgomery delayed until he had integrated reinforcements, including new American Sherman tanks, and improved the morale and training of his forces.

PLAN AND EXECUTION

According to Montgomery's plan, the offensive would open with an artillery barrage. The infantry would then clear paths through the minefields under cover of darkness, and tanks would advance down these lanes passing through the infantry and breaking into the enemy defenses. In practice, the barrage of October 23 worked, but the rest did not. Mine-clearing was too slow and traffic congestion blocked the cleared lanes. Still behind the infantry at daybreak, tank commanders refused to advance into the fire of German antitank guns. Despite the reinforcement of the line of attack and all Montgomery's urgings, by October 26 the offensive had become bogged down.

A QUALIFIED VICTORY

Churchill was furious at the lack of progress, but Montgomery kept his nerve. He knew that his army could afford the losses of attritional combat; if the British forces kept fighting they would win. While his front-line troops resisted furious Axis counterattacks, Montgomery withdrew formations to prepare for a renewed offensive, codenamed Supercharge. Skillfully varying the point of attack, he drove his army forward again, insisting that tank formations be prepared to accept heavy casualties. When the breakout came after 13 days of fighting, Montgomery failed to envelop Rommel's fleeing motorized forces. He was content to mop up and consolidate after a hard-won victory.

> ❝ ALL THAT IS NECESSARY IS THAT EACH AND EVERY OFFICER AND MAN SHOULD ENTER THIS BATTLE WITH THE DETERMINATION TO SEE IT THROUGH, TO FIGHT AND KILL, AND FINALLY TO WIN. ❞
>
> **BERNARD MONTGOMERY**, IN A MESSAGE TO THE EIGHTH ARMY ON THE EVE OF EL ALAMEIN

TIMELINE

MONTGOMERY

9:40 p.m. Montgomery launches battle with an artillery barrage and infantry advance through minefields in the northern sector and a diversionary attack in the south	**Night** Montgomery orders reluctant tank commanders to pursue the offensive as the advance stalls

Montgomery shifts troops from the southern sector to reinforce the main thrust in the north

Montgomery accepts his initial offensive has failed and begins planning a second breakthrough attempt

Night Montgomery orders Australian infantry to thrust north toward the coast road

| 1942: OCT 23 | OCT 24 | OCT 25 | OCT 26 | OCT 27 | OCT 28 | OCT 29 |

ROMMEL

Early morning General Georg Stumme, commanding Panzerarmee Afrika in Rommel's absence, dies of a heart attack

Evening Rommel returns from sick leave in Austria to resume command

Night Rommel orders the 21st Panzer Division to move from the southern sector to counterattack in the north

Afternoon Axis armored counterattack suffers heavy losses to British antitank guns

Rommel redeploys forces toward the coast to block the Australian thrust

ROMMEL

⑦ November 4: Rommel, reduced to about 30 serviceable tanks, starts retreat toward Libya

④ October 26: The 21st Panzer Division moves north to support Rommel's counterattacks

⑤ November 2: Start of Operation Supercharge. Allies make progress through minefields, despite heavy losses

⑥ November 3: Allied forces break through between the German and Italian forces

Mediterranean Sea

Tobruk

Sidi El Rahman

③ October 23–25: Allied tanks fail to find a way through Axis minefields

El Alamein

Alexandria

MONTGOMERY

① October 23: Montgomery starts the battle with artillery barrage along the whole front

② October 23: Allied forces make a series of diversionary raids in the south

Miteiriya Ridge

Ruweisat Ridge

KEY
- — Axis front line 23 October 1942
- ▪ Allied forces
- ▪ Axis forces
- • Axis minefield
- ◦ Area cleared of mines
- -- Railway

Qattara Depression

Qaret el Himeimat

0 km 5 10
0 miles 5 10

N

Desert warfare
British Churchill tanks advance through the desert sand. Churchill Mark IIIs appeared on the battlefield for the first time at El Alamein and stood up well to Axis antitank fire.

LOCATION 60 miles (100 km) west of Alexandria, Egypt
CAMPAIGN North African Campaign
DATE October 23–November 4, 1942
FORCES Allies: 195,000 men, 1,029 tanks; Axis: 104,000 men, 489 tanks
CASUALTIES Allies: 14,400; Axis: 25,000, with 30,000 taken prisoner

ERWIN ROMMEL

Withdrawn from the desert on sick leave, Rommel might never have returned to Africa but for the death of his replacement, General Stumme, on the first morning of the battle. Even then Hitler hesitated to send him back—Rommel spent the night of October 24–25 at an airport in Vienna awaiting the Führer's orders. It was late on October 25 when the Axis forces at El Alamein received the crisp message: "I have taken over the army again. Rommel."

LIMITED CHOICES
Rommel's forte was aggressive mobile warfare but Montgomery had him trapped in static defense. To regain the initiative, Rommel tried to switch his tanks rapidly to wherever in the line Montgomery was pressing and land powerful counterpunches. But his supply situation was critical. Every redeployment had to be weighed in terms of the fuel it required. He lacked air cover and his formations could not travel by day without being decimated by the RAF. Armored counterattacks on a restricted battlefield packed with enemy tanks and antitank guns proved extremely costly.

FACING THE INEVITABLE
As early as October 29, Rommel began planning a withdrawal to the west. His official communications with Axis headquarters in Rome—made available to Montgomery by the British Ultra codebreakers—consisted of a stream of appeals for more fuel and ammunition. His private letters to his wife revealed a fatalistic, death-obsessed state of mind.

On November 2, he judged the situation untenable and ordered a withdrawal. Hitler countered with a stand-fast order: "To your forces you can show no path other than to victory or death." Rommel felt he had to send an envoy to explain the situation to Hitler face-to-face.

In the end, Hitler's intervention only delayed the retreat by a day. Once on the move with his tanks—abandoning the Italian non-motorized infantry—the Desert Fox returned to form. He outpaced his enemies in the race westward, eventually reaching the Tunisian border, ready to fight again the following year.

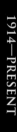

With Rommel committed to blocking the coast road, Montgomery decides to focus his next breakthrough attempt, Operation Supercharge, farther south and begins detailed plans

1 a.m. Montgomery launches Operation Supercharge

Night Montgomery reorganizes his forces in preparation for a final breakout

Morning Montgomery's forces have broken through the Axis lines and he attempts an envelopment

OCT 31 — NOV 1 — NOV 2 — NOV 3 — NOV 4

Furious counterattacks fail to dislodge the Australians. Rommel begins planning a retreat

Rommel throws in his armored reserves to block Supercharge

Night Faced with heavy losses, Rommel issues orders for a withdrawal

Hitler orders Rommel to stand firm and the retreat is halted

5:30 p.m. Rommel orders a general retreat in time for his tanks to escape envelopment

US ARMY COMMANDERS IN EUROPE

ENTERING WORLD WAR II in December 1941, the US government gave priority to the defeat of Germany rather than the war against Japan. Commanding the vast American forces sent across the Atlantic was a huge task entrusted to individuals who had little or no combat experience. Command structures were necessarily complex: in France in late 1944, General George Patton had two other generals, Omar Bradley and Dwight D. Eisenhower, above him in the chain of field command. Yet coherent leadership was maintained, great feats of organization accomplished, and tactical and operational skills developed to a high level of excellence.

MODERN COMMANDERS

OMAR BRADLEY

US ARMY GENERAL
BORN February 12, 1893
DIED April 8, 1981
KEY CONFLICT World War II
KEY BATTLES Sicily 1943, Normandy 1944, The Bulge 1944–45

Omar Bradley graduated from West Point in 1915. By the start of World War II, he was a brigadier-general specializing in infantry training and tactics. In early 1943, he was sent to North Africa to help Eisenhower iron out problems that had appeared when inexperienced US forces faced battle-hardened Germans. By the end of the Tunisian campaign, the Americans had, in his words, "learned to crawl, to walk—then run."

NORMANDY LANDINGS
Bradley continued to impress as a corps commander in the invasion and conquest of Sicily in summer 1943. His reward was command of US First Army for the Normandy landings in June 1944. Watching the near disaster at Omaha Beach from his offshore headquarters on USS *Augusta* was an uncomfortable experience, but he distinguished himself in the subsequent battle for Normandy, taking much of the credit for the eventual breakout.

Eisenhower gave him command of 12th Army Group—four armies and over 900,000 men. He excelled at the task, directing subordinates, such as Patton, without cramping their initiative. Through the battle of the Bulge, the crossing of the Rhine, and the final defeat of Germany, Bradley's lead was consistently bold but sound.

Star general
After World War II, Bradley became the first chairman of the US joint chiefs of staff and was made a five-star general.

Roman triumph
Mark Clark (in the jeep's front passenger seat) was intensely publicity conscious. He ensured that his unopposed entry into Rome on Sunday, June 4, 1944, received maximum coverage from press photographers.

MARK CLARK

US ARMY GENERAL
BORN May 1, 1896
DIED April 17, 1984
KEY CONFLICTS World War II, Korean War
KEY BATTLES Operation Torch 1942, Salerno 1943, Monte Cassino 1943–44, Anzio 1944

Mark Clark was the son of an infantry officer. He was wounded leading a company in France in World War I, and between the wars made a reputation as a staff officer and infantry instructor. In 1942, he was appointed Eisenhower's deputy for the Torch landings in French North Africa. Before the invasion, he was landed by submarine on the Algerian coast to meet pro-Allied French officers, and he negotiated ceasefire terms with the French authorities once the invasion got under way. Promoted to lieutenant-general, he was given command of Fifth Army for the invasion of Italy, landing at Salerno in September 1943.

Energetic and fearless, Clark led resistance to German counterattacks at Salerno in person, and drove forward the advance through Italy until halted by the Gustav Line defenses at Monte Cassino. He was not personally responsible for the failure of the Anzio landings, south of Rome, in January 1944, but faced criticism for an ill-judged attempt to force a passage across the Rapido River that cost the Texas Division 2,000 lives.

AGAINST ORDERS
When the breakthrough came in the spring of 1944, Clark chose to capture Rome instead of following orders to encircle retreating German forces, which consequently escaped to the north. He remained in Italy for the rest of the war, becoming army group commander in December 1944. He later served as commander of UN forces in the Korean War.

DWIGHT D. EISENHOWER

US ARMY GENERAL AND US PRESIDENT
BORN October 14, 1890
DIED March 28, 1969
KEY CONFLICT World War II
KEY BATTLES Operation Torch 1942,
Operation Overlord 1944

Eisenhower graduated from West Point in 1915. He became a staff officer and, in the 1930s, aide to General Douglas MacArthur. He was a major for 16 years before World War II.

METEORIC RISE

Catching the attention of Army Chief-of-Staff George C. Marshall, Eisenhower was catapulted into important posts in Washington and, in 1942, surprisingly chosen to command US forces in the European theater. Despite his lack of combat experience, his handling of the Torch landings and subsequent campaign in North Africa showed he had the strategic and political skills that the job required. He oversaw the invasions of Sicily and the Italian mainland before his appointment, in January 1944, as supreme commander of the Allied forces for the invasion of France.

Throughout the rest of the European campaign, he struggled to reconcile the conflicting egos of his British and US generals. His decision-making was sound, aside from the error of backing Operation Market Garden, and his firm optimism was morale-boosting. For example, he insisted that the German Ardennes offensive of December 1944 be seen as an opportunity and not as a disaster. After the war, he was the first supreme commander of NATO, and US president from 1953 to 1961.

Five stars
Eisenhower is one of only five men who have held the rank of five-star general.

KEY BATTLE

D-DAY

CAMPAIGN World War II
DATE June 6, 1944
LOCATION Normandy, France

As supreme commander of the Allied Expeditionary Force for the invasion of France (code-named Operation Overlord), Eisenhower bore a tremendous burden of responsibility. The scale of the amphibious operation was unprecedented, with over 4,000 landing craft supported by 1,200 naval warships. Eisenhower insisted that strategic bombing forces were attached to the operation, targeting roads and railroads inland of the five landing beaches. He also pushed for the use of massed airborne troops to back up the seaborne landings. D-Day was originally set for June 5, but bad weather forced a delay. Instead of opting for a long postponement, Eisenhower chose to go ahead on June 6. The weather eased, and the armada crossed the Channel. The hardest fighting was at Omaha beach, where the Americans were nearly pushed back into the sea. More than 150,000 troops landed on the day, at a cost of around 6,000 Allied lives.

Supreme commander
Eisenhower talks to US Airborne paratroopers on the eve of the D-day landings. His honesty and toughness won him respect from soldiers and officers alike.

TIMELINE

- **June 1909** Patton graduates from West Point, the US Military Academy.

- **1916–17** Patton serves as aide to General Pershing, the commander-in-chief during the American intervention in the Mexican revolution.

- **1918** In the later stages of World War I, he leads the 1st Tank Brigade at St. Mihiel and is wounded in the Meuse-Argonne Offensive.

- **1919–39** Peacetime appointments include staff jobs in Hawaii and Washington, D.C., and attendance at Army War College.

PATTON IN 1918

- **1940–42** Patton takes command of the 2nd Armored Brigade in August 1940 and, from 1941 to 1942, is promoted successively to lead the 2nd Armored Division and the 1st Armored Corps.

- **March 6, 1943** Reaching the rank of lieutenant-general, Patton takes command of US II Corps in Tunisia.

- **July 1943** Patton commands the Seventh US Army in the successful invasion and capture of Sicily, but is sidelined after he strikes two hospitalized soldiers (August 1943).

- **December 1943** As part of Fortitude South—a ploy to mislead the German high command over plans for the forthcoming D-Day landings—Patton is sent to England to command the fictitious First Army Group.

- **August 1, 1944** Patton's Third Army becomes operational and immediately joins in the breakout from the Normandy beachhead, before advancing into Brittany and moving east toward Paris.

- **August 19, 1944** Patton's forces cross the Seine and continue to the Meuse.

- **March 22, 1945** Patton sends Third Army units across the Rhine the day before Montgomery's crossing farther north and begins to advance across southern Germany.

- **August 19, 1945** The Third Army captures Pilsen in Czechoslovakia but—to Patton's disgust—is ordered to halt, allowing Soviet forces to occupy the rest of the country.

- **October 7, 1945** Patton is officially relieved of command of the Third Army and his military governorship of Bavaria after he suggests that members of the Nazi Party should be employed in administrative roles.

GEORGE PATTON

US ARMY GENERAL
BORN November 11, 1885
DIED December 21, 1945
KEY CONFLICTS World War II
KEY BATTLES Sicily 1943, Normandy 1944, The Bulge 1944–45

A controversial figure, General George Patton was feared and respected by Allied and German commanders alike. He also earned the respect of his men, who, when asked later where they served, would simply reply, "I was with Patton."

After training at the US Military Academy West Point, Patton served as an officer in a cavalry regiment. He soon attracted attention, within the army as the designer of a new cavalry sword, and to the wider public as a competitor in the modern pentathlon in the 1912 Olympics. His first active service was in the US intervention in Mexico in 1916–17. During this conflict, Patton was involved in a well-publicized shootout with a bandit leader.

TANK WARFARE

Patton next saw brave and successful service as one of his country's first tank officers in France in World War I. Always an avid student of military history and theory, Patton was quick to understand that Germany's developments in tank warfare would have to be taken up in the US armed forces. With the expansion of the US Army that began in 1940, Patton therefore decided to leave his beloved cavalry for the fledgling Armored Corps. His success in training new tank units marked him out for higher command.

TO TUNISIA

In November 1942, Patton led the Western Task Force in Operation Torch, the Anglo-American invasion of north-west Africa. His command saw little combat, but, in March 1943, he was called to the front in Tunisia, where he took over the underperforming US II Corps, transforming it with his energy and determination.

A ferocious disciplinarian, Patton always insisted on his men wearing correct uniforms. He also cultivated an inspiring presence, assiduously visiting forward units and imbuing his speeches to the troops with a charisma that transcended his surprisingly high-pitched voice. Although in private he could be sensitive and thoughtful, in public his speech was laced with obscenities and aggressive, bloodthirsty remarks.

It was during the Tunisian campaign that Patton first encountered the British general Bernard Montgomery.

Showy weapon
Patton often sported ivory-handled revolvers. This nickel-plated Colt .45 was his favorite, owned by him since 1916.

The pair would have a difficult relationship marked, on Patton's side, by an intense sense of rivalry. In general, Patton found it hard to work with British commanders, becoming paranoid that the US armed forces were being belittled and manipulated by their British allies.

The Germans and Italians in Tunisia surrendered in May 1943, and the next month Patton was given command of Seventh Army for the invasion of Sicily. The invasion was a success, but controversy endangered Patton's career. His exhortations to "kill Germans" were cited in the defense of soldiers who had murdered prisoners, and he was accused of striking two hospitalized soldiers whom he accused of malingering.

Advancing through France
American tanks transport infantry through the Normandy countryside on August 2, 1944, following the D-Day landings.

> ## ON OUR VICTORY DEPENDS THE FREEDOM OR SLAVERY OF THE HUMAN RACE. WE SHALL SURELY WIN.
>
> **GEORGE PATTON**, IN A PROCLAMATION TO HIS TROOPS, NOVEMBER 3, 1942

Allied commander-in-chief, Dwight D. Eisenhower, intervened, recognizing that Patton was too gifted a general to lose and ordered him to make amends. Eisenhower then sent Patton to Britain in December as part of Fortitude South, a plan designed to confuse the Germans about the location and timing of the D-Day landings.

NORMANDY INVASION

In January 1944, Patton took command of the Third Army, which would play a leading role in the Allied breakout from the Normandy beachhead after the D-Day landings. The Third Army's advance across France to the German border in August 1944 was spectacular and brought Patton new fame, but when the German defenses stiffened, he struggled to organize his forces for effective attacks. Patton's finest hour was undoubtedly his role in the battle of the Bulge (pp. 326–27).

In this and the final defeat of Germany in the spring of 1945, he showed that he was truly a master of rapid maneuver. Patton was made military governor of Bavaria at the end of the war, but—controversial to the last—he was formally relieved of command in early October 1945 after failing to follow denazification policies. He was fatally injured in a car accident in Germany just over two months later.

Four-star general
Patton was promoted to the rank of four-star general in April 1945, jealously aware that contemporaries—and, in his view, rivals and inferiors—had reached this rank before him.

KEY BATTLE
SICILY CAMPAIGN

CAMPAIGN Liberation of Sicily
DATE July 10–August 17, 1943
LOCATION Southern Italy

When Patton commanded the Seventh US Army in the invasion and capture of Sicily, he proved—as he had in Tunisia—that the US Army could fight well and more effectively than some senior British officers were prepared to admit. Patton's advance to capture Palermo was a remarkable achievement, albeit against limited resistance, but he was obsessed with beating Montgomery's forces to Messina. This "race to Messina" was highly counter-productive, driven more by Patton's ego than by sound military judgment.

PATTON: ON THE ATTACK

"A genius for war."

Patton, Carlo D'Este, 1995. *D'Este's biography of Patton reveals his many sides—erudite and foul-mouthed, conflicted and single-minded.*

STATUE OF PATTON AT THE PATTON MUSEUM, BLYTHE, CALIFORNIA

"From time to time there will be some complaints that we are pushing our people too hard. I don't give a good Goddamn about such complaints. I believe in the old and sound rule that an ounce of sweat will save a gallon of blood."

From Patton's pre-D-Day motivational speech to the Third Army. Patton gave the same speech on a number of occasions in May–June 1944.

GENERALS HAVE GIVEN inspiring pre-battle speeches since the earliest times. Following in their footsteps, Patton recognized that soldiers need special motivation if they are to risk their own lives in the struggle to vanquish the enemy. In his speech to the Third Army as it prepared for D-Day, Patton's sentences were peppered with obscenities and lurid references to violence, as was so often the case with his public speaking. However, when the rabble-rousing and grandstanding is stripped away, it is clear that Patton actually delivered a carefully crafted message to his troops.

Admitting that some of his listeners would not survive the fight, Patton emphasized that fear could be conquered, and lauded the feats that bravery and persistence could achieve. He made a point of mentioning not only combat troops but also support units—the Third Army was to operate as a team. Patton explained, too, how his aggressive style of command, advancing constantly and digging in only as a last resort, was designed to finish the conflict sooner, so that there would ultimately be fewer casualties. On returning home after the war, his men would be proud to have fought with Patton.

PATTON WAS A BOLD WARRIOR who would have been at home in one of history's great cavalry charges and an unruly subordinate whose mouth often got him into trouble. He was the general in a hurry who sometimes might have done better to plan a careful, considered attack in the manner of his rival, the British general, Bernard Montgomery. The clash of personalities and military tactics between Patton and his British counterparts was the cause of much hostility, and this bad feeling was not limited to Patton, extending also to other US commanders. Some senior British figures did little to hide their low opinion of the US Army's fighting prowess in Tunisia in early 1943 and failed to realize how quickly the Americans would bounce back from their mistakes. On both sides, these attitudes did the Allied cause much unnecessary harm.

"My meeting with Patton has been of great interest. I had already heard of him, but must confess that his swashbuckling personality exceeded my expectation. I did not form any high opinion of him, nor had I any reason to alter this view at any later date.

A dashing, courageous, wild and unbalanced leader, good for operations requiring thrust and push but at a loss in any operation requiring skill and judgment."

General Sir Alan Brooke, British Army Chief-of-Staff, on his first meeting with Patton (January 1943). Patton got along famously badly with his Allied colleagues.

IN MODERN ARMIES it is clearly understood that combat exhaustion and trauma are realities of warfare, and that those suffering from them deserve considerate treatment. Another school of thought states that armies with strong discipline and a "robust attitude" to such problems will end up with fewer sufferers having to be withdrawn from front-line units. Patton was certain which of these opposing views ought to be followed. He found fear revolting and dreaded exhibiting it himself. When confronted with its reality he lost control and lashed out, slapping two soldiers he believed were feigning battle fatigue.

"It has come to my attention that a very small number of soldiers are going to the hospital on the pretext that they are nervously incapable of combat. Such men are cowards and bring disgrace to their comrades, whom they heartlessly leave to endure the dangers of battle..."

Patton's order to the US Seventh Army, Sicily (August 3, 1943). Written after the first of the so-called "slapping incidents" that threatened his career.

"He liked to fight, he'd rather fight than eat."

General Paul Harkins's assessment of Patton. Harkins was Patton's assistant chief-of-staff from 1943 to 1945.

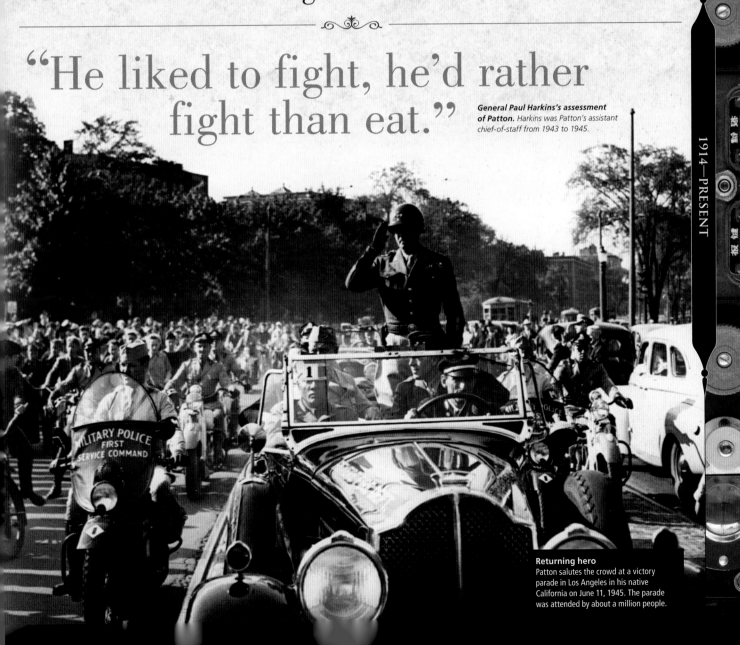

Returning hero
Patton salutes the crowd at a victory parade in Los Angeles in his native California on June 11, 1945. The parade was attended by about a million people.

PATTON AT THE BULGE

LOCATION
Ardennes region, Luxembourg, and eastern Belgium

CAMPAIGN Liberation of northwest Europe
DATE December 16, 1944–end January 1945
FORCES Allied (initially): 83,000; German: 200,000
CASUALTIES Allied: c. 100,000; German: c. 100,000

When the previously quiet Ardennes sector erupted on December 16, 1944, with a massive German attack—the last major German offensive of World War II—the top Allied commanders were taken by surprise. Three German armies smashed into a front held by a weak mix of exhausted veterans and newcomers from General Courtney Hodges' US First Army.

Allied defenses were soon broken, although some units did manage to hold on at St. Vith and Bastogne. In the hilly and heavily wooded terrain of the Ardennes, the road networks that spread out from these towns were vital. The Germans were never likely to achieve their goal of reaching Antwerp far to the northwest, but the "bulge" they were creating in the Allied front line was a serious threat.

It was only on December 19 that Allied leaders began to respond effectively. At a planning conference, General Eisenhower decided that north of the bulge Bernard

Montgomery would be responsible for halting the German advance and then counterattacking. Omar Bradley was given the corresponding role to the south, but, in effect, George Patton, commanding the US Third Army, became the driving force behind the southern operations.

At Eisenhower's conference, officers were disbelieving when Patton claimed that he could have three divisions on the attack against the German southern flank—some 90 miles (150 km) from their existing front—within 48 hours. But Patton made this happen. Over the next few days, Patton alone worked as the Third Army's forward headquarters, driving from unit to unit and hurrying them along the line of march, adjusting their deployment, and, finally, sending them into battle. The relief of Bastogne was achieved on December 26, and on January 16 the Third Army linked up at Houffalize with forces of Hodges' First Army attacking from the north.

ALLIED VICTORY

Patton's forces did not win the battle of the Bulge on their own. Even as he set his men moving, other American infantry and tank units were converging on the sector from all sides. But as a feat of generalship, Patton's achievement in planning and executing the Third Army's attack has few equals in any war. The German attack had been a costly gamble that did not pay off.

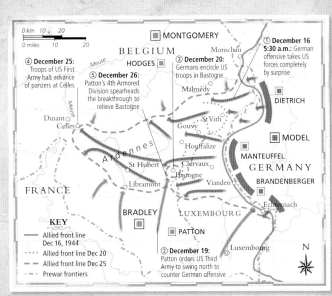

MONTGOMERY

① **December 16 5:30 a.m.:** German offensive takes US forces completely by surprise

④ **December 25:** Troops of US First Army halt advance of panzers at Celles

③ **December 20:** Germans encircle US troops in Bastogne

⑤ **December 26:** Patton's 4th Armored Division spearheads the breakthrough to relieve Bastogne

BELGIUM
Monschau
HODGES
Malmédy
DIETRICH

Dinant
Celles
Gouvy
St Vith
MODEL
Houffalize
MANTEUFFEL
St Hubert
Clervaux
GERMANY
Bastogne
Vianden
BRANDENBERGER
Libramont
Echternach

FRANCE

BRADLEY
LUXEMBOURG

KEY
— Allied front line Dec 16, 1944
···· Allied front line Dec 20
– – Allied front line Dec 25
–·– Prewar frontiers

PATTON

② **December 19:** Patton orders US Third Army to swing north to counter German offensive

Luxembourg

N

Ardennes
Meuse

0 km 10 20
0 miles 20

1914–PRESENT

Difficult conditions
An M36 tank destroyer passes another on an
icy road. The Germans hoped that the wintry
weather would stop the Allies from using their
air power, but when conditions improved,
Allied aircraft made devastating attacks.

US COMMANDERS IN THE PACIFIC

THE SURPRISE ATTACK on Pearl Harbor on December 7, 1941, and the wave of Japanese conquests that followed, left the United States fighting back across the Pacific to Japan against a tenacious enemy. Command of Allied forces in the Pacific was split by geographical area between General Douglas MacArthur and Admiral Chester Nimitz. This decision created a situation in which, at times, conflicting strategies were pursued simultaneously and inter-service rivalries were rampant. Nonetheless, in a war of dramatic sea-air battles, amphibious operations, and jungle fighting, US commanders marshaled ever-growing resources with notable skill and efficiency.

DOUGLAS MACARTHUR

US ARMY GENERAL
BORN January 26, 1880
DIED April 5, 1964
KEY CONFLICTS World War I, World War II, Korean War
KEY BATTLES Bataan 1942, Philippines 1944–45, Inchon 1950

The son of a general and first in his class at West Point, the supremely self-confident Douglas MacArthur was destined for a high-flying military career. He distinguished himself fighting with the 42nd "Rainbow" Division on the Western Front in World War I, ending the war as a brigadier-general. By 1930, he was US Army chief-of-staff, and in 1935, he undertook the building of an army for the semi-independent Philippines.

WAR IN THE EAST

Formally recalled to US service in July 1941, MacArthur was caught unprepared by the Japanese offensive after Pearl Harbor. Unable to prevent enemy landings on the Philippines, he withdrew to the Bataan peninsula. On President Roosevelt's orders, he left his troops to escape to Australia in March 1942. Installed as supreme commander of Allied forces in the southwest Pacific, he launched an offensive in New Guinea and instituted an "island-hopping" strategy, bypassing Japanese strongpoints. He used the media to press for his preferred strategic choices, invading the Philippines in 1944 against the judgment of the joint chiefs of staff.

After the war, MacArthur led the occupation forces in Japan, and at the onset of the Korean War in 1950, he was given command of UN forces. He stabilized a perimeter around the port of Pusan, then launched a brilliant counterstroke with landings at Inchon that forced a Communist withdrawal northward. In pursuit toward the Chinese border, he met with large-scale Chinese military intervention that sent his army reeling into retreat. His public advocacy of an invasion of China and the use of nuclear weapons led President Truman to dismiss him in April 1951.

Four stars
MacArthur's four-star plate was superseded in December 1944, when he became a five-star general.

A promise kept
Fleeing the Philippines in 1942, MacArthur promised to return. He did wade ashore at Leyte in October 1944, but this staged publicity shot was taken later.

HOLLAND SMITH

US MARINE CORPS GENERAL
BORN April 20, 1882
DIED January 12, 1967
KEY CONFLICT World War II
KEY BATTLES Tarawa 1943, Kwajalein 1944, Saipan 1944, Iwo Jima 1945

Known as the father of modern amphibious warfare, Holland McTyeire Smith practiced law before joining the Marines in 1905. During his early years as a junior officer in the Philippines, he acquired the nickname Howlin' Mad. Aptly reflecting his fearsome temperament, the name stuck with him for the rest of his career. When the United States entered World War I in 1917, Smith was sent to the Western Front, where he became a staff officer and was awarded the French Croix de Guerre. His career progressed satisfactorily between the wars and, by 1937, he was the Marine Corps' director of operations and training. Over the following years, Smith led the development of tactics and equipment

Marine general
A hard-hitting Marine general, Smith was largely responsible for US forces' standard of excellence in combined-arms amphibious operations during World War II.

for the conduct of opposed amphibious landings. Given command of First Marine Brigade in 1940, he began intensive training in amphibious warfare that he later extended to the rest of the Marines and other relevant Army formations.

ISLAND ASSAULTS

In 1943, Smith was able to put his doctrine into practice as commander of t h e V Amphibious Corps in the Pacific War. In the attack on the Gilbert Islands, Smith was in charge of the costly assault on Tarawa, a tiny island captured at the expense of 3,000 Marine casualties. Lessons were learned and V Corps' capture of Kwajalein in the Marshall Islands in January 1944 went more smoothly.

The following June, Smith led the assault on Saipan in the Marianas, in which the 27th Infantry Division fought alongside the Marines. In the midst of the fighting, Smith fired the army divisional commander who, he felt, lacked sufficient aggression. This caused much ill-feeling between the Army and Marines, and led to Smith being shifted to a less hands-on battlefield role as commander of the Fleet Marine Force. His final act in World War II was to mastermind the assault on Iwo Jima in February 1945.

KEY TROOPS
MARINE CORPS

In the early 20th century, the US Marine Corps was America's overseas intervention force. As such, its officers and men gained combat experience that served them well in World War I, when the Marines earned the nickname Devil Dogs. By World War II, they had developed an expertise in amphibious warfare that was applied to seizing islands in the Pacific War. Their performance in the bitter combat against the Japanese at Guadalcanal, Tarawa, Saipan, and Iwo Jima gained the Marines a reputation as an elite fighting force. By 1945, the corps had grown from two brigades to six divisions numbering almost half a million men. They confirmed their elite reputation in the toughest fighting of the Korean and Vietnam wars.

CHESTER NIMITZ

US ADMIRAL
BORN February 24, 1885
DIED February 20, 1966
KEY CONFLICT World War II
KEY BATTLES Coral Sea 1942, Midway 1942, Philippine Sea 1944, Leyte Gulf 1944, Okinawa 1945

Nimitz graduated from the US Naval Academy at Annapolis in 1905. He became an expert in submarines and diesel engines, serving as a staff officer with the US Atlantic submarine force during World War I. He broadened his career with administrative postings and surface ship commands, rising to rear-admiral in 1938.

Ten days after the Japanese attack on Pearl Harbor in December 1941, he was appointed commander-in-chief of the US Pacific Fleet and began rebuilding US naval power for the fight back. In March 1942, his command was extended to all forces in the Pacific Ocean Areas, air and ground as well as naval. He coped with this wide-ranging role by giving subordinates overall direction but avoiding interference in the detailed conduct of operations.

Provided with excellent intelligence by naval code breakers, Nimitz was able to send his carriers to engage the Japanese at the Coral Sea and Midway in 1942, turning the tide of the Pacific War. His strategy of pushing toward Japan through the Central Pacific, adopted in 1943, was clear-sighted and effective, even if in retrospect some of the islands assaulted en route—especially Iwo Jima— might have been better sidestepped.

SUBMARINE POWER

In addition to presiding over the great naval battles of the Philippine Sea and Leyte Gulf, Nimitz unleashed an unrestricted submarine war against Japanese merchant shipping that was savagely effective in the later stages of the war. He was made fleet admiral in December 1944, one of only four men to hold that rank.

Victory over Japan
Nimitz is portrayed at the signing of the Japanese surrender on board USS *Missouri*, on September 2, 1945. He always avoided stirring up inter-service rivalries, but was often at odds with General MacArthur (on the right).

AIR COMMANDERS

THE CORRECT USE of air power was a subject of intense debate both before and during World War II. The Germans saw their Luftwaffe as primarily an adjunct to ground operations, as demonstrated in the Blitzkrieg offensives of the first two years of the war. In contrast, British air commanders, believing that strategic bombing might decide the outcome of the war, focused on the defense of Britain's cities and a nighttime bombing campaign against Germany. The United States began with a commitment to the precision-bombing of military and economic targets, but in the end pursued the destruction of Japan's cities by conventional and nuclear bombing.

MODERN COMMANDERS

HUGH DOWDING

HEAD OF RAF FIGHTER COMMAND
BORN April 24, 1882
DIED February 15, 1970
KEY CONFLICT World War II
KEY BATTLES France 1940, Britain 1940

Dowding joined the Royal Flying Corps in 1913 and fought as a squadron commander in World War I. In 1936, he was chosen to lead the newly formed RAF Fighter Command. He exploited radar technology to create the world's first integrated air defense system, with coastal radar stations linked to operations rooms that directed fighter aircraft to their targets.

In spring 1940, regarding the defense of Britain as his primary concern, he limited the commitment of fighters to battles in Norway and France. Resisting a German air offensive in the Battle of Britain that summer, he exhibited a clear sense of purpose and priorities,

Defender of the skies
Known as Stuffy, Dowding was a diffident and reserved individual lacking in charisma, yet he possessed an unmatched understanding of modern air defense.

husbanding reserves while imposing maximum losses on German bombers. He realized that as long as Fighter Command was an effective defensive force, the Luftwaffe would not win. Despite his success, Dowding lost political backing, and, in November 1940, he was summarily dismissed.

ARTHUR HARRIS

HEAD OF RAF BOMBER COMMAND
BORN April 13, 1892
DIED April 5, 1984
KEY CONFLICT World War II
KEY BATTLES Cologne 1942, Ruhr 1943, Hamburg 1943, Berlin 1943–44, Dresden 1945

"Bomber" Harris fought with the Royal Flying Corps in World War I. Starting World War II in command of a bomber group, in February 1942, he was appointed head of RAF Bomber Command with orders to carry out the area bombing of German cities. He took over a demoralized force and transformed it, introducing improved heavy bombers, and refining navigational and targeting equipment that made reasonably accurate night bombing possible.

BLANKET BOMBING

Choosing targets each morning for the next night's raids, Harris sought to maximize impact by concentrated destruction. In May 1942 he staged a "Thousand Bomber" raid on Cologne, a stunt that greatly improved both morale and his public image. From 1943, he partially cooperated with the US policy of attacks on selected economic targets, but never wavered from his belief that bombing cities could win the war. He twice achieved destruction on the scale he sought: in the firestorms that devastated Hamburg in July 1943 and Dresden in February 1945. Campaigns against the cities of the Ruhr and especially Berlin in 1943–44 were costly in terms of aircraft lost and failed to achieve a decisive result.

"Bomber" Harris
Air Marshal Arthur Harris (seated) was a blunt, aggressive man who rejected suggestions that bombing German civilians was immoral. He felt his Command was badly treated after the war, when opinion turned against strategic bombing.

The Spitfire
RAF Fighter Command's most famous aircraft, the Supermarine Spitfire, went into production in 1938, appearing just in time to counter the Luftwaffe. This Mark V version was flown by a Canadian pilot.

ALBERT KESSELRING

LUFTWAFFE FIELD MARSHAL
BORN November 30, 1885
DIED July 16, 1960
KEY CONFLICT World War II
KEY BATTLES Poland 1939, France 1940, Britain 1940–41, Operation Barbarossa 1941, siege of Malta 1942, Monte Cassino 1943–44

Originally an artillery officer, in 1936, Kesselring was appointed chief-of-staff of the newly formed Luftwaffe—having learned to fly at the age of 48. He favored the use of aircraft in tactical support of ground forces, and canceled plans for a strategic heavy

Adaptable leader
A photograph taken on the Eastern Front in August 1941 shows Kesselring while still a Luftwaffe commander. A few months later, he was dispatched to Italy.

bomber. In September 1939, he led Luftflotte 1 in the invasion of Poland, and the following year commanded Luftflotte 2 from the bombing of Rotterdam in May 1940 through the battle of France, the Battle of Britain, and the Blitz, before transferring to the east for the invasion of the Soviet Union in June 1941.

In December 1941, he was switched from commanding air attacks on Moscow to controlling Axis forces in the Mediterranean as commander-in-chief south, based in Rome. His conduct of the defensive campaign in Italy from the Allied invasion of Sicily in July 1943 to the fall of 1944 was exemplary in military terms. However, war crimes committed at this time brought Kesselring a life prison sentence after the German defeat.

CURTIS LEMAY

US AIR COMMANDER
BORN November 15, 1906
DIED October 1, 1990
KEY CONFLICT World War II
KEY BATTLES Regensburg 1943, Tokyo 1945

From a blue-collar background in Columbus, Ohio, Curtis LeMay joined the US Army Air Corps via the Army Reserve and the National Guard. Originally a fighter pilot, he transferred to bombers in 1936, in time for the start-up flights of the B-17 Flying Fortress heavy bomber.

When the United States entered World War II, LeMay led a bomber group, which he trained and took to England in October 1942. In a daylight bombing campaign directed against targets in Germany, LeMay often led from the front, flying on combat missions such as the costly Schweinfurt-Regensburg raid in August 1943. He also contributed

to the evolution of bomber tactics, devising new targeting techniques and combat formations. He achieved rapid promotion and was a major-general when, in August 1944, he was sent to Asia to command newly introduced long-range B-29 Superfortress bombers in the war against Japan.

DEVASTATION OF JAPAN
In line with standard US bomber doctrine, B-29s were at first used for high-altitude daylight raids intended to achieve precision bombing of military and industrial targets. Finding these tactics ineffective, from February 1945, LeMay switched to night bombing at low altitude with incendiary bombs. On the night of March 9–10, 1945, LeMay's B-29s, flying from the Marianas, devastated Tokyo with a firestorm that killed up to 80,000 people. Over the following months, city after city

Getting results
A draconian disciplinarian with no tolerance of incompetence or weakness, LeMay always ensured his bomber crews were the best trained in the air force, achieving greater accuracy and suffering lower casualties.

was laid to waste. At least a quarter of a million people were killed by LeMay's conventional bombers before the Japanese surrender in August.

From 1948 to 1957, LeMay headed the US Strategic Air Command, creating a nuclear bomber force that was capable of hitting targets in the Soviet Union. From 1961 to 1965, he was chief-of-staff of the US Air Force. During the Cuban Missile Crisis in 1962, he forcefully argued for bombing raids to take out Soviet missile bases on the island.

> ## THE DESTRUCTION OF JAPAN'S ABILITY TO WAGE WAR LIES WITHIN THE CAPABILITY OF THIS COMMAND, PROVIDED THE MAXIMUM CAPACITY IS EXTENDED UNSTINTINGLY...
>
> **CURTIS LEMAY**, REPORT TO GENERAL LAURIS NORSTAD, APRIL 1945

The Blitz
Air raid wardens clamber over the wreckage of a bomb-damaged building in Holborn, central London, following a daylight raid on October 8, 1940. The Blitz caused 30,000 deaths and 50,000 injuries in London alone.

NAVAL COMMANDERS OF WWII

WORLD WAR II INVOLVED naval warfare of unprecedented scale and variety. In the Pacific, Japanese and American naval commanders had to devise new tactics for battles fought mainly by aircraft carriers. In the Atlantic, the Allies faced the German U-boat threat in one of the most crucial campaigns of the war.

The importance of amphibious landings and seaborne supply made naval support essential to army operations from Normandy to Okinawa. Despite all the innovations, however, some established naval traditions remained relevant—the surprise attack executed with boldness, and resolution when taking punishment from enemy firepower.

MODERN COMMANDERS

YAMAMOTO ISOROKU

JAPANESE ADMIRAL
BORN April 4, 1884
DIED April 18, 1943
KEY CONFLICT World War II
KEY BATTLES Pearl Harbor 1941, Midway 1942, Eastern Solomons 1942, Santa Cruz Islands 1942, Guadalcanal 1942

Born Takana Isoroku and adopted by the Yamamoto samurai clan, the future Japanese admiral was wounded at the battle of Tsushima during the Russo-Japanese War in 1905. He became a specialist in naval aviation and, as an admiral in the 1930s, argued for resources to be devoted to aircraft carriers, not battleships.

Yamamoto angered Japanese militarists by arguing for avoiding war with the United States, but he was still appointed as commander-in-chief of the Combined Fleet in 1939 and planned the surprise attack on Pearl Harbor in December 1941. The goal of this raid was defensive, to buy Japan time to create a far-flung protective perimeter in the Pacific, but

Yamamoto's strategy was essentially offensive. He wanted to draw the US Navy into a major action in which it could be destroyed. At Midway in June 1942, this strategy led to a major defeat for Japan. Fierce battles followed in the Guadalcanal campaign (including the battles of the Eastern Solomons and the Santa Cruz Islands), in which both sides suffered substantial losses.

In April 1943, Yamamoto's aircraft was shot down over Bougainville—a deliberate assassination, since his movements had been identified by US naval intelligence.

Careful planning
Although he masterminded the Pearl Harbor attack, Yamamoto was pessimistic about Japan's chances of winning a war against the US.

> SINKING... BATTLESHIPS IS NO CAUSE FOR CELEBRATION. THERE WILL BE TIMES OF DEFEAT AS WELL AS VICTORY.
> **YAMAMOTO ISOROKU**, IN A LETTER TO HIS SISTER AFTER PEARL HARBOR, 1941

PEARL HARBOR

CAMPAIGN Pacific Theater, World War II
DATE December 7, 1941
LOCATION Oahu Island, Hawaii

Overriding opposition from the Japanese naval staff, Yamamoto pushed through his plan for a surprise strike against the US Pacific Fleet at Pearl Harbor, without a prior declaration of war. A task force under Vice-Admiral Nagumo Chuichi, including six carriers, sailed across thousands of miles of ocean, undetected. More than 350 Japanese naval aircraft sank or crippled 18 US warships, including eight battleships. They failed, however, to sink the fleet's three carriers, which were at sea.

Fiery admiral
Cunningham embodied the fighting spirit of the Royal Navy. He once ordered his fleet to "sink, burn, and destroy" every enemy vessel.

ANDREW CUNNINGHAM

BRITISH ADMIRAL
BORN January 7, 1883
DIED June 12, 1963
KEY CONFLICT World War II
KEY BATTLES Taranto 1940, Cape Matapan 1941, Crete 1941

Andrew Browne Cunningham, known as "ABC," served with distinction on World War I destroyers. At the outbreak of World War II, he was commander-in-chief of Britain's Mediterranean Fleet. Wedded to the aggressive Nelsonian tradition, in November 1940, Cunningham launched a successful attack by carrier-borne aircraft on Italian warships in port at Taranto—a feat that helped to inspire the Japanese

attack on Pearl Harbor a year later. In March 1941, a night pursuit off Cape Matapan left five Italian warships sunk with no British losses. The arrival of the Luftwaffe in the Mediterranean theater exposed Cunningham's ships to heavy punishment, but he stuck resolutely to his task, even when nine ships were lost in the battle for Crete in May 1941.

Cunningham later commanded the naval forces for a series of amphibious operations, from the Torch landings in North Africa in November 1942 to the invasions of Sicily and mainland Italy the following year. As First Sea Lord from October 1943, he presided over the Normandy landings.

RAYMOND SPRUANCE

AMERICAN ADMIRAL
BORN July 3, 1886
DIED December 13, 1969
KEY CONFLICT World War II
KEY BATTLES Midway 1942, Philippine Sea 1944, Okinawa 1945

Spruance graduated from the US Naval Academy in 1906. By the 1930s, he had a reputation as an officer who thought deeply about naval strategy and command. When the Pacific War began, he was a rear admiral commanding a cruiser division, which in 1942 was assigned as escort to Vice-Admiral William Halsey's carrier Task Force 16. After Halsey became ill in May 1942, Spruance took command of his carriers, despite lacking naval aviation experience. Spruance consequently gained much of the credit for the decisive American

Coolness under pressure
Spruance was a quiet man, cool and decisive under pressure. After the war, he served as president of the US Naval War College and later as US ambassador in the Philippines.

victory at Midway on June 4, in which four Japanese carriers were sunk. He boldly launched his aircraft piecemeal to seize the opportunity to attack at the start of the battle, then showed cautious good sense in avoiding a night encounter with the Japanese fleet at the end of the day.

After Midway, Spruance served as chief-of-staff to Admiral Nimitz until mid-1943, when he was given command of the Central Pacific Force, later the US Fifth Fleet.

FURTHER SUCCESSES

While covering amphibious landings at Saipan with Vice-Admiral Marc Mitscher as his carrier task force commander, Spruance encountered a Japanese fleet in the Philippine Sea in June 1944. The battle was a disaster for Japanese naval aviation, savaged in the "Marianas Turkey Shoot," but Spruance again showed his caution in vetoing a headlong pursuit of the retreating Japanese warships. He remained successfully in command of the Fifth Fleet through the 1945 landings at Iwo Jima and Okinawa.

Bombers at Midway
An artist's view of Douglas Dauntless dive-bombers flying away after scoring hits on a Japanese carrier during the battle of Midway on June 4, 1942.

KARL DÖNITZ

GERMAN ADMIRAL
BORN September 16, 1891
DIED December 24, 1980
KEY CONFLICT World War II
KEY BATTLE The Atlantic 1940–45

Karl Dönitz first commanded a submarine in World War I. After Hitler's rise to power, Dönitz was entrusted with creating a new U-boat force. He believed submarines could be a war-winning weapon if used against merchant ships, but failed to win priority for U-boat production.

After the fall of France in summer 1940, Dönitz based his submarines in Brittany and began to prey on shipping in the Atlantic. As the number of U-boats increased, Dönitz deployed them in "wolf packs" coordinated by radio. They attacked on the surface by night, to avoid

Meeting the crew
Dönitz tried to maintain a close relationship with his U-boat crews, who were originally hand-picked and trained to a high standard.

convoy escorts' underwater detection devices. Dönitz usually directed operations in person, communicating by radio. By 1943, he seemed on the verge of cutting Britain's Atlantic lifeline. A grateful Hitler appointed him to replace Erich Raeder as commander-in-chief of the navy.

In spring 1943, however, tactical and technological developments allowed Allied convoy escorts and antisubmarine aircraft to get the upper hand and U-boat losses escalated to an unsustainable level.

FAILED STRATEGY

In May 1943, Dönitz was forced to withdraw his submarine fleet from the main battle area. Although U-boat operations were resumed and continued sporadically to the end of the war, Dönitz's strategy had failed. He remained a loyal supporter of the Nazi regime and briefly succeeded Hitler as German head of state in May 1945. After the war he was imprisoned for war crimes.

KEY TROOPS

U-BOAT CREW

In the early years of World War II, U-boat crews were a well-trained elite and their commanders were celebrated in Germany as "aces," competing to rack up "kills." The life expectancy of U-boat crewmembers was low, however. By the end of the war, 60 percent of men who had served on U-boats were dead.

U-BOAT SAILOR'S UNIFORM

1945—PRESENT

POST WORLD WAR II

"THAT'S THE BURDEN THE MANTLE OF LEADERSHIP PLACES UPON YOU. YOU COULD BE THE PERSON WHO GIVES THE ORDERS THAT WILL BRING ABOUT THE DEATHS OF THOUSANDS AND THOUSANDS OF YOUNG MEN AND WOMEN. IT IS AN AWESOME RESPONSIBILITY. YOU CANNOT FAIL. YOU DARE NOT FAIL."

US GENERAL NORMAN SCHWARZKOPF, MAY 15, 1991

ALTHOUGH IT WAS NOT CLEAR at the time, it now seems obvious that 1945 marked the end of the era of total war—mainly because total war had come to mean the utter devastation of all combatants by nuclear weapons. Military commanders reluctantly learned to operate within politically imposed limits, vetoing the use of certain weapons held in their increasingly powerful arsenals, and restricting the geographical extent of the fighting. For example, they sometimes ruled out the decisive invasion or conquest of the enemy's country.

The four decades after 1945 were dominated by a war that never happened. The Cold War saw much of the world divided into two blocs, one headed by the United States, the other by the Soviet Union. In this confrontation, commanders developed elaborate strategies and tactics for war between nuclear-armed powers, yet the battles for which their forces planned and trained never happened. Instead, the major Cold War conflicts were fought with conventional weapons, in Korea between 1950 and 1953, and in Vietnam in the 1960s and 70s.

GUERRILLA WARFARE

The Korean War, precipitated by a Communist North Korean invasion of the pro-American South, was fought for the most part with World War II-vintage equipment, commanders, and tactics. In Vietnam, some of the world's most skilled practitioners of guerrilla warfare took on US forces strong on firepower but weaker on the political and propaganda aspects of war. US commanders were often successful in their conduct of operations, but when it came to long-term strategy, their Communist opponents out-planned and out-maneuvered them.

Although no other conflict of this period matched Vietnam in scale, there was also a series of Arab-Israeli wars in the Middle East, in which desert terrain provided a theater for conventional tank-and-aircraft battles in which some Israeli commanders proved themselves the true successors of Rommel and Montgomery. But guerrilla war was perhaps the most characteristic form of conflict in the second half of the 20th century, featuring in wars of independence against colonial powers and revolutionary uprisings against unpopular regimes. Guerrilla leaders, such as Fidel Castro and Che Guevara, were among the most striking military commanders of the time.

By 1989, the Cold War was over, the collapse of the Soviet bloc leaving the United States as the world's sole military superpower. During the wars against Saddam Hussein's Iraq in 1990–91 and 2003, a post-Cold War generation of US generals showed their skills in handling the panoply of advanced command-and-control technology at their disposal. Both in the occupation of Iraq and in Afghanistan, however, the early 21st century showed that the world's most advanced armies still found it difficult to prevent or counter sustained insurgencies.

Vietnam War
Taken in 1964, this photograph shows a US Army special forces captain contacting his base camp via radio in the foreground. In the background, Vietnamese soldiers set fire to a Vietcong hideout.

Vought A-7 Corsair
The Corsair was a US Navy attack aircraft introduced during the Vietnam War in the 1960s and still in frontline service during the 1990–91 Gulf War.

POSTWAR COMMANDERS

THE WARS OF THE 1950s and 1960s reflected both the determination of the United States to prevent the spread of Communism and the resistance of European powers to independence movements in their colonies. Military commanders tended to pursue strategies for military success without due regard for the political complexity of the conflicts in which they were engaged. In Korea, massive firepower intelligently applied enabled America and its allies to fight Chinese and North Korean conventional forces to a standstill. Elsewhere, however, guerrilla and terrorist tactics wore down the Western powers' political will to fight.

MATTHEW RIDGWAY

US ARMY GENERAL
BORN March 3, 1895
DIED July 26, 1993
KEY CONFLICTS World War II, Korean War
KEY BATTLES Normandy 1944, Market Garden 1944, Rhine Crossing 1945, Operation Killer 1951, Imjin River 1951

Matthew Bunker Ridgway served with distinction as a commander of airborne forces in World War II. He landed in France with the 82nd Airborne Division on D-Day and commanded an Airborne Corps from Operation Market Garden through to the defeat of Germany in 1945.

In December 1950, Ridgway was sent to Korea to save the Eighth Army, demoralized after a headlong retreat from North Korea. He instantly stabilized a defensive line against the pursuing Chinese. Instituting "meatgrinder" tactics, he used the firepower of American artillery and aircraft to inflict maximum casualties on the enemy. His aggressive fighting spirit was encapsulated in the names he gave to operations, such as "Killer" and "Ripper." In April 1951, he took over from MacArthur as commander-in-chief of UN forces, a position he held until May 1952. He later served as chief-of-staff of the US Army.

Inspiring the troops
Arriving in Korea at a desperate moment in the war, Ridgway (fourth from left) made a point of visiting his men at the front, bringing a fresh resolve to the fight against the Chinese Army.

JEAN DE LATTRE DE TASSIGNY

FRENCH GENERAL
BORN February 2, 1889
DIED January 11, 1952
KEY CONFLICTS World War II, First Indochina War
KEY BATTLES Colmar Pocket 1945, Vinh Yen 1951, Hoa Binh 1951–52

De Lattre de Tassigny was a French commander in World War II. He led the French First Army from the Allied landings in Provence in August 1944 to Germany's defeat. He distinguished himself particularly in the reduction of the heavily defended Colmar Pocket in January–February 1945.

THE DE LATTRE LINE

In December 1950, with the French hold on Vietnam precarious in the face of a Viet Minh guerrilla offensive, he took over as commander-in-chief in Indochina. To hold the densely populated Red River Delta, he built a fortified line of 1,200 concrete strongpoints. He backed up this passive defense with mobile forces and paratroopers ready to respond aggressively to Viet Minh attacks.

In January 1951, de Lattre proved the effectiveness of his method by inflicting heavy losses upon a force of 20,000 Viet Minh fighters at Vinh Yen. Further attempts to breach the de Lattre Line met a similar fate. By November de Lattre felt confident enough to take the offensive, sending paratroopers and ground forces into Hoa Binh, a base outside the defensive perimeter. Ill health obliged him to return to France before a Viet Minh counteroffensive drove the French out of Hoa Binh the following year.

Determined professional
A thoroughly professional soldier, de Lattre brought intelligence and decisivenenss to the struggle in Vietnam. This was in spite of failing health and the loss of his only son, killed fighting the Viet Minh in the spring of 1951.

JACQUES MASSU

FRENCH GENERAL
BORN May 5, 1908
DIED October 26, 2002
KEY CONFLICT Algerian War
KEY BATTLE Algiers 1957

A career officer, Jacques Massu joined General de Gaulle's Free French forces in World War II and took part in the liberation of Paris. After the war, he served in Indochina and was a leader of airborne forces in the abortive Suez campaign of 1956. In 1957, he was tasked with suppressing the Algerian nationalist movement for liberation. Massu's brutal but successful crackdown became known as the battle of Algiers. In 1958, he led an uprising by hardline Algerian colonists against the policies of the French government, which was prepared to negotiate with the nationalists. The crisis triggered the collapse of France's Fourth Republic and the proclamation of the Fifth Republic with de Gaulle as president. Massu was soon at odds with de Gaulle's policy on Algeria and was shifted from his command in 1960. But he remained loyal to the Gaullist regime until his retirement in 1969.

Hard fighter
A rugged, natural warrior, Massu was adored by Algerian colonists but denounced by Arabs and by French liberals for the use of torture during the battle of Algiers.

WILLIAM WESTMORELAND

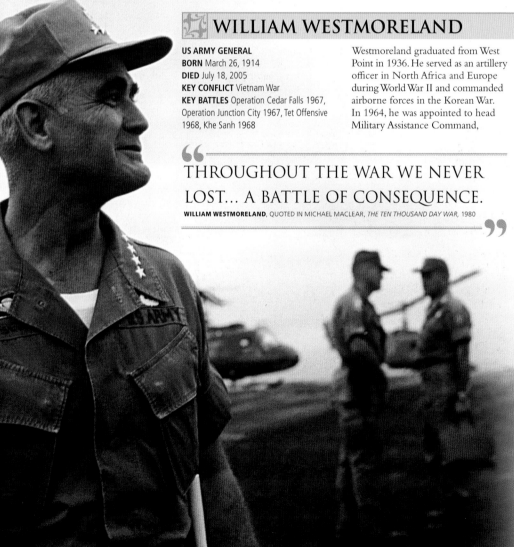

US ARMY GENERAL
BORN March 26, 1914
DIED July 18, 2005
KEY CONFLICT Vietnam War
KEY BATTLES Operation Cedar Falls 1967, Operation Junction City 1967, Tet Offensive 1968, Khe Sanh 1968

> ## THROUGHOUT THE WAR WE NEVER LOST... A BATTLE OF CONSEQUENCE.
> **WILLIAM WESTMORELAND**, QUOTED IN MICHAEL MACLEAR, *THE TEN THOUSAND DAY WAR*, 1980

Westmoreland graduated from West Point in 1936. He served as an artillery officer in North Africa and Europe during World War II and commanded airborne forces in the Korean War. In 1964, he was appointed to head Military Assistance Command, Vietnam (MACV). To stem the advance of Communist-led guerrilla forces, Westmoreland used helicopters to get troops and guns into hostile terrain and mounted large-scale "search-and-destroy" operations: infantry located enemy forces, and artillery and aircraft destroyed them.

MEDIA SCEPTICISM

Banned from invading North Vietnam or attacking bases and supply routes in neighboring Cambodia and Laos, Westmoreland used the body count of enemy dead as a measure of success. Despite an increasingly sceptical press, he demanded ever larger resources. Between 1964 and 1968, which saw two major operations—Cedar Falls and Junction City—American troop numbers in Vietnam rose from 16,000 to over half a million.

The 1968 Tet Offensive, in which Communist guerrillas attacked cities throughout South Vietnam, and the simultaneous siege of the US Marine base at Khe Sanh were disasters for Westmoreland. He argued that both brought the Communists costly defeats, but his critics knew that he had no credible strategy for winning the war. In June 1968, Westmoreland handed over his Vietnamese command to General Creighton Abrams. He was Army chief-of-staff until 1972.

Defending his honor
Westmoreland vigorously defended his record in Vietnam, arguing that the war had been a military success for the United States, thrown away by a lack of political will.

REVOLUTIONARY FIGHTERS

UNTIL THE 20TH CENTURY, guerrilla warfare was a form of piecemeal resistance to a superior force, be it a government or an invading army. In the Chinese Civil War from the 1920s to the 1940s and through various movements of World War II, guerrilla tactics became linked with revolutionary politics. This potent combination brought Communist rule to China and Fidel Castro to power in Cuba, and destabilized many other colonial regimes and ill-governed countries. The greatest triumph of revolutionary warfare came in Vietnam where, directed by General Vo Nguyen Giap, Communist-led nationalists defeated the French and then the Americans.

MAO ZEDONG

CHINESE REVOLUTIONARY LEADER
BORN December 26, 1893
DIED September 9, 1976
KEY CONFLICTS Chinese Civil War, Sino-Japanese War
KEY BATTLES Guerrilla Warfare

Mao Zedong was a founding member of the Chinese Communist Party in 1921. In 1927, conflict with Jiang Jieshi's Kuomintang (Chinese Nationalist Party) forced the Communists to flee to rural areas. They were saved from destruction by the Long March to remote Shaanxi province in 1934. During the struggle against the Kuomintang, and from 1937 against Japanese invaders, Mao became leader of the Communists and developed a systematic theory of revolutionary guerrilla warfare. In a long patient struggle—the "protracted war"—revolutionary fighters would take over rural areas then capture towns and cities. Winning the support of the peasants, the guerrillas would operate amid the rural population "like fish in the sea." Finally, when the guerrilla campaign had weakened the enemy, the revolutionaries would field regular forces to finish off the conflict with conventional war.

COMMUNIST TRIUMPH
After the collapse of Japan in 1945, the civil war with Jiang Jieshi resumed in earnest. The Communists were strengthened by Soviet support and established control over Manchuria. With a combination of guerrilla warfare and campaigns by large field armies, they defeated an increasingly demoralized enemy. The founding of the Communist People's Republic of China in October 1949 gave Mao immense prestige and his theory of revolutionary warfare became a guide to liberation movements worldwide.

Revolutionary leader
A Communist poster shows a young Mao leading Chinese peasants on the Long March. He ruled China from 1949 to his death in 1976, presiding over the violent transformation of the country.

Cuban guerrillas
Fidel Castro poses with fellow commanders at a secret guerrilla base in Cuba in 1957.

FIDEL CASTRO

CUBAN REVOLUTIONARY LEADER
BORN August 13, 1926
KEY CONFLICT Cuban Revolution
KEY BATTLES Moncada 1953, La Plata 1958, Bay of Pigs 1961

A law student from a middle-class family, Fidel Castro attempted a revolt against the Cuban dictator, Fulgencio Batista, in 1953. His attack on the Moncada army barracks failed and he was imprisoned, but released under an amnesty in 1955. Basing himself in Mexico, Castro armed a group of 81 followers and sailed for Cuba in November 1956. His arrival was intended to coincide with a revolutionary uprising, but the revolt had been suppressed by the time he landed. His men were attacked by Batista's forces, a handful surviving to regroup in the Sierra Maestra mountains. Reinforced by supporters from Cuba's cities, Castro's men began hit-and-run attacks on government targets, while urban guerrillas destabilized the regime with terrorist attacks.

In May 1958, Batista mounted a major campaign against Castro's bases in the Sierra Maestra. Poorly led government forces fell into ambushes and were defeated in firefights such as the battle of La Plata in July. Sensing victory, from August, Castro went on the offensive. Batista fled Cuba in January 1959 and Castro took power. His regime survived precariously at first, repulsing an American-backed invasion by Cuban exiles at the Bay of Pigs in April 1961. A deal between the United States and the Soviet Union after the 1962 Cuban Missile Crisis banned further American military intervention in Cuba.

ERNESTO "CHE" GUEVARA

INTERNATIONAL GUERRILLA LEADER
BORN June 14, 1928
DIED October 9, 1967
KEY CONFLICTS Cuban Revolution, Congolese Civil War, Bolivian Insurgency
KEY BATTLES Las Mercedes 1958, Santa Clara 1958

Born in Argentina, Guevara, nicknamed Che, studied medicine but became more interested in revolutionary politics. He was in Guatemala when a democratically elected reformist government was overthrown in a US-backed coup in 1954, an experience that confirmed his belief that freedom and an end to poverty in South America could only be won by fighting US imperialism.

KEY BATTLE
BOLIVIAN CAMPAIGN

CAMPAIGN Bolivian Insurgency
DATE November 1966–October 1967
LOCATION Bolivia

Che Guevara entered Bolivia in disguise in November 1966. Planning to start a guerrilla campaign against the military government of General René Barrientos, he assembled a band of 29 Bolivians, 17 Cubans, and a few foreigners. This small but well-armed group carried out two successful ambushes against army patrols in spring 1967, but failed to gain significant support from opposition groups in Bolivia's cities or from local peasants, some of whom willingly informed the authorities of the guerrillas' movements. Guevara's men became fugitives, hunted down by Bolivian special forces and their American advisers. On October 8, 1967, they were surrounded and destroyed as a fighting force. Guevara himself was wounded, taken prisoner, and executed the next day.

In Mexico, he met Fidel Castro and sailed with him to foment revolution in Cuba in 1956. Starting out as the group's doctor, he evolved into a skilled military leader, commanding one of Castro's guerrilla columns.

In the summer of 1958, he played a prominent role in resisting the Cuban government's offensive in the Sierra Maestra, extricating himself from a perilous envelopment at Las Mercedes in August. Later that year, he led his column on the offensive into central Cuba, capturing Santa Clara in December.

RISE AND FALL

In the years after the victory of the Cuban guerrillas in January 1959, Guevara filled a series of roles in the Cuban administration, executing enemies of the revolution, heading the finance ministry, and leading a delegation to the United Nations.

During this time, he developed the *foco* (focus) theory of revolutionary guerrilla warfare. This stated that a small armed band, based in a remote rural area, could bring about a revolutionary uprising in any of the world's poorer countries. In 1965, quitting Cuba with a handful of followers, Guevara set out to spread the revolution worldwide. His ultimate goal was the defeat of the United States, which he described as "the great enemy of the human race."

Guevara went first to the Congo, an African state torn apart by chaotic civil war, where his attempt to organize a guerrilla movement to oppose the American-backed government was a total failure. Although antigovernment factions were interested in power, they were indifferent to social revolution.

Guevara then moved to his native South America, somewhat arbitrarily choosing Bolivia as his target for organizing a *foco*. The Bolivian

Revolutionary hero
Guevara's good looks and idealistic outlook have made him a world-famous iconic leader.

campaign was almost equally ineffectual and ultimately fatal for Guevara. His violent death in October 1967 completed his ascent to a form of revolutionary sainthood.

AK47 assault rifle
The AK47 was adopted by the Soviet Army in 1949. Since then, more than 70 million have been produced, its robust and simple design making it a particular favorite of guerrilla fighters around the world.

> " WHEREVER DEATH MAY SURPRISE US, LET IT BE WELCOME IF... OTHER MEN COME FORWARD TO JOIN IN OUR FUNERAL DIRGE WITH THE STACCATO SINGING OF MACHINE-GUNS. "
>
> **CHE GUEVARA**, ADDRESS TO THE TRICONTINENTAL CONGRESS, JANUARY 1967

1914–PRESENT

VO NGUYEN GIAP

VIETNAMESE GUERRILLA AND ARMY COMMANDER
BORN August 25, 1911
KEY CONFLICTS Indochina War, Vietnam War
KEY BATTLES Lang Son 1950, Hoa Binh 1951–52, Dien Bien Phu 1954, Tet Offensive 1968, Easter Offensive 1972

When Vo Nguyen Giap was born, Vietnam was part of the French colony of Indochina. Giap's military career began during World War II. As a member of the Viet Minh, a Communist-led nationalist movement, he organized guerrillas who fought the Japanese occupation forces in northern Vietnam. When Japan surrendered to the Allies in 1945, Viet Minh leader, Ho Chi Minh, declared Vietnam independent. Giap became a minister in Ho's government. However, France was determined to regain its colony. After a breakdown in negotiations, in December 1946, Giap ordered his Viet Minh forces to attack the French, "destroy the invaders and save the nation." But after fighting in Hanoi, French rule was restored.

Based in the mountainous Viet Bac region, Giap patiently built up his guerrilla force. He established a main body, eventually numbering around 125,000 full-time soldiers under his direct command, while regional guerrilla forces

Map and map case
A Chinese-supplied map case was used by Vietnamese guerrillas to carry maps with detailed information on enemy bases marked on them.

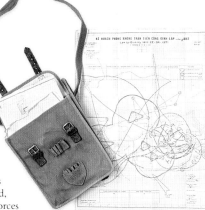

and part-time militia—villagers who turned into guerrilla fighters after dark—operated throughout Vietnam.

Although he had read military history and studied the theories of Mao Zedong, Giap had much to learn. His first substantial offensive operations, which led to the fall of a major French base at Lang Son in October 1950, were easy triumphs over exposed outposts. The following year, fielding 10,000 to 20,000 men at a time in frontal attacks on the Red River Delta, Giap was roundly defeated by well-marshaled French firepower. He drew the right conclusion: that he would have to lure the French away from their positions around the major cities and inflict military setbacks that would erode their political will to fight. Giap tried the technique at

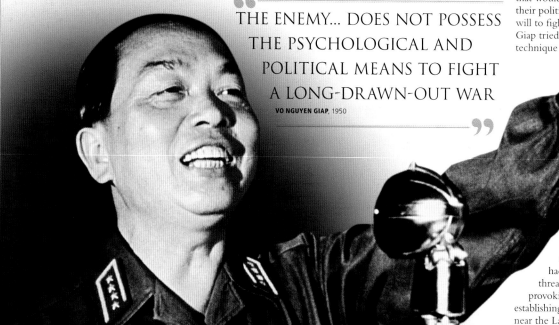

> ## THE ENEMY... DOES NOT POSSESS THE PSYCHOLOGICAL AND POLITICAL MEANS TO FIGHT A LONG-DRAWN-OUT WAR
> **VO NGUYEN GIAP**, 1950

Hoa Binh in late 1951 to early 1952, harassing supply lines to the base so effectively that the French had to withdraw. He then threatened outposts in Laos, provoking the French into establishing a base at Dien Bien Phu, near the Laotian border. The major Viet Minh victory that followed (pp. 344–45) ended French colonial rule and made Giap famous.

FIGHTING THE SOUTH

In the Communist state established in North Vietnam from 1954, Giap was defense minister, commander-in-chief of the army, and a member of the ruling politburo. In 1959,

The price of victory
Giap was a remarkably successful leader, defeating the French and the Americans, but he was wasteful of his men's lives— about a million NVA and Viet Cong were killed in the war against the United States.

MODERN COMMANDERS

■ **1931** While a student in Hanoi, Vo Nguyen Giap becomes a member of Ho Chi Minh's Indochina Communist Party founded the previous year. The party seeks to oppose French rule in Vietnam.

■ **1939** To escape a crackdown by the French colonial authorities, Giap—now an experienced journalist and activist—flees to join Ho Chi Minh in exile in China.

GIAP (LEFT) REVIEWING THE TROOPS IN 1958

■ **1941–45** Giap becomes the military leader of Viet Minh guerrillas fighting the Japanese occupation forces in Vietnam.

■ **December 1946** The reimposition of French rule in Vietnam leads to fighting with the Viet Minh, who are driven into remote rural areas.

■ **1950** Supplied with arms and training by Communist China, Giap's Viet Minh attack and seize French outposts in northern Vietnam near the Chinese border.

■ **January–June 1951** A series of Viet Minh attacks on the French in the Red River Delta, ordered by Giap, fail with heavy losses.

■ **March 13–May 7, 1954** Giap defeats the French at Dien Bien Phu, breaking their will to continue the war. After the resulting Geneva conference, he becomes a member of the government of North Vietnam (October 1954).

■ **1959** As a member of North Vietnam's ruling Communist politburo, Giap participates in the decision to start a guerrilla campaign in South Vietnam.

■ **October 1964** Giap begins infiltrating North Vietnamese Army (NVA) troops into South Vietnam. His plans for a rapid victory are blocked by the commitment of American ground forces to combat from 1965.

■ **January 1968** Giap launches the Tet Offensive against South Vietnamese cities, while besieging the US Marine base at Khe Sanh.

■ **April 1972** Giap directs the Easter Offensive, a three-pronged invasion of South Vietnam. The invasion is halted by South Vietnamese forces and American air power.

■ **1974** General Van Tien Dung, Giap's chief-of-staff, takes over as NVA commander-in-chief. The defeat of South Vietnam follows in April 1975.

the politburo decided to launch a guerrilla war in South Vietnam. Personnel from North Vietnam were infiltrated into the South to organize an insurrection. Giap set up the supply route known as the Ho Chi Minh Trail through Laos and Cambodia to feed the guerrilla war.

By 1964, the South Vietnamese guerrillas—known to the Americans as the Viet Cong—were so successful that Giap began sending North Vietnamese Army (NVA) infantry along the Ho Chi Minh Trail, anticipating a swift victory. But the US's huge commitment of forces to South Vietnam from 1965—as part of a global anti-Communism campaign—made him rethink. At first, Giap reacted cautiously to the aggressive American presence, mostly seeking to preserve his own forces by evasive action. In 1968, however, he judged the time right for a major blow that would break his enemy's will to fight. NVA troops besieged

Viet Cong briefing
Guerrillas prepare for an attack on a fortified compound by studying a scale model. The siege of Dien Bien Phu in 1954 was prepared for in this way and many other NVA attacks were based on similarly good intelligence.

the US Marine base at Khe Sanh in a manner reminiscent of Dien Bien Phu, while the Tet Offensive was unleashed on South Vietnamese cities. In military terms, both Tet and Khe Sanh proved very costly defeats for Giap, but even so they strained American morale to breaking point. This led directly to negotiations that would result in a complete US withdrawal from Vietnam in 1973.

A NATION REUNITED

Giap's final act as North Vietnam's commander-in-chief was the launch of a conventional invasion of South Vietnam in 1972. The NVA's Easter Offensive showed all Giap's usual talent for organization and logistical support of large-scale operations, but he fatally underestimated the impact of air power on conventional forces without air cover. Nor did the South Vietnamese Army collapse under pressure, as he had hoped. After suffering massive losses, the NVA was fought to a standstill. Giap was no longer army commander-in-chief when NVA tanks finally rolled into Saigon in 1975, reuniting Vietnam and completing his life's work.

KEY BATTLE
TET OFFENSIVE

CAMPAIGN Vietnam War
DATE January 31–March 2, 1968
LOCATION South Vietnam

In an offensive timed to coincide with Tet, Vietnam's New Year national holiday, more than 80,000 Viet Cong guerrillas and North Vietnamese troops attacked over 100 locations throughout South Vietnam. With many South Vietnamese soldiers away from their units for the holiday, the attacks were a total surprise. In Saigon guerrillas even penetrated the US Embassy compound. A series of counterattacks by American and South

Vietnamese forces reestablished control of most urban areas within days, but it took a month of fighting to retake Hue, the old imperial capital of Vietnam. Although the Viet Cong suffered unsustainable losses in the offensive, Tet convinced the American public that the war could not be won.

GIAP AT DIEN BIEN PHU

LOCATION
Northern Vietnam

CAMPAIGN
First Indochina War

DATE March 13–May 7, 1954
FORCES Viet Minh: c. 50,000; French: c. 20,000
CASUALTIES Viet Minh: 8,000 killed, 15,000 wounded; French: 2,000 killed, 6,000 wounded, 10,000 taken prisoner

In November 1953, the French Army began building a fortified camp at Dien Bien Phu, a remote location near Vietnam's border with Laos. General Vo Nguyen Giap ordered four divisions of regular soldiers from his Viet Minh main force to surround the camp and prepare to capture it.

PREPARING FOR BATTLE

Both sides would be fighting far from their base areas. Villagers were mobilized to supply Giap's soldiers, carrying food along jungle routes on bicycles and pack animals. Heavy artillery and antiaircraft guns were manhandled across the difficult terrain. Giap positioned his troops on the hills overlooking Dien Bien Phu and had his engineers build a warren of gun emplacements into the wooded slopes. These preparations took three months. Meanwhile, the French flew in reinforcements and built a chain of strongpoints around their camp.

Giap opened the battle with a huge artillery bombardment starting at 5:00 p.m. on March 13, 1954, stunning the French, who were anticipating an attack but did not expect their enemy to have heavy guns. Infantry attacks began that night, and by March 17 the Viet Minh had overrun three of the fortified positions defending the camp. The French fought back fiercely, mounting counterattacks and inflicting heavy casualties.

Giap's artillery had put the base's airstrip out of action almost right away. This left the French dependent on parachute supply drops, but these were rendered hazardous by Viet Minh antiaircraft fire.

Heavy fighting continued through early April. More French strongpoints were overrun, but Giap's artillery-supported infantry assaults were proving too costly and damaging to his soldiers' morale. He switched to a classic siege technique, digging zigzag lines of trenches across the open ground to advance his troops to the perimeter of the French base.

A VIETNAMESE VICTORY

By the first week of May, the French and Viet Minh had begun negotiations at a peace conference in Geneva; Giap was desperate for a quick victory to influence the course of the talks. Meanwhile, the French were pleading with the United States to rescue them by bombing the Viet Minh. But the Americans would not intervene, and, on May 7, the surviving French soldiers in Dien Bien Phu, without any prospect of relief, surrendered.

③ **March 14:** Airstrip so badly damaged that French have to drop future supplies by parachute

② **March 13:** Viet Minh infantry launch night attack on French positions

⑦ **May 1:** Giap launches an all-out attack on remaining positions

④ **March 17:** Many Vietnamese soldiers on the French side desert, forcing a French withdrawal

⑨ **May 7:** Remaining French positions overrun

① **March 13:** Daytime artillery attack weakens French base at Béatrice

⑩ **May 7:** Their supplies exhausted, French abandon Isabelle at night. Only 70 men manage to escape to Laos

⑤ **March 30:** Fierce fighting begins for Eliane and Dominique

⑧ **May 6:** Viet Minh detonate huge mine below Eliane

⑥ **March 30:** Isabelle is isolated by artillery fire, stopping reinforcements from heading north

GIAP

DE CASTRIES

Gabrielle
Béatrice
Anne-Marie
Dominique
Huguette
Eliane
Claudine
Isabelle
Airstrip
Nam Yum

KEY
Viet Minh forces
Viet Minh artillery
French fortified strongpoint

0 km   1   2
0 miles   1   2

Infantry assault
Viet Minh soldiers advance behind artillery fire. At Dien Bien Phu, Giap showed superb organizational ability, but his battle tactics mostly involved unsubtle frontal assaults.

COMMANDERS IN THE ISRAELI WARS

THE STATE OF ISRAEL has been in conflict with neighboring Arab states and Palestinian Arab groups ever since it was founded in 1948. From the outset, the Israelis saw attack as the best means of defense. The Suez War of 1956 and especially the Six-Day War of 1967 earned the Israelis a reputation as masters of aggressive mobile warfare. The Yom Kippur War of 1973, which opened with a successful Egyptian offensive, ended with a more hard-fought Israeli victory. Subsequent exercises in counterinsurgency, incursions into Lebanon, and suppression of Palestinian unrest have offered Israeli commanders few opportunities to cover themselves in glory.

YITZHAK RABIN

ISRAELI MILITARY AND POLITICAL LEADER
BORN March 1, 1922
DIED November 4, 1995
KEY CONFLICTS Arab-Israeli War 1948, Six-Day War 1967
KEY BATTLES Jerusalem 1948, Negev 1948

Born in Jerusalem, in 1941, Yitzhak Rabin joined the *Palmach* (the elite section of the Haganah Jewish militia). In 1946, he was briefly imprisoned by the British for armed resistance to their rule in Palestine. In the First Arab-Israeli War he led a brigade in the battle for Jerusalem and fought the Egyptians in the Negev Desert. Intelligent and professional, he earned an appointment as chief-of-staff of the Israeli Defense Forces (IDF) in 1964. He built up the IDF for an expected showdown with Israel's Arab neighbors and his planning lay behind the Israeli triumphs of the 1967 Six-Day War. However, Rabin, suffering from a nervous breakdown, had limited input into the conduct of operations once the conflict began. He left the army soon after. Entering politics, he twice served as Israeli prime minister. A late convert to making peace with the Palestinians, he was assassinated in 1995 by a Jewish opponent of the peace process.

The legacy of 1967
Rabin (left) planned the Six-Day War in 1967, but as prime minister in the 1990s he negotiated an Israeli withdrawal from the territories gained in that conflict.

KEY TROOPS
ISRAELI DEFENSE FORCES

Founded after Israel's declaration of independence in May 1948, the Israeli Defense Forces include the army, air force, and navy in a single integrated structure. Based on universal Jewish military service, the IDF operates with a relaxed attitude to formal discipline but achieves a high level of performance in combat. It specializes in fast-moving armored operations supported by superior air power. Its doctrine emphasizes the need for officers at all levels in the chain of command to exercise initiative and take independent action.

MOSHE DAYAN

Charismatic image
An instantly recognizable figure due to his eye patch, Moshe Dayan's swashbuckling image matched the high performance of Israeli forces in the 1950s and 60s.

ISRAELI MILITARY AND POLITICAL LEADER
BORN May 20, 1915
DIED October 26, 1981
KEY CONFLICTS Arab-Israeli War 1948, Suez War 1956, Six-Day War 1967, Yom Kippur War 1973
KEY BATTLES Sinai 1956, Jerusalem 1967

Born on a kibbutz (a collective agricultural settlement), Moshe Dayan joined the Haganah Jewish militia as a youth. In 1941, after the Haganah agreed to support Britain in World War II, Dayan lost an eye fighting the Vichy French in Lebanon. He led the defense of the Jordan Valley at the start of the First Arab-Israeli War and earned a good reputation as a fighting commander.

SUCCESSFUL CAMPAIGNS
In 1953, Dayan was made chief-of-staff of the Israeli Defense Forces (IDF). He transformed an amateurish citizen army into a disciplined modern force. Under his command, the IDF triumphed over the Egyptians in the Sinai campaign of 1956, achieving a major victory with little cost in lives. Dayan resigned from the IDF in 1958 to enter politics. In 1967, he was made defense minister and supervised the victories of the Six-Day War, involving himself most directly in the capture of east Jerusalem. Popular in Israel, Dayan was still defense minister when the Egyptians crossed the Suez Canal at the start of the Yom Kippur War in 1973. He was shocked by the losses the Israelis suffered in the war and blamed for complacency and lack of preparation. His career never recovered.

Israeli assault rifle
Modeled on the AK47, the Galil assault rifle came into service after the Yom Kippur War.

ARIEL SHARON

ISRAELI MILITARY AND POLITICAL LEADER
BORN February 26, 1928
KEY CONFLICTS Suez War 1956,
Six-Day War 1967, Yom Kippur War 1973,
Lebanon War 1982
KEY BATTLES Mitla Pass 1956, Abu Ageila
1967, Suez Canal Crossing 1973

Sharon in the Sinai Desert, 1973
Ariel Sharon's creation of a bridgehead across the
Suez Canal during the Yom Kippur War opened
the way for a possible Israeli drive on Cairo, but
this was prevented by international pressure.

Sharon was a junior officer in the First Arab–Israeli War of 1948. In the 1950s, his natural aggression found an outlet in Israel's newly founded special forces. In the Sinai campaign in 1956, he commanded a parachute brigade, exceeding his orders in an attack on Egyptian defenses in the Mitla Pass that ended in success, but at excessive cost. This move held back Sharon's career.

RESURGENT CAREER

Recovering from the controversy of Mitla, Sharon once more showed outstanding fighting qualities while commanding a tank division in the 1967 Six-Day War, achieving the vital breakthrough at Abu Ageila. He was recalled from retirement to serve in the Yom Kippur War in 1973, and led an armored division across the Suez Canal in a bold stroke that turned the initially disastrous war in Israel's favor.

Leaving the army for good in 1974, Sharon embarked on a controversial political career. As defense minister during the Israeli invasion of Lebanon in 1982, he was accused of partial responsibility for the massacres of Palestinian civilians at the Sabra and Shatila refugee camps in Beirut and forced to resign from the ministry.

Overwhelming firepower
An Israeli gun fires on enemy positions during the 1973 Yom Kippur War. Israel benefited from cutting-edge American military technology.

YASSER ARAFAT

PALESTINIAN LEADER
BORN August 24, 1929
DIED November 11, 2004
KEY CONFLICTS Anti-Israeli Campaigns,
Lebanese Civil War
KEY BATTLES Karameh 1968, Black
September 1970, Beirut 1982

Yasser Arafat was born in Egypt to Palestinian parents. Around 1959, living in Kuwait, he formed the Fatah Palestinian liberation movement. In the mid-1960s, Fatah's guerrillas made small-scale raids across the border from Jordan into Israel, but the movement was ignored when Arab states founded the Palestine Liberation Organization (PLO) in 1964.

FATAH'S RISE TO FAME

The defeat of the Arabs in the 1967 Six-Day War gave Arafat a chance to transform his status. In March 1968, Israeli forces carried out a punitive raid against a Fatah guerrilla base at Karameh in Jordan. Arafat's men stood and fought, inflicting casualties on the Israelis. The contrast with the poor performance of the Arab states in the Six-Day War made Arafat a hero. He became leader of the PLO and was seen as the representative of the Palestinian people, but his existence was precarious, surrounded as he was by faction-ridden militant Palestinian groups and insecure Arab states.

In 1970, Jordanian forces defeated Arafat's guerrillas in Black September. He shifted to Lebanon, where he narrowly survived involvement in the Lebanese Civil War in the mid-1970s, only to be driven out by an Israeli siege of Beirut in 1982. This effectively ended Arafat's career as a freedom fighter.

Palestinian fighter
Constantly aware of the importance of the image he projected, here Yasser Arafat wears his trademark *keffiyeh* headdress and carries the freedom fighter's AK-47.

> " I HAVE COME BEARING AN OLIVE BRANCH AND A FREEDOM FIGHTER'S GUN. DO NOT LET THE OLIVE BRANCH FALL FROM MY HAND. "
>
> **YASSER ARAFAT**, ADDRESS TO THE UN GENERAL ASSEMBLY, 1974

POST-COLD WAR COMMANDERS

THE END OF THE COLD WAR in the late 1980s left the United States as the world's only military superpower. The limits on the use of that power were political, especially the need to minimize casualties that would be unpopular with the voting US public. From the Gulf War of 1990–91 to the invasion of Iraq in 2003, US commanders carried out large-scale offensive operations with well-prepared professional forces that had the benefit of overwhelming technological superiority. However, they also had to cope with prolonged conflicts against guerrillas and international terrorists that were militarily frustrating and potentially demoralizing.

MODERN COMMANDERS

NORMAN SCHWARZKOPF

US ARMY GENERAL
BORN August 22, 1934
KEY CONFLICTS Vietnam War, Gulf War
KEY BATTLE Operation Desert Storm 1991

Stormin' Norman
A photograph taken during the run-up to Desert Storm captures the gritty determination that earned Schwarzkopf his nicknames, The Bear and Stormin' Norman.

Born in New Jersey, H. Norman Schwarzkopf was the son of a general. He graduated from West Point in 1956 and became an officer in an airborne regiment. In 1965, he volunteered for service in Vietnam, experiencing some fierce firefights as an adviser with the South Vietnamese airborne division. He returned to Vietnam for a second tour of duty in 1969, commanding a US infantry battalion. His insistence on a high level of discipline and training, as well as active pursuit of the enemy, was not popular, but Schwarzkopf's concern for the safety of his men and readiness to put his own life on the line were evident.

RAPID RESPONSE
After the Vietnam debacle, Schwarzkopf participated in the reconstruction of the US Army as a professional force of well-trained soldiers under highly motivated officers. In 1988, he was appointed commander-in-chief of US Central Command, with responsibility for rapid response to crises in the Middle East. After Saddam Hussein's Iraq invaded Kuwait in August 1990, Schwarzkopf was given command of forces defending Saudi Arabia in Operation Desert Shield. Half a million US troops were eventually sent to the Gulf, along with about 200,000 from a coalition of allies. Schwarzkopf impressed with his style of leadership—he inspired confidence in his troops, cooperated with coalition commanders, and handled the media comfortably. When planning began for Operation Desert Storm, he applied the principles of air-land war, therefore emphasizing rapid movement, flexibility, and shock effect. To minimize casualties, he devised an outflanking movement in the desert—a masterpiece of logistics and deception—that avoided the need for a bludgeoning head-to-head battle. The huge gap in technology, morale, and leadership between the coalition forces and the Iraqis made Desert Storm a rapid, overwhelming victory, achieved for the loss of 290 American lives. Shortly after this triumph, Schwarzkopf retired.

> **THERE'S MORE THAN ONE WAY TO LOOK AT A PROBLEM, AND THEY ALL MAY BE RIGHT.**
> GENERAL NORMAN SCHWARZKOPF

KEY BATTLE

DESERT STORM

CAMPAIGN Gulf War
DATE January 17–February 28, 1991
LOCATION Saudi Arabia, Kuwait, and Iraq

Operation Desert Storm was an offensive by a US-led coalition responding to Iraq's invasion of Kuwait in 1990. The operation opened with a prolonged aerial onslaught in which aircraft and cruise missiles destroyed a wide range of targets inside Iraq as well as striking Iraqi armed forces. On February 24, Schwarzkopf launched his land offensive: an encircling movement from the western flank forcing a precipitate withdrawal of Iraqi forces from Kuwait, during which they suffered massive casualties. The pursuit of the routed Iraqis was halted on February 28.

TOMMY FRANKS

US ARMY GENERAL
BORN June 17, 1945
KEY CONFLICTS War in Afghanistan, Iraq War
KEY BATTLES Invasion of Afghanistan 2001, Invasion of Iraq 2003

Tommy Franks enlisted in the army in 1965 and was commissioned as an officer in 1967, serving a tour as a lieutenant in Vietnam. By the time of the 1991 Gulf War, he was assistant commander of 1st Cavalry Division. In 2000, he was made commander-in-chief of US Central Command, responsible for operations in the Middle East. In 2001, the 9/11 al-Qaeda terrorist attacks in the United States thrust his command into the front line. Franks was tasked with planning military action against both al-Qaeda bases and the Taliban government in Afghanistan. He sought

66

WE'RE TAKING PART IN A GLOBAL WAR ON TERRORISM.

GENERAL TOMMY FRANKS

99

to avoid an invasion of Afghanistan, which would have risked heavy casualties. Instead, when Operation Enduring Freedom was launched in October, small numbers of special forces were inserted into Afghanistan to direct air strikes, attack al-Qaeda compounds, and act as advisers to local anti-Taliban guerrillas. Only after the Taliban collapsed under the impact of strikes by B-52 bombers did Franks begin to send in more troops. The operation, which Franks conducted from a headquarters in Florida, won praise for achieving results while minimizing US casualties. But eradicating Taliban and al-Qaeda guerrillas was to prove a near impossible long-term task.

INTO IRAQ

In 2003, Franks led the controversial Anglo-American invasion of Iraq. Contrary to the predictions of many analysts, he achieved a swift defeat of Saddam Hussein's army. Precisely targeted air and missile strikes destroyed the Iraqi command and control system. The rapid advance of allied ground forces obliged the Iraqis to concentrate their forces in response, providing an unmissable target for air strikes. The speed of the offensive gave the Iraqis no time to regroup and major military operations were completed in six weeks. Franks retired in July 2003.

Franks in Iraq
General Franks mixes with US troops in Iraq in 2003. The Oklahoma-born general had retired before the apparent successes of his operations in Afghanistan and Iraq began to unravel in the face of large-scale insurgency.

OSAMA BIN LADEN

AL-QAEDA LEADER
BORN March 10, 1957
KEY CONFLICTS War against Soviets in Afghanistan, International Terrorist Campaign
KEY BATTLE 9/11 attacks 2001

Osama bin Laden was born into a wealthy Sunni Muslim family in Saudi Arabia. After the Soviet invasion of Afghanistan in 1979, he helped found the Afghan Services Bureau, recruiting, financing, and arming volunteers to fight in the mujahideen guerrilla war against the Soviet occupation forces. When the Russians withdrew from Afghanistan in the late 1980s, bin Laden created the al-Qaeda ("the base") network to promote war on a global scale. His enemies were the Jews and Israel, the United States and its allies, Shiite Muslim "heretics," and most governments in the Muslim world, condemned for betraying true Islam. In 1998, he proclaimed that "killing the Americans and their allies— civilians and military—is an individual duty for every Muslim who can do it in any country."

A HUNTED MAN

After al-Qaeda bombings of two US embassies in Africa in 1998, the Americans tried to track down bin Laden to arrest or assassinate him. He found refuge in Afghanistan, where his fighters supported the seizure of power by the militant Islamist Taliban movement. With its skillfully coordinated use of four hijacked airliners to attack New York's World Trade Center and the Pentagon in Washington, causing almost 3,000 deaths, al-Qaeda's 9/11 onslaught in 2001 brought bin Laden to the center of world attention. The United States' response to this atrocity was to attack Afghanistan, but bin Laden avoided capture.

Media manipulator
Bin Laden's large-scale operations were calculated for maximum media impact. A number of analysts believe that he may now be dead, possibly from kidney failure.

Afghanistan War
US Soldiers exit a helicopter to search for an IED (improvised explosive device) factory in Afghanistan in September 2009. IEDs have been used extensively against coalition forces in both the Afghanistan and Iraq wars.

INDEX

INDEX

ACKNOWLEDGMENTS

The publisher would like to thank the following for their kind permission to reproduce their photographs:

(Key: a-above; b-below/bottom; c-center; f-far; l-left; r-right; t-top)

1 The Bridgeman Art Library: Church of St. Johannes, Cappenberg, Germany (c). **2-3 The Art Archive:** British Library. **4 Corbis:** Bill Ross (l). **4-5 Corbis:** Ed Darack/Science Faction. **6 akg-images:** (ftr) (br). **Ancient Art & Architecture Collection:** C.M. Dixon (tr); Uniphoto (tl). **The Art Archive:** Archaeological Museum Thasos / Alfredo Dagli Orti (ftl). **Corbis:** Arte & Immagini (fbl); The Corcoran Gallery of Art (fbr). **The Stapleton Collection:** (bl). 7 **The Art Archive:** Gianni Dagli Orti (fbl). **Australian War Memorial:** (bl). **The Bridgeman Art Library:** Art Museum, Khabarovsk, Russia (tr). **Corbis:** Christie's Images (tl). **National Maritime Museum, Greenwich, London:** (ftr). **PA Photos:** Gurinder Osan / AP (fbr). **Photo Scala, Florence:** BI, ADAGP, Paris (br). **TopFoto.co.uk:** RIA Novosti (ftl). 8-9 Corbis: Araldo de Luca. 10 akg-images: Iraq Museum, Baghdad (c). **Ancient Art & Architecture Collection:** (bl); Museo Capitolino Rome / Dagli Orti (br). **Réunion des Musées Nationaux Agence Photographique:** Droits réservés (bc). 11 akg-images: Laurent Lecat (br). **Ancient Art & Architecture Collection:** Egyptian Museum Cairo / Dagli Orti (c). **Photo Scala, Florence:** (bl) (bc). **12-13 The Art Archive:** Museo di Villa Giulia Rome / Gianni Dagli Orti (t). **13 Dorling Kindersley:** British Museum (br). **14 akg-images:** Erich Lessing (br). **Ancient Art & Architecture Collection:** (l). **15 The Art Archive:** Musée du Louvre Paris / Gianni Dagli Orti (tr). **Corbis:** Christina Gascoigne/Robert Harding World Imagery (tl); Araldo de Luca (br). **16 The Bridgeman Art Library:** Musee des Beaux-Arts, Tournai, Belgium/ Giraudon (bl). **Corbis:** Gianni Dagli Orti (c). **17 akg-images:** Erich Lessing (br). **Corbis:** Gianni Dagli Orti (bl). **Wikipedia, The Free Encyclopedia:** Cabinet des Médailles, Paris (tc). **18 akg-images:** Cameraphoto (tr); Erich Lessing (bc). **Réunion des Musées Nationaux Agence Photographique:** Droits réservés (cl). **19 Ancient Art & Architecture Collection:** Brian Wilson (l). The Art Archive: Archaeological Museum Thasos / Alfredo Dagli Orti (r). **Photo Scala, Florence:** Heritage Images (bl). **20 Corbis:** Araldo de Luca (tr). **21 Corbis:** The Gallery Collection (br). **22 The Art Archive:** Musée Archéologique Naples / Alfredo Dagli Orti (cl). **22-23 Réunion des Musées Nationaux Agence Photographique:** Daniel Arnaudet / Gérard Blot (c). **23 TopFoto.co.uk:** (cr). **24-25 The Art Archive:** Museo Capitolino Rome / Dagli Orti (t). **25 Photo Scala, Florence:** (br). **26 Photo Scala, Florence:** courtesy of the Ministero Beni e Att. Culturali (cr). **Wikipedia, The Free Encyclopedia:** schurl50 (bc). **27 akg-images:** (tr). **Alamy Images:** London Art Archive (bl). **28 Corbis:** Gianni Dagli Orti (bl) (cl). **28-29 Corbis:** Gianni Dagli Orti. **29 Alamy Images:** Mary Evans Picture Library (cr). **Glasgow University Library:** (tc). **30-31 akg-images:** Erich Lessing. **32 Photo Scala, Florence:** (br). **TopFoto.co.uk:** Luisa Ricciarini (cr). **33 akg-images:** Erich Lessing (tc). **The Bridgeman Art Library:** Louvre, Paris, France/ Giraudon (bl). **Getty Images:** Antonio Vassilacchi (br). **34 akg-images:** Herve Champollion (cr). **Ancient Art & Architecture Collection:** C.M. Dixon (l). **35 Alamy Images:** PjrStudio (cr). **The Art Archive:** Museum der Stadt Wien / Gianni Dagli Orti (b). **Dorling Kindersley:** Courtesy of the Ermine Street Guard (tc). **36 akg-images:** (tr). **The Bridgeman Art Library:** Giraudon (b). **38 The Art Archive:** Museo della Civilta Romana Rome / Gianni Dagli Orti (cl). **38-39 Corbis:** The Gallery Collection (c). **39 Photolibrary:** Vincent Leblic (cr). **40-41 Photo Scala, Florence:** Ministero Beni e Att. Culturali. **42 Alamy Images:** Interfoto (br); The Art Gallery Collection (cr). **Photo Scala, Florence:** BPK (bl). **43 akg-images:** (br). **The Bridgeman Art Library:** Musei Capitolini, Rome, Italy / Lauros / Giraudon (tc). **44 Alamy Images:** Germany Images David Crossland (bl). **The Bridgeman Art Library:** Musée des Antiquités Nationales, St. Germain-en-Laye, France / Lauros / Giraudon (c). **45 Dreamstime.com:** David Garry (tr). **Photo Scala, Florence:** (b). **46-47 Ancient Art & Architecture Collection. 47 Corbis:** Asian Art & Archaeology, Inc. (bc). **48 akg-images:** Laurent Lecat (b). **Ancient Art & Architecture Collection:** Uniphoto (c). **49 The Bridgeman Art Library:** (bc). **The Field Museum:** (tc). 50 akg-images. **52 akg-images:** VISIOARS (br). **Ancient Art & Architecture Collection:** (bl). **Dorling Kindersley:** Geoff Dann (c). **Réunion des Musées Nationaux Agence Photographique:** Château de Versailles / Gérard Blot (bc). **53 akg-images:** (bl). **The Art Archive:** Bibliothèque Nationale Paris / Harper Collins Publishers (bc). **Getty Images:** The Bridgeman Art Library (br). **54-55 The Trustees of the British Museum:** (t). **55 Ancient Art & Architecture Collection:** Interfoto Germany (b). **56 akg-images:** Erich Lessing (bl). Réunion des Musées Nationaux Agence Photographique: René-Gabriel Ojéda (br). **57 Ancient Art & Architecture Collection:** (c). **Corbis:** The Art Archive (br). 58 British Library: (r). **59 Bibliothèque Nationale De France, Paris:** (r) (bl). **The Bridgeman Art Library:** University of Edinburgh (c). 60-61 akg-images. **62 Lebrecht Music and Arts:** RA (bl). **Réunion des Musées Nationaux Agence Photographique:** (br). **63 akg-images:** (br). **The Bridgeman Art Library:** Ashmolean Museum, University of Oxford, UK (tc). **Getty Images:** Hulton Archive (clb). **64 The Art Archive:** Biblioteca Nazionale Marciana Venice / Alfredo Dagli Orti (b). **Photo Scala, Florence:** HIP (cra). **TopFoto.co.uk:** The Granger Collection (ca). **64-65 Getty Images:** Hulton Archive (b). **65 akg-images:** (tc). **The Bridgeman Art Library:** Bibliothèque Municipale, Castres, France/ Giraudon (crb). 66-67 Photo Scala, Florence. **68 Ancient Art & Architecture Collection:** C.M. Dixon (br). Getty Images: Hulton Archive (cr). **69 The Art Archive:** (bl). **Getty Images:** The Bridgeman Art Library (br). **TopFoto.co.uk:** The Granger Collection (tc). **70-71 Corbis:** Nik Wheeler. **72-73 Corbis:** The Gallery Collection (tl). **73 Dorling Kindersley:** Warwick Castle (b). **74 Photo Scala, Florence:** HIP (cr). **74-75 Dorling Kindersley:** Royal Armouries (ca). **75 akg-images:** VISIOARS (b). **Photo Scala, Florence:** White Images (tl). **76 akg-images:** (b); British Library (tl). *Photo Scala, Florence:* Ministero Beni e Att. Culturali (tr). **77 akg-images:** (r); Erich Lessing (clb). **78-79 akg-images:** Cameraphoto. **80 akg-images:** (clb); Hedda Eid (br). **81 The Art Archive:** Bibliothèque de l'Arsenal Paris / Kharbine-Tapabor / Coll. Jean Vigne (tl). **Corbis:** Charles & Josette Lenars (br). **82 Getty Images:** Hulton Archive (cl). **82-83 Getty Images:** The Bridgeman Art Library (c). **83 The Art Archive:** Galleria degli Uffizi Florence / Alfredo Dagli Orti (c). **84 Ancient Art & Architecture Collection:** Prisma (l). **85 akg-images:** British Library (tr). **Mary Evans Picture Library:** Aisa Media (bl). **86-87 Ancient Art & Architecture Collection:** Elly Beintema (t). **87 DNP Art Image Archives:** Tokyo National Museum (b). **88 Getty Images:** Massimo Pizzotti (br). V&A Images \ Victoria and Albert Museum, London: (bl). **89 akg-images:** (cb). **Ancient Art & Architecture Collection:** (cr). **90 The Bridgeman Art Library:** Lauros / Giraudon (cl). **Photo Scala, Florence:** White Images (b). **91 The Art Archive:** Victoria and Albert Museum London / Eileen Tweedy (tr). **Dorling Kindersley:** Courtesy of the Churchill College Archives, Cambridge University (cla). Getty Images: Travel Ink (b). **92 Getty Images:** DEA / C. Sappa (tr). **93 Ancient Art & Architecture Collection:** C.M. Dixon (br). **94 The Bridgeman Art Library:** Private Collection (b). **Corbis:** Asian Art & Archaeology, Inc (c). **94-95 akg-images. 95 Corbis:** Barney Burstein (crb). **96-97 Photo Scala, Florence:** HIP (t). **97 Dorling Kindersley:** Courtesy of the Wallace Collection, London (b). **98 The Art Archive:** Bibliothèque Nationale Paris / Harper Collins Publishers (b). **99 akg-images:** Robert O'Dea (cla). **The Bridgeman Art Library:** Private Collection (br). **British Library:** (tr). **Corbis:** The Art Archive (bl). **101-102 Lebrecht Music and Arts:** RA (b). **102 Getty Images:** The Bridgeman Art Library (bl) (br). **Photo Scala, Florence:** HIP (c). **103 Getty Images:** The Bridgeman Art Library (r). **104 TopFoto.co.uk:** RIA Novosti (bl). **105 Alamy Images:** Angus McComiskey (tl); John McKenna (bl); Phil Robinson / PjrFoto (tr). **Getty Images:** Hulton Archive (br). **106 Photo Scala, Florence:** BPK. **108 The Art Archive:** Moldovita Monastery Romania (bl); Museo de America Madrid / Gianni Dagli Orti (br). China Tourism Photo Library: Fotoe (bc). **Dorling Kindersley:** Courtesy of the Wallace Collection, London (c). **109 akg-images:** (bl). **The Bridgeman Art Library:** Leeds Museums and Galleries (City Art Gallery) UK (tr). **Getty Images:** The Bridgeman Art Library (bc). **National Maritime Museum, Greenwich, London:** (br). 110-111 The Art Archive: Moldovita Monastery Romania (t). **111 Dorling Kindersley:** Dave King / Courtesy of the Pitt Rivers Museum, University of Oxford (b). **112 The Bridgeman Art Library:** National Gallery, London, UK (cla). Corbis: Christie's Images (bc). **112-113 Getty Images:** The Bridgeman Art Library. **113 The Art Archive:** Topkapi Museum Istanbul / Gianni Dagli Orti (br). **Réunion des Musées Nationaux Agence Photographique:** Jean-Gilles Berizzi (tr). **114 Photo Scala, Florence:** British Library (br). **115 akg-images:** (tl). **The Bridgeman Art Library:** Bibliothèque Nationale, Paris, France (br). **116-117 Werner Forman Archive:** Kuroda Collection, Japan. **117 The Art Archive:** Europhoto (b). **118 DNP Art Image Archives:** Tokugawa Art Museum, Japan (b). **119 Corbis:** Asian Art & Archaeology, Inc. (tr). **DNP Art Image Archives:** Tokugawa Art Museum, Japan (bc). **120-121 DNP Art Image Archives:** Tokugawa Art Museum. 122 **Ancient Art & Architecture Collection:** EuroCreon (r) (bl). 123 Alamy Images: Pat Behnke (tr). **Ancient Art & Architecture Collection:** Uniphoto (br). **China Tourism Photo Library:** Fotoe (bl). 124-125 akg-images. **125 Dorling Kindersley:** Courtesy of the Wallace Collection, London (bc). **126 The Art Archive:** (br); Museo Colonial Antigua Guatemala / Dagli Orti (cl). **127 Corbis:** Herbert Kehrer (tr). **Photo Scala, Florence:** Musee Du Quai Branly (br). **128 akg-images:** Erich Lessing (bc). **Ancient Art & Architecture Collection:** (tr). **The Art Archive:** Biblioteca Nacional Madrid / Gianni Dagli Orti (cl). **Dorling Kindersley:** Board of Trustees of the Armouries (c). **129 The Art Archive:** Museo de America Madrid / Gianni Dagli Orti (b). **130-131 Getty Images:** The Bridgeman Art Library. **132 Mary Evans Picture Library:** Aisa Media (r). **Réunion des Musées Nationaux Agence Photographique:** Château de Versailles / Daniel Arnaudet / Jean Schormans (bl). **133 The Bridgeman Art Library:** Private Collection (cl). **Réunion des Musées Nationaux Agence Photographique:** Paris - Musée de l'Armée, Dist. RMN / Pascal Segrette (br). **Photo Scala, Florence:** White Images (bl). **Ullstein Bild:** Imagebroker.net (tc). **134-135 The Bridgeman Art Library:** Museo e Gallerie Nazionale di Capodimonte, Naples, Italy. **136 akg-images:** Erich Lessing (cl). **136-137 Rijksmuseum Amsterdam. 137 The Art Archive:** British Library (cra); Alfredo Dagli Orti (cla). **Lebrecht Music and Arts:** Leemage (br). **138 The Bridgeman Art Library:** Art Museum, Khabarovsk, Russia (bl). **Getty Images:** The Bridgeman Art Library (br). **Mary Evans Picture Library:** Aisa Media (c). **139 akg-images:** Erich Lessing (b). **Alamy Images:** Marc Hill (tc). **140-141 akg-images:** Erich Lessing (t). **141 Dorling Kindersley:** (br). **142 Lebrecht Music and Arts:** Interfoto (bc). **Photo Scala, Florence:** Courtesy of the Ministero Beni E Att. Culturali (c). **142-143 akg-images:** (c). **143 Getty Images:** Hulton Archive (cr). **Photo Scala, Florence:** White Images (br). **144 Dorling Kindersley:** Royal Armouries (cl). **144-145 akg-images:** (c). **145 akg-images:** (t). Nationalmuseum, Stockholm: (bc). **Photo Scala, Florence:** BPK, Bildagentur fuer Kunst, Kultur und Geschichte, Berlin (br). **146 Corbis:** The Art Archive (cla). **146-147 Getty Images:** Rischgitz (c). **147 akg-images:** (ca). **148 The Bridgeman Art Library:** Private Collection (bc). **Photo Scala, Florence:** HIP (cr). **148-149 Getty Images:** Wolfgang Kaehler (b). **149 akg-images:** Rabatti - Domingie (tc). **Mary Evans Picture Library:** (tr). **150-151 Getty Images:** The Bridgeman Art Library. **152 The Bridgeman Art Library:** Trustees of Leeds Castle Foundation, Maidstone, Kent, UK (cl). 152-153 akg-images. **153 Getty Images:** The Bridgeman Art Library (c). **154 Getty Images:** The Bridgeman Art Library (bl). National Maritime Museum, Greenwich, London: (br). **155 akg-images:** Erich Lessing (br). National Maritime Museum, Greenwich, London: (cra) (cla). **156 Rijksmuseum Amsterdam:** (bl). **156-157 National Maritime Museum, Greenwich, London:** (t). **157 akg-images:** (bl). **National Maritime Museum, Greenwich, London:** (crb). **159 TopFoto.co.uk:** Ullstein Bild. **160 akg-images:** (bc). **The Bridgeman Art Library:** The Holburne Museum of Art, Bath, UK (bl). **Dorling Kindersley:** Courtesy of the National Army Museum, London (c). **Mary Evans Picture Library:** Otto Money / AIC Photographic Services (br). **161 akg-images:** Sotheby's (bc). **The Art Archive:** Museo Bolivar Caracas / Gianni Dagli Orti (br). **The Bridgeman Art Library:** Bonhams, London, UK (t); Château de Versailles, France/ Lauros / Giraudon (bl). **Dorling Kindersley:** (cb). **162 Getty Images:** The Bridgeman Art Library (t). **163 Dorling Kindersley:** National Museums of Scotland (br). **164 akg-images:** Cameraphoto (cr). **The Bridgeman Art Library:** The Holburne Museum of Art, Bath, UK (bl). **165 akg-images:** (clb). **The Bridgeman Art Library:** Château de Versailles, France/ Lauros / Giraudon (c). **166 The Bridgeman Art Library:** National Army Museum, London (tr). **Corbis:** Steven Vidler / Eurasia Press (bl). **Dorling Kindersley:** Dave King / Courtesy of Warwick Castle, Warwick (cb). **167 Corbis:** Arte & Immagini (l). National Portrait Gallery, London: (br). **168-169 The Bridgeman Art Library:** National Army Museum, London. **170 Photo Scala, Florence:** (b). **171 akg-images:** (bl). **The Bridgeman Art Library:** Philip Mould Ltd., London (tl). **Getty Images:** The Bridgeman Art Library (br). **172 akg-images:** (t). 173 Lebrecht Music and Arts: Interfoto (b). **174 akg-images:** (c); Hervé Champollion (cr). **The Bridgeman Art Library:** Heeresgeschichtliches Museum, Vienna, Austria (br); The Trustees of the Goodwood Collection (bl). **175 akg-images:** (b). **176-176 Getty Images:** Hulton Archive (b). **177 akg-images:** (bc) (cr) (tl). 178-179 akg-images. **180 Getty Images:** Hulton Archive (bl). National Portrait Gallery, London: (cr). **181 The Art Archive:** Imperial War Museum (b). **Corbis:** Stapleton Collection (cla). **Getty Images:** Time & Life Pictures (tr). **182-183 National Gallery Of Canada, Ottowa. 184 The Frick Collection, New York:** (c). **Photo Scala, Florence:** Metropolitan Museum of Art, NY (br). **185 akg-images:** North Wind Picture Archives (br) (tl). **186 Corbis:** Bettmann (tr). **Getty Images:** Travel Ink (cl). **186-187 SuperStock:** (b). **187 The Bridgeman Art Library:** Private Collection/ Peter Newark American Picture (tr). **188-189 Photo Scala, Florence:** Yale University Art Gallery/Art Resource, NY. **190 Getty Images:** Hulton Archive/Stringer (cr). **190-191 Corbis:** Bettmann (c). **191 Corbis:** Bettmann (cr). **192 akg-images:** Erich Lessing (br). **The Stapleton Collection:** (cla). **193 Mary Evans Picture Library:** Otto Money / AIC Photographic Services (t). **The Stapleton Collection:** (br). **194-195 Getty Images:** The Bridgeman Art Library (t). **195 Dorling Kindersley:** Royal Armouries (bc). **196 The Bridgeman Art Library:** Louvre, Paris, France (b). **Corbis:** Gianni Dagli Orti (cr). **197 The Bridgeman Art Library:** Musée de la Révolution Française, Vizille, France (cl); Private Collection (cr). **Réunion des Musées Nationaux Agence Photographique:** Paris - Musée de l'Armée, Dist. RMN / Marie Bruggeman (bc). **198 The Bridgeman Art Library:** Private Collection / Photo © Bonhams (cla). **Dorling Kindersley:** (tc). **Getty Images:**

The Bridgeman Art Library (bl). **198-199 Getty Images:** The Bridgeman Art Library (c). **199 The Bridgeman Art Library:** Tretyakov Gallery, Moscow, Russia (br). **Dorling Kindersley:** Courtesy of David Edge (tc) (tr). **200 Corbis:** Araldo de luca (c). **201 Corbis:** The Gallery Collection (c). **203** akg-images: Erich Lessing (c). **204** The Art Archive: Musée du Château de Versailles / Gianni Dagli Orti (cl). **The Bridgeman Art Library:** Château de Versailles, France/ Giraudon (bc). **205 The Bridgeman Art Library:** Private Collection/ Roger-Viollet, Paris (l); The Detroit Institute of Arts, USA/ Founders Society purchase, Mr and Mrs Edgar B. Whitcomb fund (br). **206** akg-images: (bc) (c). **207** akg-images: (b); RIA Novosti (tl). **208 The Bridgeman Art Library:** Private Collection/ Mark Fiennes (r). Photo Scala, Florence: HIP (bl). **209 The Bridgeman Art Library:** National Gallery of Victoria, Melbourne, Australia/ The Bridgeman Art Library (tl). **Dorling Kindersley:** Geoff Dann (bc); Judith Miller / Wallis and Wallis (cr). **210** The Art Archive: Wellington Museum London / Eileen Tweedy (br). **210-211 Getty Images:** The Bridgeman Art Library (c). **211 Photo Scala, Florence:** The National Gallery, London (cr). **212-213 Corbis:** The Gallery Collection. **213 The Art Archive:** Private Collection Paris / Gianni Dagli Orti (bc). **214 The Art Archive:** Harper Collins Publishers (cl). **The Bridgeman Art Library:** Philip Mould Ltd., London (br). **214-215 Dorling Kindersley:** Royal Armouries (t) (cr). **215 The Bridgeman Art Library:** Château de Versailles, France/ Lauros / Giraudon (bl); Lawrence Steigrad Fine Arts, New York (tr). **216 Getty Images:** The Bridgeman Art Library (r). **National Maritime Museum, Greenwich, London:** (bl). **217** akg-images: Erich Lessing (cra). **The Bridgeman Art Library:** Walker Art Gallery, National Museums Liverpool (b). **Corbis:** Historical Picture Archive (t). **218-219** akg-images: Sotheby's. **220-221 Corbis:** The Gallery Collection (t). **221 Dorling Kindersley:** (bc). **222** akg-images: (ca). **The Art Archive:** Catholic University Quito Ecuador / Gianni Dagli Orti (br); Museo Nacional de Historia Lima / Gianni Dagli Orti (b); Museo Bolivar Caracas / Gianni Dagli Orti (bl). **223 The Art Archive:** Museo Nacional Bogota / Gianni Dagli Orti (b). **224** akg-images: North Wind Picture Archives (b). **Corbis:** Bettmann (cr). **225 The Bridgeman Art Library:** Chicago History Museum, US (c). **Getty Images:** MPI (br). **226 The Bridgeman Art Library:** Private Collection (l). **228** akg-images: **Corbis:** The Corcoran Gallery of Art (bc). **Dorling Kindersley:** Museum of Artillery, The Rotunda, Woolwich, London (c). **Getty Images:** MPI (br). **229 The Art Archive:** National Army Museum London (bl). **The Bridgeman Art Library:** Musée Condé, Chantilly, France / Giraudon (bc); Peter Newark Military Pictures (t). **Corbis:** Bettmann (br). **230-231** akg-images: (t). **231 Dorling Kindersley:** Collection of Jean-Pierre Verney (b). **232 Getty Images:** Nadar (ca). **Photo Scala, Florence:** BPK, Bildagentur fuer Kunst, Kultur und Geschichte, Berlin (bl). **233 The Art Archive:** Belvoir Castle / Eileen Tweedy (ca). **The Bridgeman Art Library:** Private Collection (b). National Portrait Gallery, London: (tr). **234** akg-images: Erich Lessing (cl). **Art Resource, NY:** Adoc-photos (br). **235** akg-images: (br). **The Art Archive:** Museo del Risorgimento, Rome / Gianni Dagli Orti (b). **Photo Scala, Florence:** Museo del Risorgimento, Turin (tr). **236-237** akg-images: Pirozzi. **238** akg-images: ullstein bild (r). **Getty Images:** Time Life Pictures (bl). **239** akg-images: (bl). **Dorling Kindersley:** Courtesy of Henri Vuillemin (t). **Réunion des Musées Nationaux Agence Photographique:** Château de Versailles / Jean-Gilles (cra). **240** akg-images: (cla). **240-241 Mary Evans Picture Library:** Rue des Archives / Tallandier (c). **241** akg-images: (ca). **242-243 Nancy Hoyt Belcher:** (t). **243 Dorling Kindersley:** Dave King / Confederate Memorial Hall, New Orleans (br). **244 Getty Images:**

Hulton Archive (c). Shawn Latta: (br). **Mary Evans Picture Library:** (bl). **245 Corbis:** The Corcoran Gallery of Art (r). Library Of Congress, Washington, D.C.: (bl). **246 The Bridgeman Art Library:** Atwater Kent Museum of Philadelphia/ Courtesy of Historical Society of Pennsylvania Collection (b). **Getty Images:** MPI (cla). **247 Alamy Images:** Chris Pondy (crb). **Corbis:** Bettmann (c); The Corcoran Gallery of Art (l). **248** akg-images: (cra). **The Art Archive:** (c). **249 Corbis:** Medford Historical Society Collection (c). **250 Corbis:** Bettmann (c). **Getty Images:** MPI (br). **251 Corbis:** Bettmann (br). **Dorling Kindersley:** Dave King / Courtesy of the US Army Heritage and Education Center (c) (cra) (r). Smithsonian Institution, Washington, DC, U.S.A.: (clb). **253 Alamy Images:** Historical Art Collection (bc). **Getty Images:** Hulton Archive (tl). **Library Of Congress, Washington, D.C.:** (bl). **254-255 Library Of Congress, Washington, D.C..** **256 The Art Archive:** National Army Museum London (c). **257 Dorling Kindersley:** Geoff Brightling (b). **258 Corbis:** (ca); Bettmann (bl). **259 Corbis:** (cr). **Dorling Kindersley:** (cl). **Getty Images:** MPI (b). **260-261 The Art Archive:** Buffalo Bill Historical Center, Cody, Wyoming. **262** akg-images: (bl). **Alamy Images:** Mary Evans Picture Library (br). **Photo Scala, Florence:** Ann Ronan / HIP (cla). **263 The Bridgeman Art Library:** Musee Conde, Chantilly, France / Giraudon (br). Corbis: Hulton-Deutsch Collection (tl). **264** akg-images: (cr). **Getty Images:** Hulton Archive (bl). **265 The Bridgeman Art Library:** Leeds Museums and Galleries (City Art Gallery) UK (r). **Corbis:** Historical Picture Archive (bl). **266-267 The Art Archive:** 17 & 21st Lancers Museum / Eileen Tweedy (b). **268 Corbis:** Bettmann (bl); Hulton-Deutsch Collection (r). **269** akg-images: (cr). Corbis: Hulton-Deutsch Collection (br). **Getty Images:** Hulton Archive (cl). **270 The Bridgeman Art Library:** Private Collection/ Peter Newark American Picture (t). **271 National Maritime Museum, Greenwich, London:** (br). **272 The Art Archive:** National Archives Washington DC (cl). **Lebrecht Music and Arts:** Interfoto (r). **273 Corbis:** Bettmann (bl). **Photo Scala, Florence:** Ann Ronan / Heritage Images (r). **274-275 Lebrecht Music and Arts:** Interfoto (b). **276 Nick Scott. 278** akg-images: (br); Erich Lessing (bc). **The Bridgeman Art Library:** Canadian War Museum, Ottawa, Canada (bl). **Dorling Kindersley:** Imperial War Museum, London / Andy Crawford (c). **279 Corbis:** David Turnley (br); Smithsonian Institution (br). **Dorling Kindersley:** Royal Armouries (c). **Getty Images:** Hulton Archive (bl). Courtesy of U.S. Navy: PH3 Daniel G. Lavoie (tr). **280-281 Corbis:** Hulton-Deutsch Collection (c). **281 Dorling Kindersley:** Royal Armouries (br). **282 The Bridgeman Art Library:** Private Collection/ Archives Charmet (bl). **Corbis:** Bettmann (r). **283 The Art Archive:** Imperial War Museum (br) (tl). **Photo Scala, Florence:** Ann Ronan / HIP (bl). **284 The Bridgeman Art Library:** Archives Larousse, Paris, France / Giraudon (br). **Corbis:** Bettmann (c). **Dorling Kindersley:** Collection of Jean-Pierre Verney (cr). **285** akg-images: (br). **The Bridgeman Art Library:** Private Collection/ Ken Welsh (l). **286-287 The Bridgeman Art Library:** Canadian War Museum, Ottawa, Canada. **288 The Bridgeman Art Library:** Canadian War Museum, Ottawa, Canada (cr). **Corbis:** Bettmann (b). **289** akg-images: (bl). **The Bridgeman Art Library:** Private Collection / © Gavin Graham Gallery, London, UK (br). **Getty Images:** Hulton Archive (tc). **290 Corbis:** The Art Archive / **Dorling Kindersley:** (br). **Getty Images:** Hulton Archive/ Stringer (bl). **291** akg-images: (tl). **The Art Archive:** Museo Storico Italiano della Guerra Rovereto / Gianni Dagli Orti (bc). **Getty Images:** Hulton Archive (br). **292 Lebrecht Music and Arts:** Leemage (cl). **292-293 Lebrecht Music and Arts:** Leemage (c). **293** akg-images: (c). **294** akg-images: (br). **Lebrecht Music and Arts:**

Leemage (c). **National Maritime Museum, Greenwich, London:** (cr). **295** akg-images: Erich Lessing (bl). **The Art Archive:** Private Collection MD (br). **Corbis:** Hulton-Deutsch Collection (c). **297 Dorling Kindersley:** Courtesy of Firepower, The Royal Artillery Museum, Royal Artillery Historical Trust, Gary Ombler (br). **298 The Art Archive:** *Domenica del Corriere* / Alfredo Dagli Orti (bc). **Corbis:** Bettmann (c). **PA Photos:** AP (bl). **299 The Art Archive:** Private Collection / Marc Charmet (tr). Corbis: Hulton-Deutsch Collection (b); Underwood & Underwood (tl). **300-301 Getty Images:** The Bridgeman Art Library. **302 The Art Archive:** Gianni Dagli Orti (br). **The Bridgeman Art Library:** Bibliothèque Polonaise, Paris, France / Bonora (cr). **Getty Images:** Hulton Archive (bl). **303 Corbis:** EFE (b). **Getty Images:** Hulton Archive (tl). **The National Archives:** (cl). **304-305 The Art Archive. 305 Dorling Kindersley:** Courtesy of the Bradbury Science Museum, Los Alamos (b). **306** akg-images: (bl). **Getty Images:** Hulton Archive (c). **307 Corbis:** Austrian Archives (tl). **Getty Images:** Hulton Archive (bl). www.historicalimagebank.com: (cr). **308-309 The Bridgeman Art Library:** SZ Photo. **310** akg-images: RIA Novosti (br). **Getty Images:** Hulton Archive (cl). **311 The Bridgeman Art Library:** SZ Photo (bl). **Dorling Kindersley:** (tr). TopFoto.co.uk: (br). **312 Corbis:** Bettmann (cl). **312-313 RIA Novosti:** (c). **313 PA Photos:** AP-Photo/Kirsche (c). **314 Corbis:** Underwood & Underwood (bl). **Getty Images:** Popperfoto (r). **Imperial War Museum:** (cl). **315** akg-images: (br). **Australian War Memorial:** (tr). **Corbis:** (bl). **Imperial War Museum:** (cl). **316 The Art Archive:** General Wolfe Museum Quebec House / Eileen Tweedy (tr). **Dorling Kindersley:** Imperial War Museum, London / Andy Crawford (br). **Getty Images:** Time Life Pictures (clb). **317 The Bridgeman Art Library:** Look and Learn (tl). **Imperial War Museum:** (br). **Lebrecht Music and Arts:** Interfoto (cl). **318 Getty Images:** Time & Life Pictures (cla). **318-319 Getty Images:** Popperfoto (c). **319 Getty Images:** Hulton Archive (ca). **320 Corbis:** Bettmann (cr); Hulton-Deutsch Collection (bl). **321 The Art Archive:** (cr). Eisenhower National Historic Site: (tl). **Getty Images:** Popperfoto (b). **322 The Art Archive:** Culver Pictures (cl). **Getty Images:** Keystone (b). **The Patton Museum:** (tr). **323 Corbis:** (bl); Bettmann (br). **324 Corbis:** Nik Wheeler (tr). **325 Corbis:** (b). **326-327 Getty Images:** George Silk// Time Life Pictures. **328 Alamy Images:** History (b). **Courtesy of The Museum of World War II, Natick, Massachusetts:** (cr). **329 Corbis:** Getty Images: (br); Time & Life Pictures (cla). **330 Corbis:** Hulton-Deutsch Collection (cl). **Dorling Kindersley:** Gary Ombler (c). **Getty Images:** Popperfoto (b). **331 Corbis:** (br). **Photo Scala, Florence:** White Images (tl). **332-333 Getty Images:** William Vanderson/Fox Photos. **334 The Art Archive:** Imperial War Museum Photo archive IWM (bl). **Corbis:** (c). TopFoto.co.uk: The Granger Collection (cr). **335 Corbis:** (bl); Smithsonian Institution (c). **Dorling Kindersley:** (br). **Getty Images:** American Stock (tc). **336 Getty Images:** Time & Life Pictures (c). **337 Corbis:** (b). **338 Corbis:** Bettmann (cl). **Photo Scala, Florence:** White Images (bc). **339** akg-images: Ullstein Bild (c). **Corbis:** Bettmann (b). **340 The Bridgeman Art Library:** Private Collection/ Archives Charmet (cr). **Corbis:** Bettmann (bl). **341 Dorling Kindersley:** (b). **Photo Scala, Florence:** BI, ADAGP, Paris (tr). **342 Corbis:** Bettmann (b) (cra). **Dorling Kindersley:** (ca). **343 Corbis:** Bettmann (tc). **Getty Images:** Hulton Archive (bl). **344-345 Corbis:** Dien Bien Phu Museum / Reuters. **346 Corbis:** Bettmann (cr). **Dorling Kindersley:** (bl). **Getty Images:** Hulton Archive (cl); Arnold Newman (br). **347 Corbis:** Geneviève Chauvel / Sygma (cla). **Getty Images:** (cla); Rolls Press / Popperfoto (cra). **348 Corbis:** David Turnley (bl); Peter Turnley (br). **349 Corbis:** Reuters (br); Sherwin Crasto / Reuters (cl). **350-351 Panos Pictures:** Adam Dean

Front Endpapers: **Corbis:** Kevin R. Morris ; Back Endpapers: **Corbis:** Kevin R. Morris

The publisher would like to thank: Caroline Hunt for the proofreading, Marie Lorimer for the index, and Sharon Southren and Mia Stewart-Wilson for picture research assistance.

All other images © Dorling Kindersley For further information see: www.dkimages.com